MILLER'S
Antiques
PRICE GUIDE

to
one
antique
from
another
lots of love at Christmas

David

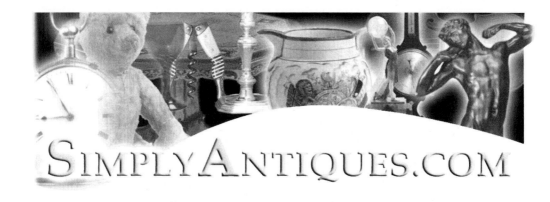

SIMPLYANTIQUES.COM

Buy & sell on the net.

- ✓ We collect secure payment for you online.
- ✓ We pick up, deliver, & insure in transit.
- ✓ We do all of the technical stuff so you don't have to.

Why make life complicated?

www.SimplyAntiques.com

Email: enq@SimplyAntiques.com

Tel. 01722 500554   Fax. 01722 503773

I-ADA
INTERNET ANTIQUE
DEALERS ASSOCIATION
MEMBER

I-ADA

INTERNET ANTIQUE
DEALERS ASSOCIATION

I-ADA is the only association specifically for the Internet antiques community.

Member benefits, discounts, news & online assistance.

Global networking opportunities.

Peace of mind.

www.I-ADA.com

Email: info@I-ADA.com   Telephone 01722 505500

MILLER'S
Antiques
PRICE GUIDE

General Editor
Elizabeth Norfolk

2001
Volume XXII

MILLER'S ANTIQUES PRICE GUIDE 2001

Created and designed by
Miller's
The Cellars, High Street
Tenterden, Kent, TN30 6BN
Tel: 01580 766411
Fax: 01580 766100

General Editor: Elizabeth Norfolk
Editorial and Production Co-ordinator: Jo Wood
Editorial Assistants: Carol Gillings, Lalage Johnstone
Assistant to General Editor: Gillian Charles
Production Assistant: Elaine Burrell
Advertising Executive: Jill Jackson
Advertising Assistants: Jo Hill, Melinda Williams
Designers: Philip Hannath, Kari Reeves
Advertisement Designer: Simon Cook
Indexer: Hilary Bird
Additional Photographers: Ian Booth, Roy Farthing, David Merewether,
Dennis O'Reilly, Robin Saker

First published in Great Britain in 2000
by Miller's, a division of Mitchell Beazley,
imprints of Octopus Publishing Group Ltd,
2–4 Heron Quays, London E14 4JP

© 2000 Octopus Publishing Group Ltd

A CIP catalogue record for this book is
available from the British Library

ISBN 1-84000-259-X

Illustrations: CK Litho, Whitstable, Kent
Colour origination: Pica Colour Separation Overseas Pte Ltd, Singapore
Printed and bound: Lego SPA, Italy

from left: A Charles II walnut and marquetry-inlaid longcase clock,
by Jacobus Markwick, London, 82in (208cm) high.
£45,000–50,000 DRA
A Chamberlain's Worcester two-handled bowl, cover and saucer,
printed red mark, c1820, saucer 6in (15cm) diam.
£500–600 HAM
An Arts and Crafts walnut and oak wardrobe, by Gillows, c1880, 52in (132cm) wide.
£1,300–1,500 S
A silver corkscrew, in the form of a fish, with garnets for eyes, early 20thC, 4in (10cm) long.
£300–400 CSK

5

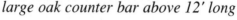

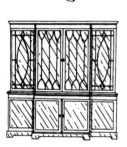

7

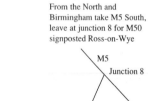
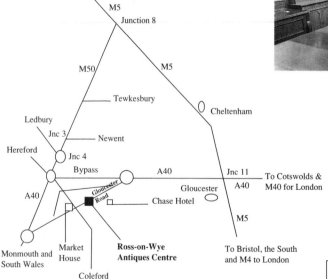

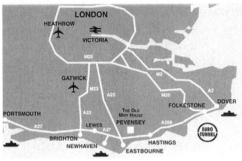

10

11

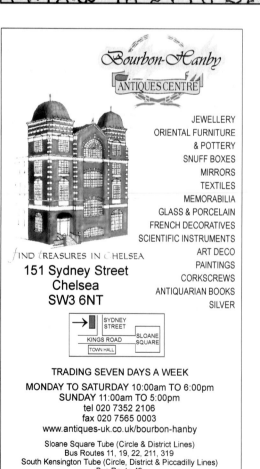

What you collect is your business; how you protect it is ours.

Invaluable Protector – the most comprehensive service for locating and retrieving stolen art, antiques and collectables.

Visit our website at www.invaluable.com
or call 0800 018 029.

Invaluable
POWERED BY THESAURUS

Know the lot.

Contents

MILLER'S

2001

Acknowledgements

The publishers would like to acknowledge the great assistance given by our consultants.
We would also like to extend our thanks to all auction houses and their press offices,
as well as dealers and collectors, who have assisted us in the production of this book.

FURNITURE: Edward Reily Collins, Hallidays,
                                        The Old College, High Street, Dorchester-
                                        on-Thames, Oxfordshire OX10 7HL

OAK & COUNTRY FURNITURE: Victor Chinnery, Wiltshire

POTTERY: Christopher Spencer, 26 Melrose Road,
                                        Merton Park, London SW19 3HG

PORCELAIN: Mark Law, Special Auction Services,
                                        The Coach House, Midgham Park,
                                        Reading, Berkshire RG7 5UG

                                        Henry Sandon, Worcester

ASIAN CERAMICS AND WORKS OF ART: Peter Wain, Glynde Cottage, Longford,
                                        Market Drayton, Shropshire TF9 3PW

GLASS: Timothy Osborne, Delomosne & Son Ltd,
                                        Court Close, North Wraxall, Chippenham,
                                        Wiltshire, SN14 7AD

SILVER: Daniel Bexfield, 26 Burlington Arcade,
                                        London W1V 9AD

CORKSCREWS: Christopher Sykes, Woburn, MK17 9QM

CLOCKS: Brian Loomes, Calf Haugh, Pateley
                                        Bridge, North Yorkshire HG3 5HW

BAROMETERS: Michael Oxley, P. A. Oxley Ltd,
                                        The Old Rectory, Cherhill, Nr.Calne,
                                        Wiltshire SN11 8UX

DECORATIVE ARTS: Fiona Baker, London

RUGS & CARPETS: Andrew Middleton, Phillips, 9 Paradise
                                        Square, Sheffield, Yorkshire S1 2DE

FANS: Paula Raven, Fantiques, London

FIREPLACES: Adrian Aiger, Ashburton Marbles,
                                        Great Hall, North Street, Ashburton,
                                        Devon TQ13 7QD

TREEN: Tony Foster, Buckinghamshire

ICONS: Christopher Richardson, Richardson &
                                        Kailas, 65 Rivermead Court, Ranelagh
                                        Gardens, London SW6 3RY

ANTIQUITIES: Joanna van der Lande, Bonhams,
                                        Montpelier Street, London SW7 1HH

TRIBAL ART: Gordon Reece, Finkle Street,
                                        Knaresborough, Yorkshire HG5 8AA

SCIENTIFIC INSTRUMENTS AND MARINE: Arthur Middleton, 12 New Row,
                                        London WC2N 4LF

ARMS & ARMOUR AND MILITARIA   John Spooner, West Street Antiques,
                                        63 West Street, Dorking, Surrey RH4 1BS

How to use this book

It is our aim to make this book easy to use. In order to find a particular item, consult the contents list on page 19 to find the main heading – for example, Furniture. Having located your area of interest, you will find that larger sections have been sub-divided. If you are looking for a particular factory, designer or craftsman, consult the index which starts on page 796.

CHESTS-ON-CHESTS

Miller's Compares

> **Miller's Compares**
> explains why two items which look similar have realised very different prices.

A George I walnut chest-on-chest, the two short and three long graduated drawers with figured banding, the lower section with a brushing slide above three further graduated drawers, later alterations and restored, 67in (171.5cm) high.
£4,500–5,500 RTo

A George III mahogany chest-on-chest, the top with pendant frieze, over two short and three long graduated drawers, the base with three long graduated drawers, with ivory escutcheons and later brass handles, 42in (106.5cm) wide.
£4,000–4,500 DA

I A George II walnut chest-on-chest, the three short and three long graduated drawers flanked by fluted canted corners, the lower section with a brushing slide and four further graduated drawers, c1740, 43in (109cm) wide.
£17,000–20,000 Bon

II A George II walnut chest-on-chest, the three short and three long graduated drawers and brushing slide flanked by reeded canted corners, the base with three further long graduated drawers, c1740, 43in (111cm) wide.
£6,000–7,000 Bon

> **Price Guide**
> these are worked out by a team of trade and auction house experts, and are based on actual prices realised. Remember that Miller's is a price guide not a price list and prices are affected by many variables such as location, condition, desirability and so on. Don't forget that if you are selling it is quite likely you will be offered less than the price range. Price ranges for items sold at auction tend to include the buyer's premium and VAT if applicable.

The quality of construction was the major factor which determined the different prices these two chests achieved in the saleroom. Item I was made in London and displays the superior skills of a cabinet-maker trained in the capital, who would have had a wealthier clientele and would therefore be able to use the best materials. It is constructed of oak, and the veneers consist of single sheets of walnut. It also has superbly crafted drawer linings and beautiful dovetailing. Item II is a provincial piece and, whilst attractive and competently constructed, it is less desirable because of its pine carcase with section veneers consisting of three or four pieces of walnut. Of equal importance is the fact that Item I retains its glorious original colour. Furthermore, Item I has a brushing slide and original drawer handles and escutcheons, which Item II lacks.

A George III mahogany chest-on-chest, the two short and three long drawers with oval brass handles, three further drawers below, 44in (112.5cm) wide.
£1,700–2,000 Bri

A George III mahogany chest-on-chest, with blind-fret frieze drawer, over two short and three long drawers with a further blind-fret drawer in the waist, the base with three long drawers, 45in (116cm) wide.
£4,000–4,500 TEN

Further Reading
Miller's Collecting Furniture: The Facts at Your Fingertips, Miller's Publications, 1995.

A George III mahogany secretaire chest-on-chest, the two short and two long drawers with secretaire drawer below, the base with three graduated drawers, 45in (116cm) wide.
£3,500–4,200 P(NW)

A George III mahogany chest-on-chest, the top with two short and three long drawers with brass handles, flanked by inlaid canted corners, 45in (114.5cm) wide.
£1,650–2,000 AH

> **Further Reading**
> directs the reader towards additional sources of information.

A late George III mahogany chest-on-chest, with two short and six long graduated drawers, the top section decorated with inlaid satinwood crossbanding, featherbanding and shell motifs with canted corners, with embossed brass handles, 44in (112cm) wide.
£1,000–1,200 AG

A George III mahogany chest-on-chest, with fluted canted corners and original handles, 36in (91.5cm) wide.
£2,000–2,200 Odi

Japanning
- Developed mid-17thC in imitation of Chinese and Japanese lacquer, which was very costly, scarce and in great demand.
- Main ingredient was shellac (an encrustation of insects which feed on the sap of trees in India and Thailand), seed-lac or gum-lac, which was dissolved in alcohol and then applied in numerous coats and usually decorated with gilt chinoiserie.
- Japanning became a popular pastime for young ladies during the late 17th and early 18thC.
- The technique was fashionable in the first half of the Victorian period for small pieces of furniture, trays, jugs, etc. Decoration often included British flowers such as roses and forget-me-nots.

Chests-on-Chests • FURNITURE 93

Caption
provides a brief description of the item including the maker's name, medium, year it was made and in some cases condition.

Information Box
covers relevant collecting information on factories, makers, care and restoration, fakes and alterations.

Source Code
refers to the Key to Illustrations on page 789 that lists the details of where the item was photographed.

21

British Dates & Periods

DATE	MONARCH	PERIOD
1558–1603	Elizabeth I	Elizabethan
1603–25	James I	Jacobean
1625–49	Charles I	Carolean
1649–60	Commonwealth	Cromwellian
1660–85	Charles II	Restoration
1685–89	James II	Restoration
1689–94	William & Mary	William & Mary
1694–1702	William III	William III
1702–14	Anne	Queen Anne
1714–27	George I	Early Georgian
1727–60	George II	Georgian
1760–1812	George III	Late Georgian
1812–20	George III	Regency
1820–30	George IV	Late Regency
1830–37	William IV	William IV
1837–1901	Victoria	Victorian
1901–10	Edward VII	Edwardian

Introduction

Towards the end of the last century, much talk centred on how our perception of antiques and collectables would change as we moved into the new one. I do not think we are yet far enough into this century to really feel like 21st century people, but to my mind there is already a marked trend in antique buying that has in fact been apparent for the past decade or so – simply that 'anything goes'.

A case in point is 1950s style, which for many of those who lived through that decade will seem like a contradiction in terms. But for a few years now the furniture and furnishings of that era have been viewed as a distinct area of design and have been researched and collected as such. A relatively short time ago any affection, let alone admiration, for the output of that time would have been dismissed as at worst bad taste and at best nostalgia. Much the same goes for the 1960s, and now even the 1970s is being collected and taken seriously by some. One man's skip fodder is another's design classic, a point vividly brought home to me at a recent sale in New York when a 1943 plywood construction by Charles and Ray Eames sold to a collector for $330,000, and designer furniture of the 1970s was fetching up to $15,000.

Post-war design is very much a field to explore. Already firmly established in Holland and the United States where there are specialist major fairs, this area of interest is picking up fast in this country and although there have been some specialist fairs there is still plenty available at keen prices at some of the showground events.

Interestingly, recent months have seen a marked resurgence of interest in items from the turn of the previous century, the years of around 1880 to the First World War which encompassed Art Nouveau and Arts and Crafts, the latter having become particularly potent on the market of late. Moreover, Art Deco is now often making stratospheric prices, especially for choice pieces of furniture, but is still accessible with shopping around.

When serious popular interest in antiques took off in the later 1960s and 1970s it was then a very different collecting world. Antiques fairs were not the ubiquitous phenomenon they now are and those that were staged often had a dateline of 1837, the accession of Queen Victoria. Victorian furniture was not highly regarded, and Edwardian was shipped out of the country by the container-load.

Now, 18th- and much 19th-century walnut and mahogany is not just at a premium, pieces of quality have almost priced themselves out of the market. As Victorian antiques get more expensive, so periods nearer to our time become increasingly acceptable as areas to collect. Edwardian furniture is a very good buy indeed and is understandably popular, but that too is getting expensive, although for your money you do get handsome, very well made pieces which probably represent as good an investment as many can afford when buying furniture.

If one is chasing bargains in furniture it is worth looking at some more quirky areas. One that I have noticed taking off in the last year is bamboo furniture: this first found favour as part of the vogue for Orientalism at the end of the 18th century and by the 1870s there was a thriving manufacturing industry centred on the Midlands and France. Tastes veered away in the 1920s but enough had been made to ensure that there is still plenty around – you can find examples from around £100 and do not have to go over £2,000. I am not the only one to have noted that increasingly at fairs, shops and auctions the buying of antiques is becoming a matter of shopping rather than connoisseurship. And there is nothing wrong with that. This is in part due to the increasing influence of the interior decorator on the antiques world, and no longer do buyers feel restricted by period or style. Be the look country house, minimalist, retro or shabby chic, feel free to mix and match as you please. The results can be stunning.

The rising interest in affordable contemporary art has been staggering over the past few years and modern work can look totally at home in an environment of country furniture and traditional antiques. Similarly contemporary pottery looks most effective when mixed with antiquities (still an underpriced area) or even icons or tribal art. All these subjects, and more, can be found in *Miller's Antiques Price Guide*.

So, one need never feel inhibited by buying a one-off that takes your fancy. Just buy what you like, and hang having to buy a load of other items to complete a conventional collection or decor. Invent your own look. However, the oldest advice is still the best – whatever you buy make sure it is the best quality you can afford.

As tastes and appreciation become ever wider there has never been a more rewarding time to buy – choice is fun and antiques are increasingly an expression of the individual's personality. This brings me to the question of buying on the web. Use it as a tool to see what is around, and certainly use it to buy a limited edition or something you must have in order to complete a collection, but for anything of lasting value that you cherish, that reflects something of yourself, then there is no substitute for touching and feeling. **David Moss**

BaCa

BRITISH antiques and collectables awards

presented by

MILLER'S

In association with

B B C HOMES & ANTIQUES MAGAZINE

Celebrating the Winners of the First Annual BACA

BACA was created to celebrate the outstanding qualities across the enormous range of goods and services that make up the world of Antiques and Collectables. The previous 12 months of planning for this event culminated in a wonderful evening of champagne and applause on Tuesday 20th June 2000 at Grosvenor House, Park Lane, London. Our second Awards will be held in June 2001 and will follow along the lines established this year.

Nominations – Who Can Vote? Who can be nominated?

Anybody from the leisure Collector to a member of the Trade itself can make a nomination for any number of the Awards in any of the categories.

How to Vote for 2001

The voting process for the 2001 Awards begins now and will end in March 2001. For a voting form, please apply to:

BACA/Miller's
2-4 Heron Quays
London E14 4JP
www.baca-awards.co.uk

The ideas, support and interest we have received for BACA have given these Awards a fascinating start and we would be very interested to hear more from you on the subject of new Categories and new Awards – but most importantly of course, we want your vote!

PROUDLY SPONSORED BY

The BACA *Winners...*

CATEGORY 1
General Antiques Dealer

LONDON *sponsored by* **Invaluable**
Patricia Harvey
42 Church Street, Marylebone,
London NW8 8ED

ENGLAND *sponsored by* **Invaluable**
Witney Antiques
96-100 Corn Street, Witney, Oxfordshire
OX8 7BU

WALES
Country Antiques
Castle Mill, Kidwelly, Carmarthen,
Wales SA17 4UW

SCOTLAND
Georgian Antiques
Pattinson Street, Leith, Edinburgh EH6 7HF

NORTHERN IRELAND
MacHenry Antiques of Jordanstown
Newtown Abbey,
BT37 0RY

CATEGORY 2
Specialist Antiques Dealers

FURNITURE
Avon Antiques
25-27 Market Street, Bradford on Avon,
Wiltshire BA15 1LL

CERAMICS *sponsored by*
Jonathan Horne
66c Kensington Church Street,
London W8 4BY

**CLOCKS, WATCHES &
BAROMETERS**
Derek Roberts
25 Shipbourne Road, Tonbridge,
Kent TN10 3DN

DECORATIVE ARTS
New Century
69 Kensington Church Street,
London W8 4BG

SILVER AND PLATE *sponsored by*
Marks Antiques
49 Curzon Street,
London W1Y 7RE

GLASS
Jeanette Hayhurst
32a Kensington Church Street,
London W8 4HA

COLLECTABLES
sponsored by **Invaluable**
Cobwebs
78 Northam Road, Southhampton SO14 0PB

ORIENTAL
S. Marchant & Sons
120 Kensington Church Street,
London W8

JEWELLERY
Wartski Ltd
14 Grafton Street, London W1X 4DE

CATEGORY 3
Auction Houses

LONDON *sponsored by* **Invaluable**
Christie's South Kensington
85 Old Brompton Road, London SW7 3LD

ENGLAND *sponsored by* **Invaluable**
Drewatt Neate
Donnington Priory, Donnington, Newbury,
Berkshire RG13 2JE

WALES
Wingetts
29 Holt Street, Wrexham,
North Wales LL13 8DH

SCOTLAND
Lyon & Turnbull
33 Broughton Place, Edinburgh EH1 3RR

NORTHERN IRELAND
Temple Auctions
133 Carryduff Road, Temple,
Lisburn BT27 6YL

CATEGORY 4
Associated Awards

FAIR OF THE YEAR AWARD
sponsored by *www.Antiquesweb.co.uk*
BADA
British Antiques Dealers Association
20 Rutland Gate,
London SW7 1BD

**ANTIQUES PERSONALITY
OF THE YEAR** *sponsored by* **HOMES & ANTIQUES** MAGAZINE
Henry Sandon

**BEST ANTIQUES TOWN/
VILLAGE** *sponsored by* **MILLER'S CLUB**
Brighton – East Sussex

Furniture

Having dealt in antiques for the last 25 years, there is one significant word that crops up every year without fail – 'quality'. I have never advised any of my clients to buy simply for investment, but rather to buy a piece because they love it and can afford it. However, it is essential to be prepared to pay a fair price rather than falling for a bargain which could turn out to be a mistake. Due in part to the incredible media interest in collecting antiques, the market is being driven ever upwards. It is a sad fact that for most people 17th-, 18th- and the finest early 19th-century furniture has become a rare and expensive commodity. Most of the best known cabinet-makers' pieces of the 18th century are now in private collections or museums.

During the Victorian era (1837–1901), the wealthy merchants who were colonizing the world were returning to this country with vast fortunes and wished to furnish their new houses in opulent style. The insatiable demand during the mid- to late 19th century for furniture inevitably led to a decline in quality as cabinet-makers cut corners to produce items quickly.

Those lucky enough to have bought good period walnut or early Georgian mahogany over the last few years have bought themselves a piece of disappearing history – although possibly having had to pay more than they anticipated (they will not regret this). These fine pieces, if absolutely 'right', are becoming harder and harder to find and are appreciating at an alarming rate.

For those without such deep pockets there is a sound reason for buying Edwardian furniture, which officially becomes 'antique' during this decade. From around 1900, people once again demanded better quality and retailers such as Edwards & Roberts began producing beautifully made revival pieces that are popular with collectors today as they are still affordable. The Edwardian Sheraton-style mahogany display cabinet on page 42, valued at £1,300–1,600, represents incredible value, as does the Edwardian bedroom suite on page 120 at £2,000–2,400. It makes sense to buy these suites and consider splitting them up within the house – one could hardly buy the veneers at that price today, let alone make them into items of furniture.

In the dining room there has been a big demand for early 20th-century mahogany Adam-style serving tables and sideboards with carvings of urns, swags and harebells. These pieces sell well as they are of solid construction and are therefore suited to everyday use. **Edward Reily Collins**

BEDS

A mahogany and cane cradle, hung from a ring-turned stand, early 19thC, 46in (117cm) wide.
£600–700 EH

A pair of Biedermeier ebonized fruitwood beds, probably Austrian, with scrolled headboards and footboards, on outswept feet, 1825–40, 37½in (95.5cm) wide.
£2,200–2,600 NOA

A William IV mahogany half-tester bed, the figured footboard with turned pilasters, bun finials and turned feet, 1830–37, 58in (147cm) wide.
£1,500–1,800 M&K

◄ A George IV mahogany four-poster bed, the posts carved with acanthus, spiral-turned and part ebonized, with associated headboard, c1830, 60in (152.5cm) wide.
£2,200–2,600 G(T)

▶ A Victorian brass double bedstead, with tubular rails and ball finials, 54in (137cm) wide.
£750–900 DD

Miller's Compares

I An American Federal mahogany carved four-poster bed, the reeded tapering posts with carved foliage above stylized pineapple carving, with accompanying tester, 19thC, 52¼in (133cm) wide.
£6,000–6,750 SK(B)

II An American Federal mahogany four-poster bed, the shaped headboard joined to the foot posts by rails fitted for roping and flat tester frame, refinished, early 19thC, 58in (147cm) wide.
£1,300–1,500 SK(B)

A Victorian mahogany half-tester bed, with panelled footboard and projecting canopy, restored, c1875, 48in (122cm) wide.
£2,300–2,600 NAW

Although these beds are similar in design and date, Item I is the more desirable because of the quality of craftsmanship. It has an attractively shaped headboard, compared with the plain example on Item II, and reeded and ribbon-tied posts on pineapple stands. The posts on Item II are simply reeded with no further decoration and, whilst appealing in its simplicity, this bed would be unlikely to attain the price of a piece such as Item I.

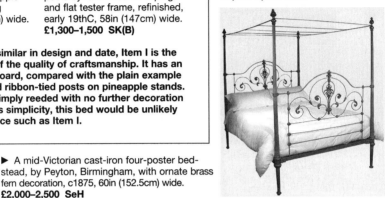

▶ A mid-Victorian cast-iron four-poster bed-stead, by Peyton, Birmingham, with ornate brass fern decoration, c1875, 60in (152.5cm) wide.
£2,000–2,500 SeH

A brass four-poster bedstead, by Lord, Birmingham, with cast crown and canopy, decorative cast plaques in front and back panels, c1880, 54in (137cm) wide.
£3,000–3,500 SeH

A late Victorian brass-mounted iron double bedstead, enamelled black, with rose-decorated porcelain ornaments to the foot, 56in (147cm) wide.
£500–600 PFK

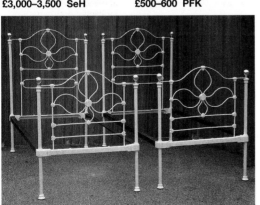

A pair of Victorian cast-iron single bedsteads, restored, c1880, 36in (91.5cm) wide.
£1,200–1,500 SeH

A Victorian brass and iron bedstead, with brass rosettes and porcelain decoration, c1895, 54in (137cm) wide.
£800–1,000 SeH

A French Napoleon III bronze-mounted boulle marquetry bedstead, the headboard flanked by gilt-bronze covered urns, the side rails fitted with gilt-bronze leaf tip borders and bearded masks, mid-19thC, 47in (119cm) wide.
£2,200–2,600 S(NY)

An Empire-style mahogany bedstead, the headboard flanked by swans on parcel-gilt columnar supports, the side rails and footboard decorated with gilt-bronze foliage, the columnar end supports topped by star-studded spheres, late 19thC, 66in (168cm) wide.
£18,000–20,000 S(NY)

The flamboyance of this bed would appeal particularly to decorators and this no doubt explains the price it achieved in the saleroom.

Cross Reference
See Colour Review

An eastern European wrought-iron four-poster single bed, c1880, 36in (91.5cm) wide.
£650–750 CF

A pair of French Louis XVI-style white-painted beds, with padded bedheads and footboards within moulded frames between fluted bulbous uprights, c1900, 44in (112cm) wide.
£1,100–1,200 P

► A French cane and painted bed, restored, c1900, 54in (137cm) wide.
£1,800–2,000 NAW

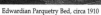

An oak bed, with carved and inlaid headboard and footboard, 1920s, 55¼in (140cm) wide.
£600–700 OOLA

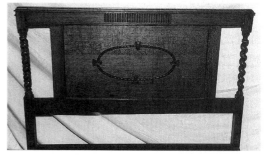

An oak bed, with carved decoration and barley-twist pillars, with footboard, 1920s, 55¼in (140cm) wide.
£450–550 OOLA

BENCHES

A Regency black-painted and parcel-gilt caned bench, with central painted panel depicting musical trophies, repaired, 1800–25, 37½in (95cm) wide.
£9,000–10,000 S(NY)

An early Victorian satinwood child's bench, with pierced ends, 21in (53.5cm) wide.
£900–1,100 NOA

A pair of Victorian mahogany and ebonized hall benches, in the manner of C. H. Tatham, the curved ends with turned ebonized roundels, 60in (152cm) wide.
£11,000–12,000 P

BONHEURS DU JOUR

▶ A Victorian burr-walnut bonheur du jour, inlaid throughout with foliate arabesques and applied with gilt-brass foliate mounts, the superstructure with mirrored recess and drawer flanked by two glazed doors, the sloping flap enclosing a fitted interior, 36¼in (92cm) wide.
£1,750–2,000 Bea(E)

A gilt-bronze-mounted mahogany and satinwood bonheur du jour, the upper section with a marble top above glazed doors revealing a shelved interior, the lower section with a sliding writing surface and single drawer, c1860, 31½in (78.5cm) wide.
£5,000–5,500 S(NY)

A Sheraton-style figured mahogany and satinwood-banded bonheur du jour, the superstructure with three stationery drawers flanked by twin cupboards, over a frieze drawer with brass oval handles, 19thC, 27½in (70cm) wide.
£1,150–1,400 Bri

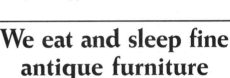

An Edwardian mahogany bonheur du jour, the raised back with two short and two long drawers flanked by a pair of cupboards with shell inlay, the hinged writing surface with long drawer under, 30in (76cm) wide.
£2,200–2,600 RBB

An Edwardian Sheraton-style rosewood bonheur du jour/work table, with boxwood line and inlaid floral motifs, the raised back with central cupboard and two small drawers, inset writing surface, fitted drawer, and tapering slide-out sewing bag, 27½in (70cm) wide.
£900–1,100 JM

BOOKCASES

A George III mahogany bookcase, the upper part fitted with adjustable shelves enclosed by a pair of moulded glazed panelled doors, the lower part enclosed by a pair of fielded panelled doors, 35in (89cm) wide.
£3,500–4,200 P(E)

A late George III mahogany breakfront library bookcase, with two pairs of astragal-glazed doors, the base with four panelled doors, each veneered with an oval, 89in (226cm) wide.
£11,500–13,500 Bea(E)

A mahogany bookcase, in the manner of Gillows, the raised superstructure with a three-quarter gallery and three graduating shelves, held by lobed reeded turned twin supports, the lower section with a pair of twin panelled cupboard doors, c1805, 57¼in (145.5cm) wide.
£8,500–10,000 Bon

A George III mahogany breakfront bookcase, the lower part with panelled cupboard doors enclosing shelves, late 18thC, 81½in (207cm) wide.
£5,000–6,000 BB(L)

A Gothic-style mahogany bookcase, with a pair of glazed and Gothic moulded trimmed doors with brass trim, flanked by narrow reeded pilasters with trefoil terminals forming cupboards, on a conforming outset base with panelled doors, and flanked by similar reeded cupboards, early 19thC, 73½in (186.5cm) wide.
£5,000–6,000 HOK

A Regency mahogany bookcase/cabinet, inlaid with ebonized arrow and dot decoration, the arched astragal-glazed doors enclosing three shelves, the lower part containing two short drawers above a pair of crossbanded panel doors, 48½in (123cm) wide.
£2,500–3,000 P

A George III mahogany breakfront library bookcase, the four astragal-glazed doors enclosing adjustable shelves, with four crossbanded panel doors below, faults, restored, c1800, 97in (246.5cm) wide.
£13,000–15,000 S(S)

A mahogany bookcase, with glazed doors on a projecting base with two panelled doors, early 19thC, 38½in (98cm) wide.
£3,000–3,500 P(L)

An American Federal mahogany bookcase, the glazed doors opening to an interior of three beaded shelves above a cupboard with a single shelf, early 19thC, 53in (134.5cm) wide.
£3,000–3,500 SK(B)

A late George III mahogany bookcase, inlaid with boxwood stringing, with astragal-glazed doors above, panelled doors below, 48in (122cm) wide.
£2,700–3,200 AG

A faux rosewood bookcase, with latticework glazed doors and two frieze drawers, two further cupboard doors below, early 19thC, 41½in (105.5cm) wide.
£4,000–5,000 TF

A William IV mahogany bookcase, the later pediment above a pair of astragal-glazed doors flanked by pilasters with lotus leaf capitals, the lower section with two frieze drawers above a pair of panelled cupboard doors, 57½in (146cm) wide.
£1,200–1,500 Bon(M)

An early Victorian mahogany bookcase, in two sections, with astragal-glazed doors flanked by half round columns, and enclosing a series of green baize-lined shelves, the base with a long serpentine-fronted drawer above a pair of cupboard doors with applied figured mahogany-veneered panels, flanked by half round pillars, 57in (149cm) wide.
£3,000–3,300 Mit

An Edwardian mahogany and satinwood cross-banded cabinet bookcase, inlaid with stringing and Tunbridge ware panels, the two astragal-glazed cupboard doors enclosing adjustable shelves, the lower section with a pair of foliate and trophy inlaid panelled cupboard doors, c1910, 31½in (80cm) wide.
£2,000–2,400 S(S)

▶ A Queen Anne-style walnut domed cabinet, enclosed by two glazed doors above four long drawers, early 20thC, 40½in (103cm) wide.
£2,000–2,400 RTo

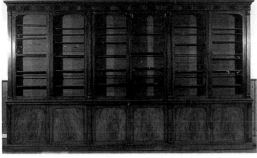

A flame-mahogany bookcase, in the style of Williams & Gibton, fitted with three pairs of arched glazed doors divided by flat pilasters with lotus leaf embellishments, the conforming outset base with panelled doors, c1840, 76¾in (195cm) wide.
£10,500–12,500 HOK

An Edwardian mahogany bookcase, with two astragal-glazed doors, on a base with an arrangement of five drawers, 27½in (70cm) wide.
£800–1,000 DN

A Victorian pollard oak and oak library bookcase, with two arched glazed panelled doors, enclosing adjustable shelves, and two panelled doors below with arrangements for adjustable shelves, 49½in (125.5cm) wide.
£900–1,100 HAM

◀ A late Victorian mahogany bookcase, the upper part fitted with four adjustable shelves enclosed by a pair of glazed doors, the cupboard under enclosed by a pair of raised panelled doors, 48in (122cm) wide.
£1,500–1,800 CAG

BUREAU BOOKCASES

A mahogany bureau bookcase, the swan-neck pierced and moulded cornice above a pierced Gothic arched frieze, astragal-glazed doors enclosing three shelves, fall-front enclosing four pigeonholes, six short drawers and a long drawer, with four long graduated drawers below, the base an early George III bureau, the top section of later date, 46in (117cm) wide.
£7,500–9,000 P

A George III mahogany bureau bookcase, the astragal-glazed doors enclosing adjustable shelves, the part-mitred fall-front enclosing a central cupboard door and stepped semi-secret shallow drawer flanked by half columns, pigeon-holes and stepped drawers, over four long graduated drawers with pierced brass lock plates, 42in (106.5cm) wide.
£2,800–3,200 Hal

A Regency mahogany bureau bookcase, with an ogee-moulded cornice and lancet frieze, a pair of panelled glazed doors, the fall-front enclosing a fitted interior of pigeonholes and shallow drawers, with three graduated drawers below, 40in (101.5cm) wide.
£2,000–2,400 BIG

A George III mahogany bureau bookcase, with two astragal-glazed doors enclosing shelves, the fall-front enclosing a fitted interior of divisions and small drawers flanking a cupboard, all above four long graduated and cockbeaded drawers with brass swan-neck drop handles, restorations, 32½in (82.5cm) wide.
£1,800–2,200 HAM

Marriages

To determine whether two- or three-part case furniture has been made up from different pieces, pay particular attention to:
- the colour, grain and quality of the timber, particularly on the sides. Backboards should closely resemble one another, both in the timber used and in the construction.
- the drawers, which should display the same constructional characteristics in all sections, ie the dovetails should be the same, and screws used in holding backboards should be identical.
- the junction of the sections – a loose fit may indicate a marriage.
- the veneer, which should not extend far beyond where the base meets the top when the latter is removed.
- indications of the use of additional moulding, intended to widen the top to correspond with the base.
- the overall appearance of the item. Married furniture is often out of proportion, showing a visual imbalance between the joined parts. All sections of a genuine piece should display stylistic union, and decorative embellishments should be identical in both design and execution.

A cylinder bureau book-case, the two glazed doors enclosing fitted shelves, above a cylinder front enclosing bird's-eye maple drawers, over two panelled doors, 19thC, 48in (122cm) wide.
£1,300–1,600 AAV

▶ An Edwardian mahogany and satinwood banded bureau bookcase, with astragal-glazed doors, the fall-front enclosing a fitted interior, with three long drawers below, faults, 35½in (90cm) wide.
£750–900 S(S)

Cross Reference
See Colour Review

▶ An Edwardian inlaid mahogany bureau bookcase, with feathered stringing, the astragal-glazed doors enclosing adjustable shelves, the fall-front with inlaid satinwood medallion and enclosing pigeonholes and a small drawer, above three graduated drawers with brass handles, 27½in (69.5cm) wide.
£600–700 PFK

OPEN BOOKCASES

A pair of Regency giltwood open bookcases, with *verde antico* marble tops, the gadroon-moulded friezes above open shelves flanked by fluted pilasters, c1810, 61¼in (155.5cm) wide.
£1,500–1,800 S

A Victorian rosewood open bookcase, the three-quarter galleried protruding top on wrythen-turned supports, 57in (145cm) wide.
£1,100–1,300 AH

▶ An Edwardian inlaid mahogany open bookcase, with harewood and boxwood ribbon and bellflower swags and wreath, framed by chequered stringing, above two shelves and a pair of cupboard doors with similar stringing, above an undershelf, 25in (63.5cm) wide.
£450–550 PFK

An early Victorian mahogany breakfront bookcase, the open front with adjustable shelves, 71½in (181.5cm) wide.
£900–1,100 L

> Miller's is a price GUIDE not a price LIST

An ebonized and parcel-gilt open bookcase, the superstructure with a pierced three-quarter brass gallery, on a shelf with turned supports and adjustable shelves below, 19thC, 71in (180.5cm) wide.
£450–550 MEA

A satinwood and mahogany-banded open bookcase, with four adjustable shelves between fluted pilasters, bearing the label of Richardson & Sons, Hull, dated '1884', 56¾in (144cm) wide.
£1,600–2,000 TEN

Richardson & Sons were prominent cabinet-makers in Hull from 1814.

REVOLVING BOOKCASES

A William IV mahogany revolving bookstand, with four graduated circular tiers mounted with *faux* leather-bound books, raised on later animal paw feet, probably reduced in height, 29in (73.5cm) diam.
£5,000–6,000 S(NY)

An Edwardian mahogany revolving bookcase, with slatted sides, c1910, 18in (45.5cm) wide.
£550–650 NAW

A padouk wood revolving bookcase, the baluster galleried top above open shelves with moulded lattice sides, the cruciform base with open brackets, early 20thC, 19¾in (50cm) wide.
£800–900 S

SECRETAIRE BOOKCASES

An early George III mahogany secretaire bookcase, with later swan-neck pediment above a pair of astragal-glazed doors enclosing a pair of shelves, the secretaire panelled drawer enclosing pigeonholes and drawers, above two short and two long graduated drawers, 45¼in (115cm) wide.
£5,000–6,000 P

A George III mahogany and rosewood-inlaid secretaire bookcase, the astragal-glazed doors enclosing shelves, the single drawer enclosing later drawers and pigeonholes, an open shelf below, 77½in (197cm) high.
£9,000–11,000 P(S)

A George III fiddleback mahogany secretaire bookcase, the astragal-glazed doors enclosing shelves, the fall-front opening to a fitted interior, above three oak-lined drawers, 46in (117cm) wide.
£2,600–3,200 WILL

A George III mahogany secretaire bookcase, the astragal-glazed doors enclosing adjustable shelves, the fall-front opening to a fitted interior of drawers and pigeonholes around a cupboard door, with three graduated drawers below, the bookcase section later, two parts associated, 46½in (118cm) wide.
£4,500–5,500 Bon

A George III mahogany secretaire bookcase, the astragal-glazed doors enclosing adjustable shelves, the dummy drawer fall-flap enclosing a fitted interior with drawers and pigeonholes, above three graduated drawers, 43¼in (110cm) wide.
£3,300–4,000 SWO

A late George III mahogany secretaire bookcase, the astragal-glazed crossbanded doors enclosing three shelves, the base with crossbanded fall-front enclosing pigeonholes, drawers and central cupboard, above two panelled doors, 41in (104cm) wide.
£1,650–2,000 JM

A William IV mahogany secretaire bookcase, the glazed doors enclosing adjustable shelves, the panelled fall-front enclosing a fitted interior of drawers and pigeon-holes, above two flame-mahogany doors flanked by turned tapering pillars, 36in (91.5cm) wide.
£3,600–4,200 WW

A late Victorian pollard oak secretaire bookcase, the glazed doors enclosing adjustable shelves, the base with secretaire drawer enclosing drawers and pigeonholes, above fielded panelled cupboard doors, the whole with stiff-leaf carved pilasters, 48¾in (124cm) wide.
£900–1,100 P(NW)

▶ A Victorian mahogany breakfront secretaire book-case, with three arched glazed doors enclosing adjustable shelves, the secretaire drawer with birch-lined interior, a later additional wing on either side with glazed doors above a drawer and cupboards, 161in (409cm) wide.
£7,500–9,000 AH

▶ A mahogany secretaire bookcase, the astragal-glazed doors enclosing three shelves, the base with secretaire drawer, above two arched panelled doors, 19thC, 47½in (120.5cm) wide.
£1,300–1,600 AH

BUCKETS

A Dutch spindle bucket, with brass rim and handle, c1790, 13in (33cm) high.
£1,750–1,950 CAT

An Irish mahogany spiral-ribbed and brass-bound plate bucket, with swing handle, c1800, 14½in (37cm) diam.
£2,500–3,000 HOK

◄ A mahogany and brass-bound bucket, with bail handle and brass liner, 19thC, 12½in (32cm) high.
£550–650 CGC

A George III mahogany and brass-bound peat bucket, with swing handle, 14¼in (36cm) diam.
£1,200–1,400 TEN

◄ A George III coopered mahogany and brass-bound peat bucket, with brass half-liner and swing handle, 14¼in (36cm) diam.
£1,200–1,400 TEN

A George III mahogany and brass-bound peat bucket, with reeded border and brass handle, 18in (45.5cm) high.
£850–1,000 DN

BUFFETS

A mahogany and satinwood-banded telescopic three-tier buffet, inlaid with stringing, the rising top revealing a lower tier above a panel drawer, c1825, 59in (150cm) wide.
£1,600–2,000 S(S)

A French Louis Philippe mahogany metamorphic buffet, the hinged top opening to form a back gallery with folding shelves, above two drawers, the lotus-carved columns bisected by a central shelf, mid-19thC, 61½in (156cm) wide.
£4,500–5,500 NOA

A Victorian mahogany buffet, the arched superstructure surmounted by a foliate scroll-carved cartouche with central carved hound's head, the central panel with a relief-carved hunting trophy, the top with two frieze drawers with flowerhead carved pulls, the undertier on baluster legs and leaf-carved feet, some moulding replaced, 65¾in (167cm) wide.
£3,200–3,800 P

This buffet is likely to have been made for a hunting lodge.

An Edwardian mahogany buffet/serving table, the raised back with brass rail, with two frieze drawers, open shelf and cupboards below with moulded doors, 54in (137cm) wide.
£775–900 DD

An oak buffet, by Moore & Hunton, maker's brand plate, c1880, 34in (86.5cm) wide.
£525–585 NET

► A Victorian mahogany three-tier buffet, each tier with a gallery and supported by reeded columns, raised on turned supports terminating in casters, 54in (137cm) wide.
£700–850 AAV

BUREAUX

A George I walnut and herringbone-banded bureau, the lipped fall-front with fitted interior of small drawers and divisions flanking a cupboard, above two short and three long drawers, with brass drop handles, 34in (86.5cm) wide.
£1,600–2,000 HAM

A George II walnut and featherbanded bureau, the fall-front enclosing drawers and pigeonholes above a well, above two short and two long drawers, restored, c1730, 36¼in (92cm) wide.
£7,000–8,500 Bon

A George II mahogany bureau, the fall-front enclosing drawers and pigeonholes, above two short and three long drawers with brass handles, 39in (99cm) wide.
£1,300–1,500 DN

▶ A George III mahogany bureau, crossbanded with string inlay, the fall-front enclosing drawers and pigeonholes, above four graduated drawers with brass drop handles, 34in (86.5cm) wide.
£1,000–1,200 AH

Miller's Compares

I A walnut and featherbanded bureau, the fall-front enclosing a fitted interior with well, small drawers, pigeonholes and central cupboard, above two short and three long drawers, later bracket feet, restored, c1720, 30in (76cm) wide.
£12,000–14,000 S(S)

II A walnut and featherbanded bureau, the fall-front with a later inset writing surface, the interior a well, small drawers and pigeonholes, above two short and two long drawers, on later bracket feet, restored, c1720, 25in (63.5cm) wide.
£5,750–7,000 S(S)

Item I has more 'presence' than Item II, perhaps due to its greater width, although in general the smaller piece would be the more desirable today to fit into modern houses. The moulding around the upper section of Item I, which acknowledges that early bureaux were often made in two pieces, is a particularly desirable feature. Although both examples have later bracket feet, those of Item I are more attractively styled. Item I has a richer golden colour than Item II and displays more extensive and pronounced crossbanding, with sophisticated cockbeaded moulding to the borders of the drawer fronts, which Item II lacks.

A George III mahogany bureau, the crossbanded fall-front enclosing a satinwood and tulipwood crossbanded and harewood-inlaid interior, centred by a figured-mahogany cupboard door flanked by foliate inlaid letter slides, pigeonholes, drawers and two semi-secret drawers, above two short and three long drawers with later stamped brass handles, 43in (109cm) wide.
£1,200–1,400 Hal

A George III mahogany and string-inlaid bureau, the fall-front with fitted interior, above four graduated drawers, 42in (106.5cm) wide.
£3,500–4,000 BERA

A late Georgian cherrywood bureau, the fall-front enclosing seven pigeonholes, above four drawers, c1800, 39in (99cm) wide.
£1,200–1,400 ESA

A Georgian mahogany bureau, the fall-front enclosing fitted interior, above four graduated drawers, 38½in (98cm) wide.
£800–950 DDM

An American Federal cherrywood bureau, the fall-front with fitted interior, above a single drawer, some imperfections, Massachusetts, c1800, 38½in (98cm) wide.
£800–900 SK(B)

A Dutch mahogany and marquetry-inlaid bureau, the fall-front with fitted interior, the three graduated drawers between shaped flat half columns, interior incomplete, cracked, veneer losses, 19thC, 42in (106.5cm) wide.
£2,300–2,750 Hal

A George IV mahogany bureau, inlaid with boxwood stringing, the fall-front with fitted interior, above four drawers with original brass handles, 38in (96.5cm) wide.
£2,000–2,200 DD

A Victorian walnut, tulipwood-crossbanded and inlaid lady's bureau, the raised back with central drawer and mirror flanked by glazed doors, above a sloping fall and sliding well, the legs with foliate gilt-metal mounts, 34¼in (87cm) wide.
£1,800–2,200 P(B)

A Victorian mahogany cylinder bureau, the fall-front with pigeonholes flanked by drawers with dummy drawers below, bird's-eye maple veneered with ebonized knob handles, the pull-out writing surface with three hinged flaps, the central one on a ratchet, above pedestals each with three drawers, 59½in (151cm) wide.
£1,000–1,200 WW

An Edwardian inlaid rosewood bureau, the pierced brass gallery above a floral and scroll-inlaid top and cylinder front enclosing pigeonholes, above a pair of frieze drawers, 30¾in (78cm) wide.
£2,000–2,400 P(L)

An Edwardian inlaid mahogany bureau, the fall-front inlaid with a conch shell enclosing a central cupboard, small drawers and pigeonholes, above four graduated drawers, 25¾in (65.5cm) wide.
£750–900 DA

◀ An Edwardian mahogany bureau, marquetry-inlaid with urns and scrolling foliage within satinwood banding, stamped 'Pratt & Son, Guildford', 36in (91.5cm) wide.
£850–1,000 Bea(E)

CABINETS

A Spanish cabinet, veneered in ebony, rosewood, cedar and tortoiseshell, decorated with inlaid and applied metal, the central door enclosing small drawers, flanked by two banks of four drawers, late 17thC, 43¾in (111cm) wide.
£3,000–3,500 TEN

Cross Reference
See Colour Review

A George III mahogany and boxwood-inlaid collector's cabinet, in the manner of Gillows, the hinged lid enclosing two trays above a dummy drawer, the pair of inlaid cupboards enclosing three drawers, on a later stand, the sides with brass carrying handles, c1795, 24in (61cm) wide.
£6,500–7,500 S

A late George III breakfront mahogany cabinet, with astragal doors enclosing adjustable shelves and three small drawers, above three graduated drawers, flanked by full-length panelled doors enclosing pegs for adjustable shelves, now converted to hanging space, 74½in (189cm) wide.
£4,000–4,500 AG

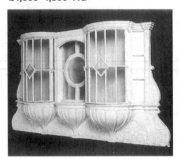

A mahogany collector's cabinet, the hinged top above an arrangement of drawers with a brass pole locking device, early 19thC, 51in (129.5cm) extended.
£550–650 P(B)

A pair of Italian neo-classical black walnut pedestal cabinets, each with a frieze drawer, with reeded columnar supports above hinged cabinet doors, on bun feet, mid-19thC, 18½in (47cm) wide.
£6,250–7,000 S(NY)

A Coalbrookdale cast-iron, glazed and mirrored wall cabinet, the central recessed niche with circular convex mirror within spandrel plates, flanked by four bowfronted display cabinets, on fluted and upswept brackets, c1902, 56¼in (143cm) wide.
£1,300–1,600 TEN

BEDSIDE CABINETS

A pair of George III mahogany bowfronted bedside cabinets, with ebonized stringing, 16in (40.5cm) wide.
£3,500–4,200 S

A George III mahogany bedside cabinet, with tambour door and fitted pull-out front, 19½in (49.5cm) wide.
£1,600–1,750 DN

A George III mahogany bedside cabinet, with pierced and shaped tray top, two doors above pull-out commode drawer, 22in (56cm) wide.
£1,350–1,600 Bea(E)

A pair of French brass-inlaid bedside cupboards, each with a marble top above a tambour shutter, and cupboard doors below, early 19thC, 13¾in (35cm) wide.
£2,700–3,000 P

A George III mahogany bedside cabinet, with pierced hand-grips, drawer handle replaced, 24¼in (61.5cm) wide.
£600–750 WW

A late Georgian mahogany bedside cabinet, with moulded panels to the sides, 18½in (47cm) wide.
£100–120 PFK

Miller's is a price GUIDE not a price LIST

A Regency mahogany low pot cupboard, with ledge back and panel door, 16½in (42cm) wide.
£400–500 P(E)

A French bedside cabinet, with original cream paint and gilt decoration, c1880, 20in (51cm) wide.
£250–300 ESA

BUREAU CABINETS

A George I walnut bureau cabinet, the crossbanded fall-front enclosing a fitted interior, altered and restored, 35½in (90cm) wide.
£3,300–4,000 HAM

A south German/Austrian walnut, ebony-inlaid and parquetry bureau cabinet, panelled with strapwork and geometric motifs, the fall-front with fitted interior, the serpentine lower part with three long drawers, c1735, 51¾in (135cm) wide.
£11,000–12,000 S

A Dutch burr-walnut and walnut bureau cabinet, the fall-front enclosing a fitted interior, above two small and two long drawers, mid-18thC, 46½in (118cm) wide.
£8,500–9,500 S(Am)

A mahogany bureau cabinet, the mirrored doors enclosing adjustable shelves, the base with fall-front enclosing fitted interior, above three short and three long drawers, between canted blind fret corners, 19thC, 49¼in (125cm) wide.
£4,000–4,800 TEN

CABINETS-ON-CHESTS

A William and Mary walnut and floral marquetry cabinet-on-chest, the base with two short and two long drawers, the upper section enclosed by a pair of glazed panel doors, replacement ogee bracket feet, some restoration, 42½in (108cm) high.
£7,000–8,000 P(WM)

A William III cabinet-on-chest, the front veneered in burr-walnut with featherbanding, the pair of doors enclosing shelves, 43in (109cm) wide.
£6,000–7,000 WW

A mahogany cabinet-on-chest, the upper section with two wire grille and fabric panelled doors enclosing shelves, early 19thC, 31in (78.5cm) wide.
£1,250–1,500 Bea(E)

CORNER CABINETS

A mahogany corner cupboard, the broken swan-neck pediment above fielded panelled doors, stop-fluted canted corners, mid-18thC, 50¼in (128cm) wide.
£4,000–5,000 P(B)

A George III mahogany standing corner cupboard, the astragal-glazed doors enclosing a shelved interior, restored, c1780, 41¼in (105cm) wide.
£2,700–3,200 S(S)

A Dutch walnut and floral marquetry standing corner cabinet, the top of shaped outline above a door with flanking elliptical panels, late 18th/early 19thC, 31½in (80cm) wide.
£850–1,000 P(S)

A mahogany bowfront corner cabinet, with boxwood and Tunbridge ware line inlay, early 19thC, 31in (78.5cm) wide.
£500–600 JM

A mahogany bowfront corner cupboard, with acorn and drop bead moulded cornice, a pair of ebony strung crossbanded doors above a central drawer flanked by dummy drawers, early 19thC, 33in (84cm) wide.
£650–800 DN

An inlaid mahogany corner cabinet, the astragal-glazed doors enclosing three shelves, the base with twin panelled doors bordered in satinwood and inlaid with musical trophies, c1900, 40¾in (103.5cm) wide.
£3,500–4,200 Bri

An early George III mahogany standing corner cupboard in two parts, with two panelled doors enclosing shelves, 34in (86.5cm) wide.
£2,700–3,250 DN

A Dutch marquetry bowfront corner cupboard, the walnut veneer inlaid with bunches of flowers and shell foliage scrolls to the tiered shelved superstructure, the top with birds flanking an urn of flowers, the interior with a shelf enclosed by a pair of doors with inlaid oval panels, the side pilasters with pendants of flowers, 19thC, 30½in (77.5cm) wide.
£2,000–2,400 WW

▶ An Edwardian mahogany and inlaid corner cabinet, the upper part with a pair of astragal-glazed doors, the lower part enclosed by panel doors, 34¾in (88.5cm) wide.
£3,200–3,800 P(B)

A George III mahogany serpentine standing corner cabinet, with two pairs of crossbanded cupboard doors, c1795, 38in (96.5cm) wide.
£5,000–6,000 Bon

A Welsh mahogany two-tier corner cupboard, the upper part fitted with three shaped shelves enclosed by a pair of astragal-glazed doors, the base fitted with one real and two dummy frieze drawers above a cupboard enclosed by a pair of arched panelled doors, 19thC, 43in (109cm) wide.
£1,400–1,700 CAG

DISPLAY CABINETS

An Italian kingwood and olive display cabinet, inlaid with kingwood banding, with glazed doors, sections of veneer and moulding missing, Piedmontese, c1750, 51¼in (130cm) wide.
£8,000–9,000 S

A late Victorian mahogany display case, with a pair of glazed doors with wooden astragals enclosing a series of cloth-lined adjustable shelves, the base with foliate scroll carved centre, 51½in (131cm) wide.
£3,750–4,250 Mit

A limed oak display cabinet, the central glazed door and canted sides enclosing glass shelves, above a deep drawer, late 19thC, 79in (200.5cm) high.
£1,800–2,200 DN

▶ A mahogany and inlaid display cabinet, the two glazed doors flanked by crossbanding and line inlay, with detachable side sections, late 19thC, 60in (152.5cm) high.
£900–1,100 AAV

A French kingwood and gilt-metal-mounted vitrine, the frieze centred with winged sphinx between trailing swags, the bevelled glazed doors enclosing three glass shelves, late 19thC, 49¼in (125cm) wide.
£4,200–5,000 P(L)

An Italian Baroque-style ivory and bone-inlaid ebony vitrine, the glazed cupboard doors flanked by string-inlaid tapering cylindrical columns, above panelled cupboard doors, late 19thC, 45¾in (116cm) wide.
£3,300–3,700 BB(L)

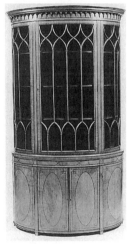

An Edwardian satinwood and ebony-strung bowfront display cabinet, the Gothic-style glazed bowed panelled door flanked by two similar panels, the base fitted with two central oval panelled doors, feet reduced, 46½in (118cm) wide.
£3,500–4,200 P(Sc)

Cross Reference
See Colour Review

◀ An Edwardian mahogany display cabinet, with satinwood crossbanding and ebony stringing, the bowed glazed central section flanked by glazed sections with marquetry panels and Prince of Wales feathers, 49¾in (126cm) wide.
£2,800–3,400 P(Ed)

An Edwardian mahogany display cabinet, with a scroll-carved frieze, twin concave glazed doors, the panelled lower part with carved rosette and garland details, 58¼in (148cm) wide.
£2,300–2,750 WL

An Edwardian mahogany display cabinet, in the Sheraton-revival style, with double astragal-glazed doors enclosing shelves, the lower section of serpentine form with two drawers, the whole having boxwood stringing and satinwood-banded details, 30in (76cm) wide.
£1,300–1,600 PFK

An Edwardian Chippendale-style mahogany display cabinet-on-stand, with twin lancet glazed doors enclosing three shelves, above serpentine-shaped base, 25½in (64.5cm) wide.
£750–900 Bri

An Edwardian Sheraton-style mahogany and marquetry display cabinet, the cornice inlaid with bell-flowers suspended from ribbon-tied bows over a glazed door enclosing shelves, the bowfront base with a single panelled door, 24¼in (61.5cm) wide.
£650–750 HYD

◄ An Edwardian mahogany and inlaid display cabinet, the pair of astragal doors above a pair of panelled doors, 43¼in 110cm) wide.
£500–600 S(S)

An Edwardian mahogany and satinwood-banded display cabinet, inlaid with stringing, the Greek key-cut cornice above a pair of astragal-glazed doors enclosing a lined and shelved interior, 50½in (128cm) wide.
£1,400–1,600 S(S)

An Edwardian mahogany serpentine display cabinet, inlaid in satinwood and ivorine with ribboned wreaths, harebells, urns and classical females with oval reserves, two glazed doors with interior shelves and two doors below, 36¼in (92cm) wide.
£550–650 M

A George V mahogany display cabinet, the frieze with bellflower swags above two glazed doors, 35¾in (91cm) wide.
£500–600 RTo

An Edwardian mahogany boxwood, chequer-strung and inlaid display cabinet, the frieze with inlaid decoration of an urn flanked by swags and ribbons above a central glazed section flanked by a pair of ogee astragal-glazed doors, enclosing three shelves, 52¼in (132.5cm) wide.
£1,350–1,600 P(L)

An Edwardian inlaid mahogany display cabinet, with raised mirrored back, decorated all over with satinwood crossbanding, boxwood stringing and fan motifs, a single drawer to the centre with a pair of panelled doors enclosing a cupboard and open recess below, flanked by a pair of glazed panelled doors enclosing lined shelves, 47⅛in (120.5cm) wide.
£600–700 AG

A mahogany-veneered display cabinet, with glazed doors over two drawers, 1920s, 72in (183cm) high.
£400–500 AAV

MUSIC CABINETS

A Victorian walnut and marquetry music cabinet, the raised mirrored back with bracket shelf, the glazed door with a marquetry panel depicting scrolling foliage centred by a vase, 21in (53.5cm) wide.
£1,100–1,200 AH

A Victorian ebonized music cabinet, with burr-walnut banding, stained boxwood stringing and gilt-brass mounts, the canted corners faced with fluted pilasters, the pair of doors centred by Wedgwood plaques and enclosing shelves, two drawers below, 26½in (67.5cm) wide.
£1,000–1,200 P(Ed)

A Victorian burr-walnut music cabinet, with a cantilevered shelf above a further shelf with mirror back flanked by fluted uprights and pierced scrolling supports, a pair of glazed panelled doors below enclosing shelves, 27in (68.5cm) wide.
£1,000–1,200 AG

A mid-Victorian amboyna-veneered and ebonized music cabinet, in the manner of Holland & Sons, the twin panelled doors each with applied gilt-metal beadwork, enclosing a shelved interior, open section below with traces of dividing slats, 30in (76cm) wide.
£900–1,100 BIG

Miller's is a price GUIDE not a price LIST

◄ An American rococo-revival rosewood music cabinet, the shaped marble top over a conforming cupboard door mounted with a mirror plate with floral carving at its base, mid-19thC, 30in (76cm) wide.
£850–1,000 NOA

SECRETAIRE CABINETS

A walnut and featherbanded escritoire, with a cushion frieze drawer above a fall, enclosing pigeonholes and short drawers around a central door, the top late 17th century, the lower section associated and partly reveneered, 48in (122cm) wide.
£3,400–4,000 P

A Queen Anne walnut and featherbanded secretaire cabinet, the cushion frieze drawer over a fall-front with internal adjustable reading slide, drawers and pigeonholes around a central cupboard, the base with two short and two long drawers, brass drop handles, 48in (122cm) wide.
£3,000–3,500 AH

A William III walnut-veneered fall-front secretaire cabinet, the interior fitted with a central crossbanded cupboard door flanked by drawers with feather-banding, open arcaded compart-ments, with two short and two long drawers, replaced open brass plate handles and escutcheons, 36in (91.5cm) wide.
£4,000–5,000 WW

A George I walnut escritoire, the cushion drawer over a line-inlaid quarter-veneered fall-front enclosing a writing surface and fitted interior, a central door enclosing three small drawers with six removable pigeonholes, flanked by drawers to either side, over two short and two long drawers, 36in (91.5cm) wide.
£5,500–6,500 P(NW)

A walnut secretaire cabinet, with cushion frieze drawer, the fall-front with matched figured veneered panels, fitted interior with secret drawers with figured veneered panels within ebony stringings and banding, some later mouldings and handles, early 18thC, 41in (104cm) wide.
£4,500–5,500 CAG

A French Louis XVI kingwood, tulipwood and purplewood-banded *secrétaire à abattant*, the grey veined marble top with canted corners above a frieze drawer and fall-front enclosing four compartments and six short drawers, above a pair of cupboard doors enclosing a shelf, late 18thC, 36¼in (92cm) wide.
£2,000–2,400 P

A George III mahogany crossbanded and line-inlaid secretaire cabinet, with two flame mahogany doors, lower sections with a satinwood fitted interior, above three long drawers, c1780, 44in (112cm) wide.
£2,000–2,400 WILL

A Dutch mahogany and marquetry-inlaid *secrétaire à abattant*, the frieze drawer above a recessed fall-front enclosing a fitted interior and writing surface, above two doors enclosing a shelf and a concealed drawer, flanked by columns and with two further drawers below, early 19thC, 38½in (98cm) wide.
£2,700–3,250 HAM

A *secrétaire à abattant* has a fall-front writing cabinet over a cupboard or chest of drawers. Fine quality timber was used, often incorporating panels of marquetry or Oriental lacquer.

◄ A Biedermeier mahogany and burrwood secretaire cabinet, the pediment with a central drawer flanked by two small drawers, above a frieze drawer and fall-front opening to reveal a fitted interior and pull-out baize-lined writing slide, above three further drawers, above three long drawers, c1810, 42in (106.5cm) wide.
£5,750–7,000 S

◄ A Continental neo-classical *secrétaire à abattant*, the fall-front enclosing a fitted writing compartment above drawers, mid-19thC, 41¼in (105cm) wide.
£1,300–1,500 SK

SIDE CABINETS

A late Georgian rosewood mirror-back chiffonier, with a long frieze drawer over a cupboard base, part fitted with pull-out linen shelves and enclosed by arched panelled doors flanked by pilasters with fluted capitals, 40in (101.5cm) wide.
£1,400–1,700 TMA

A Regency mahogany side cabinet, with two dummy frieze drawers over two shaped panelled doors enclosing shelving, flanked by ring-turned and tapering pilasters, 37¼in (94.5cm) wide.
£900–1,100 AH

Cross Reference
See Colour Review

A late George III satinwood side cabinet, the top crossbanded in partridge wood, two drawers to the frieze with later brass handles, above two glazed doors backed with pleated celadon-green silk and enclosing adjustable shelves, crossbanded in kingwood, outlined with ebony and boxwood stringing, 42½in (108cm) wide.
£11,000–13,000 HAM

A Regency rosewood side cabinet, with fitted frieze drawer over a pair of panelled doors flanked by half-turned pilasters, with pierced brass gallery and ribbon and husk mounts, 43¼in (110cm) wide.
£700–850 MCA

A rosewood breakfront side cabinet, with open shelves to top part, over central mirrored doors flanked by open mirror-backed ends, stamped 'W & G' for Williams & Gibton, c1825, 96in (244cm) wide.
£2,750–3,000 GKe

◀ A George IV rosewood chiffonier, by Holland & Sons, the shelved and mirror-back with downswept fret-pierced supports above three glazed doors, restored, c1825, 60in (152.5cm) wide.
£4,500–5,000 S(S)

A south German walnut crossbanded and parquetry side cabinet, the shaped top with re-entrant corners above a stellar and lozenge inlaid door enclosing a shelf above an apron drawer, on later bun feet, 18thC, 33½in (85cm) wide.
£2,300–2,750 P

A Regency grained rosewood chiffonier, the shelved superstructure with pierced three-quarter brass gallery on scroll uprights, over a recessed door with brass grille flanked by columns, 34in (86cm) wide.
£1,700–2,000 P(EA)

A Georgian brass-mounted mahogany campaign cabinet, the case with brass corners and inset bail handles on the sides, the interior with 12 pigeonholes, 13 drawers and a central cupboard, raised on later ivory ball feet, 30in (76cm) wide.
£1,750–2,000 NOA

An Irish rosewood low cabinet, with a white marble top, two frieze drawers with applied leaf carving and two doors with printed fabric panels flanked by turned columns, 19thC, 56in (142cm) wide.
£700–800 DN

An early Victorian mahogany chiffonier, the single shelf superstructure with a three-quarter gallery on scrolling pierced brass supports, above a pair of double arched panelled doors, on brass ball feet, 43¼in (110cm) wide.
£1,500–1,800 P

A Victorian walnut-veneered and floral marquetry serpentine-fronted side cabinet, applied with gilt-metal mounts, with a central panelled cupboard door enclosing a shelved interior, glazed panels to either side, 48¾in (124cm) wide.
£2,500–3,000 P(E)

A William IV mahogany chiffonier, the superstructure with a shelf and three-quarter gallery raised on reeded turned supports, the top above a concealed drawer and two panelled doors with beaded outlines, enclosing a shelf, flanked by reeded pilasters, 37in (94cm) wide.
£1,650–2,000 HAM

A Victorian burr-walnut and carved credenza, outlined with ebonized mouldings, the galleried mirror back with a shelf on reeded baluster supports, the flowerheaded-carved frieze above four glazed doors above foliate-carved fluted Corinthian columns, 81½in (207cm) wide.
£6,000–7,000 Bea(E)

A mid-Victorian burr-walnut side cabinet, the shaped top above a central glazed panelled cupboard door, 47½in (120.5cm) wide.
£1,100–1,300 Bon(M)

◄ A Victorian ebonized and amboyna side cabinet, with gilt-metal mounts, the frieze inlaid with stylized plant forms, above two bowed glazed doors enclosing shelves, an inlaid central panelled door, flanked and divided by reeded turned pilasters, damaged, 66¼in (168cm) wide.
£1,100–1,300 S(S)

An American mahogany side cabinet, with an ogee-moulded drawer and two cupboard doors, Boston, c1825, 40in (101.5cm) wide.
£1,100–1,300 SK(B)

A Victorian burr-walnut and marquetry credenza, boxwood strung, and with gilt-metal bands, the central panelled door enclosing shelves, flanked by tapering columns and bowed glazed doors, 65in (165cm) wide.
£3,000–3,500 DN

A Victorian figured-walnut cabinet, the ebony and amboyna-banded top over a frieze applied with carved fruiting swags, the glazed door between sunk panelled pilasters, label for Marsh & Jones, 41in (104cm) wide.
£2,400–3,000 TEN

Marsh & Jones (later Marsh, Jones, Cribb & Co) were 19thC manufacturers of furniture, based in Leeds.

An ebonized and gilt-metal-mounted breakfront cabinet, the white marble top above an acanthus frieze and three glass doors, the sides with mask motifs, c1860, 76in (193cm) wide.
£2,500–3,000 S(S)

A Victorian figured-walnut, ebonized and gilt-metal-mounted credenza, the panelled door centred by a blue jasper plaque of a Classical figure, the glazed shaped cupboard doors enclosing lined shelves, c1875, 64in (162.5cm) wide.
£2,300–2,750 HAL

A Victorian rosewood and inlaid side cabinet, the stepped and recessed top above a bowed central section enclosed by a single boxwood, harewood and bone-inlaid panelled door, flanked to either side by a galleried shelf above a cupboard, 59¾in (152cm) wide.
£520–625 P(NW)

A French kingwood and gilt-bronze side cabinet, by Fernand Kohl, the marble top with incurved frieze above four quarter-veneered doors with crossbanded borders, signed on the reverse, c1890, 87in (221cm) wide.
£3,500–4,200 S

Fernand Kohl was based at 55 rue Traversière, Paris, from 1876. He exhibited at the 1889 Exposition Universelle, where he showed furniture mainly in Louis XVI style.

A serpentine credenza, with walnut veneer and inlaid floral marquetry with stringing, the interior with a shelf, the bowfront door decorated with a vase of flowers, flanked by leaf-carved capped cabriole pilasters, the side cupboards with shelves enclosed by shaped doors, 19thC, 60in (152.5cm) wide.
£1,800–2,200 WW

A Victorian ebonized and walnut-inlaid breakfront credenza, with gilt-metal mounts, fluted column supports and central Wedgwood plaque, 59in (150cm) wide.
£750–900 LUC

A late Victorian carved mahogany side cabinet, the centre section with a pair of panelled doors with ornate brass hinges flanked by open shelves and fluted acanthus leaf carved Corinthian pilasters, three short drawers to the frieze with brass ring handles, an open recess below with carved panelled doors on either side centred by male masks in relief, 84in (213.5cm) high.
£900–1,100 AG

◄ A Edwardian George III-style mahogany and inlaid demilune side cabinet, inlaid with stringing, with three central long drawers flanked by a pair of cupboard doors, 54in (137cm) wide.
£850–1,000 S(S)

A Victorian figured-walnut and marquetry side cabinet, with gilt-metal mounts, the inverted breakfront top with out-set corners, above a pair of panelled cupboard doors centred by flowering urns, damaged, c1880, 60in (152.5cm) wide.
£5,000–5,500 S(S)

A burr-walnut, rosewood, thuya and tulipwood marquetry breakfront side cabinet, applied with gilt-metal mounts, glazed door enclosing shelves with a further panelled door to each side, flanked by baluster turned Corinthian columns, late 19thC, 74½in (189cm) wide.
£4,000–4,500 P

The quality of this piece and the profuse use of different woods would indicate that it could have originated from a firm of the calibre of Gillows or Holland & Son.

An Edwardian inlaid rosewood chiffonier, decorated with floral neo-classical designs, the upper section with mirrors and turned spindle pilasters supporting shelves, the base with drawers and bowed cupboards, 60in (152.5cm) wide.
£1,000–1,200 FHF

CABINETS-ON-STANDS

A Portuguese walnut, rosewood and ebonized escritoire, the top with a pollard oak panel, the ripple-moulded double-panelled fall-front with an adjustable writing surface, enclosing a fitted interior, damaged, c1690, stand later, 39¾in (101cm) wide.
£1,300–1,600 S(S)

A Flemish baroque-style ebonized cabinet-on-stand, the two doors opening to an interior fitted with short drawers, the case sides with iron handles, the lower part with cushion-moulded frieze fitted with a single drawer, 1875–95, 30in (76cm) wide.
£6,500–7,200 BB(S)

An early 18thC-style walnut and mahogany cocktail cabinet-on-stand, c1920, 53in (134.5cm) high.
£400–450 Doc

A Dutch William and Mary rosewood and satinwood cabinet-on-stand, the two doors inlaid with a star motif, above two drawers, alterations, early 18thC, 70in (178cm) wide.
£4,000–4,500 S(Am)

> **Cross Reference**
> See Colour Review

A French figured-walnut and kingwood-crossbanded cabinet-on-stand, with ormolu mounts, the two detachable sliding doors with floral-painted Sèvres medallions, enclosing a fitted interior, with a single long drawer below, further porcelain medallions to the handles and sides, the stand with cherub cartouches to the sides, on cabriole legs headed by caryatids and acanthus, 19thC, 30in (76cm) wide.
£3,500–4,200 P(E)

A japanned cabinet, decorated in black and gold chinoiserie, the two doors enclosing a fitted interior, on a contemporary stand, 18thC, 40¼in (102cm) wide.
£3,000–3,500 TEN

A George III penwork cabinet-on-stand, the two doors enclosing five long drawers, decorated throughout with classical scenes within leaf and flower decorated borders, c1795, 26in (66cm) wide.
£8,500–10,000 S

◄ A Dutch marquetry cabinet-on-stand, the doors and sides inlaid with a vase of flowers within laburnum crossbanding, with drawers to the interior, the stand with a single drawer, 18thC and later, 24½in (62cm) wide.
£2,300–2,750 DN

> ## Boulle marquetry
> - decorative inlay using tortoiseshell and other materials such as brass, pewter, ebony or mother-of-pearl.
> - named after the master cabinet-maker to Louis XIV, Andre-Charles Boulle (1642–1732), who perfected rather than invented the technique, there being several other workshops in Paris undertaking this type of work at the time.
> - also referred to as 'berainesque' after the architect and designer Jean Berain who worked with Boulle and was one of the principal creators of the Louis XIV style.
> - revived in Britain between c1815 and 1840 and known as 'Buhl' work, although usually spelt 'boulle' nowadays.
> - multicoloured inlay, such as blue and green with red, is particularly popular.
> - pay attention to condition when buying boulle as it can be very expensive to repair.

► A boulle marquetry cabinet-on-stand, the arched panelled doors above two drawers, on caryatid-mounted cabriole legs, 19thC, 32¼in (82cm) wide.
£600–700 WL

◄ A Charles II-style manta ray skin and ivory cocktail cabinet, on a silvered carved wood stand, the panelled doors enclosing a sycamore interior with three drawers, labelled 'Waring & Gillow Ltd', 1920s, 30½in (77.5cm) wide.
£10,000–12,000 Gam

TABLE CABINETS

► An Italian baroque specimen marble table cabinet, the central door enclosing three drawers, the sides and drawer fronts inlaid with marble panels, c1800, 40in (101.5cm) wide.
£5,000–6,000 S(NY)

A Milanese ebonized and ivory marquetry table cabinet-on-stand, the inlaid doors enclosing a central strapwork and lozenge-carved door revealing a parquetry-inlaid compartment and four secret drawers, with carrying handles to the side, 17thC, stand later, 27¼in (69cm) wide.
£3,200–3,800 P

A Victorian walnut humidor, the doors opening to drawers, the sides mounted with carrying handles, 1850–95, 13in (33cm) wide.
£950–1,150 S(NY)

◄ A Victorian burr-walnut table cabinet, the two panelled doors with rosette corners, enclosing five sliding trays, 19in (48.5cm) wide.
£1,200–1,500 DN

An early Victorian walnut collector's chest, the eight graduated drawers with turned handles, flanked by turned pilasters, one with a lock, 19in (48.5cm) wide.
£500–600 DN

CANTERBURIES

A Regency mahogany canterbury, in the manner of Gillows, with three bowed folio sections held by fluted turned corner supports, the single frieze drawer faced by a conforming false drawer, c1805, 17in (43cm) wide.
£3,500–4,200 Bon

A Regency mahogany canterbury, the four-division top above a frieze drawer, 19¼in (49cm) wide.
£1,500–1,800 P(Sc)

A Regency rosewood canterbury, the three X-framed turned divisions with brass strings above a frieze drawer, 19¼in (49cm) wide.
£3,000–3,500 P

A Regency carved mahogany canterbury, with single drawer, bearing label 'T. H. Filmers, Berners St., London', one knob missing, 18in (45.5cm) wide.
£1,400–1,600 Odi

A Victorian simulated walnut canterbury, the ends formed as stylized lyres, with turned spindles above a drawer, legs and some spindles later, 27in (68.5cm) wide.
£1,250–1,400 S(NY)

A Victorian rosewood music canterbury, the three X-divisions with stiff leaf garlands, turned ends and finials, with a frieze drawer, 19in (48cm) wide.
£1,800–2,200 DN

A figured-walnut and inlaid music canterbury, the base with three divisions and an apron drawer, c1860, 24in (61cm) wide.
£1,600–1,750 S(S)

A Victorian walnut canterbury, the top section with pierced gallery raised on turned fluted oval carved columns above a canterbury base with pierced panels and frieze drawer, 29in (73.5cm) wide.
£1,500–1,800 JAd

A Victorian burr-walnut canterbury, the three-division lower section with fretwork lyre-shaped supports, concave-moulded frieze with hidden drawer, 25in (63.5cm) wide.
£1,300–1,600 DD

A Victorian carved rosewood three-division canterbury, with shaped and pierced fret panels and flowerhead, scroll and acanthus ornament, fitted with a concave-fronted drawer below, 20¼in (51.5cm) wide.
£1,100–1,300 P(E)

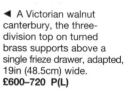
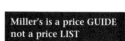

▶ A Victorian ebonized bobbin-turned two-division canterbury, 17in (43cm) wide.
£350–400 GLO

◀ A Victorian walnut canterbury, the three-division top on turned brass supports above a single frieze drawer, adapted, 19in (48.5cm) wide.
£600–720 P(L)

OPEN ARMCHAIRS

A set of three William and Mary walnut and beech high back armchairs, with padded backs, overscrolled moulded arms, bellflower and leafy carved detail with S-scroll square section supports, the padded seats on conforming legs and stretchers, restored.
£9,000–11,000 Bon

A George III mahogany armchair, with pierced vase-shaped splat and slip-in seat, c1760.
£1,000–1,200 S(S)

A Chinese-style bamboo armchair, the stepped top rail above a cock-pen motif, the upholstered seat flanked by curved arms, early 19thC.
£250–300 P(Ed)

▶ A Regency mahogany open armchair, with line inlay and solid wood seat.
£350–400 AnSh

A George I walnut open armchair, with drop-in seat, on cabriole legs, seat rails reshaped.
£1,600–2,000 S(NY)

A Chippendale-style mahogany elbow chair, c1775.
£1,300–1,500 RL

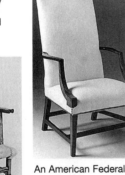

An American Federal inlaid mahogany open armchair, Massachusetts, c1795.
£2,200–2,600 S(S)

A George II mahogany carved open armchair, the pierced interlaced leaf and drop carved splat above outswept open arms with eaglehead terminals, above a drop-in seat on leaf-carved cabriole legs and claw and ball feet, possibly Irish or American.
£3,000–3,500 P

A George III Hepplewhite-style mahogany open armchair, the outward-curving arms with moulded scrolling supports and volute terminals, on moulded cabriole front legs.
£1,650–2,000 HAM

An Italian walnut armchair, the back with rococo scroll spray carving, detachable leather panel, scroll-moulded arms and a leather-covered drop-in seat, c1780.
£2,200–2,600 WW

A pair of gilt-metal-mounted hardwood armchairs, each with an oval padded back flanked by fluted pilasters surmounted by finials, with a drop-in seat, the panelled frieze mounted on three sides with scrolling foliage, probably Russian, restored, early 19thC.
£11,500–13,500 S

A set of four Regency painted and gilt open armchairs, in the manner of Thomas Hope, the bar-backs decorated with central lion masks flanked by anthemia, above X-shaped splats, on downswept scroll arms with lion paw terminals and caned seats, decoration renewed.
£13,500–15,000 P

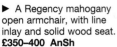

◄ A pair of mahogany open armchairs, the backs with floral and vine carved top rails above an inlaid blind-fluted tapering splat, with caned seats and bowed seat rails.
£7,000–8,000 S

A pair of French Restauration mahogany *fauteuils*, with gadrooned scrolled top rails and downswept lotus-leaf-carved arms, early 19thC.
£2,500–3,000 P

A pair of Russian neo-classical mahogany arm-chairs, with foliate scrolled top rails and acanthus-carved armrests, c1820.
£5,000–6,000 S(NY)

A George IV mahogany reclining open armchair, with a fitted wooden catch under each arm to release the back, the front seat rail sliding out to reveal an adjustable leg rest, stamped 'R Daws'.
£2,000–2,400 BIG

A pair of German/Austrian neo-classical fruitwood open armchairs, the crest rails with carved demilune ends, the reeded arms with scrolling ends over curving channelled supports, mid-19thC.
£3,300–4,000 BB(L)

A pair of Anglo-Colonial mahogany open arm-chairs, with caned seats and backs, 1825–45.
£1,800–2,000 NOA

◄ A William IV mahogany open armchair, the padded back and arms with scroll terminals, the bowed overstuffed seat on lotus-carved turned legs.
£1,800–2,200 P

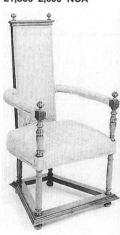

A mid-Victorian carved mahogany armchair, with original upholstery.
£400–450 NET

A Victorian walnut armchair, with a scalloped and buttoned cartouche-shaped back and serpentine seat.
£600–700 HYD

A Victorian mahogany armchair, the overstuffed seat flanked by padded arms supported by turned columns with knop finials.
£850–1,000 P(Sc)

A Victorian walnut open armchair, the balloon back carved with foliate scrolls, with serpentine-fronted seat and tapestry upholstery, on carved cabriole legs with scroll feet.
£625–750 BIG

Sets/Pairs

Unless otherwise stated, any description which refers to 'a set' or 'a pair' includes a guide price for the entire set or the pair, even though the illustration may show only a single item.

A Scottish provincial laburnum chair, the top rail carved with leaf and central star, over button-upholstered back, 19thC.
£350–420 P(Ed)

A pair of Georgian-style mahogany Gainsborough armchairs, on cabochon-carved cabriole legs, 19thC.
£4,500–5,500 HOK

A Chippendale-style mahogany open armchair, with carved and scrolled top rail and pierced splats, on claw-and-ball feet, 19thC.
£1,100–1,200 JM

A Hepplewhite-style mahogany open armchair, with leaf- and rosette-carved back rail and upholstered seat, 1880.
£250–300 RBB

A pair of mahogany low back Windsor open armchairs, the spindle backs with central vase pierced splats, late 19thC.
£700–850 MJB

A *faux* bamboo Boer War campaign chair, with original covering, c1880.
£400–500 BAB

A pair of late Victorian rosewood and boxwood armchairs, inlaid with brass, copper and ivory.
£1,600–2,000 Bon(C)

A bentwood rocking chair, with cane back and seat, c1900.
£300–350 CPA

UPHOLSTERED ARMCHAIRS

A George II walnut wing armchair, on leaf-carved front cabriole legs.
£4,000–5,000 S

A George III mahogany upholstered desk chair, covered in studded tan leather, the legs headed by paterae, c1780.
£3,500–4,000 S(S)

An American Federal mahogany armchair, on ring-turned front legs, New England, early 19thC.
£1,100–1,200 SK(B)

A William IV mahogany and leather upholstered armchair, the padded cushion seat on reeded turned tapering legs and casters, c1835.
£3,000–3,500 Bon

A Victorian walnut armchair, with pink velvet upholstery, on cabriole supports with upturned knurl feet.
£220–265 Bri

A Victorian carved mahogany and upholstered balloon-back armchair, on cabriole legs.
£575–700 S(S)

A Victorian walnut armchair, and matching occasional chair, with carved foliage to the crests, padded open arms with carved fronts, the sprung seats upholstered, buttoned backs, on carved cabriole front legs.
£1,600–2,000 WW

A Georgian-style wing armchair, on leaf-carved cabriole legs and claw-and-ball feet, 19thC.
£600–720 RBB

A wing armchair, on cabriole legs with scroll toes and casters, 19thC.
£650–800 DN

▶ A pair of William and Mary-style wing armchairs, with padded backs, shaped sides and arms, the cabriole legs joined by pierced C-scroll and leaf-carved front stretchers and block and reel H-stretchers, on scroll feet, c1910.
£2,500–3,000 P

An upholstered porter's chair, with mahogany legs, 1880.
£350–450 BAB

A pair of Liberty-style upholstered armchairs, early 20thC.
£3,200–3,500 S

A pair of French walnut armchairs, the foliate-carved frame with cresting, early 20thC.
£600–720 M

A pair of club armchairs, with cabriole legs, 1930s.
£600–650 NET

BERGERE CHAIRS

A Regency mahogany library bergère chair, with buttoned leather-covered back and seat cushions, c1815.
£5,000–5,500 S

A Regency mahogany and caned bergère chair, with scrolled arms and sabre legs, c1820.
£2,000–2,400 Bon

A George IV mahogany library bergère chair, with scrolled and close-nailed hide back, on paw feet.
£4,000–5,000 M&K

A Regency ebonized beech library armchair, with reeded frame and caned sides and back.
£1,800–2,200 DN

▶ A pair of George IV mahogany library bergère chairs, the padded backs with lotus leaf-carved scrolled arms and supports, the padded seats on turned legs with leaf-carved caps, c1825.
£16,000–20,000 S

A William IV mahogany bergère chair, with caned back and sides, the lappet and scroll-carved arms flanking a caned seat with buttoned hide squab cushion, c1835.
£5,500–6,000 S

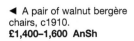

A French walnut bergère chair, with carved frame, c1880.
£600–650 GD

◀ A pair of walnut bergère chairs, c1910.
£1,400–1,600 AnSh

A Regency rosewood tub-shaped armchair, with padded back and caned seat.
£1,600–2,000 DN

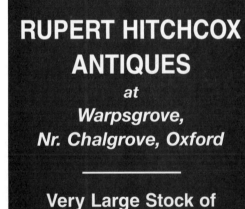

A Regency mahogany caned bergère chair, with padded back and arms, caned sides, on tapering reeded legs, c1820.
£6,500–7,000 S(NY)

A pair of late Regency mahogany bergère arm-chairs, with drop-in seats.
£12,000–14,000 P(EA)

CHILDREN'S CHAIRS

A Louis XVI grey-painted child's open armchair, with padded back and elbow rests, a bowfront stuff-over seat, reeded and carved throughout, late 18thC.
£1,650–2,000 SLN

A George III mahogany child's high chair, with adjustable footrest and later upholstered drop-in seat, some repairs, c1785.
£2,400–3,000 Hal

This and the item on the right become a separate table and chair when a winged screw is removed.

A mahogany child's high chair, with caned seat and back, c1820.
£850–950 ChA

A mahogany child's high chair, 19thC.
£150–175 ChA

An early Victorian child's chair, with turned spindle back and cane seat.
£90–110 HYD

▶ A Victorian fruitwood child's chair, the spindle back of balloon form, with caned seat.
£100–120 PFK

A mid-Victorian simulated rosewood child's chair, seat recaned.
£200–225 CSAC

CORNER CHAIRS

An American Queen Anne cherrywood corner chair, the scrolled arms on vase and ring-turned supports flanking shaped splats, above an upholstered slip seat, New England, c1750.
£2,750–3,250 SK(B)

A deep skirt like this might indicate that it is a commode chair, the skirt hiding the chamber pot which hung on rails under the lift-up seat.

An early George III walnut corner chair, with horseshoe back and pierced vase splats.
£500–600 L

A George III mahogany corner chair, with shaped curved back and scroll arms, pierced splats and drop-in seat.
£800–1,000 P(O)

A George III mahogany corner chair, with pierced vase splats and drop-in seat.
£600–700 P(L)

American styles

American furniture termed, for example, 'Queen Anne' does not necessarily date from the actual period of Queen Anne. This is because it took about 20 years for the latest fashions to cross the Atlantic, but the style is nevertheless of that period.

An Edwardian satinwood-inlaid mahogany corner chair.
£500–560 ChA

DINING CHAIRS

A pair of George I walnut chairs, with vase-shaped splats, drop-in seats and shaped aprons.
£2,000–2,400 HYD

A set of eight George III fruitwood dining chairs, with pierced Chinese-style fretwork splats and drop-in seats, restored, c1760.
£2,000–2,400 S(S)

A set of eight George III Sheraton-style chairs, including one with arms, each with three scroll-ended spindles and reeded uprights, later-upholstered drop-in seats on reeded legs and block feet.
£4,000–5,000 PFK

When one comes across an unusual number of chairs being sold together it is likely that they came from a larger set that was divided between the heirs upon the decease of the original owner. One way of proving this is to see if there are numbers on the undersides of the chairs – any figure larger than the number in the set in question will mean there are others in existence.

▶ A pair of George III carved mahogany dining chairs, with pierced vase-shaped splats and cabriole legs, c1770.
£1,000–1,200 S(S)

◀ A set of six George III mahogany dining chairs, two with arms, each with four leaf-capped upright rails, one armchair of a later date.
£1,600–2,000 DN

A Queen Anne-style walnut dining chair, with arched back rail and carved scallop motif, vase splat, drop-in upholstered seat, 18thC.
£1,600–1,800 BIG

A set of six George III mahogany dining chairs, with pierced shield-shaped splat backs carved with paterae and bowed stuffed seats, some rerailing, c1780.
£3,200–3,800 S

◀ A set of seven George III mahogany dining chairs, including one carver, with vase-shaped pierced splats and stuff-over seats.
£1,000–1,200 P(L)

A set of six George III mahogany dining chairs, the pierced vase-shaped splats carved with flower-heads and drapery, restored, c1785.
£2,200–2,500 S(S)

◀ A set of six George III mahogany dining chairs, with pierced trelliswork within fluted turned and square uprights, the padded seats on turned and reeded legs, restored, c1810.
£7,000–8,000 S

A set of eleven American Federal-style carved mahogany dining chairs, including two armchairs, the crest rails centred by a swag-carved tablet, with stuff-over seats, 19thC.
£4,000–4,500 SLN

A set of eight George III mahogany dining chairs, including two carvers, each with three narrow stylized tulip and vase-shaped splats and drop-in seat, one carver later.
£2,500–3,000 Mit

A set of twelve Regency mahogany dining chairs, including two carvers, the cresting rails decorated with oval raised panels and reeded scrolling brackets, the mid-rails with a reeded roundel supported by horseshoe-shaped motifs, drop-in seats, on sabre legs.
£13,000–15,000 AG

◀ A set of four Regency beech dining chairs, with reeded frames, each with a leaf-carved looping rail centred with a shell and a roundel, with drop-in seats, on sabre legs.
£1,350–1,600 DN

A set of twelve George IV mahogany dining chairs, including a pair of open armchairs, with reeded uprights and anthemion back bars, the floral tapestry stuff-over seats on turned and reeded tapering legs.
£12,000–14,000 P(WM)

A set of four mahogany dining chairs, including two carvers, each with a low back and central panel, moulded seat rails and baluster-turned front legs, 19thC.
£400–500 AH

A set of eight Chippendale-style mahogany dining chairs, including two carvers, with pierced wavy ladder-backs and upholstered drop-in seats, on square supports, 19thC.
£2,500–3,000 RBB

A set of six American bird's-eye maple dining chairs, the shaped scroll-back crests above vasiform splats, with old cane seats, New England, 1830–40.
£1,200–1,400 SK(B)

◀ A set of six William IV rose-wood dining chairs, each with a scroll and sheaf-carved cresting rail and horizontal splat, drop-in seats above original caned seats.
£1,600–2,000 BIG

A set of four William IV carved mahogany dining chairs, on turned supports.
£400–500 WiLP

A set of five early Victorian mahogany dining chairs, the top rails with roundel terminals above pierced acanthus horizontal splats, with drop-in seats.
£500–600 P(Ed)

A set of six early Victorian mahogany balloon-back dining chairs, the central splats carved with scrolling foliage, with stuff-over seats.
£1,150–1,400 E

A set of three American painted dining chairs, the top rails and tablet stretchers painted with geometric scrolling floral designs, the painted rush seats on ring-turned legs tied by stretchers, inscribed on the back seat rails 'L, Hitchcock, Hitchcocks-Ville, Conn, Warranted', c1830.
£1,100–1,300 Bon

A set of eight mahogany dining chairs, the backs with reeded frames, turned crest rails and padded and lattice panels, with padded seats, two with scroll arms, mid-19thC.
£3,000–3,500 DN

◀ A set of four Victorian oak dining chairs, with original leather seats, c1850.
£650–725 COLL

A set of nine Irish early Victorian mahogany frame-back dining chairs, by James Kerr & Co, Dublin, with padded backs and seats, the carver with swept arm supports.
£3,800–4,500 JAd

A set of six Elizabethan-style oak dining chairs, the padded backs with moulded boss-decorated frames and scroll-carved decoration, with padded seats, turned legs and ceramic casters, c1850.
£400–500 S

◀ A set of eight stained beech campaign chairs, with shaped splats, padded seats and turned legs, the seat rails attached to the frames by bolts, 19thC.
£800–1,000 DN

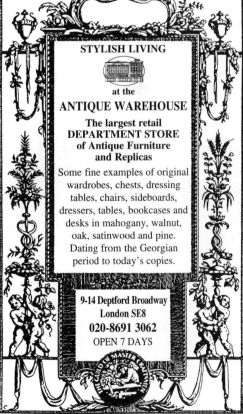

A set of six Victorian rococo-revival style walnut dining chairs, the channelled waisted backs with shaped and pierced splats and carved scrollwork, stuff-over seats.
£1,300–1,600 AH

A set of twelve Victorian Gothic-revival oak dining chairs, on square chamfered legs joined by cross-stretchers.
£5,000–5,750 P(Ed)

These chairs were designed by A. W. N. Pugin for the House of Commons.

A set of six Victorian walnut balloon-back dining chairs, the backs with shell-carved crests above C- and S-scroll infills with buttoned green velvet seats.
£1,250–1,500 Bri

A set of six Victorian mahogany balloon-back dining chairs, including one carver, the seats requiring reupholstering.
£950–1,150 LF

A set of six Victorian maple balloon-back chairs, with foliate-carved pierced splats above buttoned stuff-over seats, damaged.
£800–1,000 S(S)

▶ A set of six Victorian walnut dining chairs, the pierced and waisted backs carved with shells and scrolls, with upholstered serpentine seats.
£800–1,000 DDM

▶ A set of four Victorian walnut dining chairs, with waisted deep-buttoned backs and shell cresting in a moulded frame, above conforming buttoned seats.
£350–420 MEA

A harlequin set of four Victorian mahogany dining chairs.
£700–770 ChA

A set of four inlaid mahogany dining chairs, c1890.
£700–800 GBr

A set of six Victorian mahogany balloon-back dining chairs, the moulded top rails with square scrolls over serpentine seats.
£800–900 P(L)

A set of six Egyptian-style oak dining chairs, the padded backs above carved paterae, c1880.
£1,500–1,650 S

◀ A set of eight Georgian-style figured-walnut dining chairs, including a pair of shepherd's crook open armchairs, each with a vase splat below a looped cresting centred by a shell, with floral needlework drop-in seats, c1900.
£13,000–15,000 P(WM)

Sets/Pairs

Unless otherwise stated, any description which refers to 'a set' or 'a pair' includes a guide price for the entire set or the pair, even though the illustration may show only a single item.

A set of eleven Edwardian Chippendale-style mahogany dining chairs, including a pair of elbow chairs, with pierced baluster splats.
£4,500–5,500 P(B)

A set of eight George III-style mahogany dining chairs, including two armchairs, the shaped backs with interlaced pierced splats above drop-in seats, early 20thC.
£1,700–2,000 S(S)

A set of eight Edwardian George III-style mahogany dining chairs, including a pair of armchairs, with pierced vase-shaped splats and leather-covered stuff-over seats, on cabriole legs.
£950–1,100 S(S)

A set of eight Edwardian mahogany and satinwood crossbanded dining chairs, the reeded vertical splats above upholstered seats.
£1,600–2,000 P(Sc)

◀ A set of eight Edwardian golden oak lyre-back dining chairs, on turned tapering reeded legs.
£950–1,100 JM

A set of six Edwardian Adam-style mahogany dining chairs, including an elbow chair, the pierced leaf-carved splats above stuff-over seats, on reeded tapering legs.
£1,200–1,500 P(B)

A set of six Edwardian mahogany George III-style dining chairs, with carved pierced shell-form backs above stuff-over seats, on carved cabriole legs, c1910.
£1,500–1,800 S(S)

An Edwardian painted satinwood chair, with green upholstered seat, c1910.
£200–250 BAB

◀ A set of eight Edwardian mahogany dining chairs, each with a shaped oval back and pierced splat flanked by two conforming curved splats, above a green upholstered seat, on cabriole legs.
£1,800–2,200 MEA

HALL CHAIRS

A George III mahogany hall chair, the oval wheel back with leaf-carved spokes, a satinwood central panel and leaf-carved crest, with solid panelled seat.
£800–950 DN

A mahogany hall chair, with carved shell back, c1820.
£320–350 CAT

A set of early William IV mahogany hall chairs, with arched and reeded shield-shaped backs, on sabre front legs.
£700–850 MEA

A pair of Victorian mahogany hall chairs, the shield backs with incised roundels.
£380–450 JAd

A pair of oak hall chairs, 19thC.
£425–500 SPa

A pair of early Victorian mahogany hall chairs, with vase-carved back panels, shaped seats and sabre legs.
£400–500 TMA

An Irish mahogany hall chair, the back formed with a patera and painted crest of an *étoile*, with bowed dished seat.
£6,000–6,750 HOK

A pair of Victorian mahogany hall chairs, the moulded balloon-shaped back inset with blind shields, on turned front legs.
£700–800 WL

LIBRARY CHAIRS

A William IV mahogany library chair, the frame with a foliate and scroll-carved crest, with black leather stuff-over seat.
£1,500–1,800 WW

An early Victorian walnut and mahogany library armchair, the carved and pierced back with an oval padded panel.
£900–1,100 MEA

A limed oak swivel library chair, with red leather upholstered seat, carved padded back, candle-slide and lift-up reading tray, on quadripartite base, 19thC.
£3,400–3,750 HOK

A Victorian mahogany library chair, with new upholstery and casters.
£450–550 BAB

Cross Reference
See Reading Chairs

READING CHAIRS

A Regency simulated rosewood reading chair, with adjustable bookrest and stuff-over seat.
£1,600–2,000 P(EA)

A Victorian mahogany leather-upholstered reclining reading chair, with extending footrest and adjustable reading stand, mid-19thC.
£6,000–7,000 S(NY)

A late Regency mahogany reading chair, in the style of Morgan & Sanders, the scroll arms with brass slots for an easel or candlestand, with triple flared rails, the bell-shaped stuff-over seat covered with leather with brass nails, on front turned and ribbed tapering legs with brass casters.
£3,800–4,500 WW

A George IV mahogany reading chair, after a design by Morgan & Sanders, the horseshoe-shaped back fitted with an adjustable hinged bookrest, the shaped cane seat on turned and tapered legs headed by brass bosses, reading flap replaced, c1820.
£10,000–12,000 S

This reading chair is of a type associated with the Regency cabinet-makers, Morgan & Sanders, specialists in the manufacture of mechanical and metamorphic furniture.

Further Reading
Miller's Late Georgian to Edwardian Furniture Buyer's Guide, Miller's Publications, 1998

◄ A Victorian library armchair, the adjustable reading slope on a swivel brass arm, the upholstered seat with extending adjustable footrests, on turned tapering mahogany legs.
£900–1,100 P(Sc)

SALON CHAIRS

A set of six Victorian rosewood buckle-back salon chairs, each with a carved and pierced back and padded seat, on cabriole legs.
£2,400–3,000 CLE

A set of four Victorian walnut balloon-back salon chairs, each with a pierced scroll cresting and serpentine seat, on extended cabriole legs.
£500–600 L

A Victorian walnut salon chair, the back carved with bellflowers, acanthus leaves, swags, scrolls and leaf pendants, the serpentine-fronted upholstered seat with carved frieze, on carved cabriole legs with scroll feet.
£200–240 BIG

A pair of mahogany framed Adam-style salon chairs, upholstered in beige and floral needlework, with padded and reeded downswept arms, the tapered reeded legs headed by carved paterae, on casters, late 19thC.
£4,000–5,000 TEN

SIDE CHAIRS

A Queen Anne carved giltwood and gesso side chair, the seat rail decorated with flowerheads and trelliswork centred by a shell and flanked by scrolling acanthus leaves, the carved cabriole legs carved with acanthus and decorated with flowerheads.
£4,500–5,500 S

A Queen Anne gilt and gesso side chair, the shell and paterae-carved cabriole legs on hoof feet.
£2,200–2,650 P

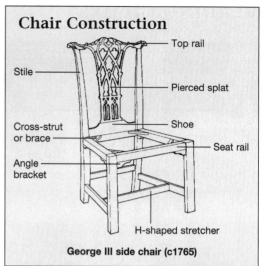

Chair Construction

Top rail
Stile
Pierced splat
Cross-strut or brace
Shoe
Seat rail
Angle bracket
H-shaped stretcher

George III side chair (c1765)

A walnut and laburnum side chair, with a padded drop-in seat, early 18thC.
£650–800 P(B)

A set of four Louis XV provincial walnut-framed side chairs, each carved with flowerheads and foliage, the upholstered serpentine seats above conforming aprons, restored, mid-18thC.
£800–1,000 Bea(E)

A pair of carved and giltwood side chairs, upholstered in tapestry-pattern fabric, decorated with bead-and-reel and incised diamond field pattern decoration, the aprons centred by scallop shells, 18thC.
£1,600–2,000 JAd

An American Chippendale-style dark stained side chair, with pierced splat and upholstered slip seat, Concord, Massachusetts, late 18thC.
£500–600 SK(B)

MISCELLANEOUS CHAIRS

An ebonized and carved prie-dieu chair, with beadwork upholstery, on turned front legs, c1850.
£350–450 OCH

A pair of Victorian ebonized and gilt-embellished parlour chairs, the padded backs flanked by turned columns, above upholstered seats with a spindle rail below.
£280–350 P(Sc)

A Victorian mahogany button-backed lady's chair, with cabriole front legs and casters, c1850.
£550–600 ChA

A mid-Victorian walnut nursing chair, the scroll-carved cresting above a spoon-back upholstered in floral needlework, over similar bowfronted seat.
£500–600 P(NW)

A George III satinwood, rosewood-crossbanded and ebonized bonheur du jour, the lower part with a fitted secretaire drawer and writing surface, 32¼in (82cm) wide.
£14,000–16,000 P

A George III polychrome-painted bonheur du jour, with removable upper section, paint refreshed, with the initials of Mary, Countess of Bute, late 18thC, 19¾in (50cm) wide.
£18,000–22,000 S(NY)

► An Italian walnut and chequer-banded bureau, the fall-front enclosing a fitted interior with a well, c1800, 40in (102cm) wide.
£2,700–3,000 S(S)

A Dutch walnut and seaweed marquetry bureau, the fall-front enclosing a central cupboard door, seven pigeonholes and two drawers, restored, late 17thC, 30in (76cm) wide.
£2,200–2,500 P

A German mahogany-veneered and gilt-brass-mounted bureau, the fall-front enclosing a concave fitted interior with pigeonholes and small drawers, 18thC, 38½in (98cm) wide.
£25,000–27,500 Bea(E)

An Irish burr-yew and walnut bureau, the fall-front enclosing a fitted interior with shaped drawers and pigeonholes surrounding a central cupboard inlaid with a figure of an Irish chieftain, c1740, 38¼in (97cm) wide.
£13,000–15,000 S

An American William and Mary maple bureau, the interior fitted with valanced pigeonholes and seven short drawers centring a prospect door above a well, 1710–30, 40in (101.5cm) wide.
£25,000–30,000 S(NY)

A French kingwood cylinder bureau, c1880, 28in (71cm) wide.
£1,000–1,200 BUSH

A painted satinwood bureau, the fall-front enclosing a fitted interior, early 20thC, 32in (81.5cm) wide.
£1,500–1,800 AH

► A Louis XVI-style mahogany and marquetry cylinder bureau, the fall-front inlaid with leather-inset writing surface, the interior enclosing four drawers, c1900, 51½in (131cm) wide.
£3,800–4,500 P

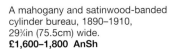

A mahogany and satinwood-banded cylinder bureau, 1890–1910, 29¾in (75.5cm) wide.
£1,600–1,800 AnSh

A mahogany and painted four-poster bed, with later silk lining hung with blue drapes, c1780, 68¼in (173.5cm) wide.
£37,000–40,000 S

This bed was formerly owned by William Waldorf Astor, 3rd Viscount Astor (1907–66), Cliveden, Buckinghamshire. The provenance helped this bed to attain the high price.

A George III mahogany and painted four-poster bed, the front posts inlaid with harewood shell and flower medallions, 64in (163cm) wide.
£8,000–10,000 S

A mahogany and brass-mounted campaign four-poster bed, by Thomas Butler, with the maker's brass plaque, parts missing, c1805, 48in (122cm) wide.
£12,500–15,000 Bon

It is reputed that Lord Byron once owned this bed.

A William IV mahogany four-poster bed, the corniced canopy with decorative fretwork, c1830, 66in (167.5cm) wide.
£8,000–10,000 SeH

A French Louis XV-style carved and gilded bedstead, c1900, 60in (152.5cm) wide.
£5,000–6,000 LaM

An American Empire Transitional full tester bed, manufactured for the southern market, early 19thC, 67in (170cm) wide.
£5,000–6,000 NOA

► A pair of Louis XV-style gilt-bronze-mounted kingwood and mahogany bedsteads, late 19thC, 83in (211cm) long.
£3,700–4,500 BB(L)

◄ An Italian burr-walnut day bed, mounted with gilt-bronze, with removable back and separate plinth, c1810, 96in (244cm) wide.
£7,000–8,500 S

A Regency mahogany and caned *méridienne*, 78in (198cm) long.
£4,500–5,000 NOA

The Regency méridienne usually had paw feet on casters.

► A Russian karelian birch and carved giltwood day bed, the curved legs with swan supports, on acanthus leaf carved bun feet, early 19thC, 87in (220cm) wide.
£12,000–15,000 S

A mahogany double-sided library bookcase, the two-drawer base with original wood handles, with turned feet on original brass casters, c1800, 36in (91.5cm) wide.
£10,000–11,000 HA

An Irish mahogany bookcase, early 19thC, 54in (137cm) wide.
£7,000–8,000 HOK

A japanned bookcase cabinet, decoration restored, early 19thC, 57in (144cm) wide.
£6,000–7,000 BB(S)

A mahogany breakfront library bookcase, the three glazed panel doors enclosing adjustable shelves, c1850, 79½in (202cm) wide.
£7,500–8,250 S(S)

A set of mahogany graduated bookshelves on a cabinet base, mid-19thC, 26½in (67cm) wide.
£1,800–2,000 HOK

A Victorian figured walnut library bookcase, the glazed doors enclosing adjustable shelves, the base with two frieze drawers, 46in (117cm) wide.
£3,400–3,750 DMC

An early Victorian mahogany double-sided 'waterfall' bookcase, 45¾in (116cm) wide.
£2,000–2,500 P

A George II mahogany-veneered bureau bookcase, the panelled doors enclosing a fitted interior, 40in (101.5cm) wide.
£12,500–14,000 HA

A mahogany-veneered bookcase, crossbanded with tulipwood, the fully-fitted secretaire with satinwood drawers, c1800, 37¾in (96cm) wide.
£15,000–17,000 BERA

A George III inlaid mahogany bureau bookcase, the fall-front enclosing a central cupboard flanked by secret drawers, pigeon-holes and other drawers, 46in (117cm) wide.
£4,000–4,500 Bri

A Regency mahogany secretaire bookcase, with glazed doors and fitted interior, 46in (117cm) wide.
£8,500–10,000 RBB

A mahogany secretaire bookcase, painted and with satinwood crossbanding, the fall-front drawer enclosing a fitted interior with leather inset, c1910, 36in (91.5cm) wide.
£10,000–11,000 S(S)

◄ A mahogany secretaire bookcase, with decorative satinwood stringing, the fall-front with fitted interior, early 19thC, 31in (78.5cm) wide.
£3,200–3,800 RBB

A Dutch neo-classical mahogany and fruitwood cabinet, with a *pietra dura* top centrally decorated with a landscape reserve, late 18thC, 28¼in (72cm) wide.
£9,500–10,500 S(NY)

A figured-walnut cabinet, the panelled doors floral painted on a gilt ground, c1860, 26in (67cm) wide.
£1,400–1,600 S(S)

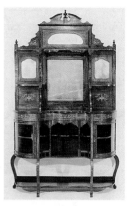

A late Victorian rosewood salon cabinet, with string inlay and floral marquetry panels, 52in (132cm) wide.
£1,200–1,400 AH

A Dutch walnut cabinet, decorated with later marquetry inlay, on ball-and-claw feet, mid-18thC, 69in (175.5cm) wide.
£7,000–8,000 S(Am)

A French ebonized and marquetry ormolu-mounted marble-topped side cabinet, in the manner of P. Somani, c1860, 47in (119.5cm) wide.
£5,000–5,750 CHE

A pair of Regency mahogany bowfront night cupboards, each with a deep drawer simulating two drawers, altered, 24¾in (63cm) wide.
£11,500–13,500 P

Although these cupboards have been adapted, they are of high value owing to their age.

A Louis XV-style parcel-gilt and painted cabinet, in two sections, late 19thC, 44in (112cm) wide.
£3,000–3,500 BB(S)

A French Louis XVI-style mahogany *table de nuit,* with a grey marble top, brass moulding and gilt inlay, late 19thC, 35in (89cm) wide.
£2,000–2,200 NOA

A north Italian bone-inlaid walnut and olive bureau cabinet, the fall-front enclosing a shelved interior, restored, the inlay possibly later, 17th/18thC, 50½in (128cm) wide.
£12,000–15,000 Bon

◄ A Continental mahogany seaweed marquetry corner cupboard, the upper section with panelled doors enclosing three shaped shelves, early 19thC, 47¼in (120cm) wide.
£5,000–5,500 P(G)

► A Gothic-style figured-mahogany hanging corner cupboard, with castellated cornice and rope-twist uprights, c1820, 29in (73.5cm) wide.
£4,500–5,000 RL

A Queen Anne walnut bureau cabinet, the fall-front headed by a pair of candleslides and enclosing stationery compartments, 40¾in (104cm) wide.
£35,000–40,000 S

An American Queen Anne carved and inlaid cherry-wood bonnet-top bureau cabinet, the panelled doors opening to three shelves, the lower section opening to a fitted interior with pigeonholes and drawers, restored, c1750–70, 36in (91.5cm) wide.
£20,000–22,000 S(NY)

An Edwardian inlaid mahogany and satinwood-crossbanded display cabinet, 30in (76cm) wide.
£6,000–6,500 P(L)

An Edwardian serpentine-fronted mahogany and ivory-inlaid cabinet, the associated mirrored back with applied shell and scroll carving, 39½in (100cm) wide.
£3,000–3,500 P(G)

A Queen Anne figured-walnut escritoire-on-chest, the fitted interior containing removable pigeonholes enclosing secret drawers, 41in (104cm) wide.
£3,000–3,500 CLE

An early George III mahogany secretaire, surmounted by a detachable fretwork superstructure, the secretaire drawer as one long and two short cockbeaded false drawers, opening to reveal a fitted interior of divisions and small drawers, with gilt tooled leather writing surface, 29¾in (75.5cm) wide.
£30,000–33,000 HAM

A stained walnut and gilt-bronze cabinet-on-stand, attributed to Gabriel Viardot, Paris, inset with black lacquer panels inlaid with mother-of-pearl, the upper part with a pagoda and a gilt-bronze Burmese lion, c1870, 35½in (90.5cm) wide.
£9,500–10,500 S

A George II japanned cabinet, the interior fitted with ten scarlet lacquered drawers, all faced with Oriental vignettes, mid-18thC, on a later stand, 41in (104cm) wide.
£3,000–3,500 NOA

A George III mahogany serpentine-fronted side cabinet, the top inlaid with a bat's wing patera to the centre, on square tapering legs and pad feet, 26¾in (68cm) wide.
£5,000–6,000 HAM

A Regency rosewood and brass-inlaid chiffonier, the pair of mirrored doors enclosing a shelf, 32⅜in (83cm) wide.
£2,750–3,000 P

A French kingwood and marquetry serpentine credenza, with a white marble top, on a shaped plinth, mid-19thC, 52in (132cm) wide.
£3,000–3,500 P(L)

A Victorian ebonized and marquetry-inlaid side cabinet, with ormolu mounts and glazed bowed ends, 57½in (146cm) wide.
£850–1,000 TMA

A Regency rosewood and parcel-gilt side cabinet, with a later white marble top above a pair of pleated silk panel doors, the sides with open shelves, 57in (145cm) wide.
£5,500–6,000 S

A Regency rosewood chiffonier, the base fitted with two doors with brass grilles and silk pleats, 35¾in (91cm) wide.
£5,500–6,500 P(Ed)

A Victorian walnut and ormolu-mounted breakfront side cabinet, with inlaid floral and scroll designs, 64in (162.5cm) wide.
£1,600–1,750 RBB

A French mahogany, walnut and marquetry breakfront side cabinet, with cast brass mounts and white marble top, late 19thC, 46in (117cm) wide.
£2,500–3,000 CAG

A Regency rosewood and brass marquetry side cabinet, the later *verde antico* marble top above a pair of mirror-panelled doors enclosing four shelves, restored, 54¼in (138cm) wide.
£6,000–7,000 P

A George IV rosewood secretaire side cabinet, the Siena marble top above a writing drawer with fall-front panelled to simulate two drawers, four further graduated drawers below, on a plinth, c1820, 61in (155cm) wide.
£4,000–5,000 S

An inlaid amboyna and gilt-metal-mounted side cabinet, the top with a pierced brass gallery above a central cupboard door with a porcelain medallion, on a plinth base, c1870, 59in (150cm) wide.
£5,250–5,750 S(S)

A Louis XVI-style walnut, kingwood and marquetry credenza, applied with gilt-metal mounts, the central door decorated with a parrot within a tropical landscape heightened in mother-of-pearl and ivory, enclosing a mirror-lined interior, on a shaped plinth base, late 19thC, 60¾in (154cm) wide.
£3,200–3,800 P

A French walnut armchair, with carved arms, upholstered in material commissioned by the Museum of Krefield in 1888–95, c1670–80.
£2,500–3,000 DBA

A Louis XIV walnut *fauteuil mécanique,* later upholstered in velvet, 1780–1820.
£3,200–3,500 BB(S)

A pair of Louis XV-style painted armchairs, 18thC.
£1,800–2,000 P(B)

An early George III mahogany Gainsborough open armchair, with blind fret carved supports and legs.
£3,000–3,500 HAM

A set of four painted, parcel-gilt and carved giltwood armchairs, two carved with an eagle, the other two with a cockerel, possibly Russian, c1820.
£9,000–10,000 S

A set of six Russian neo-classical mahogany and parcel-gilt armchairs, mid-19thC.
£17,500–20,000 S(NY)

A mahogany reclining armchair, the shaped sides with leaf-carved decoration, c1840.
£7,500–8,250 S

An Edwardian mahogany salon armchair, with pierced scrollwork back.
£400–450 PFK

A carved giltwood armchair, in the form of an eagle, carved with lapped feathers, with claw and segmented ball feet, possibly Russian, early 19thC.
£11,500–14,000 S

A Louis XV carved beechwood and caned bergère chair, c1750.
£7,000–8,000 S

An Edwardian satinwood and painted bergère chair, with floral decoration.
£1,000–1,200 P

A pair of French button-back armchairs, with later upholstery and ebonized decoration, c1860.
£1,000–1,100 BAB

A pair of Louis XV-style giltwood wing chairs, c1860.
£5,000–5,500 CHE

◄ A northern European neo-classical fruitwood bergère chair, mid-19thC.
£700–800 NOA

A Louis XVI-style walnut bergère chair, c1910.
£650–750 CF

A mahogany hall seat, in the manner of Mack, Williams & Gibton, the frame with central splat and spindle-filled back, mid-19thC, 34¾in (88cm) wide.
£3,000–3,500 P

A mahogany library armchair, with scroll supports, c1820.
£2,800–3,200 S

◄ An early Victorian Gothic revival oak metamorphic library armchair, the padded arms and seat covered with needlework.
£5,500–6,500 WW

A set of four Regency ebony-inlaid oak side chairs, attributed to George Bullock, restored, early 19thC.
£8,000–9,000 S(NY)

A George IV mahogany reclining library armchair, by George Minter, with pull-out footrest, later brass and mahogany pivoted reading rest and tray, c1825.
£15,000–16,500 S

A pair of William IV rosewood library chairs, with upholstered tub backs and seats.
£7,000–8,000 P(Ed)

► An American Second Empire painted side chair, attributed to Leon Marcott, New York, the upholstered backrest within a frame painted with stylized palmettes, c1860.
£3,000–3,500 BB(L)

A set of six Portuguese walnut and embossed leather high-back dining chairs, late 17th/early 18thC.
£4,000–5,000 Bon(C)

A set of 11 Regency mahogany dining chairs, in the manner of Thomas Hope, including a pair of elbow chairs.
£11,000–15,000 P(EA)

A Regency rosewood and brass-inlaid dining chair, in the manner of George Oakley, cut down in height.
£750–900 P

◀ A set of six mahogany dining chairs, with cabriole legs, c1850.
£2,200–2,600 GBr

A matched set of 13 George III mahogany dining chairs, each with an interlocking heart-shaped moulded pierced back carved with Prince of Wales feathers, including a pair of armchairs with later fitted arms, altered and restored.
£15,000–18,000 Bon

A set of eight Regency mahogany dining chairs, the top rails strung with ebony, early 19thC.
£7,000–8,500 TF

A set of six early Victorian Louis XV-style hide-upholstered mahogany dining chairs, by G. I. Morant.
£3,200–3,800 P

A set of 12 mahogany dining chairs, including two open armchairs, c1900.
£2,200–2,600 HOK

A set of eight late George III mahogany dining chairs, including two armchairs, all inlaid with brass stringing.
£3,200–3,800 CAG

A set of eight American Federal mahogany dining chairs, with reeded stiles centring a moulded tablet and pierced backrests, c1805.
£7,500–9,000 S(NY)

A set of six George IV mahogany dining chairs, c1820.
£4,000–5,000 S

A set of eight rosewood dining chairs, with carved crest rails and moulded cabriole legs, 19thC.
£1,500–1,800 TF

◀ A set of eight Edwardian mahogany dining chairs, c1900.
£2,800–3,200 S(S)

A William and Mary chest of drawers, inlaid with sycamore, boxwood, bog oak and holly, on replaced bun feet, c1690, 23in (58.5cm) wide.
£12,000–13,500 HA

A nailed hide-covered chest, the hinged top centred by the initials 'W R' beneath a crown, on a later oak stand, late 17thC, 45in (106cm) wide.
£4,500–5,500 S

A Queen Anne yew wood chest of drawers, c1715, 38in (96.5cm) wide.
£12,500–13,800 HA

A walnut chest of drawers, in two sections, early 18thC, 40in (101.5cm) wide.
£3,200–4,000 RBB

An Italian inlaid walnut commode, the upper drawer with a trompe l'oeil chequer pattern, reduced in height, late 18thC, 51¼in (130cm) wide.
£4,000–5,000 TEN

An Italian provincial rococo commode, with palissander, mahogany and fruitwood parquetry, mottled marble top, possibly Piedmontese, now fitted with later ormulu mounts, mid-18thC, 46in (117cm) wide.
£8,000–9,000 S(NY)

A south German walnut crossbanded *deux corps*, the cupboard enclosing a slide, four secret drawers and eight pigeonholes, on later feet, the lower part with a later top and feet, restoration and replacements, probably previously with a central bureau, 18thC, 52in (132cm) wide.
£1,700–2,000 P

A George III yew wood and walnut chest-on-chest, with geometric inlay to the sides, 42½in (107cm) wide.
£40,000–45,000 P

Early walnut furniture is particularly popular at present.

A Dutch burr-walnut and walnut marquetry serpentine linen press on chest, with several press plates above one drawer and a sliding leaf, c1725, 35½in (90cm) wide.
£2,800–3,200 S(Am)

A George I walnut chest-on-chest, with a brushing slide, c1720, 42in (106.5cm) wide.
£22,500–25,000 HA

A George III mahogany secretaire chest-on-chest, the secretaire drawer enclosing drawers and pigeonholes, around a central cupboard inlaid with a star motif and flanked by a pair of tall drawers applied with turned columns, c1785, 45¼in (115cm) wide.
£7,000–8,000 S

A Georgian mahogany press cupboard, the upper section with slides enclosed by oval panelled doors, 1800–10, 48in (122cm) wide.
£3,250–3,750 RBB

▶ An Edwardian gentleman's mahogany breakfront press/wardrobe, the central panelled doors enclosing sliding trays, flanked by cupboard doors enclosing hanging space, 96in (244cm) wide.
£5,500–6,500 P(S)

A George I walnut featherbanded and crossbanded chest-on-chest, handles replaced, 41¾in (106cm) wide.
£6,750–8,000 P(WM)

A walnut and fruitwood chest-on-stand, restored, early 18thC, stand later, 36¾in (93cm) wide.
£2,500–3,000 P

A Victorian olive, walnut and ebonized linen press, the upper panelled doors enclosing two shelves, the lower doors enclosing three slides and a shelf, the lower part cut at the back possibly to accommodate a dado, 50in (127cm) wide.
£3,300–4,000 P

A George II walnut chest-on-chest, c1750, 39¼in (100cm) wide.
£10,000–11,000 S

A Dutch mahogany and marquetry tall chest, with projecting frieze drawer, early 19thC, 43¼in (110cm) wide.
£2,000–2,200 Bea(E)

A Louix XV walnut armoire, on later compressed bun feet, mid-18thC, 60½in (154cm) wide.
£3,200–3,800 BB(S)

A Renaissance revival painted armoire, decorated in 16thC Italian style, c1865, 59in (150cm) wide.
£40,000–45,000 S

◀ A Victorian burr-walnut piano top davenport, the sprung rising top with stationery rack, the hinged flap top revealing a pull-out slide with inset gilt tooled leather, with two frieze drawers above one which releases the stationery rack, 23¼in (59cm) wide.
£3,000–3,500 WW

A Regency mahogany library davenport, with a pair of brass candle sconces and snuffers, 22¾in (58cm) wide.
£7,500–9,000 P

A mid-Victorian satinwood, sycamore, kingwood and marquetry davenport, by Holland & Sons, the fall-front inset with a writing surface, flanked by two lift-up compartments, 32in (81cm) wide.
£11,000–12,000 P

▶ A flame-mahogany partners' desk, with a lined top, early 19thC, 60in (152.5cm) wide.
£10,000–12,000 CRI

A bird's-eye maple metamorphic library desk, by William Bertram, c1850, 66in (167.5cm) wide.
£25,000–28,500 BERA

This desk was made for the 12th Earl of Pembroke.

An Italian neo-classical-style painted and parcel-gilt desk, late 19thC, 37in (94cm) wide.
£8,000–9,000 S(NY)

An Edwardian satinwood Carlton House desk, decorated with flowers and female portraits, 41in (104cm) wide.
£8,500–9,500 AG

A George III settee, painted and parcel-gilt, with later silk brocade upholstery, c1778, 93in (235cm) wide.
£50,000–56,000 HA

A George III mahogany triple chairback settee, repaired, late 18thC, 60in (152cm) wide.
£5,000–6,000 S(NY)

A pair of late George III painted sofas, with shaped top rails and button backs, on square tapering legs, 69in (175cm) wide.
£12,000–14,000 P

A late George III green decorated sofa, painted with leaf foliate and beaded chains, one leg later, restorations to seat rails, 79in (201cm) wide.
£2,500–3,000 P

A Russian Empire mahogany and bronze-mounted canapé, the top rail inlaid with swans and laurel wreaths, the armrests in the shape of carved swans, c1805, 89in (224cm) wide.
£18,000–20,000 S(Am)

A George IV rosewood sofa, on fluted bun feet, 63in (160cm) wide.
£1,600–1,800 RBB

A Dutch neo-classical mahogany and marquetry sofa, 84in (215cm) wide.
£4,000–4,500 BB(S)

A William IV simulated rosewood and parcel-gilt sofa, c1835, 98½in (250cm) wide.
£4,500–5,000 S

A Biedermeier fruitwood sofa, the backrest and seat with needlepoint upholstery, mid-19thC, 81½in (205cm) wide.
£3,300–3,600 BB(L)

A French button-back sofa, c1890, 56in (142cm) wide.
£625–700 BAB

A Victorian mahogany settee, the frame carved with scrolling foliage, 90in (228cm) wide.
£1,300–1,600 SWO

A Hungarian sofa, with original upholstery, c1880, 67in (170cm) wide.
£720–800 MIN

A Geoerge III inlaid mahogany
sideboard, c1790, some inlay
possibly later, 66in (167.5cm) wide.
£16,000–20,000 S

A George III inlaid mahogany
bowfronted sideboard,
60in (152.5cm) wide.
£2,700–3,000 Odi

A George III mahogany demilune
sideboard, with segment veneered
top and satinwood crossbanding,
84in (213cm) wide.
£7,000–8,000 RBB

◄ A George III
mahogany side-
board, with
satinwood cross-
banding and
string inlay,
possibly Scottish,
some alterations,
73in (185.5cm) wide.
£1,500–1,800 AH

A mahogany and boxwood-banded
serpentine sideboard, c1790,
69¾in (177cm) wide.
£2,700–3,300 HOK

An American Federal mahogany and
line-inlaid kidney-shaped sideboard,
Philadelphia, c1800, 64in (193cm) wide.
£3,300–4,000 BB(S)

A George III mahogany breakfront
sideboard, inlaid throughout with
crossbanding and stringing, with
a brass rail to the back, one end
with a pot cupboard door, c1795,
64in (198.5cm) wide.
£12,500–15,000 S

A late Regency mahogany sideboard,
the concave-fronted drawer flanked
by a deep drawer and a cupboard,
50in (127cm) wide.
£3,800–4,500 M

A Dutch marquetry side cabinet,
the double-moulded lid with
inlaid slides to the sides, 19thC,
48¾in (124cm) wide.
£3,500–4,200 P

A William IV mahogany twin
pedestal sideboard, one pedestal
enclosing a drawer above four
trays and cupboard space below,
the other with drawer above a
cupboard and a deep drawer,
50in (127cm) wide.
£800–1,000 PFK

An early Victorian mahogany
sideboard, with four ogee-moulded
frieze drawers and twin cupboard
doors, flanked by cellaret and cutlery
cupboards, 84in (241cm) wide.
£2,200–2,400 Bri

A Victorian inlaid oak and marquetry
sideboard, by Marsh & Jones,
Leeds, design attributed to
J. P. Seddon, the top formerly with
mirror back, 90in (228cm) wide.
£2,000–2,400 P(L)

A late Victorian carved pollard oak
sideboard, the base fitted with a
central drawer above a fall-front
cupboard, flanked by cupboards,
84in (213cm) wide.
£1,700–2,000 CAG

A carved and inlaid oak sideboard,
by Gillows of Lancaster, design
attributed to Bruce Talbert, c1870,
84in (210cm) wide.
£12,000–15,000 HAM

A William IV rosewood tilt-top parquetry breakfast table, the tapering facet column with a ring-turned collar, on a tripartite platform base, 50in (127cm) diam.
£4,000–4,500 TMA

A French mahogany and marquetry centre table, with cast brass leaf mounts, marquetry-inlaid with musical trophies, late 19thC, 53in (134.5cm) wide.
£3,800–4,500 CAG

A Regency mahogany breakfast table, in the manner of William Trotter, with radially veneered and crossbanded snap top, 51½in (130cm) wide.
£5,000–5,500 P

A George IV goncalo alves tilt-top centre table, attributed to Gillows, c1825, 52in (132cm) diam.
£5,750–7,000 S

▶ An Italian cherrywood extending dining table, with two extra leaves and four extra detachable tapering legs, c1830, 79in (200cm) wide.
£10,000–12,000 S

A Danish neo-classical mahogany and parcel-gilt centre table, the frieze fitted with two short drawers with later ormolu and gilt-metal mounts, early 19thC, 66in (167.5cm) wide.
£8,000–9,500 S(NY)

A George III mahogany pedestal dining table, the top with triple tilting action, with four additional leaves, some parts later, 202in (512cm) extended.
£11,500–14,000 S

◄ A William and Mary walnut crossbanded and feather-banded card table, the hinged top enclosing a baize-lined interior, restored, the legs and lower platform probably later or reconstructed, 23¾in (60cm) wide.
£6,000–7,000 P

A George II mahogany card table, the top lined in red baize, on one hinged and three fixed legs, c1740, 33¾in (85.5cm) wide.
£1,300–1,600 HAM

An early Victorian satin-wood and ash card table, in the manner of Richard Bridgens, with swivel top, 36¼in (92cm) wide.
£1,100–1,300 P

A Regency mahogany and rosewood-inlaid card table, with fold-over top, c1815, 35½in (90cm) wide.
£4,750–5,500 BB(L)

A French walnut card table, with baize-lined interior and ormolu mounts, late 19thC, 40¼in (102cm) wide.
£1,500–1,800 DDM

A mid-Victorian rosewood fold-over card table, 36in (91.5cm) wide.
£1,600–2,000 TMA

A satinwood card table, stamped 'Edwards & Roberts', the fold-over top painted with a central medallion depicting Seneca, damaged, c1910, 32in (81cm) wide.
£3,700–4,200 S(S)

The firm of Edwards & Roberts were prolific furniture makers. Normally when one finds a stamped piece it was because it was made for stock, whereas if they were producing furniture for private clients they didn't bother – the client knew who made it!

A Russian neo-classical brass-mounted fruitwood and parquetry games table, the hinged top supported on a gate leg and opening to reveal four elliptical wells, late 18thC, 36½in (92.5cm) wide.
£18,000–22,000 S(NY)

A Regency rosewood and brass-inlaid games table, the sliding tooled leather inset top adjustable and reversible, the central well inlaid for backgammon, the chessboard below, previously with work basket, 28½in (72cm) wide.
£3,500–4,000 P

A William IV yew wood games table, with drop leaves, the top inlaid with a chessboard, mid-19thC, 36in (91.5cm) wide.
£3,000–3,500 S(NY)

A French mahogany tric-trac table, the top inset with green felt on one side and brown tooled leather on the reverse, with an ivory-inlaid rosewood recessed backgammon board, the frieze fitted with a drawer and false drawer, mid-19thC, 44¼in (112.5cm) wide.
£3,000–3,500 NOA

A late Regency pollard oak games table, with reversible chessboard sliding top, 28in (71cm) wide.
£3,400–4,000 P(B)

A George III satinwood and harewood marquetry Rudd's patent dressing table, the frieze fitted with a central drawer and two flanking drawers with hinged and pivoted rising mirrors fitted with divisions and lidded compartment, c1780, 41¾in (106cm) wide.
£11,500–14,000 S

This table supposedly derives its name from a once popular character, for whom it was reputedly designed.

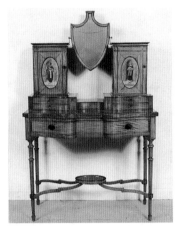

A satinwood dressing table, the serpentine base with a frieze drawer, 19thC, 39in (99cm) wide.
£1,200–1,500 RBB

A Regency rosewood library table, with two drawers and two false drawers, edged with boxwood stringing, 27½in (70cm) wide.
£16,000–20,000 HAM

A Milanese ivory-inlaid walnut writing table, mid-19thC, 42¾in (109cm) wide.
£2,800–3,200 BB(L)

An American rococo revival rosewood dresser, with marble top, probably Philadelphia, mid-19thC, 53in (134.5cm) wide.
£7,000–8,000 NOA

A Regency mahogany and rosewood drum table, with a gilt-tooled leather-lined surface over four drawers alternating with simulated drawers, basically early 19thC, 47in (119.5cm) wide.
£4,500–5,500 HYD

An Edwardian mahogany drum occasional table, the top with an interlacing harebell and laurel border, with the signs of the zodiac, above four drawers and four false drawers, 29½in (75cm) diam.
£3,500–4,000 P(Ed)

A George III inlaid mahogany writing table, with later tooled leather inset top, 44in (112cm) wide.
£2,000–2,400 P

A decorated dressing/work table, the frieze drawer flanked by a pair of small drawers above a slide for a workbag, 19thC, 33½in (85cm) wide.
£2,000–2,400 P

A Gothic revival oak extending drum table, with an arrangement of two opposing frieze drawers and four dummy frieze drawers, stamped 'Gillows of Lancaster', c1855, 67¾in (172cm) extended.
£4,000–5,000 S

A pair of rosewood library tables, attributed to Williams & Gibton, the panelled friezes with acanthus-carved scrolled brackets, c1830, 48½in (123cm) wide.
£13,500–15,000 HOK

A Louis XV/XVI rosewood, tulipwood-crossbanded and parquetry *table liseuse*, incorporating a slide with later tooled leather, 39in (99cm) wide.
£9,000–11,000 P

◄ A George III inlaid mahogany writing table, with later tooled leather inset top, 44in (112cm) wide.
£2,000–2,400 P

A George III satinwood and giltwood console table, the top crossbanded in mahogany and decorated with swags of beads filled with anthemia, legs possibly reduced in height, c1775, 46in (116cm) wide.
£8,500–10,000 S

A Biedermeier parcel-ebonized burr-poplar and ash console table, early 19thC, 30in (78cm) wide.
£2,200–2,600 BB(S)

A French Empire mahogany console table, in the manner of Jacob-Desmalter, applied with gilt-metal mounts, with grey fossil marble top, early 19thC, 56in (142cm) wide.
£1,500–1,800 P

◀ An Italian gilt-wood serpentine console table, with green marble top, mid-19thC, 76in (193cm) wide.
£7,000–8,000 Bon

▶ A pair of Edwardian satinwood and marquetry console tables, the tops inlaid with panels of musical instruments and putti, centred by an inlaid fan patera, c1910, 53in (134cm) wide.
£17,000–18,500 S

An early Victorian mahogany hall table, with boot rack, and with later back rail and feet, 45in (114cm) wide.
£2,000–2,400 P

A Queen Anne burr-walnut side table, the top inlaid with geometric strapwork within a featherbanded border, 32¾in (83cm) wide.
£10,000–12,000 P(Sc)

A George III mahogany serving table, the banded top above an inlaid panelled frieze, c1790, 50in (127cm) wide.
£5,500–6,000 S

A George IV mahogany serving table, the inverted breakfront top with a brass gallery surmounted by urn finials, gallery replaced, c1825, 102¼in (260cm) wide.
£10,500–11,500 S

A George II carved pine side table, with a mottled marble top, c1745, formerly painted, 32½in (82cm) wide.
£8,500–10,000 S

A George II Irish carved mahogany side table, the later top above a scrolling leaf-carved frieze centred by a grinning mask, 56¼in (143cm) wide.
£17,000–20,000 P

An early Victorian mahogany side table, with a cushion-shaped drawer, 26in (66cm) wide.
£1,200–1,400 Bon(M)

A George III marquetry table, inlaid with sprays of flowers, c1775, 25in (63cm) wide.
£4,500–5,500 S

A French Directoire oyster-veneered marquetry laburnum, plane, yew, elm, mahogany, cherrywood and parquetry tilt-top *guéridon*, late 18thC, 28¼in (72cm) wide.
£8,000–9,000 S

A George III green-painted Pembroke table, by Thomas Chippendale, decorated throughout with ivory bandings within black strung outlines, c1772, 42in (107cm) extended.
£11,500–14,000 S

A label in the drawer states that this table formerly belonged to David Garrick and was used by him in the Green Room at the Garrick Theatre.

A Russian pearwood and marquetry *table à rognon*, with brass-bound top, possibly St Petersburg, restored, late 18thC, 39in (99cm) wide.
£6,000–7,000 P

A painted and gilded table, with replaced marble top, late 19thC, 29in (74cm) wide.
£630–700 NET

A mahogany Pembroke table, with boxwood stringing and central inlaid motif, 18thC, 31in (78.5cm) wide.
£2,400–2,700 CRU

A Regency mahogany sofa table, with boxwood stringing, the two frieze drawers with brass handles opposing false drawer fronts, 66in (168cm) extended.
£3,500–4,000 DN

◀ A Regency rosewood sofa table, the two short and two false drawers with turned brass handles, 38½in (98cm) wide.
£15,000–16,500 AG

A pair of George III carved giltwood tables, the tops centred by hand-coloured curled paper prints and painted borders within leaf-cast brass edges, formerly polescreens, 15¼in (39cm) wide.
£8,000–9,000 S

A mahogany occasional table, with satinwood inlay, c1890, 24in (61cm) wide.
£520–575 GBr

A George III burr-yew Pembroke table, in the manner of Mayhew & Ince, the top inlaid with a fan and central flower, above a bowfront end drawer and dummy drawer opposite, later handles, 28in (71cm) wide.
£8,500–9,500 DN

A Regency rosewood and brass marquetry sofa table, applied with gilt-bronze mounts, the pair of frieze drawers opposed by simulated drawers, 62½in (159cm) wide.
£23,000–28,000 P

A Regency rosewood work table, inlaid with satinwood, 29in (73.5cm) wide.
£4,250–4,750 CRU

A Regency mahogany work table, with boxwood stringing, on turned legs and original casters, c1815, 18in (45.5cm) wide.
£2,000–2,500 RL

A Regency rosewood drop-flap work table, the hinged top containing two drawers and a pleated silk compartment, 32½in (82cm) extended.
£2,000–2,400 P

A William IV painted and parcel-gilt work table, the hinged glazed top inset with a floral needlework panel above a frieze decorated with Vitruvian scrolls, mid-19thC, 20in (51cm) wide.
£1,800–2,200 BB(S)

A Charles rosewood *guéridon à ouvrage*, the lifting top inlaid with satinwood arabesque marquetry, mid-19thC, 16in (40.5cm) diam.
£1,600–1,800 NOA

A William IV octagonal rosewood, maple and pine parquetry work table, the hinged top enclosing a lined and compartmented interior, c1835, 17¾in (45cm) wide.
£1,100–1,300 S(S)

A Regency Tunbridge ware combined teapoy and work table, containing two lidded boxes and apertures for mixing bowls, c1815, 15¼in (39cm) wide.
£3,000–3,500 S

A Victorian rosewood firescreen, fitted with a beadwork panel, mid-19thC, 35½in (90cm) wide.
£650–775 NOA

A George II chestnut stool, with drop-in floral needlework seat, c1730, 20½in (52cm) wide.
£9,000–11,000 S

A French giltwood stool, with original tapestry, c1885, 23in (58.5cm) wide.
£1,000–1,200 RL

A pair of Napoleon III carved giltwood stools, in the manner of A. M. E. Fournier, 23in (58cm) wide.
£5,500–6,000 P

◄ A mahogany five-tier whatnot, in the manner of Gillows, two tiers fitted with drawers, 17¾in (45cm) wide.
£6,500–7,500 S

► A Victorian figured-walnut whatnot, with three serpentine shelves and drawer to base, 21¾in (55.5cm) wide.
£900–1,100 M

A pair of late Regency mahogany window seats, each with a moulded roundel and lotus-leaf carved frame, later decorated, 49¼in (128cm) wide.
£17,000–20,000 P

CHAISES LONGUES & DAY BEDS

A Louis XV French provincial carved walnut *duchesse brisée*, the bergère chair with padded back, sides, arms and loose cushion seat, the top rail, seat rail and knees carved with flowers and leaves, the serpentine stool with loose cushion seat.
£8,000–9,000 S

A *duchesse brisée* is of French origin, popular in England during the late 18thC. It consisted of one or two tub-shaped chairs and a stool to extend the length. Sheraton's design consisted of two rounded settees joined by a stool.

A George IV rosewood chaise longue, with reeded show frame and one scroll end, padded side, back and seat, 72in (183cm) wide.
£1,000–1,200 DN

A walnut chaise longue, mid-19thC, 77in (195.5cm) long.
£2,800–3,200 ChA

A rococo-revival walnut and button-upholstered *recamier*, on cabriole legs and scrolling toes, 1880–90, 77in (195.5cm) long.
£1,500–1,800 SK

A Biedermeier walnut *recamier,* with outscrolling upholstered headrest applied with roundels, early 19thC, 80in (203cm) wide.
£4,000–5,000 BB(S)

The *recamier* was named after Madame Recamier who was depicted in a painting reclining on a day bed with scroll ends.

A George IV rosewood chaise longue, with reeded and rosette-carved frame, the back and out-scrolled sides caned above a squab cushion seat, 80in (203cm) long.
£1,500–1,800 DN

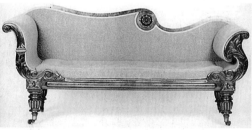

A George IV carved mahogany chaise longue, the scrolling top rail with rosette motif above padded back and arms, with carved floral and scrollwork decoration, 78in (198cm) long.
£1,200–1,400 P(L)

A Victorian walnut chaise longue, the serpentine button-upholstered back with leaf and scroll carving, with overstuffed serpentine seat, 69in (175.5cm) long.
£1,400–1,700 AH

CHESTS OF DRAWERS & COMMODES

A William and Mary walnut chest of drawers, the top with an inlaid panel, the drawers below with conforming inlaid decoration, damaged and restored, some veneers later, c1690, 39¾in (101cm) wide.
£3,400–3,750 S(S)

A William III oyster olivewood chest of drawers, strung and beaded with holly, the sides veneered with figured ash, on later turned feet, restored, 36½in (92.5cm) wide.
£4,000–5,000 TEN

A Queen Anne walnut and feather-banded chest of drawers, with two short and three long drawers, on replacement bun feet, 40in (101.5cm) wide.
£2,000–2,400 RBB

A George I walnut crossbanded chest of drawers, with oak drawer linings and bottoms, on replacement bracket feet, 32in (81.5cm) wide.
£1,800–2,200 WILL

An oyster veneer walnut chest of drawers, early 18thC, 38in (96.5cm) wide.
£7,000–8,000 RBB

Despite missing handles and feet and requiring extensive repair to the veneers, the unrestored condition of this chest of drawers, with its inlaid boxwood top in an unusual geometric design, resulted in fierce telephone bidding between seven people. The final price was more than ten times the top estimate.

A George II mahogany chest of drawers, with a caddy top over a slide and two short and three long drawers, on bracket feet, restored, 33in (84cm) wide.
£1,700–2,000 TEN

A George II mahogany chest of drawers, with a caddy top over a slide and two short and three long drawers, on bracket feet, restored, 33in (84cm) wide.

A Portuguese mahogany and rosewood serpentine commode, with two short and three graduated long drawers, mid-18thC, 46in (117cm) wide.
£1,600–2,000 Bea(E)

A George III mahogany chest of drawers, the four oak-lined long graduated drawers with original brass swan-neck handles, 34in (86.5cm) wide.
£2,000–2,400 DMC

A French Louis XV *bois satiné* and purpleheart commode, the marble top over two short and three long drawers, between rounded stiles headed by gilt-metal mounts, on stile feet, 18thC, 50½in (128.5cm) wide.
£2,600–3,200 TEN

◄ A mahogany bachelor's chest, with a brushing slide above four long graduated drawers, flanked by fluted canted corners, 18thC, 31in (78.5cm) wide.
£2,600–3,000 RBB

A George III mahogany chest of drawers, with two short and three long drawers with original beaded brass swan-necked bale handles, between fluted quadrant corners, 45½in (115.6cm) wide.
£750–900 PFK

An ebonized chest of drawers, chinoiserie-decorated with birds, figures and foliage, with brass handles, raised on later bracket feet, 18thC, 41in (104cm) wide.
£400–500 AG

This piece was formerly the top section of a tallboy.

An American Chippendale mahogany bowfront chest of drawers, the top with inlaid edge above a cockbeaded base of four drawers, replaced brasses, Massachusetts, c1780, 37¾in (96cm) wide.
£3,500–4,000 SK(B)

A Maltese marquetry commode, the reserves purplewood-banded and inlaid with boxwood lines and with 'love bird' inlaid oval panels, the top inlaid with a panel above a frieze drawer and three long drawers, the sides inlaid with cockerels and foliage, 18thC, 59½in (151cm) wide.
£6,000–7,000 P

An Italian kingwood and walnut-veneered commode, with pink marble top, the two long drawers and sides with geometric banding and inlaid star motifs, marble top damaged, late 18th/early 19thC, 53¼in (135.5cm) wide.
£7,000–8,500 Bea(E)

A south German rosewood and floral marquetry commode, the top with projecting corners, inlaid with a central panel of a parrot eating fruit, flanked by floral sprays, above three long drawers, the sides inlaid, late 18thC, 56in (142cm) wide.
£4,000–5,000 P

A pair of Regency mahogany bowfront commodes, the three long graduated drawers flanked by reeded columns, c1805, 39in (99cm) wide.
£9,500–11,500 Bon

A mahogany crossbanded and line-inlaid chest of drawers, with two short and three long graduated drawers, a secretaire slide and covered pen well, with two side carrying handles, early 19thC, 39in (99cm) wide.
£1,100–1,200 TMA

An Irish mahogany tall chest, on bracket feet, c1800, 67in (170cm) wide.
£1,800–2,200 HOK

Cross Reference
See Colour Review

► An American early Empire mahogany chest of drawers, the superstructure surmounted by a scrolled backboard, the front with an outset frieze drawer raised on columnar stiles flanking three recessed drawers, early 19thC, 42¼in (107.5cm) wide.
£1,000–1,100 SLN

An Empire ormolu-mounted ebonized chest of drawers, with grey mottled marble top above seven drawers, flanked by Egyptian terms, early 19thC, 31in (78.5cm) wide.
£3,700–4,000 S(NY)

A European mahogany chest of drawers, with gadrooned decoration and moulded marble top, c1840, 50in (127cm) wide.
£3,000–3,500 HA

A Scottish walnut chest of drawers, the frieze drawer over a hat drawer, flanked by four small drawers over three long drawers, c1850, 60in (152.5cm) wide.
£675–750 NAW

A Dutch neo-classical mahogany chest of drawers, the top inlaid with ebony and boxwood, the pair of drawers over three graduated drawers with original handles cast with lions, the canted corners decorated with parquetry, early 19thC, 40½in (103cm) wide.
£2,000–2,200 NOA

A Spanish walnut commode, with quarter-veneered and banded top, the frieze drawer diagonally inlaid with stringing lines, above graduated drawers flanked by carved shells and foliage, mid-19thC, 46½in (118cm) wide.
£7,000–8,500 BB(S)

A German gilt-metal-mounted walnut commode, the serpentine top over two drawers and a shaped apron, 19thC, 26in (66cm) wide.
£850–1,000 P

◄ A Baltic neo-classical-style gilt-bronze-mounted walnut chest of drawers, the top over a pair of drawers and two recessed drawers, flanked by columns, c1900, 35¾in (91cm) wide.
£650–800 SK

A George IV mahogany bowfront chest of drawers, the three short and four graduated long drawers with turned mahogany handles, over a shaped and ebony-strung apron, 47½in (120.5cm) wide.
£550–650 TRM

A burr-walnut chest of drawers, c1860, 41in (104cm) wide.
£1,200–1,350 GBr

A Victorian Scottish mahogany chest of five drawers, with three hidden drawers, on bun feet, 50in (127cm) wide.
£400–500 AAV

An Edwardian satinwood and inlaid chest, with a dentil-moulded top over two short and three long drawers, between outset canted stop-fluted stiles, 43¼in (110cm) wide.
£1,800–2,200 TEN

CHESTS-ON-CHESTS

A George I walnut chest-on-chest, the two short and three long graduated drawers with figured banding, the lower section with a brushing slide above three further graduated drawers, later alterations and restored, 67¼in (171.5cm) high.
£4,500–5,500 RTo

The purchase invoice, dated 11th July 1950, from Philip & Richard Parker, 98 Fulham Rd, London, states that the piece was 'originally in the Gatehouse of Hampton Court Palace'.

A George III mahogany chest-on-chest, the two short and three long drawers with oval brass handles, three further drawers below, 44¼in (112.5cm) wide.
£1,700–2,000 Bri

▶ A George III mahogany chest-on-chest, with fluted canted corners and original handles, 36in (91.5cm) wide.
£2,000–2,200 Odi

A George III mahogany chest-on-chest, the top with pendant frieze, over two short and three long graduated drawers, the base with three long graduated drawers, with ivory escutcheons and later brass handles, 42in (106.5cm) wide.
£4,000–4,500 DA

A George III mahogany chest-on-chest, with blind-fret frieze drawer, over two short and three long drawers with a further blind-fret drawer in the waist, the base with three long drawers, 45¾in (116cm) wide.
£4,000–4,500 TEN

Miller's Compares

I A George II walnut chest-on-chest, the three short and three long graduated drawers flanked by fluted canted corners, the lower section with a brushing slide and four further graduated drawers, c1740, 43in (109cm) wide.
£17,000–20,000 Bon

II A George II walnut chest-on-chest, the three short and three long featherbanded drawers and brushing slide flanked by reeded canted corners, the base with three further long graduated drawers, c1740, 43¾in (111cm) wide.
£6,000–7,000 Bon

The quality of construction was the major factor which determined the different prices these two chests achieved in the saleroom. Item I was made in London and displays the superior skills of a cabinet-maker trained in the capital, who would have had a wealthier clientele and would therefore be able to use the best materials. It is constructed of oak, and the veneers consist of single sheets of walnut. It also has superbly crafted drawer linings and beautiful dovetailing. Item II is a provincial piece and, whilst attractive and competently constructed, it is less desirable because of its pine carcase with section veneers consisting of three or four pieces of walnut. Of equal importance is the fact that Item I retains its glorious original colour. Furthermore, Item I has a brushing slide and original drawer handles and escutcheons, which Item II lacks.

A George III mahogany secretaire chest-on-chest, the two short and two long drawers with secretaire drawer below, flanked by fluted quarter columns, the base with three long graduated drawers, 45¾in (116cm) wide.
£3,500–4,200 P(NW)

A George III mahogany chest-on-chest, the top with two short and three long drawers with brass handles, flanked by inlaid canted corners, 45in (114.5cm) wide.
£1,650–2,000 AH

A late George III mahogany chest-on-chest, with two short and six long graduated drawers, the top section decorated with inlaid satinwood crossbanding, featherbanding and shell motifs with canted corners, with embossed brass handles, 44in (112cm) wide.
£1,000–1,200 AG

A Regency mahogany and ebony-strung bowfront chest-on-chest, the arched reeded pediment above two short and three long drawers, the base with three further long drawers, c1805, 44½in (113cm) wide.
£4,500–5,500 Bon

A mahogany bowfront chest-on-chest, with Gothic arcade frieze, eight drawers and a brushing slide, on splay feet, early 19thC, 46in (117cm) wide.
£3,000–3,500 RBB

Miller's is a price GUIDE not a price LIST

A George III-style mahogany chest-on-chest, the egg-and-dart dentilled frieze with three short and three long graduated drawers below, flanked by fluted angled pilasters, the base with four long graduated drawers, late 19thC, 47¼in (120cm) wide.
£1,400–1,700 P(Ed)

CHESTS-ON-STANDS

A William and Mary walnut chest-on-stand, with crossbanded top over two short and three long graduated drawers, the stand with a drawer over an undulating frieze, on later turned bun feet, late 17th/early 18thC, 39¼in (99.5cm) wide.
£2,800–3,200 HYD

A walnut and feather-banded chest-on-stand, the top containing three frieze drawers and long graduated drawers, on later associated stand, early 18thC, 37½in (95.5cm) wide.
£1,100–1,300 P

Cross Reference
See Colour Review

A George I walnut chest-on-stand, the two short and three long feather-banded drawers with brass pierced lock plates and swing handles, the stand with a bevelled long drawer, sides of cornice replaced, both back legs replaced, restored, 38in (96.5cm) wide.
£3,500–4,200 HAL

A George I japanned chest-on-stand, decorated overall with figures and birds in Oriental landscapes on a black ground, the moulded cornice above a bolection drawer, two short and three long drawers with brass handles and escutcheons, the base with one short and two deep drawers, parts replaced, 42in (106.5cm) wide.
£3,300–4,000 DN

A walnut chest-on-stand, with two small and three graduated drawers with crossbanding and drawer-fronts of seaweed marquetry, on later stand of period design, early 18thC, 37in (94cm) wide.
£1,500–1,800 RBB

Japanning

- Developed mid-17thC in imitation of Chinese and Japanese lacquer, which was very costly, scarce and in great demand.
- Main ingredient was shellac (an encrustation of insects which feed on the sap of trees in India and Thailand), seed-lac or gum-lac, which was dissolved in alcohol and then applied in numerous coats and usually decorated with gilt chinoiserie.
- As shellac was weak and permeable to water, it was necessary to build up raised areas in sawdust and gum arabic in order to replicate the depth of relief obtainable with lacquer.
- Japanning became a popular pastime for young ladies during the late 17th and early 18thC, stimulated by the publication in 1688 of John Stalker and George Parker's 'Treatise on Japanning and Varnishing', which included recipes, instructions and designs.
- The technique was fashionable in the first half of the Victorian period for small pieces of furniture, trays, jugs, etc. Decoration often included British flowers such as roses and forget-me-nots.

MILITARY CHESTS

A George III mahogany brass-bound campaign chest, in two parts, raised on original acorn-design feet, c1800, 32in (81.5cm) wide.
£3,200–3,500 CAT

A camphorwood and brass-bound campaign chest, in two sections, the fall-front secretaire drawer enclosing a fitted interior of a panelled door flanked by pigeonholes and small drawers, with two short and two long drawers below, brass carrying handles, 19thC, 38½in (98cm) wide.
£1,300–1,600 P

A late Victorian walnut-veneered and teak military chest, in two parts, with brass mounts and recessed handles, the hinged and panelled top enclosing four hinged shelves with brass supports and finials flanking a mirror, above an arrangement of five short and four long drawers, one fitted with an adjustable writing slope, a stationery rack and two lidded compartments, lacking the feet, 42in (106.5cm) wide.
£2,700–3,000 DN

A Regency mahogany campaign-type chest, the top with a reeded three-quarter ledge back and a reeded and ebony-strung edge, with two long drawers and a cupboard below enclosed by a pair of panel doors, the sides with brass carrying handles, 30¼in (77cm) wide.
£1,250–1,500 P(E)

Further Reading

Miller's Collecting Furniture: The Facts at Your Fingertips, Miller's Publications, 1995

A teak and brass-bound military chest, with a central fitted secretaire drawer, flanked by a small drawer on each side, with three further drawers below, 19thC, 39in (99cm) wide.
£1,500–1,800 E

A Victorian teak and brass-bound military chest, the top with six drawers, the lower section with two long drawers, c1860, 39in (99cm) wide.
£550–650 Bon(G)

A Victorian mahogany and brass-bound military chest, in two parts, with two short and three long drawers, 24in (61cm) wide.
£2,600–3,200 P

By repute, this chest was made for the Paris Exhibition of 1889, and won an award.

▶ A mahogany brass-bound two-part military chest, fitted with two short and three graduated long drawers, 19thC, 40in (101.5cm) wide.
£1,500–1,800 G(B)

A teak and brass-bound secretaire campaign chest, in two parts, with a central fitted secretaire drawer containing small drawers and pigeonholes around a cupboard flanked by four short drawers with three long drawers below, 19thC, 41in (104cm) wide.
£2,300–2,750 P(S)

SECRETAIRE CHESTS

A late George III mahogany and rosewood-crossbanded chest, the secretaire drawer enclosing a fitted interior, 31in (78.5cm) wide.
£1,500–1,800 P

LOCATE THE SOURCE
The source of each illustration in Miller's can be found by checking the code letters below each caption with the Key to Illustrations, pages 789–795.

A late Georgian oak and mahogany crossbanded secretaire chest, the secretaire drawer fitted with drawers and pigeonholes, above three other long drawers, all with brass swan-neck bale handles, 44in (112cm) wide.
£700–850 PFK

▶ A French Charles X mahogany and gilt-metal-mounted secretaire commode, the fall-front enclosing a fitted interior of drawers and pigeonholes above three long drawers flanked by turned columns, c1830, 56in (142cm) wide.
£1,600–2,000 Bon

A late George IV inlaid mahogany secretaire chest, the upper section with two long dummy drawers enclosing a writing surface and fitted interior, above three long conforming drawers flanked by cluster column-type pilasters, 47in (119.5cm) wide.
£1,600–2,000 MEA

WELLINGTON CHESTS

A Regency bird's-eye maple Wellington chest, with ten drawers and locking pilaster, on later feet, 26in (66cm) wide.
£1,700–2,000 S(S)

◀ A Victorian mahogany Wellington chest, the eleven drawers with brass handles, with a hinged locking pilaster, 27in (68.5cm) wide.
£1,250–1,500 JAd

A Victorian pollard oak Wellington chest, with six drawers flanked by pilasters, one locking, with acanthus-carved corbels, 20in (51cm) wide.
£1,100–1,300 P(S)

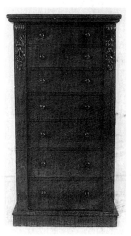

A Victorian figured-mahogany Wellington chest, the seven graduated drawers with turned knob handles, the centre drawer fitted with a panel perhaps for writing, all flanked by pilasters with bold acanthus scroll and flower pendant capitals, one lockable, 25in (63.5cm) wide.
£1,600–2,000 HAM

▶ An Irish rosewood Wellington chest, with eight drawers and a locking pilaster, some moulding missing, 19thC, 45in (114.5cm) wide.
£1,200–1,500 DN

A Victorian mahogany Wellington chest, with seven drawers and hinged locking upright, 25¼in (64cm) wide.
£2,500–3,000 P(G)

CLOTHES & LINEN PRESSES

A George II mahogany clothes press, with a pair of panelled doors enclosing a series of pull-out trays, above two short and one long drawer with brass swan-neck drop handles and brass escutcheons, 50in (127cm) wide.
£2,800–3,200 **Mit**

A George III mahogany linen press, with two panelled doors above two short and three long drawers, 51in (129.5cm) wide.
£1,350–1,600 **E**

A George III mahogany linen press, with swan-neck pediment above a pair of panelled doors enclosing sliding shelves, two short and two long graduated drawers with brass handles, 52in (132cm) wide.
£2,400–3,000 **AG**

A George III figured-mahogany linen press, with later ogee-moulded cornice above twin oval-banded panelled doors, 59½in (150cm) wide.
£1,250–1,500 **Bri**

▶ A late George III inlaid mahogany linen press, with satinwood crossbanding throughout, the two panelled doors enclosing sliding trays, two short and two long drawers, 49¾in (126.5cm) wide.
£2,300–2,750 **Bea(E)**

A mahogany linen press, with two panelled doors enclosing trays, above two short and two long drawers, late 18thC, 48in (122cm) wide.
£1,500–1,800 **MJB**

A mahogany linen press, with two panelled doors above two short and two long drawers, c1800, 48in (122cm) wide.
£1,250–1,500 **HOK**

A Victorian figured-mahogany linen press, with twin shaped-top panelled doors enclosing three linen trays, the base with two short and two long graduated drawers with wooden knob handles, 51¾in (131.5cm) wide.
£600–700 **Bri**

A mahogany clothes press, in the style of Gillows, the panelled doors enclosing slides, above two short and two long drawers with replaced wooden knob handles, flanked by narrow long cupboards fitted for hanging, c1830, 66in (167.5cm) wide.
£2,300–2,750 **PFK**

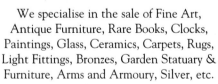

DAVENPORTS

A George III mahogany davenport, the swivel top with three-quarter brass gallery and central handle, a pen drawer to one side and two drawers to the interior, the side fitted with four drawers, the reverse side with a slide and four false drawers, 15in (38cm) wide.
£5,000–6,000 P(B)

A late Regency rosewood davenport, with pierced three-quarter gallery above a leather-lined slope enclosing four short drawers, above stationery compartment and slides to each side, the four long drawers flanked by simulated drawers, 23¼in (59cm) wide.
£2,000–2,400 P

A William IV rosewood davenport, with sliding top, inset writing slope enclosing small drawers, four dummy and four real drawers to the sides, the front with half-round pilasters and leaf-carved capitals, 21in (53.5cm) wide.
£1,600–2,000 RBB

A Victorian rosewood and boxwood-strung harlequin davenport, with a meta-morphic stationery rack, the piano lid with fitted sliding writing surface, four drawers to one side and opposing dummy drawers, 23¼in (59cm) wide.
£1,600–2,000 P(NW)

A walnut davenport, with boxwood inlay, the pen compartment with three-quarter gallery, c1870, 21in (53.5cm) wide.
£1,800–2,000 GBr

A Victorian mahogany davenport, the hinged sloping lid inset with leather writing surface, a hinged door to the rear, above a cupboard to the rear and scroll-ended carved cabriole supports, 25½in (65cm) wide.
£320–385 PFK

A Victorian walnut davenport, the hinged stationery compartment above a leather-covered writing slope, on carved scrolling supports with four short and four false drawers to the sides, 21½in (54.5cm) wide.
£900–1,100 AG

A Victorian walnut davenport, the pen compartment with a three-quarter pierced gallery, the serpentine slope over four real and four dummy drawers, 22in (56cm) wide.
£1,200–1,400 Bri

A Victorian walnut davenport, the hinged top enclosing a fitted interior above a leather-inset fall-front, over four real and four opposing dummy drawers, with bobbin and ring-turned columns, faults, one drawer stencilled 'Maple and Co...', 20½in (52cm) wide.
£850–950 S(S)

A Victorian inlaid rosewood davenport, the brass-galleried box fitted with cubbyholes, the slope with tooled leather writing surface, the front panel centred by a marquetry patera, one side with a bank of drawers, the reverse with dummy drawers, 20¾in (52.5cm) wide.
£1,000–1,200 NOA

A late Victorian rosewood davenport, the pen compartment with a three-quarter brass gallery, over four real and four dummy drawers, on ceramic casters, damaged, 22in (56cm) wide.
£650–800 S(S)

▶ A Victorian inlaid walnut davenport, with four drawers, casters missing, 22in (56cm) wide.
£800–900 S(S)

A Victorian burr-walnut davenport, with carved serpentine supports, and four real and four false drawers, 21in (53.5cm) wide.
£800–1,000 Bri

DESKS

A George II walnut kneehole desk, with seven drawers and kneehole cupboard, top veneers and feet replaced, 30¼in (77cm) wide.
£3,200–3,850 TEN

A German walnut pedestal desk, with leather inset top, nine cedar-lined herringbone-banded drawers, the sides with geometric banding, late 18thC, 52in (132cm) wide.
£3,000–3,500 DN

A late George II mahogany kneehole desk, by Giles Grendey, with cockbeaded frieze drawer, a recessed cupboard below enclosing a single shelf with arched drawer above, three graduated drawers to either side, paper label of Giles Grendey to frieze drawer, 30in (76cm) wide.
£3,800–4,500 P(NW)

Giles Grendey, or Grindey, (1693–1780) traded from St. John's Square, Clerkenwell. He was elected to the Livery of the Joiners' Company in 1729 and became Master in 1766. He is known for his superb japanned work as well as his general cabinet-making and mirrors.

A George III mahogany kneehole desk, with two frieze drawers, six further drawers and a cupboard, 36in (91.5cm) wide.
£600–700 RTo

An early Victorian mahogany-veneered desk compactum, with sliding leather-inset writing top, a folio compartment above three graduated drawers with brass locks and turned wood knob handles, the reverse with dummy drawers, 45in (114.5cm) wide.
£1,250–1,500 WW

A Victorian mahogany partners' desk, the leather-inset top over a long drawer, flanked by two short drawers, the pedestals with three short drawers, turned wood handles, 60in (152.5cm) wide.
£2,200–2,650 Doc

A late Victorian walnut pedestal desk, the top inset with black leather, over two slides and three frieze drawers, each panelled pedestal swivelling to reveal a fitted nest of lacewood drawers, metal label inscribed 'The Shannon Limited, Ropemaker Street, London, E.C.', 60¾in (153.5cm) wide.
£6,000–7,000 TEN

A Victorian mahogany cylinder desk, by Holland & Sons, with three-quarter pierced brass gallery, the sliding tambour fall revealing a fitted interior of drawers and pigeonholes and a pull-out leather-lined writing slide, the frieze with three drawers, the pedestals each with three further drawers, central frieze drawer stamped 'Holland & Sons, Mount Street, London', c1865, 53½in (136cm) wide.
£5,000–5,500 S

The firm of Holland & Sons was founded c1803 as Taprell, Stephen & Holland and became one of London's most distinguished cabinet makers in Victorian times. They worked extensively for the Royal family and the government and employed some of the leading designers of the day.

A Victorian walnut-veneered writing desk, the top with nests of five drawers divided by a spindle gallery, over two small drawers and writing slope, with turned handles, damaged, 50in (127cm) wide.
£750–900 DA

A late Victorian mahogany kneehole desk, the inset leather-lined writing surface above seven short drawers, with moulded brass handles, 50in (127cm) wide.
£800–1,000 AG

▶ An Edwardian satinwood-banded mahogany and marquetry Carlton House desk, made to a design retailed by Maple & Co, with a pull-out leather-lined writing surface, 54in (137cm) wide.
£9,000–10,000 G(L)

A Victorian mahogany Wooton desk, by Gillows of Lancaster, the shaped three-quarter gallery mounted with turned finials above a pair of panelled cupboard doors flanked by fluted pilasters, the cylinder-shaped projecting mid-section with four panelled sections opening to a fitted interior, the base with a drawer, the pediment stamped 'Gillows of Lancaster', c1870, 39¼in (99.5cm) wide.
£18,000–22,000 S

This desk is based on a design patented in 1874 by William S. Wooton, a manufacturer of school desks and office furniture based in Indianapolis. The success of the design led to other firms of cabinet-makers producing furniture of a similar type in both America and England.

A teak railway desk, the top centred by the East Indian Railway arms beneath a crown, now glazed, late 19thC, 31in (78.5cm) wide.
£3,200–3,500 S

The East Indian Railway was founded by Rowland MacDonald Stephenson on 1 June 1845. The first section of the line was built between Calcutta and Mirzapur, later extending to Delhi.

A walnut Wooton desk, the two doors with central handle, letterbox and fully fitted interior, maker's plaque marked 'Pat.Oct.6.1876', 39½in (100.5cm) wide.
£6,000–6,500 CLE

A Victorian mahogany desk, 60in (152.5cm) wide.
£2,200–2,650 WILL

A walnut desk, with Moorish carved panels and friezes, the inset leather top over two frieze drawers and open sections to either side of the kneehole, each end fitted with a deep drawer, on square tapering legs, 1880, 43¾in (106cm) wide.
£2,700–3,250 GH

An Edwardian mahogany Carlton House desk, decorated in the neo-classical manner with rosettes, swags, bellflowers and rams' heads, the top section with central cupboard, four pigeonholes, six short drawers and quadrant cupboards above three drawers, 48in (122cm) wide.
£1,500–1,800 JAd

An Edwardian mahogany kidney-shaped writing desk, with boxwood stringing and marquetry decoration, the top with tooled leather insert above a frieze drawer flanked by pedestals of four graduated drawers, 51½in (131cm) wide.
£3,500–4,200 P(Ed)

An Edwardian satinwood and mahogany-crossbanded pedestal desk, inlaid with tulipwood, boxwood and ebonized lines, the top inset with a tooled green leather writing surface, the three frieze drawers above a recessed cupboard door and flanked by six further drawers, 54¼in (138cm) wide.
£1,800–2,200 P

A mahogany kidney-shaped desk, by Whytock & Reid, the top inset with a panel of green leather above a central frieze drawer with carved decoration, flanked by ten short drawers with acanthus-carved capitals, the sides and back panelled with flame veneers, gilt-metal trade plate inscribed 'Whytock & Reid, Edinburgh', leather distressed, early 20thC, 60¼in (153cm) wide.
£8,500–10,000 P

Whytock & Reid of Edinburgh can trace their origins to the early 19thC, originally specializing in textile manufacture. By the 1870s, cabinet-making was their major concern and by the end of the 19thC they were the most prominent art manufacturers and retailers in Edinburgh. In the early 20thC they produced pieces in both historical styles and in the more contemporary Arts and Crafts and Art Deco styles.

An Edwardian inlaid satinwood writing desk, with shaped leather-inset top over a central drawer flanked by banks of three graduated drawers, stamped 'Edwards & Roberts', minor damage, c1900, 42in (106.5cm) wide.
£2,000–2,200 SK

An Edwardian mahogany pedestal partners' desk, with inset writing surface above four drawers flanking arched kneeholes, the pedestals each with three drawers and panelled cupboard doors, on plinth bases, faults, 72in (183cm) wide.
£1,800–2,200 S(S)

◄ An Edwardian mahogany serpentine kneehole desk, by Maple & Co, the leather-inset top with boxwood, ebony and satinwood cross-banding, over a concave central drawer between four convex drawers, 42in (106.5cm) wide.
£1,300–1,600 EH

► An Edwardian mahogany and satinwood-crossbanded writing table, inlaid with stringing, with inset leatherette writing surface, damaged, 39½in (100.5cm) wide.
£630–700 S(S)

◄ An Edwardian oak pedestal desk, by Maple & Co, the reverse breakfront with deep-moulded leaf-carved edge, stamped 'Maple & Co', 48in (122cm) wide.
£850–1,000 HAM

DUMB WAITERS

A George II mahogany dumb waiter, with three revolving graduated tiers and turned and spiral-knopped baluster supports, on lappet-carved tripod base, c1755, 24in (61cm) diam.
£6,500-7,000 S

An early George III mahogany three-tier dumb waiter, the dished graduated top with ring-turned and wreathed supports, on cabriole legs, 23¾in (60.5cm) diam.
£2,000-2,400 P

> Miller's is a price GUIDE not a price LIST

A George III mahogany dumb waiter, the graduated dished tiers supported by a faceted baluster-shaped standard, on cabriole legs, late 18thC, 23in (58.5cm) diam.
£1,800-2,200 S(NY)

A George IV mahogany two-tier dumb waiter, the revolving trays with moulded edges, on reeded cabriole legs, 24in (61cm) diam.
£1,700-2,000 WW

A William IV mahogany three-tier metamorphic dumb waiter, the adjustable tiers on square section end standards, with scroll-carved brackets, 48in (122cm) wide.
£900-1,100 TMA

An early Victorian mahogany metamorphic dumb waiter, the three tiers with a sash cord action joining to form a table with an edge-moulded top, 38¼in (97cm) wide.
£800-900 DN

An oak telescopic dumb waiter, on a lotus leaf-carved pillar and tricorn plinth, c1845, 22in (56cm) diam.
£1,100-1,300 S

A mahogany folding two-tier dumb waiter, each twin drop-leaf tier with raised stringing to the edge, on ring-turned column, and splayed tripod base, 19thC, 41¼in (105cm) high.
£1,200-1,400 P(L)

FRAMES

A Florentine carved, pierced and gilded frame, with stepped sight, acanthus ogee, and scrolling acanthus, 18thC, 13 x 20in (33 x 51cm).
£850-1,000 Bon

A south German carved giltwood rococo frame, bordered with rocaille-shaped acanthus leaves, single roses and other blooms, early 18thC, 18½ x 21¼in (47 x 54cm).
£1,800-2,200 DORO

A north Italian polychrome carved gilt pine frame, with pierced white and dark green leaf and tendril decoration, c1750, 15¼ x 12½in (38.5 x 31.5cm).
£850-1,000 DORO

A carved giltwood fluted frame, with an inner beaded border, egg-and-dart and laurel leaf outer border, c1770, 42 x 38in (106.5 x 81.5cm).
£1,500–1,800 WW

A carved and gilded Carlo Maratta-style frame, with cavetto sight, cushion-moulded top edge, 18thC, 29 x 18¼in (73.5 x 46.5cm).
£600–720 Bon

An Italian School carved giltwood frame, surrounded by foliate scrolls and cherubs' heads, 19thC, 44 x 36in (112 x 91.5cm).
£800–950 P(EA)

This is a replica of the frame made for Raphael's 'Madonna Della Sedia'.

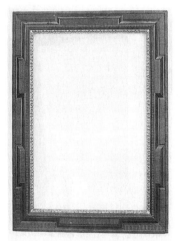

A Dutch parcel-gilt and ebonized ripple-moulded frame, 19thC, 43 x 29¾in (109 x 75.5cm).
£550–650 Bon

A gilded composition frame, with stepped sight and bound laurel leaf and berry D-section top edge, late 19thC, 21¼ x 15¼in (54 x 38.5cm).
£140–170 Bon(C)

A French gilded composition frame, with stepped sight, and laurel leaf and berry D-section top edge, early 20thC, 27½ x 21⅛in (70 x 54.5cm).
£350–420 Bon(C)

HALL STANDS

◄ A Victorian cast-iron hall stand, the pierced trellis-formed frame applied with coat hooks, the lower section with a stick stand, on twined branch-moulded feet, 55in (139.5cm) high.
£400–450 GAK

A straight grain walnut hall stand, c1870, 45in (114.5cm) high.
£750–825 GBr

A Victorian brass-mounted hall stand, attributed to James Shoolbred & Co, the drawer stamped for 1883, 39¾in (101cm) wide.
£4,000–4,500 S

The firm of James Shoolbred & Co was established c1870, later expanding to become one of the first great department stores in London on the Tottenham Court Road. The firm was renowned for the quality of its wares and was issued with a Royal warrant in the mid-1880s.

JARDINIERES

A George III mahogany jardinière, with a twin-handled metal liner and brass carrying handles to the sides, 22¾in (58cm) wide.
£2,000–2,200 P

A Regency mahogany jardinière, with replaced brass liner, c1825, 30in (76cm) high.
£2,800–3,250 CAT

A Dutch mahogany and marquetry jardinière, with brass carrying handles and brass liner, 18thC, 21in (53.5cm) high.
£400–500 PFK

A French Louis XV-style jardinière, veneered in satinwood and kingwood with gilt-metal mounts of flowers and foliage, late 19thC, 27in (68.5cm) high.
£1,000–1,100 RBB

A George III mahogany jardinière, with two divisions, waved top edge and cut-out carrying handles, fitted with two metal liners, c1770, 15½in (39.5cm) wide.
£4,500–5,000 S

A George IV rosewood jardinière, with a baluster and lotus-leaf carved column, triform base and bun feet, 29in (73.5cm) high.
£750–900 HYD

◀ An Edwardian mahogany jardinière, 36in (91.5cm) high.
£320–350 NAW

A Dutch neo-classical mahogany and marquetry jardinière, outlined in diagonal ebony and box-wood inlay, with arcaded brass gallery, the frieze with marquetry panels within brass mouldings, damaged, late 18thC, 23¾in (60.5cm) wide.
£1,500–1,800 NOA

An Italian walnut jardinière, the *verde antico* top enclosing a removable copper liner, with a handle at each side, on lion monopodia supports surmounted by a satyr mask, joined by a concave-sided triform stretcher, c1820, 21½in (54.5cm) diam.
£3,500–4,200 S

LOWBOYS

A Queen Anne walnut lowboy, the serpentine top with incurved corners above one narrow and two deep frieze drawers, the drawer fronts with chevron banding, 34¼in (87cm) wide.
£2,000–2,200 Oli

A George I walnut lowboy, the top crossbanded and herringbone-banded, with brass drop handles, the legs resited, 30in (76cm) wide.
£2,000–2,400 HAM

A George I walnut lowboy, herringbone-banded and with a crossbanded top, one long and two short drawers with brass handles, 33in (84cm) wide.
£1,800–2,200 DN

MINIATURE FURNITURE

A Portuguese miniature rosewood chest of drawers, the ripple-moulded cornice above two short and one long cushion-moulded drawer, damaged, c1700, 19in (48.5cm) wide.
£500–600 S(S)

A Queen Anne walnut miniature chest of drawers, inlaid with stringing and burr-yew bandings, the cleated top above two short and three long graduated drawers, early 18thC, 9½in (24cm) wide.
£5,500–6,000 S

A south German miniature marquetry commode, of serpentine form, inlaid in fruitwood with figures and animals, with two drawers, c1740, 25¼in (64cm) wide.
£1,800–2,200 S(Z)

A Victorian Scottish miniature mahogany chest, fitted with three deep frieze drawers above three long graduated drawers, flanked by spreading pilasters, 12½in (32cm) wide.
£500–600 P(Sc)

An Italian miniature walnut-veneered commode, decorated with parquetry banding, with three long drawers, early 19thC, 13¾in (35cm) wide.
£950–1,150 Bea(E)

A Victorian miniature mahogany breakfast table, the tilt-top with radiating parquetry segments of rosewood and sycamore, the baluster-turned stem on a circular parquetry base, with brass ball feet, 7½in (19cm) wide.
£100–120 WW

CHEVAL MIRRORS

A George III mahogany cheval mirror, the counter-weighted plate between box supports on sabre legged bases, with square tapered feet, 24¾in (63cm) wide.
£1,600–1,800 TEN

A late George III mahogany cheval mirror, with a crossbanded frame, the supports with urn finials, on downswept legs with brass terminals, casters and a stretcher, 25½in (65cm) wide.
£1,100–1,200 DN

A Regency mahogany cheval mirror, with a crossbanded frame, the turned supports with reeded bands capped by roundels, 31in (78.5cm) wide.
£1,800–2,200 DN

A Regency mahogany cheval mirror, with a ring-turned frame, on swept supports with brass paw caps and casters, parts later, 63in (160cm) high.
£1,600–2,000 P(B)

A French Empire ormolu and mahogany cheval mirror, with gilt-bronze stylized leaves, flanked by columns surmounted by classical urns, c1810, 44in (112cm) wide.
£2,800–3,200 S(Am)

A George IV mahogany cheval mirror, the reeded adjustable frame rising on sash cords, with a gilt-metal handle, 22¾in (58cm) wide.
£2,000–2,400 DN

A William IV brass-mounted mahogany cheval mirror, with turned supports and adjustable candle-arms, c1835, 26in (66cm) wide.
£1,200–1,400 SK

A Victorian Georgian-style inlaid satinwood cheval mirror, decorated with inlaid trailing foliage, on square tapering side supports with brass urn finials, 26½in (67.5cm) wide.
£1,600–2,000 JAd

DRESSING TABLE MIRRORS

A Queen Anne gilt gesso dressing mirror and bureau, decorated with acanthus leaves and scrolls, the mirror plate within a moulded frame and later squared tapered uprights, the bureau base with fall-front enclosing a green and gilt japanned interior, on a punched ground, c1710, 19½in (49.5cm) wide.
£3,200–3,850 S

A mahogany dressing table mirror, on a concave-fronted platform base, with three drawers, c1740, 17in (43cm) wide.
£1,100–1,300 RL

A George III satinwood dressing table mirror, decorated with rosewood crossbanding and stringing, the three short drawers with turned ivory knob handles and lock escutcheon, 18in (45.5cm) wide.
£320–380 AG

◀ A George III mahogany and chequer-strung dressing table mirror, the supports with brass urn finials, 16¼in (41.5cm) wide.
£360–420 DN

A George II mahogany dressing table mirror, the moulded and parcel-gilt frame flanked by tapered uprights with brass finials, c1750, 22½in (57cm) wide.
£1,400–1,700 S

A walnut dressing table mirror, inlaid with chequer stringing, c1750–60, 17¼in (44cm) wide.
£220–260 L

▶ A mahogany and ebony-strung dressing table mirror, the box base with three drawers, early 19thC, 31¼in (79.5cm) wide.
£180–220 DN

A George III satinwood-veneered and rosewood-crossbanded dressing table mirror, with later glass plate, 14in (35.5cm) wide.
£1,100–1,300 Bea(E)

A mahogany dressing table mirror, on a marble base, c1860, 17in (43cm) wide.
£235–260 GBr

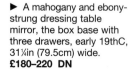

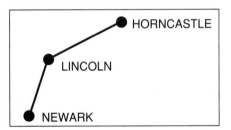

A carved walnut wall mirror, the two-piece plate within a cushion frame, with scrolled and leaf-carved surmount centred by a shell, 17thC, 21½in (54.5cm) wide.
£500–600 AH

A walnut oyster-veneered cushion-framed wall mirror, inset with a bevelled plate within a moulded slip, early 18thC, 27½in (70cm) wide.
£2,200–2,600 P(E)

A George I carved giltwood wall mirror, the plate within a leaf-moulded border surmounted by a broken arch cresting with central Prince of Wales feathers, candle sconces missing, 25¼in (64cm) wide.
£2,200–2,600 P

A pair of George II mahogany wall mirrors, the arched and bevelled plates within an egg-and-dart carved moulded frame, the scrolled lower sides carved with leaves, 29½in (74.5cm) wide.
£3,500–4,200 S

An American Chippendale walnut wall mirror, the ogee-moulded cross-banded frame surmounted by a pierced and scrolled crest with a central rosette, the corners with further scrolls, mid-18thC, 20in (51cm) wide.
£600–720 SLN

A George II walnut and parcel-gilt wall mirror, with a scrolled pediment and gilt slip, parts later, 21½in (54.5cm) wide.
£1,300–1,600 TEN

A George III walnut and parcel-gilt wall mirror, re-glazed, c1760, 31in (78.5cm) high.
£350–400 AnSh

A George III wall mirror, the leaf and scroll-moulded frame with scrolled cresting and apron, c1770, 21¾in (55.5cm) wide.
£2,750–3,000 S

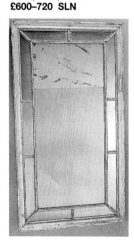

A Louis XVI giltwood wall mirror, surmounted by a carved crest with floral and tied ribbon motifs, late 18thC, 12½in (32cm) wide.
£320–380 SLM

◄ A George III wall mirror, the two-piece plate within a beaded gilt and mirrored frame, 27in (68.5cm) wide.
£500–600 DN

An American Chippendale inlaid mahogany wall mirror, the scrolled frame with a pierced crest of a gilt carved phoenix, above a string-inlaid liner, possibly New England, c1780, 22¾in (58cm) wide.
£1,500–1,800 SK(B)

An Irish carved giltwood wall mirror, c1790, 33in (84cm) wide.
£5,500–6,500 GKe

Cross Reference
See Colour Review

A convex wall mirror, with ebonized reeded slip and surmounted by a carved ebonized eagle, the base with a leaf spray, early 19thC, 25½in (65cm) wide.
£1,150–1,350 WW

An early Victorian gilt painted wood and gesso overmantel mirror, surmounted by a cartouche of scallop shell and acanthus leaf scrolls, flanked by a pair of turned uprights supporting a pair of scrolling candle sconces, 66in (167.5cm) wide.
£2,400–3,000 AG

A pair of gilt-bronze girandoles, the bevelled plates set within a pierced scrolling acanthus-cast frame, with candle sconces, one plate missing, late 19thC, 15½in (39.5cm) wide.
£800–1,000 P

▶ A French painted pier mirror, with deep stucco relief, with original glass plate and backing, late 19thC, 42½in (108cm) wide.
£700–800 OFM

A Regency giltwood wall mirror, the stiff-leaf border fitted with a plain ebonized liner, early 19thC, 30¼in (77cm) diam.
£1,700–2,000 NOA

A pair of neo-classical-style pier mirrors, the carved wood and gesso frame with stiff-leaf and husk banding, originally gilded, 19thC, 49½in (125.5cm) wide.
£3,500–4,200 AH

A giltwood wall mirror, the frame applied with vine and scroll carvings, late 19thC, 27in (68.5cm) wide.
£400–500 DN

A late Regency giltwood overmantel mirror, the later plate above a moulded inverted front cornice with *faux* bamboo edging and side pilasters, the back stencilled 'C. Hindley & Sons, 134 Oxford St, London', 63¼in (160.5cm) wide.
£1,600–2,000 WW

C. Hindley & Sons, furniture-makers, were recorded in the 1820s and 1830s.

A giltwood wall mirror, the bevelled plate surmounted by a carved foliate scrolling frame, with a cartouche, labelled 'Ciceri and Co, Edinburgh', 19thC, 34¼in (87cm) wide.
£2,000–2,400 P(Ed)

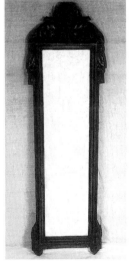

A French wall mirror, with carved wooden frame, Bordeaux, c1890, 14in (35.5cm) wide.
£380–420 BAB

A William IV giltwood overmantel mirror, the frame with rounded top corners carved with acanthus, scroll and flowers, the crest detached, 59½in (151cm) wide.
£600–720 DN

A pair of giltwood pier mirrors, the foliate slip flanked by columns joined with flowerheads and hung with fruit, the acanthus-carved cresting centred by a seated putto under a foliate and fruit arch, the apron scroll-carved with grapes, late 19thC, 16½in (42cm) wide.
£1,800–2,200 P(NW)

A French giltwood wall mirror, with beaded surround and red gesso showing through gold leaf, c1900, 26¼in (67.5cm) wide.
£125–150 OFM

PEDESTALS

A pair of George IV oak pedestals, the tops with outset moulded and rounded corners above arched panels with columnar corners and moulded collars, one pedestal fitted with a slide, c1820, 25½in (65cm) high.
£7,000–8,000 S

This pair of pedestals is designed in the Gothic-revival style popular at the time and promoted by well-known designers and cabinet-makers, such as George Bullock and Gillows.

A kingwood, mahogany and rosewood pedestal, with a fluted tapering column supporting a square red marble stand, with gilt-metal mounts, 19thC, 42½in (108cm) high.
£1,300–1,500 AH

A pair of French green-painted and parcel-gilt pedestals, with paterae-carved friezes, the panelled sides carved with steer's head motifs and entwined wreaths, damaged and restored, late 19thC, 58¼in (148cm) high.
£1,500–1,650 S(S)

A pair of French Napoleon III gilt-bronze-mounted and ebonized pedestals, each decorated with opposing roundels, the upper inlaid with a bird, the lower with a butterfly flanked by *faux* lapis and tortoiseshell panels, the sides inlaid with musical trophies within canted corners headed by putti, 52½in (133.5cm) high.
£6,500–7,200 S(NY)

SCREENS

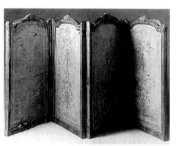

A French painted screen, each outer leaf decorated with a cartouche enclosing mythological figures in landscapes, the inner panels with oval cartouches enclosing similar mythological scenes, the reverse of the panels decorated with oval or urn-shaped cartouches painted with landscapes enclosed by scrolling foliage and ribbon-tied swags, early 18thC, 98in (249cm) wide.
£4,500–5,500 S

Reputedly this is a wedding screen painted in 1734 for the daughter of Bertin, Finance Minister of Louis XV, Governor of Perigord at the Château de Bourdeille, on the occasion of her marriage to the Marquis le Feyolle.

▶ An Edwardian mahogany four-fold screen, the upper section with shaped cresting and lattice glazing over gold and silver floral fabric panels, 70in (178cm) high.
£900–1,100 DA

A French Louis XVI-style silk-upholstered giltwood four-panel screen, each panel carved with berried foliage, enclosing floral silk panels, c1900, 50½in (128.5cm) high.
£500–600 S(NY)

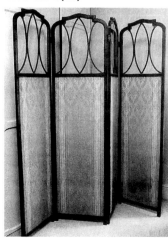

A Victorian ebonized and parcel-gilt four-fold screen, the spindle-turned and pierced brass gallery surmount headed by ivory-capped finials, each fold with twelve glazed panels inset with wood-block prints, c1890, 41¾in (106cm) wide.
£575–700 S(S)

A Victorian walnut-framed four-fold scrap screen, with carved scrolling foliage and birds to the pierced surmounts, chased gilt-brass and glass handles, 84in (213.5cm) high.
£1,500–1,800 WW

FIRE SCREENS

A Regency black lacquer pole screen, the adjustable chinoiserie-painted panel on a brass pole, the turned standard on a triangular plinth, 54½in (138.5cm) high.
£700–800 NOA

A William IV bird's-eye maple fire screen, c1835, 16in (40.5cm) wide.
£340–385 GBr

A mahogany pole screen, with later gros-point floral needlework inset, on Chippendale-style tripod base, 19thC, 56in (142cm) high.
£200–240 PFK

A Victorian rosewood pole screen, the needlepoint panel set in a rococo-style foliate and scroll-carved frame, supported by a twist-turned column, 65½in (166.5cm) high.
£550–600 NOA

◀ A Victorian fire screen, the carved giltwood frame enclosing a floral needlework panel on trestle ends with plate of 'J. J. Byrne, Dublin', 53in (134.5cm) high.
£850–1,000 L

SETTEES & SOFAS

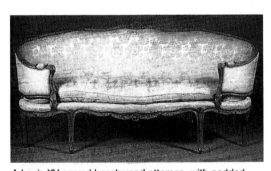

A Louis XV carved beechwood ottoman, with padded back, scrolled arms and serpentine seat on a leaf-carved seat rail, c1770, 81in (205.5cm) wide.
£2,000–2,400 P

A Georgian settee, covered in floral tapestry, raised on turned and reeded tapering mahogany legs, 76in (193cm) wide.
£1,600–2,000 AG

◀ A George III sofa, with square tapering front legs on block feet, 77in (195.5cm) wide.
£1,500–1,800 DN

An Italian mahogany and carved giltwood sofa, probably Lucca or Siena, the rear stiles with leafy finials on fluted supports, the arms carved with lions' masks on fluted supports, the sides applied with ribbon-tied branches of acorns, oak and laurel leaves, c1800, 80in (203cm) wide.
£5,750–7,000 S

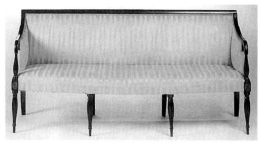

An American Federal mahogany and parcel-gilt sofa, with convex crest rail flanked by downswept, leaf-capped padded arms with baluster-turned reeded supports, the serpentine-fronted stuff-over seat raised on turned and reeded legs headed by gilt sunbursts, c1800, 72½in (184cm) wide.
£2,700–3,250 SLN

A Georgian mahogany-framed settee, on six slender square tapering supports with understretchers, outswept back supports, 1810, 96in (244cm) wide.
£2,700–3,250 RBB

A Regency black-painted and parcel-gilt sofa, with reeded ends and seat rail on outscrolled legs joined by turned stretchers, early 19thC, 85½in (217cm) wide.
£6,500–7,000 S(NY)

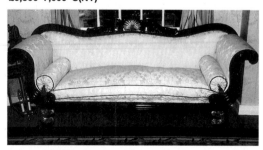

A Regency settee, with scroll arms, on hairy paw feet with carved eagles' heads, c1830, 90in (228.5cm) wide.
£6,750–7,500 HA

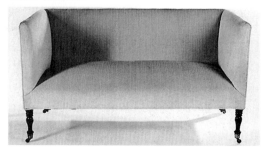

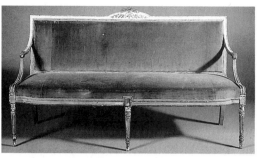

A late George III painted and parcel-gilt sofa, the padded back surmounted by a quill and foliate-decorated crest, the acanthus-carved downswept arms and bowed stuff-over seat on fluted turned tapering legs, 64½in (164cm) wide.
£3,700–4,000 P

A Dutch Empire mahogany settee, with slightly curved top rail, padded back and seat, down-curved reeded armrests, on sabre legs, with yellow fabric upholstery, early 19thC, 64¼in (163cm) wide.
£1,200–1,500 S(Am)

Formerly in the collection of HRH Anna Paulowna of Orange, Queen of the Netherlands 1795–1865.

An Italian neo-classical cherry settee, the upholstered backrest flanked by fluted outscrolled upholstered sides, raised on rounded legs, early 19thC, 84in (213.5cm) wide.
£3,000–3,500 S(NY)

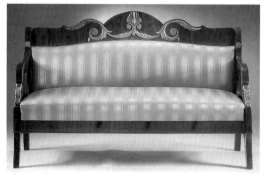

A Russian satin birch canapé, with gilt mounts, upholstered in blue, c1800–20, 74in (188cm) wide.
£3,200–3,850 S(Mon)

◄ An American late Federal walnut sofa, the stuff-over seat raised on baluster-turned legs with casters, early 19thC, 61in (155cm) wide.
£700–850 SLN

A three-seater settee, with scroll arms, the cabriole legs acanthus-carved to knees and with hoof feet, 19thC, 83in (211cm) wide.
£1,650–2,000 DA

A Victorian rosewood button-upholstered settee, with foliate and shell-carved exposed rosewood centre and foliate-carved scrolling arms, serpentine front rail and scrolling carved cabriole legs, 78in (198cm) wide.
£1,350–1,500 Mit

An American Louis XV-revival mahogany sofa, with floral upholstery, 19thC, 75½in (192cm) wide.
£350–420 FBG

A Victorian walnut twin chair-back sofa, with carved rococo splat, on cabriole legs and volute toes, 73½in (186.5cm) wide.
£1,200–1,500 M&K

An Edwardian mahogany and satinwood-inlaid settee, 74in (188cm) wide.
£900–1,000 ChA

An Edwardian mahogany two-seater cottage sofa, inlaid with boxwood and satinwood banding and stringing, the top rail supported by three X-framed splats, 41½in (105.5cm) wide.
£300–350 GAK

SHELVES

A George III inlaid harewood hanging shelf, with three graduated shelves, above two drawers, replacements, 27in (68.6cm) wide.
£1,800–2,000 S(NY)

► A set of mahogany hanging shelves, with gilded mounts, the raised panelled back with applied beading over four mirror-backed shelves, on ring-turned supports with turned finials, applied paterae and stiff-leaf banding, panelled base with applied festoon, 19thC, 8½in (21.5cm) wide.
£500–600 AH

A mahogany wall shelf, the three tiers on slender turned supports, the boxwood-strung base with two drawers, on later pierced C-shaped brackets, 19thC, 17¼in (44cm) wide.
£900–1,100 Bea(E)

SIDEBOARDS

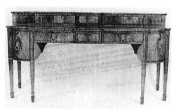

A George III mahogany sideboard, with bowed frieze drawer, flanked to both sides by a deep cellarette drawer, inlaid with boxwood bands, the legs headed by blind flutes and inlaid paterae, c1795, 70½in (179cm) wide.
£8,000–9,000 S

A Dutch mahogany sideboard, inlaid with brass stringing and satinwood floral urn motifs, the hinged top revealing two folding shelves and a pair of fold-over panels, the frieze drawer above a pair of panelled doors flanked by canted corners, c1800, 42in (106.5cm) wide.
£1,800–2,200 S(S)

A George III Scottish mahogany and ebony-strung bowfronted sideboard, the stage back fitted with two sliding doors, over two frieze drawers, flanked by two deep drawers, 85½in (217cm) wide.
£3,500–4,200 P(Ed)

An American Federal inlaid mahogany sideboard, the single central drawer flanked by two small drawers over four cupboard doors and two-sectioned bottle drawers, each outlined in stringing with ovolo corners, some restoration, New England, c1800, 67½in (171.5cm) wide.
£7,500–9,000 SK(B)

► A mahogany bowfronted sideboard, crossbanded and ebony-strung, with two drawers and a door around an arch, 19thC, 60½in (153.5cm) wide.
£2,000–2,400 DN

A Georgian inlaid mahogany bowfronted sideboard, with frieze drawer above a curtained interior, flanked by two cellarette drawers, sliding tambour missing, 60in (152.5cm) wide.
£3,000–3,500 WILL

A Regency mahogany breakfront sideboard, with a pair of ebony-strung drawers over a secret apron drawer between a pair, with revolving right hand bottle drawer, 79in (200.5cm) wide.
£1,650–2,000 EH

A Regency mahogany-veneered pedestal sideboard, on ring-turned legs, c1815, 88in (223.5cm) wide.
£9,000–10,000 HA

Pedestal sideboards are currently fashionable as they suit today's smaller houses. This piece has original features and colour.

A Victorian mahogany pedestal sideboard, with carved centre shell and scroll pediment, the central figured mahogany drawer with shell and scroll applied mouldings, flanked by panelled cupboard doors, 87in (221cm) wide.
£1,500–1,650 Mit

A late Victorian Renaissance-style sideboard, the pediment centred by a mask over a deep coved frieze and mirror, flanked by carved panelled cupboards raised on gadrooned balusters, the base with a bowed centre, three frieze drawers and carved panelled cupboards below, stamped 'Gillows', 90¼in (229cm) wide.
£2,800–3,200 TEN

An Edwardian inlaid mahogany and satinwood-banded sideboard, of broken bowed outline, with curtain-rail above a central frieze drawer, flanked to one side by a drawer, a cupboard door enclosing a single shelf to the other, 66in (167.5cm) wide.
£4,000–4,500 P(NW)

A George IV mahogany breakfront sideboard, the mirror back surmounted by a bishop's mitre, the sides with panels bearing cross motifs, the panelled and crossbanded frieze with bowfront central drawer, mirror back altered, 119⅜in (304cm) wide.
£6,000–6,500 Bea(E)

By repute, this item originated from the Bishop's Palace, Exeter.

A Victorian mahogany sideboard, the arched back crested with acanthus leaf mount and applied with scrolls, the serpentine central drawer flanked on either side by two plain drawers over two pedestals, each with panelled doors enclosing cupboards, 58in (147.5cm) wide.
£700–850 GAK

A walnut baroque-revival buffet, the arched panels with carved masks, flanked by mirrors and turned reeded columns and gallery, above a marble surface with three frieze drawers and open shelves, turned three-quarter gallery and carved columns, 19thC, 66in (167.5cm) wide.
£1,400–1,700 RTo

▶ An American mahogany sideboard, the top surmounted by a mirrored back, the base with a pair of drawers over a pair of cupboard doors, flanked by scrolling columns, late 19thC, 67¼in (171cm) wide.
£900–1,100 NOA

A William IV mahogany sideboard, c1835, 43in (109cm) wide.
£1,250–1,500 GBr

A late Victorian Sheraton-revival satinwood, kingwood-crossbanded and line-inlaid demilune sideboard, the top inlaid with harewood ovals, the frieze drawer over a shaped apron flanked by a pair of dummy front cupboard doors, 54in (137cm) wide.
£3,400–4,000 P(WM)

An American carved walnut sideboard, with a marble top over two short and one long drawer and a pair of panelled cupboard doors, maker's label 'Carrollton Furniture Manuf'g Co./Carrollton, Ky.', late 19thC, 50½in (128.5cm) wide.
£600–720 SLN

STANDS

A mahogany rosewood and boxwood-strung sheet music stand, with galleried top over four open racks between Ionic pillared sides, late 18thC, 22in (56cm) wide.
£10,000–11,000 EH

This item is very unusual and consequently sold for approximately ten times its pre-sale estimate.

► An American walnut plant stand, attributed to George W. Hunziger, New York, painted in cream with gilt highlights, c1875, 37¼in (94.5cm) wide.
£1,500–1,800 SK(B)

A Victorian Georgian-style mahogany cutlery canterbury, with a tapering spiral twist column, 22½in (57cm) wide.
£600–720 Gam

A Victorian figured-walnut dressing stand, the mirror between moulded lyre-shaped supports, with two small drawers in the frieze, raised on a turned pillar with a carved tripod cabriole base, 63in (160cm) wide.
£1,300–1,600 TEN

► An Edwardian inlaid cake-stand, stamped 'Harrison', 34in (86.5cm) high.
£270–300 CSAC

An oak cake stand, c1900, 34in (86.5cm) high.
£100–115 GBr

HAT & STICK STANDS

A Bavarian carved fruitwood hat and stick stand, in the form of a bear clinging to a tree with its cub in the branches, another cub at its feet, on a base with vegetation around a metal drip tray, mid-19thC, 81in (205.5cm) high.
£5,000–6,000 BIG

A walnut stick stand, with drip tray, c1870, 29in (73.5cm) high.
£270–300 GBr

A Victorian beech stick stand, turned to simulate bamboo, with a detachable drip tray to the base, 19in (48cm) high.
£240–300 DN

◄ A Coalbrookdale black-painted cast-iron umbrella stand, cast as a Chihuahua dog, with front paws crossed, holding a bull whip, raised on a pedestal base with leaf-shaped drip tray, c1880, 24¾in (63cm) high.
£1,600–2,000 HAM

A Victorian mahogany hat and coat stand, the turned column with scroll hooks and a central stick support, ending in a moulded base with drip tray, faults, restored, 72½in (184cm) high.
£750–825 S(S)

LUGGAGE STANDS

A George IV mahogany luggage stand, by Gillows of Lancaster, with a spindle back and slatted top, stamped, 25¼in (64cm) wide.
£5,000–5,500 P(E)

An early Victorian mahogany luggage stand, the moulded slats with rounded ends, raised on bulbous turned legs, mid-19thC, 30½in (77.5cm) wide.
£850–1,000 NOA

An elm and oak luggage stand, with a slatted top, on tapering outswept legs, c1900, 32½in (82.5cm) wide.
£380–450 NOA

Miller's is a price GUIDE not a price LIST

MUSIC STANDS

A George III mahogany duet stand, the central spindle headed by an urn finial, with four later articulated brass candlearms, c1795, 55in (140cm) high.
£7,500–8,250 S

A Regency mahogany music stand, with adjustable octagonal top, on three later downswept splayed legs with lead ball feet, 13in (33cm) wide.
£370–450 Bea(E)

◄ A William IV duet stand, the dual ratcheted top with lyre supports, raised on brass adjustable shaft and reeded turned column, 59in (150cm) high.
£800–1,000 P(EA)

► An early Victorian rosewod duet music stand, with lyre decoration, on an adjustable brass column, alterations and faults, 17in (43cm) wide.
£650–800 RTo

A Regency mahogany duet music stand, with two adjustable flaps inset with lyre splats, a brass candle bracket to each side, 19¾in (50cm) wide.
£2,500–3,000 Bea(E)

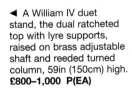

A Regency rosewood duet stand, the lattice-pierced easel flanked by hinged brass candle sconces above a ring-turned reeded adjustable column, on later bun feet, 17¼in (44cm) wide.
£3,300–4,000 P

A William IV mahogany double music stand, the adjustable lyre-form rests attached to a moveable pole within a reeded stem, mid-19thC, 14in (35.5cm) wide.
£3,800–4,200 NOA

STEPS

A set of walnut library steps, probably south German, in the form of a desk, with a rectangular leather-lined top, above a frieze containing a drawer, the lower section of serpentine form concealing a false drawer pulling out to reveal a chair and a set of steps, the whole carved with recessed cartouches, 18thC, open 58¼in (148cm) high.
£11,500–13,500 S

A set of Regency mahogany metamorphic library steps, in the manner of Morgan & Sanders, with reeded over-scrolled arms and caned seat on sabre legs, c1815, the steps 28¼in (72cm) high.
£5,500–6,500 Bon

A set of jarrah wood library steps, early 19thC, 37in (94cm) high.
£2,200–2,500 CRU

A set of late Georgian mahogany bed steps, with green leather treads and two hinged compartments, 27in (68.5cm) long.
£500–600 JM

A pair of bed steps, in the manner of Gillows of Lancaster, raised on four turned and reeded legs, c1810, 24in (61cm) wide.
£8,500–9,500 CAT

A Victorian mahogany step commode, the three leather-inset treads with studded borders, 19in (48.5cm) wide.
£400–500 DN

STOOLS

A George I walnut stool, the needlework-covered drop-in seat centred by a spray of flowers within a cartouche, the burr-walnut veneered seat rails on cabriole legs carved with shells, husks and scrolls, c1725, 23¾in (60.5cm) wide.
£9,000–10,500 S

A George II mahogany stool, the floral needlework seat on shell and acanthus leaf-carved cabriole legs with claw-and-ball feet, 19in (48.5cm) wide.
£1,300–1,500 S

An early George III mahogany stool, the apron with shell-carved centres and raised upon cabriole legs with shell- and harebell-carved knees and gros point upholstered top, 26in (66cm) wide.
£2,500–3,000 TEN

A George II walnut long stool, with a tapestry seat, on plain turned legs united by squared stretchers, 78½in (199.5cm) wide.
£1,000–1,200 HYD

An American mahogany footstool, with a foliate-carved scalloped apron and original needlepoint upholstery, mid-19thC, 18in (45.5cm) wide.
£700–800 NOA

A pair of William IV mahogany stools, each with beaded edge moulding to the upholstered top, confronting S-scroll end supports joined by a bobbin-turned pole stretcher and on trestle feet, 19¼in (49cm) wide.
£1,450–1,750 Bea(E)

A pair of giltwood stools, after a design by A. M. E. Fournier, with button-upholstered tops, over rope-twist seat rails and similar knotted legs, united by a knotted stretcher, 19thC, 22in (56cm) diam.
£5,000–6,000 P(Ed)

A. M. E. Fournier traded initially from Blvd. Beaumarchais in Paris, and from 1867 from Blvd. des Capucines. That year he exhibited at the Exposition Universelle where for the first time exhibitors of fine furniture described themselves as upholsterers. Fournier's stools inspired the Baccarat glass factory to produce some glass seats.

An early Victorian mahogany stool, with button-upholstered top, inset carved foliate pendant frieze, octagonal and turned legs joined by X-shaped stretchers, 32in (81.5cm) wide.
£340–400 DD

A Victorian rosewood stool, with serpentine-shaped apron, raised on four moulded cabriole legs, 39in (99cm) wide.
£900–1,100 MEA

A pair of Biedermeier birchwood stools, with ebony ball finials and stuff-over seats, 19thC, 20in (51cm) wide.
£600–720 AH

A walnut stool, the top upholstered in old velvet and beadwork embroidered panels, with carved aprons and on rosette-capped moulded cabriole legs, mid-19thC, 43¼in (110cm) wide.
£2,200–2,600 HOK

A Victorian rosewood stool, with padded seat and arcaded and beaded seat rails, on turned legs carved with stylized leaves, 20in (51cm) wide.
£600–720 DN

A Victorian ebonized and gilt stool, 17in (43cm) wide.
£170–200 Ber

MUSIC STOOLS

A William IV mahogany piano stool, the inverted Ionic capital raised on a lotus-clad stem, mid-19thC, 18in (45.5cm) wide.
£800–900 NOA

Miller's is a price GUIDE not a price LIST

◄ A walnut adjustable music seat, with carved tripod, late 19thC, 27in (68.5cm) high.
£340–385 CSAC

A late Victorian mahogany duet stool, with later upholstered seat enclosing music well, on turned legs with turned H-stretcher, 40in (101.5cm) wide.
£320–380 PFK

A Victorian adjustable piano chair, the shell-form cushioned seat on four reeded and flared legs joined by a cruciform stretcher centred by an urn, 27⅜in (70.5cm) high.
£300–350 NOA

BEDROOM SUITES

An Edwardian satinwood bedroom suite, comprising a kidney-shaped dressing table, a matching dressing table, a three-part wardrobe and two single beds, dressing table 54⅛in (138cm) wide.
£2,000–2,400 P(NW)

A painted chinoiserie-style bedroom suite, decorated and polychrome highlighted with gilt, comprising a dressing table, two single beds, a wardrobe, a bowfront chest of drawers, a mirror, a cane-backed chair and side chair, early 20thC.
£1,150–1,350 P(NW)

A Victorian four-piece walnut and burr-walnut bedroom suite, comprising a wardrobe, a pot cupboard with panelled door, a dressing table and a washstand with a later mahogany top, wardrobe 72in (183cm) wide.
£1,250–1,500 TRM

DINING ROOM SUITES

A Queen Anne-style walnut dining room suite, comprising a set of six dining chairs, including a pair of armchairs, an extending dining table with two additional leaves, a serving table and a sideboard, early 20thC.
£2,000–2,200 S(S)

A Renaissance-style oak dining room suite, comprising an extending round table with seven additional leaves, twelve chairs, a large and a small sideboard, c1900.
£2,200–2,650 BRH

A light oak dining room suite, comprising sideboard with cocktail unit, table and four chairs, c1930–35.
£1,750–2,100 OOLA

Condition

The condition is absolutely vital when assessing the value of an antique. Damaged pieces on the whole appreciate much less than perfect examples.

However a rare desirable piece may command a high price even when damaged.

SALON SUITES

A Louis XV salon suite, by Matthäus Funk and his workshop, comprising a sofa and two *fauteuils*, upholstered in yellow silk worked in green, c1760, sofa 63in (160cm) wide.
£3,800–4,500 S(Z)

A Louis XV-style giltwood salon suite, comprising three seater sofa and a pair of elbow chairs, the backs all crested with rosettes and buds, decorated with scrolls and terminating in splayed arms, all with foliate moulded aprons, 19thC.
£650–800 GAK

An American Second Empire-style mahogany and ormolu-mounted parlour suite, comprising a settee, an armchair, and a sidechair, the gilt-ormolu mounts bearing the stamp of P. E. Guerin, each raised on carved circular paw feet, New York, late 19thC, settee 61¼in (155.5cm) wide.
£2,700–3,000 NOA

An American rococo-style carved and laminated rosewood three-piece parlour suite, by John Henry Belter, New York, in the 'Rosalie' pattern, comprising a settee and a pair of side chairs, the cresting carved with flowers and fruit amid foliage, all upholstered in velvet, c1860, settee 72in (183cm) wide.
£3,700–4,500 BB(L)

John Henry Belter (1804–63) was born in Germany and emigrated to the United States in 1833. He developed a range of sumptuously carved and heavily proportioned furniture which was intended to grace the houses of the country's nouveau riche. This is said to have given rise to the expression 'a Belter of a piece'.

An Italian walnut salon suite, comprising a table, eight chairs including two side chairs, a sofa and a bergère chair, 1890–1900, chair 37½in (95.5cm) high.
£2,700–3,000 BAB

A painted salon suite, comprising a sofa and three armchairs, each piece decorated with blue trailing flowers on a black ground, 19thC, distressed, sofa 38½in (98cm) wide.
£4,500–5,500 P(Sc)

 A walnut and upholstered suite, comprising a settee and two matching armchairs, covered in red damask, and with scroll arms carved with swans' masks above stuf-over seats, early 20thC, settee 69in (175.5cm) wide.
£1,100–1,200 S(S)

A French salon suite, comprising four side chairs, two open armchairs and a sofa, the arms carved with acanthus with spiral-fluted and leaf-carved baluster supports, the white and gilt decorated frames carved with guilloche crests and bands of stiff leaves, late 19th/early 20thC, sofa 71in (180.5cm) wide.
£3,200–3,850 DN

ARCHITECTS' TABLES

A George III mahogany architect's desk, the leather-lined double easel top above a drawer containing a hinged writing surface and compartments, stamped 'Gillows, Lancaster', signature of Henry Walling, cabinet-maker, late 18thC, 52in (132cm) wide.
£13,000–15,000 NOA

A George III mahogany architect's table, the hinged ratcheted top with brass candle slides to the sides, above a frieze drawer with hinged baize-lined writing slide, containing a fitted interior, 35¾in (91cm) wide.
£3,300–4,000 P(EA)

A George III mahogany architect's table, the adjustable top with an applied rest and pull-out frieze extending to reveal divided wells, late 18thC, 35in (89cm) wide.
£2,200–2,600 BB(S)

Insurance Values

Always insure your valuable antiques for the cost of replacing them with similar items, regardless of the original price paid. Both dealers and auctioneers will provide a valuation service for a fee.

◄ A French Louis XVI fruitwood architect's table, with a pull-out writing slide on one side, stamped 'C. Mauter Jme', with later gilt-bronze sabots, c1780, 32in (81.5cm) wide.
£5,000–5,500 S

A Regency mahogany architect's table, the drop-flap top containing a double ratcheted slide, with brass-hinged circular candle stands, above a frieze drawer, 35¾in (91cm) wide.
£3,700–4,000 P

BREAKFAST TABLES

A George III mahogany breakfast table, the top crossbanded and on a baluster support with four reeded sabre legs, 52⅛in (133.5cm) wide.
£11,500–13,500 TEN

This table is of particularly good quality and is in superb condition.

A George III mahogany snap-top breakfast table, crossbanded in rosewood, on a baluster-turned column, 44½in (113cm) wide.
£2,600–3,200 P(C)

A late George III mahogany breakfast table, the tilt-top on a ring-turned shaft and downswept reeded legs, 35½in (90cm) wide.
£1,250–1,500 P

◄ A George III satinwood breakfast table, with rosewood and satinwood banding within string-inlaid borders, c1800, 55½in (141cm) wide.
£7,000–8,000 S

A Regency rosewood breakfast table, the top inset with an outer band of foliate brass, raised on a pierced lyre and platform base, with four brass-strung sabre legs, 47¾in (121.5cm) wide.
£9,000–11,000 DMC

A George IV mahogany breakfast table, on a baluster-turned column with four splayed legs, 63in (160cm) wide.
£2,000–2,400 DN

A George IV faded mahogany breakfast table, the tilt-top with rosewood crossbanding, the turned stem on four panelled splayed legs, 46in (117cm) wide.
£1,500–1,800 WW

A mid-Victorian walnut and marquetry breakfast table, on a carved baluster column, 54in (137cm) diam.
£6,500–8,000 Bon(C)

A Regency mahogany satinwood-banded breakfast table, on four splayed legs edged with stringing, some alteration, 56in (142cm) wide.
£1,500–1,800 WW

A George IV mahogany breakfast table, with tilt-top and turned column, with a concave tripod platform and turned feet, 45in (114.5cm) diam.
£350–420 TRM

A William IV rosewood breakfast table, with a gadroon-moulded edge, the chamfered baluster pillar with a leaf-carved collar, on a moulded tricorn plinth with scroll-carved paw feet, 54¾in (139cm) diam.
£4,500–5,500 S

A Victorian rosewood breakfast table, on a lotus turned and C-scroll carved column, the trefoil base on carved scrolling feet, 54in (137cm) diam.
£2,300–2,750 P

▶ A Victorian figured-walnut breakfast table, on four fluted turned supports, and moulded downswept legs, restored, 48in (122cm) wide.
£500–600 S(S)

A Regency mahogany and rosewood crossbanded breakfast table, inlaid with boxwood lines, 41in (104cm) wide.
£2,200–2,600 P

A William IV Irish mahogany breakfast table, on a plain turned column and moulded base with three scroll legs and carved rosettes, 54in (137cm) diam.
£1,000–1,200 DN

A burr-walnut tilt-top breakfast table, on carved quadripartite legs, 19thC, 60in (152.5cm) wide.
£1,100–1,200 AAV

A Victorian mahogany breakfast table, on a bulbous column with four scrolling legs, 51in (129.5cm) diam.
£500–600 AG

CARD TABLES

A Colonial hardwood combined tea and card table, the fold-over top enclosing a tooled green velvet playing surface, within a foliate carved border with counterwells, c1750, 31½in (80cm) wide.
£4,000–4,500 S(S)

A George III inlaid harewood and satinwood demilune card table, the hinged top inlaid with a half patera and a garland of flowers within a double crossbanded edge, the deep band frieze with further floral inlay, on tapered legs headed by bellflower inlay, 22¼in (56.5cm) wide.
£6,500–7,500 Bon

A George III mahogany demilune card table, the crossbanded fold-over top on square tapering legs, 36in (91.5cm) wide.
£850–1,000 CRI

▶ An American Federal carved and figured-mahogany serpentine-front card table, the hinged top above a conforming frieze, Salem, Massachusetts, c1815, 34¾in (88.5cm) wide.
£1,800–2,200 S(NY)

A George II Colonial padoukwood card table, the top enclosing a baize-lined interior with counter pockets and coasters, opening to reveal a well, 32¾in (83cm) wide.
£3,200–3,850 Bon

A mahogany card table, with cabriole legs and centre drawer, 18thC, 34in (86.5cm) wide.
£4,000–4,500 CRU

An Irish rosewood, yew wood and satinwood-banded fold-over card table, with boxwood trim, the plain frieze with geometric inlay, on tapering legs headed by trellis-inlaid panels, probably Cork, c1800, 36¼in (92cm) wide.
£5,000–6,000 HOK

A George III mahogany card table, in the manner of John Linnell, the flap-top inlaid with satinwood marquetry with a border of satinwood with paterae in elliptical stringing, the crossbanded tulipwood edge with chequer stringing, baize-lined, an oval panel of burr-yew and sycamore, 39in (99cm) wide.
£8,000–9,500 WW

A walnut fold-over card table, with a single frieze drawer, on carved cabriole legs, some restoration, 18thC, 28in (71cm) wide.
£1,600–2,000 RTo

A rosewood card table, on a pedestal base, early 19thC, 34in (86.5cm) wide.
£900–1,100 WILL

A Regency mahogany crossbanded fold-over top card table, raised on balustered and ring-turned supports, terminating in quadriform base, 36in (91.5cm) wide.
£730–800 GAK

A Regency rosewood card table, crossbanded in satinwood and tulipwood, the frieze with a boxwood and ebony key design, one back leg replaced, 35½in (90cm) wide.
£600–700 DN

A Regency rosewood and brass-inlaid card table, inlaid with a foliate brass border and enclosing a baize playing surface, on a splayed column support ending in four sabre legs, faults, 36in (91.5cm) wide.
£3,000–3,500 S(S)

A late Regency rosewood card table, with gadrooned border, on a fluted and acanthus-carved centre column, ending in a quadriform platform base with scroll feet, 37in (94cm) wide.
£1,300–1,600 P(S)

An American mahogany card table, the fold-over top on a carved support, on carved paw feet, Philadelphia, c1825, 38in (96.5cm) wide.
£3,200–3,500 SK(B)

A pair of mahogany card tables, the flame-veneered swivel flap-over top with rosewood crossbanding, on hipped splayed legs, stems replaced, c1830, 36in (91.5cm) wide.
£5,500–6,500 WW

A William IV mahogany fold-over card table, on a central carved pedestal, with four turned feet, 36in (91.5cm) wide.
£700–850 WilP

A mahogany card table, the half-round fan-inlaid top with a radiating design of paterae and anthemia linked by swags, 19thC, 29in (73.5cm) wide.
£2,600–3,200 TEN

A rosewood fold-over card table, the swivel top opening to a baize lining, on a concave-sided platform base with turned feet, 19thC, 36in (91.5cm) wide.
£800–1,000 AH

A Victorian Gothic revival walnut fold-over card table, attributed to a design by William Burges, the frieze inlaid with card suits, the carved base comprising two pierced end standards, 36in (91.5cm) wide.
£22,500–25,000 MJB

Furniture designed by Burges is very rare because his Gothic Florentine style went out of fashion and many known examples have been lost, perhaps destroyed. His designs are now very sought after by collectors and consequently achieve high prices.

A Victorian rosewood swivel-action card table, the hinged top opening to reveal a circular baize-lined playing surface, with waved scroll-carved frieze, on faceted column and circular platform with scroll carved feet, 36¼in (92cm) wide.
£1,000–1,200 P(NW)

◄ A Victorian walnut loo table, the quarter-veneered top boxwood-strung, the base with four turned gadrooned supports, on four downswept scrolling legs, 41in (104cm) wide.
£2,000–2,200 Mit

A rosewood folding card table, the hinged top opening to reveal a baize-lined playing surface, 19thC, 31in (78.5cm) wide.
£1,750–1,950 CRU

A mid-Victorian mahogany fold-over card table, revolving to reveal a well, on a scroll-moulded support with a baluster-turned column, supported on four leaf and scroll-carved legs with scrolling feet, 36½in (92.5cm) wide.
£850–1,000 TMA

◄ An Edwardian mahogany envelope card table, with satinwood and ivory arabesque inlay, with a drawer and shaped apron, the cabriole legs joined by a pierced fret stretcher, 22in (56cm) wide.
£1,250–1,400 S(S)

▶ An Edwardian satinwood crossbanded and strung demilune card table, the hinged top with a baize-lined interior, on square tapering legs headed by shaped spandrels with spade feet, 36¼in (92cm) wide.
£500–600 P

A mahogany fold-over top card table, c1860, 38in (96.5cm) wide.
£350–400 MIL

CENTRE TABLES

A George II walnut centre table, with a later marble panel, on cabriole legs terminating in carved trefoil feet, 31½in (80cm) wide.
£3,200–3,850 P(B)

A French Restauration mahogany centre table, with gilt-metal mounts, white marble top, on carved paw feet and triform base, c1820, 39½in (100.5cm) diam.
£4,000–4,500 P

A George III tulipwood and amboyna centre table, the serpentine top with quarter veneers and crossbanding above a shaped frieze fitted with a chevron-veneered drawer, 22½in (57cm) wide.
£3,200–3,500 S

A late Regency rosewood centre table, crossbanded and boxwood-strung, on scrolled pedestal supports joined by a scroll and turned stretcher centred by a lyre, 34½in (87.5cm) wide.
£5,000–5,500 SK

A mahogany centre table, with rounded rectangular top, on a baluster column and quadruple base with brass paw toe-caps, early 19thC, 56in (142cm) wide.
£900–1,100 RBB

A William IV pollard oak centre table, branded 'Johnstone, Jupe and Co, New Bond Street, London', 55in (139.5cm) diam.
£9,500–10,500 NOA

Robert Jupe is best known for his expandable or capstan tables. His establishment was located at 67 New Bond Street, in the heart of London's furniture stores. The top quality name Johnstone, Jupe and Co was synonymous with superlative and innovative cabinet-making.

A William IV rosewood centre table, on lotus-carved turned tapering end supports, 50¾in (129cm) wide.
£1,400–1,600 P

A Victorian satinwood-inlaid rosewood centre table, the top with a central stylized geometric floral pattern and crossbanded edge, on a faceted column and inlaid triform base, 48½in (123cm) diam.
£6,000–7,000 Bon

An early Victorian rosewood centre table, with a panelled frieze, on turned end pillars joined by a turned stretcher, on trestle bases with scrolled feet, 60¼in (153cm) wide.
£1,000–1,200 TEN

An early Victorian faded rosewood centre table, the top with a heavy gadroon edge, 49in (124.5cm) diam.
£800–1,000 WW

An early Victorian walnut centre table, the top inset with figured marble, on ribbed and turned end supports and cabriole legs, 36in (91.5cm) diam.
£500–600 WW

A Victorian walnut and marquetry-inlaid centre table, the tilt-top inlaid with flowers and a butterflies against an ebony ground, on an acanthus-carved baluster column and foliate-carved legs with knurled feet spaced by floral inlaid panels, restored, 49½in (125.5cm) diam.
£5,000–5,500 HAL

A Gothic revival ash centre table, attributed to A. W. N. Pugin and manufactured by Holland & Sons, with a pair of frieze drawers, carved with a Gothic letter 'M', stamped 'Holland & Sons', c1855, 48in (122cm) wide.
£3,000–3,500 Bon

Augustus Welby Northmore Pugin (1812–52), one of the country's leading architects of the 19thC, is probably best remembered for his use of the Gothic revival style in his designs as well as being one of the two designers of the New Palace of Westminster. In the 1850s the two leading cabinet-makers of the time, Gillow and Holland & Sons, were both supplying large quantities of furniture, designed by Pugin, to the Houses of Parliament. After Pugin's death, both firms still produced a number of items modelled closely on Pugin's designs, and continued to manufacture pieces to his designs for domestic clients well into the 1870s.

A Victorian walnut centre table, by Gillow & Co, with a kingwood-crossbanded oval tilt top, fluted and foliate carved stem and on four acanthus-carved moulded splayed legs, the block stamped 'Gillow & Co', 51¼in (130cm) wide.
£2,300–2,750 Bea(E)

A French centre table, inlaid with a panel of flowers, crossbanded in kingwood with ormolu mounts and mask end decorations, on cabriole supports, 19thC, 45in (114.5cm) wide.
£1,400–1,700 RBB

A Victorian walnut centre table, the oval tilt top above a turned tapering column with quadrupartite base, each leg with gadroon roundel decoration terminating in feet with square scroll decoration, with paper label inscribed 'W. M. Johnson & Sons, Cabinet Makers, Upholsterers, Sheffield', 47¾in (121.5cm) diam.
£850–950 P(L)

An Edwardian inlaid and crossbanded mahogany centre table, on square tapered supports, 39½in (100.5cm) diam.
£300–350 WilP

CONSOLE & PIER TABLES

A George III mahogany pier table, painted with figures after Angelica Kauffman's 'Dormic Innocuas', restored, 39¾in (101cm) wide.
£1,250–1,500 TEN

An Adam-style stripped pine console table, surmounted by a white marble top of broken outline, on tapered fluted legs, 18thC, 42⅛in (108cm) wide.
£2,300–2,750 P(EA)

A George IV stained pine console table, with a serpentine-shaped grey marble top, the front legs as winged lion monopodia, 48in (122cm) wide.
£2,800–3,200 DN

A William IV mahogany console table, with grey mottled marble top, 40¼in (102cm) wide.
£1,500–1,800 Bea(E)

A pair of Victorian gilt gesso bracket pier tables, each with red velvet tops, 25½in (65cm) wide.
£650–800 DN

A Louis XVI-style giltwood console table, with breccia marble top, on turned and fluted legs, stamped in ink to the reverse 'Maison Herbert & Pointeaux Reunies, E. Bardin & Cie Successeurs, 24 Avenue Daumesnil', early 20thC, 52in (132cm) wide.
£1,800–2,200 P

DINING TABLES

A George III mahogany three-part dining table, comprising two demilune ends and a drop-leaf section, with a crossbanded top above a line-inlaid frieze, on inlaid tapering square legs, 122in (310cm) extended.
£2,500–3,000 BB(S)

A mahogany extending dining table, in three sections, each demilune end flanking the central two-flap drop-leaf section, late 18thC, 95in (241.5cm) extended.
£650–800 PF

A late George III mahogany two-pillar dining table, on cannon-barrel turned columns, with sabre legs, 91½in (232.5cm) extended.
£5,000–6,000 HAM

A Georgian mahogany dining table, with demilune ends, on square moulded legs, 47¾in (121cm) long.
£1,300–1,600 P

A George III mahogany extending dining table, the centre drop-leaf table with a pair of half round side tables, on square moulded and chamfered legs, 111in (282cm) extended.
£2,600–3,000 WW

A late George III mahogany dining table, comprising a pair of rounded rectangular ends on square tapering legs and central drop-leaf section, 109½in (278cm) wide.
£1,500–1,800 P(L)

An American Federal extending dining table, in two parts, the top with a reeded edge, the tulip-turned reeded tapering legs with bun feet, early 19thC, 93¾in (238cm) long.
£1,300–1,500 SLN

An American Federal cherry drop-leaf dining table, with hinged leaves and square tapering legs, repaired, New England, early 19thC, 53in (134.5cm) extended.
£800–1,000 SK(B)

A mahogany extending dining table, supported on twelve fluted ring-turned tapering legs, with four extra leaves, two of which are later replacements, early 19thC, 130in (330cm) extended.
£3,000–3,500 TMA

A Regency mahogany dining table, by Morgan & Sanders, the top with a reeded edge, fitted with brass handles, on slender tapering baluster reeded legs, including two extra leaves, 107½in (273cm) extended.
£8,500–10,000 P(B)

The partnership of Thomas Morgan and Joseph Sanders produced an extensive range of patent furniture in the early years of the 19thC. Their designs were widely published by Rudolph Ackermann in his monthly periodical *The Repository of Arts* and their claim to have supplied furniture to Nelson is supported by a payment of £549 in 1810.

Auction or Dealer?

All the pictures in our price guides originate from auction houses and dealers. When buying at auction, prices can be lower than those of a dealer, but a buyer's premium and VAT will be added to the hammer price. Equally, when selling at auction, commission, tax and photography charges must be taken into account. Dealers will often restore pieces before putting them back on the market.

Both dealers and auctioneers will provide professional advice, so it is worth researching both sources before buying or selling your antiques.

A late Georgian mahogany D-end extending dining table, raised on reeded square-shaped tapering legs, 88in (223.5cm) long.
£2,000–2,400 AG

A George IV mahogany extending dining table, in the manner of Gillows, with three leaf insertions, on turned tapered and reeded legs, 105½in (268cm) extended.
£5,500–6,000 S(S)

A George IV mahogany drop-leaf dining table, the top with rounded corners, on turned legs with casters, 68½in (174cm) long.
£750–900 DN

A Biedermeier walnut dining table, the top with radiating figured veneers, on a columnar standard raised on an incurving tripartite under-scrolled base, mid-19thC, 47in (119.5cm) diam.
£2,500–3,000 BB(S)

A Sheraton-style mahogany and satinwood-banded dining table, on central urn support with lotus leaf-carved hipped quadripartite downswept legs, 19thC, 69in (175cm) diam.
£12,000–14,000 HOK

A William IV dining table, the radially veneered top raised on a lotus-carved pillar and concave triform base with scrolled feet, 53¼in (135cm) diam.
£3,400–4,000 TEN

A William IV mahogany triple pillar dining table, with two leaf insertions, the top on baluster-shaped octagonal column supports ending in platform bases with carved paw feet, restored, c1835, 136in (345.5cm) extended.
£7,000–8,500 S(S)

An early Victorian mahogany extending dining table, the wind-out top with four leaves, on ring-turned and reeded tapering legs, one leaf of a later date, 134¼in (341cm) extended.
£5,500–6,500 P

◄ A mahogany dining table, on lappet-carved turned tapering legs, previously with additional leaves, mid-19thC, 47¼in (120cm) square.
£1,100–1,300 PFK

This table would be worth approximately £3,000 if the purchaser had been able to acquire two of the leaves pictured right.

An early Victorian mahogany table, with two D-shaped end sections and three leaves, one table top bears label to underside 'E. W. Bonham Esq., Her Britannic Majesty's Consul, Calais', 142in (360.5cm) extended.
£3,800–4,500 CAG

Recognizing decent timber when he saw it, a Dover resident paid £7 for this table top and leaves 30 years ago, but never got around to using them. When he was told they would realize at least £1,500–2,000 at auction, the vendor thought the auctioneer was joking, but proceeded anyway. In fact, it realized more than double that figure, because old timber is very sought-after by dealers. If an extending table is missing a leaf, it is always preferable to use period timber for the additional leaf.

▲ ► An early Victorian extending dining table (above), with three leaves, contained in a mahogany cabinet (right) fronted by a what-not with four shelves, 136¼in (164cm) extended.
£2,500–3,000 Bon(G)

A Victorian oak and pollard oak extending dining table, including three leaves and two winding handles, on five ebonized ring-turned and fluted legs, c1870, 126in (321cm) extended.
£2,500–3,000 S(S)

A Victorian mahogany wind-out dining table, on reeded turned tapering legs, 87in (223cm) long.
£1,500–1,800 P

A Victorian walnut extending dining table, the top with burr-walnut veneered frieze, the central support with lotus-carved turned elements and splayed scroll-carved feet, lacking extra leaves and winder mechanism, stamped 'Gillow', 65½in (166cm) diam.
£5,000–6,000 Bea(E)

A late Victorian mahogany extending dining table, with three loose leaves, on turned and reeded legs, some damage to leaves, 124¾in (317cm) extended.
£2,800–3,200 DN

A walnut extending dining table, with three leaves, on four ring-turned baluster supports, lacking casters, late 19thC, 100in (254cm) extended.
£1,100–1,300 Bri

▶ An Edwardian mahogany extending dining table, including two leaf insertions, on foliate carved cabriole legs ending in claw-and-ball feet, c1910, 118¼in (300cm) extended.
£2,700–3,000 S(S)

A Georgian-style mahogany D-end dining table, in three sections, on tapering moulded supports, early 20thC, 112¾in (286cm) extended.
£1,400–1,700 Wilp

DISPLAY TABLES

A German satinwood and inlaid display table, with a glazed top and plush-lined interior, raised on square tapered legs with brass ball feet, 19thC, 32¼in (82cm) diam.
£1,700–2,000 TEN

A French kingwood display table, with chased brass mounts, the hinged serpentine-shaped top with a glazed bevelled panel, glazed sides and cabriole legs, late 19thC, 32in (81.5cm) wide.
£2,000–2,400 DN

An Edwardian satinwood display table, painted with floral swags and harebells, raised on square tapered splay legs united by an undertier, 24¾in (63cm) diam.
£1,200–1,500 TEN

An Edwardian simulated rosewood octagonal display table, the glazed top enclosing a plush-lined interior, painted throughout with rosettes and sprigs of flowers, 11½in (29cm) wide.
£500–600 GAK

◄ An Edwardian satinwood heart-shaped display table, strung throughout in ebony and boxwood, the top painted with flowers, with a silk-lined interior, on three cabriole legs painted with trails of husks, 18in (45.5cm) wide.
£900–1,100 HAM

◄ An Edwardian satinwood display table, with diced inlaid borders, square tapered legs and cross stretchers, 25in (63.5cm) wide.
£1,100–1,200 FHF

DRESSING TABLES

A George III Sheraton-style faded mahogany gentleman's dressing table, the divided top banded in purple wood and satinwood, opening and resting on brass scroll brackets, enclosing an adjustable mirror and fitted interior, 33in (84cm) wide.
£2,000–2,400 HAM

A walnut kneehole dressing table, the later galleried top above an arrangement of seven cockbeaded and featherbanded drawers around the apron drawer and cupboard in the recess, lacking part of gallery, early 18thC, 32¼in (83cm) wide.
£2,700–3,250 Bea(E)

An American Queen Anne walnut dressing table, the central drawer with a lunette, on cabriole legs, replaced brass, Boston, 1730–50, 34½in (87.5cm) wide.
£6,500–7,500 SK(B)

> **Cross Reference**
> See Colour Review

► A late George III mahogany dressing table, the twin flap top enclosing a plain interior with a counterbalanced mirror, above three drawers and a tambour shutter flanked by drawers, 28¼in (72cm) wide.
£700–850 P(Sc)

A mahogany serpentine-fronted dressing table, with two deep drawers flanking a central drawer, early 19thC, 36in (91.5cm) wide.
£2,200–2,600 DN

A mahogany dressing table, crossbanded and boxwood-strung, the two hinged covers enclosing a fitted interior, 19thC, 27½in (70cm) wide.
£500–600 DN

An American Renaissance revival rosewood dresser, with gilt incising, the mirror surmounted by a carved winged female mask and supported by a pair of marble-topped pedestals, the cupboards enclosing drawers, New York, mid-19thC, 62½in (159cm) wide.
£3,200–3,500 NOA

A maple bowfront dressing table, the frieze with cane panels, the hinged cover with a triple folding mirror, interior with fitted accessories, with silver mounts by Henry Clifford Davies, Birmingham, 1927, 27in (68.5cm) wide.
£7,000–8,000 S(S)

A previous owner provided the history of this item. He explained that it was intended for Princess Elizabeth's Wendy House but was not suitable and was then exhibited in the first Ideal Home Exhibition.

A French fruitwood *poudreuse*, with marquetry banding and floral inlay, the centre top panel lifting to reveal a mirrored vanity, 19thC, 38in (96.5cm) wide.
£500–600 BG

◀ An Edwardian inlaid mahogany bowfront dressing table, with five drawers, 40½in (103cm) wide.
£300–350 Wilp

DROP-LEAF TABLES

A George II mahogany double-action drop-leaf table, on tapered legs ending in pad feet, restored, c1750, 67¼in (171cm) wide.
£1,600–1,750 S(S)

A George II mahogany drop-leaf dining table, on cabriole legs with claw-and-ball feet, 55in (140cm) wide.
£900–1,100 Bri

A George III mahogany drop-leaf dining table, with shaped end frieze, on cabriole legs and pad feet, c1760, 64in (162.5cm) wide.
£2,200–2,600 Bon

An American Queen Anne mahogany drop-leaf table, Rhode Island, restored, 1790s, 48⅛in (123cm) wide.
£1,300–1,500 SK(B)

A Regency mahogany drop-leaf table, the top with reeded edge, the secretaire drawer with baize writing slope, 40½in (103cm) wide.
£800–1,000 P(Ed)

An American Empire carved mahogany drop-leaf table, the top with scalloped corners, the frieze with gilt-metal moulding, with a drawer at one end and an opposing dummy drawer, with leaf-capped hairy-paw feet, possibly New York, c1825, 58½in (148.5cm) long.
£1,400–1,700 SLN

DRUM TABLES

A George III mahogany library drum table, the tooled leather-inset top above eight frieze drawers, c1790, 57⅛in (146cm) diam.
£4,000–5,000 Bon

A Regency brass-mounted mahogany drum table, the maroon leather-inset top with alternate real and dummy drawers, 48in (122cm) diam.
£5,500–6,000 BB(L)

A Regency mahogany drum table, the leather-inset top above four real and four dummy drawers, 46¾in (119cm) diam.
£4,000–5,000 TEN

An Irish mahogany drum table, the leather-inset top above real and dummy drawers, labelled 'Miller & Beatty', 19thC, 45¾in (116cm) diam.
£2,700–3,250 HOK

A mahogany revolving drum table, the leather-inset top above drawers, c1850, 48in (122cm) diam.
£2,000–2,250 CHE

A painted satinwood drum table, with four dummy and four small drawers, early 20thC, 24in (61cm) diam.
£2,500–2,750 NOA

GAMES TABLES

A George II red walnut games table, the shaped frieze with centre drawer and long side drawer, c1760, 26in (66cm) wide.
£1,600–2,200 WILL

An Italian rococo-style kingwood and walnut triangular games table, the fold-over top enclosing leather-lined playing surface, resting on a pull-out leg, with one small drawer, late 18thC, 44¼in (112.5cm) wide.
£2,500–2,750 NOA

A George IV rosewood games table, in the style of Gillows, with a central slide revealing a backgammon board, and reversing to an inlaid chessboard, above a false frieze drawer, c1825, 42in (106.5cm) wide.
£3,000–3,500 Bon

LOCATE THE SOURCE
The source of each illustration in Miller's can be found by checking the code letters below each caption with the Key to Illustrations, pages 789–795.

◄ A George IV penwork games table, the tilt-top decorated as a games board, with sprays of flowers and leaves throughout, c1820, 19¼in (49cm) wide.
£5,000–6,000 S

An American mahogany fold-over games table, with crossbanded top over fitted interior, 19thC, 42in (106.5cm) wide.
£250–300 FBG

An early Victorian walnut and floral marquetry games/work table, the top inlaid with a chequer board above a frieze drawer and wool slide, 22in (56cm) wide.
£750–900 P(Sc)

A Victorian papier mâché tripod table, the top inlaid with a chessboard and flower sprays in mother-of-pearl and painted in colours, 22½in (57cm) diam.
£400–500 P(C)

► A Victorian burr-walnut games table, decorated with crossbanding and boxwood stringing, the hinged swivel top opening to reveal inlaid boards in ebony, bird's-eye maple, tulipwood and sycamore for chess, backgammon and cribbage, with frieze drawer, 26½in (67.5cm) wide.
£2,300–2,750 AG

LIBRARY TABLES

A mahogany three-drawer library table, with leather-inset top, on end column supports united by a stretcher, early 19thC, 72in (183cm) wide.
£2,300–2,500 Odi

A George IV mahogany library table, the top inset with tooled black leather, over two frieze drawers and opposing dummy drawers, raised on turned and moulded end supports with gadrooned collars joined by a turned stretcher, on trestle bases with carved paw feet, 65¾in (167cm) wide.
£7,000–8,000 TEN

An American Federal carved and figured-mahogany library table, in the manner of Duncan Phyfe, the top flanked by trefoil leaves above a panelled frieze with pendant finials, on four leaf-carved columnar supports and acanthus-carved downswept legs, repairs to two legs, c1815, 51in (129.5cm) wide.
£1,800–2,200 S(NY)

Duncan Phyfe (1768–1854) is one of the best-known makers of American Federal furniture. He was Scottish by birth, but lived in New York and specialized in elegant seat furniture.

A Regency rosewood library table, the top above two real and two opposing dummy drawers, the panelled splayed end supports with pierced fan angle brackets, on platform bases with scroll feet, underside stamped 'G. I. Morant, 81 New Bond Street', 51in (129.5cm) wide.
£2,600–3,200 S(S)

G. I. Morant was a well-known firm of London decorators and cabinet-makers, founded in 1790. On the recommendation of the Duke of Gloucester, George Morant successfully applied for Royal Appointment in the early years of Queen Victoria's reign.

◀ A mahogany double-sided library table, with leather-inset top, the frieze with three drawers to each side, on ropetwist tapering legs with leaf-carved bulbous feet and casters, mid-19thC, 62¼in (158cm) wide.
£7,000–8,000 HOK

NESTS OF TABLES

A nest of four mahogany tables, with crossbanding and ebony stringing, c1820, largest 19in (48.5cm) wide.
£2,500–3,000 DOA

A nest of four inlaid mahogany tables, c1890, largest 23in (58.5cm) wide.
£2,000–2,250 CHE

A George IV mahogany nest of three tables, each with a pair of bamboo-turned supports, on a bulbous-turned plinth, headed by concentric bosses, ending in turned feet, largest 22¼in (56.5cm) wide.
£900–1,100 NOA

A set of Edwardian walnut and amboyna quartetto tables, each on four down-curved feet, with two pairs of ringed tapering columns and a crossbanded top, largest 19½in (49.5cm) wide.
£900–1,100 Gam

▶ A set of Edwardian figured-mahogany oval quartetto tables, satinwood-inlaid and crossbanded, largest 20½in (52cm) wide.
£450–550 M

▶ A nest of Edwardian mahogany and satinwood-crossbanded quartetto tables, inlaid with stringing, on slender ring-turned legs ending in downswept feet, 20½in (52cm) wide.
£2,500–2,750 S(S)

OCCASIONAL TABLES

A walnut wine table, with turned column, mid-18thC, 18in (45.5cm) diam.
£3,000–3,350 DaH

A Napoleon III gilt-bronze mounted walnut occasional table, possibly by Gabriel Viardot, the shelves etched with Chinese foliage and landscapes, inlaid with mother-of-pearl figures and flowers, one side with a bronze dragon, 31½in (80cm) wide.
£1,500–1,800 S(NY)

Viardot specialized in exotic furniture of Chinese and Japanese inspiration. He was a participant and jury member at the Expositions Universelles of 1867 where he acquired four medals, 1878 where he acquired a silver medal and 1889 where he was awarded a gold medal.

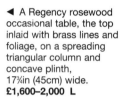

A late Georgian mahogany wine table, on an associated octagonal stem and triform platform base with button feet, 15in (38cm) wide.
£220–250 PFK

◀ A Regency rosewood occasional table, the top inlaid with brass lines and foliage, on a spreading triangular column and concave plinth, 17¾in (45cm) wide.
£1,600–2,000 L

A Victorian walnut occasional table, with a drawer, raised on shaped fretwork end supports and trestles with scrolled feet, joined by pole stretchers, 21¼in (54cm) wide.
£500–600 AH

An American Federal cherry occasional table, the frieze with a drawer, raised on turned, tapered and reeded legs, 17¼in (44cm) wide.
£650–800 SLN

An occasional table with a later parcel-gilt tripod base, early 19thC, 18in (45.5cm) wide.
£1,600–2,000 DOA

An Edwardian satinwood occasional table, crossbanded with string and parquetry banding, the top inlaid with husks and flowerheads, the frieze with inlaid panels, raised on four slender turned and fluted supports, 18in (45.5cm) diam.
£850–1,000 AH

◀ An Edwardian satin-wood occasional table, with crossbanded decoration, the string-inlaid top with musical floral marquetry panel, square tapering legs and under-shelf, 27in (68.5cm) diam.
£1,300–1,600 JM

An American Federal mahogany and birch table, with a drawer, and on four square tapering legs, New England, 17in (43cm) wide.
£1,800–2,200 SK(B)

A William IV rosewood and parquetry occasional table, with foliate-moulded brass edge, over one long frieze drawer, 20in (51cm) wide.
£1,600–1,750 BG

An Edwardian mahogany occasional table, the top with a fret frieze, the legs in groups of four slender turned spindles united by a shaped undertier, 30in (76cm) wide.
£340–400 DA

An oak occasional table, with barley-twist legs, c1930s, 20in (51cm) square.
£65–75 TAC

PEMBROKE TABLES

An early George III mahogany butterfly Pembroke table, with two drop flaps, a cockbeaded drawer to the frieze with brass swan-neck drop handles, on chamfered square legs, 30in (76cm) wide.
£1,600–2,000 HAM

A George III Hepplewhite-style satin-wood and tulipwood-crossbanded serpentine Pembroke table, the top with a foliate marquetry medallion within a riband-tied border above a frieze drawer, 38½in (98cm) extended.
£5,000–6,000 P

A George III inlaid kingwood Pembroke table, the hinged top with an inlaid oval patera to each side above a single end frieze drawer fitted with a slide, c1785, 37½in (95.5cm) extended.
£2,500–3,000 Bon

A George III crossbanded and ebony-strung satinwood Pembroke table, the top with a lily engraved border above a real and opposing dummy drawer with banded decoration and later handles, on tapering supports with ebonized spade feet, minor restorations, 32in (81.5cm) extended.
£1,500–1,700 Bri

An American Federal inlaid mahogany Pembroke table, the top and leaves with stringing, the legs inlaid with floral motifs above husk inlays, on square tapering legs, New York, c1800, 21½in (54.5cm) extended.
£5,000–5,500 SK(B)

A Regency faded mahogany Pembroke table, with frieze drawer and opposing dummy drawer, with ebony stringing and brass floret knob handles, on a baluster stem with a reeded collar and four reeded splay legs, 36in (91.5cm) extended.
£450–550 WW

A George IV mahogany Pembroke table, the top with a frieze drawer opposing a dummy drawer front, on ring-turned tapering legs, 41¾in (106cm) extended.
£350–420 DN

A late Regency mahogany Pembroke table, with a drawer to one end, on a turned stem and four reed-edged swept legs with turned paterae surmounts, 44½in (113cm) extended.
£500–600 PFK

A Regency mahogany and rosewood-crossbanded Pembroke table, inlaid with boxwood and ebonized lines, the reeded top above a hinged fall-front enclosing a pair of small drawers, flanked by an opposing simulated drawer, on reeded turned and tapering legs, 29½in (75cm) extended.
£1,200–1,500 P

▶ An Edwardian mahogany Pembroke table, with serpentine border, inlaid with musical instruments and ribbon swags, with a single frieze drawer, on square tapering legs, 30¼in (77cm) wide.
£800–1,100 RTo

READING TABLES

A William IV mahogany reading table, the adjustable top on a telescopic turned column support ending in a triform platform base with lobed bun feet, restored, c1830, 21¼in (54cm) wide.
£800–1,000 S(S)

An early Victorian rosewood reading table, the divided top with two hinged rachet-action book rests with a hinged cover to the side enclosing former pen tray and inkwell recesses, a frieze drawer to one side opposed by a pair of candle slides, 32½in (82.5cm) wide.
£500–600 P(NW)

A Victorian part-ebonized amboyna library table, with a hinged ratcheted top, above a frieze drawer opposed by a false drawer, over an open centre section with a shelf, 1870–80, 33in (84cm) wide.
£4,750–5,250 S(NY)

SERVING TABLES

A mahogany bowfront serving table, the crossbanded and string-inlaid top above three frieze drawers with replaced oval brass plate swing handles, late 18thC, 66in (167.5cm) wide.
£2,800–3,200 WW

A Gothic revival carved oak serving table, the blind Gothic tracery frieze incorporating three drawers, the end supports with cluster column pilasters headed at the front by earlier carved grotesque masks, c1840, 84¼in (214cm) wide.
£3,700–4,000 S

The inclusion of genuine Gothic carvings is unusual at this date, marking this out as a rare early example of antiquarian furniture-making. Carvings of this type were collected by several of the designers most closely associated with the Gothic revival, including Pugin and Cottingham.

A Regency mahogany serving table, in the style of Gillows, on four turned reeded legs, 83in (211cm) wide.
£6,250–7,000 CHE

An Irish William IV mahogany serving table, by Williams & Gibton, the top with a deep lappet-carved edge above a cavetto bead-moulded frieze, on lappet clad Corinthian column supports, formerly with a rear mirror, stamped 'Williams & Gibton', c1835, 63¾in (162cm) wide.
£7,000–8,000 S(S)

The firm of Williams & Gibton was formed in Dublin in 1829, evolving from a company started by John Mack in the late 18thC. Gibton had many strings to his bow, being also an auctioneer, a seller and maker of trunks, portmanteaux, gun cases and musical instrument cases. In 1844, two years after his death, the firm changed its name to Williams & Son, finally ceasing business in 1852.

A Regency mahogany bowfront serving table, the top with reeded edge above three frieze drawers, on reeded tapering legs terminating in spool feet, 50¼in (127.5cm) wide.
£1,650–2,000 P(L)

Prices

The price ranges quoted in this book reflect the average price a purchaser might expect to pay for a similar item. The price will vary according to the condition, rarity, size, popularity, provenance, colour and restoration of the item and this must be taken into account when assessing values.

A Victorian carved oak serving table, the back carved with central shell motif flanked by S-scrolls above the top with ogee-shaped frieze drawer, on carved cabriole supports with lion paw feet, 57in 145cm) wide.
£1,100–1,200 Bri

SIDE TABLES

A William and Mary walnut and crossbanded side table, with frieze drawer, on bobbin-turned legs joined by an X-shaped stretcher and on bun feet, restored, 28in (71cm) wide.
£3,500–4,000 S(S)

A walnut side table, with a drawer, c1720, 28in (71cm) wide.
£2,000–2,275 RED

A George III oak bowfront side table, with mahogany crossbanding, 29in (73.5cm) wide.
£1,600–1,750 CRU

An oyster walnut side table, the crossbanded laburnum top above a frieze drawer, on baluster turned legs united by an X-stretcher and on bun feet, reduced in height, late 17thC, 30¼in (77cm) wide.
£1,100–1,300 P(S)

A George III mahogany side table, the satinwood-banded top with fan centre inside garlands of flowers above an ornate frieze, on square tapering inlaid legs, 49in (124.5cm) wide.
£5,500–6,500 MEA

A painted pine side table, with original decoration and parcel gilt, attributed to John Linnell, c1776, 55in (139.5cm) wide.
£8,000–9,000 CAT

John Linnell worked for the family firm of William & John Linnell. It was established in London c1730 and John took over the business in 1763. Their reputation for quality was on a par with the Chippendales, Ince & Mayhew, Cobb etc.

A Continental walnut side table, with frieze drawer, on ring and block-turned legs joined by turned stretchers, ending in ball feet, top reset, late 17thC, 37in (94cm) wide.
£2,200–2,500 S(NY)

A George III satinwood eliptical table, banded in tulipwood or purpleheart, the top inlaid with a marquetry chrysanthemum segment in an elliptical panel, above painted frieze of ribbon and tied swags of flowering laurel, on tapering legs capped by lyres and bellflower pendants, 39½in (100.5cm) wide.
£2,500–3,500 WW

A Dutch walnut side table, marquetry-inlaid with flowers and foliage, the two quadrant drawers hinged to open outwards, on three square tapering legs, late 18thC, 31in (78.5cm) wide.
£900–1,100 RBB

◀ A Dutch mahogany, rosewood-crossbanded and marquetry side table, the trapezoidal top above a chequer-banded frieze drawer and sides, on fluted tapering legs and brass ball feet, late 18th/early 19thC, 26in (66cm) wide.
£2,800–3,200 P

By repute this table was given to Brigadier Verre Stone by Queen Victoria in recognition for various alterations and colour schemes which the Brigadier, who was also an architect, had carried out to the Queen's summer residence, Osborne House, on the Isle of Wight. The Queen was so pleased with the ornate painting work carried out by Peter Van de Pol, a craftsman brought over from Amsterdam by Brigadier Stone, that she decided to present him with this Dutch table.

A late George III inlaid mahogany bowfront side table, with brass handles, 28½in (72.5cm) wide.
£220–260 PFK

A Regency japanned pine side table, the top decorated in Chinese style with figures, the frieze panelled with flowers on a cream ground, 48in (122cm) wide.
£2,000–2,400 DN

A George IV fruitwood and yew wood side table, the crossbanded top above a pair of frieze drawers, on a splayed faceted column and concave quadripartite base, on scrolled feet, 30in (76cm) wide.
£4,000–5,000 Bon

A mid-Victorian walnut side table, the waisted top with carved edge, on barley-twist supports, formerly a sewing table, 26in (66cm) wide.
£700–850 P(L)

A late Victorian rosewood occasional table, with boxwood stringing, c1890, 21in (53.5cm) square.
£650–700 OTT

An Irish 18thC-style mahogany side table, the green mottled top over a frieze with a vitruvian scroll and with two flush drawers to the front, on shell-capped moulded cabriole legs with rosette brackets, on claw-and-ball feet, 19thC, 66in (167.5cm) wide.
£2,500–3,000 HOK

SILVER TABLES

A George III mahogany silver table, the galleried top above a frieze raised on cluster column legs ending in block feet, top possibly associated, 33¾in (85.5cm) wide.
£2,500–3,000 S(NY)

A Dutch mahogany silver table, the galleried top containing a cushion frieze drawer on cabriole legs and pad feet, 19thC, 33¾in (85.5cm) wide.
£750–900 P

◄ A mahogany silver table, the top with undulating raised rim, over a pierced Chinese fretted frieze with pierced spandrels, on clustered, pierced and carved legs, restored, 18thC, 32in (81.5cm) wide.
£1,700–2,000 TEN

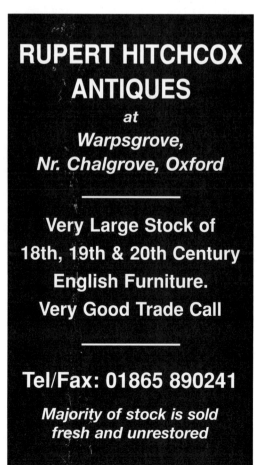

SOFA TABLES

A Georgian mahogany sofa table, the two short and two dummy frieze drawers with turned knob handles, 43in (109cm) extended.
£2,000–2,400 AG

A Regency rosewood sofa table, with single drawer, on cheval frame with fluted quarter roundels, 42in (106.5cm) extended.
£3,800–4,500 RBB

A Regency satinwood and ebony-strung sofa table, the hinged top above two frieze drawers and two dummy drawers, on lyre-shaped solid end supports, c1820, 55in (139.5cm) extended.
£1,400–1,700 Bon

A mahogany sofa table, with brass line inlay, with alternate real and dummy drawers on each side, c1835, 58¼in (148cm) extended.
£1,350–1,600 HOK

A George III mahogany sofa table, inlaid with stringing and geometric banding, with alternate real and opposing dummy drawers, one with pen compartment, 57in (145cm) wide.
£4,000–4,500 S

A Regency rosewood gilt-metal-mounted sofa table, with satinwood stringing, on a lyre-shaped column, 51in (129.5cm) extended.
£2,500–3,000 RBB

A Danish mahogany and string-inlaid sofa table, the frieze inlaid with drapery swags centred by a female mask and incorporating a drawer, c1830, 55in (139.5cm) extended.
£1,400–1,700 S(S)

An Italian walnut and Sorrento marquetry sofa table, the hinged top inlaid with a central panel of peasants, above a frieze drawer, mid-19thC, 48in (122cm) extended.
£1,800–2,200 P

An early Regency mahogany sofa table, with amaranth narrow band inlay, two short drawers with brass ring handles, small pieces of veneer missing, 58½in (148.5cm) wide.
£1,500–1,800 MCA

A late Regency mahogany sofa table, the hinged top above two frieze drawers, raised on five turned pillars with swept quadruped base, 58¼in (148cm) wide.
£1,800–2,200 P(B)

A George IV mahogany sofa table, the faded flame-figured top crossbanded in rosewood, the friezes with alternate drawers and dummy drawers with replaced brass handles, carved side panels, 42in (106.5cm) extended.
£3,000–3,500 WW

An Edwardian mahogany sofa table, by Edwards & Roberts, the top with a reeded edge above two frieze drawers with two opposing dummy drawers, painted with foliage, festoons and ribbon bows in colours, one drawer stamped and also with an ivory plaque inscribed with maker's name, 63in (160cm) wide.
£2,500–3,000 P(O)

The firm of Edwards & Roberts, cabinet-makers and dealers in antiques, modern furniture and reproductions, was established in London in 1845.

SUTHERLAND TABLES

A Victorian burr-walnut Sutherland table, raised on moulded and scrolled dual end supports joined by a turned stretcher, on carved cabriole legs with scrolled toes, 50¾in (129cm) wide.
£2,800–3,200 TEN

A Victorian burr-walnut Sutherland table, with scroll feet and casters, 35in (89cm) wide.
£900–1,000 S(S)

A Victorian rosewood Sutherland table, marquetry and string-inlaid, on twin turned tapering end supports and trestles, 21¼in (54cm) wide.
£450–550 AH

TEA TABLES

A George III walnut tea table, with hinged fold-over top enclosing a well, 26in (66cm) wide.
£3,200–3,500 CRU

A George III boxwood and ebony-strung mahogany fold-over tea table, the top opening to a well, the frieze with a central drawer, on four tapered legs, probably Scottish, 38in (96.5cm) wide.
£1,750–2,000 Mit

A George III mahogany tea table, the fold-over top above a wavy apron, on straight chamfered legs, 30¾in (78cm) wide.
£450–550 DN

A mahogany swivel-action tea table, the hinged top above a carved frieze on a turned column and lion-carved feet, early 19thC, 36¼in (92cm) wide.
£400–500 P(NW)

An American Federal mahogany and tiger-maple fold-over tea/card table, the top with a rosewood crossbanded edge, the bird's-eye maple frieze centred by an inlaid rosewood panel with an oval satin-birch cameo, Massachusetts, 1800–10, 39¾in (101cm) wide.
£4,500–5,000 SLN

◄ An American Federal mahogany tea table, the swivelling and folding flap top on a carved pineapple stem with a moulded circular base, on four moulded outline scroll legs and ebonized bun feet, c1825, 35in (89cm) wide.
£1,400–1,700 WW

A George IV mahogany tea table, the reeded fold-over top on a leaf-carved lotus pillar and quadripartite base, 34in (86.5cm) wide.
£2,200–2,600 M&K

An early Victorian peacock-grained mahogany tea table, with fold-over swivel top, 38in (96.5cm) wide.
£700–850 DD

TRIPOD TABLES

A mahogany tripod table, the tip-up top on a bird-cage support, mid-18thC, 24¾in (63cm) diam.
£1,250–1,500 Bea(E)

A mahogany tilt-top table, with Chippendale-style piecrust rim and bird-cage support, on a leaf carved tripod base, mid-18thC, 30¾in (78cm) diam.
£850–1,000 HOK

A George II mahogany tripod table, the tilt-top with a piecrust rim, on a turned, tapered and fluted column with claw-and-ball feet, restored, c1755, 19½in (49.5cm) diam.
£4,500–5,500 S

A George II mahogany tripod table, the dished tilt-top on a ring-turned column with cabriole legs, on pad feet, probably Scottish, 26in (66cm) high.
£800–1,000 P

Tilt-Top Tables

Tilt-top tables invariably have a hinged 'bird-cage' attached to the top, consisting of two parallel platforms joined by columns, through which the top of the shaft or column could be inserted and then fixed by a wedge to the neck.

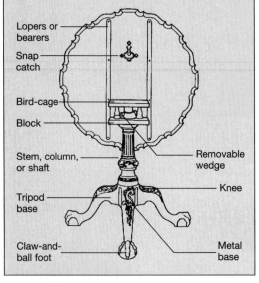

Lopers or bearers
Snap catch
Bird-cage
Block
Stem, column, or shaft
Removable wedge
Knee
Tripod base
Claw-and-ball foot
Metal base

An American Chippendale mahogany tilt-top candlestand, with a bird-cage support, damaged, Pennsylvania, c1760–80, 21¾in (55.5cm) diam.
£3,300–3,600 SK(B)

A Victorian mahogany tilt-top table, 21in (53.5cm) diam.
£700–775 NAW

A George III yew wood tilt-top pedestal tripod table, the baluster column supported on three splayed cabriole legs with pad feet, in need of restoration, 27in (68.5cm) diam.
£850–1,000 TMA

A Georgian elm tilt-top tripod table, c1790–1800, 18in (45.5cm) square.
£885–985 CAT

A Regency mahogany tripod table, attributed to Gillows, the top with a beaded edge, with brass plaque inscribed 'This belonged to George Gordon, 6th Lord Byron', c1820, 19¼in (49cm) wide.
£3,800–4,500 Bon

A French mahogany tripod table, c1890, 16in (40.5cm) diam.
£1,000–1,200 RL

▶ A Victorian mahogany wine table, 22in (56cm) diam.
£270–300 NAW

An inlaid mahogany wine table, c1890, 18in (45.5cm) diam.
£700–800 GBr

TWO-TIER TABLES

A Sheraton-style painted satinwood two-tier occasional table, with shaped gallery and on square supports, late 19thC, 25in (63.5cm) wide.
£1,000–1,200 RBB

A French Louis Philippe two-tier table, with frieze drawer, the legs joined by an undertier, 19in (48.5cm) diam.
£6,700–7,500 S(Mon)

The age, small size and decorative lacquerwork of this table contribute to its high value.

◄ An Edwardian inlaid rosewood two-tier table, with pierced side splats each flanked with half-reeded and turned supports on conforming ebonized ring-turned legs, 20in (51cm) diam.
£370–450 MEA

◄ A mahogany coin 'guinea changing' table, by J. C. Cox, with a central glazed coin counter, bell ringing and locking, flanked by twelve sectioned shelves, the table top with coin wells, late 19thC, 27in (68.6cm) wide.
£700–850 TMA

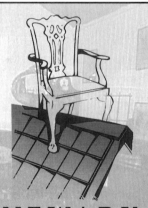

WORK TABLES

An American Federal carved mahogany work table, the hinged top above a cockbeaded fitted drawer, with a deep drawer below, on vase and ring-turned legs with tapering feet, replaced brasses, New York or Philadelphia, c1815, 24½in (62cm) wide.
£1,600–2,000 SK(B)

A Regency rosewood work table, the lyre-shaped undercarriage with two drawers and a shaped workbox, c1820, 30in (76cm) wide.
£3,200–3,600 NAW

A Regency mahogany work table, in the style of Gillows, on four reeded legs, c1815, 36in (91.5cm) extended.
£2,500–2,650 CHE

A Regency rosewood work/card table, the fold-over top with baize lining, with a drawer below and pouch, on U-shaped support, 28in (71cm) wide.
£1,200–1,400 RBB

A Regency mahogany lift-top work table, on a turned central pedestal, 26¾in (68cm) wide.
£600–700 WilP

A Regency mahogany sewing table, with a drawer, c1820, 13in (33cm) wide.
£2,500–3,000 DOA

Miller's is a price GUIDE not a price LIST

A William IV inlaid calamander games/work table, the drop-leaf top with pierced brass semi-circular galleries and lift-out central section inlaid with a foliate panel, with a chessboard on the reverse, the frieze with a drawer above a sliding work bag, 34½in (87.5cm) wide.
£2,000–2,200 Bea(E)

An early Victorian work table, the serpentine amboyna top with rosewood crossbanding and ebony mouldings, with a drawer above a pull-out workbox, lock missing to drawer, 26in (66cm) wide.
£2,700–3,250 CAG

An inlaid burr-walnut games/work table, c1860, 28in (71cm) wide.
£2,750–3,000 CRU

A rosewood and mother-of-pearl-inlaid work table, the top enclosing a fitted interior with a frieze drawer below, 19thC, 22in (56cm) wide.
£1,350–1,600 TEN

A Victorian walnut work table, the boxwood-strung top enclosing a fitted interior, 20in (51cm) wide.
£2,500–2,750 Mit

A Victorian walnut trumpet-shaped work table, the hinged top with a parquetry-inlaid chessboard and enclosing a fitted interior, 17¾in (45cm) wide.
£900–1,100 WL

A Victorian walnut trumpet-shaped work table, with segmented veneered top, opening to reveal a fitted interior and central well, 20in (51cm) wide.
£320–380 DOM

► An Irish inlaid yew wood work table, the hinged top with a fitted interior, on a baluster shaft and base, with paw feet, Killarney, 19thC, 22½in (57cm) wide.
£1,100–1,300 P(EA)

WRITING TABLES

A Spanish walnut writing table, with three twin-ended frieze drawers, on barley-twist legs tied by stretchers and with iron supports, late 17thC, 65in (165cm) wide.
£4,000–5,000 Bon(C)

An inlaid and crossbanded mahogany writing table, brass handles replaced, late 18thC, 34in (86.5cm) wide.
£2,600–3,200 WW

A George III rosewood and kingwood-crossbanded work/writing table, inlaid with stringing, the top with a rear rising screen above one frieze drawer, with a leather-inset ratchet-adjustable writing slope, c1790, 22in (56cm) wide.
£1,750–2,000 S(S)

This type of writing table was mostly used by ladies because of its small size, and the screen at the back would shield her face from the fire as the heat might cause her make-up to run.

A French Directoire mahogany *bureau plat*, the later top inset with a leather-lined writing surface flanked by a pair of candle slides, restored, stamped 'G. Kemp', late 18thC, 51in (129.5cm) wide.
£7,000–8,000 S(NY)

A Regency rosewood writing table, with a frieze drawer and brass gallery, c1820, 42in (106.5cm) wide.
£4,500–5,000 CHE

Cross Reference
See Colour Review

A George IV rosewood writing table, with two frieze drawers and opposing dummy drawers, 50¼in (127.5cm) wide.
£4,000–5,000 WW

A George IV rosewood writing table, the end supports linked by a turned stretcher, 56in (142cm) wide.
£2,200–2,650 HAM

A William IV mahogany writing table, with inset leather top above cockbeaded frieze drawers, c1835, 72in (183cm) wide.
£5,000–5,500 BB(L)

A William IV rosewood writing table, with two frieze drawers and central raised tablet, 51½in (131cm) wide.
£1,700–2,000 WW

A Napoleon III gilt-bronze-mounted boulle marquetry *bureau plat*, with two frieze drawers and opposing dummy drawers, signed 'Diehl Paris, 19 r Michele Comte', late 19thC, 54¼in (137.5cm) wide.
£5,000–5,500 S(NY)

In 1840 German born Charles-Guillaume Diehl (1811–58) moved to Paris where he established his workshops at 39 rue Saint-Sebastien. By 1870 more than 600 workers were in his employ. Diehl exhibited in the Great Exhibition of 1851, was awarded a medal at the 1861 Exposition des Arts Industriels and the *hors-concours* at the 1878 Exhibition.

A Napoleon III boulle and gilt-metal-mounted *bureau plat*, after a model by Bernard II van Risen Burgh, with writing slide, two short drawers and a dummy drawer, 38½in (98cm) wide.
£3,500–4,000 P

The original desk by van Risen Burgh is now in the Louvre, Paris.

A Louis XV-style mahogany and floral marquetry writing table, with inset leather writing surface above a frieze drawer, 19thC, 38in (96.5cm) wide.
£900–1,100 AH

A maple writing table, with inset leather top above two frieze drawers, c1870, 39in (99cm) wide.
£900–1,000 GBr

A Napoleon III ebonized and metal marquetry *bureau plat,* in the manner of Andre Charles Boulle, with frieze drawer, c1870, 45¾in (116cm) wide.
£500–600 P

A Victorian mahogany writing table, with inset leather top above two frieze drawers, 41½in (105.5cm) wide.
£700–850 DN

A rosewood writing table, with inset leather top above two moulded panel frieze drawers, locks replaced, late 19thC, 49½in (125.5cm) wide.
£1,100–1,200 P

◀ An Edwardian mahogany serpentine writing table, inlaid with stringing, with a three-quarter pierced brass gallery and ratchet-adjustable writing surface, damaged, c1910, 37in (94cm) wide.
£800–1,000 S(S)

A Louis XV-style walnut and marquetry *bureau plat*, inlaid with stringing, late 19thC, 47¼in (120cm) wide.
£1,300–1,500 S(S)

TEAPOYS

A late George III black japanned teapoy, the hinged lid enclosing four mixing bowls and bottles, with brass carrying handles, 16½in (42cm) wide.
£2,000–2,400 P

A thuyawood teapoy, bowls not original, early 19thC, 16in (40.5cm) wide.
£3,200–3,500 CRU

◄ A Victorian rosewood octagonal teapoy, the hinged top enclosing four lidded divisions, 19½in (49.5cm) wide.
£500–600 DN

► A Victorian rosewood teapoy, the hinged top enclosing two caddies and two cut-glass bowls, on cabriole legs, 14½in (37cm) wide.
£1,100–1,200 Gam

A Regency rosewood and brass-inlaid teapoy, with fitted interior and brass lion's mask handles, 16½in (42cm) wide.
£1,400–1,600 P(E)

A Regency mahogany teapoy, on turned tapering column with an acanthus-carved capital and foot, the platform base applied with rosettes, on paw feet, 19¾in (50cm) wide.
£1,500–1,800 P(Sc)

A rosewood teapoy, c1835, 15in (38cm) wide.
£675–750 NAW

TORCHÈRES

A pair of Victorian ebonized torchères, 45in (114.5cm) high.
£900–1,100 JAd

LOCATE THE SOURCE

The source of each illustration in Miller's can be found by checking the code letters below each caption with the Key to Illustrations, pages 789–795.

A pair of mahogany torchères, adapted from bed posts, c1830, 51in (129.5cm) high.
£750–950 BUSH

A pair of carved giltwood torchères, the circular lotus-edged tops on fluted and acanthus-carved pillars, 19thC, 59¾in (151.8cm) high.
£2,000–2,400 TEN

An Italian carved stained wood, giltwood and gesso torchère, the top supported by a carved cherub, restored, c1900, 53in (134.5cm) high.
£2,300–2,500 S(S)

TOWEL RAILS

A mahogany quilt rail, c1870,
48in (122cm) wide.
£1,150–1,275 CAT

**This item is unusual because of its
large size.**

A Victorian mahogany towel rail,
27in (68.5cm) wide.
£250–275 COLL

An Edwardian oak towel rail, c1910,
32½in (82.5cm) wide.
£85–95 NAW

TRAYS

A George III mahogany butler's tray,
on plain folding stand with hinged
leaf, 26in (66cm) wide.
£1,350–1,600 CAG

A mahogany butler's tray, the hinged
sides with cut-out handles, on later
stand, late 18thC, 31½in (80cm) wide.
£3,000–3,300 S

A mahogany tray, on later stand,
c1790, 34in (86.5cm) wide.
£2,200–2,450 CAT

A Victorian ebonized, mother-of-
pearl-inlaid and polychrome papier
mâché tray, stamped 'Jennings &
Bettridge, London', on later stand,
25½in (65cm) wide.
£1,500–1,800 NOA

A satin birch butler's tray, on original
stand, c1850, 28in (71cm) wide.
£1,100–1,200 GBr

A French Louis Philippe octagonal
tôle peinte tray, in black and orange,
on later *faux* bamboo stand, mid-
19thC, 18in (45.5cm) diam.
£700–850 NOA

A Victorian papier mâché tray,
on later stand, 30in (76cm) wide.
£850–950 P

A Victorian black lacquer and parcel-
gilt papier mâché tray, marked
'Deanes London Bridge', on later
stand, 31in (78.5cm) wide.
£1,300–1,500 S(NY)

◀ A trolley tray, with a gilt floral
border, on later stand, c1870,
30in (76cm) wide.
£2,200–2,500 HA

WARDROBES

A Dutch walnut ebonized and parcel-gilt armoire, the ripple-moulded frieze doors flanked by bobbin-turned split pilasters, dated '1657', restored, 74¾in (190cm) wide.
£1,000–1,200 S(S)

A Biedermeier birch and fruitwood armoire, mid-19thC, 63in (160cm) wide.
£2,000–2,400 BB(S)

A French painted and gilded mirrored armoire, late 19thC, 80in (203cm) wide.
£1,200–1,500 CF

▶ A Victorian figured-mahogany breakfront wardrobe, with brass knob handles, 92in (233.5cm) wide.
£1,250–1,500 M

A French Louis XVI walnut armoire, with carved shaped skirt, on scrolling feet, late 18thC, 52in (132cm) wide.
£2,000–2,400 BB(S)

A William IV mahogany breakfront wardrobe, the central doors enclosing shelves with drawers below, c1835, 91¼in (232cm) wide.
£2,000–2,400 S

A flame mahogany sentry box wardrobe, c1849, 70in (178cm) wide.
£2,000–2,200 GBr

A George IV mahogany breakfront wardrobe, the central doors with three drawers below, flanked by free-standing columns, stamped 'Wilkinson Ludgate Hill 14597', 98in (249cm) wide.
£3,200–3,500 S

The firm of Wilkinson was established c1790 by William Wilkinson, working in partnership with a relation, Thomas Wilkinson. By 1808, William had established a business of his own at 14 Ludgate Hill. From this prime location in the heart of the City, Wilkinson built up a flourishing trade, winning significant commissions from such distinguished clients as the Goldsmith's Company. A versatile designer and craftsman, Wilkinson worked in a variety of styles, producing furniture in the Egyptian, rococo and Grecian manner.

An early Victorian mahogany breakfront pedestal wardrobe, the centre with panelled doors enclosing shelves and a drawer, with panelled doors on each side, 99in (251.5cm) wide.
£800–950 AG

A French-style mahogany breakfront armoire, with shaped mirrored door flanked by concave doors, c1900, 94½in (240cm) wide.
£1,800–2,200 HOK

WASHSTANDS

A George III mahogany shaving stand, the hinged lid enclosing a cut out basin stand, mirror, bowls and compartments, with drawers below, 27in (68.5cm) wide.
£3,300–4,000 AG

A George III mahogany washstand, the hinged top enclosing compartments and a mirror, above a dummy frieze drawer, cupboard and frieze drawer, with brass carrying handles to the sides, 16½in (42cm) wide.
£800–950 P(L)

A George III mahogany washstand, the lid enclosing recesses and a mirror, the panelled door above a drawer, 16¾in (42.5cm) wide.
£650–800 L

A George III mahogany washstand, with tray gallery, doors and drawer below, altered, 20¼in (51.5cm) wide.
£500–600 L

A George III three-tier mahogany corner washstand, with drawer, the fitted top with blue and white Ironstone jug and basin, 24in (61cm) wide.
£220–265 RID

A George III mahogany washstand, with later top, c1800, 14in (35.5cm) wide.
£300–340 RPh

A late George III mahogany washstand, with flaps enclosing cut-out basin and beaker stands, with mirror, false and real drawers and tambour slide below, 18in (45.5cm) wide.
£450–550 AG

A mahogany corner washstand, with ebony stringing and one drawer, late 19thC, 24½in 62cm) wide.
£300–350 DN

A mahogany washstand, the hinged top enclosing mirror and wells for washbowl and glasses, the sides with drawers for pull-out bidet, early 19thC, 64in (162.5cm) wide.
£1,650–2,000 S(Z)

An American Federal mahogany washstand, the pierced top and turned supports joining a valanced skirt, with a shelf and drawer, New England, c1815–25, 20½in (52cm) wide.
£1,300–1,500 SK(B)

A Victorian mahogany washstand, with two drawers and raised gallery, on turned legs joined by a stretcher, 45¼in (115cm) wide.
£600–700 WilP

An American Empire cherry and bird's-eye maple corner washstand, the undertier with two drawers flanking a dummy drawer, early 19thC, 24½in (62cm) wide.
£350–420 SLN

Condition

The condition is absolutely vital when assessing the value of an antique. Damaged pieces on the whole appreciate much less than perfect examples. However, a rare desirable piece may command a high price even when damaged.

WHATNOTS

A George III mahogany whatnot/music stand, in the style of Gillows, the hinged top with ratchet mechanism and slope, the lower tier fitted with a drawer, c1800, 18in (45.5cm) wide.
£4,000–4,500 S

This model was designed to store sheets of music flat and the slope was used as a music stand.

A George IV mahogany four-tier étagère, with three-quarter gilt-metal pierced galleries and a drawer, mid-19thC, 20½in (52cm) wide.
£3,700–4,500 S(NY)

▶ A George IV rosewood four-tier whatnot/music stand, the adjustable ratcheted slope fitted with a ledge, with a drawer below, 19¼in (49cm) wide.
£1,700–2,000 P(E)

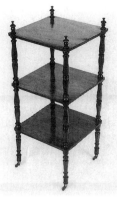

A Regency mahogany three-tier whatnot, on original brass casters, c1815, 14in (35.5cm) wide.
£2,000–2,200 RL

A George IV mahogany four-tier whatnot, with three-quarter gallery and a drawer below, 19¼in (49cm) wide.
£1,350–1,500 P(EA)

A mahogany whatnot, early 19thC, 14in (35.5cm) wide.
£1,100–1,250 CRU

A mahogany four-tier whatnot, on ring-turned columns, with a drawer below, early 19thC, 17in (43cm) wide.
£1,000–1,200 P

◀ A pair of early Victorian walnut semi-eliptical whatnots, each with three tiers and baluster turned supports and finials, 39in (99cm) wide.
£1,650–2,000 DN

A Victorian rosewood three-tier whatnot, with pierced three-quarter gallery, mirror-panelled doors below, 36in (91.5cm) wide.
£1,250–1,500 AG

A William IV rosewood three-tier whatnot, 19¼in (49cm) wide.
£1,200–1,500 P(O)

A Victorian figured-walnut canterbury whatnot, with three-quarter gallery above three divisions and drawer, 22¼in (56.5cm) wide.
£800–1,000 M

A Victorian rosewood whatnot, with four shelves divided by spiral twist columns, 22in (56cm) wide.
£800–1,000 P(Sc)

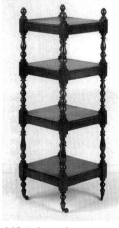

A Victorian mahogany four-tier whatnot, with turned supports, 13½in (34.5cm) square.
£800–900 S(S)

A mid-Victorian rosewood whatnot, the graduated tiers on barley-twist supports, 34in (86.5cm) wide.
£400–500 PFK

A Victorian inlaid walnut corner whatnot, with three bowfront tiers, on turned supports, 39½in (100.5cm) wide.
£170–200 PFK

An ebonized canterbury whatnot, late 19thC, 18in (45.5cm) wide.
£400–425 NET

WINDOW SEATS

A George III window seat, with black and gold painted frame and cane panelled ends, 49¼in (125cm) wide.
£5,500–6,500 TEN

A pair of George III cream-painted window seats, repainted, 34½in (87.5cm) wide.
£3,700–4,500 S(NY)

A Swiss carved walnut window seat, c1800, 25½in (65cm) wide.
£1,000–1,200 S(Z)

A mahogany window/hall seat, designed by Charles Heathcote Tatham, c1810, 66in (167.5cm) wide.
£10,000–12,000 CAT

Charles Tatham was a well-known 19thC architect. Pieces such as this are sought after today by interior decorators.

A pair of Continental mahogany window seats, with scroll and turned armrests, 19thC, 25½in (65cm) wide.
£4,500–5,000 S

A mahogany window seat, with serpentine apron and cabriole legs, c1890, 32in (81.5cm) wide.
£420–470 GBr

WINE COOLERS

A George III inlaid mahogany wine cooler, with a brass tap at the base and brass handles, 20½in (52cm) wide.
£3,200–3,500 P(E)

A George III mahogany wine cooler, with lead-lined interior and brass handles, 19in (48.5cm) wide.
£1,600–2,000 P(Sc)

A George III mahogany wine cooler, with brass handles, restored, late 18thC, 22in (56cm) wide.
£2,200–2,500 NOA

A George III brass-bound wine cooler, with lead-lined interior, damaged, c1780, 18in (46cm) wide.
£2,200–2,500 S(S)

► A late George III mahogany cellaret, inlaid with boxwood lines, with carrying handles, 17¾in (45cm) wide.
£650–800 P

A sarcophagus-shaped cellaret, with fitted interior, marked 'Gillows Lancaster', early 19thC, 31½in (80cm) wide.
£2,000–2,400 TEN

A Georgian-style mahogany wine cooler, on scroll-carved cabriole legs and ball-and-claw feet, late 19thC, 26in (66cm) wide.
£475–525 RBB

◄ A William IV sarcophagus-shaped mahogany cellaret, with lead-lined fitted interior and lion's mask handles, 24in (61cm) wide.
£900–1,100 P(S)

► A Victorian mahogany cellaret, with Gothic-style brass mounts and side carrying handles, on four short leaf-carved feet, 24in (61cm) wide.
£1,300–1,500 AP

◄ A Victorian sarcophagus-shaped oak cellaret, the top surmounted by fruit and foliage, the sides with applied flower-heads, on claw-and-ball feet, 27¼in (69cm) wide.
£500–600 Bea(E)

Oak & Country Furniture

REGIONAL STYLES

Until a few years ago, the interest in regional patterns was restricted to a small group of academics, but today the growing awareness of localized differences lends a new dimension to the popularity of early and country-made furniture. The market has responded enthusiastically by placing a premium on furniture with a strong regional identity.

In the Middle Ages, only the affluent could afford furniture of any quality or pretension. These people were relatively mobile, with access to the international trade in luxury goods. Their furnishings tended to reflect the tastes of Anglo-Flemish and German traders, who were influenced in turn by the spread of Renaissance styles from northern Italy.

The earliest groups of furniture with any strong regional identity in England appeared in the second half of the 16th century. London was served by its own community of craftsmen and by immigrant cabinet-makers and inlayers who settled in Southwark. In the provinces, production was dominated by the joiners, who made carved and panelled oak furniture, concentrated in the large ports and cathedral towns such as Bristol and Salisbury. The list of identifiable urban styles is still remarkably short, despite a surge of interest in the 1970s and '80s. Much work remains to be done in charting and publishing local trends in the major cities and rural southern England.

In the second half of the 17th century, the fashion for carved oak furniture lasted much longer in the north of England, serving the affluent farming and clothing communities of Yorkshire, Lancashire, Cheshire, the North Pennines and the Lake District. The furniture from these areas has survived in large quantities, often with sufficient provenance to identify its origin, without which regional identification becomes mere guesswork. It is now possible to chart local preferences, but reliable written records for this period are rare, so individual makers are virtually unknown.

In the 18th century and later, joiners still made panelled furniture but in a plain style that lent itself less readily to regional variations. As a result, regional identification relies heavily on distinctive forms (such as the Welsh *cwpwrdd tridarn*) or esoteric applied detail (such as local preferences for crossbanding, inlaid motifs or quarter-column corners). A useful source of comparative information for 18th-century case furniture is clock case design, where named clockmakers bought their cases from neighbouring cabinetmakers. The 18th and early 19th centuries also saw a popularization of cheap, turned rush-seat chairs and Windsor chairs, the makers of which can be identified from sources such as the published trade directories and other written records.   **Victor Chinnery**

Late 17th century panel back armchairs are often the most distinctive examples of regional types, easily identifiable by their profile and decoration. The Cheshire/Lancashire chair on the left has a typical low square profile, with the floral-carved panel and small pyramid finials found in this area. On the right is the taller south Yorkshire chair with its elaborate scrolled cresting and earpieces above a bold diamond-carved panel.

Credits:

l The Fardon Collection, r St. John's Church, Leeds (courtesy of Temple Newsam House)

BEDS

A carved oak crib, restored, late 17thC, 38in (96.5cm) wide.
£650–780 S(S)

An oak tester bedstead, the back panels carved with figures, restored, early 17thC and later, 56in (142cm) wide.
£10,000–12,000 SeH

An oak tester bed, the headboard carved with two gadrooned arcades with central floral motifs, altered and restored, early 17thC, 54in (137cm) wide.
£4,500–5,500 BIG

An American red-painted low post press bed, the hinged rails fitted for roping, New England, early 19thC, 49¾in (126.5cm) wide.
£500–600 SK(B)

A French provincial fruitwood rocking cradle, Alsace, late 19thC, 45½in (115.5cm) wide.
£350–420 NOA

An oak tester bed, the six-panel headboard with foliate-carved frieze, with twelve-panel wainscot canopy, restored, 17thC, 51in (129.5cm) wide.
£1,800–2,200 TRL

BOXES

An oak box, the front carved with flowerheads and initials 'I B', late 17thC, 29in (73.5cm) wide.
£500–600 EH

A Welsh oak candle box, c1780, 20in (51cm) high.
£750–850 CoA

An oak candle box, 18thC, 17in (43cm) high.
£325–360 AEF

◄ A north Italian incised and inlaid cedarwood box, decorated with flowers and mythological animals, 17thC, 51½in (131cm) wide.
£1,200–1,400 P(E)

BOOKCASES

A Welsh oak bureau bookcase, with astragal-glazed door above a fall-front enclosing an inlaid fitted interior, Carmarthenshire, c1790, 43in (109cm) wide.
£4,400–4,850 CoA

A Flemish oak cupboard bookcase, with astragal-glazed doors above two panelled doors, flanked by canted corners, late 18thC, 50¾in (129cm) wide.
£2,500–2,750 S(S)

A Welsh oak cupboard, with mahogany embellishments, the glazed doors above five drawers, c1840, 38in (96.5cm) wide.
£3,800–4,250 CoA

BUFFETS

A French Louis XV-style oak buffet, the doors with parquetry inlay, Normandy, c1880, 59in (150cm) wide.
£850–1,000 LPA

A Flemish carved fruitwood buffet, with two moulded and carved cupboard doors, early 18thC, 54½in (138.5cm) wide.
£1,700–2,000 JAd

A French chestnut buffet, with two asymmetrically panelled doors, 18thC, 44½in (113cm) wide.
£700–850 DN

> **Miller's is a price GUIDE not a price LIST**

BUREAUX

An oak bureau, the fall-front enclosing a fitted interior, early 18thC, 33in (84cm) wide.
£3,000–3,500 BIG

A George I oak bureau, the fall-front enclosing a stepped, fitted interior, c1720, 38in (96.5cm) wide.
£3,750–4,500 PHA

A Queen Anne oak bureau, the fall-front enclosing a fitted, stepped interior, faults, restored, early 18thC, 30in (76cm) wide.
£1,700–1,850 S(S)

Miller's Compares

I A George III ash bureau, with mahogany crossbanding, chequer stringing and quartered veneers, the fall-front with a fan marquetry corners, 39in (99cm) wide.
£4,000–4,500 DN

II A George III mahogany bureau, the fall-front with a fitted interior, 34¼in (87cm) wide.
£1,000–1,100 DN

A George III oak bureau, the fall-front enclosing a fitted interior, on bracket feet, 35¾in (91cm) wide.
£1,200–1,400 P

It is the scarcity factor which led to these bureaux achieving such different prices at auction. The state of preservation of both pieces is similar, but furniture in ash, such as Item I, is seldom found, while similar examples to Item II are seen quite frequently.
Item I has good colour and patination, distinctive figuring and attractive fan marquetry in the corners of the fall-front. It has also not been adapted or improved, which further enhances its appeal to the prospective purchaser.

Insurance Values
Always insure your valuable antiques for the cost of replacing them with similar items, regardless of the original price paid. Both dealers and auctioneers will provide a valuation service for a fee.

◀ An oak bureau, c1790, 36in (91.5cm) wide.
£2,500–2,850 RED

An oak bureau, the fall-front enclosing a fitted interior, 18thC, 27¼in (69cm) wide.
£1,600–1,750 P(L)

BUREAU CABINETS

A George III provincial oak bureau cabinet, the lower section with fall-front enclosing a fitted interior, restored, 36½in (92.5cm) wide.
£2,000–2,400 BB(L)

A George III oak bureau cabinet, the fielded panelled doors enclosing shelves, the fall-front enclosing a fitted interior, top and base associated, faults and restorations, 39in (99cm) wide.
£1,200–1,400 S(S)

A French provincial oak bureau cabinet, 19thC, 40in (101.5cm) wide.
£2,000–2,400 SWO

An oak bureau cabinet, the fielded panelled doors enclosing a shelved interior, over two drawers, the fall-front enclosing a fitted interior, 18thC, 35½in (90cm) wide.
£1,000–1,200 P(L)

CHAIRS

A pair of oak backstools, with shaped top rails and board seats, late 17thC.
£1,250–1,500 BIG

An American Pilgrim turned maple carver chair, with rush seat, right arm and stretcher probably replaced, Rhode Island, 1670–1700.
£4,750–5,250 S(NY)

▶ A set of five ash ladder-back chairs including one carver, with panelled seats, 18thC.
£1,500–1,800 WL

A pair of oak backstools, with carved C-scrolls to the crest rails, late 17thC.
£800–1,000 P

Backstools did not become common until the 17thC, and were essentially chairs without arms, midway between stools and armchairs.

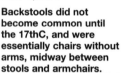

An oak backstool, the arched top rail and panelled back carved with leaves and flowerheads, over a panelled seat, Lancashire, late 17thC.
£850–1,000 P(L)

An oak backstool, with turned front legs, c1710.
£750–900 SWG

A set of six George III elm dining chairs, the horizontal centre rails with turned balls between, drop-in rush seats.
£800–1,000 L

An oak backstool, the moulded slatted back with heart-scroll pierced surmount, with board seat, late 17thC.
£400–500 PFK

A George I oak armchair, c1720.
£1,800–2,000 PHA

A pair of oak backstools, with scrolled crestings over caned panels between turned posts, the caned seat raised on 'horsebone' front legs with C-scrolls in the front rail, early 18thC.
£2,400–3,000 TEN

Country Chairs

Windsor chairs and spindleback chairs are both types made in antiquity, the former with board seats and stake legs, the latter formed entirely of turned parts made on the lathe.

In the 18thC, turners and wheelwrights began producing updated versions of these ancient types, mainly to compete with the more expensive framed chairs made by the joiners. The new chairs were cheap and strong, appealing to the less affluent members of society for whom hitherto the stool had been the only form of seat furniture. Regional styles evolved quickly, with each region producing distinctive variations on the basic type.

Windsor chairs normally had seats of elm, with ash, sycamore or beech forming the legs, arms and back. Turned chairs were mostly made of ash, with seats of woven rush or ash board. The best chairs of both types were made from yew or fruitwood, still the most sought after by collectors.

A Welsh oak and fruitwood armchair, with pierced apron, c1770.
£2,500–3,000 PHA

A Welsh primitive oak armchair, c1790.
£1,250–1,500 PHA

A set of six George III oak dining chairs, including two elbow chairs, of country Sheraton style, with pierced vertical splat backs and stuff-over seats.
£800–900 HYD

An ash and elm primitive comb-back Windsor armchair, the bowed top rail with eared corners above turned spindles, with solid saddle seat, minor restorations, West Country, late 18thC.
£600–720 Bon(C)

An American Federal carved birch armchair, with three shaped incised splats on panelled beaded stiles with shaped arms, painted wooden seat, probably New England, 1790–1800.
£500–600 SK(B)

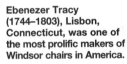

An American chestnut and maple braced continuous arm Windsor chair, stamped 'E. B. Tracy', Lisbon, Connecticut, 1780–1803.
£700–800 SK(B)

Ebenezer Tracy (1744–1803), Lisbon, Connecticut, was one of the most prolific makers of Windsor chairs in America.

A George III ash wavy-line ladderback armchair, c1800.
£900–1,100 PHA

A set of three elm and yew Windsor armchairs, by John Amos, each with a bowed top rail and pierced splat back, with solid saddle seats, stamped 'Amos, Grantham', early 19thC.
£5,000–5,500 Bon(C)

An Irish ash sugán chair, with original paint and later string seat, 19thC.
£100–120 CPA

A Welsh elm rocking chair, Cardiganshire, c1800.
£500–600 CoA

A harlequin set of eight elm and ash ladderback chairs, with rush seats, early 19thC.
£3,200–3,500 DeG

▶ A yew, elm and beech Windsor armchair, with pierced splat and solid seat, early 19thC.
£850–1,000 Bea(E)

▶ An elm comb back Windsor chair, with central solid vase-shaped splat, and solid saddle seat, early 19thC.
£1,800–2,200 P(S)

A pair of American black-painted stencilled gilt and polychrome side chairs, the horizontal splats with foxhunting scenes, rush seats, Hitchcocksville, Connecticut, c1825–30.
£750–825 SK(B)

An elm highback Windsor chair, c1840.
£550–600 MIN

A deal and sea grass chair, c1850.
£400–500 EON

A set of four ash and elm spindle back country chairs, c1840.
£1,800–2,000 SEA

A yew wood Windsor arm-chair, with pierced shaped splat, elm saddle seat and crinoline stretcher, 19thC.
£1,000–1,200 AH

An ash chair, with rush seat, c1840.
£120–135 OCH

A set of six yew wood low splat Windsor chairs, with elm seats, Nottinghamshire, mid-19thC.
£3,500–4,200 P(S)

An ash and elm Windsor armchair, with shaped pierced splat and solid seat, 19thC.
£750–900 BIG

A set of six French fruit-wood chairs, with rush seats, c1860.
£1,700–1,900 DeG

A beech elbow chair, with original paint finish and rush seat, c1890.
£800–900 RL

An ash Windsor armchair, with pierced splat, hoop back and solid seat, 19thC.
£350–420 BIG

A stained beech chair, with rush seat, c1910.
£65–75 OLM

▶ A set of six oak dining chairs, with pierced centre rails and solid seats, late 19th/ early 20thC.
£900–1,100 JM

◀ An American Shaker Production No. 3 rocking chair, with red and green taped seat, one splat impressed with '3' another with decal used on Mount Lebanon Community production chairs, Mount Lebanon, New York, 1875–80.
£300–350 SK(B)

CHILDREN'S CHAIRS

An American black-painted turned maple and chestnut child's high chair, with plank seat replacing original rush seat, New England, probably Rhode Island, 1700–30.
£2,750–3,250 S(NY)

An ash and elm child's Windsor chair, on baluster turned legs, 19thC.
£250–300 WL

An American Shaker Production No. 1 maple child's armchair, Mount Lebanon, New York, late 19th/early 20thC.
£700–800 SK(B)

An American maple child's high chair, with slat back and rush seat, probably Massachusetts, mid-18thC.
£1,000–1,100 SK(B)

▶ An American black-painted and decorated child's highchair, the legs with gold stencilled highlights, red and black taped seat, New England, 1820s.
£500–550 SK(B)

An early Victorian yew wood and elm child's Windsor armchair, with pierced shaped central splat and solid seat.
£750–900 P(Sc)

An elm child's chair, early 20thC.
£80–90 CSAC

A Regency oak, elm and mahogany child's chair, with hinged seat and original chamber pot.
£650–800 PHA

A child's oak rocking chair, c1850–1900.
£600–675 DBA

An elm and beech child's chair, early 20thC.
£70–80 CSAC

A yew and elm child's Windsor chair, with pierced and shaped splat and solid seat, 19thC.
£550–650 P

A child's oak chair, c1900.
£90–100 CSAC

An elm and ash child's chair, c1940.
£70–80 CSAC

CHESTS OF DRAWERS

An oak enclosed chest of four drawers, c1670, 35in (89cm) wide.
£5,000–6,000 PHA

An oak chest of drawers, on bun feet, late 17thC, 37in (94cm) wide.
£1,800–2,200 BIG

An oak chest of drawers, with later applied beaded moulding, late 17thC, 37½in (95.5cm) wide.
£1,200–1,400 P(NW)

A joined oak chest of drawers, in two parts, late 17thC, 45¼in (115cm) wide.
£1,800–2,200 TEN

An oak chest of drawers, on bracket feet, late 17thC, 38in (96.5cm) wide.
£1,400–1,700 PFK

An oak chest of drawers, with painted decoration, c1690, 35½in (90cm) wide.
£3,000–3,500 PHA

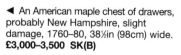

A George III oak and crossbanded chest of drawers, with six dummy and three real drawers, Lancashire, late 18thC, faults, 61½in (156cm) wide.
£1,600–1,800 S(S)

◄ An American maple chest of drawers, probably New Hampshire, slight damage, 1760–80, 38½in (98cm) wide.
£3,000–3,500 SK(B)

A William and Mary oak chest of drawers, with stile supports, 44½in (113cm) wide.
£1,800–2,200 HYD

An oak chest of drawers, with panelled sides, late 17thC, 43in (109cm) wide.
£1,500–1,800 TF

An oak chest of drawers, c1690–1700, 35in (89cm) wide.
£2,500–2,800 SWG

A George III oak chest-on-stand, with shaped apron and cabriole legs, c1760, 38in (96.5cm) wide.
£7,500–9,000 PHA

◄ A George III oak chest-on-chest, with mahogany veneer to cornice, 44in (112cm) wide.
£550–650 LUC

An oak chest of drawers, with wooden handles, early 19thC, 45¼in (115cm) wide.
£450–550 PFK

A French provincial fruitwood chest of drawers, the three serpentine drawers carved with a central cartouche, 18thC, 45in (114.5cm) wide.
£3,300–3,600 BG

An oak chest of drawers, on bracket feet, early 19thC, 41in (104cm) wide.
£350–420 WBH

A George IV elm chest of drawers, 37in (94cm) wide.
£550–650 MEA

CHESTS & COFFERS

◄ An oak chest, early 17thC, 48in (122cm) wide.
£400–500 MSW

An oak boarded chest, the front panel carved with continuous broad strapwork, early 17thC, 64½in (164cm) wide.
£2,200–2,500 P(NW)

◄ A Charles I joined oak chest, with triple panelled top and carved front and sides, c1650, 48in (122cm) wide.
£2,200–2,600 HAL

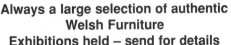

An oak chest, with four-panel top and front, mid-17thC, 50in (127cm) wide.
£1,350–1,600 BIG

An American red and black painted oak and maple Pilgrim chest, attributed to the Symonds Shop tradition, Salem, Massachusetts, restored, 1670–1700, 47in (119.5cm) wide.
£4,000–4,500 S(NY)

A Charles II oak child's chest, c1685, 20in (51cm) wide.
£3,500–4,200 PHA

◄ A Charles II carved oak chest, restored, late 17thC, 47¼in (120cm) wide.
£1,000–1,200 S(S)

An oak panelled chest, 17thC, 38in (96.5cm) wide.
£1,200–1,400 Mit

A Welsh carved oak chest, Monmouthshire, c1690, 57in (145cm) wide.
£2,000–2,300 CoA

An oak panelled chest, with original loop hinges, c1690, 38in (96.5cm) wide.
£1,350–1,500 SWG

An oak chest, the frieze carved with S-scrolls, above three flowerhead and foliate carved panels, 17thC, 48⅛in (123cm) wide.
£900–1,100 P

An oak chest, the top rail carved with S-scrolls, the panels with a leafy quatrefoil, 17thC, 44⅛in (113cm) wide.
£900–1,100 TF

An oak chest, with plain top and deeply recessed triple panelled front, altered, 17thC, 53½in (136cm) wide.
£400–500 L

◄ An Italian baroque walnut chest, with leaf-carved arcaded panels, 17thC, 58in (147.5cm) wide.
£3,500–3,850 BB(S)

► An oak chest, early 18thC, 38in (96.5cm) wide.
£400–500 WW

A German oak coffer, with painted crests, original iron-work and handles, 18thC, 42in (106.5cm) wide.
£1,600–1,800 HA

A Welsh painted *coffor bach*, c1770, 15in (38cm) wide.
£1,500–1,650 SEA

A George III painted oak and inlaid mahogany 'captain's' or carpenter's chest-on-stand, enclosing an arrangement of fixed and adjustable drawers, hidden wells and cupboards, the hinged lid painted with a panel depicting French and British men-of-war, the reverse with Horatio Nelson's coat-of-arms, the front with 'H. N.' flanked by Union Jack trophies, c1790, later decorations, 43in (109cm) wide.
£5,000–6,000 Bon

This chest was probably commissioned by an admirer of Lord Nelson after his death in 1805 at the battle of Trafalgar. Between 1780 and 1930, joiners and cabinet-makers would often make chests to contain their tools. Many of these were elaborately fitted and decorated, such as this example. They were generally plain externally, built of oak or pine, and made to stand rough travel by carriage or ship.

A yew wood and oak joined chest, 18thC, 67in (170cm) wide.
£1,400–1,700 DN

An oak chest, with a three-plank top and two drawers to the base, 18thC, 40in (101.5cm) wide.
£600–720 BIG

◀ A George III oak chest, with cross-banded decoration, and low raised back, Lancashire, 64in (162.5cm) wide.
£1,700–2,000 JM

An elm boarded chest, the front marked 'IB 1794', 46in (117cm) wide.
£500–600 DN

An oak chest, with four flower and lozenge-carved front panels and two base drawers, carving possibly later, 18thC, 55½in (141cm) wide.
£500–600 P(L)

CUPBOARDS

An oak livery cupboard, the panels with marquetry-inlaid decoration depicting a vase of flowers and birds, restored, early 17thC, 53½in (136cm) wide.
£15,000–16,500 P

This press cupboard is illustrated in Victor Chinnery's book *Oak Furniture The British Tradition*. Chinnery has chosen this piece as an example of early 17thC inlaid furniture in his discussion on inlay, parquetry and marquetry techniques.

An oak *cwpwrdd deuddarn*, with geometric moulded upper doors and ventilation design on lower doors, north-east Wales, c1680, 55in (139.5cm) wide.
£5,200–5,800 CoA

An oak press, with two arched panelled doors and two drawers below, late 17th/early 18thC, 63in (160cm) wide.
£1,500–1,800 GAK

An oak press cupboard, with frieze decoration, initialled and dated '1640', North Wales, 62in (157.5cm) wide.
£8,000–9,250 CoA

An oak press cupboard, the panel carved 'ERS 1694', North Wales, unrestored, 62in (157.5cm) wide.
£1,100–1,200 BG

An oak press cupboard, with panelled doors, the frieze carved with date '1691', 52in (132cm) wide.
£1,400–1,700 BIG

A Queen Anne press cupboard, the frieze carved with '1709', Westmorland, 90in (228.5cm) wide.
£2,200–2,600 Mit

A joined oak press cupboard, with panelled doors, North Country, 64¼in (163cm) wide.
£13,000–15,000 Bon(C)

A Charles II oak food hutch, the door punched with 'AD 1671', basically late 17thC, 36½in (92.5cm) wide.
£800–1,000 HYD

A Welsh oak *cwpwrdd deuddarn*, early 18thC, 55½in (141cm) wide.
£3,200–3,800 HAM

A carved oak press cupboard, early 18thC, 65¾in (167cm) wide.
£1,800–2,200 P(Ed)

An early Georgian oak press cupboard, 54in (137cm) wide.
£1,500–1,800 BIG

A George I cupboard, painted with armorial decoration, c1720, 18in (45.5cm) wide.
£2,200–2,600 PHA

An oak panelled cupboard, c1750, 45in (114.5cm) wide.
£3,700–4,000 SWG

A George III oak and rosewood-banded hanging corner cupboard, with an acorn and bell moulded frieze, faults, restored, late 18thC, North West, 37in (94cm) wide.
£2,200–2,500 S(S)

A George III oak joined cupboard, with later brass handles, 63in (160cm) wide.
£2,800–3,200 DN

An oak cupboard, with later cornice, 18thC, 61½in (156cm) wide.
£1,300–1,600 AG

An elm hanging corner cupboard, with original brass escutcheon and iron hinges, c1770, 26in (66cm) wide.
£1,250–1,400 SWG

A George III oak hanging corner cupboard, with dentil cornice and fluted frieze, 33½in (85cm) wide.
£600–720 PFK

▶ A George III oak hanging corner cupboard, with single panelled door and H hinges, 29in (73.5cm) wide.
£340–375 LUC

A Welsh oak press cupboard, 18thC, 45in (114.5cm) wide.
£1,600–2,000 CLE

Cupboards • OAK & COUNTRY FURNITURE 169

A French provincial chestnut armoire, the carved panelled doors with marquetry-inlaid geometric panels, late 18th/early 19thC, 68in (172.5cm) wide.
£1,500–1,800 HYD

A French cherrywood armoire, late 18thC, 50in (127cm) wide.
£2,200–2,500 CF

A Welsh oak *cwpwrdd deuddarn*, Cardiganshire, c1820, 52in (132cm) wide.
£5,000–5,500 SEA

A French chestnut armoire, the doors carved with flowers and foliage and with brass decoration, c1826, 59in (150cm) wide.
£6,500–7,200 HA

An oak cabinet on stand, in the 16thC French Henri II style, the two doors carved with saints over two frieze drawers carved with lions masks, 19thC, 43¾in (111cm) wide.
£1,400–1,600 P

A French cherrywood armoire, in the Louis XV style, south Brittany, c1850, 58in (147.5cm) wide.
£1,250–1,500 LPA

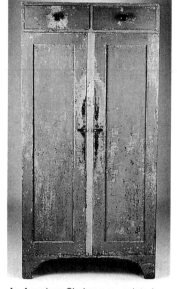

An American Shaker grey-painted poplar cupboard, with two drawers above two panelled doors, Mount Lebanon, New York community, 1850–60, 36¾in (93.5cm) wide.
£1,800–2,000 SK(B)

An American cherrywood standing corner cupboard, the upper section with a pair of glazed doors, mid-19thC, 54¾in (139cm) wide.
£1,250–1,400 SLN

A carved oak sideboard, carved with kings, queens, a hound, bird, horse and stylized leaf and scroll patterns, 19thC, 48in (122cm) wide.
£500–600 LF

DRESSERS

A oak Welsh dresser, Harlech, c1720, 57in (145cm) wide.
£18,000–20,000 CoA

This dresser is particularly desirable because of its fine colour and early features such as turned legs and triple pendants.

A George III oak Welsh dresser, with two shelves enclosing two ogee headed panelled cupboard doors, Denbighshire, 55½in (144cm) wide.
£6,500–7,800 P(NW)

This Denbighshire dresser is unusual as it has three different shapes of panels in the base and a further design in the rack.

An early Georgian oak Welsh dresser, with three drawers, on Tuscan column supports and undertier, 63in (160cm) wide.
£5,000–6,000 JAd

A George III elm dresser, with three frieze drawers above a wavy apron, 56¾in (144cm) wide.
£2,500–3,000 CGC

An oak dresser, restored, 18thC, 54¼in (138cm) wide.
£2,200–2,600 G(T)

A Georgian fruitwood dresser, the three shelves flanked by cupboards, 66in (167.5cm) wide.
£4,500–5,500 RBB

An oak dresser, with six drawers, on turned supports, 18thC, 72in (183cm) wide.
£6,000–7,000 RBB

A joined oak Welsh dresser, late 18thC, 51in (129.5cm) wide.
£700–850 Bri

A French Louis XV carved elm and chestnut dresser, the shelves flanked by small cupboards, on short cabriole legs, late 18thC, 54in (137cm) wide.
£3,300–3,600 BB(S)

A George III oak and mahogany dresser, with crossbanding and ebony stringing, c1790, 83in (211cm) wide.
£3,200–3,850 Hal

Facts in Brief

- Name derives from French *dressoir*, a medieval sideboard used for preparing (or 'dressing') dishes of food in the kitchen, or for displaying food, drink and plates in the dining room.
- Early kitchen dressers consisted of a side table for food preparation, often with a rack of shelves hanging on the wall above.
- Early dining room dressers consisted of a standing cupboard with a superstructure formed by steps of shelves under a forward-sloping canopy, often with a low shelf at base level.
- In the 17thC dressers were often made without a superstructure of shelves (a low dresser), or the rack of shelves might now be attached to the base (forming a high dresser).
- From the late 17thC dressers were made with turned legs below the drawers (an open dresser) or with cupboards below the drawers (an enclosed dresser), and sometimes with a bank of drawers between the cupboards, or filled completely with drawers.
- The fashion for cheap tin-glazed earthenware from the later 17thC led to the introduction of the 'delft rack' for displaying plates and decorative wares - similar to the dresser rack, but completely detached and hanging independently on the wall.

An oak dresser, the base with three frieze drawers, with brass knob handles, late 18th/early 19thC, 65½in (166.5cm) wide.
£3,200–3,850 AH

An oak high dresser, Shropshire, late 18thC, 74¾in (190cm) wide.
£2,300–2,750 P(S)

A late George III oak dresser, on ring-turned baluster legs, 64½in (164cm) wide.
£4,500–5,500 Bea(E)

An oak Welsh dresser inlaid with rosewood and maple, Anglesey, early 19thC, 65¾in (167cm) wide.
£3,400–4,000 P(NW)

A French chestnut dresser, western Brittany, 19thC, 55in (139.5cm) wide.
£1,800–2,400 MTay

A French provincial oak dresser, the frieze carved with a central star, with three galleried shelves below, late 19thC, 53½in (136cm) wide.
£2,500–2,750 P

◄ A Regency oak and elm dresser, c1820, 72in (183cm) wide.
£5,000–5,750 SEA

A French provincial-style walnut side cabinet, with carved foliate decoration, the top with carved cresting, early 20thC, 56in (142cm) wide.
£700–850 P(Sc)

LOW DRESSERS

A William and Mary oak open low dresser, restored, late 17thC, 72¾in (185cm) wide.
£2,200–2,600 Bon(C)

An oak and walnut-crossbanded dresser, c1770, 72in (183cm) wide.
£7,500–8,500 RYA

▶ An oak and mahogany-crossbanded low dresser, mid-18thC, 90in (229cm) wide.
£2,000–2,400 BIG

An oak low dresser, with brass escutcheons and handles, early 18thC, 71in (180.5cm) wide.
£4,700–5,500 AG

A low dresser, with three drawers and turned front legs, c1720, 79in (202cm) wide.
£4,500–5,000 ANV

A George III elm low dresser, with three drawers, on square tapering legs, 78in (198cm) wide.
£3,000–3,500 L

An oak low dresser, 18thC, 74in (188cm) wide.
£2,500–3,000 SWO

A George III oak dresser base, with three frieze drawers, and with chequer banding above cupboards, Lancashire, 61¾in (157cm) wide.
£1,600–2,000 RTo

◄ An oak low dresser, mid-18thC-style, with three frieze drawers crossbanded in mahogany, 19thC, 72¼in (183.5cm) wide.
£2,000–2,400 DN

An oak low dresser, with three drawers and straight square legs, early 19thC, 77½in (197cm) wide.
£3,200–3,850 TEN

An oak enclosed low dresser, with plank top and four central drawers flanked by ogee panelled cupboard doors, 18thC, 69in (175.5cm) wide.
£1,600–2,000 AH

LOWBOYS

A George I oak lowboy, c1720, 29in (73.5cm) wide.
£3,000–3,300 RED

A George I oak lowboy, with three frieze drawers and shaped apron, top later, 28in (71cm) wide.
£400–500 RTo

An elm lowboy, with three frieze drawers, c1760, 30in (76cm) wide.
£2,700–3,000 RED

An oak lowboy, with three frieze drawers and a shaped arched apron, mid-18thC, 31½in (80cm) wide.
£1,000–1,200 P

A George III oak lowboy, with scroll-shaped apron, 33in (84cm) wide.
£850–1,000 CLE

An oak William and Mary-style lowboy, with one long drawer, the shaped apron with turned acorn drop finials, early 20thC, 27in (68.5cm) wide.
£700–850 Mit

SETTLES

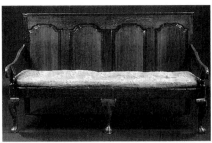

A George II oak settle, the back with four truncated ogee fielded panels inlaid with black and white chevron banding, 72¾in (185cm) wide.
£1,000–1,200 TEN

An oak settle, with later high back over a hinged solid seat, the front carved rail enclosing three rosette-centred lozenge-carved panels, 17thC, 48½in (123cm) wide.
£1,000–1,200 P(NW)

A panelled oak settle, with plank seat, early 18thC, 38¾in (98.5cm) wide.
£1,700–2,000 Bon

A panelled oak box settle, c1760, 64in (162.5cm) wide.
£3,500–4,200 PHA

A fruitwood curved panelled settle, c1800, 50in (127cm) wide.
£7,500–8,750 DBA

An oak curved bacon settle, with a solid seat and panelled cupboard doors below, the reverse with a pair of four-panelled doors, early 19thC, 63in (160cm) wide.
£3,000–3,500 P(NW)

▶ A mid-Georgian oak settle, with four fielded panels to the back, the front with three panels, 61in 155cm) wide.
£1,000–1,200 PFK

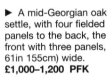

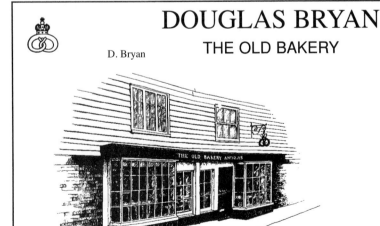

STOOLS

An oak boarded stool, the chip-carved seat above shaped boarded sides, reduced in height, faults, restored, early 17thC, 22in (56cm) wide.
£2,000–2,400 S(S)

A pair of oak jointed stools, with turned spreading legs joined by understretchers, early 18thC, 19in (48cm) wide.
£3,000–3,500 P(Sc)

An oak pig bench, 18thC, 28in (71cm) wide.
£1,200–1,400 PHA

A turned elm stool, with dished top and remnants of original paint, c1830, 13in (33cm) high.
£140–175 CPA

▶ A Welsh sycamore three-legged turned stool, with ash legs, 19thC, 13in (33cm) wide.
£140–160 CoA

TABLES

◀ An oak joined dining table, the three-plank cleated removable top on cannon-barrel shaped turned legs, with later H-stretchers, mid-17thC, 82½in (209.5cm) wide.
£4,000–5,000 PFK

A Charles II oak table, the cleated plank top above a gadrooned frieze dated '1661', faults, later alterations, 102¾in (261cm) wide.
£4,500–5,500 S(S)

A joined frame walnut tavern table, c1680, 55in (139.5cm) long.
£4,000–4,500 RYA

A Charles II oak folding coaching table, the oval planked top supported by a gateleg action, faults, late 17thC, 35in (89cm) wide.
£900–1,100 S(S)

A William and Mary oak gateleg table, the oval hinged top with a waved frieze to each end, late 17thC, 62½in (159cm) wide.
£3,800–4,500 Bon(C)

An oak bobbin-turned side table, c1690, 29in (73.5cm) wide.
£2,750–3,250 RED

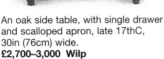

An oak side table, with single drawer and scalloped apron, late 17thC, 30in (76cm) wide.
£2,700–3,000 Wilp

An oak joined table, on turned legs, restored, late 17thC, 19¾in (50cm) wide.
£500–600 Bea(E)

A Queen Anne oak and ash oval table, with ogee arched friezes, early 18thC, 26¾in (68cm) wide.
£4,500–5,000 S(S)

A Queen Anne oak gateleg table, on barrel turned legs and Braganza feet, c1714, 27in (68.5cm) wide.
£3,000–3,500 PHA

An oak gateleg dining table, on baluster supports, with square moulded stretchers and inverted cup feet, early 18thC, 50¾in (129cm) wide.
£3,800–4,500 TEN

An oak serving table, with three plank top and a moulded front frieze, 17thC, 69½in (176.5cm) wide.
£2,000–2,400 HAM

A George I oak side table, with a single drawer, c1730, 30in (76cm) wide.
£3,000–3,500 PHA

An oak tripod table, with gunbarrel turned stem, c1730, 23in (58.5cm) wide.
£900–1,100 SWG

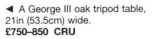

◀ A George III oak tripod table, 21in (53.5cm) wide.
£750–850 CRU

A yew wood drop-leaf table, c1770, 42in (106.5cm) wide.
£2,200–2,500 DeG

A dish-top tripod table, with drawers, c1780, 21in (53.5cm) wide.
£3,400–3,750 SEA

A French fruitwood side table, with one drawer and square tapering legs, c1800, 29in (73.5cm) wide.
£700–800 DeG

A Georgian oak cricket table, the two-piece top on triangular chamfered legs, with platform base, 29¼in (74.5cm) diam.
£750–900 PFK

A George III oak table, the triple-plank cleated top on square chamfered legs joined by a moulded H-stretcher, late 18thC, 73in (185.5cm) long.
£3,400–3,750 S(S)

An elm side table, c1820, 30in (76cm) wide.
£300–335 AL

An oak cricket table, c1820, 33in (84cm) diam.
£400–450 MIL

A French walnut and cherrywood table, legs shortened, c1860, 40in (101.5cm) long.
£275–325 OLM

A French cherrywood farmhouse table, with a single drawer, on octagonal shaped legs, c1820, 66in (167.5cm) long.
£3,300–3,700 HA

A French cherrywood farmhouse table, northern Brittany, 19thC, 29in (73.5cm) wide.
£1,200–1,400 MTay

An oak side table, with three frieze drawers, on turned legs, restored, c1880, 72in (183cm) long.
£275–300 DFA

► A French provincial oak table, with two frieze drawers, on baluster turned legs joined by H-stretchers, restored, 19thC, 66¼in (168cm) wide.
£1,600–1,800 P

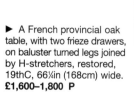

A sycamore butcher's table, c1880, 26in (66cm) long.
£450–550 GD

Pine

BEDS

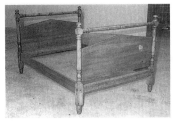

An Irish pine bed, 19thC,
50in (127cm) wide.
£400–500 Sam

▶ A Continental pine bed, c1890,
36in (91.5cm) wide.
£250–325 Sam

A Czechoslovakian pine crib, c1900,
30in (76cm) wide.
£150–185 P&T

BENCHES

An American pine bucket bench,
with remains of old red paint,
possibly New England, early 19thC,
55½in (141cm) wide.
£2,500–2,750 SK(B)

A Romanian pine and oak bench,
c1890, 83in (211cm) wide.
£650–700 MIN

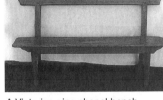

A Victorian pine chapel bench,
60in (152.5cm) wide.
£200–250 DEE

A pine folding work bench, c1900,
41½in (105.5cm) wide.
£90–100 AL

A pine bench, c1890,
36in (91.5cm) wide.
£50–60 AL

A Hungarian pine bench, c1900,
41in (104cm) wide.
£350–400 MIN

BOXES

A Victorian pine tool chest, with a
shelf, 32in (81.5cm) wide.
£140–175 P&T

A Victorian iron-bound pine box,
22in (56cm) wide.
£150–180 DEE

▶ A painted pine box, c1860,
28in (71cm) wide.
£145–160 AL

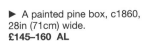

A pine slope-fronted box, with iron
fittings, c1850, 37in (94cm) wide.
£175–200 P&T

CHAIRS

A Victorian beech
Suffolk chair.
£80–100 DEE

A child's beech chair, c1900.
£30–35 MIL

A Scottish provincial
pine and elm armchair,
with solid seat, 19thC.
£320–380 P(Ed)

A Victorian child's stained
pine lambing rocker chair,
with hinged seat, late
19thC, 26in (66cm) high.
£270–300 NAW

CHESTS & COFFERS

A painted pine plank chest, c1800, 51in (129.5cm) wide.
£340–375 MIL

An American red-painted pine chest, New England,
late 18thC, 51in (129.5cm) wide.
£1,000–1,100 SK(B)

An American pine blanket chest,
with two false drawers, New England,
late 18thC, 38½in (98cm) wide.
£1,100–1,200 SK(B)

▶ An American six-board pine chest,
old red and yellow paint simulating fan
inlay at the corners, Ohio or Pennsylvania,
1830s, 45in (114.5cm) wide.
£1,200–1,300 SK(B)

**Pine furniture is currently popular
in America.**

A painted pine panelled coffer,
c1800, 40in (101.5cm) wide.
£450–500 MIL

A Regency polychrome-painted
pine chest, with naive figures and
palm trees in a tropical landscape,
the front and sides with a country
house and its grounds, a large
fox to the reverse, early 19thC,
36¼in (92cm) wide.
£4,500–5,000 M&K

◀ An American
blue-painted
pine chest,
the hinged top
enclosing a lidded
till, New England,
early 19thC,
50in (127cm) wide.
£1,100–1,200 SK(B)

An early Victorian pine mule chest,
39in (99cm) wide. **£350–400 P&T**

A Victorian pine blanket chest, enclosing a candle tray, 37in (94cm) wide.
£200–240 P&T

A pine mule chest, enclosing a candle box, c1860, 36in (91.5cm) wide.
£800–880 AL

A pine blanket chest, c1865, 28in (71cm) wide.
£175–200 P&T

A pine chest, enclosing a candle box, c1880, 41½in (105.5cm) wide.
£300–335 AL

A German dome top chest, c1880, 38in (96.5cm) wide.
£125–150 NOTT

◀ A pine blanket chest, 1880, 33in (84cm) wide.
£130–150 MIL

▶ A Continental pitch pine dome top chest, c1890, 39in (99cm) wide.
£150–200 BAB

A pine military chest, with brass and copper fittings, c1880, 38in (96.5cm) wide.
£700–800 AL

▶ A pine blanket chest, 1900, 36in (91.5cm) wide.
£120–150 NOTT

A pine chest, c1900, 39in (99cm) wide.
£250–300 MIN

▶ A Dutch pine dome top blanket chest, c1900, 37in (94cm) wide.
£200–235 P&T

CHESTS & FLIGHTS OF DRAWERS

An American pine chest of drawers, painted red and black to simulate grain mahogany, New England, early 19thC, 39½in (100.5cm) wide.
£800–1,000 SK(B)

A pine chest of drawers, c1820, 36in (91.5cm) wide.
£450–500 TPC

An American pine chest of drawers, painted dark blue-grey with later polychrome decoration, New England, replaced brasses, early 19thC, 39½in (100.5cm) wide.
£1,000–1,100 SK(B)

A Victorian pine chest of drawers, with simulated bamboo mouldings, faults, c1870, 42in (106.5cm) wide.
£750–900 S(S)

A Continental pine chest of drawers, c1890, 41in (104cm) wide.
£350–400 TPC

A Victorian pine chest of drawers, 41in (104cm) wide.
£350–400 P&T

▶ A painted pine flight of 38 drawers, c1870, 25in (63.5cm) wide.
£500–550 MIL

A Victorian pine plan chest, c1880, 69in (175.5cm) wide.
£1,000–1,250 ESA

◀ A Victorian pine chest of drawers, 55in (139.5cm) wide.
£500–575 P&T

A pine dressing chest, c1870, 42in (106.5cm) wide.
£450–500 AL

A pine dressing chest, the marble-topped washstand with tiled back, c1870, 38in (96.5cm) wide.
£320–350 MIL

A pine dressing chest, with tiled back, c1880, 38in (96.5cm) wide.
£450–500 AL

A pine chest of drawers, with white porcelain knobs, c1880, 41in (104cm) wide.
£350–400 MIL

A set of six pine drawers, c1890, 9in (23cm) wide.
£55–60 AL

▶ A pine dressing chest, c1890, 36in (91.5cm) wide.
£450–500 AL

◀ An American Queen Anne pine chest of drawers, the top opening to a well above two short and one long false drawers and two real drawers, remains of blue-green paint, Middle Atlantic States, restored, late 19thC, 21½in (54.5cm) wide.
£1,300–1,500 SK(B)

Cross Reference
See Colour Review

A set of three pine drawers, 1900, 12in (30.5cm) wide.
£12–15 AL

An eastern European pine chest of drawers, c1920, handles replaced, 29in (73.5cm) wide.
£175–200 WaH

A oak box on stand, mid-Wales, c1780, 25in (63.5cm) wide.
£3,400–3,800 CoA

An elm candle box, c1820, 15in (38cm) wide.
£340–375 SEA

A cherrywood bureau, with inlaid starburst pattern to bottom drawer, c1760, 40in (101.5cm) wide.
£4,500–5,000 RED

A George III oak bureau, with mahogany crossbanding, the fall-front enclosing a fitted interior with secret drawers, c1760, 36in (91.5cm) wide.
£3,500–4,200 PHA

A fruitwood bureau, the fall-front enclosing a fitted interior, c1760, 30in (76cm) wide.
£2,800–3,200 BIG

A chequer-inlaid oak bureau, North Wales, 1770–1800, 36in (91.5cm) wide.
£6,000–6,500 RYA

Paul Hopwell Antiques

Early English Oak

Dressers, tables and chairs always in stock

A pair of William and Mary walnut tall back side chairs. English.　　c1695

A Queen Anne oak single drawer side table. English.　　c1710

A Charles II oak carved and panelled hanging cupboard. English.　　c1685

A rare 17th century oak carved and panelled cupboard. English.　　c1640-70

Paul Hopwell Antiques

A Charles II oak
geometrically
moulded dresser
base.
English.   c1685

A mid-18th century oak
inlaid mule chest.
Welsh.   c1730

A Charles II oak
cupboard dresser base
with moulded front.
English.   c1680

A Charles I oak panel back armchair, damaged and restored, mid-17thC.
£7,000–8,000 S(S)

The underside of this chair bears a letter claiming that it was once sat in by Bonnie Prince Charlie on his way to Culloden.

A child's oak high chair, c1650–70, 17thC, 36in (91.5cm) high.
£3,400–3,750 DBA

A Charles II carved oak wainscot chair, Yorkshire, c1685.
£3,500–4,200 PHA

A Charles II child's armchair, Lancashire/Cheshire, c1680.
£8,000–9,000 S

A Scottish oak armchair, the fielded panel with flowerheads, initials 'TK' and dated '1694'.
£5,500–6,500 PFK

A pair of Welsh turned ash chairs, c1740.
£2,800–3,250 CoA

A pair of elm chairs, with upholstered seats, c1770.
£1,500–1,700 SWG

A fruitwood carver chair, c1770.
£1,300–1,450 DeG

A Chippendale elm chair, 1780.
£250–285 ANV

A George III Hepplewhite-style child's elm armchair, c1795.
£3,000–3,500 PHA

A George III walnut, ash and elm Windsor chair, damaged and restored, early 19thC.
£2,000–2,200 S(S)

A comb-back Windsor chair, c1800.
£475–525 RED

◀ A yew, fruitwood and ash Windsor armchair, with roundel splat, probably Thames Valley, c1820–60.
£1,000–1,150 DBA

▶ A yew and elm high-back Windsor chair, with shepherd's crook arms and crinoline stretcher, c1820.
£1,800–2,250 SEA

A set of six French cherrywood chairs, with rush seats, c1920.
£650–750 CF

Robert Young Antiques

e Country Furniture & Folk

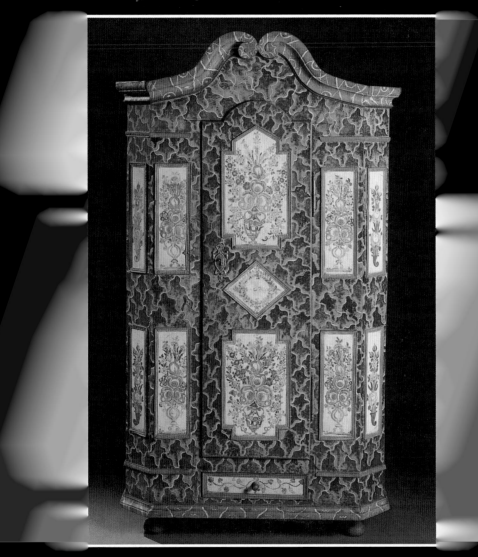

Robert and Josyane Young

Battersea Bridge Road, London SW11 3A
Tel: 020 7228 7847   Fax: 020 7585 048

THUSIASTIC BUYERS OF F
TRY FURNITURE AND FOL

A James I oak chest, carved with lions' masks and dragons, early 17thC, 60in (152.5cm) wide.
£5,500–6,000 TAM

A joined oak chest, with inlaid arched panels, early 17thC, 55½in (141cm) wide.
£1,800–2,200 TEN

A small joined oak chest, with one-piece top, c1620–50, 38in (96.5cm) wide.
£4,500–5,000 DBA

A Charles I oak chest, with carved panels, Gloucestershire, c1640, 57in (145cm) wide.
£3,000–3,500 PHA

A Charles II oak chest, with flowerhead and leaf-carved panels, c1660, 50¾in (129cm) wide.
£1,000–1,200 S

An oak chest, with carved panels, c1660, 43in (109cm) wide.
£2,000–2,250 SEA

An oak boarded chest, with scratch-carved decoration, West Country, c1680, 43in (109cm) wide.
£2,000–2,200 RYA

An oak chest, with rosette-carved panels and initials 'B. T.', 17thC, 57in (145cm) wide.
£1,000–1,200 RBB

A German marquetry-inlaid oak chest, the front with birds and flowers, on later bun feet, early 18thC, 45in (114.5cm) wide.
£2,200–2,500 BB(S)

An oak panelled chest, with double doors enclosing four plain drawers, late 17thC, 43½in (110.5cm) wide.
£7,500–8,250 PFK

A William and Mary oak chest-on-stand, with frieze drawer, c1695, 40in (101.5cm) wide.
£11,000–13,000 PHA

An oak chest, inlaid with bog oak and holly, the top drawers inlaid '1709' and 'W H', 43½in (110.5cm) wide.
£2,000–2,400 TF

A Welsh oak *coffor bach*, with original handles, 1730, 23in (58.5cm) wide.
£2,500–2,750 SEA

▶ A George III oak and mahogany-crossbanded chest, north west of England, 61in (155cm) wide.
£900–1,100 S(S)

A George III oak chest, c1800, 40in (101.5cm) wide.
£750–850 MIL

A oak livery cupboard, West Country, 1650–80, 55in (139.5cm) wide.
£9,000–11,000 PHA

An oak press cupboard, Cardiganshire, 18thC, 56in (142cm) wide.
£4,000–5,000 RBB

An oak potboard dresser, 1720–30, 71in (180.5cm) wide.
£10,000–12,000 SWG

A oak press cupboard, the top carved with 'E W' and '1687', Lake District/Westmorland, 84¼in (214cm) wide.
£6,000–7,200 P(Ed)

A French Louis XV provincial oak *dressoir*, mid-18thC, 98½in (250cm) wide.
£17,000–20,000 BB(S)

An oak potboard dresser, 1720–30, 71in (180.5cm) wide.
£10,000–12,000 SWG

An oak Welsh dresser, inlaid with fan motifs and with mahogany banding, frieze rail reduced in height, c1800, 72½in (184cm) wide.
£2,300–2,750 CAG

◀ A French Louis XVI inlaid oak and burr-elm *buffet à deux corps*, late 18thC, 78in (198cm) wide.
£7,500–9,000 BB(S)

A Charles II oak and chequer-banded hanging livery cupboard, late 17thC, 32¼in (82cm) wide.
£6,500–7,200 S(S)

A French oak two-door armoire, Normandy, 19thC, 54in (137cm) wide.
£1,200–1,400 MTay

A George III oak dresser, with six spice drawers, North Wales, c1770, 72in (183cm) wide.
£22,000–27,000 PHA

A George III oak dresser, the five base drawers with mahogany crossbanding, 75½in (192cm) wide.
£4,500–5,500 P(L)

A Charles II oak dresser, c1685, 53in (134.5cm) wide.
£11,000–13,000 PHA

A George III oak and mahogany crossbanded breakfront dresser base, north west of England, late 18thC, 71½in (181.5cm) wide.
£4,500–5,000 S(S)

An oak dresser base, c1780, 68in (172.5cm) wide.
£4,500–5,000 RYA

A Queen Anne oak side table, c1705, 22in (56cm) wide.
£6,000–7,200 PHA

An oak lowboy, handles replaced, c1770, 32in (81.5cm) wide.
£1,550–1,700 SWG

An oak dresser base, c1740, 68in (172.5cm) wide.
£5,000–5,500 RED

A George II oak, ash and burr-elm dresser base, faults, restored, 52¼in (132.5cm) wide.
£2,000–2,400 S(S)

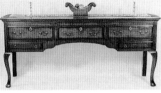

A George III oak dresser base, crossbanded with mahogany, Shropshire, c1785, 80in (203cm) wide.
£9,000–11,000 PHA

An oak lowboy, mid-18thC, 34in (86.5cm) wide.
£1,350–1,500 ANV

A George II oak dresser base, Wales, c1735, 49in (124.5cm) wide.
£7,500–9,000 PHA

A George III oak dresser base, Yorkshire, c1760, 84in (213.5cm) wide.
£11,000–13,000 PHA

A oak cupboard, Denbighshire, late 18thC, 63in (160cm) wide.
£6,000–6,800 CoA

◄ A French Louis XV provincial oak cupboard, the frieze carved with trailing flowerheads, 100in (254cm) wide.
£4,500–5,000 BB(L)

A George III oak lowboy, with original brass handles, Wales, c1780, 30in (76cm) wide.
£5,500–6,500 PHA

◄ A George III oak lowboy, crossbanded in mahogany and with ebony stringing and boxwood cockbeading, c1785, 34in (86.5cm) wide.
£5,000–6,000 PHA

A Charles II oak table/settle,
Gloucestershire, c1680,
72in (1183cm) wide.
£6,750–8,000 PHA

A figured-elm bacon settle,
with hinged doors to the reverse,
18thC, 58in (147.5cm) wide.
£4,500–5,000 HA

◄ A Charles II oak gateleg table,
late 17thC, 60in (152.5cm) wide.
£8,000–9,500 Bon(C)

A George III fruitwood and elm
concave settle, the curved panelled
back with a central fall, late 18thC,
84in (213.5cm) wide.
£10,000–12,000 Bon

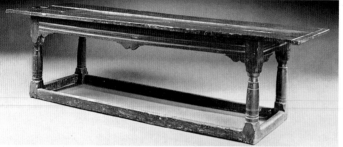

A joined oak refectory table, feet reduced, late 17thC, 112½in (286cm) wide.
£6,000–7,000 Bon(C)

A Charles II oak side table, with
reel and bobbin turning, handles
replaced, c1680, 24in (61cm) wide.
£5,000–6,000 PHA

A Spanish walnut side table,
with geometrically carved drawers,
sides and back, 17thC,
71½in (181.5cm) wide.
£5,500–6,500 P(Ed)

A Charles II oak bobbin turned gateleg
table, c1680, 18in (45.5cm) wide.
£4,500–5,500 PHA

A fruitwood and walnut gateleg
table, with barley-twist legs, possibly
Scottish, c1700, 36in (91.5cm) wide.
£6,750–8,000 PHA

► An oak side table, on turned legs,
early 18thC, 36½in (92.5cm) wide.
£1,200–1,375 ANV

A George I oak side table,
on baluster turned legs, c1720,
38in (96.5cm) wide.
£3,500–4,200 PHA

An oak table, with a cleated three-plank top, on ring-turned and square
supports and square stretchers, early 18thC, 108in (274.5cm) wide.
£4,000–4,500 RBB

An elm side table, with gun barrel turned legs and original brassware, 1720–30, 32in (81.5cm) wide.
£2,000–2,400 SWG

A sycamore drop-leaf table, with a drawer, c1840, 53in (134.5cm) wide.
£2,200–2,500 DeG

A partridge wood coaching table, c1820, 41in (104cm) diam.
£4,250–4,750 SEA

A French provincial walnut refectory table, with a drawer to each end, late 18th/early 19thC, 123in (312.5cm) long.
£7,500–9,000 BB(S)

A George II oak side table, with baluster turned legs, c1730, 32in (81.5cm) wide.
£4,500–5,000 PHA

An oak gateleg table, with baluster turned legs, c1730, 44in (112cm) extended.
£1,500–1,650 SWG

An oak cricket table, with three turned legs, c1740, 27in (68.5cm) diam.
£2,250–2,500 DBA

A George III oak side table, 34½in (87.5cm) wide.
£1,250–1,375 ANV

An elm X-frame tavern table, c1780, 42in (106.5cm) wide
£3,500–3,800 RYA

An elm cricket table, with undertier and three tapering legs, c1780, 28in (71cm) diam.
£1,300–1,500 SWG

A George III oak side table, with fretwork frieze, handles replaced, c1790, 36in (91.5cm) wide.
£4,500–5,500 PHA

A George III elm gateleg table, c1780, 26in (66cm) extended.
£1,800–2,200 PHA

▶ A Continental provincial fruitwood farmhouse table, with two end drawers and one small side drawer, late 18thC, 78¼in (199cm) wide.
£1,400–1,600 NOA

A Victorian painted pine chest of drawers, late 19thC, 34¼in (87cm) wide.
£650–750 Bon

A paint-decorated pine lodging box, North Country, c1820, 40in (101.5cm) wide.
£1,200–1,400 RYA

An Austrian Empire painted pine chest, c1840, 49in (124.5cm) wide.
£2,000–2,200 DeG

A Bohemian painted Baltic pine cupboard, c1830, 40in (101.5cm) wide.
£2,500–3,000 DeG

A painted pine corner cupboard, c1770, 40in (101.5cm) wide.
£7,000–8,000 RYA

A Swiss painted armoire, dated '1797', 54¼in (138cm) wide.
£7,000–8,000 S(Z)

A Continental polychrome armoire, possibly Alsatian, mid-19thC, 55¾in (141.5cm) wide.
£550–650 NOA

A painted pine corner cupboard, c1880, 27in (68.5cm) wide.
£250–275 OLM

An Irish painted pine dresser, Co Meath, c1860, 50in (127cm) wide.
£750–825 DFA

▶ A German painted pine cupboard, dated '1919', 56¼in (143cm) wide.
£1,200–1,400 S(Am)

A painted pine miniature wardrobe, 1890, 16in (40.5cm) wide.
£270–300 OLM

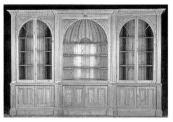

A George III Irish pine breakfront cabinet, the open central section flanked by cupboards with glazed doors, 161in (409cm) wide.
£10,000–11,000 BB(L)

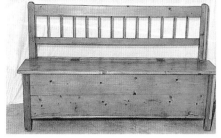

A Continental pine box bench, c1900, 61in (155cm) wide.
£280–350 Sam

A pine glazed bookcase, with a frieze drawer above two panelled cupboard doors, c1860, 39in (99cm) wide.
£580–650 MIL

A pine sheep bench, c1880, 60in (152.5cm) wide.
£275–300 AL

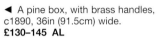

A Victorian pine grain box, with split lid, 32in (81.5cm) wide.
£150–175 P&T

◄ A pine box, with brass handles, c1890, 36in (91.5cm) wide.
£130–145 AL

► A beech stick back chair, c1890.
£60–65 AL

A Georgian pine chest of drawers, 36in (91.5cm) wide.
£400–500 TPC

An early Victorian pine chest of drawers, 45in (114.5cm) wide.
£450–500 P&T

A German pine chest of drawers, c1840, 39in (99cm) wide.
£250–300 NOTT

A Victorian pine chest of drawers, 47in (119.5cm) wide.
£400–450 P&T

A Victorian pine chest of drawers, with gallery, 40in (101.5cm) wide.
£250–300 P&T

A Victorian pine chest of drawers, 38in (96.5cm) wide.
£330–400 P&T

► A pine flight of drawers, with brass handles, c1870, 49in (124.5cm) wide.
£425–475 AL

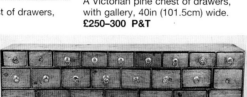

A pine chest of drawers, with white ceramic knobs, c1880, 41in (104cm) wide.
£520–565 AL

An eastern European pine chest of drawers, c1875, 38in (96.5cm) wide.
£450–500 Sam

A Victorian pine chest of drawers, 35in (89cm) wide.
£320–350 P&T

A pine chest of drawers, with brass handles, c1880, 40in (101.5cm) wide.
£500–565 AL

A pine chest of drawers, c1880, 43in (109cm) wide.
£350–400 MIL

A Victorian pine chest of drawers, 34in (86.5cm) wide.
£300–330 P&T

► A Victorian pine chest of drawers, 41in (104cm) wide.
£300–350 P&T

A pine chest of drawers, with wooden knobs, on turned legs, c1880, 36in (91.5cm) wide.
£340–375 MIL

A Victorian pine chest of drawers, with wooden knobs, on a shaped plinth base, 41in (104cm) wide.
£275–300 P&T

An Irish pine chest of drawers, with galleried back and overhanging top, on a shaped plinth base, c1880, 31½in (80cm) wide.
£180–220 Byl

A pine chest of drawers, on a shaped plinth base, c1890, 38in (96.5cm) wide.
£300–350 TPC

A pine miniature chest of drawers, with brass knobs, c1880, 11in (28cm) wide.
£90–100 MIL

A Hungarian pine chest of drawers, c1900, 44in (112cm) wide.
£800–900 MIN

A pine corner cupboard, with Gothic arched glazed doors, c1800, 48in (122cm) wide.
£2,000–2,500 TPC

An Irish pine cupboard, c1800, 50in (127cm) wide.
£1,300–1,500 TPC

A Georgian pine corner cupboard, with shaped shelves, 40in (101.5cm) wide.
£1,400–1,800 TPC

A Georgian pine cupboard, with drawer under, c1800, 30in (76cm) wide.
£700–800 TPC

A Georgian pine four-door cupboard, 49in (124.5cm) wide.
£900–1,000 P&T

A pine bread and cheese cupboard, with simulated oak finish, Caernarfon, c1820, 51in (129.5cm) wide.
£3,300–3,700 CoA

An Irish pine cupboard, with sunburst-decorated doors and panelled sides, Co Galway, c1840, 53in (134.5cm) wide.
£1,600–1,800 HON

An Irish pine four-door food cupboard, c1865, 46in (117cm) wide.
£550–650 Byl

A pine cupboard, with carved and moulded panelled doors, c1850, 48in (122cm) wide.
£600–665 AL

A Victorian pitch pine vestry cupboard, 43in (109cm) wide.
£360–400 P&T

A pine huffer, or proving cupboard, c1860, 43in (109cm) wide.
£700–800 AL

◄ A pine corner cupboard, c1870, 26in (66cm) wide.
£350–400 MIL

► A Continental pine food cupboard, c1880, 38in (96.5cm) wide.
£275–300 Sam

▶ A Hungarian pine larder cupboard, c1890, 29in (73.5cm) wide.
£630–700 MIN

A pine pot cupboard, c1880, 15in (38cm) wide.
£200–220 AL

An Irish pine cupboard, with three shelves, c1880, 27in (68.5cm) wide.
£115–130 Byl

An Irish pine two-door cupboard, with book shelves above two panelled doors, Newquay, Co Clare, c1870, 25in (63.5cm) wide.
£450–550 HON

An Irish pine wall cupboard, c1890, 29in (73.5cm) wide.
£250–300 MIN

A Romanian pine food cupboard, c1890, 27in (68.5cm) wide.
£350–400 MIN

A pine dresser, Montgomeryshire, restored, late 18thC, 67¼in (171cm) wide.
£2,000–2,400 S(S)

An Irish pine dresser, with sledge feet, c1840, 62in (157.5cm) wide.
£1,400–1,600 TPC

A pitch pine dresser, c1860, 42in (106.5cm) wide.
£600–675 MIL

A deal dresser, with a plate rack, early 19thC, 72¼in (184cm) wide.
£2,500–3,000 PFK

An Irish pitch pine dresser, c1840, 84in (213.5cm) wide.
£1,600–1,800 Byl

An Irish pine dresser, Co Clare, doors replaced, c1850, 45in (114.5cm) wide.
£675–750 Byl

▶ An Irish pine dresser, 19thC, 50in (127cm) wide.
£850–950 DEE

An early Victorian pine dresser, 72in (183cm) wide.
£1,400–1,600 P&T

A pine dresser, c1850, 92in (233.5cm) wide.
£1,600–1,800 TPC

An Irish pine dresser, c1850, 113in (287cm) wide.
£1,800–2,000 Byl

A Continental pine dresser, c1875, 47in (119.5cm) wide.
£500–600 Sam

A pine dresser, c1880, 57in (145cm) wide.
£700–780 MIL

A Hungarian pine dresser, c1910, 59in (150cm) wide.
£550–650 MIN

A Hungarian pine dresser, with glazed upper doors, c1900, 50in (127cm) wide.
£500–550 MIN

A Continental pine dresser, with spice drawers, 1900, 48in (122cm) wide.
£650–775 Sam

An early Victorian pine sideboard, 60in (152.5cm) wide.
£1,200–1,300 P&T

A Victorian pine chiffonier, 47in (119.5cm) wide.
£800–900 DEE

A pine butler's serving cupboard, c1840, 42in (106.5cm) wide.
£350–450 TPC

A Victorian pine chiffonier, 70in (178cm) wide.
£800–900 P&T

A Victorian pine dresser base, Lincolnshire, 54in (137cm) wide.
£475–525 P&T

A Victorian pine chiffonier, 51in (129.5cm) wide.
£550–650 P&T

◄ A pine low dresser, c1860, 31in (78.5cm) wide.
£350–400 Sam

A pine sideboard, with sycamore top, c1860, 62in (157.5cm) wide.
£580–650 MIL

A pine dresser base, with central candle drawer and original sliding doors, c1890, 62in (157.5cm) wide.
£800–900 TPC

A pine low dresser, with potboard, c1880, 38in (96.5cm) wide.
£480–535 AL

A Hungarian pine buffet, c1890, 43in (109cm) wide.
£450–550 MIN

◄ An eastern European pine dresser base, c1900, 38in (96.5cm) wide.
£220–240 P&T

An Irish pine serving cupboard, c1865, 37in (94cm) wide.
£180–220 Byl

An eastern European pine chiffonier, c1900, 39in (99cm) wide.
£350–425 Sam

A Welsh pine tavern table,
with X-frame and lower shelf,
c1780–1800, 52in (132cm) wide.
£2,400–2,750 RYA

A Welsh drop-leaf pine table,
with bobbin-turned legs, c1810,
43in (109cm) diam.
£500–600 TPC

A Georgian pine writing table,
37in (94cm) wide.
£350–400 P&T

A Victorian pine table, with two
drawers and turned pitch pine legs,
53in (134.5cm) wide.
£400–450 P&T

A pine Pembroke table, c1860,
36in (91.5cm) wide.
£250–300 TPC

A Victorian pine drop-leaf table,
with turned legs, 35in (89cm) wide.
£150–175 P&T

A pine cricket table, c1880,
31¼in (79.5cm) diam.
£350–400 AL

An Irish pine wardrobe, restored,
c1880, 48in (122cm) wide.
£320–350 DFA

A pine wardrobe, c1860,
54in (137cm) wide.
£650–800 TPC

A pine wardrobe, c1880,
47in (119.5cm) wide.
£600–650 MIL

▶ A pine compactum, with
bevelled mirrored door, c1900,
49in (124.5cm) wide.
£850–950 TPC

A Continental pine wardrobe,
with drawer under, c1880,
47in (119.5cm) wide.
£320–400 Sam

A pitch pine box pew, c1860, 35in (89cm) wide.
£340–375 MIL

▶ A pine luggage rack, c1920, 30in (76cm) wide.
£60–75 AL

A Victorian pine settle, 46in (117cm) wide.
£200–240 P&T

A Victorian pine washstand, 36in (91.5cm) wide.
£250–300 P&T

A pine towel rail, c1880, 25in (63.5cm) wide.
£70–80 AL

An Edwardian pine washstand, 36in (91.5cm) wide.
£200–240 P&T

▶ A pine washtub, on a stand, c1870, 32in (81.5cm) wide.
£125–140 MIL

A ceramic bread barrel, with wooden lid, 19thC, 22in (56cm) high.
£275–325 B&R

A cast-iron egg timer, c1880, 3in (7.5cm) high.
£45–50 SMI

A French copper tart mould, c1880, 8¼in (21cm) diam.
£220–250 MSB

A ceramic sugar storage jar, c1880, 7in (18cm) high.
£50–55 SMI

A painted tin flour bin, c1880, 20in (51cm) high.
£180–200 AL

A copper jelly mould, mid-19thC, 9in (23cm) high.
£180–200 OCH

A set of spice drawers, c1890, 8in (20.5cm) wide.
£180–200 WeA

A ceramic flour shaker, c1930, 5in (12.5cm) high.
£45–50 AL

A Buttercup Dairy Co butter crock, c1900, 7in (18cm) wide.
£180–200 WeA

A copper fish kettle, c1860, 23in (58.5cm) wide.
£180–200 AL

An oak spoon rack, c1750, 24in (61cm) high.
£600–650 SEA

A Royal Winton Grimwades ceramic sugar jar, c1920–30, 6½in (16.5cm) high.
£25–30 AL

CUPBOARDS

A painted pine hanging corner cupboard, c1790, 24in (61cm) wide.
£850–950 DeG

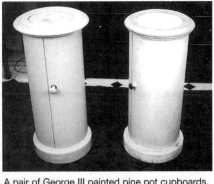

A pair of George III painted pine pot cupboards, stamped 'Mack, Williams & Gibton', c1810, 16in (40.5cm) diam.
£1,100–1,300 GKe

An American yellow pine corner cupboard, decorated with blue, green and yellow wash, the open top with shaped shelves, Shenandoah Valley, repaired, late 18thC, 41in (104cm) wide.
£2,000–2,200 SK(B)

A pine pot cupboard, c1800, 17in (43cm) wide.
£180–200 MIL

A Victorian pine cupboard, with shelves, c1860, 38in (96.5cm) wide.
£350–400 TPC

Miller's is a price GUIDE not a price LIST

◄ A Romanian painted pine hanging cupboard, dated '1855', 39in (99cm) wide.
£650–700 MIN

An Irish pine cupboard, c1860, 38in (96.5cm) wide.
£375–450 Byl

An Irish pine panelled cupboard, 1875, 51in (129.5cm) wide.
£450–550 Byl

◄ An Irish pine cupboard, c1875, 46in (117cm) wide.
£180–220 Byl

A Victorian pine cupboard, with glazed doors and eight drawers, 60in (152.5cm) wide.
£720–800 P&T

A pine corner cupboard, 19thC, 37¾in (96cm) wide.
£900–1,100 DN

A Victorian pine linen press, 48in (122cm) wide.
£1,100–1,300 DEE

A Victorian pine cupboard, 42in (106.5cm) wide.
£450–500 P&T

An Irish pine four-door cupboard, with central drawer, c1880, 44in (112cm) wide.
£500–550 Byl

A pine cupboard, c1880, 35in (89cm) wide.
£350–400 AL

A pine three-door cupboard, c1880, 54in (137cm) wide.
£300–350 AL

A pine glazed wall cabinet, c1880, 23in (58.5cm) wide.
£175–200 Sam

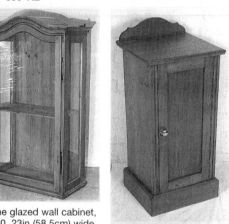

A pine pot cupboard, c1880, 15½in (39.5cm) wide.
£200–220 AL

A pair of pine pot cupboards, 1880, 16in (40.5cm) wide.
£180–200 MIL

► A pine hall cupboard, c1890, 38in (96.5cm) wide.
£350–400 AL

A pine pot cupboard, with drawer, c1890, 15½in (39.5cm) wide.
£180–200 AL

A late Victorian rustic pine cupboard, 38in (96.5cm) wide.
£375–450 DEE

◀ A Hungarian pine corner cupboard, with a candle box, c1900, 42in (106.5cm) wide.
£550–600 MIN

▶ A pine Southern Railway telephone cupboard, c1920, 23in (58.5cm) wide.
£130–160 WaH

A Hungarian pine cupboard, painted green and brown, c1900, 37in (94cm) wide.
£550–600 MIN

A pair of Continental pine pot cupboards, c1900, 18in (45.5cm) wide.
£240–280 Sam

A pine pot cupboard, c1930, 17in (43cm) wide.
£65–80 NOTT

DESKS

An early Victorian pine desk,
by Maples of London,
48in (122cm) wide.
£600–700 P&T

A Victorian pine kneehole desk,
36in (91.5cm) wide.
£450–500 P&T

A pine clerk's desk, with fitted
interior, c1790, 36in (91.5cm) wide.
£500–600 TPC

A pine desk, c1890, 48in (122cm) wide.
£675–750 MIL

A French pine desk, painted blue,
1890, 33in (84cm) wide.
£250–275 OLM

An Irish pine shopkeeper's desk,
c1880, 24in (61cm) wide.
£80–100 Byl

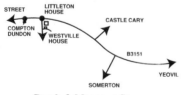
DRESSERS

◀ A George II
pine dresser,
with later cavetto-
moulded cornice
and waved frieze,
restored, 84¾in
(215.5cm) wide.
£1,400–1,600 S(S)

An Irish pine dresser, with
panelled doors, mid-18thC,
56¼in (143cm) wide.
£450–550 M

A late George III painted pine
dresser, 59in (150cm) wide.
£3,000–3,500 P(NW)

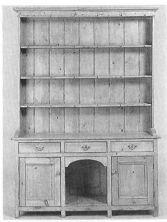

A pine dresser, with arched recess, early 19thC, 64¼in (163cm) wide.
£900–1,100 P

A Cornish painted pine dresser, c1830, 58in (147.5cm) wide.
£5,000–5,500 RYA

A pine dresser, c1840, 52in (132cm) wide.
£1,200–1,500 TPC

A Victorian pine dresser, 57in (145cm) wide.
£500–550 P&T

A Victorian pine farmhouse dresser, 87in (221cm) wide.
£2,250–2,500 P&T

A pine dresser, 19thC, 64in (162.5cm) wide.
£775–875 HOA

A pine dresser, 19thC, 54in (137cm) wide.
£1,100–1,200 DN

An Irish pine dresser, 19thC, 56in (142cm) wide.
£775–875 HOA

▶ An Irish pine dresser, with red and white painted top and yellow base, Co Tipperary, c1850, 54in (137cm) wide.
£380–420 DFA

An Irish pine dresser, mid-19thC,
56in (142cm) wide.
£775–850 HOA

An Irish painted pine dresser, Co
Galway, c1860, 49in (124.5cm) wide.
£575–650 DFA

► An Irish pine chicken coop
dresser, 19thC, 52in (132cm) wide.
£850–950 HOA

A Hungarian white-painted pine
dresser, c1880, 40in (101.5cm) wide.
£450–500 A&H

A French pine dresser, c1870,
54in (137cm) wide.
£900–1,000 P&T

A Dutch glazed pine dresser, c1900,
45in (114.5cm) wide.
£630–700 P&T

A Victorian pine dresser,
60in (152.5cm) wide.
£675–750 P&T

► An Edwardian pine mirror-backed
dresser, 55in (139.5cm) wide.
£700–800 DEE

An Irish pine dresser, Co Donegal,
c1870, 78in (198cm) wide.
£1,200–1,400 HON

A pine dresser, with carved panels,
c1890, 65in (165cm) wide.
£1,200–1,350 AL

DRESSER BASES & SIDE CABINETS

A pine dresser base, early 19thC, 74in (188cm) wide.
£500–550 HOA

A pine sideboard, with gallery back, c1880, 54in (137cm) wide.
£350–385 HOA

A pine sideboard, with gallery back, 1870–80, 60in (152.5cm) wide.
£400–450 HOA

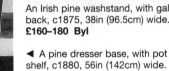

A pine sideboard, 19thC, 54in (137cm) wide.
£500–550 HOA

An Irish pine washstand, with gallery back, c1875, 38in (96.5cm) wide.
£160–180 Byl

◄ A pine dresser base, with pot shelf, c1880, 56in (142cm) wide.
£500–565 AL

◄ A Danish pine dresser base, c1880, 45in (114.5cm) wide.
£500–600 BOR

A pine sideboard, 19thC, 57in (144.8cm) wide.
£380–425 HOA

▶ A pine dresser base, c1930, 42in (106.5cm) wide.
£350–400 P&T

RACKS & SHELVES

A pine bookshelf, c1880,
33in (84cm) wide.
£180–200 AL

◄ A late Georgian pine bookshelf, 29in (73.5cm) wide.
£350–400 MIN

A pine hanging cabinet,
19thC, 17in (43cm) wide.
£120–150 DEE

A pair of pine racks, c1900,
41in (104cm) wide.
£350–400 AL

SETTLES

An Irish pine settle, restored, early 19thC,
72in (183cm) wide.
£380–420 DFA

An American painted pine settle, Pennsylvania,
early 19thC, 60½in (153.5cm) wide.
£1,500–1,650 SK(B)

A George III pine bacon
settle, faults, restored, early
19thC, 31in (78.5cm) wide.
£1,000–1,200 S(S)

A Welsh pine settle, with cupboards
below, c1830, 46in (117cm) wide.
£350–400 P&T

A pine pew, c1880, 39in (99cm) wide.
£320–350 MIL

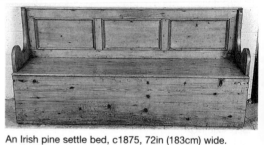

An Irish pine settle bed, c1875, 72in (183cm) wide.
£450–500 Byl

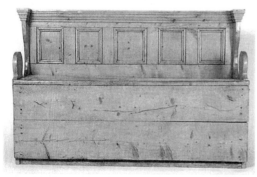

A Continental pine box settle, 19thC,
73½in (186.5cm) wide.
£450–550 SLM

► An eastern European pine settle, c1900, 72in (183cm) wide.
£300–350 P&T

STEPS

A Victorian pine step ladder, 24in (61cm) high.
£55–70 DEE

A pine step ladder, 1920, 28in (71cm) high.
£35–40 AL

▶ A pine step ladder, c1920, 69in (175.5cm) high.
£50–60 AL

STOOLS

A Gothic-style pine stool, 1865, 20in (51cm) wide.
£80–100 OLM

A Welsh pine high stool, 1860, 27½in (70cm) high.
£50–55 OLM

A pine stool, c1880, 12in (30.5cm) wide.
£50–60 MIL

A beech stool, c1890, 27in (68.5cm) wide.
£50–55 AL

A three-legged milking stool, with octagonal seat, c1890, 12in (30.5cm) wide.
£30–35 AL

A pine stool, c1890, 16in (40.5cm) wide.
£40–45 MIL

A pine stool, c1900, 22in (56cm) wide.
£50–55 MIL

◀ A three-legged milking stool, c1900, 16in (40.5cm) high.
£25–30 AL

▶ A pine stool, c1900, 18½in (47cm) high.
£35–40 AL

A pine stool, c1900, 22½in (57cm) high.
£40–50 AL

TABLES

A pine refectory table, with six legs joined by stretchers, c1800, 120in (305cm) long.
£1,000–1,200 TPC

A French pine farmhouse table, with cleated top and large draw-leaf, on tapered legs, c1800, 108in (274.5cm) wide.
£800–900 TPC

An American painted pine chair/table, New Jersey, early 19thC, 76in (193cm) long.
£6,000–7,000 SK(B)

An American pine sawbuck table, New England, early 19thC, 45in (114.5cm) wide.
£500–600 SK(B)

An early Victorian pine table, with drop-leaf and three drawers, 44in (112cm) wide.
£350–400 P&T

An American pine and tiger maple chair/table, New England, restored, late 18thC, 52in (132cm) diam.
£3,200–3,500 SK(B)

An American painted chair/table, the tilt-top above a dark-green painted plank seat, New England, late 18thC, 42in (106.5cm) wide.
£2,500–2,750 SK(B)

A pine refectory table, early 19thC, 102in (259cm) wide.
£2,000–2,200 TAM

A Welsh pine cricket table, c1800, 19in (48.5cm) wide.
£1,350–1,500 CoA

A Welsh pine cricket table, c1820, 27½in (68.5cm) diam.
£630–700 RED

An American red-painted pine table, with ring-turned tapering legs, Massachusetts, 1820–30, 96in (244cm) long.
£6,000–7,000 SK(B)

An Irish pine table, reduced in height, c1870, 26in (66cm) wide.
£100–120 DFA

A Victorian pine farmhouse table, 66in (167.5cm) long.
£470–520 DEE

A Victorian pine serving table, 54in (137cm) long.
£230–260 P&T

A pine table, with one drawer, on reeded legs, c1880, 48in (122cm) long.
£350–400 AL

► A pine table, with turned and reeded legs, c1880, 48½in (123cm) long.
£300–335 AL

◄ A pine table, c1880, 40½in (103cm) long.
£280–320 AL

A Victorian pine serving table, with two drawers and shaped apron, 59in (150cm) long.
£320–400 P&T

◄ A pine table, c1880, 50in (127cm) long.
£220–250 AL

► A pine draw-leaf table, the cabriole legs with lion's paw feet, 19thC, 81in (205.5cm) extended.
£400–450 HOA

A pitch pine side table, c1880, 36in (91.5cm) wide.
£120–150 MIL

A pine primitive-style three-legged table, c1890, 24½in (61cm) wide.
£80–100 AL

A pine lamp table, c1880, 25in (63.5cm) long.
£160–180 AL

► A pine table, with two drawers, c1890, 64in (162.5cm) long.
£350–400 AL

Further Reading

Miller's Pine & Country Furniture Buyer's Guide, Miller's Publications, 1995

► A Victorian pine table, with one drawer, on turned legs, 48in (122cm) wide.
£400–450 TPC

A pitch pine table, with cleated top, the legs joined by stretchers, c1900, 62in (157.5cm) long.
£400–450 TPC

► A Hungarian pine table, with fold-over top, c1900, 28in (142cm) wide.
£250–300 MIN

WARDROBES

A Victorian pine compactum,
71in (180.5cm) wide.
£1,800–2,000 P&T

A Hungarian pine miniature wardrobe,
c1890, 21in (53.5cm) wide.
£250–300 MIN

A pine wardrobe, c1890,
47in (119.5cm) wide.
£575–650 MIL

A Continental pine wardrobe, c1900,
82in (208.5cm) wide.
£800–900 TPC

A pine compactum, c1900,
46in (117cm) wide.
£850–950 TPC

A Continental pine knock-down
wardrobe, with central mirror, c1900,
56in (142cm) wide.
£675–750 P&T

A German pine triple knock-down
wardrobe, 1900, 68in (172.5cm) wide.
£650–775 Sam

A German pine knock-down wardrobe,
c1920, 49in (124.5cm) wide.
£400–450 NOTT

◄ A Continental pitch pine
knock-down wardrobe, c1920,
56in (142cm) wide.
£630–700 P&T

A Czechoslovakian pine knock-down
wardrobe, c1920, 62in (157.5cm) wide.
£675–750 P&T

Prices

The price ranges quoted in this
book reflect the average price a
purchaser might expect to pay
for a similar item. The price will
vary according to the condition,
rarity, size, popularity, provenance,
colour and restoration of the item
and this must be taken into
account when assessing values.

WASHSTANDS

An American painted and gilt-stencilled pine washstand, the bowfront top with two drawers painted black, with original light blue-green paint and apple-green striped border, possibly Vermont, 1825–35, 18½in (47cm) wide.
£1,500–1,650 SK(B)

A Victorian pine washstand, with a single drawer, 36in (91.5cm) wide.
£250–300 P&T

A Victorian pine washstand, with a shaped undertier, 36in (91.5cm) wide.
£175–200 P&T

▶ A French pitch pine washstand, with a marble top and ceramic basin, c1910, 39in (99cm) wide.
£650–800 CF

A pine washstand, with two drawers, c1800, 38in (96.5cm) wide.
£250–275 TPC

A pine washstand, with a gallery, c1890, 34in (86.5cm) wide.
£200–220 AL

A Victorian pine washstand, with a single drawer, 35in (89cm) wide.
£175–200 P&T

A Regency pine washstand, c1810, 20in (51cm) wide.
£200–240 TPC

A Victorian pine washstand, with a gallery, 36in (91.4cm) wide.
£180–200 OLM

A Victorian pine washstand, 32in (81.5cm) wide.
£150–175 P&T

A German pine washstand, with a lift-up top, c1900, 26in (66cm) wide.
£130–150 NOTT

Kitchenware

An American cast-iron apple peeler, c1880, 9in (23cm) long.
£80–100 MSB

An American pottery spongeware bowl, decorated in brown, green and cream, c1900, 9½in (24cm) diam.
£85–95 MSB

A wooden butter mould, 19thC, 2½in (6.5cm) high.
£30–32 OCH

An American tin biscuit shaper, with wooden plunger and two extra heads, c1890, 12¼in (31cm) long.
£90–110 MSB

An Irish hanen, or bread warmer, 18thC, 14in (35.5cm) high.
£160–185 SEA

A wooden butter roller, with marker, c1880, 5in (12.5cm) long.
£115–130 WeA

A set of French enamel kitchen canisters, largest 10in (25.5cm) high.
£270–300 AL

An American biscuit cutter, in the shape of a leaf, c1930, 2¼in (5.5cm) diam.
£35–40 MSB

An American set of shell pattern cake tins, c1880, 8¼in (21cm) long.
£70–80 MSB

A cast-iron cauldron, c1870, 6in (15cm) high.
£100–120 WeA

An American cast-iron cherry stoner, by Enterprise Mfg Co, Philadelphia, c1880, 11¾in (30cm) long.
£100–120 MSB

A Continental enamel coffee percolater, decorated in green and red, c1930, 13½in (34.5cm) high.
£60–70 B&R

▶ A ceramic crock, impressed 'Cooper & Co, Glasgow, London and Liverpool', c1890, 8in (20.5cm) high.
£135–150 WeA

A Kleen Ware ceramic colander, by Saddler, decorated with green bands, c1930, 10½in (26.5cm) diam.
£80–90 B&R

A brass and steel food chopper, c1870, 4in (10cm) wide.
£160–180 WeA

An American cast-iron food grinder, by Rollerman Manufacturing Co, Joy, Pennsylvania, c1880, 6¾in (17cm) long.
£80–100 MSB

An oak hanging cutlery box, inlaid with a knife and fork, c1780–90, 22in (56cm) high.
£320–350 AnSh

◀ An iron meat fork, dated '1783', 17in (43cm) long.
£225–250 SEA

A reversible toasting fork, c1790, 27in (68.5cm) long.
£350–390 SEA

A German cast-iron French bean slicer, by Harris, c1880, 10in (25.5cm) long.
£110–125 MSB

An iron game hook, 19thC, 13in (33cm) wide.
£270–300 SEA

A wooden grain measure, c1850, 6in (15cm) high.
£90–100 SEA

An iron griddle, c1750, 25in (63.5cm) long.
£160–175 SEA

A cast-iron and enamel griddle, by Kendricks, c1900, 24in (61cm) long.
£110–125 B&R

An Irish wrought-iron meat fork, and a copper-bowled ladle, 18thC, ladle 20in (51cm) long.
Ladle £110–125
Fork £35–40 EON

A ceramic ham stand, marked 'Parnall & Sons Ltd', c1910, 9¼in (23.5cm) diam.
£90–100 AL

A pine lug, late 19thC, 8½in (21.5cm) high.
£50–65 ChA

A lug is a container for vegetables or fruit, with a capacity of 28–40 lbs.

A cast-iron 'Magic Marmalade' orange shredder, for making marmalade, c1900, 16½in (42cm) long.
£100–110 MSB

An Irish copper-on-tin milk cooling pan, 18thC, 11¼in (28.5cm) diam.
£65–75 EON

A milk saver, by Kent, c1880, 5in (12.7cm) high.
£90–100 WeA

A tin chocolate mould, in the shape of a hen, c1920, 4⅝in (11.5cm) wide.
£35–40 AL

A brown salt-glazed jelly mould, c1830, 7½in (19cm) diam.
£35–40 IW

A copper jelly mould, mid-19thC, 6in (15cm) wide.
£60–70 OCH

A Victorian copper jelly mould, 4in (10cm) wide.
£65–75 OCH

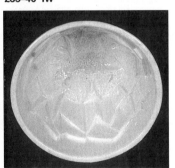

A jelly mould, with fish design, c1880, 5in (12.5cm) wide.
£60–70 SMI

Two copper jelly moulds, 19thC, 5in (12.5cm) wide.
£160–220 each DEN

A copper jelly mould, in the shape of a turret, 19thC, 5in (12.5cm) high.
£130–150 GAK

A copper oval jelly mould, late 19thC, 6½in (16.5cm) wide.
£100–120 GAK

A copper mould, for iced puddings, with Star of David top, c1880, 3½in (9cm) high.
£250–275 MSB

> **Cross Reference**
> See Colour Review

◄ An American copper-on-tin pudding mould, with melon design, c1880, 4¾in (12cm) long.
£35–40 MSB

A sheet metal nutmeg grater, 19thC, 4¼in (11cm) diam.
£70–80 AnSh

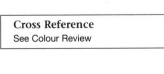

A nutmeg grater, c1880,
8in (20.5cm) long.
£100–120 WeA

A Continental bronze cooking pot,
inscribed in relief 'Re mi Jia paez',
16th/17thC, 12in (30.5cm) diam.
£220–250 F&C

A pudding basin, with brass plaque
inscribed 'The Lord Mayor's pudding
basin', c1860, 7¼in (18.5cm) diam.
£60–70 AL

A pine cheese/meat safe, 19thC,
22in (56cm) wide.
£80–100 DEE

An American pine six-drawer spice
chest, painted red, 19thC,
15½in (39.5cm) wide.
£1,200–1,400 SK(B)

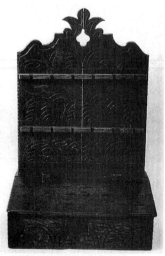

A spice tin, with brass handle,
c1850, 6in (15cm) diam.
£60–70 AL

A George III silver spice rasp,
by T. Phipps and E. Robinson, with
shell and leaf formed handle and
armorial crest to reverse, London
1810, 4⅛in (11.5cm) high.
£1,000–1,200 GAK

A black-glazed storage pot,
mid-19thC, 12in (30.5cm) high.
£100–120 IW

An oak hanging spoon rack, the
sloping box with iron hinges, late
18th/early 19thC, 31½in (80cm) wide.
£340–400 MSW

◀ An enamelled yeast tray,
late 19thC, 12in (30.5cm) wide.
£60–70 SMI

A cast-iron tin opener, modelled as a sea creature,
c1880, 5in (12.5cm) long.
£60–70 SMI

An milkmaid's elm yoke, c1850, 35in (89cm) long.
£100–120 MIL

◀ A cast-iron and wrought-iron wafering iron, 19thC,
30in (76cm) long.
£130–145 SEA

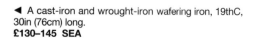

Pottery

ANIMALS & BIRDS

A salt-glazed stoneware model of a lion, c1745, 6in (15cm) high.
£1,500–1,650 JHo

A Staffordshire creamware model of a spaniel, with brown, green and ochre markings, minor chipping to base, late 18thC, 3¼in (8.5cm) high.
£370–420 P

A salt-glazed bear jug and cover, decorated with shards and brown slip, 18thC, 7in (18cm) high.
£700–800 P(O)

A pair of Whieldon models of a cow and bull, decorated with brown mottled glaze, the bases applied with green-glazed leaves and flowers, restored extremities, c1760, larger 8¼in (21cm) wide.
£6,000–7,000 Bon

A pair of Staffordshire models of cats, with green and yellow sponging and painted faces, c1800, 5in (12.5cm) high.
£500–600 HYD

A Yorkshire Prattware cow group, in cane-coloured pottery with black and mauve sponging, restored, c1800, 6in (15cm) wide.
£450–550 P

A Prattware deer vase, decorated in brown, green and fawn, c1800, 8in (20.5cm) high.
£850–950 JHo

Prattware

Prattware evolved in the last quarter of the 18th century and is similar to pearlware in colour and weight. Made in Staffordshire, north-east England and in Scotland, Prattware is distinguished by a bold, high-temperature palette that comprises yellow-ochre, blue, green and muddy brown. These colours were normally used to heighten relief decoration on wares such as jugs, or details on figures. Types of Prattware include figures, allegorical subjects, animals and domestic hollow wares; flatwares are rare.

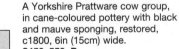

A Staffordshire pearlware model of a hound, with liver-spotted body, supported by a mottled green tree trunk and base, restored, early 19thC, 7in (18cm) wide.
£1,100–1,300 P

A pearlware model of a grey stallion, probably Leeds, the base picked out in Pratt colours, 1820–30, 16¾in (42.5cm) wide.
£11,000–12,000 S

This model is seldom seen.

A Staffordshire model of a fox attacking a hen, decorated in yellow, blue, red and purple, on a green washed base, some damage, c1820, 5½in (14cm) wide.
£600–675 P

A Staffordshire model of a deer, in brown, green, red, yellow and blue, c1820, 10in (25.5cm) high.
£900–1,000 JHo

A Staffordshire model of a cow under a tree, in green, brown and red, c1820, 5in (12.5cm) high.
£250–300 JHo

A Yorkshire model of a bird, decorated in yellow, black and brown, c1820, 4in (10cm) high.
£350–400 JHo

A pair of Staffordshire models of sheep, decorated in green and brown, c1825, 7in (18cm) high.
£1,200–1,400 DAN

A pair of Staffordshire models of spaniels, with iron-red body markings and gilt collars, the bases in green and black with a gilt band, both slightly damaged, 1845–50, 7¾in (19.5cm) high.
£2,500–3,000 DN

Ex-Rev Harry Bloomfield collection. The Reverend Bloomfield was a collector of Staffordshire models during the late 20thC. His collection included some rare pieces, such as these examples.

A Staffordshire model of a leopard, in yellow and black, on a green base, c1850, 7¼in (18.5cm) high.
£2,700–3,200 DN

A pair of Staffordshire models of spaniels, with black markings and gilt collars, c1850, 8in (20.5cm) high.
£180–200 SER

A Staffordshire model of a greyhound, with black markings, mid-19thC, 10½in (26.5cm) high.
£500–550 S(S)

A pair of Staffordshire spill vases, modelled as a lion or lioness with cubs before a tree stump, 1850–60, 11¼in (28.5cm) high.
£2,500–3,000 DN

A Staffordshire model of a zebra, on a green base, c1850, 6in (15cm) wide.
£120–140 SER

▶ A pair of Staffordshire models of lions with lambs, decorated in green, brown and yellow, c1860, 10¼in (26cm) high.
£5,000–5,500 DN

Ex-Rev Harry Bloomfield collection.

A pair of Staffordshire models of goats, decorated in black, red and green, c1860, 11in (28cm) high.
£650–750 DN
Ex-Rev Harry Bloomfield collection.

A pair of Continental majolica blue-glazed models of birds, probably French, tiny chips, c1870, 11in (28cm) wide.
£1,200–1,400 S(NY)

A majolica model of a pug dog, with detachable head, decorated in mottled brown with a blue collar, late 19thC, 9in (23cm) high.
£200–240 P(E)

Cross Reference
See Colour Review

A Staffordshire cow and milkmaid group, decorated in black, green and yellow, restored, late19th/early 20thC, 7in (18cm) wide.
£200–240 Hal(C)

A pair of Staffordshire models of spaniels, with lustre decoration, c1860, 9½in (24cm) high.
£150–175 OD

A Staffordshire or American majolica brown-glazed model of an elephant, entitled 'Jumbo', supported on a mottled green and brown glazed base, chips, c1880, 11in (28cm) wide.
£1,200–1,400 P

Already a national favourite, this London Zoo elephant achieved even greater fame when he was exported to the USA by the American showman Phineas T. Barnum in 1882. His Stateside career was tragically cut short, however, when he died after charging a train in Ontario in 1885. Few models of Jumbo exist.

A pair of Staffordshire models of lions, with glass eyes, late 19thC, 12½in (32cm) wide.
£130–160 L

A Wedgwood black basalt model of a bulldog, by E. W. Light, 1915, 5in (12.5cm) wide.
£180–200 CoCo

A Victorian Staffordshire model of a lop-eared rabbit, with black and pink markings, nibbling a green cabbage leaf, 10in (25.5cm) wide.
£1,500–1,800 PF

A pair of Austrian models of deer, decorated in shades of brown, 19thC, 47¼in (120cm) high.
£5,000–6,000 P(Ed)

An Austrian model of a pug dog, decorated in naturalistic colours, with glass eyes, restored, late 19thC, 12½in (32cm) long.
£650–800 S

A pair of models of seated cats, with lemon bodies and green and black eyes, seated on green cushions with gilded borders, early 20thC, 7in (18cm) high.
£230–275 GAK

Many fakes exist of this style of cat model, especially those 4–5in (10–12.5cm) high. Check for wear and scratches. Fakes are often unblemished apart from dust, dirt and induced glaze cracks.

BOTTLES

A Rhenish salt-glazed stoneware
wine vessel, with blue scroll
decoration, chips, late 17th/early
18thC, 9in (23cm) high.
£120–150 PFK

A Liverpool blue and white pearlware
vase, rim restored, c1780,
9½in (24cm) high.
£300–350 IW

An Italian maiolica bottle, decorated
with two saints, inscribed 'SS Delice
et Adavto MM', probably Savona,
18thC, 9½in (24cm) high.
£450–550 S(S)

BOWLS

An English delft bowl, decorated in
polychrome enamels, probably Bristol,
minor chips, c1720, 7in (18cm) diam.
£3,700–4,100 S

A Mason's Ironstone bowl, reserved
with Oriental figures and a scene of
islands, on a turquoise ground,
impressed marks, repaired, c1840,
21in (53.5cm) diam.
£2,200–2,600 S(S)

► A Verwood Pottery bowl,
the inside with brown glaze,
early 20thC, 16½in (42cm) diam.
£75–85 IW

An English delft blue and white bowl,
c1760, 8in (20.5cm) diam.
£320–360 JHo

A Wedgwood black basalt orange
bowl, impressed mark, 19thC,
8¾in (22cm) diam.
£700–800 SK(B)

A pair of creamware baskets,
impressed 'Fell' on base, late
18th/early 19thC, 9½in (24cm) diam.
£350–420 FBG

An earthenware brown-glazed
porringer, possibly Verwood Pottery,
19thC, 6in (15cm) wide.
£35–40 IW

An American Morton Pottery set of
three bowls, decorated with daisies,
1900–30, largest 6in (15cm) diam.
£130–160 NSA

BUILDINGS

A Scottish pearlware cottage money-box, painted in bright colours with sponged decoration, early 19thC, 5in (12.5cm) high.
£750–825 S

A Staffordshire spill vase, modelled as a fort, entitled 'Malakoff', on yellow and green base, c1854, 9¼in (23.5cm) high.
£650–720 JO

A Staffordshire pastille burner, modelled as a cottage, with orange detail, c1860, 6in (15cm) high.
£150–180 DAN

CANDLESTICKS & CHAMBERSTICKS

A Spode stoneware chamberstick, the brown ground with blue sprigging, impressed 'Spode', c1820, 2in (5cm) high.
£275–320 DIA

◀ A candlestick, modelled as a tree, decorated in green, blue and brown, c1760, 12in (30.5cm) high.
£3,000–3,300 JHo

A majolica chamberstick, modelled as bindweed, decorated in green, white and browns, probably by George Jones, c1880, 4in (10cm) high.
£6,000–6,750 HAM

> **Miller's is a price GUIDE not a price LIST**

CENTREPIECES

A Mason's centrepiece, with ram's head handles, the interior enamelled with flowers and leaves, some minor chips, c1820, 15¼in (38.5cm) wide.
£200–240 DN

A majolica centrepiece, modelled as two female figures supporting a basketware dish, restored, late 19thC, 17in (43cm) wide.
£300–350 P(E)

◀ A Minton pierced majolica centrepiece, model number 874, the base with three pigeons, impressed marks, c1871, 12½in (32cm) diam.
£3,500–4,000 S

A Wedgwood Queen's Ware Sunderland centrepiece, with pierced bowl, the support modelled as three putti alternating with shell form sweetmeat dishes, impressed mark, c1879, 12¾in (32.5cm) high.
£1,400–1,600 SK

CLOCKS

A Dutch Delft clock case, polychrome painted and decorated with scattered blooms, applied to each side with putti, 18thC, 11¾in (30cm) high.
£2,500–3,000 S(Am)

A Wedgwood light blue jasper mantel clock case, clock parts missing, impressed mark, early 19thC, 9¾in (25cm) high.
£1,250–1,500 SK(B)

A Dutch Delft striking mantel clock, the blue and white case painted with a lake scene, with French movement, minor damage, late 19thC, 11in (28cm) high.
£180–220 Bea(E)

A Wedgwood dark blue jasper clock case, with applied white classical and foliate relief and motto 'Tempus Fugit' above a relief of Father Time, impressed mark, c1900, 8in (20.5cm) high.
£550–620 SK(B)

COW CREAMERS

A creamware cow creamer, decorated in beige, on green base, cover missing, c1800, 7in (18cm) long.
£450–500 OCH

A creamware cow creamer, decorated with manganese, yellow and blue, on green base, cover replaced, restored, early 19thC, 6½in (16.5cm) long.
£750–900 S(NY)

A pair of lustre cow creamers, decorated with purple and red, on green bases, some damage, early 19thC, 7in (18cm) long.
£370–440 MJB

CRUETS

A pearlware mustard pot, decorated in underglaze blue, lid missing, base cracked, 1790, 4½in (11.5cm) high.
£100–120 IW

A Wedgwood creamware cruet, with pierced sides, blue Greek key pattern in relief and painted blue flowers, impressed mark, one cruet bottle slightly chipped, late 18thC, 8¼in (21cm) high.
£750–900 AG

A pair of Dutch Delft oil and vinegar jugs, with fitted stand, decorated in blue, chipped, marked for De porcelyne Klaauw, c1800, 7in (18cm) high.
£1,100–1,250 S(Am)

Prices

The price ranges quoted in this book reflect the average price a purchaser might expect to pay for a similar item. The price will vary according to the condition, rarity, size, popularity, provenance, colour and restoration of the item and this must be taken into account when assessing values.

CUPS

A salt-glazed cup, enamelled in green, blue, red and yellow, c1765, 3in (7.5cm) high.
£1,000–1,150 JHo

A pink lustre cup and saucer, c1840, cup 2½in (6.5cm) high.
£45–50 SER

A salt-glazed stoneware cup, enamelled in red, blue and green, c1765, 3in (7.5cm) high.
£3,300–3,650 JHo

An American Dedham Pottery crackle-glaze cup and saucer, decorated with blue bands and moulded elephant pattern, early 20thC, saucer 6¼in (16cm) diam.
£250–300 JMW

A cup, hand-painted with leaves and 'George' in brown, green and black, c1830, 2½in (6.5cm) high.
£400–500 NSA

A Wedgwood jasper dip coffee can and saucer, the black ground decorated in white and yellow, impressed mark, mid-19thC, saucer 5¼in (13.5cm) diam.
£1,600–1,800 SK(B)

DISHES

An Italian Deruta dish, decorated in blue and red on a yellow ground, c1620, 7½in (19cm) diam.
£525–625 JNic

An Italian Faenza maiolica dish, decorated in blue and yellow, early 17thC, 10in (25.5cm) diam.
£1,600–2,000 S

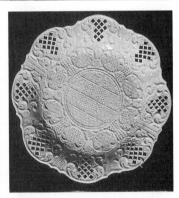

A salt-glazed dish, the rim with pierced panels, c1760, 11½in (29cm) diam.
£275–325 OCH

A Staffordshire oval dish, with green moulded cabbage leaf pattern, c1765, 7in (18cm) wide.
£1,100–1,300 JHo

A Derbyshire creamware dish, the rim with pierced panels, painted with green flowers and swags, c1770, 10in (25.5cm) wide.
£450–500 JHo

A pair of square dishes, painted with flowers in green, yellow and brown, c1825, 9in (23cm) wide.
£550–620 DAN

A pink lustre dish, c1840,
8in (20.5cm) diam.
£40–45 SER

Cross Reference
See Colour Review

A majolica dish, moulded in relief
with holly and a robin in green,
yellow and brown, with turquoise
ground and yellow rope border,
some damage, 19thC,
11in (28cm) wide.
£140–160 WL

A French earthenware tambourine-
shaped dish, probably Clement
Massier, modelled with a mask,
fan, beads and flowers, some
damage and restoration, c1880,
10½in (26.5cm) diam.
£750–900 S(NY)

COVERED DISHES

A white salt-glazed stoneware
butter dish and cover, with
applied decoration, the knop
modelled as a cow, c1750,
4in (10cm) wide.
£1,600–1,850 JHo

A Wedgwood caneware game
pie dish and cover, the knop
modelled as a rabbit, c1820,
12¼in (31cm) wide.
£300–350 AnSh

A George Jones majolica 'Daisy'
butter dish and cover, pattern
number 5205, the blue ground
moulded with a railed fence,
wheat ears and daisies, with
turquoise interior, handle chipped,
c1870, 7½in (19cm) diam.
£2,000–2,400 TEN

**See Colour Review for a
cheese dome decorated
in the same pattern.**

A game pie dish, c1860,
7in (18cm) wide.
£220–250 WeA

A Wedgwood majolica cheese
dish and cover, impressed mark,
c1871, 7¾in (19.5cm) high.
£300–350 SK

A George Jones majolica Argenta
ware game dish and cover, moulded
with hares, grasses, ferns and oak
leaves, the knop modelled as a quail,
enamelled in autumnal colours,
late 19thC, 13½in (34.5cm) wide.
£800–1,000 Bea(E)

◀ A Minton
majolica 'lobster'
tureen and cover,
date code for
1870, 13½in
(34.5cm) wide.
£7,000–8,500 CAG

A George Jones majolica cheese
dish and cover, pattern number
3241, the cobalt blue glazed cover
moulded with flowering cherry
branches, impressed mark, c1880,
9¾in (25cm) high.
£1,800–2,000 S(S)

FIGURES

A Staffordshire figure of Venus in the waves and a putto, decorated in green and brown, c1770, 5in (12.5cm) high.
£800–900 JHo

A Prattware figure of a woman, decorated in orange, brown and green, small chip on base, c1790, 5in (12.5cm) high.
£300–350 DAN

A Staffordshire figure of a boy, decorated in blue, yellow and brown on a green base, c1800, 7in (18cm) high.
£250–300 DAN

A Yorkshire Prattware figure of a lady, with blue spotted dress and orange spotted apron, seated on a green chair, restored, c1800, 4in (10cm) high.
£320–380 P

A Staffordshire figure of a woman leaning against an obelisk, decorated in yellow, blue and red, c1810, 8in (20.5cm) high.
£500–550 JHo

◄ A pair of black basalt figures of Lord Rodney and Admiral Hood, swords missing, incised 'Stephan', late 18th/early 19thC, 12in (30.5cm) high.
£9,000–10,000 WW

These figures were made to commemorate the Battle of the Saints in 1782 and no other example of this pair is recorded. Each is signed 'Stephan', by either Pierre Stephan or his son who was also a modeller. Stephan senior worked for the Derby factory, but because he also did freelance work, and the figures bear no factory marks, the place of origin is not known.

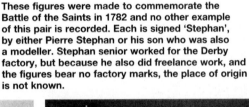

A pair of Staffordshire Walton-type groups, enamelled in overglaze colours, early 19thC, 9½in (24cm) high.
£2,000–2,400 HYD

A pair of Staffordshire pearlware groups entitled 'The Sailor's Farewell' and 'The Sailor's Return', decorated in naturalistic colours, 1815–25, each 9in (23cm) high.
£1,000–1,200 Hal(C)

A Staffordshire pottery figure of a farmer with a goose, decorated in green, yellow and brown, c1815, 9in (23cm) high.
£470–550 DAN

◄ A pearlware figure of a Clan Chief's piper, possibly Rathbone's Pottery, Portobello, decorated in brightly coloured tartan, c1820, 9in (23cm) high.
£2,750–3,250 S

▶ A Staffordshire pottery figure, entitled 'Old Age', decorated in maroon, yellow and blue, c1815, 9in (23cm) high.
£200–240 DAN

Staffordshire Figures

Victorian Staffordshire figures were intended to be viewed on a mantelpiece from the front only, and consequently the backs were neither modelled nor painted; hence the name 'flatbacks' for such pieces. Many figures were simple, but highly decorative, images of children or lovers. However, from the 1840s there was a demand for portraits of famous people, whose features were copied from journals or the covers of popular printed music. In an age when the public rarely knew what famous people truly looked like, potters sometimes reused discontinued moulds to represent more topical individuals. Some figures were even wrongly named, such as a portrait of Benjamin Franklin labelled as George Washington. Some popular figures were produced for many years and often require a close examination to determine whether they are earlier or later examples; this can greatly affect the value. As there are many fake Staffordshire figures on the market it is important to learn the correct 'feel' of genuine pieces, and it is advisable to buy only from reputable dealers and auctioneers.

A Staffordshire figure entitled 'Fire', decorated in yellow, green, brown and red, restored, c1820, 7in (18cm) high.
£380–450 DAN

This piece is entitled 'Fire' because the figure holds in his right hand a magnifying glass with which he is starting a fire.

A Staffordshire figure of a cherub, decorated in blue, yellow and green, c1820, 5in (12.5cm) high.
£220–260 DAN

A Staffordshire group, entitled 'Sunday Best', decorated in maroon, pink, green and yellow, c1820, 6in (15cm) high.
£450–500 JHo

A Staffordshire group entitled 'Faithful Friend', decorated in blue, green and brown, c1820, 7½in (19cm) high.
£450–500 JHo

A Staffordshire spill vase entitled 'Band of Hope', c1850, 14in (35.5cm) high.
£350–420 DN

Ex-Harry Bloomfield collection. The Band of Hope was a temperance organisation, formed in 1847, for children who had taken the pledge.

A pair of Staffordshire figures, each standing beside a chair and holding a parrot, decorated in bright colours, damaged and repaired, mid-19thC, 10¼in (26cm) high.
£400–450 P

A Staffordshire watch stand, in the form of Britannia with a lion, flanked by a musician and companion, decorated in pink, yellow, beige and green, some restoration, c1850, 13¾in (35cm) high.
£1,250–1,400 DN

Ex-Harry Bloomfield collection.

◄ A Staffordshire group of a girl with a goat, decorated in brown, green and pink, c1850, 6in (15cm) high.
£150–175 SER

A Staffordshire figure of a Turk, decorated in green, brown and red, c1840, 7in (18cm) high.
£200–230 DAN

► A Staffordshire watch stand, in the form of a monk and a nun flanking a church door, decorated in enamels and gilt, c1860, 12¾in (32.5cm) high.
£550–650 DN

Ex-Harry Bloomfield collection.

A pair of Staffordshire pepper pots in the form of portly gentlemen, decorated in blue and orange, c1860, 6in (15cm) high.
£230–270 DAN

A Victorian Staffordshire group of the Madonna and Child, on a marbled base, 13½in (34.5cm) high.
£400–500 HYD

A pair of Continental figures of a Tyrolean man and woman, decorated in naturalistic colours, late 19thC, 19¾in (50cm) high.
£350–420 Bea(E)

A Victorian Staffordshire group of a Scottish courting couple, 14¼in (36cm) high.
£100–120 WilP

A pair of Wedgwood figures of Cupid and Psyche, decorated in turquoise enamel, impressed marks, c1860, 7¾in (19.5cm) high.
£700–800 SK(B)

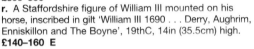
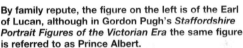

l. A Staffordshire figure of the Earl of Lucan mounted on his horse, 19thC, 12⅛in (32cm) high.
£300–350
r. A Staffordshire figure of William III mounted on his horse, inscribed in gilt 'William III 1690 . . . Derry, Aughrim, Enniskillon and The Boyne', 19thC, 14in (35.5cm) high.
£140–160 E

By family repute, the figure on the left is of the Earl of Lucan, although in Gordon Pugh's *Staffordshire Portrait Figures of the Victorian Era* the same figure is referred to as Prince Albert.

A Continental group of Mr Punch in a boat-shaped vase and his seated dog, possibly by Theodore Deck, decorated in yellow, red, blue and brown, c1880, 15½in (39.5cm) wide.
£300–350 HAM

◀ A Victorian Staffordshire group of a young lady with a greyhound, painted in blue, green and yellow, 9¼in (23.5cm) high.
£200–240 PFK

▶ A coronation souvenir jug in the form of Queen Mary, decorated in yellow, brown, red and gilt, 1911, 6in (15cm) high.
£25–30 IW

A Staffordshire group of a couple embracing beneath an umbrella, decorated in mauve, green, iron-red and blue, 19thC, 6in (15cm) high.
£120–140 GAK

A pair of Austrian busts of a gallant and companion, each wearing fashionable clothes, decorated in polychrome enamels, impressed numerals, late 19thC, 20in (51cm) high.
£1,400–1,650 S

FLATWARE

A Brislington blue and white plate, c1685, 14in (35.5cm) diam.
£2,000–2,200 JHo

Brislington was one of the most important centres of British delftware production, the others being Southwark, Aldgate and Lambeth in London, Norwich, Bristol, Liverpool, Glasgow and Wincanton.

A Bristol delft blue and white plate, decorated with a Chinese scene, 1740, 8¾in (22cm) diam.
£85–95 IW

An English delft blue and white plate, decorated with vases of flowers and a floral border, interspersed with cartouches, 1750, 8¾in (22cm) diam.
£120–140 IW

▶ An English delft dish, decorated with a central panel enclosing a peony in red, blue and green, mid-18thC, 13½in (34.5cm) diam.
£450–500 S(S)

A London delft blue and white plate, depicting King William and Queen Mary, c1690, 9in (23cm) diam.
£3,500–4,000 JHo

An English delft blue and white charger, decorated with a Chinese scene, probably Liverpool, c1750, 12¾in (32.5cm) diam.
£400–500 Bon(C)

A pair of Staffordshire green-glazed creamware dishes, moulded with a central chequered roundel within leaf-scroll cartouches, c1760, 10¼in (26cm) diam.
£1,500–1,800 DN

A Bristol delft plate, polychrome decorated with a bridge and a tree in blue and brown, c1730, 8in (20.5cm) diam.
£200–220 JHo

An English delft plate, probably Bristol, polychrome decorated with a Chinese scene in blue, green and puce, 1750, 9in (23cm) diam.
£150–180 IW

An English delft dish, painted with a Chinese scene in manganese and blue, cracked, c1760, 13in (33cm) diam.
£575–650 S(S)

A salt-glazed stoneware plate, transfer-printed with a pastoral scene in orange, c1765, 7½in (19cm) diam.
£2,200–2,500 JHo

A Liverpool delft blue and white plate, decorated with a Chinese scene, c1765, 8½in (21.5cm) diam.
£160–180 JHo

A Bristol tin-glazed charger, decorated with flowers and leaves in manganese, blue, red and green, 18thC, 13¾in (35cm) diam.
£700–800 Mit

A London delft plate, polychrome decorated with a Chinese lake scene in blue, yellow and brown, c1770, 7½in (19cm) diam.
£340–375 JHo

A white salt-glazed basket-weave plate, damage to rim, 1770, 8in (20.5cm) diam.
£90–100 IW

A English creamware plate, Dutch-decorated with a crucifixion scene within a foliate border in browns, greens and yellow, c1785, 10in (25.5cm) diam.
£400–450 JHo

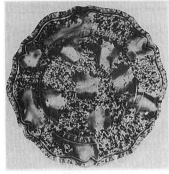

A Whieldon plate, abstractly decorated in yellow and green on a brown speckled ground, 18thC, 9in (23cm) diam.
£140–160 GAK

A Dutch Delft dish, decorated with a fisherman standing by a river and a sailing vessel, in iron-red, blue and green, 18thC, 8¾in (22cm) diam.
£300–350 S(Am)

A Dutch Delft charger, polychrome decorated with stylized flowers in green, blue and manganese, c1735, 12in (30.5cm) diam.
£170–200 HYD

A Dutch Delft plate, polychrome decorated with a bird and foliage in blue, c1760, 8½in (21.5cm) diam.
£125–150 GAK

A creamware plate, Dutch-decorated with a scene of the baptism of Christ in reds, green and brown, c1800, 9½in (24cm) diam.
£180–200 JHo

A pair of Spode New Stone armorial plates, decorated in green, brown, reds and gilt, c1810, 8in (20.5cm) diam.
£500–600 HA

A French faïence plate, decorated with flowers in red, blue, green and yellow, c1850, 9½in (24cm) diam.
£100–110 IW

A set of 12 Wedgwood green-glazed dessert plates, decorated with sunflower heads, c1850, 8½in (22cm) diam.
£380–450 RTo

A Saint Antony's Pottery christening plate, for John Williamson, born 1854, decorated with salmon and copper lustre, 8in (20.5cm) diam.
£180–200 TRM

A George Jones *pâte-sur-pâte* charger, decorated with maidens in a wooded landscape in white slip on a brown ground, signed 'Schenk', impressed mark, 1880, 12in (30.5cm) diam.
£800–1,000 SK

An American Dedham Pottery plate, the rim decorated with swans amid rushes in underglaze blue, glaze damaged, 1896–1906, 8½in (21.5cm) diam.
£200–220 JMW

A majolica bread plate, decorated in green, yellow and mauve, inscribed 'waste not, want not', 1880–90, 12in (30.5cm) diam.
£120–135 CoCo

An Henriot Quimper plate, painted in blue, green, orange and yellow, c1930, 9in (23cm) diam.
£65–75 SER

FLASKS

A Savona maiolica blue and white flask, painted with flowers and foliage, late 17thC, 9½in (24cm) high.
£380–420 S(S)

▶ A Continental brown slipware costrel, 19thC, 7½in (19cm) wide.
£90–100 IW

A costrel is a drinking vessel that is carried on the shoulder, a strap being threaded through the integral loops.

A stoneware gin flask, in the form of a clock, inscribed 'Patent Chronometer', c1840, 7½in (19cm) high.
£220–250 JHo

A Scottish flask, in the form of a potato, painted blue, c1840, 7in (18cm) high.
£180–200 DAN

A Taylor, Tunnicliffe brown stoneware flask, late 19thC, 6in (15cm) high.
£85–100 CoCo

A Scottish brown and cream agate ware flask, 19thC, 5½in (14cm) high.
£85–100 IW

FLOWER BRICKS

A Bristol delft blue and white flower brick, decorated with a boy and his dog, c1740, 5½in (14cm) wide.
£1,400–1,600 JHo

A pair of English delft blue and white flower bricks, probably Liverpool, restored, 1756, 6¼in (16cm) wide.
£900–1,000 IW

An English delft blue and white bulb pot, painted with Chinese scenes, c1760, 5in (12.5cm) wide.
£1,800–2,000 P

FOOTBATHS

A Mason's Ironstone footbath, decorated in underglaze blue and iron-red, 1815–20, 16in (40.5cm) wide.
£1,400–1,600 DN

A Samuel Allcock & Co footbath, transfer-printed in blue with a laburnum pattern, c1840, 19¾in (50cm) wide.
£400–500 Bea(E)

A creamware footbath, decorated with blue borders and a band of flowers and foliage in pink and green, inscribed 'No. 861', 19thC, 20in (51cm) wide.
£600–700 E

GARDEN SEATS

A pair of Copeland & Garrett earthenware garden seats, moulded in relief with panels of butterflies and flowers enamelled in bright colours on a brown ground, the fluted sides picked out in yellow and blue, impressed crown, printed 'COPELAND' and painted pattern number 8338, c1850, 17¾in (45cm) high.
£3,200–3,600 S(NY)

A Victorian Minton's garden seat, decorated with stylized blue flowerheads within a trailing leaf and flower border, 18½in (47cm) high.
£700–800 TRM

A Wedgwood majolica St Louis garden seat, moulded with prunus and stylized chrysanthemums picked out in turquoise, impressed WEDGWOOD and year code for 1864 or 1890, 17½in (44.5cm) high.
£600–700 S(NY)

INKSTANDS

A Savona maiolica inkwell, decorated with a bird, trees and a building in blue, chipped, 17thC, 3in (7.5cm) high.
£3,000–3,300 P

A Wedgwood black basalt inkstand with pots, impressed marks, 19thC, 3¾in (9.5cm) high.
£550–600 SK(B)

A French faïence inkstand, with two lift-out inkwells, a heart-shaped pounce pot, drawer and two integral candle holders, polychrome decorated with Oriental figures, yellow and gilt line borders, restored, late 19thC, 9½in (24cm) wide.
£200–240 WW

JARS

A Deruta maiolica syrup jar, decorated with exotic birds in ochre, blue and puce, early 17thC, 10½in (26.5cm) high.
£800–900 S(S)

A Savona wet drug jar, decorated in blue, inscribed 'Sir: del Ducha', late 17thC, 8in (20.5cm) high.
£700–800 P

A pearlware jar, with blue rim and swirling lines, impressed 'London', restored, c1800, 4½in (11.5cm) high.
£75–90 IW

An earthenware tobacco jar, slip-decorated in brown and cream, South Wales or West Country, 1890, 8in (20.5cm) high.
£80–100 IW

► A Sicilian drug jar, decorated in colours on a blue ground, base missing, 17thC, 11½in (29cm) high.
£550–600 P

► A Wedgwood *rosso antico* potpourri jar and cover, enamelled with tropical birds and floral sprays, impressed mark, 19thC, 12in (30.5cm) high.
£1,000–1,100 SK

JARDINIERES

A Nevers faïence blue and white jardinière, with moulded mask handles, foot restored, late 18thC, 18in (45.5cm) high.
£3,000–3,500 S(NY)

A Minton majolica jardinière, moulded in high relief with stylized pine trees in green and brown on a cobalt blue ground, with ochre rim and turquoise interior, impressed factory marks, c1881, 20½in (52cm) wide.
£600–700 S

A Wedgwood jasper planter, decorated with oval lilac medallions and applied white classical figures on a green ground, impressed mark, late 18th/early 19thC, 17in (43cm) high.
£5,500–6,000 SK(B)

A Minton earthenware jardinière, painted with fish in blue, brown and purple, with stiff-leaf moulded border in olive green and gilt, foot repaired, red printed factory mark, c1888, 15½in (39.5cm) high.
£1,800–2,000 S

A majolica jardinière, applied in high relief with female caryatids alternating with horned masks hung with laurel swags, picked out in bright colours on a turquoise ground, minor restoration, late 19thC, 11¾in (30cm) diam.
£2,000–2,200 P

A majolica planter, the single tier over three planters, decorated with oak branches, leaves and acorns, late 19th/early 20thC, 10½in (26.5cm) high.
£240–270 FBG

JUGS

A Dutch Delft blue and white wine jug, 1695, 8in (20.5cm) high.
£700–780 IW

A stoneware jug, with mottled brown glaze, c1720–30, 7½in (19cm) high.
£350–400 SEA

An English delft puzzle jug, painted with a verse, floral sprays in pale blue, the neck pierced with flowers and petals, the loop handle dotted, probably Liverpool, damaged, c1750, 7¼in (18.5cm) high.
£500–600 Bri

► A creamware jug, painted in coloured enamels with a version of a New Hall porcelain pattern showing two Chinese figures by a fence, with a red border, c1780, 6½in (16.5cm) high.
£300–330 P

A salt-glazed jug, enamelled with flowers in pink, yellow and green, c1760, 3in (7.5cm) high.
£1,000–1,200 JHo

Puzzle Jugs

Puzzle jugs were first produced in medieval times as potters' jokes. The neck is pierced to confuse the drinker, who must obtain the liquor through one of a number of nozzles around the rim that are connected to a hidden tube. All English delftware factories made them, and they are found in various forms. In the mid-to late 18thC decoration with European scenes became common.

A creamware Masonic jug, transfer-printed in magenta, restored, 1795, 7¼in (18.5cm) high.
£250–300 IW

A brown jug, decorated in yellow with an Oriental scene, glaze defect inside, 1810–20, 4½in (11.5cm) high.
£80–100 IW

A Staffordshire clobbered jug, in blue, mauve, brown and green, 1810–30, 5in (12.5cm) high.
£85–100 CoCo

A creamware satirical jug, the neck with a puce rim and inscribed 'Bonaparte Dethron'd April 1st 1814', the body transfer-printed in black and overpainted in colours, early 19thC, 6¼in (16cm) high.
£470–550 MJB

A creamware jug, transfer-printed and coloured with 'Duke Wellington' and 'One of the 71st taking a French Officer prisoner in Portugal 1814', with silver lustre and red vine and grape border, damaged, c1815, 10¼in (26cm) high.
£380–450 TEN

A creamware jug, transfer-printed in black with an eagle perched on a sword and cannon beside a United States flag above the motto 'Peace and Independence', the reverse printed with a woman standing beside two Native Americans and gesturing to portrait medallions including Washington, Raleigh and Columbus, a further vignette below, probably Liverpool, c1815, 9¾in (25cm) high.
£1,750–2,000 S(S)

The prints refer to the American war with England, which concluded with the signing of a treaty at Ghent on Christmas Day, 1814. The two-year war assured American peace and independence, despite international trade still being monitored by the British navy, and Canada remaining a secure part of the British Empire. The English potteries, particularly in the Liverpool region, had been making pieces for American merchants since the signing of the Treaty of Paris in 1783, and following the war they had to produce very pro-American pieces to counter the antipathy towards all things of English manufacture.

A Mason's Ironstone jug and bowl set, decorated with naive flowers and urns in Imari colours, c1825, bowl 12in (30.5cm) diam.
£700–800 HAL

A Daniel O'Connell commemorative creamware jug, transfer-printed in reddish-brown with a profile portrait and encircled with the inscription 'Daniel O'Connell Esqr M.P. for the County of Clare, The Man of the People', and on the reverse 'Rejoice, sons of Erin Rejoice', some damage, c1828, 6in (15cm) high.
£1,000–1,100 P

A hero of the cause of Catholic emancipation, O'Connell stood for election to the County Clare seat against the established landowner and sitting MP Vesey Fitzgerald. O'Connell won, although his religion barred him from taking up his seat in the House.

A John & William Ridgway Japan Flowers stoneware water jug, the body with polychrome flower panels, interspersed with a gadroon border in relief, c1830, 12in (30.5cm) high.
£180–220 BIG

► A Staffordshire jug, moulded and lustre decorated with a sporting scene, with green and puce detail, 19thC, 7½in (19cm) high.
£85–100 GAK

A brown and white salt-glazed stoneware jug, with metal rim, c1840, 11in (28cm) high.
£580–650 OCH

A pink lustre jug, c1840, 5¾in (14.5cm) high.
£100–120 SER

A creamware balustered milk jug, decorated with silver lustre foliate design, 19thC, 6½in (16.5cm) high.
£175–200 GAK

◄ A pink lustre jug, transfer-printed in black with 'North Shields the mouth of River Tyne', c1850, 8½in (21.5cm) high.
£520–580 IS

This jug is attributed to John Carr, North Shields Lowlights Pottery. The factory's kiln can be clearly seen on the lower right-hand side.

A Minton Silenus dark green jug, moulded with figures and vines, impressed '19', moulded 'M', mid-19thC, 11in (28cm) high.
£230–275 Mit

► A Victorian set of four Mason's Ironstone graduated jugs, transfer-printed and overpainted in enamel colours, largest 5¼in (13.5cm) high.
£280–320 PFK

A set of 12 Mason's Ironstone graduated jugs, decorated in the Japan pattern in underglaze blue and iron-red, printed marks, damaged, mid-19thC, tallest 9½in (24cm) high.
£750–825 S(S)

A majolica green and yellow 'corn on the cob' jug, 1880s, 7in (18cm) high.
£100–120 CoCo

A Minton ewer, with mask-moulded spout, decorated in ochre with clover designs on a deep blue ground, incised mark and date cipher for 1871, 9½in (24cm) high.
£120–150 GAK

◄ A Scottish jug, painted with 'Frae Edinburgh' and green and maroon thistles, c1900, 5in (12.5cm) high.
£75–85 FQA

MUGS & TANKARDS

A brown and white salt-glazed hunting mug, probably Mortlake, 18thC, 8in (20.5cm) high.
£675–750 OCH

A creamware mug, commemorating George III's recovery to good health in 1789, the rim lined in green and printed in iron-red, minor damage, 2¾in (7cm) high.
£700–800 SAS

In an effort to counter Whig propaganda, the Tories promoted a campaign advocating 'Health to The King' to underline his role as the legal head of the nation. A service of thanksgiving for the Royal recovery was held at St Paul's on 15th March 1789.

◀ A pearlware mug, transfer-printed in black, c1780, 6in (15cm) high.
£250–300 JHo

A Bacchus mug, decorated with Prattware colours, c1810, 5in (12.5cm) high.
£200–230 DAN

A frog mug, with pink lustre rim and foot, transfer-printed with 'Sailors Farewell', attributed to Anthony Scott, c1840, 5in (12.5cm) high.
£350–400 IS

A blue printed mug, with a portrait of a gentleman taking snuff, his breast pinned with the Garter Star, the reverse with a lady in an elaborate hat and a ruff collar, the underside printed with 'Antiques', some damage, c1830, 4in (10cm) high.
£450–500 SAS

This previously unrecorded mug dates from the time of George IV's death, when the potter's ability to lampoon is well documented. These mugs are perhaps intended to represent George IV as a dandy with Queen Caroline in an absurd hat and outlandish collar.

A pink lustre mug, c1840, 2in (4cm) high.
£55–65 SER

A mug commemorating the Great Exhibition of 1862, transfer-printed in puce, 1862, 3¾in (9.5cm) high.
£70–80 IW

A tankard and cover, with relief figures of mounted huntsmen attacking a den of lions, the cover with raised leaf and berry decoration and a seated lion to the centre, printed crowned N, late 19thC, 10¾in (27.5cm) high.
£400–450 Mit

A mug, commemorating the birth of Ambrose Nosworthy in 1876, decorated in green and gilt, 4in (10cm) high.
£100–120 Ber

PEDESTALS

A Wedgwood majolica Argenta ware 'Corinthian' pedestal base, decorated with neo-classical portrait pendants suspended by ribbons, impressed mark, restored, c1878, 33½in (85cm) high.
£1,500–1,650 SK

A Minton majolica pedestal, naturalistically coloured on a turquoise ground, impressed 'Mintons', shape No. 891, c1880, 37in (94cm) high.
£1,100–1,300 S(NY)

A Minton earthenware pedestal, in four sections, decorated with stylized floral bands on a grey simulated marble ground, impressed marks, shape No. 2179, some damage, c1889, 40½in (103cm) high.
£800–1,000 S

A pair of late Victorian majolica jardinière pedestals, glazed in turquoise, red, green and mustard, 40in (101.5cm) high.
£400–500 DD

PLAQUES

A Dutch Delft blue and white plaque, painted with a cow and two hares in a wooded landscape, early 18thC, 12¼in (31cm) wide.
£650–800 P

A Belleek earthenware wall plaque, painted in black on a white ground, 1863–90, 9½in (24cm) wide.
£700–800 MLa

A Sunderland pink lustre plaque, printed in black with a portrait of William IV, inscribed 'The Only Royal Refermer (sic) since Alfred', c1832, 6¾in (17cm) diam.
£320–380 SAS

A Villeroy & Boch Mettlach plaque, decorated by Schlitt with a Greek soldier playing a lyre to a maiden, in brown and beige on a black ground, signed 'Schlitt', c1898, 15½in (39.5cm) diam.
£600–675 PGA

POT LIDS

'Genuine Russian Bears Grease For Increasing the Growth of Hair', printed in sepia, 19thC, 2¾in (7cm) diam.
£370–450 BBR

'Grand International Buildings of 1851', framed, mid-19thC, 4½in (11.5cm) diam.
£100–120 GAK

'Our Home', No. 241, c1852, 3¾in (9.5cm) diam.
£160–200 SAS

'New York Exhibition 1853', No. 142, damaged, 5¼in (13.5cm) diam.
£200–220 SAS

'Wellington', by F. & R. Pratt, framed, 19thC, 4in (10cm) diam.
£100–120 Hal

'Charing Cross', No. 193, by F. & R. Pratt, c1865, 4in (10cm) diam.
£65–80 BBR

'Queen Victoria and the Prince Consort', No. 152, with matching base, c1868, 4¾in (12cm) diam.
£120–140 SAS

'F M Lord Raglan and General Canrobert, the Allied Generals', by F. & R. Pratt, in an ebonized frame, 19thC, 4½in (11.5cm) diam.
£45–55 Hal

'Dr Johnson', No. 175, framed, 19thC, 6in (15cm) diam.
£65–75 GAK

'Decker's Sulphur Scurf Pomade, D & Co London & Paris', 19thC, 2½in (6.5cm) diam.
£55–65 BBR

'Victoria Areca Nut Tooth Paste', 19thC, 2½in (6.5cm) diam.
£90–110 BBR

'Fortnum & Mason's Mushroom Savoury', 19thC, 3¼in (8.5cm) diam.
£55–65 BBR

Pot Lid Numbers

The numbers in the captions refer to the system used by A. Ball in his reference work *The Price Guide to Pot Lids*, Antique Collectors Club, 1980.

SERVICES

A Wedgwood creamware part dinner service, comprising 30 pieces, decorated in brown and green, impressed marks, some damage, late 18thC.
£1,300–1,500 P

A Miles Mason part tea and coffee service, comprising 35 pieces, printed and enamelled with the Boy in the Door pattern, 1805–10.
£1,400–1,600 Bon(C)

A Spode pearlware part dessert service, comprising 10 pieces, painted in colours with mixed summer flowers, insects and butterflies within a gilt line rim, impressed marks, pattern No. 2648, c1810.
£800–1,000 TEN

◄ A Mason's Ironstone dinner service, comprising 48 pieces, painted in underglaze blue, iron-red, green, pink and gilding, printed and impressed marks, damaged, c1820.
£6,750–7,500 S(S)

A Mason's Ironstone dinner service, comprising 65 pieces, printed and painted with Oriental-style exotic birds among flowers, printed and impressed marks, mid-19thC.
£1,750–2,000 WL

A Copeland Spode Ironstone dinner service, comprising 50 pieces, transfer-printed and hand-painted in Japanese style in blue, red and gilt, printed and impressed marks, 19thC.
£1,150–1,400 BLH

A Real Stone dinner service, comprising 48 pieces, decorated in Imari-style colours, probably Hicks, Meigh & Johnson, Ridgway, c1830.
£2,200–2,500 M

A Victorian ironstone part dinner service, comprising 71 pieces, decorated with an Oriental design in blue, rust and gilt, c1840.
£1,100–1,300 WilP

A majolica part dessert service, comprising 11 pieces, decorated in green, rose, blue and yellow, marked 'GJ', pattern No. 3403, 19thC.
£3,000–3,500 CGC

A Gien faïence dinner service, comprising 126 pieces, brightly painted with flowers, exotic birds and insects, printed marks, some damage, late 19th/early 20thC.
£850–1,000 S(S)

A Wedgwood creamware part dessert service, comprising 26 pieces, decorated with flowers in Chinese *famille rose* palette, mid-19thC.
£700–800 Bea(E)

An Ashworth Real Ironstone dinner service, decorated with pink and rust flowers and gilt foliate scrolls on a blue ground, pattern No. B2349, late 19thC.
£2,800–3,200 B&L

STRAWBERRY SETS

A Victorian Wedgwood majolica strawberry set, the bowl with high relief strawberry leaf decoration, impressed 'Wedgwood BOA' and registration mark for 1869, 8in (20.5cm) wide.
£550–650 Mit

A George Jones majolica strawberry dish, modelled as a lily pad, with sugar-sifting and cream ladles, impressed monogram and registration mark for 1876, 9¾in (25cm) wide.
£850–1,000 P(E)

A George Jones faïence strawberry set, moulded and painted with strawberries and leaves, printed and impressed marks, 1885–90, 14½in (37cm) wide.
£380–450 DN

Items in the Pottery section have been arranged in date order within each sub-section.

TEA & COFFEE POTS

A Staffordshire redware teapot, applied with the Royal coat-of-arms and inscription in white relief, possibly by Thomas Whieldon, c1740, 4in (10cm) wide.
£400–500 P

A German Westerwald stoneware teapot, the body incised with flowers and foliate sprays, restored, 1750–60, 5¼in (13.5) high.
£500–600 S(NY)

A Wedgwood creamware teapot, transfer-printed in red-brown with three ladies playing with a dog, the reverse with classical ruins, 1765–70, 5½in (14cm) high.
£600–675 P

A Staffordshire teapot, with black and green glaze, c1765, 4in ((10cm) high.
£1,000–1,150 JHo

A Leeds creamware teapot, decorated in polychrome enamels with flowers, c1770, 4¾in (12cm) high.
£250–300 Mit

A creamware teapot, Dutch-decorated with a couple by a tree in browns, green and blue, c1785, 5in (12.5cm) high.
£575–650 JHo

A Joseph Holdcroft majolica teapot, modelled as a coconut with a Chinese boy climbing up the side, decorated in bright colours, some damage, c1880, 5¼in (13.5cm) high.
£900–1,100 P

A Scottish teapot, inscribed 'Frae Dunmore', glazed with brown and cream, 1880–1900 5in (12.5cm) high.
£160–175 SAA

A Mintons earthenware teapot, modelled as a fish, painted in pale blue and pink, with a green seaweed handle, moulded diamond registration mark, early 20thC, 7¼in (18.5cm) high.
£950–1,100 S(NY)

TEA CANISTERS

A creamware pierced and double-walled tea canister, cover missing, c1770, 4½in (11.5cm) high.
£1,100–1,250 P

A William Greatbatch Fruit Basket tea canister, moulded and picked out in underglaze green, blue, brown and ochre, cover missing, 1770–82, 4¼in (11cm) high.
£275–325 P

A creamware tea canister, black transfer-printed in Liverpool with a portrait of Minerva and an owl, inscribed 'Let Wisdom Unite Us', the reverse with pigeons, cover missing, c1775, 4½in (11.5cm) high.
£400–450 P

A tea canister, transfer-printed in blue with pheasants, c1790, 4in (10cm) high.
£175–200 IW

A tea canister, transfer-printed in blue, 1795, 3¾in (9.5cm) high.
£125–150 IW

◀ A Prattware tea canister, moulded with two gentlemen, painted in red, green and blue, c1810, 5in (12.5cm) high.
£180–215 JHo

A tea canister, with brown body and inlaid underglaze blue band, early 19thC, 4in (10cm) high.
£125–150 IW

TILES

A tile, decorated in yellow with a lion rampant, 16th/17thC, 6in (15cm) square.
£100–120 BAC

> Miller's is a price GUIDE not a price LIST

A Bristol tile, polychrome decorated in red, blue and grey, c1760, 5¼in (13.5cm) square.
£160–180 JHo

▶ An Henriot Quimper tile, painted in red, blue, yellow and green, c1922, 4½in (11.5cm) square.
£40–45 SER

A set of nine Dutch Delft blue and white tiles, with mainly tavern scenes, 18thC, each 5in (12.5cm) square.
£200–240 Mit

TOBY JUGS & CHARACTER JUGS

A black basalt Toby jug, pipe stem lacking, restored, c1790, 9½in (24cm) high.
£700–800 P

A Prattware Toby jug, painted in blue, yellow, brown and green, c1820, 8in (20.5cm) high.
£800–1,000 DAN

A blue and white Toby jug, in the form of a snuff-taker, 19thC, 10½in (26.5cm) high.
£280–340 CoCo

A Scottish Toby jug, painted in blue, black and yellow and with a red face and a moustache, damaged and restored, early 19thC, 7¾in (19.5cm) high.
£320–380 S

It is thought that this jug was modelled on a local Leith character, possibly a sea-captain.

TUREENS

A Wedgwood creamware soup tureen, with mushroom finial, decorated with chocolate highlights, c1790, 16½in (42cm) wide.
£650–750 SLN

A creamware tureen and cover, in the form of a marrow, early 19thC, 9½in (24cm) wide.
£500–550 S(S)

A Scottish pottery porridge tureen and cover, decorated in grey sand dash with blue rim, possibly Oban, c1890, 6½in (16.5cm) high.
£60–70 JEB

VASES

A London delft blue and white vase, decorated with a Chinese scene, late 17thC, 12in (30.5cm) high.
£2,700–3,000 JHo

A Savona vase and cover, painted in blue with lambrequin motifs and scrolls, the gadroons and knop also shaded in blue, early 18thC, 8¼in (21cm) high.
£1,600–1,800 P

A pair of Dutch Delft vases, with blue Chinese-style alternating panels of figures and flowers, c1760, 9½in (24cm) high.
£750–900 DN

A pair of Nove vases and stands, decorated with scenes of a romantic couple, the reverse with flowers, between scrolling winged griffin-head handles, bases possibly matched, some damage, marked, early 19thC, 23½in (59.5cm) high.
£1,700–2,000 Bon(C)

A Wedgwood Queen's Ware figural vase, decorated by Emile Lessore with landscapes including a shepherd and farmer with animals, supported by two putti, impressed mark, c1872, 11in (28cm) high.
£1,250–1,400 SK

> Miller's is a price GUIDE not a price LIST

▶ A majolica basket vase, moulded with a bird and inset design on a blue ground, with pale blue interior, some damage, c1880, 10in (25.5cm) wide.
£100–120 RBB

A Wedgwood black basalt Portland vase, decorated with figures in white relief, impressed upper case mark, 19thC, 10¾in (27.5cm) high.
£1,400–1,600 P

A Mettlach punchbowl, with Greek-type medallion on one side, Oriental on the other, in red, yellow and blue on a cream ground, c1892, 17¼in (44cm) high.
£800–900 PGA

A Mason's Ironstone vase and cover, transfer-printed in blue and overpainted in red, pink, and green, with dragon handles and dolphin finials, blue painted mark and impressed 'BS', 19thC, 18½in (47cm) high.
£700–850 RBB

A Victorian Ironstone vase, decorated in Imari pattern, with a wavy rim, twin lion mask and ring handles, 17in (43cm) high.
£2,000–2,200 JAd

A Delphine Massier majolica vase, moulded with flowers in red, yellow, blue and green, late 19thC, 11in (28cm) high.
£550–600 MLL

A Royal Bonn vase, decorated with a scene of Aphrodite emerging from the sea, c1900, 23in (58.5cm) high.
£800–900 SK

A Maling Cetem ware three piece garniture, comprising a pair of two-handled vases and a jardinière, all decorated with flowering azaleas and a moon on a black ground, pattern Nos. '9481' and '9480', jardinière with sunburst and castle mark, slight damage, c1913, vases 9½in (24cm) high.
£1,000–1,200 AG

WALL POCKETS

A Staffordshire wall pocket, in green and ochre glaze, c1765, 9in (23cm) high.
£1,500–1,650 JHo

A Wedgwood majolica nautilus shell wall pocket, with insert lid, in brown, yellow and green translucent glazes, c1863, 10in (25.5cm) wide.
£450–550 SK

◀ A pair of Prattware wall pockets, representing Autumn and Winter, moulded with putti drinking from a bottle or carrying a brazier, in green, blue, brown and yellow, probably Scottish, some damage, c1808, 10½in (26.5cm) high.
£550–650 Bon(C)

BLUE & WHITE TRANSFER WARE

A Spode blue and white earthenware tureen and cover, transfer-printed with the Tower pattern, after an engraving of the Bridge of Salaro, cracked, c1800, 11in (28cm) wide.
£100–120 Hal

A blue and white pearlware serving dish, decorated with a child feeding ducks and a dog before a manor house and walled city, early 19thC, 13½in (34.5cm) diam.
£475–525 SK(B)

A Ridgway blue and white serving dish, transfer-printed with the Mosque at Latachia pattern from the Ottoman Empire Series, c1820, 16in (40.5cm) wide.
£450–500 GN

▶ A blue and white serving dish, transfer-printed with St Woolston's, Kildare, from the Picturesque Views series, 1820, 14in (35.5cm) wide.
£340–375 GN

A blue and white chinoiserie transfer-printed cow creamer, one horn re-glued, early 19thC, 8in (20.5cm) wide.
£170–200 EH

A blue and white pearlware bowl, inscribed 'Rum and Water', c1805, 6½in (16.5cm) diam.
£300–350 SCO

An Endsleigh Cottage Devon blue and white transfer-printed plate, from the Acorn and Leaf Border series, 1810–35, 10in (25.5cm) diam.
£150–175 OCH

◀ A Robinson Wood & Brownfield blue and white jug and bowl, transfer-printed with Zoological pattern, 1830, bowl 22in (56cm) diam.
£600–660 GN

A Spode blue and white transfer-printed egg strainer, decorated with Forest Landscape pattern, c1805, 3½in (9cm) diam.
£100–120 SCO

A blue and white plate, transfer-printed by William Adams with Alnwick Castle Northumberland c1820, 10in (25.5cm) diam.
£180–200 OCH

A pair of blue and white side plates, with pierced arcaded edge, transfer-printed with Willow pattern to the centre, early 19thC, 7½in (19cm) diam.
£150–180 Mit

A Spode blue and white plate, transfer-printed with the Italian pattern, 1820–30, 9½in (24cm) diam.
£20–25 OD

A blue and white footbath, transfer-printed with a maid drawing water from a pump and figures in a punt by a river, early 19thC, 16in (40.5cm) wide.
£800–1,000 GAK

A Brameld blue and white transfer-printed plate, decorated with Woodman pattern, early 19thC, 25¼in (64cm) diam.
£575–700 DDM

A blue and white commemorative flask, transfer-printed with 'Her Gracious Majesty Queen Victoria' and stylized foliage, c1837, 6in (15cm) wide.
£800–900 SCO

A Staffordshire blue and white footbath, transfer-printed with Trellis & Plants pattern, c1840, 19½in (49.5cm) wide.
£1,200–1,400 S(S)

A Wedgwood blue and white pearlware footbath, transfer-printed with a Tower of London scene, impressed mark, early 19thC, 19¼in (49cm) wide.
£1,250–1,400 SK(B)

A Staffordshire blue and white milk jug, transfer-printed with a man on a horse in a rural landscape, 19thC, 5½in (14cm) high.
£120–150 CoCo

 ◄ A Staffordshire blue and white soup tureen, cover and stand, transfer-printed in underglaze-blue with floral decoration, marked '2', 19thC, 15½in (39.5cm) wide.
£140–170 PFK

A blue and white transfer-printed cup and saucer, inscribed 'The Ruby Day and Sunday Schools', impressed 'Edwards', 1870, saucer 5¾in (14.5cm) diam
£25–30 OD

A Wedgwood blue and white dinner service, comprising 79 pieces, transfer-printed with Raphael pattern, late 19thC.
£500–600 WBH

WEMYSS

Wemyss Ware was first produced in 1882 when Robert Heron, the owner of the Fife Pottery, brought a group of Bohemian craftsmen to Scotland, one of whom, Karel Nekola, became Heron's master painter. Wemyss Ware quickly assimilated lifelike natural subjects into its decorative range, painted freehand in bold underglaze colours. Designs included the well-known Roses and Cocks and Hens but also every imaginable type of flower, fruit and farmyard animal, and were applied to an extensive range of shapes, including the famous cats and pigs. The striking new wares were initially sold through Thomas Goode's Mayfair china shop.

Karel Nekola died in 1915, and was succeeded by Edwin Sandland. Nekola's son, Joseph, became senior artist in 1928, and the Fife Pottery continued until 1930, when the economic depression forced it to close.

In 1930 the directors of The Bovey Pottery Company, Bovey Tracey, Devon, which had been producing unmarked Wemyss-style wares since about 1916, employed Joseph Nekola with the intention of continuing the Wemyss tradition. Many of the Fife Pottery moulds, and remaining undecorated biscuit pottery were also transferred, as were the rights to the goodwill in the Wemyss name. Changing fashions kept down the level of sales of Wemyss Ware during the 1930s, as the company maintained its traditional style and did not adapt to meet modern needs.

Some confusion is caused by wares marked Plichta or Plichta London England. Jan Plichta was an importer and wholesaler of pottery and glass, who began to purchase Wemyss Ware from The Bovey Pottery in 1939 when supplies of decorative wares from his native Czechoslovakia dried up. It should be noted that not all Plichta-marked wares are Wemyss, as he purchased Wemyss-style wares from other sources.

Distinguishing between wares from the Fife period and the Bovey period can be difficult. Wemyss Ware made at Bovey is less prone to glaze crazing and is generally whiter in appearance than the Fife Pottery products. Some of the pink and lighter green colours used at Fife were rarely used at Bovey, where reds and dark greens predominated. There is less variety in painting style at Bovey.

Joseph Nekola died in 1952, but Wemyss Ware continued to be produced at Bovey until the pottery closed in 1957. Many Wemyss animal moulds were transferred to the Pountney Pottery, Bristol, and were produced with printed decoration, while other moulds were acquired by potteries in Devon. **Christopher Spencer**

A Wemyss white pig, c1895, 6½in (16.5cm) long.
£350–380 RdeR

A Wemyss pig, painted with Flowering Clover pattern in pink and green, the snout, trotters and tail tinged in pink, early 20thC, 11½in (29cm) long.
£1,350–1,600 Bea(E)

A Wemyss pig, painted with Shamrocks pattern in green and ochre, the face and trotters tinged in pink, marked 'Wemyss' in green, 1900–30, 6¼in (16cm) long.
£400–450 P

A Wemyss pig, painted with Flowering Clover pattern in pink and green, early 20thC, 18in (45.5cm) long.
£1,800–2,000 BG

A Wemyss black and white pig, with pink ears and toes, ears and tail restored, painted mark in black, c1920, 18½in (47cm) long.
£900–1,100 DN

A Wemyss Bovey Tracy pig, painted with Shamrock pattern in green, marked 'Wemyss Made in England' in green, 1930–36, 17¾in (45cm) long.
£1,300–1,500 P

Further Reading

Miller's Ceramics Buyer's Guide, Miller's Publications, 2000

A Wemyss Gallé-style cat, restored, c1900, 13in (33cm) high.
£6,000–7,000 S

A Wemyss green-glazed cat, with yellow and green glass eyes, impressed 'Wemyss Ware R.H. & S.', c1900, 13in (33cm) high.
£3,500–3,850 S

A Wemyss black-glazed cat, with green glass eyes, some restoration, painted 'Wemyss' in black, early 20thC, 13in (33cm) high.
£6,500–7,200 S

A Wemyss Plichta cat, painted with Thistle pattern in green and pink, picked out in black, 1940–50, 5¼in (13.5cm) high.
£280–320 SAA

A Wemyss basket, painted with Raspberry pattern, impressed mark, c1890, 8in (20.5cm) wide.
£675–750 Fai

A Wemyss button, painted with Violets pattern, in purple with a green scalloped border, impressed 'Wemyss', early 20thC, 1¼in (3cm) diam.
£650–800 S

A Wemyss covered jar, painted with Plum pattern, in purple, blue and green, lid damaged, impressed mark, retailer's stamp 'T. Goode', c1910, 6¼in (16cm) high.
£60–70 PFK

◄ A Wemyss vessel with two handles, painted with Strawberry pattern in red and green, impressed mark, c1900, 6in (15cm) diam.
£140–170 TRM

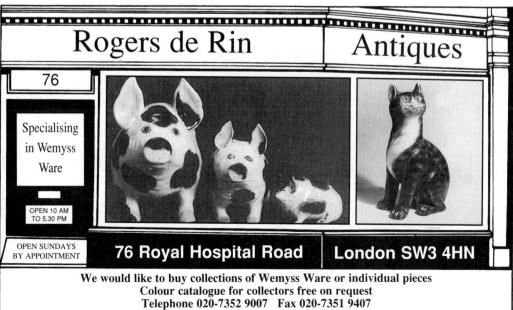

A Wemyss match striker, painted with Fishing Vessels (Fifies) pattern in brown, yellow and green, c1900, 5in (12.5cm) wide.
£600–700 RdeR

A Wemyss mug, by Edwin Sandland, painted with Iris pattern in green, pink, mauve and yellow, unmarked, c1910, 5½in (14cm) high.
£180–200 Fai

A Wemyss mug, painted with Roses pattern in pink, blue, green and yellow on a multi-coloured ground, 1920–30, 7in (18cm) high.
£165–185 Fai

A Wemyss Gordon plate, painted with Raspberry pattern in green and red, c1890, 8in (20.5cm) diam.
£250–300 RdeR

A Wemyss plate, painted with Cock pattern in brown, green, and red, with green rim and and inscribed 'Bon Jour', c1900, 4¼in (11cm) diam.
£130–150 Fai

A Wemyss plate, painted with Dog Roses pattern in green, black and pink, 1900–20, 5in (12.5cm) diam.
£160–200 RdeR

A Wemyss 'Gypsy' pot, by Karel Nekola, painted with Cabbage Roses pattern in pink and green on a green washed ground, on three brown-glazed feet, restored, signed, 'Wemyss' script mark in yellow, 1915, 10½in (26.5cm) diam.
£2,200–2,500 S

This piece is dated 1915, the year of Karel Nekola's death.

A Wemyss Bovey Tracy teapot, decorated with Cherries pattern in green and red, the handle, cover and spout picked out in green, 1930–40, 6½in (16.5cm) high.
£225–250 Fai

A Wemyss beaker vase, painted with Honeysuckle pattern in red and green, impressed 'R H & S Wemyss Ware', c1895, 6in (15cm) high.
£370–400 P

A Wemyss tray, painted with Roses pattern, c1900, 10in (25.5cm) wide.
£300–340 RdeR

A Wemyss Coombe tray, painted with Cock and Hens pattern in black, green and red, c1900, 10in (25.5cm) wide.
£350–400 RdeR

▶ A Wemyss fan-shaped vase, with two flowerhead handles, decorated with a cockerel and a fly, puce painted mark, early 20thC, 15in (38cm) high.
£1,200–1,400 JBe

Porcelain

ANIMALS & BIRDS

A pair of Samuel Alcock models of seated spaniels, each picked out in brown and black, on yellow glazed bases, each impressed '121', 1830–40, 5¼in (13.5cm) high.
£750–900 DN

A Derby model of a pug, decorated in brown, the base picked out in turquoise, green and gilt, c1780, 2½in (6.5cm) high.
£450–520 DAN

A Meissen model of a bison, minor restoration, crossed swords in underglaze blue, c1750, 5in (12.5cm) wide.
£1,100–1,200 S

A pair of Bow models of white pug dogs, some damage, c1755, 5in (12.5cm) wide.
£2,000–2,400 SWO

A Derby model of a ram, the white body with red markings, the green-glazed base applied with coloured flowers, marked in red, 1785–90, 5½in (14cm) wide.
£900–1,000 P

A Derby duck sauce boat, the feet and bill picked out in orange and black, crown, crossed batons and 'D' mark in red, c1815, 4¼in (11cm) wide.
£400–450 P

A Meissen partridge tureen, naturalistically coloured, cover restored, crossed swords in underglaze blue, c1750, 6in (15cm) wide.
£900–1,100 S

◄ A Marcolini Meissen swan box and cover, the plumage picked out in bright gold, crossed swords, star mark and impressed numeral, c1810, 5¼in (13.5cm) wide.
£750–825 P

A Chelsea quail tureen, picked out in puce, yellow, brown and iron-red on a yellow ground, restored, red anchor mark, 1755–58, 5½in (14cm) wide.
£2,000–2,200 DN

A pair of Derby models of sheep, the white bodies with red markings, on pale green bases, c1790, 3in (7.5cm) high.
£500–600 DMa

Items in the Porcelain section have been arranged in factory order, with non-specific pieces appearing at the end of each sub-section.

A Longton Hall model of a sheep, the white body with brown and cream markings, the face picked out in red and black, 1752–56, 3¼in (8.5cm) high.
£950–1,100 P

Ex-Bernard Watney collection. Bernard Watney was one of the foremost collectors and researchers of early English porcelain, and the recent auction of his extensive collection was arguably the most significant porcelain sale in London for decades. Many enthusiasts were keen to acquire pieces from this important source and as a result prices of some of the common pieces commanded a premium.

A Meissen model of a lobster, decorated in naturalistic colours, underglaze crossed swords mark, late 19thC, 9in (23cm) long.
£3,500–4,000 DORO

A Meissen model of a peacock, crossed swords in underglaze blue, incised No. '227', minor restoration, 9in (23cm) wide.
£1,600–1,750 S

A Meissen model of a polar bear, underglaze and impressed marks, early 20thC, 4¼in (11cm) high.
£140–160 DORO

A Nymphenburg model of a parrot, with green plumage, initialled 'RB 1929', impressed mark and incised number, 11¼in (28.5cm) high.
£700–850 TEN

A Plymouth model of a sheep, c1768, 2in (5cm) high.
£750–900 DMa

A St Cloud silver-mounted bonbonnière, modelled as a bird with brightly coloured plumage, the interior painted with flowers, c1740, replacement cover c1750, 3in (7.5cm) wide.
£2,300–2,750 S

A pair of Staffordshire models of bulls, each picked out in iron-red, black, puce and gilt, horns and ears chipped, 1830–40, 2¾in (7cm) high.
£340–400 DN

A pair of Staffordshire models of poodles, 1840–50, 4¼in (11cm) high.
£150–180 OD

A pair of Staffordshire models of begging poodles, c1840, 4¼in (11cm) high.
£850–1,000 DAN

LOCATE THE SOURCE
The source of each illustration in Miller's can be found by checking the code letters below each caption with the Key to Illustrations, pages 789–795.

A Staffordshire model of a poodle, on a blue base, c1840, 3in (7.5cm) wide.
£160–200 DAN

A German Meissen-style figure, entitled 'The Tailor on a Goat', slight damage, restored, underglaze blue crossed swords mark to base, c1870, 9¼in (23.5cm) high.
£650–800 CAG

A Vienna model of an English show-jumper, brightly coloured, underglaze blue marks, c1930, 8¼in (21cm) high.
£750–900 DORO

BASKETS

A Belleek Henshaw shape basket, First Period, c1862, 4¼in (11cm) high.
£1,800–2,000 DeA

A Belleek three-strand oval basket, First Period, c1862, 12in (30.5cm) wide.
£900–1,000 DeA

A pair of Berlin reticulated baskets, each painted in the centre with Watteau-style musicians and lovers in a landscape, underglaze blue sceptre marks, incised and impressed numerals, c1790, 9½in (24cm) wide.
£1,800–2,000 S(NY)

A Chelsea basket, with green stem handles, the interior painted with damsons on a branch, small repair, brown anchor mark, c1755, 4in (10cm) wide.
£450–550 P

A pair of Derby yellow-ground baskets, the exterior with basket-weave moulding, the interior painted with colourful flower sprays, restored, 1760–65, 8in (20.5cm) wide.
£1,250–1,400 P

A Du Paquier Meissen-style two-handled basket, the interior painted with trailing sprays of Oriental flowers, the handles terminating in male and female masks, c1740, 10in (25.5cm) wide.
£1,500–1,800 S(NY)

Du Paquier (1718–44)

Europe's second porcelain factory was founded in Vienna by Claudius du Paquier after he had bribed a Meissen decorator, Christoph Hunger, to teach him the formula for hard-paste porcelain. When it became obvious that Hunger did not know as much as he pretended, du Paquier offered an even larger inducement to the Meissen kilnmaster, Samuel Stölzel, and the factory made its first successful hard-paste porcelain in 1719. However, frustrated by his failure to pay him, Stölzel soon returned to Meissen with du Paquier's best painter, Johann Gregor, who went on to develop the exquisite decorations and palette that were to make Meissen famous. In time, du Paquier was to lose the secret as easily as he had gained it. His daughter fell in love with Joseph Ringler, one of his painters, whom she helped to obtain the formula, which he in turn took on to Höchst, Frankenthal, Ludwigsburg and Ellwangen.

A Meissen basket, the interior decorated with brightly coloured animals and insects, the exterior moulded with basketweave, underglaze blue crossed swords mark, c1740, 10¼in (26cm) wide.
£1,000–1,200 S(NY)

BOWLS

A Berlin *sucrier* and cover, with a flower finial, painted in puce with Roman landscapes on a bright green ground, sceptre mark, incised, early 19thC, 3½in (9cm) wide.
£1,200–1,400 P

A Caughley bowl, printed in underglaze blue with the Fisherman pattern, impressed 'Salopian' and blue 'S', c1775, 10in (25.5cm) wide.
£320–385 DD

A Coalport jug and bowl set, decorated with floral sprays and sprigs within gilt borders, c1860, bowl 10in (25.5cm) diam.
£160–180 Hal

Items in the Porcelain section have been arranged in factory order, with non-specific pieces appearing at the end of each sub-section.

A Davenport miniature guglet and basin, painted in coloured enamels on a blue ground, c1820, guglet 2in (5cm) high.
£600–700 DN

A guglet is a form of water bottle, used with a small basin for minor ablutions.

A Du Paquier bowl, painted in brown with a battle scene, c1730–40, 15¼in (38.5cm) diam.
£3,000–3,500 DORO

A Meissen slop bowl, each side painted in the style of C. F. Herold with a scene of merchants and their wares by a quayside, underglaze blue crossed swords mark, impressed numeral, 1740–45, 7in (18cm) diam.
£1,300–1,500 S

A Sèvres footed bowl, printed marks and incised letters and numerals, c1915, 18in (45.5cm) diam.
£3,300–3,650 S(NY)

A Sèvres bowl, decorated in pink and green, painter's and gilder's marks, dated '1777', 9in (23cm) diam.
£2,500–2,750 S(NY)

A Vienna covered bowl, decorated in naturalistic colours with a portrait of a lady, with a mauve and white floral border, c1900, 5in (12.5cm) diam.
£150–175 DSG

BUILDINGS

A Goss model of Huer's House, Newquay, Cornwall, 1910–20, 3in (7.5cm) wide.
£175–200 MGC

A Staffordshire box and cover, enamelled and gilt, 1830–40, 4¼in (11cm) high.
£340–400 DN

Ex-Rev Harry Bloomfield collection.

A Goss model of Sulgrave Manor, 1910–30, 5in (12.5cm) wide.
£1,000–1,200 G&CC

The Goss factory first introduced its models of cottages in 1893, and soon extended to a range of 42 historic buildings. Sulgrave Manor is very rarely found in perfect condition, and substandard examples are worth less than half this price range.

BUSTS

A parian bust of Admiral Lord Nelson, possibly Copeland, marked 'Josh. Pitts, Sc., London, 1853', 9½in (24cm) high.
£750–900 MCA

▶ A Copeland parian bust of Princess Alexandra, by F. M. Miller, for the Crystal Palace Art Union, early version with earrings, 1863, 12in (30.5cm) high.
£200–240 Bri

A Copeland parian bust, entitled 'Veiled Bride', by Raphael Monti, on a socle base impressed 'Crystal Palace Art Union', impressed factory marks, date and artist's signature, c1861, 14½in (37cm) high.
£3,000–3,300 S

A Copeland parian bust of Clytie, c1870, 13in (33cm) high.
£500–550 JAK

A Copeland parian bust of Ophelia, by W. Calder Marshall, c1860, 11in (28cm) high.
£425–475 JAK

A Copeland parian bust, entitled 'Hop Queen', c1875, 14in (35.5cm) high.
£600–700 JAK

▶ A Minton parian bust of Jenny Lind, by Samuel Joseph, c1847, 14in (35.5cm) high.
£1,000–1,150 JAK

A Derby bust of George IV, wearing a jacket with gilded Garter star, wrapped in a red shroud, on a reeded column with gilded bands, repaired, crown, crossed batons, 'D' mark and '53' in red, c1820, 4½in (11.5cm) high.
£900–1,100 P

◀ A Ridgway Bates & Co parian bust of Handel, dated and marked 'B', 1859, 10½in (26.5cm) high.
£160–200 OD

A Robinson & Leadbeater parian bust of Beethoven, wearing a green jacket, the details picked out in gilding, raised on a socle, impressed mark, late 19thC, 17¾in (45cm) high.
£700–800 S(S)

CANDLESTICKS & CHAMBERSTICKS

A Bow chamber candlestick, modelled as two buntings perched on a flower-encrusted tree stump, brightly decorated in coloured enamels, restored, c1764, 9¼in (23.5cm) high.
£600–700 DN

A Brown-Westhead Moore chamberstick, the white ground with gilt and floral strapping, registration marks for 1870, 1¾in (4.5cm) high.
£275–325 DIA

A pair of Derby candlesticks, each in the form of two lambs beneath a flower encrusted tree stump, decorated in coloured enamels, some damage, c1758, 8¼in (21cm) high.
£900–1,100 DN

A pair of Derby Cupid and Flora candelabra, each clad with drapery and a garland of pink and green flowers, c1775, 10¾in (27.5cm) high.
£3,000–3,500 S

◄ A pair of Derby candlesticks, each in the form of a putto supporting a candle nozzle, picked out in gold and green, c1770, 6¼in (16cm) high.
£400–500 P

A Spode chamberstick, pattern No. 1166, decorated with flowers on a dark blue and gilt ground, c1820, 1¾in (4.5cm) high.
£750–850 DIA

CENTREPIECES

A Belleek centrepiece, First Period, 1863–90, 11¾in (30cm) high.
£700–800 MLa

It is unusual to find such a piece from the First Period.

A Copeland centrepiece, with a pierced and gilded basket painted with landscape ovals supported by a parian ware group of two putti allegorical of Summer and Autumn, printed mark, late 19thC, 18¼in (46.5cm) high.
£2,000–2,200 P

A Derby centrepiece, modelled as a boy wearing a turquoise jacket holding a scallop shell on his head, surrounded by six scallop shells, all painted with coloured enamels with gilded details, restored, c1765, 9½in (24cm) high.
£800–1,000 WW

► A Royal Vienna Turn centrepiece, gilt decorated with a maiden and two cherubs, c1900, 15in (38cm) wide.
£800–1,000 ANO

A Meissen centrepiece, the pierced basket encrusted and painted in turquoise and pink with flowers, supported on a stem modelled with a gentleman and his female companion, c1880, 19in (48.5cm) high.
£1,600–1,800 S

CLOCKS

A Berlin mantel clock, with panels enclosing blossoms and foliage in pink, red, green and white, surmounted by a putto, 19thC, 27in (68.5cm) high.
£4,500–5,000 BB(L)

A Berlin clock and stand, with gilt-metal frame and numerals, one side applied with a putto, underglaze blue sceptre mark, impressed and incised number, c1900, 17¼in (44cm) high.
£1,400–1,700 S

A Minton *pâte-sur-pâte* clock case, by L. M. Solon, the eleven panels with white figures allegorical of time on a brown ground, signed, c1880, 21¾in (55.5cm) high.
£9,000–11,000 S

A Meissen mythological clock, modelled with naturalistically coloured figures of Prometheus, Hercules, Jupiter and a putto, crossed swords and dot mark, 1763–74, 28in (71cm) high.
£4,250–4,750 P

◀ A Paris clock, painted in pink, yellow and green with sprigs of flowers, 19thC, 25¼in (64cm) wide.
£2,200–2,500 S(Am)

▶ A Sèvres bisque clock garniture, with ormolu mounts, applied overall with cherubs and classical figures, 19thC, 24⅛in (62cm) high.
£4,500–5,500 AH

A Bow polychrome teapot, decorated in iron-red and manganese with Chinese figures, c1765, 5¼in (13.5cm) high.
£500–600 Mit

A Philip Christian & Co teapot, with blue Chinese-style borders, restored, 1765–70, 5¾in (14.5cm) high.
£350–420 P

Ex-Bernard Watney collection.

A Derby coffee pot and domed cover, painted with insects and flowers, crack to body, 1758–60, 9in (23cm) high.
£1,500–1,650 S(S)

A Du Paquier coffee pot, painted on each side with figures among classical ruins, cover missing, c1735, 7½in (19cm) high.
£3,500–4,000 S(NY)

A Lowestoft teapot, painted on each side in underglaze blue with a Chinese landscape, c1780, 6in (15cm) high.
£750–900 S

A Meissen teapot, the two panels with scenes of merchants, crossed swords and 'KPM' marks in blue and gilt numerals, restored, 1725–30, 5in (12.5cm) high.
£3,500–4,200 P

A Meissen teapot, moulded with sprays of trailing vines highlighted in mauve and green enamels and gilt, underglaze blue crossed swords mark, mid-18thC, 4½in (11.5cm) high.
£900–1,000 BB(S)

A New Hall coffee pot, painted with a pale apricot band above flower sprays, some damage, 1782–87, 10¼in (26cm) high.
£320–380 P

A New Hall teapot and stand, painted in underglaze blue with a band of floral swags, restored, 1782–87, 7in (18cm) high.
£700–800 P

A New Hall coffee pot, printed and painted with the Window pattern, c1800, 10¼in (26cm) high.
£440–480 S(S)

A Sèvres teapot, with painted floral panels on a turquoise ground, crossed 'L' mark, 18thC, decoration 19thC, 4¾in (12cm) high.
£400–450 P

A William Lowe teapot, commemorating Queen Victoria's Diamond Jubilee, the yellow ground printed in sepia and enamelled in colours, 1897, 6½in (16.5cm) high.
£250–300 SAS

COFFEE & TEA SERVICES

A Belleek Tridacna cabaret set, comprising 12 pieces, with pink washed border, Second Period, 1891–1926, tray 15¾in (40cm) wide.
£750–900 HOK

A Belleek part cabaret set and tray, comprising 10 pieces, shell and coral moulded, the rim and handles painted pale green, Second Period, 1891–1926, tray 16in (40.5cm) wide.
£700–800 DA

A Royal Crown Derby cabaret set, comprising 12 pieces, with blue trellis and scroll borders hung with floral swags, printed mark, date code for 1897, tray 18½in (47cm) wide.
£900–1,100 TEN

A Coalport tea service, comprising 30 pieces, each with gilt fruiting vine pattern, puce printed mark, c1820.
£230–275 Mit

A Grainger tea service, by John Stinton, comprising 16 pieces, painted in naturalistic colours with cattle in a landscape, dated '1902'.
£1,600–1,800 P

While a great many tea and coffee services were painted by Harry Stinton, it is very rare to find small cups and saucers painted by his father, John.

A Meissen part tea service, comprising 13 pieces, painted with *deutsche Blumen* within iron-red rim bands, some damage, crossed swords marks in blue, late 18thC.
£600–700 DN(H)

▶ A Sèvres coffee service, comprising 14 pieces, decorated in gold with stylized leaf motifs on a dark blue ground, red printed marks, c1813.
£1,300–1,500 WW

Vienna 1744–1864

Du Paquier's factory in Vienna was run by the Austrian state from 1744–84. It continued to produce many of Du Paquier's shapes and patterns and introduced new rococo table wares in the manner of Meissen, many of them decorated by some of the best enamellers of the day. The most important products during the State period were figures, especially those by Johann Niedermayer. By 1784 the factory was in such serious financial difficulty that it was unsaleable. Konrad Sorgel von Sorgenthal was appointed director and he abandoned the rococo style in favour of refined neo-classicism, especially in the Sèvres style with solid coloured grounds and sumptuous gilt scrollwork. The factory became particularly famous for its *tête-à-tête* services and solitaires. Although Sorgenthal died in 1805, the factory continued to use and develop his innovations until its closure in 1864.

A Spode part tea and coffee set, comprising 29 pieces, decorated with Chinese landscapes and flowers, pattern number 488, early 19thC.
£1,100–1,200 G(B)

A Vienna coffee service, comprising 10 pieces, decorated in bright colours with flowers and butterflies, c1785.
£1,200–1,400 DORO

CRUETS

A Belleek churn cruet, the handle and rims moulded as logs and tied with pink rope, all picked out in pink, Second Period mark in black, 1891–1920, 5¼in (13.5cm) high.
£500–600 P

A Bow shell-shaped triple salt, picked out in brightly coloured enamels, the interiors painted with sprays of flowers and leaves, c1762, 4½in (11.5cm) high.
£600–700 DN

A Derby table salt, painted in blue with flower sprigs, handles missing, c1765, 2in (5cm) diam.
£600–675 P

Ex-Bernard Watney Collection.

CUPS

A Caughley teacup and saucer, decorated with an undulating gold line and a pale turquoise ground, the recesses with miniature female heads in colours on a brown ground, 1780–90, cup 2¼in (5.5cm) high.
£630–700 P

A Coalport trio, decorated with pink and blue flowers in cartouches on a deep blue ground and embellished with gilt, c1820, saucer 6in (15cm) diam.
£220–250 HA

A Copeland & Garrett trio, each piece painted with named river landscapes, on a turquoise ground, printed marks and pattern number, c1840, saucer 4in (10cm) diam.
£250–300 S(S)

A Nantgarw-style cabinet cup and saucer, each painted with panels of flowers within gold reserves on a decorated cream band, early 19thC, saucer 5in (12.5cm) diam.
£230–250 Bea(E)

A 'Sèvres' coffee can and saucer, the can painted in coloured enamels with portraits within gilt and jewelled panels on a *bleu céleste* ground, the saucer with flowers and musical trophies, c1880, saucer 4in (10cm) diam.
£850–1,000 DN

A Derby coffee cup, painted in *famille rose* style with Chinese figures, 1765–70, 2½in (6.5cm) high.
£380–420 P

Ex-Bernard Watney collection.

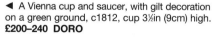

A Spode 4 trio, transfer-printed in black within gilt borders, c1810, saucer 6in (15cm) diam.
£180–220 DAN

◀ A Vienna cup and saucer, with gilt decoration on a green ground, c1812, cup 3½in (9cm) high.
£200–240 DORO

▶ A Minton teacup and saucer, each painted with a landscape panel within a gilt border, c1800.
£100–120 S(S)

DESSERT & DINNER SERVICES

An Aynsley part dessert service, painted by R. J. Keeling, comprising 13 pieces, decorated with titled landscape scenes within gilt rims on a cobalt blue ground, marked, c1900.
£1,800–2,200 S

A Brown, Westhead & Moore part dessert service, comprising 14 pieces, painted with a landscape within a blue-ground border with gilt Greek key details, c1870.
£1,700–1,850 S(S)

A Berlin dinner service, comprising 111 pieces, the central flowers within borders of floral sprigs and insects, cancelled sceptre mark in underglaze blue, late 19th/early 20thC.
£5,000–5,500 S(NY)

A Thomas Barlow part dessert service, comprising 15 pieces, painted in coloured enamels with a spray of flowers and leaves, the turquoise ground border pierced with leaf-shaped panels and picked out in gilt, impressed mark and number, c1865.
£450–550 DN

A Coalport dessert service, comprising 17 pieces, each piece decorated with a hand-painted scene of exotic birds in a landscape within a blue and gilt border, printed, impressed and painted marks, 1903–4.
£1,400–1,600 P

A Coalport part dessert service, comprising 23 pieces, decorated with classical figures in bronze tones heightened by gilding, 1805–10.
£6,500–7,200 S(NY)

A porcelain dessert service, possibly Coalport, comprising 15 pieces, each piece painted in the centre with a flower within a gilt-edged rim and apple-green-ground gilt foliate scroll border, c1825.
£1,600–1,800 S(NY)

◄ A Copeland Sèvres-style dessert service, comprising 22 pieces, the centre initialled 'AOV' in gilt within pink rosebud borders, the dark blue rim with panels of pink roses, printed marks, 1850–60.
£1,500–1,650 P

A Davenport part dessert service, comprising 16 pieces, the centres painted with lakeland scenes within gilt scroll borders on a grey ground, printed and impressed marks, c1860.
£1,200–1,400 S

A Copeland dessert service, comprising 17 pieces, decorated in Imari style, impressed marks for 1897.
£700–850 Mit

A Davenport dessert service, comprising 39 pieces, painted with a central bouquet of flowers within gilt foliate scroll and turquoise pierced border, printed marks, c1870.
£1,300–1,500 P(E)

A Dresden dessert service, comprising 12 pieces, painted with bouquets of brightly coloured flowers within gilt and puce pierced borders, blue cross and script mark and impressed numerals, late 19thC.
£1,200–1,500 P(E)

An M. Redon, Limoges, dessert service, comprising 28 pieces, painted with wild flowers on a blush ivory ground, the details picked out in gilt, c1900.
£900–1,100 S(S)

A Minton dessert service, comprising seven pieces, each piece painted with a brightly coloured bird within a broad turquoise band and acid-etched gilt border, c1870.
£500–600 S(S)

A Naples part table service, comprising 11 soup plates and 21 dinner plates, painted with a circle of flowers surrounded by single flowers, the rim with a band of flower swags, damaged and restored, 'N' marks in underglaze blue, c1790.
£3,200–3,500 S

A New Hall dessert service, comprising 18 pieces, the borders with flowersprays on a blue ground gilded with fruiting vine, the centre painted with a flowerspray, 1825–30.
£2,000–2,200 P

Items in the Porcelain section have been arranged in factory order, with non-specific pieces appearing at the end of each sub-section.

► A Paris Sèvres-style part dinner service, comprising 68 pieces, incised numerals and pseudo-Sèvres marks in blue, late 19thC.
£2,300–2,750 S

A Stone, Coquerel et Le Gros, Paris, part dinner service, comprising eight pieces, printed in brown monochrome with a landscape or townscape within a border of gilt bands and printed grapevines, c1815.
£2,500–2,750 S(NY)

A Sèvres-style part dinner service, comprising 47 pieces, painted with birds in a landscape within a border set with vignettes on a *bleu céleste* ground, some damage and repair, pseudo Sèvres marks in underglaze blue, mid-19thC.
£6,750–7,500 S

► A Staffordshire porcelain dessert service, comprising 16 pieces, painted in iron-red, blue, green and gilt with a vase of flowers, the border with a cornucopia of flowers and leaves, c1830.
£800–900 DN

DISHES

A pair of Bow moulded scallop dishes, painted in colours with floral sprays, some damage, c1760, 5¼in (13.5cm) wide.
£575–650 P

A Chelsea cabbage leaf-shaped dish, painted in coloured enamels with a spray of flowers and leaves, the veining picked out in puce, within a yellow and green banded border, red anchor mark, c1755, 9½in (24cm) high.
£600–700 DN

A Spode dish, painted in coloured enamels with flowers and leaves, the blue-ground border decorated with flowerheads, leaf scrolls and lanterns in orange and gilt, script mark and pattern number, c1820, 11in (28cm) wide.
£450–550 DN

A Caughley blue and white dish, painted with Chinese pagodas on islands, c1785, 11in (28cm) wide.
£160–200 DN(H)

A pair of Chelsea-Derby dishes, painted in colours with fruit and insects, with blue enamelled borders, anchor and 'D' marks in gold, c1770–80, 11½in (29cm) wide.
£1,100–1,250 P

In 1770, the owners of the Derby factory, John Heath and William Duesbury, bought the Chelsea works, which had closed the previous year. The two concerns operated together until the factory was finally closed in 1784.

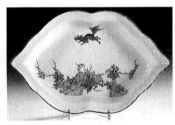

A Meissen dish, painted with the Flying Fox pattern in browns and blues, with a brown rim line, crossed swords in underglaze blue, c1735, 8in (20.5cm) wide.
£1,700–1,850 S

A Vienna dish, painted in colours with flowersprays and leaves, c1767, 17¾in (45cm) wide.
£425–475 DORO

A pair of Chelsea oval dishes, painted in polychrome with sprays of flowers, with apple-green rims and edged in puce, red anchor period, c1755, 8½in (21.5cm) wide.
£700–850 HYD

A Stevenson & Hancock dish, decorated in colours with a Japanese pattern, marked in iron-red with crossed batons, crown and 'D' and the letters 'S. H.', late 19thC, 11in (28cm) wide.
£160–200 GAK

A Ridgway footed dish, richly gilded and painted with colourful flowers, c1850, 16in (40.5cm) wide.
£500–550 JAK

A Sèvres platter, painted with the Arrival of Louis XIV at Dunkerque within a pink-ground border decorated with bands of 'jewelling' within a gilt rim, mid-19thC, 13¼in (33.5cm) wide.
£1,650–1,800 S(NY)

FIGURES

An Ansbach figure of Pierrot, by Carl Gottlob Laut and Johann Friedrich Scherber, wearing a gilt-edged white costume and yellow shoes with blue ribbons, his face painted in flesh tones, some chips, impressed shield mark, c1765, 4¾in (12cm) high.
£11,000–12,000 S

The Ansbach manufactory produced only six figures from the Italian Comedy.

A Bow figure of Harlequin, painted in blue, pink and green, c1755, 5in (12.5cm) high.
£1,200–1,500 DMa

A Copeland parian group of Paul and Virginia, by C. Cumberworth, c1860, 12in (30.5cm) high.
£800–900 JAK

A Copeland parian figure, entitled 'The Pets', by F. Miller, c1875, 17in (43cm) high.
£675–750 JAK

A Copeland parian figure, entitled 'Go To Sleep', by J. Durham, c1865, 18in (45.5cm) high.
£1,300–1,450 JAK

◄ A pair of Derby figures of a gallant and his companion, decorated in bright colours, 1760–65, 11in (28cm) high.
£2,300–2,600 HA

A set of four Bow figures of putti, emblematic of the Seasons, each decorated in coloured enamels, the bases picked out in blue, puce and gilt, some damage, c1765, 5¾in (14.5cm) high.
£800–950 DN

A pair of Chelsea sweetmeat vases, in the form of a gentleman and a lady each holding an oval basket, decorated in coloured enamels and gilt, some restoration, c1765, 8in (20.5cm) high.
£2,400–2,750 DN

A Fürstenberg figure of Spring, by Jean Desoches, wearing a puce bodice and yellow flowered skirt, script 'F' mark in underglaze blue, c1775, 7in (18cm) high.
£650–720 S(NY)

This figure is from a set of the four seasons first modelled in 1773 and listed in the factory archives as 'Four Seasons in the form of French farmers'.

▶ A Meissen group of a young man presenting flowers to his companion, crossed swords mark in underglaze blue, late 19thC, 7in (18cm) high.
£500–600 DORO

A Russian Imperial Porcelain Manufactory, St. Petersburg figure of a peasant girl, wearing a flowered blue apron and holding a flower-encrusted water jug, 1855–81, 13½in (34.5cm) high.
£2,500–3,000 S(NY)

A pair of Staffordshire pearlware models of a lion and lioness, 18thC, 7½in (19cm) long.
£3,700–4,500 SWO

A Staffordshire stirrup cup, in the form of a hound's head, 1830–40, 4¾in (12cm) long.
£350–400 OD

A pair of Staffordshire models of lions, on imitation marble bases, c1820, 6in (15cm) long.
£2,500–3,000 JHo

A Scottish cow creamer, cover replaced, c1840, 6in (15cm) long.
£600–700 DAN

A Staffordshire model of a rabbit, one ear restored, 1850, 10in (25.5cm) long.
£4,000–4,500 DN

A Staffordshire model of a cat, c1880, 6in (15cm) long.
£180–200 SER

A Royal Winton Grimwades teapot, in the form of a chicken, c1936, 6¾in (17cm) high.
£160–180 CoCo

A pair of Scottish models of spaniels, c1890, 10½in (26.5cm) high.
£180–200 IW

A pair of Dutch Delft figures, restored, c1760, 4¾in (12cm) high.
£6,000–7,200 S(Am)

A Staffordshire group, entitled 'Charity', c1810, 9in (23cm) high.
£400–500 DAN

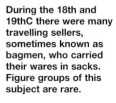

A pair of Staffordshire groups of shoe sellers, c1820, 9in (23cm) high.
£1,600–1,800 JHo

During the 18th and 19thC there were many travelling sellers, sometimes known as bagmen, who carried their wares in sacks. Figure groups of this subject are rare.

A Staffordshire pearlware figure of a lady reading, c1825, 9in (23cm) high.
£800–1,000 S

A Staffordshire pearlware group of a mother and child, early 19thC, 14½in (37cm) high.
£900–1,100 RBB

◄ A Staffordshire figure of Benjamin Franklin, c1850, 13½in (34.5cm) high.
£800–1,000 OD

A Staffordshire cauliflower tea canister, cover replaced, c1770, 5in (12.5cm) high.
£1,200–1,350 JHo

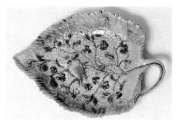

A Staffordshire leaf dish, handle repaired, c1765, 11in (28cm) wide.
£850–950 JHo

A Marseilles faïence stand, late 18thC, 13½in (34.5cm) wide.
£1,400–1,600 S

A Davenport creamware dish, painted with *Rosa mundi*, c1800, 11in (28cm) wide.
£400–450 JAK

A Minton majolica Christmas dish, made for the Crystal Palace Art Union, c1859, 15½in (39.5cm) diam.
£2,000–2,200 S(NY)

A Minton majolica bread dish, c1873, 15¾in (40cm) diam.
£1,650–2,000 S

A Quimper dish, by Paul Fouillon, c1900, 12in (30.5cm) wide.
£180–200 SER

A Minton majolica game pie dish and cover, date code for 1866, 14in (35.5cm) wide.
£4,000–4,500 CAG

A George Jones majolica Daisy cheese dome and stand, cracked, c1870, 10¼in (26cm) diam.
£5,000–6,000 TEN

A George Jones majolica cheese bell, c1880, 10¼in (26cm) diam.
£1,300–1,500 P

An English delft flower brick, probably London, c1750, 5¾in (14.5cm) wide.
£5,500–6,000 JHo

A pair of Minton majolica jardinières and stands, one stand replaced, minor cracks, c1865, 19¼in (49cm) high.
£11,000–12,000 S(NY)

A majolica jardinière, with raised birds, foliage and flowers, interior cracks and crazing, 19thC, 17½in (44.5cm) wide.
£800–1,000 AG

An English delft charger, decorated in Chinese style, c1710, 13⅝in (34.5cm) diam.
£1,000–1,200 DN

An English delft charger, decorated with Adam and Eve, probably Liverpool, c1725, 13½in (34.5cm) diam.
£1,100–1,250 S

A Dutch Delft biblical charger, minor repair and hairline crack, early 18thC, 13¾in (35cm) diam.
£2,200–2,500 S(Am)

A Dutch Delft polychrome plate, mid-18thC, 9in (23cm) diam.
£120–140 IW

A Staffordshire salt-glazed plate, c1765, 7½in (19cm) diam.
£575–650 JHo

A pair of English delft plates, probably Bristol, mid-18thC, 8¾in (22cm) diam.
£650–750 DD

A Liverpool delft polychrome plate, c1765, 11in (28cm) diam.
£200–220 JHo

A Lambeth delft polychrome plate, decorated with Vincenzo Lunardi's balloon, c1785, 10¼in (26cm) diam.
£2,400–2,650 JHo

A Strasbourg faïence dish, by Paul Hannong, 18thC, 9½in (24cm) diam.
£4,500–5,000 S(Am)

A label to the underside reads 'Exposition la faïence Pavillion de Marsau Louvre, 1932 No. 2069'.

A set of six Dutch Delft dishes, 18thC, 11in (28cm) diam.
£1,200–1,350 S(Am)

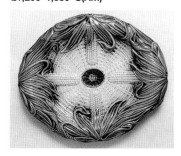

A creamware Dutch-decorated plate, c1800, 10in (25.5cm) diam.
£200–220 JHo

◄ A majolica corn-on-the-cob plate, 1880–1900, 13in (33cm) wide.
£130–150 CoCo

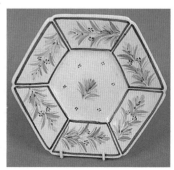

An Henriot Quimper hexagonal plate, c1922, 7in (18cm) wide.
£35–40 SER

A Wedgwood creamware jelly mould, c1800, 9in (23cm) high.
£1,650–1,850 S(NY)

A Mayer & Newbold jug, 1817–33, 5¼in (13.5cm) high.
£165–185 CoCo

A lustre Masonic jug, 1820–65, 6½in (16.5cm) high.
£160–180 SER

A Fifeshire pottery mug, with sponged decoration, c1885, 4¼in (11cm) high.
£65–75 SAA

A Mettlach stoneware tankard, with pewter cover, c1895, 8½in (21.5cm) high.
£325–375 PGA

A Staffordshire plaque, restored, c1800, 9in (23cm) high.
£750–850 DAN

A Brown-Westhead, Moore & Co plaque, with ebonized frame, impressed mark, c1870, 25½in (65cm) diam.
£700–850 TEN

A Portuguese Palissy-style reptile plaque, early 20thC, 9½in (24cm) diam.
£600–700 NOA

An English delft posset pot and cover, probably Bristol, early 18thC, restored, 7½in (19cm) high.
£2,000–2,200 S

An agate ware sauce boat, c1755, 4in (10cm) wide.
£3,000–3,500 JHo

A pearlware sauce boat, probably Liverpool, c1750, 7½in (19cm) wide.
£100–120 IW

▶ A Staffordshire Whieldon-style sauce boat, c1765, 7in (18cm) wide.
£1,500–1,750 JHo

A Minton Henri Deux ware salt, by Charles Toft, dated '1874', 7in (18cm) high.
£1,500–1,800 P

A Mason's Ironstone dessert service, comprising 33 pieces, printed and impressed marks, c1820.
£6,000–6,750 P

A Staffordshire dinner service, by Ashworth & Bros, comprising 67 pieces, decorated with flowers, c1840.
£3,500–4,000 RBB

A Staffordshire creamware cauliflower teapot, tea canister and milk jug with cover, 18thC, canister 4¼in (11cm) high.
£650–900 each SWO

▶ A Staffordshire teapot, with enamel decoration, c1765, 5in (12.5cm) high.
£1,800–2,000 JHo

A Wedgwood creamware teapot, some damage, c1770, 5½in (14cm) high.
£800–900 P

A Swansea pearlware teapot, late 18thC, 9½in (24cm) high.
£1,300–1,500 Bri

A Staffordshire salt-glazed teapot, depicting Frederick of Prussia, c1765, 3½in (9cm) high.
£650–800 Mit

A George Jones majolica teapot, in the form of a cockerel, c1870, 6½in (16.5cm) high.
£6,250–7,000 JEA

A Brussels faïence tureen, cover and stand, by Philippe Mombaers, modelled as a cabbage, c1750, stand 13½in (34.5cm) diam.
£4,000–4,500 S(NY)

A Minton majolica pigeon tureen and cover, dated '1867', 9½in (24cm) diam.
£6,000–7,000 P

A Wedgwood blue jasper bamboo vase, some damage, c1790, 8¼in (21cm) high.
£3,700–4,200 P

◀ A Copeland earthenware urn, depicting the goddess Diana driving a chariot, restored, marked, late 19thC, 29in (73.5cm) high.
£2,000–2,400 BB(S)

▶ A Copeland vase, signed by Charles Ferdinand Hürten, c1875, 24in (61cm) high.
£2,500–2,800 JAK

A set of four blue and white transfer-printed saucer dishes, c1810, 6¼in (16cm) diam.
£280–320 OD

A blue and white transfer-printed coffee pot, c1810, 10in (25.5cm) high.
£150–165 OD

A Heathcote blue and white transfer-printed bread bin, decorated with Cattle and River pattern, c1815, 15in (38cm) high.
£800–1,000 SCO

A Brameld Pottery blue and white meat plate, transfer-printed with the Castle at Rochefort pattern, early 19thC, 20¾in (52.5cm) wide.
£330–400 AH

A blue and white platter, transfer-printed with hop pickers, c1820, 17in (43cm) wide.
£800–1,000 SCO

A Ridgway blue and white meat dish, transfer-printed with Leeds Castle, Kent, c1820, 23in (58.5cm) wide.
£800–900 GN

A Spode meat platter, decorated with the Castle of Boudron, c1810, 17in (43cm) wide.
£750–900 SCO

A Don Pottery blue and white plate, transfer-printed with the Monastery at Castagne, c1820, 8½in (21.5cm) diam.
£120–145 OCH

A Staffordshire blue and white pearlware meat dish, 19thC, 14in (35.5cm) wide.
£280–350 CoCo

A blue and white jug, transfer-printed with Ponte Molle pattern, c1820, 12in (30.5cm) high.
£550–600 GN

A pair of Thomas Forrester blue and white vases, transfer-printed with flowers, c1910, 9¼in (23.5cm) high.
£180–220 CoCo

◄ A Minton blue and white footbath and jug, transfer-printed with Verona pattern, c1830, footbath 22in (56cm) wide.
£3,200–3,600 GN

A Stevenson & Williams blue and white plate, transfer-printed with Beehive and Vase pattern, c1825, 10in (25.5cm) diam.
£180–200 OCH

A Wemyss tabby cat, restored, c1900, 13in (33cm) high.
£8,500–9,500 S

A Wemyss flower pot, painted with Goose pattern, impressed mark, c1890, 3in (7.5cm) high.
£450–500 Fai

A Wemyss mug, painted with a stag, retailer T. Goode, c1890, 3½in (9cm) high.
£900–1,000 Fai

A Wemyss Bute vase, with Roses pattern, c1900, 12in (30.5cm) high.
£600–700 RdeR

A Wemyss pig, Bovey Tracey period, painted with Clover pattern, c1930, 6½in (16.5cm) high.
£500–550 SAA

A Wemyss Coombe flower pot, painted with Dog Roses pattern, c1920, 7in (18cm) high.
£350–400 RdeR

A Wemyss mug, painted with Roses pattern, c1890, 5½in (14cm) high.
£180–220 AOT

A Wemyss teapot, painted with Buttercups pattern, 1890–1900, 4in (10cm) high.
£400–500 RdeR

A Wemyss biscuit barrel and lid, painted with Sweet Pea pattern, painted mark, c1890, 5in (12.5cm) high.
£400–450 Fai

A Wemyss water jug, painted with Roses pattern, late 19thC, 9½in (24cm) high.
£600–700 BIG

A Wemyss mug, painted with Tulip pattern, impressed mark, retailer's stamp 'T. Goode', c1900, 5½in (14cm) high.
£300–330 Fai

A Wemyss plate, painted with Pheasant pattern, c1900, 5in (12.5cm) diam.
£200–240 RdeR

◄ A Wemyss tray, by Edwin Sandland, painted with Roses on a multi-coloured background, painted mark, c1925, 10in (25.5cm) wide.
£150–170 Fai

A Bow model of a squirrel, repaired, c1760, 8½in (21.5cm) high.
£4,500–5,000 S

A Derby Fable candlestick group, depicting a fox and cockerel, c1775, 9½in (24cm) high.
£600–700 DMa

A Meissen duck tureen and cover, restored, 1790–1810, 11¼in (28.5cm) high.
£4,000–4,500 S(NY)

A Chelsea figure of Autumn, c1756, 5¼in (13.5cm) high.
£4,000–4,500 P

A set of four Derby figures of the Classical Seasons, each attended by a putto, c1765, 9½in (24cm) high.
£4,300–4,750 DN

A pair of Chelsea figures of a gentleman and companion, from the gold anchor period, c1765, 9in (23cm) high.
£2,000–2,500 DMa

A Derby figure of a huntsman with his dog, 1770–80, 7¼in (18.5cm) high.
£450–500 Mit

A Lowestoft model of a pug dog, repaired, forelegs and paws missing, 1700–72, 7½in (19cm) high.
£1,100–1,300 P

Ex-Bernard Watney collection.

A Derby figure of Edmund Kean as Richard III, c1835, 12in (30.5cm) high.
£1,200–1,400 DMa

A Meissen allegorical group, entitled 'Evening', 19thC, 13¾in (35cm) high.
£1,500–1,800 AH

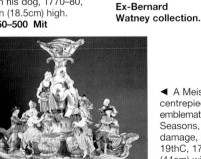

◄ A Meissen centrepiece, emblematic of the Seasons, some damage, mid-19thC, 17¼in (44cm) wide.
£5,000–6,000 P

A Mennecy silver-mounted bonbonnière, modelled as a woman, c1765, 2¼in (5.5cm) high.
£2,800–3,500 S

A Volkstedt model of a woman in a sedan chair, with a pug dog on her knee, mid-20thC, 11½in (29cm) high.
£500–600 DORO

A Derby chestnut basket with
pierced cover and knop, c1765,
8in (20.5cm) high.
£1,500–1,800 DN

A Nymphenburg *sucrier* and cover,
c1820, 3in (7.5cm) high.
£180–200 HA

A Meissen gilt-bronze-mounted
centrepiece, c1750, mounts 19thC,
13in (33cm) high.
£6,000–7,000 DORO

A Derby bowl, the interior painted
in Japanese style, 1760–65,
8¾in (22cm) diam.
£900–1,100 DN

A Mennecy silver-gilt-mounted snuff
box, c1760, 2½in (6.5cm) wide.
£800–900 S

A French gilt-metal-mounted
Sèvres-style centrepiece, 19thC,
16in (40.5cm) high.
£2,750–3,250 LJ

A Chelsea dish, painted with an
orange and gilt tiger entwined
around a blue bamboo cane in
pursuit of a butterfly, c1752–55,
6¾in (17cm) diam.
£6,000–7,000 S(NY)

◄ A pair of Derby dessert dishes,
c1825, 11in (28cm) wide.
£350–400 DAN

► A Stevenson & Hancock dessert
dish, painted by H. S. Hancock,
c1930, 11in (28cm) wide.
£1,600–1,800 S

A Coalport Etruscan-shape *sucrier*
and cover, c1820, 5½in (14cm) diam.
£340–400 DAN

A candlestick, probably Minton,
c1840, 5in (12.5cm) high.
£200–240 DAN

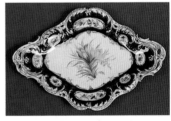

A Coalport dish, by Stephen Lawrence,
c1845, 14¼in (36cm) wide.
£350–400 JAK

A Du Paquier deep dish, c1735,
13in (33cm) wide.
£8,000–9,000 S(NY)

A Derby coffee can, by Richard Askew, crown, crossed batons and 'D' mark, c1794, 2½in (6.5cm) high.
£1,800–2,000 P

A Nantgarw teacup and saucer, London decorated, some wear to gilding, 1817–22, saucer 4¾in (12cm) diam.
£450–500 S(S)

A Jacob Petit shell-shaped cabinet cup and saucer, c1850, saucer 7in (18cm) diam.
£900–1,000 NOA

A Sèvres orange-ground coffee can and saucer, c1786, saucer 4¼in (11cm) diam.
£1,700–2,000 S

A Vienna gilt cup and saucer, 1809, cup 2¾in (7cm) high.
£525–600 DORO

A Sèvres cup and saucer, gilded and enamelled in the Etruscan style, dated 1816, cup 3¼in (8.5cm) high.
£1,000–1,200 P

A pair of Russian Popoff ewers, early 19thC, 8¾in (22cm) high.
£2,500–2,750 NOA

A jug, with unusual handle terminal, c1835, 6in (15cm) high.
£200–250 DAN

A Bow teapot, 1765–68, 4½in (11.5cm) high.
£700–800 P

Ex-Bernard Watney Collection.

A Meissen coffee pot and cover, c1735, 9in (23cm) high.
£3,000–3,500 S

A Meissen tea and coffee service, comprising 10 pieces, c1860, coffee pot 8¼in (21cm) high.
£7,500–9,000 DORO

A Copeland Sèvres-style cased presentation 'jewelled' *tête-à-tête*, c1854, teapot 4¼in (11cm) high.
£2,200–2,500 S

▶ A Paris royal armorial part service, comprising 34 pieces, decorated by Jacquel with the arms of King Leopold I of Belgium, c1856.
£5,750–7,000 S

A Belleek teapot stand, hand-painted by Cerial Arnold, 1863–90, 4¾in (12cm) diam.
£350–400 DeA

A Longton Hall moulded strawberry plate, c1758, 9in (23cm) diam.
£2,000–2,300 DAN

A Tournai tobacco leaf dish, small firing crack, c1775, 9½in (24cm) diam.
£3,200–3,850 S(Am)

A Plymouth lobed sauce boat, painted in Kakiemon palette, c1768, 8in (20.5cm) wide.
£1,100–1,250 JUP

A Spanish Alcora tureen, cover and stand, gilt 'A' mark, c1780, stand 13in (33cm) diam.
£11,500–13,000 S

A Chelsea Warren Hastings-style, platter, 1752–56, 13in (33cm) wide.
£2,500–2,750 P

A Minton charger, painted by A. Holland with a view of Balmoral Castle, signed, c1951, 14in (35.5cm) diam.
£350–420 S

A West Pans plate, with scalloped rim, 1764–70, 6in (15cm) diam.
£450–500 P

▶ A Berlin dessert service, comprising 13 pieces, 19thC.
£1,000–1,200 TEN

A Du Paquier Imari pattern tureen and cover, 1730–35, 9¼in (23.5cm) wide.
£15,000–16,500 S(NY)

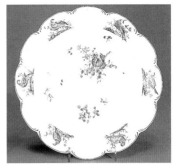

A pair of Chelsea plates, c1755, 8½in (21.5cm) diam.
£900–1,100 DN

A serving dish, probably Strasbourg, 18thC, 15½in (39.5cm) wide.
£2,700–3,000 S(Am)

A Bow sauce boat, painted in *famille rose* palette, c1755, 7in (18cm) wide.
£1,500–1,800 DAN

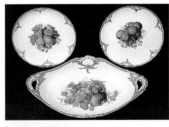

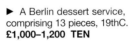

◀ A Coalport dinner service, comprising 111 pieces, damaged, restored, c1810.
£17,000–20,000 P

A 'Sèvres' two-handled *écuelle*, cover and stand, restored, late 19thC, stand 9½in (24cm) wide.
£1,400–1,600 S

A pair of Coalbrookdale-style vases and covers, c1860, 13¾in (35cm) high.
£2,000–2,400 HAM

A Derby Frill vase and cover, pierced and applied with flowers, restored, 1760–65, 11½in (29cm) high.
£1,300–1,500 S

A Meissen Augustus Rex vase and cover, cover restored, c1730, 15¾in (40cm) high.
£7,500–8,250 S

► A Russian gilt and bisque porcelain urn with cover, c1900, 32in (81.5cm) high.
£8,000–9,000 S(NY)

A pair of Chelsea vases and covers, restored, c1765, 10¾in (27.5cm) high.
£2,500–2,750 P

A Royal Crown Derby vase and cover, painted by D. Leroy, signed, cover restored, c1899, 9½in (24cm) high.
£5,000–5,500 S

A Meissen vase, cover missing, c1740, 6½in (16.5cm) high.
£6,000–7,000 Bon(C)

► A pair of Vienna vases and covers, enamelled with classical scenes by A. Heer, signed, c1900, 14¼in (36cm) high.
£1,750–2,000 DN

A Coalport pot pourri vase and cover, c1900, 6in (15cm) diam.
£1,200–1,400 JUP

A Royal Crown Derby vase, painted by Albert Gregory, repaired, c1902, 16in (40.5cm) high.
£3,200–3,600 JUP

A Minton *pâte-sur-pâte* vase, decorated by L. M. Solon, signed, gold printed Paris Exhibition mark for 1878, c1876, 16¾in (42.5cm) high.
£18,000–20,000 S

A Coalport vase and cover, painted with loch scenes within gilt reserves, the domed cover with floral finial, c1900, 6¼in (16cm) high.
£400–500 TMA

A pair of Derby vases, 1820–25, 16in (40.5cm) high.
£8,500–9,500 CAT

A pair of richly gilded Paris vases, early 19thC, 12¾in (32.5cm) high.
£2,500–2,750 NOA

A Chamberlain's Worcester beaker, 1800–10, 4in (10cm) high.
£1,000–1,200 S

A Worcester punchbowl or tureen, cracked, 1758–60, 16in (40.5cm) wide.
£4,500–5,000 P

A Worcester cream boat, with lobed foot, c1754, 4¼in (11cm) wide.
£10,000–11,000 WoR

A Worcester saucer, with Chinese figures, 1768–70, 4¾in (12cm) diam.
£650–720 P

Ex-Bernard Watney Collection.

A pair of Kerr & Binns Worcester Sèvres-style dessert plates, printed mark in puce, c1857, 9¼in (23.5cm) diam.
£200–240 RBB

A Worcester bowl, painted with exotic birds in a river scene, 1775–80, 7½in (19cm) diam.
£550–650 SWO

A Worcester chamberpot, hatched crescent mark, c1770, 5½in (14cm) high.
£4,000–5,000 DN

A Worcester coffee cup, painted in *famille rose* palette, c1753, 2¾in (7cm) high.
£1,200–1,400 JUP

▶ A Chamberlain's Worcester armorial platter, c1830, 19in (48.5cm) wide.
£1,350–1,500 JAK

A Chamberlain's Worcester inkwell decorated with Jabberwocky pattern, c1810, 2¼in (5.5cm) high.
£275–325 DIA

A Royal Worcester centrepiece, impressed mark, c1870, 7in (18cm) high.
£750–850 JEA

A Royal Worcester figure of a dancing bacchante, tambourine missing, pattern No. 1441, date code for 1901, 28¼in (72cm) high.
£1,700–2,000 TEN

A Worcester Barr, Flight & Barr inkstand, inscribed to base 'Chepstow Castle', 1804–13, 6in (15cm) high.
£700–850 HOK

A Royal Worcester reticulated milk jug, c1871, 5½in (14cm) high.
£1,250–1,400 JUP

A Worcester mug, decorated with Banded Hedge pattern, cracked, 1753–54, 3in (7.5cm) high.
£650–750 P

A Worcester gilded Imari pattern scent bottle, c1892, 2in (5cm) diam.
£550–620 BHa

A Chamberlain's Worcester scent bottle, allegorical of remembrance, c1790, 4in (10cm) wide.
£900–1,000 LeB

A Worcester Barr, Flight & Barr part dessert service, comprising 37 pieces, gilded and painted with fruiting vines, 1804–13.
£5,500–6,500 HOK

A Royal Worcester majolica stick stand, c1875, 27in (68.5cm) high.
£4,000–5,000 S(NY)

A Worcester teapot, c1758, 5in (12.5cm) high.
£700–800 P

A Worcester Barr, Flight & Barr triple spill vase, probably by Samuel Smith, c1810, 5¾in (14.5cm) high.
£6,500–7,200 P

A pair of Royal Worcester reticulated vases, by George Owen, dated '1878', 7¼in (18.5cm) high.
£17,000–20,000 P

A Chamberlain's Worcester vase, small chip, c1815, 9in (23cm) high.
£1,400–1,600 DAN

▶ A Royal Worcester vase, painted by Harry Davis, signed, c1912, 8½in (21.5cm) high.
£2,000–2,400 WW

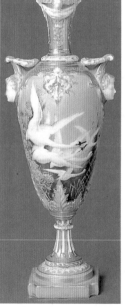

A pair of Royal Worcester vases, by Charley Baldwyn, both signed, dated 1904, 11½in (29cm) high.
£7,000–8,000 P

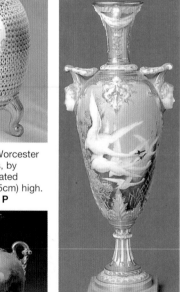

A pair of Royal Worcester vases, by C. H. C. Baldwyn, c1899, 12in (30.5cm) high.
£2,400–2,700 JUP

A pair of glazed pottery roof tiles, modelled as galloping horses, Ming Dynasty, 11½in (29cm) long.
£2,200–2,650 S(Am)

A biscuit model of a Buddhist lion, Kangxi period, 14¼in (36cm) high.
£2,000–2,200 S

A pair of gilt-metal-mounted porcelain models of parakeets, Kangxi period, 9in (23cm) high.
£2,000–2,400 P

A pair of *famille verte* biscuit parrots, Kangxi period, 7in (18cm) high.
£2,500–3,000 GeW

A biscuit model of a junk, Kangxi period, 11½in (29cm) high.
£6,000–7,000 S

A Chinese *famille rose* figure of Buddai Ho Shang, seated with a rosary in his right hand, c1900, 10¼in (26cm) high.
£100–120 WW

A pair of *famille rose* porcelain candlesticks, moulded as standing Chinese figures, restored, late 18thC, 18in (45.5cm) high.
£20,000–22,000 S(NY)

A Canton porcelain set of the Eight Immortals, Qianlong period, 9½in (24cm) high.
£4,000–5,000 P(B)

A *famille rose* tea bowl and saucer, Yongzheng period, saucer 4in (10cm) diam.
£350–400 GLD

A Chinese Canton *famille rose* bough pot and cover, with canted corners and loop side handles, painted with panels of figures, birds and foliage on a relief-moulded ground, hairline cracks, 19thC, 9¾in (25cm) high.
£400–450 WW

◄ A Longquan celadon stem cup, early Ming Dynasty, 7in (18cm) high.
£1,500–1,800 GLD

► A Chinese export blue and white butter dish, Qianlong period, 5in (12.5cm) wide.
£3,000–3,500 GLD

A Junyao stoneware bowl, Yuan Dynasty, 7in (18cm) diam.
£1,200–1,400 GLD

A Chinese export *famille rose* porcelain bowl,
Qianlong period, 13½in (34.5cm) diam.
£900–1,100 P(B)

A *wucai* basin, Wanli period,
11¾in (30cm) diam.
£15,000–16,500 S

A blue and white barber's bowl, hairline
crack, 18thC, 5½in (14cm) diam.
£600–700 Mit

A Longquan celadon twin
fish dish, Song/Yuan Dynasty,
10in (25.5cm) diam.
£1,200–1,500 GLD

A Canton *famille rose* porcelain
bowl, with ormolu mounts,
mid-19thC, 17½in (44.5cm) wide.
£1,400–1,600 AH

A Chinese Canton *famille rose* bowl,
decorated with two panels of figures
in an interior and two of birds and
butterflies, rim chip, mid-19thC,
10⅛in (26.5cm) diam.
£500–550 WW

A Longquan celadon tripod censer,
Yuan/early Ming Dynasty,
6¼in (16cm) diam.
£9,000–10,000 S

A green-glazed circular box with
cover, Han Dynasty, 4in (10cm) diam.
£700–850 GLD

A pair of Junyao tripod censers,
Song Dynasty, 2¼in (5.5cm) diam.
£10,000–11,000 S

A painted pottery cocoon jar,
Han Dynasty, 19in (48.5cm) wide.
£3,000–3,500 S(Am)

A dragon jar, Qianlong period,
7¼in (18.5cm) high.
£6,000–7,000 S(HK)

A *famille verte* ginger jar and carved
wooden cover, Kangxi period,
9¾in (25cm) high.
£1,400–1,700 P

A dragon dish, Kangxi period, 14¾in (37.5cm) diam.
£6,500–7,200 S(NY)

A *famille verte* charger, Kangxi period, 13¾in (35cm) diam.
£4,500–5,500 P

A *famille verte* charger, Kangxi period, 15in (38cm) diam.
£2,800–3,400 GLD

A *famille rose* dish, Qianlong period, 9in (23cm) diam.
£12,500–15,000 S

This plate is very rare and unusual, probably being a sample piece, the design incorporating the rim used for a famous 18thC service, and the central coat-of-arms of an unknown prospective client.

A Kakiemon-style dish, Kangxi period, 7in (18cm) square.
£1,500–1,800 GLD

A Chinese Imari export dish, decorated with trees and flower-filled urns, 18thC, 12½in (32cm) diam.
£700–850 TEN

A *famille rose* part dinner service, comprising 27 pieces, painted in Twin Peacock pattern, Qianlong period.
£24,000–30,000 P

A plaque, painted with birds on a waterlily by Chen Yiting, c1930, 9 x 5in (23 x 12.5cm).
£850–1,000 Wai

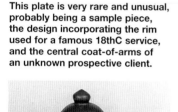

A Chinese Yixing 'Zisha' teapot, c1845–50, 7in (18cm) wide.
£2,500–3,000 Wai

A blue and white mallet vase, Yongzheng period, 7in (18cm) high.
£16,000–17,500 S

A *famille rose* vase, Qianlong period, 19¼in (49cm) high.
£9,000–10,000 S

A pair of Canton vases, with gilded moulded animal mounts, 19thC, 24in (61cm) high.
£1,000–1,200 RBB

A relief-decorated celadon porcelain vase, restored, 19thC, 16¾in (42.5cm) high.
£650–800 NOA

A Satsuma beaker, Meiji period,
2in (5cm) high.
£800–885 MER

A Satsuma censer and cover, signed
Kaburagi, c1880, 2¼in (5.5cm) high.
£550–600 MCN

A Ko-Imari bowl, c1740,
8in (20.5cm) diam.
£1,200–1,400 GLD

An Arita model of a *shishi*,
restored, early 18thC,
17in (43cm) high.
£2,500–3,000 S(Am)

A pair of Arita fish dishes, c1700,
11in (28cm) long.
£1,000–1,200 GLD

A set of four Imari scalloped dishes, 18thC,
11in (28cm) long.
£3,500–4,000 S(L)

An Imari porcelain dish,
gilding rubbed, early 18thC,
18⅓in (47cm) diam.
£1,300–1,500 TEN

► An Imari porcelain charger,
19thC, 22in (56cm) diam.
£500–600 AH

A teapot, by Makuzu Kozan, decorated with
fish, c1900, 6in (15cm) high.
£800–1,000 MCN

► A pair of
Imari plaques,
one damaged,
late 17thC,
21¼in (54cm) diam.
£1,600–2,000
Bea(E)

A pair of Imari floor
vases, on carved wooden
stands, Meiji period,
49½in (125.5cm) high.
£5,500–6,500 LJ

A Satsuma vase, c1920,
25in (63.5cm) high.
£300–350 TMA

A porcelain *koro* and cover,
by Makuzu Kozan, Meiji
period, 9¾in (25cm) high.
£3,500–4,000 S

► A Satsuma vase,
by Yabu Meizan, late Meiji
period, 10in (25.5cm) high.
£1,800–2,000 MBO

A Venetian enamelled and gilt glass bowl, c1500, 11in (28cm) diam.
£11,000–13,000 S

A Murano opaque white glass bowl, attributed to the Brussa workshop, mid-18thC, 5in (12.5cm) diam.
£20,000–22,000 P

A turquoise glass finger bowl, c1840, 4¾in (12cm) diam.
£100–125 CB

A blue glass sugar bowl and cream jug, c1820, jug 4in (10cm) high.
£320–400 GS

A pair of amethyst glass finger bowls, with waisted bodies and flared rims, c1840, each 3¾in (9.5cm) high.
£220–240 Som

A set of eight double-lip cranberry glass rinsers, c1870, each 5½in (14cm) wide.
£650–750 CB

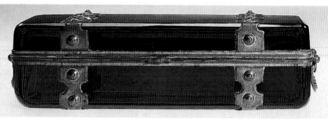

A Bohemian ruby glass casket, with gilt-metal mounts and swing handles, c1850, 10½in (26.5cm) wide.
£750–825 S

▶ A yellow amber glass iris bowl, marked 'Webb', 1930s, 3in (7.5cm) high.
£100–120 JHa

A Bohemian engraved cranberry glass casket, with gilt-metal mounts, c1850, 11¼in (28.5cm) wide.
£5,000–5,500 S

A 'Nailsea' light green glass cream jug, c1810, 4½in (11.5cm) high.
£325–360 Som

A blue glass baluster-shaped cream jug, 1760–70, 3½in (9cm) high.
£400–450 Del

A Bohemian engraved glass jug, 1840, 5in (12.5cm) high.
£100–120 PIL

A club-shaped blue glass port decanter, c1800, 9¼in (23.5cm) high.
£800–900 Som

A blue glass rum decanter, c1800, 10in (25.5cm) high.
£200–240 Del

A set of four mallet-shaped green glass decanters, c1810, each 9¼in (23.5cm) high.
£800–1,000 DN

An onion-shaped amber glass carafe, c1840, 8in (20.5cm) high.
£160–180 Som

An onion-shaped green glass carafe, engraved with fruiting vine motif, c1840, 9in (23cm) high.
£250–280 Som

A 'Nailsea' blue glass flask, c1860, 7in (18cm) high.
£130–150 Som

A yellow amber glass whisky flagon, with metal mounts, c1860, 9in (23cm) high.
£120–140 JHa

A Beilby armorial enamelled opaque-twist glass goblet, the bowl extensively repaired, c1765, 7½in (19cm) high.
£5,750–7,000 S

A green wine glass, with double ogee bowl, c1770, 6in (15cm) high.
£1,500–1,800 Del

A glass, with tulip bowl, c1820, 5in (12.5cm) high.
£40–50 JHa

A pear-shaped peacock green glass rummer, c1790, 5in (12.5cm) high.
£400–450 Del

▶ A pair of wine glasses, with conical bowls, c1825, 5¼in (13.5cm) high.
£125–140 Som

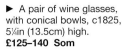

A Venetian enamelled glass goblet and cover, c1500, 10¼in (26cm) high.
£40,000–45,000 S

A Dresden enamelled and gilded glass beaker, by Ludwig Mohn, signed and dated '1816', 4¼in (11cm) high.
£8,000–9,000 S

A cameo glass perfume bottle, with enamelled gold mount, c1880, 10½in (26.5cm) high.
£5,000–6,000 ALiN

A *façon de Venise* glass beaker, possibly Spanish, late 16th/early 17thC, 5¾in (14.5cm) high.
£2,200–2,650 P

A Bohemian *Lithyalin* glass beaker, from the Friedrich Egermann workshop, c1835, 4¼in (11cm) high.
£2,800–3,200 DORO

A southern Netherlands *façon de Venise* serpent-stemmed glass goblet, mid-17thC, 7in (18cm) high.
£4,500–5,000 S(Am)

A Bohemian green and gilt footed glass beaker, minor rim chips, c1845, 4¾in (12cm) high.
£400–500 DORO

A Nuremburg engraved glass goblet, by Adam Renneisen, stem repaired, signed, c1675, 11¼in (28.5cm) high.
£8,000–9,000 S

An amethyst cut glass toilet water bottle, c1765, 7in (18cm) high.
£650–750 Del

A black glass scent bottle, decorated with enamelled flowers, the opaque white borders with rosettes, with silver-gilt mount, c1880, 3½in (9cm) high.
£900–1,000 Som

A French turquoise opaline glass scent bottle, decorated with gilt, late 19thC, 2in (5cm) diam.
£280–320 BHa

A double-ended ruby glass scent bottle, with central vinaigrette, and silver-gilt mounts, late 19thC, 5in (12.5cm) long.
£1,100–1,250 BHa

A cranberry glass bell-pull, overlaid in white, with brass fittings, c1865, 4⅛in (11.5cm) long.
£200–240 GS

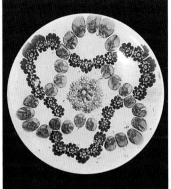

A Baccarat garlanded double clematis paperweight, mid-19thC, 3in (7.5cm) diam.
£2,200–2,500 P

A Clichy millefiori paperweight, c1850, 3in (7.5cm) diam.
£1,800–2,000 S

A New England faceted double-overlay millefiori paperweight, c1845–60, 2⅛in (6.5cm) diam.
£1,400–1,600 WoW

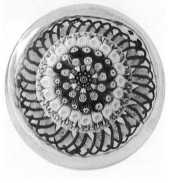

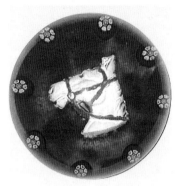

A St Louis mushroom paperweight, 1845–60, 3¼in (8.5cm) diam.
£2,400–2,650 SWB

A St Louis paperweight, the fruit on a latticino ground, c1845–60, 3in (7.5cm) diam.
£800–950 WoW

A Paul Ysart paperweight, with 'PY' cane, c1930, 2¾in (7cm) diam.
£850–950 SWB

A pair of Victorian ruby glass lustres, with white overlay, hung with prism drops, 11¾in (30cm) high.
£1,200–1,400 P(G)

A German enamelled milchglas tankard and cover, c1780, 8⅓in (21.5cm) high.
£900–1,000 S

A Bohemian enamelled and gilt blue overlay opaline glass vase, c1850, 14in (35.5cm) high.
£1,600–1,800 S

An opaline glass vase, c1850, 9½in (24cm) high.
£160–180 PIL

A pair of Baccarat enamelled opaline glass vases, attributed to Jean-François Robert, c1850, 17½in (44.5cm) high.
£5,500–6,000 S

A glass celery vase, cut with steps and flat flutes, c1830, 6in (15cm) high.
£400–450 Del

A Stourbridge cameo glass vase, c1885, 2in (5cm) high.
£800–900 BELL

A pair of Continental blue opaline glass vases and covers, decorated with enamelled silvered scrolling foliage, c1860, 10½in (26.5cm) high.
£800–1,000 GSP

▶ A pair of ruby-flashed cut to clear glass cornucopiae, with gilded mounts, on alabaster bases, c1870, each 6½in (16.5cm) high.
£900–1,000 CB

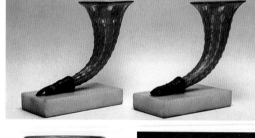

A pair of Bohemian ruby glass vases, with white overlay, 19thC, 11in (28cm) high.
£1,000–1,100 Mit

A pair of blue satin glass vases, late 19thC, 14⅛in (37cm) high.
£2,200–2,600 AH

▶ A pair of green glass vases, with gilt-bronze-mounts, late 19thC, 16¼in (41.5cm) high.
£1,750–2,000 S(S)

A Meissen biscuit figure of a bacchante, by C. J. Jüchtzer, incised crossed swords within a triangle, restored, c1785, 10in (25.5cm) high.
£800–900 S

▶ A Meissen group of a winged figure surrounded by putti, enamelled and gilt, some damage, mark in blue and incised 'D82', c1880, 8¾in (22cm) high.
£600–700 DN

A Meissen figural group, in the form of 18thC-style children playing on stilts, c1880, 11in (28cm) high.
£800–1,000 HAM

Meissen Marks

Rare marks found on some wares after 1724 are the initials KPM (Königliche Porzellan Manufaktur).

The initials AR (Augustus Rex) are also found on some, usually larger, Kakiemon wares.

After 1725, the most common mark is the crossed swords in underglaze blue, from the arms of Saxony.

From 1730 onwards, the angle between the swords becomes noticeably more acute.

From c1740 onwards, the mark is smaller – on most pieces it is less than 0.7in (1.5cm) long.

A Minton parian group, entitled 'The Amazon', after J. Feuchère, c1851, 15in (38cm) high.
£1,650–1,850 JAK

A Minton parian centrepiece, after an original model by A. Carrier-Belleuse, decorated in green enamel and gilding, impressed factory marks, incised number, c1856, 10½in (26.5cm) diam.
£1,750–2,000 S

A Naples figure of Hercules, resting on a gilt club and with a lion's skin draped across his leg, crowned 'N' in underglaze blue, late 18thC, 8¼in (21cm) high.
£4,500–5,500 S

Miller's is a price GUIDE not a price LIST

A pair of Royal Dux figures of a Reaper and a Sower, both dressed in green, pink and fawn, highlighted with gold, impressed triangles and printed marks, c1920, 11¼in (28.5cm) high.
£340–400 P

A St James seal, in the form of a boy playing a flute, wearing blue-plumed pink hat and pink jacket over a flowered waistcoat and yellow breeches, head restuck, 1752–55, 1¼in (3cm) high.
£370–400 P

A Sitzendorf group of a shepherd with his sheep and dog, early 20thC, 9¾in (25cm) high.
£200–240 DORO

A German figure of a lady, possibly Sulzbach, her dress decorated with flower chains and sprigs in gilding and purple on a green ground, on a moulded base, underglaze blue monogram 'CT', c1771, 6in (15cm) high.
£2,000–2,400 S

A Vienna figure of a bagpipe player, wearing a leather waistcoat over a puce jacket and breeches, some restoration, shield mark in underglaze blue, c1770, 8in (20.5cm) high.
£300–350 S

A Vienna figure of a young girl combing her hair, her yellow skirt decorated with sprigs of flowers, c1845, 5¼in (13.5cm) high.
£350–400 DORO

A Vienna figure of a baby in swaddling clothes, the robe decorated with green leaf borders and puce bows, gilt lines, early 19thC, 4¾in (12cm) high.
£500–600 P

A Vienna figure of a chicken fryer, early 20thC, 7½in (19cm) high.
£280–320 DORO

A Volkstedt figure, entitled 'Wind', underglaze blue marks, early 20thC, 13¼in (33.5cm) high.
£150–180 DORO

A Volkstedt figure of a young man, wearing green floral breeches and a striped waistcoat, underglaze blue sunburst mark, early 20thC, 11in (28cm) high.
£130–150 P(EA)

An early Victorian parian figure of the Duke of Wellington, 10¾in (27.5cm) high.
£300–350 MCA

A pair of French bisque child groups, representing Summer and Winter, underglaze blue monogram, 19thC, 6¼in (16cm) high.
£400–500 AG

A pair of French bisque figures, each wearing brightly painted and gilt 18thC-style costume, impressed 'L' and 'M', c1860, largest 22¾in (58cm) high.
£575–700 P

A parian group, entitled 'One More Shot – Wounded To The Rear', by John Rogers, New York, depicting the American Civil War, c1864, 22in (56cm) high.
£1,700–1,900 JAK

A pair of Continental bisque figures of a couple in evening dress, painted with purple and gilt floral sprays on a cream ground, early 20thC, 16½in (42cm) high.
£300–350 DA

FLATWARE

A set of ten Samuel Alcock dessert plates, painted with flowers, and with cream, green and gilt borders, puce number, c1840, 9¼in (23.5cm) diam.
£600–700 DN

A Bow plate, decorated in Kakiemon-style with Quail pattern in iron-red and with a gilt scroll band, 1753–55, 8¼in (21cm) diam.
£450–550 DN

A Du Paquier or Vezzi plate, painted in black with gilt details, c1720, 8¼in (21.5cm) diam.
£2,200–2,600 DORO

Miller's Compares

I A Samuel Gilbody plate, painted in blue with two crane-like birds, 1755–59, 9in (23cm) diam.
£9,000–10,000 P

Ex-Bernard Watney collection.

II A Samuel Gilbody plate, painted with two crane-like birds, damage to rim, 1755–59, 9in (23cm) diam.
£2,800–3,200 P

These two plates are almost identical, but there was a big difference in the prices they realized. Item I had an excellent provenance but also, and more importantly, it was in extremely good condition, whereas Item II had a large piece missing from the rim. Few early pieces in undamaged condition are found these days, and when one does turn up it sells very much at a premium.

A pair of Copeland Spode plates, each with a central crest within a turquoise border, impressed marks for 1896, 10in (25.5cm) diam.
£600–700 JAK

A Frankenthal dish, painted in bright colours with chickens, flowers and fruit, gilt border, underglaze blue mark, 1770–93, 9in (23cm) diam.
£1,000–1,200 DORO

◄ A Russian Imperial Porcelain Manufactory, St Petersburg, plate, painted in colours with infantry soldiers before a cathedral, with gilt border, 1876, 9¾in (25cm) diam.
£4,000–5,000 BB(L)

A Derby dessert plate, painted with Moss Province Rosebuds, with gilt rim line, crowned crossed batons, c1795, 9in (23cm) diam.
£750–825 S(S)

A Russian Imperial Porcelain Manufactory, St Petersburg, dinner plate, from the Kremlin service, decorated with red, green and blue strapwork, the border with four black Imperial eagles, with gilding, underglaze blue cypher mark, 1825–55, 9½in (24cm) diam.
£1,000–1,200 S(NY)

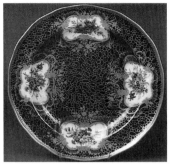

A Russian Imperial Porcelain Manufactory, St. Petersburg, Alexander III plate, decorated in Sèvres style, the blue ground reserved with four panels painted with floral sprays, bordered with gilt, printed mark, 1825–55, 10in (25.5cm) diam.
£370–400 P

A Minton plate, the centre painted in colours with a cathedral within a turquoise border and hand-pierced and gilded rim, impressed and printed marks with date code for 1877, 9¾in (25cm) diam.
£150–180 Bea(E)

A Meissen plate, in the style of A. F. von Löwenfink, painted with a mythical beast, the rim with butterflies and purple flowers, crossed swords mark in underglaze blue, c1740, 9½in (24cm) diam.
£800–1,000 S

A set of eight Minton dessert plates, each painted in colours with scenes of children, impressed and puce-printed factory marks and year cyphers, c1883, 9½in (24cm) diam.
£2,500–3,000 S(NY)

There were a number of decorators at the Minton factory specializing in child subjects of this type, including Antonin Boullemier, Rebecca Coleman and William Coleman.

A pair of Sèvres cabinet plates, each painted with a maiden and young boy in pastoral landscapes, within raised gilt and cobalt-ground borders, green and red printed marks, c1870, 9in (23cm) diam.
£350–420 Hal

A Bohemian Pirkenhammer plate, painted by Josef Freund with an italianate harbour scene within a gilt rim, signed, c1840, 9¼in (23.5cm) diam.
£1,600–1,800 S

A plate, decorated and signed by G. R. Pain, with Cork city coat-of-arms in brown, with gilt border, 1828, 10¾in (27.5cm) diam.
£300–360 STA

A Vienna plate, painted with a young woman, the border with a band of foliage in gold and enamel colours, late 19thC, 9¾in (25cm) diam.
£750–825 Bea(E)

A Sèvres dessert plate, painted by François Binet, with colourful floral sprays, the border with green scrolls, crossed 'L' mark, dated 1758, 9½in (24cm) diam.
£250–300 P

A Zürich plate, painted with a landscape vignette, with gilt rim line, marked 'Z' in underglaze blue, c1775, 9¾in (25cm) diam.
£1,400–1,600 S

A Continental ribbon plate, printed in colours with a portrait entitled 'Prince Edward of Wales Our Future King', within a pierced and gilded border, hairline crack, c1902, 7in (18cm) diam.
£75–90 SAS

ICE PAILS & WINE COOLERS

A Berlin bisque and glazed porcelain wine cooler, moulded in relief with a Bacchus head, the reverse with Pan, each handle modelled as a bacchante, underglaze blue sceptre and heraldic eagle mark, late 19thC, 12½in (32cm) high.
£2,500–2,750 BB(S)

A pair of Derby ice pails and covers, painted with speedwell and with gilt bullrush handles, c1810, 10in (25.5cm) high.
£1,600–1,800 TEN

A pair of Derby ice coolers and covers, the bodies painted with botanical specimens all titled in red, with gilt scroll borders, damaged, early 19thC, 10¼in (26cm) high.
£1,600–1,800 WW

INKSTANDS

A Coalbrookdale flower-encrusted inkstand, reserved with flowers and butterflies within green and gilt raised foliate scroll borders, containing two ink pots and covers, restored, c1830, 8in (20.5cm) wide.
£450–550 Hal

A strawberry-shaped inkwell, with lilac glaze and highlighted with gilt, c1835, 6in (15cm) wide.
£350–400 DAN

A Ludwigsburg inkstand, painted in puce and embellished in gilt, surmounted by two putti, with fitted sander and inkpot, monograms in underglaze blue and puce and impressed numerals, 1760–65, 8in (20.5cm) high.
£3,500–4,200 S(Am)

Miller's is a price GUIDE not a price LIST

◄ A Minton inkstand, of 'Triple Bucket Ink' shape, comprising an inkwell, central pot with taperstick lid and one other pot, all with applied flowers and gilt, c1830, 11½in (29cm) wide.
£750–850 DIA

JARDINIERES

A Belleek Lipton footed jardinière, 1891–1926, 10in (25.5cm) high.
£1,100–1,200 MLa

A Coalport jardinière, applied with goat's mask handles, decorated with roses within cobalt and gilt borders, restored, pattern number in red enamel, 1900–20, 7½in (19cm) diam.
£120–150 Hal

A Meissen jardinière, painted on one side with a tulip, a daffodil and a rose, the reverse with a flowerspray tied with an iron-red ribbon, with green twig handles, crossed swords mark, c1740, 4¼in (11cm) diam.
£2,500–3,000 P

A Bow polychrome sparrow beak cream jug and cover, decorated with floral sprays and insects, 1765–68, 4¼in (11cm) high.
£230–275 Mit

A Richard Chaffers & Co jug, painted in bright colours with fancy birds, damaged and repaired, 1756–60, 9½in (24cm) high.
£950–1,100 P

A Champion's Bristol sparrow beak jug, painted with colourful flowers, c1775, 3¼in (8.5cm) high.
£300–350 WW

A Derby jug, with gilt highlights and borders, the body painted with flowers and foliage, puce mark, early 19thC, 6½in (16.5cm) high.
£100–120 E

A Derby jug, painted in enamels with a bird perched among flowers and foliage, c1758, 8in (20.5cm) high.
£800–900 S

A Samuel Gilbody cream jug, painted in colours with a floral spray, 1758–60, 3¼in (8.5cm) high.
£2,000–2,200 P

Ex-Bernard Watney collection.

A Longton Hall sparrow beak cream jug, painted with colourful flowers, 1755–58, 3in (7.5cm) high.
£2,000–2,200 P

Ex-Bernard Watney collection.

A Liverpool blue and white sparrow beak jug, attributed to Seth Pennington, c1785, 3¼in (8.5cm) high.
£100–120 Mit

A Meissen Schneeballen milk jug and cover, applied with flowerheads and trailing green leaves, gilt rims, restored, crossed swords in underglaze blue, c1745, 5¾in (14.5cm) high.
£1,000–1,200 S

A George Grainger & Co reticulated ewer, the cream ground pierced with flowerhead and leaf-scroll bands, picked out in gilt, printed mark in brown for 1891, 9in (23cm) high.
£800–900 DN

▶ A Sèvres milk jug, the *bleu lapis* ground reserved with an exotic bird in foliage, by François Joseph Aloncle, and with gilding, date letter within crossed 'L's, 1763, 4¾in (12cm) high.
£900–1,000 P

◀ A Sèvres-style jug, the body painted with portraits of ladies of the French court including Madame de Pompadour, on a dark blue ground, gilded with 'jewelled' flowers and foliage, pseudo-Sèvres marks, 19thC, 7in (18cm) high.
£300–350 P

MIRRORS

A pair of Dresden wall mirrors, white-glazed and encrusted with flowers, blue crossed swords mark, 19thC, 16in (40.5cm) high.
£250–300 Bri

A Bohemian or Thuringian mirror, surmounted by putti and encrusted with flowers, early 19thC, 20½in (52cm) wide.
£850–1,000 DORO

A pair of Sitzendorf girandoles, with a putto, flowers and leaves, decorated in coloured enamels and gilt, painted marks in blue, two candlearms missing, c1890, 19¼in (49cm) high.
£400–500 DN

A German easel mirror, applied with trailing roses and surmounted by a pair of embracing cherubs, c1900, 14¼in (36cm) high.
£300–350 S(S)

MUGS

A Bow baluster mug, decorated with a pink peony, slight damage, c1755, 4¾in (12cm) high.
£250–280 WW

A Longton Hall mug, painted with a version of the Root and Peony pattern, 1757–60, 4¾in (12cm) high.
£600–700 P

Ex-Bernard Watney collection.

A Cookworthy Plymouth or Bristol mug, with a ribbed loop handle, painted with a spray of flowers, 1768–72, 5in (12.5cm) high.
£550–600 P

PLAQUES

A pair of Berlin plaques, impressed 'KPM', 19thC, 7 x 5in (18 x 12.5cm).
£1,700–1,850 CAG

A Continental painted plaque, depicting a young lady wearing a feathered hat, 19thC, 3¼in (8.5cm) high.
£280–320 AH

A plaque, by Doulton artist Leslie Johnson, c1915, 7in (18cm) diam.
£500–600 JE

▶ A plaque, painted by J. E. Dean after J. F. Herring, probably Minton, dated '1921', 15½in (39.5cm) diam.
£2,500–3,000 LT

SAUCE BOATS & CREAM BOATS

A pair of Bow sauce boats, painted in blue with a pattern of pagodas, the interiors with peonies, one footrim restuck, c1765, 7¾in (19.5cm) long.
£550–600 P

A Chelsea sauce boat, painted with flowersprays, some damage, red anchor mark, c1755, 7½in (19cm) long.
£650–750 DN

A Chelsea sauce boat, painted with flowersprays and gilt, brown anchor mark, c1760, 7in (18cm) long.
£800–1,000 DAN

A Philip Christian & Co sauce boat, painted in blue with willow and peonies, restored, 1768–75, 5¾in (14.5cm) long.
£250–280 P

Ex-Bernard Watney collection.

A Lowestoft cream boat, painted with coloured flowers, red enamel rim, c1780, 4in (10cm) long.
£850–950 P

A Longton Hall sauce boat, probably decorated at West Pans with peach and green flowers beneath a green border, c1755, decorated 1770, 5¼in (13.5cm) long.
£800–900 JUP

A Plymouth sauce boat, decorated in dark blue with flowers and Chinese gardens, cracked, 1768–70, 8¼in (21cm) long.
£500–550 S(S)

A Vauxhall sauceboat, painted with blue flowers, the handle moulded with a monkey, damaged, 1755–78, 8¼in (21cm) long.
£600–700 P

Ex-Bernard Watney collection.

SCENT BOTTLES

A Derby scent bottle, painted in coloured enamels with figures in mountainous landscapes, gilt borders and stars, later brass cover, 1790–1800, 2in (5cm) high.
£900–1,100 DN

A Du Paquier scent bottle, painted in lime green, purple, yellow, blue, iron-red and gilding with a European figure in Oriental-style costume, c1740, 2in (5cm) high.
£2,500–2,750 S(NY)

A novelty scent bottle, in the form of a hazelnut, with silver stopper, 19thC, 1½in (4cm) high.
£250–280 LBr

> **Cross Reference**
> See Colour Review

A Meissen scent bottle, painted each side with a quay scene, gilt-metal stopper, c1750, 4½in (11.5cm) high.
£2,300–2,600 P

TEA CANISTERS

A Höchst tea canister and cover, painted with a horseman, the reverse with a bird attacking a hare, the cover with a vignette of animals, wheel mark in underglaze blue, incised letters, c1770, 5¼in (13.5cm) high.
£1,800–2,000 S

A Meissen tea canister and cover, the blue-scale ground with two painted panels of Watteauesque figures in landscapes, the gilt-metal-mounted cover with a flower-form knop, c1755, 4in (10cm) high.
£2,750–3,000 S(NY)

A Meissen tea canister and cover, the fluted body painted in polychrome with exotic birds and scattered insects, the domed cover with a floral knop, underglaze blue mark, 18thC, 5½in (14cm) high.
£1,500–1,800 HYD

A Vienna tea canister and cover, painted front and back in colours with scenes from classical mythology, each panel signed 'C. Heer', the puce side panels and yellow shoulders enriched with gilt, beehive mark in underglaze blue, 19thC, 6¾in (17cm) high.
£750–900 TEN

TRAYS

A Minton pen tray, in the Dresden shape, with encrusted flower decoration, on four shell feet, crossed swords mark, c1830, 9½in (24cm) wide.
£300–350 DIA

◄ A Minton *pâte-sur-pâte* pen tray, decorated with a cherub in salmon-pink, gold printed crown and globe mark, c1890–1900, 12in (30.5cm) wide.
£1,400–1,600 S

► A Pinxton cabaret tray, decorated with a broad band enclosing four floral panels divided by swags, c1800, 16½in (42cm) wide.
£1,000–1,100 S(S)

A Caughley spoon tray, painted in underglaze blue and enriched with gilt, c1785, 7in (18cm) wide.
£300–350 DAN

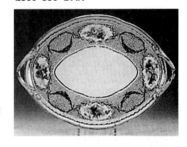

TUREENS

A pair of Derby sauce tureens, covers and stands, painted in coloured enamels with named views within gilt flower, leaf-scroll and anthemion borders, red crowned crossed batons marks, 1815–20, tureens 9in (23cm) wide.
£2,200–2,500 DN

A Sèvres-style *écuelle*, cover and stand, painted in enamels with reserves of exotic birds within gilt foliate borders and on a pink ground, 1850–60, 5in (12.5cm) diam.
£400–500 HAL

A Caughley sauce tureen, cover and stand, decorated in underglaze blue with flowers and leaves and embellished with gilt, c1785, tureen 9in (23cm) wide.
£630–700 JUP

VASES

A cornucopia-shaped vase, possibly by Samuel Alcock, the red ground with floral reserves and gilt rim, c1835, 4in (10cm) high.
£200–250 DAN

A pair of Bow vases and covers, painted with exotic birds within gilt cartouches reserved against a powder-blue ground, some damage and repair, c1770, 11in (28cm) high.
£900–1,100 S

A Coalport vase and cover, the blue ground reserved with a panel painted in colours with a country landscape, the reverse with a smaller version, the upper portion and remainder of the vase in ivory, all picked out in gold, hairline crack near rim, printed and impressed marks, c1900, 12½in (32cm) high.
£575–700 P

A Belleek pink-tinted cob vase, First Period, c1853, 6in (15cm) high.
£350–400 DeA

A Berlin KPM vase and cover, the cobalt-blue ground with ribbed sections to either side, the cover with a finial modelled as two putti, early 20thC, 26in (66cm) high.
£2,000–2,400 Bon(C)

A Copeland parian vase and cover, moulded with putti, the knop formed as a cherub, printed mark, 19thC, 15¾in (40cm) high.
£300–350 AH

A pair of Belleek lotus pattern vases, decorated with applied flowers and leaves in low relief, Second Period, 13in (33cm) high.
£600–700 JAd

A pair of Chelsea vases, each painted in polychrome with flowers, gilt line rims, restored, gold anchor marks, c1760, 7in (45.5cm) high.
£900–1,100 WW

A pair of Coalport vases and covers, each painted with oval landscape vignettes within raised gilt, yellow and cobalt ground borders, finials restuck, 1900–20, 5¾in (14.5cm) high.
£1,300–1,500 Hal

▶ A Coalport vase and cover, painted by E. Ball with a view of Loch Katrine, reserved on a dark blue ground between cream-coloured borders and gilt with scrolls and foliage, mark in green, early 20thC, 6½in (16.5cm) high.
£250–275 P

A Belleek Roscor vase, Third Period black mark, 6½in (16.5cm) high.
£160–200 SLN

A pair of Chelsea Derby cassolettes and reversible covers, each modelled with stiff-leaf and laurel garlands, picked out in gilt, on a puce ground, candle sconces missing, c1775, 6¼in (16cm) high.
£700–850 DN

A pair of Royal Crown Derby spill vases, painted with the Old Witches pattern in bright Japan colours, with gilded and moulded borders, printed marks in red, 1904, 4¼in (11cm) high.
£400–450 P

A pair of Derby vases and covers, applied overall with blue blossom and with swags of holly leaves and berries, covers damaged, c1780, tallest 11in (28cm) high.
£220–250 JAK

A pair of Royal Crown Derby vases and covers, painted with reserves of colourful flowers on a dark blue ground, embellished with gilt, mark for 1902, 13in (33cm) high.
£1,150–1,350 AAV

A Royal Crown Derby vase and cover, by Albert Gregory, painted with flowers around a gilt tablet, the neck, cover and foot with turquoise 'jewelled' and gilt decoration, printed mark, date code for 1910, 17¼in (44cm) high.
£7,000–8,500 TEN

A Royal Crown Derby vase, by W. E. J. Dean, the dark blue ground reserved with a marine painting, bordered with gilt, c1915, 6¼in (16cm) high.
£600–700 JE

A pair of Minton Sèvres-style vases, moulded with gilded rope festoons and painted with floral swags, covers missing, 1855–60, 12in (30.5cm) high.
£2,300–2,750 S

A Minton vase and cover, with *Rose de Pompadour* ground reserved with painted shipping and river scene within gilt cartouches, knop restuck, puce printed mark, c1860–9, 14½in (37cm) high.
£1,750–2,000 S

A Russian Imperial Porcelain Manufactory, St Petersburg, vase, painted in naturalistic colours with putti, the handles in the form of gilded bacchic heads, with gilded rim and foot, green cypher mark, 1855–81, 17¾in (45cm) high.
£3,200–3,500 S(NY)

A Minton *pâte-sur-pâte* vase, by Lawrence Birks, the chocolate ground decorated with three cupids, with gilded rim and base, printed and impressed marks, signed 'LB', c1885, 8¼in (21cm) high.
£1,500–1,650 P

Lawrence was one of the famous Birks family of modellers at Minton, and was one of the few artists allowed to sign his work. Trained under Solon, he developed a style very similar to his master.

A pair of Continental vases and covers, probably Paris, each reserved with fruit, some damage, mid-19thC, 5¼in (13.5cm) high.
£370–400 S(S)

A pair of German Potschappel covered vases, by Carl Thieme, each painted in colours with a panel depicting a classical building, late 19thC, 17in (43cm) high.
£1,700–1,850 NOA

A Sèvres-style vase and pierced cover, painted in enamels with figures and a wooded landscape, within gilt scroll and trophy cartouches, on a *bleu celeste* ground, pseudo-Sèvres mark in blue, c1880, 24in (61cm) high.
£1,250–1,500 DN

A Rockingham vase, decorated either side with a torch and foliate scrolls in enamel and gilt, puce mark, c1830, 5¾in (14.5cm) high.
£400–500 M&K

► A pair of Regency vases, each printed in brown with a fisherman, the reverse with a gilt flower, with beaded gilt borders, c1820, 5¼in (13.5cm) high.
£300–350 TEN

A Vauxhall vase, painted in colours with floral sprays and insects, cover missing, 1758–60, 4in (10cm) high.
£1,600–1,800 P

A Vienna vase, painted on one side with a maiden seated in a landscape, and the other with a maiden and cupid, each reserved within a gilt border on a gilt-patterned green ground, restored, blue painted shield mark, c1900, 12½in (32cm) high.
£1,650–1,800 S(NY)

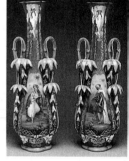

A vase, painted with a floral bouquet to either side, the gilded handles modelled as swans, scrolled gilding to the neck and foot, c1825, 11¼in (28.5cm) high.
£850–950 P

A pair of Continental blue and white striped vases and covers, with gilt borders and bud finials, late 19thC, 15½in (39.5cm) high.
£1,800–2,200 NOA

A tulip-shaped vase, the body veined with gilt and applied with moulded flowers and leaves, c1840, 8in (20.5cm) high.
£500–600 DAN

A pair of French vases, applied with vine handles with cascades of bellflowers, painted in Middle Eastern style, one with a woman by a well, the other a man in princely attire, the reverse with colourful birds, all reserved on a rich polychrome and gilt embellished ground, late 19thC, 29in (71cm) high.
£2,200–2,500 BB(S)

WALL POCKETS

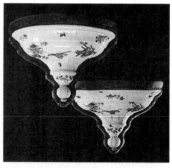

A pair of M. E. Claus cornucopia-shaped wall pockets, each with a pierced vine rim, brightly painted in coloured enamels with flowers and leaves, painted marks in blue, c1900, 8¼in (21cm) high.
£600–700 DN

A pair of Meissen Kakiemon wall brackets, converted from tureen covers, painted with dragons, cranes and insects, mounted on red velvet brackets, both damaged, c1740, 10in (25.5cm) high.
£800–1,000 S

A Meissen cornucopia-shaped foliate scroll wall vase, decorated in colours, and with a floral painted panel, repaired, late 19thC, 8½in (21.5cm) high.
£230–275 MCA

WORCESTER

The 250th anniversary of the founding of the Worcester Porcelain Company in 1751 offers a chance to contemplate the changes in collecting habits over the last 30 years. Prices for the very early pieces (1751–58) have escalated but, conversely, those for the very ornately decorated items of the 1760s to '80s have hardly kept up with inflation (except for those decorated in London by James Giles) and must show great potential for increase. At last the superb wares of Barr Flight & Barr, Flight Barr & Barr and early Chamberlain are fully appreciated, although faults as minor as slight wear to the gold can greatly lower the value, but I would sooner have a damaged piece painted by Thomas Baxter or Samuel Smith than a mint piece by a lesser artist and factory. Late Chamberlain and Kerr & Binns are other periods for which prices have not gone ahead as fast as they might, so look for these.

The second half of the 19th century was a period of recovery for Royal Worcester, whose designers adapted and anglicized ceramic shapes and decorations from Japan, Persia, and Medieval Europe, utilizing their craftsmanship to produce superb parian and majolica wares and collectable items such as candle extinguishers. The greatest explosion in price has been for the reticulated work of George Owen – breathtaking and mind-bendingly impossible to do.

The turn of the century brought forth the flowering of incredibily talented artists: Baldwyn, the Stintons, Hawkins, Sebright and the greatest of the lot, Harry Davis. The 1910s and '20s were difficult years financially for Royal Worcester but led to the three great modellers of the 1930s: Freda Doughty produced lovely studies of children, her sister Dorothy superb life-sized birds and flowers, and Doris Lindner the finest imaginable studies of horses and bulls. It is strange that the limited editions of the two latter modellers took a fall in price in the 1980s and '90s but they are going up again and must represent great prospects for the future.

To show how collecting and values have changed over 30 years, I remember Harry Davis asking me to ascertain the price of one of his superb large vases painted with Highland Sheep in a Worcester antique shop. £28 was the answer and Harry could not afford it. What would the price be now? Perhaps £5,000? It makes you think.

Henry Sandon

A set of 43 glass phials of powdered overglaze enamelling colours, two bottles of medium and one of turpentine, a glass-grinding slab and miller, palette knife with carved ivory handle and a porcelain sample plaque, by Reeves & Sons for Hancock & Son, Worcester, unused, late 19thC, in a mahogany case, 13¾in (35cm) wide.
£600–700 PFK

A Worcester blue and white basket, printed with a pine cone pattern, the exterior with applied florets, hatched crescent mark, c1780, 8¾in (22cm) diam.
£450–550 TEN

A pair of Royal Worcester busts of George V and Queen Mary, puce mark, 1935, 4½in (11.5cm) high.
£250–300 SAS

◀ A Chamberlain's Worcester model of a bird, embellished with gilt, c1830, 4in (10cm) high.
£350–450 DMa

A Worcester parian bust entitled 'Charity', c1860, 14in (35.5cm) high.
£575–650 JAK

A Worcester bough pot, the panels painted in Kakiemon style with birds and flowering plants reserved on a scale blue ground, restored, square mark, c1770, 6¾in (17cm) diam.
£1,400–1,600 P

A Royal Worcester bowl, decorated with Oriental style foliage on a blush ground, within gilded borders, printed and impressed marks and date cipher for 1888, 9in (23cm) diam.
£220–260 GAK

A Royal Worcester majolica centrepiece, modelled as shells on a fish-form base, decorated in bright colours, impressed mark, 1870–80, 6½in (16.5cm) high.
£1,800–2,000 JEA

A Worcester egg cup, painted with Music pattern in underglaze blue and gold, c1790, 2¼in (5.5cm) high.
£380–420 P

Ex-Bernard Watney collection.

A Worcester 'Chelsea Ewer' cream jug, painted in pink in Chinese style with two figures before a pavilion, the reverse with a flowerspray, c1760, 3½in (9cm) high.
£800–900 DN

A Worcester Cabbage Leaf pattern jug, printed in blue with Parrot Pecking Fruit pattern, underglaze blue mark, c1770, 8½in (21.5cm) high.
£350–420 CAG

A Royal Worcester ewer, the body inset on either side with shell-moulded plaques, painted in the centres with spring flowers, printed marks and date cipher for 1893, 7in (18cm) high.
£380–450 GAK

▶ A Royal Worcester porcelain-mounted hair brush, painted by James Stinton with a cock pheasant, with silver rim, Birmingham 1927, 4in (10cm) wide.
£700–850 AH

A Chamberlain's Worcester ice pail, decorated by George Davis, reserved on each side with gilt cartouches painted with fancy birds, within cobalt-ground gilt foliate borders, on three gilded dolphin supports, cover missing, handles damaged, 1800–10, 11in (28cm) high.
£1,000–1,200 Hal

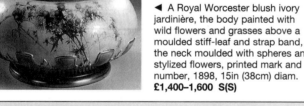

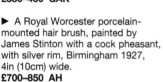

◀ A Royal Worcester blush ivory jardinière, the body painted with wild flowers and grasses above a moulded stiff-leaf and strap band, the neck moulded with spheres and stylized flowers, printed mark and number, 1898, 15in (38cm) diam.
£1,400–1,600 S(S)

Worcester: What's in a Name?

Worcester is classified according to the factory's owners:

1751–74	Dr Wall or First period (Dr John Wall, William Davis and other partners).
1774–83	Davis period (William Davis principal manager).
1783–92	Flight period (John and Joseph Flight).
1792–1804	Flight & Barr period (Joseph Flight and Martin Barr senior).
1804–13	Barr, Flight & Barr period (Martin Barr senior, Joseph Flight and Martin Barr junior).
1813–40	Flight, Barr & Barr period (Joseph Flight, Martin Barr junior and George Barr).
1840–52	Chamberlain & Co period (Chamberlain's and Flight, Barr & Barr amalgamated).
1852–62	Kerr & Binns period (W. H. Kerr and R. W. Binns joint owners).
1862–present	Worcester Royal Porcelain Co Ltd (known as Royal Worcester).

A Royal Worcester wall plaque, painted in enamels with a portrait of a Pre-Raphaelite girl, the wall behind her textured in tooled gold, within a border of turquoise foliage and gilt keyfret, impressed and printed factory marks, dated '1879', 14½in (37cm) diam.
£800–1,000 P

This most unusual plaque is probably the work of brothers James and Thomas Callowhill, who specialized in portraits and chased gilding.

A Worcester First Period dry blue platter, c1770, 17in (43cm) wide.
£850–1,000 DAN

A pair of Royal Worcester wall plates, one painted with sheep in a wooded landscape, the other with cattle in a landscape, within finely gilt decorated surrounds, signed 'H. Davis', early 20thC, 10¾in (27.5cm) diam.
£525–600 MCA

A Worcester sauceboat, painted in underglaze blue with a chrysanthemum, 1765, 7¼in (18.5cm) wide.
£450–500 JUP

◄ A Worcester sifter spoon, painted in underglaze blue with the Maltese Cross Flower pattern, c1770, 5¼in (13.5cm) long.
£630–700 JUP

A Worcester blue and white sauceboat, painted with a fisherman in a boat near a lakeside pavilion, c1760, 7½in (19cm) wide.
£800–1,000 TEN

A Royal Worcester teapot, by Scottie Wilson, transfer-printed with exotic birds, castles and trees, signed, c1960, 5in (12.5cm) high.
£220–250 DAD

A Worcester Flight & Barr teapot, decorated with gilt, c1800, 7in (18cm) high.
£300–350 DAN

> **Cross Reference**
> See Colour Review

A Worcester vase and cover, decorated with a bouquet of flowers on a ground of further sprigs, repaired, knop restored, c1760, 9in (23cm) high.
£275–300 S(S)

A Worcester Flight & Barr jardinière or vase, painted with a panel of cattle before a wooded cliff within gilded borders, c1800, 6in (15cm) high.
£450–550 HAM

A pair of vases, each painted in the style of Myles Birkett Foster with a rustic country scene within gilt ivy surrounds, on a deep blue ground, printed marks, dated '1866', 12½in (32cm) high.
£2,000–2,400 TEN

A pair of Royal Worcester vases, in Eastern style, coloured to imitate ivory, decorated in raised paste gilding with ferns and grasses on a semi-matt ground, printed marks, restored, dated '1889', 10¾in (27.5cm) high.
£250–300 P

A Royal Worcester vase, with polychrome wheat sheaf and poppy decoration highlighted with gilding, with gilt rope-tie moulded to the neck, printed mark, incised number, 19thC, 7¾in (19.5cm) high.
£150–180 Mit

A Selection of Chinese Dynasties & Marks
Early Dynasties

Neolithic	10th – early 1st millennium BC	Tang Dynasty	AD 618–907
Shang Dynasty	16th Century–c1050 BC	Five Dynasties	AD 907–960
Zhou Dynasty	c1050–221 BC	Liao Dynasty	AD 907–1125
Warring States	480–221 BC	Song Dynasty	AD 960–1279
Qin Dynasty	221–206 BC	*Northern Song*	AD 960–1127
Han Dynasty	206 BC–AD 220	*Southern Song*	AD 1127–1279
Six Dynasties	AD 222–589	Xixia Dynasty	AD 1038–1227
Wei Dynasty	AD 386–557	Jin Dynasty	AD 1115–1234
Sui Dynasty	AD 581–618	Yuan Dynasty	AD 1279–1368

Ming Dynasty Marks

Hongwu
1368–1398

Yongle
1403–1424

Xuande
1426–1435

Chenghua
1465–1487

Hongzhi
1488–1505

Zhengde
1506–1521

Jiajing
1522–1566

Longqing
1567–1572

Wanli
1573–1619

Tianqi
1621–1627

Chongzhen
1628–1644

Qing Dynasty Marks

Shunzhi
1644–1661

Kangxi
1662–1722

Yongzheng
1723–1735

Qianlong
1736–1795

Jiaqing
1796–1820

Daoguang
1821–1850

Xianfeng
1851–1861

Tongzhi
1862–1874

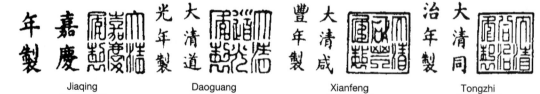

Guangxu
1875–1908

Xuantong
1909–1911

Hongxian
1916

Chinese Ceramics

ANIMALS & BIRDS

A green lead-glazed model of a pottery dog, Han Dynasty, 206 BC–AD 220, 17in (43cm) high.
£6,500–8,000 GLD

A *sancai*-glazed buff pottery model of a Bactrian camel, Tang Dynasty, AD 618–907, 22½in (57cm) high.
£2,400–2,800 P

An amber and white *sancai*-glazed pottery horse and rider, restored, Tang Dynasty, AD 618–907, 14½in (37cm) high.
£1,800–2,000 SK

▶ A pair of Cantonese candleholders, modelled as dogs, the bodies decorated in iron-red with gilt details, damaged, Qing Dynasty, 19thC, 6in (15cm) long.
£260–300 LAY

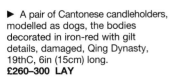

A painted grey pottery model of a horse and rider, Western Han Dynasty, 206 BC–AD 220, 22¾in (58cm) high.
£10,000–11,000 S

A painted pottery model of a horse, traces of red, brown, black and green pigment throughout, Tang Dynasty, AD 618–907, 21¾in (55.5cm) high.
£4,500–5,000 S(NY)

A pair of bisque models of dogs of Fo, with *famille verte* decoration, losses, Qing Dynasty, 18th/19thC, 19in (48.5cm) high.
£4,500–5,000 SK

A grey pottery model of a horse, traces of red pigment, Northern Wei Dynasty, AD 386–557, 9in (23cm) high.
£9,500–10,500 S(NY)

A chestnut-glazed buff pottery model of a horse and rider, restored, Tang Dynasty, AD 618–907, 16in (40.5cm) high.
£3,000–3,500 P

A pair of *blanc de Chine* models of cockerels, Kangxi period, late 17thC, 7½in (19cm) high.
£4,500–5,000 S

Blanc de Chine is a white, or near white, porcelain with a thick, rich glaze. It was used in the Dehua area of China from the late Ming Dynasty, particularly in the manufacture of figures for export during the 17th and 18thC.

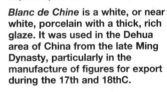

A pair of models of phoenixes, with *famille rose* decoration, Qing Dynasty, 19thC, 24in (61cm) high.
£3,000–3,500 SK

BOWLS

A moulded amber-glazed bowl, with green-glazed interior, Tang Dynasty, AD 618–907, 3½in (9cm) diam.
£650–800 GLD

A *kraak porselein*-type barbed-rim bowl, the centre painted with a recumbent beast resting in a fenced garden, Wanli period, 1573–1619, 8½in (21.5cm) diam.
£650–750 P

A blue and white porcelain bowl, the interior painted with scrolling lotus, the exterior with scrolling hibiscus, six character Chenghua mark, Kangxi period, 1662–1722, cracked, 6in (15cm) diam.
£2,800–3,200 Hal

A blue and white bowl, painted with scenes of figures at various pursuits between sprays of lotus and prunus blossom, Kangxi period, 1662–1722, 7¾in (19.5cm) diam.
£450–550 P

A moulded Yaozhou bowl, sealed crack, Song Dynasty, circa AD 1100, 6½in (16.5cm) diam.
£500–600 GLD

A *wucai* bowl, painted in red, yellow and green, Transitional period, c1650, 6in (15cm) diam.
£1,500–1,800 GLD

A bowl, with *sang-de-boeuf* glaze and orange peel surface, underglaze blue six character mark, Kangxi period, 1662–1722, 6in (15cm) diam.
£2,300–2,750 Hal

A Chinese export blue and white basket, the centre painted with a tree and peony issuing from rocks, chipped, Qing Dynasty, late 18thC, 15in (38cm) wide.
£1,200–1,400 L

A rust-splashed blackware bowl, Song/Jin Dynasty, 12thC, 6¼in (16cm) diam.
£2,000–2,400 S

A blue and white *kraak porselein* bowl, with Dutch silver handle, Shunzhi period, c1650, 5½in (14cm) diam.
£550–650 GeW

A pair of *famille verte* bowls, decorated with panels of flowers and mythological beasts, the interior with flowers and floral borders, both cracked, Kangxi period, 1662–1722, each 7¼in (18.5cm) diam.
£700–850 DN

A punchbowl, decorated with Fitzhugh pattern, painted with scrolled lappets interspersed with peony sprays to form a band on both sides, Qing Dynasty, 1800–20, 15¾in (40cm) diam.
£2,750–3,000 S

Fitzhugh is a particular export pattern for the USA market, named after the person who first ordered it. It is characterized by a border of four split pomegranates and butterflies.

◄ A *famille verte* bowl, the interior enamelled in polychrome with a mountainous landscape, the exterior with a lakeland landscape, Qing Dynasty, 19thC, 21¼in (54cm) diam.
£2,300–2,750 HYD

A Canton bowl, decorated with panels of figures, Qing Dynasty, mid-19thC, 16in (40.5cm) diam.
£1,200–1,400 HOK

A set of three blue and white graduated bowls, the exteriors decorated with lotus flowers below the eight Buddhistic emblems, the interiors painted in Japanese Satsuma-style with groups of sages and boys at play, some repair, Qing Dynasty, 19thC, largest 9in (23cm) diam.
£400–500 P

A pair of *famille rose* bowls, the exteriors each with Buddhist decoration of seven throned emblems, the interiors each with a lotus, Qing Dynasty, 19thC, 9¼in (23.5cm) diam.
£550–650 SK

A porcelain chestnut basket, decorated with panels of figures and flowers in yellow, blue and salmon pink, with pierced sides and gilt rope handles, Qing Dynasty, late 19thC, 11in (28cm) wide.
£200–240 Hal(C)

A pair of yellow-ground bowls, painted in bright yellow on a biscuit body, incised with dragons chasing a flaming pearl, with carved wooden stands, underglaze blue mark, Guangxu period, 1875–1908, 4in (10cm) diam.
£1,400–1,600 P

CUPS

A celadon stem cup, incised with flowers, Song Dynasty, AD 960–1279, 4½in (11.5cm) high.
£1,600–1,750 Hal

A blue and white teabowl and saucer, Kangxi period, 1662–1722, saucer 3½in (9cm) diam.
£180–200 GLD

▶ A pair of Meissen-style coffee cups, each painted in iron-red, puce, grey, green and yellow enamels and gilt with a European country scene, Qianlong period, 1736–95, 2½in (6.5cm) high.
£280–340 P

A blue and white stem cup, the interior decorated with Zhang Qian on a raft, Ming Dynasty, 1368–1644, 4½in (11.5cm) high.
£4,500–5,500 Hal

Zhang Qian (died 114 BC) was a traveller. He became famous for the improvement of geographical knowledge, opening up new trade routes and the introduction to China of seeds of hitherto unknown plants.

A blue and white teabowl and saucer, decorated with a hunting scene, Kangxi period, 1662–1722, saucer 3in (7.5cm) diam.
£200–220 GLD

A Chinese export teabowl and saucer, decorated in black and gilt, Qianlong period, c1740, saucer 4in (10cm) diam.
£380–450 DAN

DISHES

A celadon dish, with deep sea green glaze, the centre incised with a trellis within a band of scrolling lotus, the reverse finely incised with an Arabic inscription, Ming Dynasty, late 14thC, 17½in (44.5cm) diam.
£2,000–2,200 DN

A blue and white *kraak porselein* dish, the centre decorated with flowers, Ming Dynasty, early 17thC, 18in (45.5cm) diam.
£2,000–2,500 GLD

A blue and white plate, made for the Indian or Tibetan market, Kangxi period, c1700, 13½in (34.5cm) diam.
£1,500–1,800 GeW

A pair of blue and white saucer dishes, Wanli period, 1573–1619, 5in (12.5cm) diam.
£650–800 GLD

A *Ko-sometsuke* blue and white dish, Tianqi period, 1620s, 5in (12.5cm) diam.
£550–700 GLD

***Ko-sometsuke* (old blue and white) wares were made particularly for the Japanese market where they were used as part of the tea ceremony.**

A blue and white saucer dish, made for the European market, Kangxi period, c1700, 14in (35.5cm) diam.
£800–900 GeW

◀ A *doucai* dish, the interior painted with deer beside a pine tree, the border with bats and cloud scrolls in red, green, yellow and blue, the exterior with four *lingzhi* sprigs, Chenghua mark, Kangxi/Yongzheng period, late 17th/early 18thC, 8in (20.5cm) diam.
£2,300–2,750 S(HK)

Lingzhi is a type of fungus or mushroom used as a motif on Chinese porcelain.

Chinese Imari

Chinese Imari wares were copies or pastiches of Japanese Imari, made largely for export from the early 18thC. The decoration involved Japanese brocade designs and the typical Imari palette of dark underglaze blue, iron-red and gilt.

A Chinese Imari saucer dish, painted with flowerheads and foliage in underglaze blue, iron-red and gilt, Kangxi period, 1662–1722, 15½in (39.5cm) diam.
£230–275 CGC

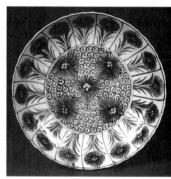

A pair of Chinese export blue and white saucer dishes, painted with stylized chrysanthemums, Kangxi period, c1700, 10in (25.5cm) diam.
£750–900 GeW

A Chinese Imari saucer dish, decorated in iron-red, underglaze blue and gilt, incised Dresden inventory mark, Qing Dynasty, early 18thC, 8¾in (22cm) diam.
£370–450 P

The inventory mark indicates that this piece originates from a sale of superfluous items from the Dresden factory in the early 20thC, although fake marks are known to exist.

A pair of *famille rose* Tobacco Leaf dishes, painted with flowers and leaves, Qianlong period, 1736–95, 11in (28cm) diam.
£2,200–2,500 P

A pair of Chinese export *famille rose* saucer dishes, the centres painted with peacocks, surrounded by peony and chrysanthemum borders, Qianlong period, 1736–95, 10in (25.5cm) diam.
£700–800 S(S)

Further Reading

Miller's Chinese & Japanese Antiques Buyer's Guide, Miller's Publications, 1999

▶ A deep dish, painted in coloured enamels with figures in a landscape with a dragon and cloud scroll border, Qing Dynasty, 19thC, 15in (38cm) wide.
£350–420 L

A *doucai* saucer dish, the exterior painted with stylized lotus on scrolling stems, the interior with a central medallion, rim crack, restored chip, Qianlong mark and of the period, 1736–95, 7½in (19cm) diam.
£800–900 P

A *famille rose* tureen stand, the centre painted with a woman and two attendants, Qianlong period, 1736–95, 14½in (37cm) wide.
£550–650 P

Famille Rose

Coloured enamelling on Chinese porcelain became popular in the early 18thC and was named after the predominant background colour – *famille verte* (green), *famille jaune* (yellow) and the rare *famille noire* (black). *Famille rose* enamelling, the opaque pink of which was derived from colloidal gold (ultramicroscopic particles of gold held in suspension in the glaze) was not used until c1720. It was one of the few ceramic innovations to be introduced to China by Europeans, and by the mid-18th century the demand for this type of decoration for export wares almost equalled that for blue and white. Orders for huge *famille rose* dinner services, often decorated with a family coat-of-arms or crest, were received from Europe and consequently many pieces have survived to this day.

A *famille rose* basin, the centre painted with a coat-of-arms, restored, Qianlong period, c1755, 14½in (37cm) diam.
£800–900 P

FIGURES

◀ A tilework figure of Buddha, decorated in green, yellow and aubergine, Ming Dynasty, 16thC, 17¾in (45cm) high.
£3,200–3,800 S

▶ A *blanc de Chine* figure of Guanyin, Qing Dynasty, 18thC, 15½in (39.5cm) high.
£1,800–2,200 S(Am)

A pair of *famille rose* figures of female deities, decorated in bright enamels, minor damage, Qing Dynasty, mid-19thC, 18½in (47cm) high.
£3,700–4,000 P

FLATWARE

A *famille verte* Birthday plate, Kangxi mark, 1662–1722, 9¾in (25cm) diam.
£7,500–9,000 S(NY)

A *famille verte* plate, the centre decorated with a bird among flowering branches, the rim with a green band, Kangxi period, 1662–1722, 9¾in (25cm) diam.
£600–700 P

An armorial plate, bearing the Lauder family coat-of-arms, decorated in pink, green, blue and gilt, the centre painted with a peacock, Qianlong period, c1760, 9in (23cm) diam.
£450–500 C&C

A *famille rose* Tobacco Leaf dish, painted with leaves and flowers, Qianlong period, 1736–95, 13½in (34.5cm) wide.
£2,500–3,000 P

A blue and white landscape dish, painted with figures in a rocky landscape, underglaze blue six character Chenghua mark, early Kangxi period, 1662–1722, 10in (25.5cm) diam.
£750–900 Hal

A Chinese Imari plate, painted with La Dame au Parasol in iron-red, blue and gilt after a design by Cornelis Pronk, Qianlong period, c1737, 9½in (24cm) diam.
£600–700 P

Made in 1734, this was the first design by Pronk for the Dutch East India Company and the original drawing is held in the Rijksmuseum, Amsterdam. It represents Pronk's interpretation of a Chinese blue and white prototype. In addition to those in the Chinese Imari palette, as illustrated here, examples exist in both later Chinese *famille rose* enamels, and also in Japanese porcelain. No other such subjects are found on either Chinese or Japanese porcelain.

A Chinese export charger, decorated in underglaze blue with entwined flowers, Qianlong period, 1736–95, 17¾in (45cm) wide.
£600–700 DN

A pair of Chinese export plates, enamelled with the arms of De Knyff, Burgomaster of Antwerp, Qianlong period, c1740, 19in (48.5cm) diam.
£9,500–10,500 C&C

These plates were commissioned through the Ostend Company which was in existence for only 20 years.

A set of three Chinese export meat dishes, decorated in underglaze blue with river landscapes, Qianlong period, largest 14¼in (36cm) wide.
£800–950 DN

A blue and white dish, painted with a stag and doe in a landscape, Qianlong period, 1736–95, 13¾in (35cm) wide.
£340–400 P(O)

GARDEN SEATS

A pair of Canton *famille rose* garden seats, enamel decorated with panels of figures within landscapes alternating with pierced panels, Qing Dynasty, late 19thC, 18¼in (46.5cm) diam.
£3,500–4,200 Bri

A pair of blue and white barrel seats, painted and pierced with cash coins, scrolling lotus blossoms, *ruyi*-heads and florets, Guangxu period, c1900, 18¼in (446.5cm) diam.
£2,200–2,650 TEN

A pair of *famille rose* garden seats, painted with flowers within geometric borders, Qing Dynasty, 19thC, 19in (48.5cm) diam.
£2,000–2,200 SK(B)

JARS

A grey pottery jar, impressed with bands of overlapping keyfret, Western Zhou Dynasty, 1050–221 BC, 19¼in (49cm) high.
£3,500–4,000 S(NY)

A green lead-glazed hill jar and cover, Han Dynasty, 206 BC–AD 220, 10in (25.5cm) high.
£1,400–1,800 GLD

The cover is moulded to represent a hill.

A green-glazed pottery jar, supported on three feet, Han Dynasty, 206 BC–AD 220, 14½in (37cm) high.
£275–300 P

A Cizhou jar, decorated in sgraffito black and white, Song Dynasty, AD 960–1280, 3¼in (8.5cm) high.
£2,700–3,250 Hal

Cizhou is a generic term for a type of stoneware. Cixian (Cizhou) itself was the most important site for this type of decoration which came from many different kilns in northern China. It is characterized by bold shapes and decoration on a slip-covered body.

A brown-glazed Henan jar, decorated with white slip, Song Dynasty, AD 960–1279, 8¾in (22cm) high.
£2,000–2,400 S(Am)

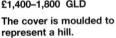

A Longquan celadon jar and cover, Yuan Dynasty, c1300, 4½in (11.5cm) diam.
£650–800 GLD

Longquan is a kiln site in southern China, famous for its celadons during the Yuan and early Ming Dynasties.

A blue and white jar, the exterior decorated with a kilin before mountainous landscapes, Transitional period, mid-17thC, 11½in (29cm) high.
£600–650 P

◄ A *wucai* jar, painted with a dignitary and two attendants, cracked, Transitional period, mid-17thC, 7¼in (18.5cm) high.
£320–380 P

A blue and white jar and cover, decorated with a scholar and an attendant in a mountainous landscape, Kangxi period, 1662–1722, 9¼in (23.5cm) high.
£1,600–2,000 S(Am)

◄ A dragon jar, painted in underglaze blue and copper-red with four dragons amid bats and fire scrolls, Qing Dynasty, 19thC, 15½in (39.5cm) high.
£3,500–4,000 S(HK)

TEAPOTS

A *famille rose* teapot, decorated with two scenes of a falconer attended by children in a garden, applied with a gilt bracket handle and S-shaped spout, the cover with a peach-shaped finial, Qianlong period, 1736–95, 7½in (19cm) high.
£500–550 P

A *famille rose* teapot, decorated with a river scene, Qianlong period, 1780, 5¼in (13.5cm) high.
£800–900 GeW

Both English pottery and Chinese export porcelain teapot shapes followed European silver shapes.

A teapot, by Wu Youyin, decorated with vegetables in green, red and mauve, the cover with an inscription from an ancient bronze *ding* tripod, dated '1946', 3¼in (8.5cm) high.
£1,000–1,200 Wai

TUREENS

◀ A blue and white tureen and cover, with pomegranate finial, stand missing, damaged, Qianlong period, 1736–95, 13in (33cm) wide.
£150–180 Hal

A Chinese export *famille rose* tureen, cover and stand, with floral sprays within pink drapes and scrolling foliate bands, cover restored, Qianlong period, 1736–95, stand 14¾in (37.5cm) wide.
£1,500–1,800 Bea(E)

A *famille rose* tureen and cover, decorated with floral sprays, Qianlong period, c1750, 10in (25.5cm) diam.
£3,200–3,500 C&C

◀ A blue and white tureen and cover, Qianlong period, c1780, 13in (33cm) wide.
£1,200–1,500 GeW

A Chinese export *famille rose* tureen, cover and stand, decorated with flowersprays within an orange scale pattern border, Qianlong period, late 18thC, stand 15in (38cm) wide.
£3,000–3,300 S(NY)

VASES

▶ A Yingqing funerary vase, the shoulders, neck and cover applied with figures and animals, all covered under a greyish glaze with iron-brown streaks, small chips, AD 960–1279, 13in (33cm) high.
£320–380 S(Am)

Yingqing (also known as Qingbai) is a type of porcelain first produced during the Song Dynasty from Jingdezhen, Jiangxi Province. Jingdezhen is still the 'porcelain' capital of China.

A Warring States vase, with incised pattern, 475–221 BC, 16in (40.5cm) high.
£1,000–1,200 GLD

A *kraak porselein* bottle vase, Wanli period, c1600, 10½in (26.5cm) high.
£1,500–1,800 GeW

A blue and white vase, painted in cobalt blue with mounted warriors in a mountain river scene, Chongzhen period, 1628–44, 17¼in (44cm) high.
£4,500–5,000 S

A turquoise-glazed bottle vase, applied on the shoulder with a moulded cartouche, Ming Dynasty, 16thC, 8in (20.5cm) high.
£150–180 P

It is uncommon to encounter vessels of this type and date bearing captions. The inscription may indicate this vessel was made to equip a temple.

A *doucai* vase and cover, decorated with ladies and children, Transitional period, c1650, 16in (40.5cm) high.
£2,500–3,000 DN

An underglaze blue and white vase, painted in outline and wash with an attendant boy proffering a book to a scholar, Transitional period, mid-17thC, 6¾in (17cm) high.
£1,600–2,000 P

An underglaze blue and white vase, decorated with figures in a pavilion, early Kangxi period, 1662–1722, 18in (45.5cm) high.
£2,500–3,000 DN

A blue and white vase and cover, the handles moulded with lion masks and *ruyi*-heads, Kangxi period, 1662–1722, 11in (28cm) high.
£5,500–6,000 S(S)

This vase is particularly desirable because of its rare shape and superb quality and condition, even retaining its original cover.

A *famille verte* beaker vase, painted with a scene of two ladies attending a maiden in a wheeled chair and scenes of figures, gardens, precious objects and calligraphy, with ormolu mounts, Kangxi period, 1662–1722, 18¼in (46.5cm) high.
£5,000–5,500 S(NY)

A *famille verte* vase and cover, decorated with mythical beasts and birds, Kangxi period, 1662–1722, 15½in (39.5cm) high.
£1,400–1,700 HYD

An inscribed blue and white vase, painted with variations of the *shou* character in 16 vertical lines, the neck inscribed with further wishes of longevity, Kangxi mark and of the period, 1672–1722, 17¾in (45cm) high.
£4,000–5,000 S(HK)

A blue and white vase, painted with a mountain lake landscape, Kangxi period, 1662–1722, 17¼in (44cm) high.
£2,200–2,600 S

A pair of blue and white vases, decorated with Long Elizas and flowers, Kangxi period, 1662–1722, 1½in (4cm) high.
£200–240 Hal

In the early 18thC it was very popular in Europe to collect miniatures, and many such small pieces were ordered from China to meet the demand.

A *yenyen* vase, painted in underglaze blue with a scene of scholars and fishermen in a rocky lake landscape, Kangxi period, 1662–1722, 18in (45.5cm) high.
£2,000–2,400 S

A blue and white triple gourd vase, Kangxi period, c1700, 6in (15cm) high.
£1,100–1,250 GeW

A blue-glazed vase, the neck applied with loop handles, Qianlong period, 1736–95, 5½in (14cm) high.
£350–420 P

A pair of *famille rose* vases, decorated with a willow tree emerging from a craggy rock among a profusion of flowers beside a fence, lids missing, Qianlong period, 1736–95, 10in (25.5cm) high.
£650–720 P

A bottle vase, with deep copper-red ground below a graduated white-glazed neck, Qing Dynasty, 18thC, 9in (23cm) high.
£350–420 Hal

A mauve flambé-glazed bottle vase, streaked in creamish-grey over a raspberry-coloured ground, Qing Dynasty, 19thC, 16¼in (41.5cm) high.
£500–550 P

A pair of Canton *famille rose* vases and covers, painted with panels of dignitaries and attendants, the shoulder applied with four lug handles in the form of animal masks, the cover surmounted by a lion dog knop, damaged and repaired, Qing Dynasty, 19thC, 17in (43cm) high.
£2,000–2,200 S(S)

A *famille rose* vase, with *millefleur* design on a gilt ground, turquoise-glazed interior and foot, early 20thC, 16in (40.5cm) high.
£1,600–1,800 SK

A pair of Canton celadon vases, decorated with birds, insects and flowers on a green ground, Qing Dynasty, late 19thC, 15½in (39.5cm) high.
£700–850 JNic

A Chinese export garniture set, comprising two vases and three covered urns with dogs of Fo finials, decorated in the Cabbage Pattern, Qing Dynsasty, 19thC, largest 14½in (37cm) high.
£2,200–2,500 SK(B)

A pair of bottle vases, applied with dragons and decorated with court figures, Qing Dynasty, late 19thC, 12in (30.5cm) high.
£250–300 BIG

◄ A *famille noire* five-piece garniture, with prunus decoration, Qing Dynasty, late 19thC, largest 15in (38cm) high.
£1,500–1,800 SK

A sepia painted vase, with unrecorded studio seal mark 'Yong shi shan fang: The Mountain Retreat of Eternal Truth', Republic period, 1916–20, 13in (33cm) high.
£1,000–1,200 Wai

MISCELLANEOUS

A *doucai* brushpot, decorated in shades of green, iron-red and yellow with courtiers approaching an inebriated scholar seated on the floor, Kangxi period, 1662–1722, 6in (15cm) high.
£5,000–6,000 S(HK)

A Chinese Imari chamber pot and cover, Qing Dynasty, early 18thC, 9in (23cm) diam.
£1,450–1,750 GeW

A *famille rose* mug, Qianlong period, c1760, 5in (12.5cm) high.
£350–420 DAN

A Chinese export chocolate pot, Qing Dynasty, late 18thC, 7½in (19cm) high.
£600–700 Wai

A Chinese export *famille rose* mug, painted with panels of birds perched on branches above diaper and flower designs, Qing Dynasty, 18thC, 5¾in (14.5cm) high.
£250–300 P(B)

A jardinière, painted in underglaze blue and white with chrysanthemums, Qianlong period, 1736–95, 13¾in (35cm) high.
£1,600–2,000 P

◄ A Chinese Imari hexagonal salt cellar, Kangxi period, c1720, 2½in (6.5cm) high.
£650–800 GeW

A plaque, decorated with a lakeside landscape, painted in the Qianjiang palette and signed by Liu Yin Chang, Guangxu period, c1880, 11in (28cm) diam.
£800–1,000 Wai

The 'impressionist' style of the painting is typical of the work being carried out at that time.

A lemon-yellow glazed snuff bottle, pierced and incised with a writhing dragon, Qing Dynasty, 19thC, 3in (7.5cm) high.
£500–600 P

◄ A Chinese export *famille rose* snuff box, modelled as a European shoe, painted with flowersprays within iron-red, black and gilt borders, cover missing, Qianlong period, 1736–95, 3¾in (9.5cm) wide.
£1,250–1,500 S

A pair of sauce boats, painted with stylized floral medallions amid flowers and leaves, restored, Qianlong period, 1736–95, 7¾in (20cm) wide.
£1,750–2,000 P

A 'beehive' waterpot, incised with three medallions of dragons and applied with a copper-red glaze, Kangxi mark and of the period, 1662–1722, 5in (12.5cm) diam.
£7,000–8,000 S

Japanese Ceramics

Japanese Chronology Chart

Jomon period (Neolithic)	circa 10,000–100 BC	Muromachi (Ashikaga) period	1333–1568
Yayoi period	circa 200 BC–AD 200	Momoyama period	1568–1600
Tumulus (Kofun) period	AD 200–552	Edo (Tokugawa) period	1600–1868
Asuka period	AD 552–710	*Genroku period*	*1688–1703*
Nara period	AD 710–794	Meiji period	1868–1911
Heian perio	AD 794–1185	Taisho period	1912–1926
Kamakura period	1185–1333	Showa period	1926–1989

ANIMALS

A Hirado model of a puppy, Meiji period, c1890, 4in (10cm) high.
£1,000–1,200 GLD

A porcelain model of a recumbent deer, the blueish glaze over a textured body, the head with sockets to receive real antlers, 19thC or earlier, 27¾in (70.5cm) high.
£11,500–14,000 WW

A Hirado model of a monkey holding a brown and blue nut, c1900, 5¾in (14.5cm) high.
£1,200–1,300 MCN

▶ A red earthenware model of a monkey with a persimmon, late 19thC, 5½in (14cm) high.
£250–275 SK

BOWLS & DISHES

An Imari barber's bowl, painted in enamel colours and gold with a vase of peonies, the rim with landscapes, some damage, early 18thC, 10¾in (27.5cm) diam.
£250–300 Bea(E)

A Kakiemon-style bowl, decorated in blue with panels of flowers, the interior with a landscape roundel below birds, insects and flowers, restored, late 17th/early 18thC, 7in (18cm) diam.
£1,000–1,200 S(Am)

An Arita underglaze blue and white bowl, the interior painted with two *ho-o* separated by peonies, the exterior with two trailing floral sprays, early 18thC, 11in (28cm) diam.
£1,250–1,500 P

A *ho-o* is a mythical bird similar to a phoenix, symbolising wisdom and energy.

▶ A pair of Imari bowls, each painted in a rich palette, one depicting a *shishi*, the other a pair of cranes, reserved on a deep blue ground with gilt scrolling, lacking covers, 18thC, 8½in (21.5cm) high.
£850–950 P

LOCATE THE SOURCE

The source of each illustration in Miller's can be found by checking the code letters below each caption with the Key to Illustrations, pages 789–795.

A pair of Arita blue and white saucer dishes, each decorated with the figure of a scholar, with gilt rims, c1740, 5in (12.5cm) diam.
£650–800 GLD

A pair of Imari dishes, the centre painted with a vase of flowers, the rim painted with chrysanthemum heads and leafy sprigs, 18thC, 8½in (21.5cm) diam.
£550–650 P

A set of five Arita dishes, with underglaze blue decoration of a bird and flowering prunus tree, early 19thC, 5½in (14cm) diam.
£350–400 SK

An underglaze blue basin, decorated with morning glories and chrysanthemums, 19thC, 21in (53.5cm) diam.
£600–720 SK

▶ An Imari porcelain bowl, with a pierced gilt-metal rim, decorated overall with fan-shaped panels enclosing exotic birds in cobalt, iron-red and gilt, some damage, late Edo period, mid-19thC, 12½in (32cm) diam.
£400–450 NOA

A set of four Arita bowls, the interiors with central dragon roundels within floral borders, the exteriors with formalized scrolls, *fuku* mark, 19thC, 7in (18cm) wide.
£600–700 SK

The *fuku* mark symbolizes happiness.

A Satsuma earthenware bowl, by Yabu Meizan of Osaka, the interior painted with a landscape of a lake and mountains, Mount Fuji in the far distance, the exterior with a band of flowers, signed, Meiji period, 1868–1911, 8¼in (21cm) diam.
£6,500–7,500 S(L)

A Satsuma bowl, the interior painted with a scene of women and children at a well, the exterior with fan-shaped panels of figures on a frieze of flowers, signed 'Hozan' on base, Meiji period, 1868–1911, 4¼in (11cm) diam.
£1,500–1,800 P

An Imari bowl, decorated in underglaze blue with red and green enamels and gilt highlights, 19thC, 8½in (21.5cm) diam.
£200–240 SK

A Satsuma dish, signed 'Kozan', Meiji period, 1868–1911, 4¼in (11cm) square.
£800–885 MER

An Arita blue and white dish, in the Nabeshima style, Meiji period, c1900, 5in (12.5cm) diam.
£750–900 GLD

FLATWARE

A charger, decorated in blue, yellow and brown with an exotic bird standing in front of a basket of flowers, late 19thC, 31in (78.5cm) diam.
£1,000–1,200 DD

An Arita blue and white plate, the interior decorated with figures of children, surrounded by a brocade and calligraphy border, the exterior with flowering branches, 18thC, 11¼in (28.5cm) diam.
£700–850 SK

> **Cross Reference**
> See Colour Review

An Imari charger, painted with a vase of flowers encircled by panels of flora and fauna, reserved on a dark blue ground interspersed with iron-red medallions, Meiji period, 1868–1911, 24½in (62cm) diam.
£450–550 P

▶ A Satsuma plate, signed 'Shizan', Meiji period, 1868–1911, 6in (15cm) diam.
£550–600 MCN

JARS

An Arita jar, decorated in underglaze blue and white with pavilions in a mountainous landscape, drilled, late 17thC, 11in (28cm) high.
£750–825 P

A pair of Arita Imari jars, decorated with gilt and painted in iron-red over underglaze blue, late 17th/early 18thC, 10¾in (27.5cm) high.
£900–1,000 P

A Satsuma jar, the brown ground decorated in gilt and iron-red with a family of three long-legged *kirin*, signed 'Kinkozan' on base, Meiji period, 1868–1911, 4¾in (12cm) high.
£1,200–1,400 RTo

A Satsuma jar and cover, painted with scenes of figures crossing a bridge, and of quail among flowers, signed 'Ryuzan' on base, Meiji period, 1868–1911, 8¾in (22cm) high.
£3,500–4,200 P

VASES

◀ An Imari vase and cover, painted in underglaze blue with gilt, black, iron-red and green enamels, with alternating panels of cranes among bamboo and lions crouched on rocks, the cover surmounted by a gilt lion finial, finial restored, late 17thC, 24¾in (63cm) high.
£1,700–2,000 P

An Arita vase, enamelled in aubergine, green, yellow and black, mid-17thC, 11½in (29cm) high.
£11,000–12,000 HYD

This is a superb early piece of Arita ware.

An Arita blue and white vase, relief decorated with a dragon around the body, and in blue with birds and flowers, late 19thC, 19in (48.5cm) diam.
£900–1,000 SK

A Hirado blue and white vase, decorated with four panels moulded and painted in underglaze blue depicting fish and birds, reserved on an incised ground of interlocking keys, 19thC, 9in (23cm) high.
£1,000–1,200 P

A pair of Imari vases, decorated with birds, floral panels, chrysanthemums and landscapes, each cover applied with a robed female figure, 19thC, 36in (91.5cm) high.
£2,500–3,000 Mit

A pair of Satsuma vases, decorated with panels of Samurai and scholars, Meiji period, 1868–1911, 14½in (37cm) high.
£250–300 P(E)

A pair of Imari vases, with moulded ties to the centre and ribbed body, late 19thC, 7in (18cm) high.
£400–450 Mit

A pair of Kutani vases, painted in iron-red, black, green, yellow and blue with panels of figures reserved on a ground of flowers and scattered hexagonal cells, six-character mark, Meiji period, c1900, 30¾in (78cm) high.
£800–1,000 P

A Satsuma vase, decorated with panels on a blue flower-strewn ground, one with a cockerel and a hen in a grassy landscape, the other with carp swimming among water weeds, signed 'Kinkozan', Meiji period, 1868–1911, 12½in (32cm) high.
£2,500–3,000 WW

▶ A pair of Satsuma pottery vases, painted with birds among flowering branches on a pale grey ground, the base with four felines, the neck applied with feline handles and painted in gilt and colour, slight damage, Meiji period, 1868–1911, 16in (40.5cm) high.
£450–550 P

Hirado

Hirado porcelain was produced at Mikawachi, close to the Arita kilns. Founded in about 1770, the kiln became famous for its fine quality underglaze blue decorated porcelain. Made to the highest technical standard, with a white glassy body and fine painting, it became very popular in the west. The body was often cut with fine openwork or applied in high relief. At the beginning of the 20thC the Hirado factory was taken over by the Fukagawa Company.

A Satsuma earthenware vase, decorated in coloured enamels and gilt with scattered stylized *kiku* and *kiri mon*, Meiji period, 1868–1911, 14½in (37cm) high.
£3,000–3,300 S

A Satsuma vase, the cobalt blue ground decorated with butterflies and gilt floral scrolls framing reserves of the sun goddess and a banquet scene, signed 'Kinkozan', late 19thC, 12in (30.5cm) high.
£1,400–1,600 SK

A Satsuma earthenware vase, decorated in coloured enamels and gilt with three monkeys and trailing wistaria, signed 'Yabu Meizan', Meiji period, 1868–1911, 7¼in (18.5cm) high.
£13,000–15,000 S

Yabu Meizan (1853–1934) was a famous pottery decorator, with a studio in Osaka. He painted in Satsuma 'brocade' style and won many prizes in international exhibitions. His work was very poplar in the west and he made several trips to Europe and America.

A pair of vases, painted in the Satsuma style with figures in a landscape, Meiji period, 1868–1911, 9¾in (25cm) high.
£900–1,000 MCN

Glass

In the past year prices for drinking glasses have reached new highs and for the rarest examples it is more or less impossible to predict at auction where the bidding will stop. This is due to increased competition for new acquisitions and a shortage of goods on the market. Until recently there were regular sales of glass in London comprising several hundred lots, but now they are few and far between.

It is the perennial favourites that have seen the most dramatic increases. Baluster glasses with the rarer knops have increased in price the most. For example when acorn, mushroom or cylinder knops occur in a goblet-sized glass, a price of £5,000 to £10,000 can be expected. Even the minor baluster glasses which until recently sold for £300 to £500 are now fetching £600 to £900.

Colour twist prices are mostly still strong, but a rare form, colour or colour combination can result in prices soaring into five figures. In the case of Beilby enamelled glasses, only the finest enamelling will command a higher price.

One category of drinking glass that has seen an increase in value recently, and is long overdue, is the facet stem with fine engraving on the bowl. In the past facet stems tended to be somewhat sidelined by collectors. Received wisdom taught that these glasses in some way represented the twilight of a golden age, and that with the demise of the opaque twist there was little else of any interest made in the remaining years of the 18th century. This view is inaccurate for two reasons. Firstly, the facet stem as a style was undoubtedly introduced earlier than hitherto supposed and by the same token opaque twists were made a good deal later. There was, in fact, almost certainly a much greater overlap of these styles than is generally thought. Secondly, a great deal more work went into the making of a facet stem and, if finely engraved with landscapes or historical subjects, they can be nothing short of little masterpieces. At last these better glasses are achieving the recognition they deserve and this is reflected in the prices now being asked.

As a word of warning, it cannot be stressed too strongly that collectors should buy from a specialist source. As the prices go up so do the temptations to repair glasses in ways that are hard to detect. A slight trim to the edge of the foot of a glass to remove a small chip probably does not matter too much, but there are many instances where glasses have been re-cut under the foot and this sort of repair can greatly decrease the value. Glasses that have been repaired by joining two parts that may not have started life together are also a great hazard to buyers. **Timothy Osborne**

ALE & WINE GLASSES

A *façon de Venise* wine glass, the rounded funnel bowl moulded around the base with gadroons, below three finely trailed threads, above a hollow double-knopped stem, early 17thC, 5¼in (13.5cm) high.
£400–450 P

Façon de Venise means 'in the Venetian style' and is a term used to describe high quality glassware, with Venetian influence, which was made throughout Europe in the 16th and 17th centuries.

A mead glass, the incurved round funnel bowl gadrooned at the base, set on the stem with an inverted baluster knop, and with a base knop, c1690, 4½in (11.5cm) high.
£1,500–1,700 Som

> **Cross Reference**
> See Colour Review

A baluster cordial glass, with a knopped baluster stem enclosing a tear, c1720, 5¾in (14.5cm) high.
£1,000–1,200 GS

▶ A wine glass, the bell bowl set on a knop over inverted baluster stem with base knop and folded foot, c1720, 6½in (16.5cm) high.
£750–900 JHa

A heavy baluster goblet, the round funnel bowl on a teared, inverted baluster stem with a folded foot, c1700, 6¾in (17cm) high.
£2,000–2,200 Som

A Newcastle glass, the bowl Dutch-engraved with the figure of Liberty, on a multi-knopped baluster stem enclosing a tear, small chip to base, 18thC, 7½in (19cm) high.
£1,000–1,100 S(Am)

The popular use of the figure of Liberty on both glass and ceramics during the 18thC derives from a version of 'the Dutch maid', a political symbol that was claimed by both sides in the controversy over the competence of William Prince of Orange.

A balustroid wine glass, with a bell bowl and plain stem, a three-ring annulated knop at the base on a domed and folded foot, c1735, 5¼in (13.5cm) high.
£450–500 P

Balustroids are glasses made in the baluster form after c1720. More elegant than balusters, their stems are taller and thinner. Balustroids have fewer and more delicate knops, often separated by lengths of plain stem.

A baluster wine glass, with round funnel bowl, on a stem with cushion-inverted baluster and base ball knops, c1730, 5½in (14cm) high.
£620–680 Som

A wine glass, the round funnel bowl set on an inverted baluster stem with base knop and folded foot, c1730, 6in (15cm) high.
£280–350 JHa

A wine glass, the bell bowl engraved with grapes and vine leaves, on a light baluster stem with a domed and folded foot, c1730, 6½in (16.5cm) high.
£500–600 JHa

A wine glass, the bell bowl with composite stem, the air-beaded ball shoulder knop above an inverted baluster and small base knop, c1730, 3¼in (8.5cm) high.
£800–900 Som

A baluster wine glass, with round funnel bowl on a cushion knop above a six-sided pedestal stem and folded foot, c1730, 6¼in (15cm) high.
£400–450 P

A balustroid wine glass, the pan-topped bowl on a teared double-knopped stem and conical folded foot, c1740, 6in (15cm) high.
£700–800 BELL

A light baluster wine glass, the engraved bowl set on a multi-knopped stem and plain conical foot, c1740, 7in (18cm) high.
£1,000–1,100 Som

A wine glass, with drawn trumpet bowl, the plain stem with centre knop, on a folded foot, c1745, 6¾in (17cm) high.
£450–500 GS

A light baluster goblet, with bell bowl, multi-knopped stem and conical foot, c1750, 7½in (19cm) high.
£1,000–1,150 GS

Light baluster glasses were made in the second quarter of the 18th century. They are characterized by a wider variety of bowl shapes including bell, thistle and trumpet, and longer more complex stems with smaller, lighter and less defined knop shapes.

A Dutch diamond-point light baluster wine glass, engraved with an inscription and a tulip, dove and laurel branch, set on a multi-knopped stem and conical foot, foot chips, dated '1767', 7¾in (19.5cm) high.
£1,600–2,000 S

A Dutch shipping wine glass, the round funnel bowl with solid teared base and engraved with two ships joined by a roundel with the lion rampant of the Netherlands, on a ball knop and six-pointed pedestal stem, early 19thC, 6¾in (17cm) high.
£2,300–2,600 P

A dwarf ale glass, the conical bowl with flammiform wrythen-moulded decoration, c1740, 4¾in (12cm) high.
£300–350 Som

A Dutch wine glass, the funnel bowl engraved with a gentleman in a nightcap, on a hollow knop and basal knop with a domed foot, mid-18thC, 7in (18cm) high.
£550–600 P

◀ A Silesian goblet, Dutch-engraved with the arms of Leyden, c1750, 7in (18cm) high.
£1,200–1,500 Del

A wine glass, with bell bowl, the plain stem with a hollow central knop, c1730, 6in (15cm) high.
£550–600 P

A wine glass, the drawn ovoid bowl engraved with grape and vine pattern, on a plain stem and folded foot, c1730, 5in (12.5cm) high.
£120–150 JHa

A wine glass, the bell bowl engraved with two fruiting trees surrounded by sea, on a plain stem, c1720, 6½in (16.5cm) high.
£900–1,100 BrW

◀ A wine glass, with a drawn trumpet bowl, on a plain stem and conical foot, c1740, 7in (18cm) high.
£140–180 JHa

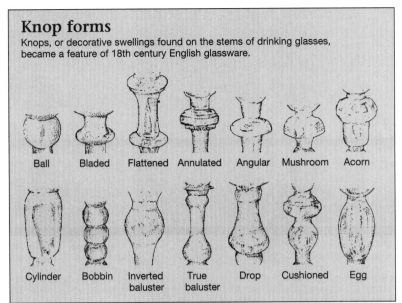

A wine glass, with a round funnel bowl, on a plain stem and folded foot, c1740, 5½in (14cm) high.
£100–120 JHa

A firing glass, with plain stem and terraced foot, c1740, 4in (10cm) high.
£120–140 JHa

A firing glass was used for toasts, and hammered on the table to make a sound like gunfire. They were produced in Britain from c1740 until the 19thC.

A wine glass, the trumpet bowl engraved with a chinoiserie scene, on a plain tapering stem, mid-18thC, 6in (15cm) high.
£700–800 WW

A Dutch wine glass, the round funnel bowl engraved with a country house, above an annulated knop, the stem with teared and basal knops, mid-18thC, 8¼in (21cm) high.
£1,500–1,800 S(S)

An ale glass, with a deep round funnel bowl lightly flute-moulded to lower half, c1750, 6½in (16.5cm) high.
£180–200 Som

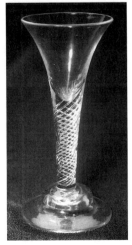

A drawn trumpet wine glass, on multi-spiral air twist stem and domed foot, c1740, 6in (15cm) high.
£500–550 Som

A tall goblet, with round funnel bowl, on a multi-spiral air twist stem with shoulder and central knops, c1745, 8¼in (21cm) high.
£700–800 Som

A wine glass, the bowl engraved with fruiting vine, on a multi-spiral air twist stem, c1745, 6¼in (16cm) high.
£400–450 Som

A Jacobite engraved wine glass, with round funnel bowl, on a double knopped multi-spiral air twist stem, c1745, 7in (18cm) high.
£1,000–1,200 JHa

A wine glass, with round funnel bowl and incised twist stem, c1750, 6in (15cm) high.
£650–750 Del

Incised twist stems were made to imitate the air twist with spiral or wrythen moulding on the outside of the stem.

A Jacobite wine glass, with a drawn trumpet bowl engraved with a six-petalled rose, on a multi-spiral air twist stem, c1750, 6in (15cm) high.
£900–1,000 BELL

A wine glass, with a waisted bucket bowl, on a single series corkscrew gauze air twist stem, c1750, 7in (18cm) high.
£350–400 JHa

A wine glass, with a round funnel bowl, on a double series air twist stem, c1750, 6in (15cm) high.
£400–450 JHa

A wine glass, with a round funnel bowl with honeycomb moulding, on a double series air twist stem, c1750, 5¾in (14.5cm) high.
£420–480 GS

A wine glass, with bell bowl, on a shoulder-knopped multi-spiral air twist stem, c1750, 6¾in (17cm) high.
£275–325 P

A pan-topped wine glass, with a double series air twist stem, c1750, 8in (20.5cm) high.
£500–600 WW

A wine glass, the bell bowl engraved with the fruiting vine, on a shoulder-knopped multi-spiral air twist stem, c1750, 6½in (16.5cm) high.
£500–600 GS

An ale glass, with a round funnel bowl, on a multi-spiral air twist stem, 1750–60, 7½in (19cm) high.
£350–400 Del

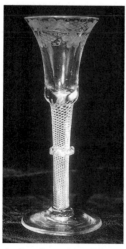

A wine glass, the bell bowl engraved with fruiting vine pattern, on a multi-spiral air twist stem with vermicular collar, c1755, 6¾in (17cm) high.
£500–600 GS

A firing glass, with a round funnel bowl, on a double series opaque twist stem, c1760, 4¼in (11cm) high.
£340–380 Som

◄ A pan-topped bucket bowl wine glass, engraved with a border of fruiting vines, on a multi-spiral air twist stem, 1750–60, 6¾in (17cm) high.
£450–550 P

A cordial glass, with ogee bowl, on a double series opaque twist stem, c1760, 5¾in (14.5cm) high.
£350–400 Som

A ratafia glass, with a lightly fluted narrow bowl, on a double series opaque twist stem, c1760, 7in (18cm) high.
£850–950 Som

Ratafia was an almond and fruit liqueur, popular during the last half of the 18thC.

A wine glass, with a bell bowl, on a mixed twist stem composed of an air thread within two solid opaque spirals and an outer multi-ply band, c1760, 6¾in (17cm) high.
£300–350 P

Twisted stems

Air twist stems proliferated between 1750 and 1760, as craftsmen sought to find a way to produce drinking glasses that were both light in weight and sufficiently decorative to have consumer appeal. Air twists were formed by denting a gather of molten glass and placing another gather on top, thereby creating air bubbles. The pattern made by the air was then elongated and twisted by drawing and rotating the molten glass until it assumed the length and breadth needed for a stem. Various stem patterns were produced, the simplest being the multi-spiral twist, composed of twelve even filaments. Single twists, or single series, feature filaments that are intertwined to create a single spiral; double series twists are more complex, with one spiral contained within another.
Mercury twist stems were made from two tears pulled into two flattened spirals and then twisted around one another.
Opaque twist stems became popular between 1770 and 1780. Rods of opaque white glass were placed in the unfinished stem and then pulled and twisted into the desired pattern.

A goblet, with an ogee bowl engraved with a band of stars and printies, on a triple opaque twist stem, c1760, 7in (18cm) high.
£450–500 Som

A wine glass, with an ogee bowl, on a multi-spiral opaque twist and double knop stem, c1760, 6½in (15cm) high.
£550–600 Som

A pan-topped wine glass, engraved with a border of flowerheads, on an air twist stem with a pair of mercurial corkscrews, c1760, 6½in (15cm) high.
£450–550 P

A goblet, the square bucket-shaped bowl engraved 'Justice' within a flower and leaf-scroll cartouche, on an opaque corkscrew stem, c1760, 9¼in (23.5cm) high.
£1,600–2,000 DN

A wine glass, with a waisted ogee bowl on a double series opaque twist stem, c1765, 6in (15cm) high.
£250–300 JHa

A wine glass, with a round funnel bowl, on a double series opaque twist stem, c1765, 7in (18cm) high.
£300–350 GS

A Beilby wine glass, the ogee bowl enamelled in white with a fruiting vine, on a double series opaque twist stem, c1765, 6in (15cm) high.
£2,200–2,500 Som

A wine glass, with a round funnel bowl, on a single series corkscrew gauze opaque twist stem, c1765, 6in (15cm) high.
£250–350 JHa

A wine glass, with an ogee bowl, on a double series opaque twist stem, c1765, 6in (15cm) high.
£200–250 Del

A wine glass, with a lipped ogee bowl, on a centre-knopped double series opaque twist stem, c1765, 6in (15cm) high.
£350–400 JHa

◄ A wine glass, the ogee bowl gilded with fruiting vines, on a double series opaque twist stem, probably from the studio of James Giles of London, c1770, 6¼in (16cm) high.
£1,800–2,000 BrW

A ribbed wine glass, the ogee bowl moulded with eight slightly curving ribs, on a double series opaque twist stem with a central gauze encircled by two pairs of spiral threads, 1765–70, 6¼in (16cm) high.
£275–300 P

A wine glass, the ogee bowl with diamond moulding, on a double series opaque twist stem, c1765, 6in (15cm) high.
£400–450 JHa

A wine glass, the ogee bowl engraved with a border of flowers between wrigglework, the double series opaque twist stem with a pair of heavy spiral threads enclosed by a pair of multi-ply corkscrews, 1770–75, 5¾in (14.5cm) high.
£350–400 P

A wine glass, the round funnel bowl engraved with a basket of flowers, on a single series lace opaque white twist stem, c1770, 6in (15cm) high.
£320–400 JHa

A wine glass, the ogee bowl engraved with fruiting vine, on an opaque twist gauze within translucent-blue twist stem, c1770, 6in (15cm) high.
£1,600–2,000 BELL

A wine goblet, with a round bowl, on a single knop air twist stem, 18thC, 8¾in (22cm) high.
£700–850 WW

▶ A wine glass, the ogee bowl with light basal fluting, engraved with a border of cross-hatched festoons hung with formal sprigs, the opaque twist stem with four spiral gauzes, c1770, 5¾in (14.5cm) high.
£275–300 P

A blue bonnet glass, with a double ogee reticulated bowl, c1760, 2¾in (7cm) high.
£90–110 Som

A diamond-moulded bonnet glass, on a petal foot, c1780, 3in (7.5cm) high.
£40–60 JHa

A wine glass, the ovoid bowl engraved with flowers, on a centre-knopped facet-cut stem, c1765, 5½in (14cm) high.
£280–320 JHa

The fashion for facet stems gathered strength in the last quarter of the 18thC and continued until the mid-19thC.

A champagne glass, the bowl engraved with fruiting vine, on a centre-knopped facet-cut stem, c1770, 8in (20.5cm) high.
£500–600 Del

A wine glass, the bowl engraved with a landscape, on a facet-cut stem, c1770, 6in (15cm) high.
£600–700 Del

A wine glass, the ogee bowl with a band of engraving, on a centre-knopped facet-cut stem, c1770, 6in (15cm) high.
£220–280 JHa

A wine glass, with a drawn ovoid bowl, on a facet-cut stem, c1770, 5in (12.5cm) high.
£100–120 JHa

A wine glass, with a drawn ovoid bowl, on a facet-cut stem, c1770, 6½in (16.5cm) high.
£130–160 JHa

A wine glass, with drawn trumpet bowl on a facet-cut stem, c1770, 6in (15cm) high.
£300–350 JHa

A wine glass, the bell bowl cut with small lenses on a centre-knopped diamond-faceted stem, the foot also slice-cut and with a barbed rim, c1785, 6in (15cm) high.
£370–400 P

A pair of rummers, the ovoid bowls engraved and with monograms, on square 'lemon-squeezer' feet, c1800, 5¼in (13.5cm) high.
£200–240 Som

A rummer, the bucket bowl engraved with Masonic symbols, on a moulded square pedestal foot, c1800, 4½in (11.5cm) high.
£450–500 GS

A pair of rummers, with flute cut bucket bowls, on bladed knop stems, c1820, 5½in (14cm) high.
£125–140 Som

A rummer, the ovoid bowl engraved with a hunting scene, on a waisted stem, c1850, 8in (20.5cm) high.
£600–675 DN

◀ A pair of flutes, the trumpet bowls engraved with stylized tulip decoration, with flute-cut bases, c1790, 7¼in (18.5cm) high.
£145–160 Som

A rummer, with a straight-sided bucket bowl, on a short plain collared stem, c1820, 4½in (11.5cm) high.
£80–100 GS

A firing glass, the trumpet bowl engraved with a Masonic square and calipers, c1780, 3½in (9cm) high.
£160–180 Som

A pair of rummers, each with a tapered bowl engraved with Masonic symbols, c1830, 6in (15cm) high.
£300–350 Bon(G)

Cross Reference
See Colour Review

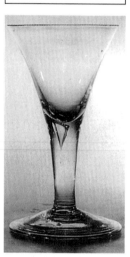

A wine goblet, with a trumpet bowl, on a plain tear-drop stem, 18thC, 9½in (24cm) high.
£500–600 WW

A goblet, with a U-shaped bowl, on a multi-knopped stem, 18thC, 11½in (29cm) high.
£1,200–1,300 WW

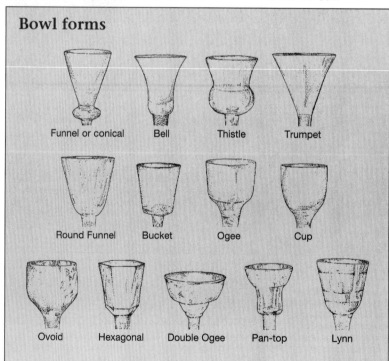

Bowl forms

Funnel or conical   Bell   Thistle   Trumpet

Round Funnel   Bucket   Ogee   Cup

Ovoid   Hexagonal   Double Ogee   Pan-top   Lynn

A ribbed dram glass, late 18thC, 4in (10cm) high.
£40–50 JHa

◄ An ale glass, engraved with hops and barley, on a 'lemon-squeezer' foot, c1790, 5½in (14cm) high.
£100–120 JHa

A Bohemian yellow glass goblet, with a faceted bowl, c1850, 6¼in (16cm) high.
£280–320 DORO

An intaglio-engraved wine glass, c1900, 5½in (14cm) high.
£65–80 JHa

BEAKERS & TUMBLERS

A Nuremberg beaker, the bowl engraved with a panoramic scene, moulded with gadrooning around the base and supported on three ball feet, late 17thC, 4¼in (11cm) high.
£4,000–5,000 P

Miller's is a price GUIDE not a price LIST

A Nuremberg tumbler, engraved on one side with a classical scene, the reverse with a coat-of-arms, in a silver-gilt mount, lacking three bun feet, late 17thC, 3½in (9cm) high.
£1,700–2,000 P

An American clear blown tumbler, by John Frederick Amelung, New Bremen Glass Manufactory, Maryland, decorated with copper-wheel engraved floral and vine wreath encircling 'Federal', 1788–89, 6¼in (16cm) high.
£33,000–40,000 SK(B)

This tumbler, and another in the collection of Jerome Strauss with similar decoration and the word 'Liberty', were made to commemorate the ratification of the American Constitution in 1788.

A tumbler, engraved with initials in an elaborate cartouche, c1790, 5in (12.5cm) high.
£300–350 Del

A footed tumbler, engraved with leafy branches and fish in water, c1880, 5in (12.5cm) high.
£100–120 JHa

A tumbler, engraved with Alnwick Castle, c1820, 4½in (11.5cm) high.
£400–450 Del

A Bohemian yellow-stained footed beaker, with four engraved medallions enclosing symbols for Health, Luck and Happiness and a floral garland, c1860, 5¼in (13.5cm) high.
£250–300 DORO

◄ A Vienna friendship beaker, with a silvery yellow band around the rim and green painted four-leaf clover, c1920, 4in (10cm) high.
£400–450 DORO

BOTTLES & DECANTERS

A *façon de Venise* diamond-point engraved flask, in the style of Willem Mooleyser, engraved with figures of Venus and Cupid, with gilt-metal mounts, damaged, late 17thC, 8¾in (22cm) high.
£1,750–2,000 P

An Austrian grey glass brandy bottle, with tin mounts, stopper missing, 17th/18thC, 7in (18cm) high.
£1,000–1,200 DORO

A pint-sized octagonal glass serving bottle, c1730, 9in (23cm) high.
£500–600 JHa

An opaque glass oil bottle, enamelled with flowers, probably Staffordshire, c1765, 6¼in (16cm) high.
£600–700 S(S)

A pint-sized mallet-shaped decanter, engraved with rose and bud design, with faceted stopper, c1770, 9in (23cm) high.
£350–450 JHa

A mallet-shaped decanter, engraved 'MADEIRA', with lozenge-shaped stopper, c1770, 11in (28cm) high.
£500–600 Del

A pair of decanters, engraved 'CYDER' and 'BEER', with diamond faceted stoppers, c1770, 14¼in (36cm) high.
£2,700–3,000 P

A club-shaped decanter, with neo-classical engraving and a lozenge-shaped stopper, c1780, 11½in (29cm) high.
£320–400 Del

A pair of Bristol blue glass decanters, with pear stoppers, gilt labels, inscribed 'Hollands' and 'Rum', late 18th/early 19thC, 9½in (24cm) high.
£450–500 GAK

◄ A pair of plain half-bottle decanters, with triple rings, c1795, 10in (25.5cm) high.
£400–450 Del

A glass spirit bottle, with diamond cut shoulder, engraved 'Rum' within a cartouche, with mushroom cut stopper, c1800, 7in (18cm) high.
£180–200 Som

An Austrian clear glass brandy bottle, painted in red, blue and yellow with flowering branches, two doves and a heart, the reverse with inscription, 18thC, 6in (15cm) high.
£250–300 DORO

A glass decanter, engraved with a view of Sunderland Bridge, with target stopper, c1800, 11in (28cm) high.
£700–800 Del

A decanter, with three neck rings and mushroom stopper, c1840, 10in (25.5cm) high.
£100–120 JHa

A decanter, engraved with a leaf patterned band, with facet-cut neck and ball stopper, 1880–1900, 8¼in (21cm) high.
£80–100 Som

A pair of cut-glass decanters, with triple neck rings and target stoppers, 1810–20, 11in (28cm) high.
£750–850 Del

A globe and shaft decanter, with slice-cut neck and printies and blazes to the body, c1870, 10in (25.5cm) high.
£60–80 JHa

A decanter, rock crystal and intaglio-engraved, with panels of stylized water lilies, 1900–10, 12¾in (32.5cm) high.
£900–1,000 JHa

The expression 'rock crystal' is used when parts of the item have been cut and polished to form deep reliefs in the same way as on early real rock crystal carved items. 'Intaglio' engraving refers to polished instead of matt engraving.

A Prussian-style decanter, with broad base fluting and three neck rings, plain mushroom stopper, c1830, 8¼in (21cm) high.
£180–200 Som

▶ A pair of French or Bohemian decanters, overlaid in opaque pink and cut around the base with six stiff leaves with gilt veining within gilt reserves, the stopper supporting a pink overlay tulip-shaped cup, c1850, 9in (23cm) high.
£1,300–1,500 S

A cut-glass decanter, with three neck rings and cut mushroom stopper, c1830, 10in (25.5cm) high.
£140–180 JHa

BOWLS

An Irish turn-over cut-glass fruit bowl, with pedestal foot, c1790, 10in (25.5cm) wide.
£2,000–2,500 Del

A gold-trailed cranberry glass bowl, with under dish, c1890, 5½in (14cm) diam.
£85–100 CB

A Bohemian amber-flashed stem bowl, engraved with five panels of animals, the stem and foot decorated in black enamel with stylized Gothic tracery and foliage, mid-19thC, 11in (28cm) high.
£700–850 WW

Cross Reference
See Colour Review

▶ A blue opal glass bowl, with threaded trailing and wavy rim, c1900, 5in (12.5cm) diam.
£120–140 JHa

A pair of rock crystal finger bowls and stands, by William Fritsche, carved with a frieze of paisley-type motifs and a spray of flowers on a simulated 'crushed ice' ground, signed, c1897, bowl 4¾in (12cm) diam.
£900–1,100 P

William Fritsche (1853–1924) is widely regarded as the greatest of the Bohemian engravers working in England at Thomas Webb & Sons in Stourbridge from 1868 onwards, and also in America.

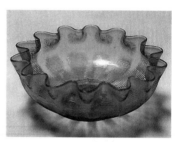

BOXES

A blue glass casket, decorated with white enamelled figures, 1890, 9in (23cm) wide.
£700–800 CB

A French sugar box, the clear glass marbled inside with deep red, early 20thC, 6¾in (17cm) wide.
£500–600 DORO

◀ A Bohemian sugar box, clear glass with white enamel overlay, c1840, 5in (12.5cm) wide.
£200–240 DORO

JARS

A pair of Irish cut-glass preserve jars and covers, c1815, 8in (20.5cm) high.
£500–600 Del

◀ A Dublin silver-mounted honey jar, by C. Haines, 1792, 8in (20.5cm) high.
£850–950 WELD

The Irish silver stopper greatly contributes to the value of this piece.

▶ A pair of Continental cut-glass jars, 1870–1900, 16in (40.5cm) high.
£550–650 JAd

JELLY & SWEETMEAT GLASSES

A Silesian sweetmeat glass, the double ogee bowl on a ribbed domed foot, c1750, 6½in (16.5cm) high.
£500–550 BrW

A hexagonal jelly glass, c1770, 4¼in (11cm) high.
£100–120 JHa

A jelly or punch glass, the trailed handle with a decorative terminal, on an opaque twist stem containing loose spiral threads, 1770–90, 4¾in (12cm) high.
£450–550 P

A sweetmeat glass, the double ogee bowl on a teared inverted baluster stem, with triple annulated and base knops, c1830, 6¼in (16cm) high.
£1,000–1,100 Som

JUGS

An Irish water jug, cut with large diamonds and brickwork, c1785, 6in (15cm) high.
£500–550 Del

An ale jug, engraved with hops and barley and with star-cut badge initialled 'WB', late 18thC, 8in (20.5cm) high.
£500–600 EH

An Irish water jug, flute-moulded below an engraved band of ribbon swags and bows, probably Cork, c1810, 6½in (16.5cm) high.
£450–500 Som

A Nailsea olive green glass jug, with white splashed decoration, c1810, 5in (12.5cm) high.
£350–400 Som

A Bohemian light blue glass water jug, c1860, 9¾in (25cm) high.
£150–180 DORO

A Stourbridge wine ewer, c1860, 13¼in (33.5cm) high.
£1,300–1,500 S

This piece is from the collection of the singer, Roger Whittaker.

► An American blown glass jug and six tumblers, the blue glass trailed with opalescent swirl pattern, late 19thC, jug 8¾in (22cm) high.
£100–120 DuM

A pair of cranberry glass water jugs, applied with clear glass reeded handles, late 19thC, 7½in (19cm) high.
£350–420 GAK

A Venetian amber-tinted glass jug, the handle with a lion mask terminal, the body and neck applied with white raised trails, c1870, 8¼in (21cm) high.
£230–275 WW

An intaglio-engraved water jug, c1910, 9in (23cm) high.
£170–200 JHa

An oil lamp, with gadrooned base, c1740, 3½in (9cm) high.
£450–500 Del

A Regency ormolu-mounted cut-glass candelabrum, with a central acorn knop and baguette and icicle drops, 14½in (37cm) high.
£350–420 GSP

◄ A pair of single light candelabra, c1765, 20in (51cm) high.
£6,000–7,000 Del

► A pair of cut-glass candlesticks, each with a knopped faceted stem and domed petalled foot, late 18thC, 9½in (24cm) high.
£2,000–2,200 S(S)

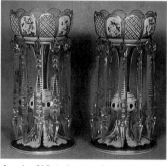

A lacemaker's lamp, with incised twist stem, c1810, 4in (10cm) high.
£100–120 BrW

A pair of cut-glass candle lustres, with fan cut borders and hung with triangular icicles, c1815, 8½in (21.5cm) high.
£900–1,000 Del

A pair of Victorian cut-glass candle lustres, with tulip-shaped sconces, 10in (25.5cm) high.
£650–720 EH

A pair of Victorian cranberry glass candle lustres, overlaid and painted, with cut-glass drops, 11½in (29cm) high.
£1,250–1,500 TRM

A pair of Victorian cranberry tinted glass table lustres, overlaid in white and cut with shaped panels, picked out in gilt, and hung with faceted drops, 9½in (24cm) high.
£800–900 DN

A pair of Victorian dark green glass lustres, with gilt decoration and prism drops, 12in (30.5cm) high.
£600–700 Mit

◄ A pair of Victorian blue/grey opaline glass lustres, enamelled and gilded with water birds, reeds and flowering branches, hung with cut-glass spear drops, 10¾in (27.5cm) high.
£650–720 RTo

► An American Astral lamp, the frosted shade with wheel-cut floral decoration on a brass standard and marble base, 19thC, 19¾in (50cm) high.
£650–720 SK(B)

PAPERWEIGHTS

A Baccarat millefiori mushroom paper-weight, with cobalt blue, white, red and green canes, 1845–60, 3in (7.5cm) diam.
£2,000–2,300 WoW

A Baccarat paperweight, with red, blue, green and yellow spirals, 1845–60, 3in (7.5cm) diam.
£225–250 SWB

A Baccarat faceted double-overlay concentric millefiori mushroom paperweight, overlaid in white and cobalt blue, c1850, 3in (7.5cm) diam.
£1,500–1,650 S

A Clichy faceted paperweight, with garlands of millefiori in mauve, green and red, minor damage, mid-19thC, 2¾in (7cm) diam.
£500–600 Bea(E)

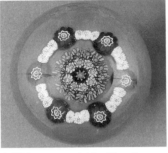

A Clichy paperweight, with red, white and green millefiori on a turquoise ground, mid-19thC, 2½in (6.5cm) diam.
£450–550 P

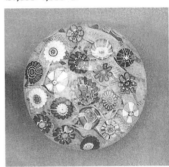

A Clichy millefiori paperweight, with brightly coloured canes on a muslin ground, mid-19thC, 2½in (6.5cm) diam.
£500–600 Bon(C)

A St Louis multi-coloured paperweight, in green, red, blue and yellow, 1845–60, 3in (7.5cm) diam.
£475–525 SWB

A St Louis millefiori paperweight, in green, pink and blue, 1845–60, 2in (5cm) diam.
£250–280 SWB

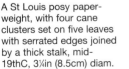

A St Louis posy paper-weight, with four cane clusters set on five leaves with serrated edges joined by a thick stalk, mid-19thC, 3¼in (8.5cm) diam.
£160–200 Bon(C)

A Paul Ysart thistle paperweight, with pink and green canes on a deep blue ground, 'PY' signature cane, c1930, 3in (7.5cm) diam.
£575–650 P

Cross Reference
See Colour Review

PICTURES

A pair of Georgian glass pictures, depicting women and children in landscapes, inscribed Autumn, Winter, Spring and Summer, 9½ x 13½in (24 x 34.5cm).
£1,350–1,500 AH

A pair of prints on glass, depicting 2nd Earl of Bedford and Robert Devereux, in reeded frames, 19thC, 17¾ x 12¼in (45 x 31cm).
£900–1,000 P

A Victorian painted glass panel, depicting Queen Elizabeth, 20¼ x 16½in (51.5 x 42cm).
£200–240 AH

Insurance Values

Always insure your valuable antiques for the cost of replacing them with similar items, regardless of the original price paid. Both dealers and auctioneers will provide a valuation service for a fee.

◀ A set of five Continental paintings on glass, each depicting figures in a landscape, in later giltwood frames, late 18thC, each 13 x 17in (33 x 43cm).
£9,000–10,000 S

SCENT BOTTLES

A façon de Venise scent bottle, the purple flask dashed with white, with pewter screw top, 17th/18thC, 3¾in (9.5cm) high.
£1,000–1,200 S(Am)

A light blue opaline glass scent bottle, with chased silver cage, chain and finger ring, c1870, 2¼in (5.5cm) high.
£400–450 Som

A Bohemian scent bottle, with coral and white glass double overlay, silver top, c1880, 4in (10cm) high.
£550–600 BHa

▶ A Victorian Stourbridge Burmese glass scent bottle, attributed to Thomas Webb & Son, the enamelled body graduating from brown to primrose and decorated with berries and a butterfly, the silver-gilt cap by Samson Mordan, in original fitted case, 1886, 4in (10cm) long.
£380–420 P

A Webb's cameo glass scent bottle, with ruby ground and gold top, c1880, 7in (18cm) high.
£1,800–2,000 BHa

A novelty screw-shaped scent bottle, with silver mount, marked for Joseph Braham 1885, 10½in (26.5cm) long.
£2,200–2,500 ALiN

A pair of milk glass scent bottles, with gilt-metal stands, overlay and tops, late 19thC, each 6¼in (16cm) high.
£800–900 S(S)

TANKARDS

A plain baluster-shaped tankard, on a low foot, c1765, 5in (12.5cm) high.
£250–300 Del

A tankard, engraved with floral sprigs and initials 'BL', with folded rim and reeded handle, late 18thC, 4½in (11.5cm) high.
£400–450 GS

A Bohemian faceted glass tankard, engraved with stags in a forest, on a lobed foot, c1845, 8in (20.5cm) high.
£600–700 P

VASES

A cut-glass celery vase, with bands of flute, prism and diamonds, c1810, 6¾in (17cm) high.
£350–400 Som

A pair of French opaline glass vases, each brightly painted with parrots on flowering branches on a peach-coloured ground, dated '1875', 17½in (44.5cm) high.
£750–825 S(S)

A pair of French Louis Philippe opaline vases, each with a stiff-leaf-decorated ormolu foot, top mounts missing, mid-19thC, 12½in (32cm) high.
£750–900 NOA

A straw opal glass vase, with wavy rim, c1890, 8in (20.5cm) high.
£100–120 JHa

◄ A Venetian red glass vase and stand, decorated with gilt, late 19thC, 8¼in (21cm) high.
£300–350 DORO

► An amethyst glass cornucopia, with clear printies, the gilt mount in the form of a hand, on an alabaster base, c1870, 7½in (19cm) high.
£200–220 CB

A Stourbridge cameo glass vase, the orange-tinted ground decorated with opaque white and carved palm leaves, the reverse with a moth, possibly Stevens & Williams, c1890, 12in (30.5cm) high.
£1,400–1,600 S

A blue opal glass vase, c1890, 3½in (9cm) high.
£70–80 JHa

A pair of cut-glass and gilt-bronze-mounted vases, 19thC, 13in (33cm) high.
£1,500–1,800 P

◄ A pair of Continental overlaid glass vases, painted with flowers and highlighted with gilding, 19thC, 8in (20.5cm) high.
£650–720 HYD

Silver

BASKETS

A George II silver chinoiserie cake basket, by Samuel Herbert & Co, centrally engraved with a crest, the handle with old repairs, London 1754, 13½in (34.5cm) wide.
£2,500–3,000 DN

**Samuel Herbert's first mark was entered in 1747, and he took an unnamed partner into the business at Foster Lane in 1750.
He specialized in pierced work, in particular baskets.**

A George III silver basket, by Robert Sharp, with armorial engraving below a bright-cut band, London 1795, 14½in (37cm) wide, 34oz.
£3,500–4,000 S

The arms are those of Mark Sprot, one of the founders of the London Stock Exchange.

▶ A Victorian silver sugar basket, by the Barnards, pierced and engraved with foliate and arabesque designs, with blue glass liner, London 1870, 4in (10cm) high.
£275–325 GAK

A George III silver basket, maker's mark partially worn, London 1780, 14¾in (37.5cm) wide, 29oz.
£1,600–2,000 Bon

A Victorian silver bonbon basket, by Yapp & Woodward, embossed at the centre with a view of York Minster, the sides embossed with fruit, flowers and foliage, Birmingham 1847, 6½in (16.5cm) diam, 4½oz.
£400–450 Bea(E)

A George III silver sugar basket, by George Gray, with bright-cut engraving of foliage, lacking glass liner, 1790, 4½in (11.5cm) wide, 5oz.
£300–350 P(O)

A Victorian silver sugar basket, by J. and E. Bradbury, with swing handle, 1869, 6in (15cm) wide, 7½oz.
£250–300 L

A pair of George V silver baskets, by William Comyns, with cast and pierced foliate decoration, London 1913, 6¼in (16cm) wide, 29oz.
£1,250–1,500 Bea(E)

These baskets sold for well in excess of their estimate because they are of a good weight, and pairs are always desirable. Furthermore, they are not too large for a modern table.

An Edwardian silver bread basket, Sheffield 1907, 10in (25.5cm) wide.
£250–275 ASAA

◀ An Edwardian silver sugar basket, by Richard Martin and Ebenezer Hall, with blue glass liner, Sheffield 1904, 5¼in (13.5cm) high overall.
£200–240 P(O)

Beware
Collectors should always look very carefully for damage to baskets and other pierced work, as this could affect the value.

BOWLS

A silver porringer, with wrythen, fluted and punched decoration, London 1699, 3½in (9cm) high, 6oz.
£900–1,100 GAK

An American silver porringer, by Elias Pelletreau, Southampton, New York, marked 'EP', c1760, 5¾in (14.5cm) diam, 7oz.
£3,300–3,650 S(NY)

A set of three silver rose bowls, by Wakely & Wheeler, each with embossed bead and reeded borders, London, 1905 and 1907, largest 10½in (26.5cm) diam, total 72oz.
£1,000–1,200 P(Ed)

A Queen Anne silver porringer, by Nathaniel Lock, the front with a vacant cartouche repoussé-decorated and surmounted by a cherub's head, London 1710, 2in (5cm) high, 11oz.
£1,150–1,400 WW

An Edwardian silver rose bowl, by the Goldsmiths & Silversmiths Co, chased and embossed with floral and foliate designs, with vacant cartouche, London 1901, 8in (20.5cm) diam, 32oz.
£550–650 GAK

◄ An Edwardian silver fruit bowl, by Walker & Hall, formerly with inscription, Sheffield 1905, 15¾in (40cm) wide, 68oz.
£900–1,100 WW

◄ A pierced silver centre bowl, with traces of gilding, inscribed, maker's mark worn, 1919, 11in (28cm) wide, 19½oz.
£400–450 P(B)

► A silver fruit bowl, with radial-engraved dished centre, Birmingham 1933, 8in (20.5cm) diam, 15oz.
£175–200 GAK

A George II Irish silver bowl, by Samuel Walker, the sides chased with trees, trailing vines and grape clusters, Dublin 1752–53, 7½in (19cm) diam, 18oz.
£5,000–6,000 P

A George III Irish silver sugar bowl, by John Clark & Jacob West, the sides embossed with flowers, the front with a cartouche engraved with a crest, Dublin 1806, 5½in (14cm) diam, 8½oz.
£450–500 P

A silver porringer, of Queen Anne design, with repoussé cable and scale pattern and vacant cartouche, Sheffield 1891, 9½in (24cm) wide, 20oz.
£400–450 L

A silver fruit bowl, by William Hutton & Sons, with blue glass liner, Sheffield 1912, 12¼in (31cm) wide, 26½oz.
£950–1,150 WW

BOXES

A Dutch silver tobacco box, by Jan Buysen, engraved with an undulating scroll border, with detachable cover, Amsterdam 1800, 6in (15cm) high.
£3,800–4,200 S(Am)

A George III silver toothpick box, by Samuel Pemberton, engraved with ray decoration on a prick-dot ground, vacant and foliate-filled cartouches, the red velvet lining and mirror both intact, Birmingham 1809, 3in (7.5cm) wide.
£500–550 P

An Austrian silver cigarette box, c1900, 4¾in (12cm) wide.
£2,200–2,500 SFL

A Russian parcel-gilt silver box, by Semenow/Saminkow, the sides engraved with cartouches enclosing a view of the Kremlin, with silver-gilt interior, Moscow 1874, 5¼in (13cm) high.
£950–1,150 S(Z)

A silver box, embossed with hunting scenes, London 1903, 3¼in (8.5cm) wide.
£1,100–1,250 SHa

A silver double cigar and cigarette box, by John Newton Mappin, monogrammed in one corner and enamelled in dark blue 'Cigars' and 'Cigarettes', with cedarwood lining, 1894, 9½in (24cm) wide.
£1,300–1,500 P

An Edwardian silver biscuit box, by Thomas Hayes, in mid-18thC style, the sides embossed with flowers, leaves and scrolls around a large cartouche, with a gilt interior, Birmingham 1905, 8¾in (22cm) wide, 21oz.
£500–600 P(S)

◄ A silver dressing table ring box, by William Comyns, the top with mother-of-pearl, gold and silver-inlaid tortoiseshell panel, London 1907, 3½in (9cm) wide.
£280–320 GAK

CADDY SPOONS

A George III silver caddy spoon, by Joseph Taylor, the bowl pierced with quatrefoil motifs, the handle with a vacant cartouche, Birmingham 1799.
£250–275 P

◄ A George IV silver fiddle-pattern caddy spoon, by Joseph Taylor, the bowl with foliate and floral-engraved central panel, Birmingham 1822.
£175–200 P

► A George III silver caddy spoon, by Thomas James, the bowl engraved with a floral branch, the terminal with a vacant cartouche in the shape of a flowerhead, London 1813, 4¼in (11cm) long.
£600–675 Bon

CANDLE SNUFFERS

◀ A pair of George III silver candle snuffers, with engraved and beaded decoration, probably by John Baker, London 1787, 2¾oz.
£330–400 P(E)

▶ A pair of George III silver candle snuffers, with steel cutter and box, by Jos. Craddock & Wm. Reid, London, and a George III tray by R. Gainsford, Sheffield, 1813, tray 9½in (24cm) wide, 5¼oz.
£650–750 DD

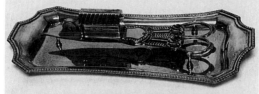

Two pairs of George IV candle snuffers, by Emes & Barnard, with a pair of snuffer trays, by Robert Garrard, 1826, snuffers 9¼in (23.5cm) long.
£2,800–3,200 P

CANDLESTICKS & CHAMBERSTICKS

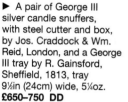

A pair of Scottish silver table candlesticks, with turned stems, maker's mark 'I.C.', c1700, 5in (12.5cm) high, 14½oz.
£6,000–7,000 L

A George II silver chamberstick, by John Priest, engraved with a coat-of-arms, with detachable nozzle, London 1752, 6¼in (16cm) diam, 14oz.
£700–800 Bea(E)

A pair of George III silver candlesticks, by Ebenezer Coker, London 1761, 10½in (26.5cm) high, 48oz.
£3,500–3,850 Mit

A pair of loaded silver candlesticks, London 1771, 9in (23cm) high.
£1,800–2,000 DIC

Loaded candlesticks

The development of mechanization during the Industrial Revolution resulted in a proliferation of machine-made loaded candlesticks produced to meet the growing demands of the newly affluent merchant classes. Less metal was used to make a loaded candlestick than a cast one, as the stem was hollow and filled with pitch or sand for weight and stability, and therefore loaded candlesticks could be sold for a significantly lower price. Collectors should be careful when buying filled candlesticks as they often have holes worn through on edges and corners, due to the thinness of the silver.

A pair of silver neo-classical candlesticks, by Joseph Heriot, one nozzle replaced, with raised festoon and ram's head decoration, weighted with wood, London 1775, 12in (30.5cm) high.
£1,600–2,000 MJB

▶ A Victorian silver taper stick, by Charles Stuart Harris, modelled as a drum, London 1887–88, 4in (10cm) high.
£1,500–1,650 BEX

▶ A silver harlequin taper stick, by Joseph Willmore, with a foliate chased base, Birmingham 1837, 5½in (14cm) high, 5oz.
£400–500 DN

Taper sticks are small versions of candlesticks and were used primarily on a writing desk for holding a taper used to melt sealing wax. They are only found as single items and not pairs, as with candlesticks.

A Victorian silver chamber-stick, by William Comyns, on a heart-shaped tortoiseshell base, London 1890, 3½in (9cm) wide.
£380–450 GTH

A pair of Victorian silver candlesticks, by John Dickson & Son, with Corinthian columns, Sheffield 1895, 8¾in (22cm) high.
£600–700 TRM

A pair of Edwardian silver candlesticks, embossed with Adam-style urns, damaged, Sheffield 1898, 6½in (16.5cm) high.
£380–450 GAK

A pair of Edwardian silver loaded candlesticks, by Walker & Hall, with Corinthian columns, the bases embossed with wheat husk garlands draped with rams' heads, Sheffield 1903, 13½in (34.5cm) high.
£1,300–1,500 P(L)

CANISTERS

A Dutch silver tea canister, the sides chased with sunflowers and acorns, Leeuwarden 1711, 5¼in (13.5cm) high, 7oz.
£4,000–4,500 S(Am)

A George III silver tea canister, by Albartus Schurman, 1760, 5¾in (14.5cm) high, 9½oz.
£850–1,000 P

A George III silver tea canister, by John Carter, with Adam-style design, London 1773, 5in (12.5cm) high, 14oz.
£4,000–5,000 S

A Portuguese silver tea canister and cover, engraved with a coat-of-arms, 19thC, 8in (20.5cm) high, 18oz.
£950–1,150 Bea(E)

CARD CASES

A Victorian silver card case, by George Unite, embossed with a relief of the Scott memorial, the reverse with an initialled cartouche, Birmingham 1844, 4in (10cm) high, 2oz.
£800–900 S

A Victorian silver card case, engraved in the Japanesque style and with a monogram, in fitted leather case, Birmingham 1890, 4in (10cm) high.
£130–150 P(S)

A Victorian silver card case, embossed with a cartouche among flowers and scrolls, the interior fitted with a pen and an ivory sheet, Chester 1899, 4in (10cm) high, 3oz.
£100–120 EH

A Maltese silver card case and purse, with blue velvet lining, engraved with scrollwork around a monogram, marked for Francis Meli, late 19thC, 4½in (11.5cm) high.
£300–350 P

CASTERS

A George II Irish silver sugar caster, the body engraved with an armorial, maker's mark mis-struck, possibly William Betagh or Byrne, Dublin 1737, 7½in (19cm) high.
£5,000–5,500 DN

Irish silver is selling well at the moment and unusual items are particularly popular. There is a scarcity of material on the market and also great demand, not only from the Irish but also from Irish Americans.

A silver sugar caster, by Sam Wood, London 1740, 7in (18cm) high.
£850–950 DIC

A silver sugar caster, Birmingham 1937, 6¼in (16cm) high, 7oz.
£140–170 P(B)

A George III silver sugar caster, by Thomas and Jabez Daniell, monogrammed, 1772, 6¼in (16cm) high, 4oz.
£320–380 P(O)

A George III silver muffineer, with reeded decoration, damaged, London 1795, 5½in (14cm) high.
£180–220 GAK

A muffineer is a small caster for sprinkling sugar, spice or salt on muffins. The holes are often finer than those on standard casters.

◄ A pair of silver sugar casters, by the Goldsmiths & Silversmiths Co, in George III classical style, with rococo husk and foliage repoussé decoration, London 1898–1902, 9¼in (23.5cm) high, 31½oz.
£1,400–1,700 WW

CENTREPIECES

A silver-gilt tazza, probably German, the plaquette embossed and chased with 'The Binding of Isaac', on a later foot chased in conforming style, 17thC and later, 10in (25.5cm) diam, 38oz.
£5,000–6,000 S

Miller's is a price GUIDE not a price LIST

A Victorian silver centrepiece, by Stephen Smith, 1866, 29in (73.5cm) high, 103oz.
£3,000–3,500 G(L)

A silver-gilt sweetmeat dish, by Sebastian Henry Garrard, the base with claw feet, supporting eggs of the Rufons Tinamon parrot, inscribed 'Laid at Lilford 1915', 5½in (14cm) high, 11½oz, with a fitted wooden carrying case.
£400–500 P(B)

An Edwardian silver epergne, by Deakin & Deakin, with three small detachable vases and a larger central vase, Sheffield 1908, 14½in (37cm) high, 33oz.
£900–1,100 P(B)

COFFEE POTS & TEAPOTS

A George II silver coffee pot, with ebony scrolled handle, London 1738, 7½in (19cm) high, 15oz.
£1,200–1,400 AH

A George III silver teapot, by Peter and Anne Bateman, with bright-cut neo-classical design, and an oval teapot stand, London 1794, 8in (20.5cm) wide.
£1,500–1,800 HYD

A William IV silver coffee pot, with embossed panels of foliate decoration on a matted background, maker's mark 'E.B.', 10¼in (26cm) high, 36oz.
£800–1,000 Bon

A Victorian silver coffee pot, by Robert Garrard, engraved with a crest, London 1854, 6¾in (17cm) high, 20oz.
£550–650 WW

A George II silver teapot, by Gabriel Sleath, the body engraved with a band of scrollwork and masks and contemporary monogram, 1752, 5in (12.5cm) high, 15oz.
£1,600–2,000 L

A George IV silver coffee pot, by Emes & Barnard, with lobed body and melon finial, 1828, 8¾in (22cm) high, 28oz.
£600–700 L

> **Cross Reference**
> See Colour Review

A Victorian silver teapot, by MacKay & Chisholm, decorated with scrolls, flowers and scalework, Edinburgh 1848, 7in (18cm) high.
£330–400 Bea(E)

A Victorian silver coffee pot, by William Hunter, engraved with hatched scrolling and vacant cartouches, London 1855, 11in (28cm) high, 24oz.
£450–550 WW

An Irish bright-cut silver teapot, by Jane Williams, the body with a monogram within a contemporary cartouche, engraved at the top with oak leaves, Cork, c1790, 12¼in (31cm) wide.
£1,100–1,300 HOK

A George III silver teapot, by Paul Storr, the body with ribbed girdle above fluting, 1813, 13½in (34.5cm) wide, 37¼oz.
£2,000–2,200 P

A Dutch silver coffee pot, by Bennewitz & Son, the partly ribbed spout ending in a panther's head, with later fitted burner, Amsterdam 1834, 13¼in (33.5cm) high, 34½oz.
£2,000–2,200 S(Am)

A Victorian silver teapot, by J. MacKay, embossed and chased with C-scrolls and floral design around a cartouche, engraved with a crest and motto, Edinburgh 1858, 12¼in (31cm) wide, 26oz.
£400–500 AG

COFFEE & TEA SERVICES

A George III silver four-piece tea and coffee service, by John Emes, with bright-cut border and cartouche engraved with a crest, London 1798, 52oz.
£1,600–2,000 L&T

A silver three-piece tea service, by Thomas Smily, embossed with flowers and leaves, London 1858, teapot 6in (15cm) high, 45oz.
£600–700 CCG

An American silver three-piece coin tea service, by Taylor & Hinsdale, New York, monogrammed, early 19thC, teapot 9½in (24cm) high, 90oz.
£1,600–2,000 SK

A silver four-piece tea and coffee service, by John Edward Terrey, with all-over repoussé decoration, the cartouches to the teapot and coffee pot engraved with a boar's head crest, London 1844, 75oz.
£1,300–1,500 WW

An American silver five-piece tea and coffee service, by Dominick & Haff, with repoussé design of flowers and leaves, St Louis 1882, coffee pot 8¾in (22cm) high, 89½oz.
£1,500–1,800 SLN

A Victorian silver four-piece tea service, by CE & Co, with half-reeded design, the tea and coffee pots with pearwood handles, Sheffield 1894–99, 59oz.
£600–700 PFK

An Edwardian silver three-piece tea service, by the Goldsmiths & Silversmiths Co, with vacant cartouches and repoussé foliage, the milk jug and sugar basin with gilded interiors, London 1901, 40oz.
£400–500 WW

A silver four-piece tea service, by Joshua Vander, with half-reeded design, London 1892, 70oz.
£700–800 P(Ed)

An Edwardian silver three-piece tea service, by the Goldsmiths & Silversmiths Co, with half-reeded design, London 1902, 32oz.
£350–420 Bea(E)

An Edwardian silver four-piece tea service, decorated with scrolling foliage, water jug 8in (20.5cm) high, 54oz.
£700–850 Mit

A silver five-piece tea service and tray, each piece on four leaf-and-scroll supports, maker's mark JF, Glasgow 1908.
£2,000–2,400 P(Ed)

CONDIMENT POTS

A Dutch silver salt cellar, chased with tulips, flowerheads and leaves, with gilt interior, c1660, 6¼in (16cm) high, 8½oz.
£2,700–3,200 S(Am)

A set of four George II silver salts, by David Hennell, each engraved with two armorials within cartouches, later clear glass liners, London 1754, 2½in (6.4cm) high, 11oz.
£900–1,100 WW

A George III silver mustard pot, by Jabez Daniell & James Mince, London 1768, 3¼in (8.5cm) high, 4oz.
£1,400–1,600 S(S)

A pair of George III silver salts, with trellis and foliate pierced sides, blue glass liners, London 1809, 3½in (9cm) long.
£175–200 GAK

A George IV silver mustard pot, by Joseph Angell, engraved with a crest, with blue glass liner, London 1825, 3in (7.5cm) high, 4oz.
£500–550 S(S)

A pair of George IV silver salts, by William Elliott, each with shell and leaf scroll rims, above foliate embossed bands, with gilt interiors, 1825, 3¼in (8.5cm) diam, 12oz.
£240–280 P(S)

CRUET STANDS

A George II silver cruet stand, with a cartouche, with three casters and two mounted and crested cut-glass oil bottles, maker's mark of Samuel Wood, London 1749, 8¼in (21cm) high, 36oz.
£2,000–2,400 Bon

▶ A Victorian silver dinner cruet, by Elkington & Co, the stand stamped with a frieze of stylized bulrushes, fitted with seven cut glass bottles including three with silver mounts, Birmingham 1881, 10in (25.5cm) wide, 32oz.
£900–1,100 P(L)

A George II silver cruet stand, by Samuel Wood, with foliate cartouche reserve, with two later cut-glass bottles and stoppers, 1751, 4in (10cm) high, 11oz.
£450–550 P(O)

A George III silver triangular cruet stand, by Robert Piercy, the stand with a pierced anthemion gallery, cartouche engraved with a stag, containing seven bottles, London 1774, 7in (18cm) wide, 21oz.
£4,500–5,000 S

▶ A Victorian silver cruet stand, by Clift Alexander Clark, modelled as a sprig of thistle, the salt, pepper and mustard pots as flowers, with two spoons, London 1894, 4½in (11.5cm) wide, 7oz.
£800–900 S

A Regency silver cruet stand, by Thomas Robinson, the base engraved with an initial, the frame with four reeded branches linked by rings for the cut glass bottles and with rests for the stoppers, London 1815, 11¼in (28.5cm) wide.
£220–260 WW

CUPS & GOBLETS

A Charles II silver tumbler cup, by Thomas Mangy, York 1677, 2in (5cm) high, 4oz.
£4,000–4,500 P(L)

A William and Mary silver tumbler cup, by Robert Timbrell, with engraved initials, 1700, 2½in (6.5cm) diam, 2¾oz.
£3,200–3,500 P

A Queen Anne silver cup and cover, London 1712, 9½in (24cm) high, 40oz.
£3,000–3,500 HYD

A George II silver tot cup, by Paul de Lamerie, London 1736, 2in (5cm) high, 3oz.
£3,200–3,500 WW

A George III sterling silver cup and cover, engraved with a coat-of-arms, maker's mark for Charles White, London 1774, 14¼in (36cm) high, 52½oz.
£1,300–1,500 LJ

A silver-mounted coconut wine goblet, on a hollow trumpet base, maker's mark 'H' over 'T', 18thC, 5in (12.5cm) high.
£500–550 TMA

A silver-mounted coconut cup, with Masonic decoration, London 1802, 6in (15cm) high.
£900–1,000 DIC

A George III Scottish silver goblet, by George McHarrie, with gilt interior, Edinburgh 1813, 8¼in (21cm) high, 13½oz.
£300–350 Bea(E)

An Irish silver bright-cut presentation cup and cover, by James Le Bass, Dublin 1816, 13in (33cm) high.
£1,800–2,000 SIL

A silver cup and cover, by Robert Garrard, London 1936, 8in (20.5cm) high.
£350–400 CoHA

DISH RINGS

A George III Irish silver dish ring, by John Lloyd, the sides pierced with bands of foliate scrolls, semi-circles and overlapping navettes, the centre cartouche engraved with a boar's head crest below and a shield charged with the hand of Ulster, Dublin c1775, 7in (18cm) wide, 11¼oz.
£2,700–3,000 P

It would appear that the engraver was not familiar with dish rings as he has engraved the crest upside down, erroneously assuming that the wider part was the top rather than the base.

▶ An Edwardian silver dish ring, by West & Sons, the body pierced, chased and engraved with various motifs, Dublin 1906, 6¾in (17cm) diam, 9oz.
£1,750–2,000 JAd

An Edwardian silver dish ring, by Nathan & Hayes, embossed and pierced with a fox, dolphin, birds and scrolling foliage, Chester 1901, 8¼in (21cm) diam, 14¼oz.
£600–700 CGC

An Edwardian silver Irish-style dish ring, by the Goldsmiths & Silversmiths Co, the pierced sides with repoussé and chased foliate scrolls, animals and birds, London 1903, 8¼in (21cm) diam, 11¼oz.
£700–800 WW

A George III-style silver dish ring, by Thomas Weir, pierced and chased with bands of scrolling foliage, geometric design, scrolling foliate swags within six plaques, with blue glass liner and fitted case, Dublin 1917, 9in (23cm) diam, 12oz.
£1,400–1,600 JAd

DISHES

A set of three George III silver shell-form butter dishes, each engraved with a crest, maker's mark of Henry Green, London 1792, 5¾in (14.5cm) long, 9oz.
£700–850 Bon

An Edward VII sweetmeat dish, with rococo-style chased floral and diaper-pierced border, marked 'TL & EM', Chester 1903, 8in (20.5cm) wide, 8oz.
£200–240 PFK

A Victorian silver entrée dish and cover, by Benjamin Smith III, the dish with an oak leaf and acorn chased border, the cover engraved with armorials, the base with a liner, London 1847, 16in (40.5cm) wide, 73½oz, with a plated stand.
£2,000–2,200 DN

▶ A set of six silver and cut-glass butter dishes and knives, by Mappin & Webb, Birmingham 1906, in fitted case 14in (35.5cm) wide.
£225–250 NAW

A Victorian breakfast turnover dish with liner, by Walker & Hall, decorated with shells, applied crest with motto, Sheffield 1891, 15½in (39.5cm) wide, 73¼oz.
£1,250–1,500 Bea(E)

◀ A set of three George V 'Celtic' silver dishes, each with knotted dragon and boss band to the rim, Dublin 1920 and 1921, largest 13in (33cm) wide, 71oz.
£1,650–2,000 DN(H)

EWERS & JUGS

A George II Scottish cast silver cream jug, by John Main, chased with rococo scrolls and flowers above an applied girdle, with engraved dragon crest, gilt interior, Assay Master Archibald Ure, Edinburgh, 1730, 4½in (11.5cm) high, 7¼oz.
£7,000–8,000 P

This cream jug attracted enthusiastic bidding because it is cast, Scottish, of early date and an unusual shape.

A George II silver ale jug, with later repoussé decoration of a coursing scene, mark indistinct, London 1745, 8¼in (21cm) high, 27¾oz.
£850–1,000 WW

A George III silver hot water jug, by John Scofield, applied with classical medallions above fluting, London 1781, 12in (30.5cm) high, 22oz.
£1,200–1,400 S

A silver Cellini ewer, 1879, 13in (33cm) high.
£1,500–1,700 DIC

The Cellini pattern ewer was a standard design of claret jug made throughout the second half of the 19thC. They are often gilded and tend to be relatively small, follow the same shape, and may have self-opening lids. Many Cellini jugs were made in Glasgow.

A silver hot water jug, chased and embossed with floral garlands and ribbon ties and with reeded band, Birmingham 1892, 7in (18cm) high.
£145–175 GAK

◄ A Victorian silver ewer, by William Smily, with a fruiting vine handle, engraved with oval panels, flowers and scrolling leaves, London 1856, 13¾in (35cm) high, 25oz.
£850–1,000 DN

A George V silver hot water jug, by Elkington & Co, with spiral fluting and leaf-shaped spout, London 1910, 8in (20.5cm) high, 17oz.
£200–240 Bea(E)

An American silver jug, by Marshall Field & Co, with repoussé scenes of putti in scroll cartouches surrounded by flowers and rocaille, early 20thC, 10¼in (26cm) high, 41oz.
£1,000–1,100 SK

INKSTANDS

A George III silver partners' inkstand, by Richard Morton & Co, with blue cut-glass bottles, two with pierced silver covers, the third engraved with a crest above a motto, Sheffield 1775, 9½in (24cm) wide, 12oz.
£800–1,000 WW

A silver presentation inkstand, the tray engraved with scrolls, with two silver-mounted faceted glass inkwells with hinged lids and a taper stick, damaged, London 1856, 10in (25.5cm) wide.
£300–350 GAK

A silver inkstand, by Henry Wilkinson & Co, the base pierced with scrolls and diaper, with two silver-mounted faceted glass bottles and a taper stick, Sheffield 1860, 9½in (24cm) wide, 17oz.
£320–385 P(L)

A silver inkstand, by William Smily, engraved with a border of 'C' scrolls, acanthus leaves and stylized motifs, with two silver-mounted faceted glass bottles and detachable taper stick, 1865, 11¾in (30cm) wide, 31¼oz.
£1,300–1,500 P

A silver inkstand, by Richard Hennell, with engraved foliate scroll decoration and initials, two silver-mounted cut-glass inkwells and a taper stick, maker's mark 'R.H.', London 1869, 8½in (21.5cm) wide, 9oz.
£425–500 MCA

An Edwardian silver standish, by Walker & Hall, with a cast openwork three-quarter gallery of foliate scrolls, monogrammed cartouche and an inscription, with silver-mounted cut-glass inkwells and scroll pen holder, Sheffield 1901, 12¾in (32.5cm) wide, 43oz.
£1,350–1,500 P(C)

An Edwardian silver inkstand, by the Goldsmiths and Silversmiths Co, the two inkwells with clear glass liners between two depressions for pens, London 1903, 8½in (21.5cm) wide, 19oz.
£600–720 GAK

An American George III-style silver inkstand, by William B. Meyers Co, Newark, New Jersey, with two silver-mounted, spiral-fluted glass inkwells and central seal box topped by a removable chamberstick, c1930, 10¾in (27.5cm) wide, 36oz.
£900–1,000 S(NY)

A George V silver inkstand, with two silver-mounted cut-glass inkwells, inscribed, maker's mark 'B.B SLs', Birmingham 1935, 8¾in (22cm) wide, 13oz.
£350–420 Bea(E)

KETTLES

◄ A George II rococo kettle-on-stand, by David Willaume II, decorated with flowers, scrolls, shells and molluscs, with two vacant cartouches, 1739, 14¼in (36cm) high, 87½oz.
£7,000–8,000 P

► A George III silver kettle-on-stand, by Andrew Fogelberg & Stephen Gilbert, with later armorial engraving below handle, London 1785, 12in (30.5cm) high, 51oz.
£800–1,000 S

A Victorian silver kettle-on-stand, by Garrard & Co, with ivory and double-scrolled handle, London 1860, 15¾in (40cm) high, 68oz.
£1,300–1,500 B&L

LETTER OPENERS & PAPER KNIVES

A silver-mounted paper knife, by Francis Higgins, with Albany-pattern handle and plain ivory blade, marked, London 1883, 14¼in (36cm) long.
£150–180 Bon

A silver ruler letter opener, London 1899, 8½in (21.5cm) long.
£340–375 SHa

► A silver and tortoiseshell paper knife, 1901, 17¾in (45cm) long.
£380–450 GIO

MIRRORS

A Victorian cast silver-gilt dressing table mirror, by Hunt & Roskell, with a monogrammed cartouche flanked by children, 1881, 14½in (37cm) wide.
£7,000–8,000 P

A silver-framed mirror, with central cartouche, pierced and embossed with scrolling foliage, Birmingham 1901, 18in (45.5cm) wide.
£1,800–2,200 TEN

An Edwardian silver-framed mirror, pierced with scrolling flowers and foliage, the top with a cartouche, Birmingham 1903, 15½in (39.5cm) wide.
£550–650 DN(H)

A silver-framed mirror, by John Septimus Beresford, embossed with stylized chinoiserie decoration, engraved with a monogram of Princess Adelaide, London 1889, 26½in (67.5cm) high.
£3,000–3,500 B&L

MODELS

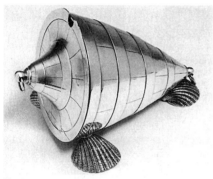

A Victorian silver spoon warmer, by Archer, Machin & Marsh, modelled as a buoy, decorated to simulate wood bound with metal bands, with gilded interior, Sheffield 1871, 8in (20.5cm) wide, 16½oz.
£1,500–1,650 P

A pair of Russian silver-gilt salts, modelled as chairs, the covers engraved with calligraphy, the interiors with cockerels, Moscow 1873–74, 3in (7.5cm) high.
£650–800 WW

A Victorian silver condiment set, by Asprey, modelled as a street lamp and three bollards, the base engraved with initials, in original case, London 1877, 7¾in (19.5cm) high.
£1,750–2,000 AH

A pair of late Victorian silver glove stretchers, by George Heath, modelled as a duck's head, with glass eyes, realistically engraved with feathers, marked, London 1887, 8in (20.5cm) long.
£300–350 Bon

◀ A Dutch silver cow creamer, with red glass eyes, her tail raised to brush off the fly applied to the cover, c1900, 11in (28cm) long, 17½oz.
£1,750–2,000 P

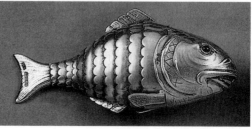

A cast silver clockwork table bell, by Joseph Braham, modelled as a tortoise, activated by the head or tail, 1903, 6¼in (16cm) long, 14oz.
£2,200–2,600 TEN

A Continental silver box, modelled as a carp with hinged head and mouth and articulated body, imported by J. G. Piddington, 1904, 5in (12.5cm) long.
£750–900 TEN

A pair of Dutch silver pepperettes, modelled as pigs, import mark for London, 1895–1904, 4in (10cm) long, 6oz.
£1,200–1,300 S(S)

A pair of German silver table ornaments, modelled as a hen and cock pheasant, with articulated wings, early 20thC, largest 18in (45.5cm) long, 52oz.
£1,700–2,000 SK

A silver pincushion modelled as a duck, by Crisford & Norris, cushion replaced, Birmingham 1906, 2¼in (6.5cm) high.
£375–425 THOM

A silver pincushion, modelled as a dog with a mother-of-pearl cart, Birmingham 1909, 4¾in (12cm) long.
£500–600 RBB

A pair of Edwardian silver dog casters, by William Edward Hurcomb, modelled as West Highland Terriers, London 1906, 2¼in (5.5cm) high, 4½oz.
£1,100–1,300 P(Ed)

Further Reading
Miller's Silver & Sheffield Plate Marks, Miller's Publications, 1993

A silver pepperette, modelled as a smiling cat, Birmingham 1911, 2½in (6.5cm) high.
£350–420 RBB

A pair of silver peppers, each modelled as Little Tommy Tucker, marked, Chester 1913, 2½in (6.5cm) high.
£575–650 SHa

MUGS & TANKARDS

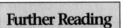

A Charles II silver tankard, engraved with a contemporary lady's armorial, marked 'MK', London 1681–82, 5¼in (13.5cm) high, 13oz.
£5,500–6,500 PFK

A George I silver mug, by John Elston, with reeded girdle and scroll handle, Exeter 1716, 3¼in (8.5cm) high, 4¾oz.
£600–720 Bea(E)

A silver tankard, by Langlands & Goodrich, handle initialled, cover possibly replaced, Newcastle 1756, 7¼in (18.5cm) high, 23oz.
£1,300–1,600 MJB

◀ A late 17th century-style silver tankard, by Frank Finlay Clarkson, Chester 1908, 5in (12.5cm) high, 16oz.
£400–500 TEN

▶ A silver tankard, commemorating the coronation of George V and Queen Mary, marked, Sheffield 1910, 3¼in (8.5cm) high.
£500–550 SHa

RATTLES

A George II child's silver rattle and whistle, engraved with a crest and motto, with coral teething stick, marked, probably EL, c1740, 4¼in (11.5cm) high.
£900–1,000 P

A silver rattle and whistle, with engraved decoration, coral teether and carrying ring, maker's mark W.T., late 18thC, 6in (15cm) long.
£700–850 Bea(E)

A George III silver rattle and whistle, by Peter and Ann Bateman, engraved with floral and foliate swags and monogram, with coral teether, London 1804, 5in (12.5cm) high.
£800–1,000 Bon

A George III silver rattle and whistle, engraved with stylized vertical banding, two of the eight bells and teething piece missing, London 1811, 4¼in (11cm) long.
£150–180 P(E)

A silver rattle and whistle, c1910, 4in (10cm) long.
£220–250 BaN

SALVERS & TRAYS

A George II silver salver, by William Peaston, with rococo rim, the centre with an armorial capped by a bull's head crest, on lion's paw feet, 1746, 7in (18cm) diam, 10oz.
£520–580 P

An Irish silver tray, with inscription on reverse, Dublin 1806, 6in (15cm) diam.
£800–900 SIL

▶ A late Victorian silver tray, by Elkington & Co, the raised moulded borders with rococo leaf sprays and scrolls, London 1899, 31in (78.5cm) wide, 162 oz.
£1,500–1,800 WW

A Russian silver tea tray, with pierced border, Assay Master Alexander Yashinkov, maker's mark 'T.P.', St. Petersburg 1808, 25¼in (64cm) wide, 87oz.
£2,000–2,200 S(NY)

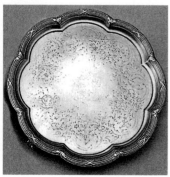

A pair of Victorian silver salvers, by John Samuel Hunt, each engraved with a band of flowers and an armorial, on four cast scroll feet, London 1847, 10in (25.5cm) diam, 42oz.
£650–750 DN

An Irish silver salver, with Celtic strapwork border incorporating mythical beasts and with applied bosses, possibly by West & Co, maker's mark obscured, Dublin 1913, 24in (61cm) diam, 148oz.
£2,500–3,000 L&E

A silver salver, by W. & S. S. Ltd, with scroll and pie-crust border, on four scrolled feet, Sheffield 1915, 17¾in (45cm) diam, 68½oz.
£700–800 WL

SAUCE & CREAM BOATS

A George II-style silver sauce boat, with heavy gadrooned rim and three shell and hoof feet, London 1902, 7in (18cm) wide, 9oz.
£170–200 GAK

A George II cream boat, by Stephen Buckle, with wavy rim and hoof feet, York, 1745, 5¼in (13.5cm) wide.
£450–500 P

The York Assay Office ceased in 1716 and, until its re-opening in about 1776, local makers were obliged to use other assay offices. Stephen Buckle of Spurriergate, York, registered his distinctive mark at the Newcastle Assay Office in 1738. By 1761, he had taken over his father's business in York where he traded until 1774.

A pair of George III silver sauce boats, by Daniel Smith and Robert Sharp, engraved with an armorial, London 1765, 8¾in (22cm) wide, 29oz.
£2,500–2,750 S

A pair of George III-style sauce boats, on three feet, 1931, 6¼in (16cm) wide, 8oz.
£240–280 L

SCENT BOTTLES

◄ A Continental silver-gilt Pilgrim flask-shaped scent bottle, chased in relief with chinoiserie figures on both sides, possibly French, c1720, 3¾in (9.5cm) high.
£600–700 P

► A Victorian silver scent bottle, enamelled on the front with a spray of dog roses in pink and white, in original fitted case, maker's mark 'H & A', Birmingham 1882, 4in (10cm) high.
£900–1,100 P

A Continental silver-gilt scent bottle, embossed with figural scenes and scroll borders, unmarked, 18thC, 4¼in (11cm) high, 3oz.
£400–500 Bon

SERVICES & CANTEENS

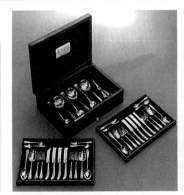

A silver Fiddle & Thread pattern part-canteen of cutlery, by Eley, Fearn & Chawner, comprising 103 pieces, 1809, including a pair of basting spoons and a soup ladle by Thomas Northcote, 1790, 107oz.
£1,400–1,700 P(B)

A silver canteen of cutlery, by Chawner & Co, comprising 125 pieces, decorated with stylized scroll pattern, in oak presentation case, London 1850s, 202oz.
£4,500–5,000 DD

A Victorian silver-gilt Elizabethan pattern dessert service, by George Adams, comprising 39 pieces, in fitted oak box, London 1858–75, 63oz.
£1,000–1,200 WW

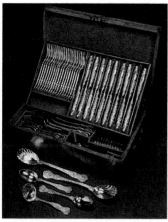

A silver-gilt Stag Hunt pattern dessert service, by George Adams, comprising 54 pieces, London 1874, 191oz, in a fitted oak case.
£8,500–10,000 TEN

Miller's is a price GUIDE not a price LIST

A silver Fiddle & Thread pattern part table service, by George Adams, comprising 28 crested pieces, London 1881, 57oz.
£1,200–1,400 Bea(E)

A set of twelve pairs of silver fish knives and forks, by J. H. Potter, each ivory handle carved as a boy or girl in a variety of costumes, with engraved blades and tines, Sheffield 1897, in a fitted wooden case.
£4,000–4,500 P

◄ An Edward VII silver Onslow pattern canteen of cutlery, by Mappin & Webb, comprising 133 pieces, Sheffield 1906, in a fitted oak table-top cabinet with three drawers.
£4,000–4,500 Bea(E)

A Scottish silver Old English pattern canteen of cutlery, by Jas Crichton & Co, comprising 18 monogrammed place settings, Edinburgh 1886, in an oak and banded case.
£4,500–5,500 HYD

An American silver Wave Edge pattern table service, by Tiffany & Co, comprising 60 initialled pieces, New York c1900, 67oz.
£3,200–3,500 S(NY)

SERVING IMPLEMENTS

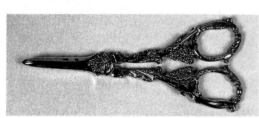

A pair of silver grape scissors, by William Hutton & Sons, London 1888, 6¼in (16cm) long, 4oz.
£530–585 TC

A pair of Scottish silver harlequin sugar nips, Edinburgh, c1870, 4½in (11.5cm) long.
£400–445 BEX

A pair of George III silver-gilt Fiddle, Thread & Shell pattern salad servers, by Eley, Fearn & Chawner, 1808–09, 9in (23cm) long, 11oz.
£800–1,000 P

A William IV silver sugar sifter, by George Adams, London 1845, 6in (15cm) long.
£90–100 ASAA

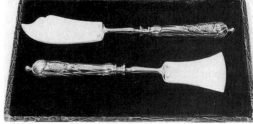

A pair of French silver servers, c1885, in a fitted case, 9in (23cm) wide.
£100–110 ASAA

A silver 'saw' cake knife, by Martin, Hall & Co, Sheffield 1921, in a fitted case, 11in (28cm) wide.
£1,100–1,250 BEX

SPOONS

To be 'born with a silver spoon in your mouth' is a familiar saying, suggesting that you come from a privileged family. The roots of this proverb date back to the 16th century when a silver spoon was given at christenings. It was a special and revered gift and would remain with you throughout your life.

When you were invited to dinner, even to a country house, it was expected that you brought your own silver spoon to eat with. This continued until the first quarter of the 17th century when place settings were being introduced: if you did not have your own, a pewter or wooden spoon might be supplied.

There is enormous scope for the amateur or experienced collector of silver spoons as, at the lower end of the market, they can be bought for just a few pounds while, at the opposite end of the scale, a single example can command many thousands of pounds. There are many styles and patterns to be found, such as the apostle spoon with its fig-shaped bowl and apostle figure as its finial, the Trefid, Dog Nose, Whip Lash, the plain Puritan, Old English, Fiddle, Kings and Queens patterns. These might then be combined with further decoration and patterns such as shells, thread, beading, bright-cut or feather-edge decoration and, furthermore, crests or initials.

The town where the spoon was made can be of great significance to the collector. Those from provincial towns such as Chester, York and Norwich, and Scottish and Irish towns such as Dumfries, Elgin, Banff, Cork, Galway and Limerick, all carry a premium as they are very sought-after. Pieces from small towns command higher prices as the output was not as great. Names such as Paul De Lamerie, Paul Storr, Hester Bateman and the prolific George Adams are in demand, but there were many thousands of talented silversmiths that are registered in the Assay offices of Great Britain that are not as popular.

The price of a spoon does not always relate to its age, which means that it is possible to build a comprehensive collection without an enormous outlay. However, overall condition, quality of hallmark, rarity of pattern or style, maker and source, all contribute to an increase in price.

The inexperienced collector can be misled by prices achieved at auction, when two people, fuelled by the 'I must have' factor, fight over a single item resulting in an unrepresentative final price. Moreover, some very fine collections have been sold over the last few years that have aroused more interest and inevitably increased values.

Daniel Bexfield

A Henry VIII silver *lion séjant affrontée* spoon, by William Simpson, London 1530, 6¾in (17cm) long.
£21,000–23,000 S

This spoon is very early, and therefore rare, and has the added distinction of coming from the singer Roger Whittaker's collection. Spoons that come from known collectors have been selling extremely well.

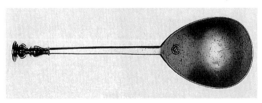

An Elizabeth I silver-gilt seal-top spoon, by Christopher Easton, the bowl later prick-dot engraved with '1641' over 'T.I.', Exeter, c1590, 6in (15cm) long.
£2,000–2,200 P

▶ A Charles I silver slip-top spoon, by Edward Hole, the finial engraved with initials, London 1633, 5in (12.5cm) long.
£850–1,000 RBB

A Henry VIII silver maidenhead spoon, by William Simpson, the terminal bearing traces of gilding, London 1543, 6in (15cm) long.
£2,300–2,750 S

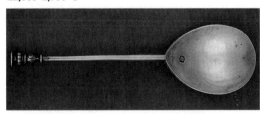

A James I silver seal-top spoon, by Daniel Cary, prick-engraved with ownership initials, London 1606, 7in (18cm) long.
£1,400–1,600 PFK

A Charles I silver seal-top spoon, by Richard Crosse, London 1636, 6½in (16.5cm) long.
£700–800 S

Apostle spoons

Apostle spoons first appeared during the reign of Henry VIII and for many people were the only item of silver they possessed. Large quantities were made in both London and the provinces.
They are so-named because the finials are headed by apostles and saints, each one identifiable by the emblems they hold in their right hand, although these can be difficult to discern. Very few full sets of Christ and all the apostles survive; they should all be made by the same maker in the same year. Production of London apostle spoons ceased in the reign of Charles I, but provincial spoons continued to be made for another 20 years.

from top left: St Matthias, St James the Greater, St Jude, St Matthew, St Andrew, St Simon, St Thomas, St John, St Peter, St James the Less, St Philip and St Bartholomew

A James I silver apostle spoon, St Matthew, provincial c1620, 7¼in (18.5cm) long.
£2,200–2,500 S

A Charles I silver apostle spoon, St Bartholomew, London 1636, 7¼in (18.5cm) long.
£1,400–1,600 S

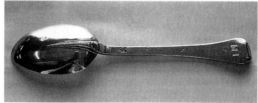

A silver trefid spoon, by Katherine Mangey, Hull, 1675–1700.
£900–1,100 DDM

◀ A James II silver trefid spoon, by John Smith, the bowl with a plain rat tail, worn, London 1688, 7¼in (18.5cm) long, 1oz.
£280–320 Bon

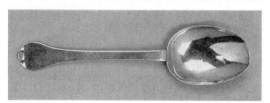

A William and Mary silver trefid spoon, the handle end with engraved initials, the bowl with beaded rat tail, maker's mark WM, 1689, 7½in (19cm) long.
£850–1,000 L

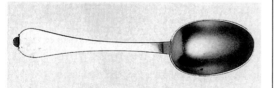

A William III silver trefid spoon, by Isaac Davenport, with ribbed rat tail, 1700, 7½in (19cm) long.
£350–400 P

This spoon is interesting as it demonstrates the transitional period between trefid and wavy end spoons.

A Queen Anne silver trefid spoon, by John Elston, Exeter 1706, 8in (20.5cm) long.
£370–400 S(S)

Miller's Compares

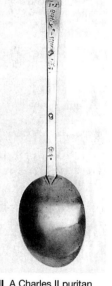

I A Charles II puritan spoon, by John King, London 1666.
£1,600–1,750 P

II A Charles II puritan spoon, by John Smith, with a baptismal inscription on stem, 1666.
£900–1,100 P

These two spoons are very similar in design and made in the same year, but Item I fetched considerably more in the auction room because the hallmarks are extremely clear. The marks on Item II are considerably worn and it was therefore a less desirable piece.

A Queen Anne silver dog nose spoon,
by Isaac Davenport, 1703, 7½in (19cm) long.
£130–150 P(EA)

A Dutch silver dog nose spoon, by Adriaan Stratenius,
Rotterdam 1735, 7¾in (19.5cm) long.
£100–120 S(Am)

An American silver dog nose spoon, by Daniel Boyer,
Boston, c1735, 7½in (19cm) long.
£1,000–1,200 S(NY)

A William III silver Hanoverian pattern spoon,
by Geo Cox, c1698, 8in (20.5cm) long.
£160–200 CoHA

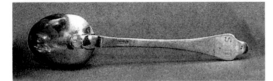

A George I silver Hanoverian pattern basting spoon,
by Thomas Mann, engraved on the underside with
a coat-of-arms, 1718, 14¼in (36cm) long.
£900–1,100 L

**By the end of the 18th century serving spoons and
basting spoons were often included in services,
but in the early part of the century they were
produced individually.**

A George II silver basting spoon, by Richd. Gosling, with
shell motif back, London 1753, 12¼in (31cm) long, 5¼oz.
£250–275 DD

A George IV silver basting spoon, by John, Henry and
Charles Lias, London 1825, 12in (30.5cm) long.
£200–235 BEX

A George III Irish silver hook-end basting spoon,
probably by Michael Keating, with a griffin crest,
Dublin 1778, 11½in (29cm) long.
£320–350 P

A George III silver Hanoverian pattern teaspoon, the bowl
decorated with a bird and cage and 'I Love Liberty' in
relief, engraved letters 'T.H.I.' to terminal, date marks
rubbed, maker's mark unclear, c1770.
£110–130 AG

**This spoon refers to the celebrated case of
John Wilkes, the English agitator and reformer,
who secured the great reforms of the abolition of
general warrants, the freeing of the press and the
freedom of choice for the electors. Support of Wilkes'
cause became national after his imprisonment in
1768 and on his discharge in 1770, the same symbol
being found on Wilkes' seals and glasses.**

A set of six silver teaspoons, by Hester Bateman,
London 1786, 5in (12.5cm) long.
£350–400 BEX

A George III silver spoon, with later embossed
decoration, London 1794, 9in (23cm) long.
£80–90 ASAA

A Victorian silver christening spoon and fork, engraved
with floral pattern, London 1885, 6in (15cm) long.
£55–60 ASAA

◀ A set of four Scottish silver tablespoons, by William
Constable, Dundee, c1800, 11½in (29cm) long.
£2,250–2,500 JBU

SNUFF BOXES

A Charles II silver and piqué snuff box, unmarked, c1680, 3½in (9cm) wide.
£1,800–2,000 BEX

Piqué is inlaid decoration of gold and silver, used on small objects such as boxes and fans.

A silver and mother-of-pearl snuff box, 1680, 3in (7.5cm) wide.
£200–225 MB

A William IV silver snuff box, the cover chased with a hunting scene incorporating a later inset panel of a coach and horses, the gilt interior with inscription, maker's mark I.J., London 1831, 5oz.
£800–1,000 Bea(E)

A William IV silver-gilt snuff box, by Taylor & Perry, the cover with cast and chased hunting scene, Birmingham 1834, 3½in (9cm) wide, 5oz.
£2,300–2,500 S

A William IV silver regimental mess table snuff box, by Benjamin Smith, the cover with foliate scroll borders, 6in (15cm) wide, 21oz.
£2,500–2,750 P

A Victorian silver table snuff box, by W. R. Smily, the cover with hunting scene in relief, 1844, 3¼in (8.5cm) wide.
£1,000–1,200 P

A silver snuff box, by Nathaniel Mills, engraved with scrolls, the base with a small scene, Birmingham 1839, 3½in (9cm) wide.
£400–450 TEN

A silver snuff box, engraved with scrolls, makers F.H. & F., Birmingham 1857, 4in (10cm) wide.
£320–385 TEN

◄ A Victorian silver-mounted ram's horn snuff mull, c1860, 3½in (9cm) long.
£500–550 SHa

VASES

◄ A Victorian silver campana-shaped vase, decorated with stylized foliate scrolls, maker's mark F.B.s Ltd, Sheffield 1896, 9in (23cm) high.
£200–240 Bea(E)

► A pair of silver neo-classical-style vases and covers, by Hutton & Sons, with ram's mask handles, Sheffield 1911, 11½in (29cm) high.
£1,600–1,750 P(C)

A pair of silver spill vases, with foliate rims, Birmingham 1926, 9½in (24cm) high.
£140–170 G(B)

VINAIGRETTES

A William IV silver vinaigrette, engine-turned, with pierced grille, maker's mark indistinct, possibly E.J., Birmingham 1834, 1½in (4cm) wide.
£160–200 P(Ed)

Miller's Compares

I A William IV silver vinaigrette, by Nathaniel Mills, depicting Abbotsford House, the grille with the remnants of a sterling lion punch, mostly lost in the piercing, Birmingham 1836, 1¾in (4.5cm) wide.
£975–1,100 P

II A William IV silver vinaigrette, by Francis Clark, depicting Abbotsford House, the grille decorated with a basket of flowers and struck with a sterling lion only, Birmingham 1836, 1¾in (4.5cm) wide.
£575–650 P

These two vinaigrettes were made in the same year and depicted the same building, but the price realized for Item I was almost double that of Item II. This is mainly because Item I is more sharply executed, with a fuller, more attractive design that includes trees and a bridge. Item II is rather sparse in comparison. Furthermore, Item I is by the famous specialist maker of silver boxes, Nathaniel Mills, whose work is keenly collected.

A silver vinaigrette, by Nathaniel Mills, depicting Windsor Castle, with foliate pierced grille within, Birmingham 1839, 1½in (4cm) wide.
£500–600 GAK

A Victorian silver vinaigrette, by Nathaniel Mills, decorated with York Minster, 1841, 1¾in (4.5cm) wide.
£1,100–1,300 G(L)

A silver vinaigrette, engraved with Osborne House, with pierced scrolling foliate grille, maker's mark D.P., Birmingham 1853, 1¾in (4.5cm) wide.
£900–1,100 P(Ed)

A Victorian silver vinaigrette, by Nathaniel Mills, engraved with scrolling foliage, the grille pierced with flowering foliage, Birmingham 1845, 1¾in (4.5cm) wide.
£280–320 P(Ed)

◄ A silver vinaigrette, by E. H. Stockwell, modelled as a rose bud with petal hinged for access, 1881, 4½in (11.5cm) long, 3oz.
£1,200–1,400 TEN

Further Reading

Miller's Silver & Plate Antiques Checklist, Miller's Publications, 1994

Silver Plate

A Regency silver-plated telescopic candlestick, c1810, 10in (25.5cm) high extended.
£80–90 AnSh

A William IV silver-plated centrepiece, the central basket above a column formed by three semi-draped classical females, one branch incomplete, 21½in (54.5cm) high.
£700–800 MJB

A pair of Elkington silver-plated table centrepieces, modelled as palm trees with a deer and giraffe, marked for 1857, 18in (45.5cm) high.
£1,350–1,500 RBB

A late Victorian silver-plated table centrepiece, 24in (61cm) high.
£800–1,000 CoHA

A pair of Sheffield plate entrée dishes and covers, probably by J. Watson & Sons, each supported on a two-handled warmer base with wooden detachable insulated feet, monogrammed, 1820–30, 13½in (34.5cm) wide.
£350–420 CGC

A George IV Sheffield plate coffee pot, with ribbed and foliate capped repoussé swan neck spout and scroll wood handle, 11in (28cm) high.
£120–140 WW

A Sheffield plate fish slice, the blade pierced with foliate scroll decoration, with green stained ivory handle, unmarked, c1780, 12½in (32cm) long.
£450–500 Bon

A pair of Sheffield plate sauce tureens, c1820, 8in (20.5cm) wide.
£1,200–1,400 DIC

A Sheffield plate three-piece teaset, with leaf-cast edges and scrolled fruitwood handle, with matching sugar pot and cream jug, c1835, teapot 7¾in (19.5cm) high.
£150–180 CGC

A silver-plated toast rack, c1900, 7in (18cm) high.
£55–65 ASAA

A pair of glass and silver-mounted vases, c1920, 6¾in (17cm) high.
£140–160 RUL

A pair of Sheffield plate wine coolers, early 19thC, 9in (23cm) high.
£1,400–1,700 AG

◀ An American silver-plated wine cooler, by Gorham Mfg Co, with Greek key bands and two stag's head handles, interior bottle sleeve, late 19thC, 10in (26.5cm) high.
£2,500–2,750 SK

Wine Antiques

An iridescent wine bottle, c1700, 7in (18cm) high.
£100–110 BAC

A silver-plated double wine coaster, on spoked wheels, 19thC, each coaster 6in (15cm) diam.
£220–260 GAK

◄ A sealed dark olive-green glass squat cylinder bottle, dated '1769', 9¾in (25cm) high.
£900–1,000 BBR

A Victorian Sheffield plate magnum coaster, with pierced sides, 9½in (24cm) diam, on a wooden base.
£130–160 Mit

A French corking machine, c1880, 17¼in (44cm) long.
£600–700 EMC

A pair of American silver-mounted decanters, by T. B. Starr, with stamped foliate base and collar, initialled, c1900, 12in (30.5cm) high.
£800–900 S(S)

A Victorian silver-mounted claret jug, modelled as a seal, the central loop carrying handle linking front and back flippers, 1881, 6½in (16.5cm) long.
£10,000–12,000 Bri

This decanter is particularly desirable because the glass is original.

A late Georgian burr-walnut and brass-mounted decanter box, with four glass decanters with stoppers, the lid with initials, 8½in (21.5cm) wide.
£400–500 WL

A Victorian silver-topped hip flask, the hobnail cut-glass body with gilt-lined integral cup, London 1885, 5½in (14cm) high.
£150–180 EH

A liqueur set, comprising four decanters and 14 glasses, the ebonized rosewood case brass-inlaid and crossbanded with mother-of-pearl, 19thC, 13¾in (35cm) wide.
£1,400–1,700 AH

A silver wine taster, unmarked, c1660, 2½in (6.5cm) diam.
£1,650–1,850 BEX

▶ A George III set of four gold wine labels, by J. Teake, Dublin 1810, 1¾in (4.5cm) wide.
£675–750 WELD

CORKSCREWS

Collecting wine antiques has become more and more popular over the years, with many items to look out for such as silver wine funnels, decorative corks, decanter labels, port-tilters, champagne taps etc. Above all, what could be more useful than the instrument for drawing the cork – the corkscrew! Although simple bottle screws, as they were first called, were used throughout the 18th century, the great age of the corkscrew is undoubtedly the 19th century.

In 1795, the Reverend Samuel Henshall, a London clergyman with a well-developed taste for wine, was the first person to patent a 'New Method for Constructing and Improving Corkscrews'. This was a functional tool with a circular concave disc fixed at the bottom of a turned steel shank just above the helix.

Over the next 100 years, England became a frenzy of industrial revolution and over 300 patents were taken out on corkscrews. A notable inventor and manufacturer was Sir Edward Thomason of Birmingham (1759–1849). In 1802 Thomason patented his brass double-action corkscrew, the mechanism of which was quite revolutionary, and its importance can be ascertained by the fact that the design was still in use well into the 20th century.

Up until about 1900, corkscrews that had either a turned bone or wooden handle were fitted at one end with a bristle brush to remove loose particles of sealing wax, cobwebs or dust on bottles that had been lying in cellars for years.

In the latter half of the 19th century there was a multiplicity of patents on all-steel lever and concertina types, many made by James Heeley & Sons of Birmingham and Lund of London. The Victorian and Edwardian period saw an array of corkscrews combined with other items including penknives, walking sticks etc. Bar cork drawers, permanently fixed by either clamp fittings or directly screwing onto the bar top, were efficient and speedy and made to survive heavy use in pubs and wine bars. Brass novelty 'figural' corkscrews also came into their own in the 1930s.

America, France, Germany, Italy, Scandinavia and Ireland all have their own corkscrew inventions, and as with English examples, have proved to be either highly successful or disastrous.

Today there is an increasing interest in collecting corkscrews, not only for use but also for investment. As much fun can be obtained in the search as in the finding and, regardless of the value, the result is the same – the joy of opening a bottle of fine wine! **Christopher Sykes**

A silver and steel pocket corkscrew, c1780, 3in (7.5cm) long.
£575–650 BEX

A double-action corkscrew, with bone handle and brass embossed barrel, c1810, 8½in (21.5cm) long.
£130–150 CS

A silver pocket corkscrew, maker's mark of Samuel Pemberton, late 18th/early 19thC, 3¼in (8.5cm) long.
£600–700 Bon

Miller's Compares

I A double-action corkscrew, with bone handle and brass barrel, applied with royal coat-of-arms, marked 'Thomason & Son Ne Plus Ultra', c1810, 7in (18cm) long.
£200–240 CS

II A double-action corkscrew, of the type patented by Sir Edward Thomason in 1802, with turned bone handle, hanging ring and dusting brush, central hermaphrodite raising screw contained in outer brass barrel, applied with royal coat-of-arms, c1820, 6½in (16.5cm) long.
£110–130 CS

These corkscrews appear almost identical, but Item I bears the maker's name of Thomason, which increases its value. Item II is a slightly later copy which hoped, no doubt, to cash in on Sir Edward Thomason's invention.

◄ A compound folding bow corkscrew, the faceted bow with ten tools, c1810, 3¼in (8.5cm) wide.
£100–120 CS

A Thomason Variant corkscrew, with turned nickel driving handle and turned walnut raising handle, applied with royal coat-of-arms, c1810, 7in (18cm) long.
£240–280 CS

A King's Screw mechanical corkscrew, with wide rack and bone driving and raising handles, c1820, 7½in (19cm) long.
£175–200 CS

A brass open-frame mechanical corkscrew, with bone handle, 1840, 7½in (19cm) long.
£400–450 EMC

A Presto ratchet mechanism corkscrew, by Charles Hull, with wooden handle, brass shank and steel corkscrew, c1870, 8in (20.5cm) long.
£400–450 CS

A London Rack mechanical corkscrew, with turned wood handle and steel frame, c1885, 6¾in (17cm) long.
£60–70 CS

A German corkscrew, in the form of a pair of lady's legs, c1890, 2½in (6.5cm) long.
£100–120 CS

A brass-mounted corkscrew, the handle in the form of a crouching man with goat's legs, probably French, 19thC, 5½in (14cm) high.
£900–1,000 S&S

◄ A Rotary Eclipse brass bar cork drawer, with walnut winder handle, c1890, 16in (40.5cm) long.
£350–400 CS

► A Merritt brass bar corkscrew, with turned wood handle, 1890, 16in (40.5cm) long.
£300–340 EMC

◄ A silver-plated corkscrew, modelled as a dog, 1930s, 3½in (9cm) long.
£50–55 BEV

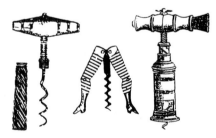

Clocks

BRITISH BRACKET, MANTEL & TABLE CLOCKS

An ebony and brass-mounted table clock, by Joseph Knibb, London, the two-train fusee movement with verge escapement, rack hour striking and quarter repeating on two bells, restored, late 17thC, 13in (33cm) high.
£13,000–15,000 DN

An ebonized and brass-mounted bracket clock, by A. M. Cressener, London, the movement with anchor escapement striking on a bell and repeating the quarters on six bells, early 18thC, 21in (53.5cm) high.
£5,000–6,000 P

Movements

• bracket, carriage, skeleton, novelty and some wall clocks are spring-driven, by the release of energy in a coiled spring. Many have a device known as a fusee, a conical spool used to even out the pull of the spring, thus spreading power over the running time of the clock, making it more accurate.
• lantern, longcase and some wall clocks are weight-driven, by the pull of hanging weights.

A George III ebony bracket clock, by Thomas Pierce, London, striking on two bells, c1750, 15½in (39.5cm) high.
£3,200–3,800 JNic

A George III inlaid mahogany bracket clock, signed Thomas Best, London, with twin fusee verge movement, 14½in (37cm) high.
£5,000–6,000 GH

A walnut bracket clock, signed Samuel Whichcote, London, the eight-day movement converted from verge to anchor escapement, striking on a bell, c1765, 20in (51cm) high.
£1,500–1,800 WW

Samuel Whichcote worked from 175 Fleet Street in the mid-18thC.

A George III mahogany and brass-mounted musical bracket clock, signed Barraud's, London, with selection of seven airs, with triple fusee movement and anchor escapement, playing 12 bells via 12 hammers, 23in (58.5cm) high.
£3,800–4,200 P

Jeffrey Formby Antiques

Specialist in Quality English Clocks and Horological Books

Longcase, Bracket, Skeleton and Lantern Clocks

Visitors welcome by appointment
Orchard Cottage, East Street,
Moreton-in-Marsh, Glos. GL56 0LQ
Telephone: 01608 650558
Internet: www.formby-clocks.co.uk

An ebonized bracket clock, by Percival Man, London, the twin-train fusee movement with later anchor escapement, striking on a bell, c1770, 17in (43cm) high.
£2,500–3,000 P(EA)

A George III Scottish ebonized bracket clock, by John Curle, Kelso, with eight-day fusee movement striking on a bell, 1770–80, 16¾in (42.5cm) high.
£1,200–1,500 HYD

An ebonized fruitwood bracket clock, by William Owen, London, the five-pillar twin fusee movement with verge escapement striking on a bell, backplate with foliate engraving, c1775, 20in (51cm) high.
£6,500–7,000 JIL

An ebonized bracket clock, by Peter Mason, London, the twin fusee movement with verge escapement, bell top and cone finials, 1770–80, 18½in (47cm) high.
£3,200–3,500 P

A mahogany bracket clock, by John Taylor, London, the twin fusee movement striking on a bell, c1780, 19½in (49.5cm) high.
£5,500–6,500 Bon

An ormolu clock, by Thos. Brown, London, in the form of a bacchante, with verge escapement, 1788–1800, 12in (30.5cm) high.
£1,100–1,400 GOL

▶ A George III brass-mounted mahogany table clock, signed Daniel Ray, Battle, the eight-day two-train fusee movement with verge escapement, c1790, 17in (43cm) high.
£3,800–4,500 DN

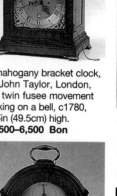

A mahogany bracket clock, by Stephens & Havelland, London, with twin fusee movement striking on a bell, c1790, 17½in (44.5cm) high.
£3,800–4,500 Bon

A musical bracket clock, by Gravell & Tolkien, with three-train anchor escapement and a selection of six airs, c1800, 27¾in (70.5cm) high.
£9,500–11,500 TEN

A mahogany bracket clock, by John Hughes, with pull repeat, c1800, 17½in (44.5cm) high.
£5,750–6,500 JeF

A mahogany and brass-inlaid bracket clock, by MacGregor, Edinburgh, with twin fusee bell striking movement, the panelled front with applied carving, and a matching bracket, c1800, 16½in (42cm) high.
£1,800–2,200 Bon

◀ A mahogany table clock, the two-train fusee movement with verge escapement, c1800, 17in (43cm) high.
£3,500–3,850 S(S)

A mahogany striking bracket clock, signed James Stone, Windsor, with twin fusee movement striking on a bell, c1800, 17in (43cm) high.
£2,200–2,600 Bon

An ebonized and brass-inlaid bracket clock, by Septimus Miles, London, with original bracket, c1805, 27in (68.5cm) high.
£5,500–6,000 JeF

A mahogany bracket clock, signed James McCabe, London, the eight-day movement striking the hours and quarters on one and eight bells, with anchor escapement, c1810, 17in (43cm) high.
£7,500–8,750 PAO

A satinwood and inlaid balloon clock, by Parker, London, with crossbanded edge decoration inlaid to the centre with three feathers, the twin fusee movement now converted to anchor escapement striking on a bell, early 19thC, 15¾in (40cm) high.
£4,000–4,500 P

A Regency mahogany bracket clock, by John Grant, London, with eight-day double fusee movement striking on a bell, c1810, 14in (35.5cm) high.
£1,600–2,000 Hal

A bronze and ormolu mantel clock, by Thos. Hawley, London, with chain fusee movement and anchor escapement, early 19thC, 12in (30.5cm) high.
£4,000–4,500 P

◀ A mahogany bracket clock, by Panchaud & Cumming, London, the eight-day movement with anchor escapement striking the hours on a bell, c1810, 16in (40.5cm) high.
£5,500–6,200 PAO

A mahogany brass-inlaid bracket clock, by R. Restell, Croydon, with twin fusee movement, c1810, 20½in (52cm) high.
£1,150–1,400 P(S)

A late Georgian ebonized bracket timepiece, by Thomas Mudge, London, the circular fusee movement with anchor escapement, the case with some alterations, 14½in (37cm) high.
£2,200–2,500 P

A Regency ebonized bracket clock, by Dwerrihouse, Carter & Son, London, c1815, 17in (43cm) high.
£4,250–4,750 JeF

A Regency mantel clock, by W. Nicoll, London, the eight-day twin fusee movement striking on bells, 11in (28cm) high.
£1,350–1,500 WW

An ebony bracket clock, by J. Bramble, London, with painted dial and twin fusee movement, strike/silent dial, c1830, 15½in (39.5cm) high.
£5,500–6,000 ALS

A Regency ebony and brass-inlaid bracket clock, by John Palmer, London, with eight-day movement striking on a bell, c1830, 16½in (42cm) high.
£3,200–3,600 HYD

When sold at auction, clocks have sometimes had alterations to their movements or are in unrestored condition, which may be reflected in the prices realized.

A Regency mahogany and brass-inlaid bracket clock, signed E. Moseley, London, with white dial, the eight-day fusee movement striking on a bell, c1830, 19¾in (50cm) high.
£2,000–2,200 HYD

A rosewood and brass-inlaid bracket clock, by Richard House, Marlborough, with twin fusee movement, c1830, 15in (38cm) high.
£3,250–3,750 BL

An Irish mahogany bracket clock, by Robert Shaw, Belfast, the eight-day two-train fusee movement with anchor escapement striking the hours on a bell, c1830, 17¾in (45cm) high.
£850–1,000 DN

A mahogany and brass-inlaid bracket clock, by E. Handscomb, Woburn, with eight-day double fusee striking movement, on brass ball feet, c1830, 22½in (57cm) high.
£1,350–1,500 E

A Regency mahogany bracket clock, with cream painted dial, the twin fusee movement chiming on two bells, c1830, 19½in (49.5cm) high.
£1,300–1,500 Bea(E)

A Regency mahogany and brass-inlaid bracket clock, by Edward Pearce, Crewkerne, with twin fusee movement striking on a bell, c1830, 19¼in (49cm) high.
£2,500–3,000 P(B)

▶ A William IV mahogany mantel clock, the case inlaid with brass design of war horses and rider, with eight-day movement striking on a rod, glass lacking, 20in (51cm) high.
£500–600 RBB

A rosewood mantel clock, with eight-day fusee movement, 1830–40, 12½in (32cm) high.
£850–1,000 E

A mahogany and brass-inlaid bracket clock, by Alstons & Hallam, London, the twin fusee movement with anchor escapement, striking on a gong, c1840, 16in (40.5cm) high.
£1,750–2,000 P

A walnut mantel timepiece, by Brockbank & Atkins, London, with single fusee movement, the case with carved foliage and ogee side mouldings, c1850, 13in (33cm) high.
£380–450 Bon

A mahogany bracket clock, by Dent, London, the eight-day fusee movement striking on a bell, with anchor escapement, c1840, 16¾in (42.5cm) high.
£1,800–2,200 DN

An ormolu thirty-day mantel timepiece, by Thomas Cole, London, the centre with an aneroid barometer and Cole's pendulum locking arrangement, two-tier month-going movement, deadbeat escapement and separately suspended pendulum with roller suspension, original numbered double-ended winder, the base with engraved flowers and scrolls, with glass dome and mahogany stand, c1851, 20in (51cm) high.
£8,500–9,500 S

◀ An ormolu nautical desk clock, by Vincent, Weymouth, c1865, 10in (25.5cm) high.
£450–550 HAL

A mahogany bracket clock, by Dent, London, with eight-day movement, c1840, 17in (43cm) high.
£4,500–5,000 JeF

◀ An oak five-glass mantel timepiece, by Dent, London, the fusee movement with anchor escapement and maintaining power, c1850, 9in (23cm) high.
£2,000–2,200 S(S)

▶ A patent winding slate and lacquered and patinated brass-mounted mantel clock, by R. Houdin/ Dent, London, 19thC, 16in (40.5cm) high.
£800–950 P

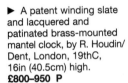

A rosewood and brass-inlaid mantel timepiece, the fusee movement with circular plates and anchor escapement, c1840, 11¾in (30cm) high.
£2,700–3,000 S

An ebonized table clock, with cylinder escapement, striking on the hour and the half hour, c1870, 8in (20.5cm) high.
£1,350–1,500 PTh

A Gothic revival gilt-brass mantel clock, the design attributed to Bruce James Talbert, the circular plated going-barrel movement with platform lever escapement, c1870, 12¼in (31cm) high.
£2,000–2,400 S

Originally a carver, Bruce James Talbert (1838–81) later trained as an architect, but is best known as a designer and decorator.

◄ An ebonized bracket clock, the movement striking on two coiled gongs, with floral cast gilt-metal inlay, late 19thC, 22½in (57cm) high.
£900–1,100 P(L)

A mahogany bracket clock, signed Thomas Leeming, Settle, with double fusee movement, c1870, 17in (43cm) high.
£1,500–1,700 BL

A tortoiseshell mantel clock, inlaid with silver stringing, c1900, 8in (20.5cm) high.
£1,500–1,750 CHAP

A silver boudoir timepiece, the front with engine-turned bead and linear decoration, the top applied with ribbon-tied swags of flowers, silver by William Comyns, 1910, 4in (10cm) high.
£700–800 P

A Smith's Astral thuyawood mantel clock, with lever movement, c1920, 6in (15cm) high.
£450–500 PTh

A carved oak bracket clock, the three-train fusee movement striking on eight bells and four gongs, late 19thC, 20in (51cm) high.
£1,350–1,500 Mit

An Edwardian inlaid mahogany bracket clock, 12½in (32cm) high.
£370–450 AAV

A mahogany mantel clock, by Mappin & Webb, the eight-day French movement striking on a gong, early 20thC, 12½in (32cm) high.
£300–350 Hal

A silver and tortoiseshell desk clock, by E. S. Barnsley & Co, Birmingham, 1919, 4½in (11.5cm) high.
£1,250–1,450 BEX

CONTINENTAL BRACKET, MANTEL & TABLE CLOCKS

A French green shell and gilt-bronze bracket clock, by Le Faucheur, early 18thC, 47¼in (120cm) high.
£8,500–9,500 S(Mon)

A French Empire ormolu and green marble clock, by Dubuc le Jeune, Paris, with eight-day movement, c1805, 13in (33cm) high.
£1,800–2,000 JIL

A French Empire ormolu mantel clock, by Michelez, Paris, the movement with countwheel strike on a bell, regilded, early 19thC, 18in (45.5cm) high.
£1,200–1,400 TMA

A French white marble and ormolu mantel clock, the bell striking movement contained in a drum case surmounted by the figure of a Roman warrior flanked by two obelisks, late 18thC, 22in (56cm) high.
£2,800–3,200 Bon

A French ormolu-mounted bisque porcelain mantel clock, by Bourrel, Paris, with eight-day single-barrel movement, c1810, 12in (30.5cm) high.
£1,800–2,000 JIL

A French ormolu-mounted mahogany portico clock, by Thomas Monginot, Paris, with full calendar indication, the movement with anchor escapement and outside countwheel strike on a bell, the heavy gridiron pendulum with micrometer regulation, early 19thC, 29in (73.5cm) high.
£5,000–6,000 P

A Swiss painted Neuchâtel bracket clock, by Fred. L. S. Huguenin, with pull repeat, striking the three quarters on two bells, and with separate alarm, c1800, 34in (86.5cm) high.
£2,500–3,000 S(Z)

▶ A French ormolu-mounted white bisque porcelain mantel clock, by Gavelle, Paris, the bell striking movement with an outside countwheel, early 19thC, 17¼in (44cm) high.
£1,650–2,000 Bon

A Viennese neo-classical ormolu mantel clock, in an arched case enclosing birds, surmounted by a bee on a basket, with three-train movement, early 19thC, 10⅜in (27.5cm) high.
£1,800–2,200 S(NY)

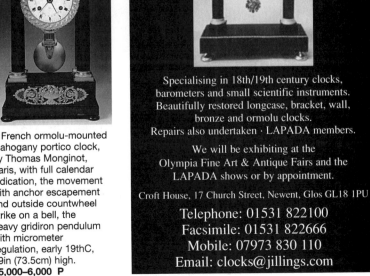

A French gilt-bronze commemorative mantel clock, with a figure of Alexander I of Russia, c1815, 17½in (44.5cm) high.
£2,800–3,200 S

A French bronze and ormolu mantel clock, the eight-day two-train movement with outside countwheel strike on a bell, the case surmounted by a seated Roman, c1840, 25in (63.5cm) high.
£1,000–1,200 DN

A French Napoleon III gilt-bronze figural mantel clock, mounted with a female figure, mid-19thC, 18½in (47cm) high.
£600–675 NOA

A French alabaster and gilt-brass portico clock, by Bechot, Paris, the movement with outside countwheel strike on a bell, with gridiron pendulum, early 19thC, 21½in (54.5cm) high.
£2,300–2,750 P

An Austrian ebonized and gilt short duration *grande sonnerie* mantel clock, the triple-train movement striking on the quarters on two gongs, mid-19thC, 24in (61cm) high.
£600–720 Bon

◀ A French gilt and ormolu mantel clock, with striking mechanism, c1840, 11in (28cm) high.
£750–850 BLA

A French burr-cedar mantel clock, by Jacot, Paris, the bell striking movement with anchor escapement, c1830, 13in (33cm) high.
£2,500–2,750 S

A French Louis Philippe inlaid rosewood and bronze-mounted portico clock, mid-19thC, 19¾in (50cm) high.
£1,000–1,200 NOA

A French *Capucine* clock, signed Montadon, Paris, the eight-day movement with double hour strike, manual repeat facility and alarm, 1830, 11¾in (30cm) high.
£1,400–1,700 S(Z)

A French mahogany portico clock, with cast and chased brass decoration, mid-19thC, 25½in (65cm) high.
£3,400–3,750 ALS

A French porcelain mantel clock, with eight-day movement striking on a bell, 19thC, 15in (38cm) high.
£600–720 DDM

◀ A French ebonized and inlaid four-pillar mantel clock, the movement inscribed Linetaine, Paris, 19thC, 19in (48cm) high.
£250–300 P(L)

Complicated striking

Clocks that strike the half or quarter hours as well as the hours have a third train, a third weight (or spring), and three winding holes. Cleaning and repair of complex striking requires expert attention. Clocks with complicated striking are more valuable than those with simple hour striking.
The principal types of striking clock are:
• grande sonnerie – repeats the last hour after each quarter-hour
• petite sonnerie – strikes the hours and quarter-hours only
• repeat mechanism – appears as a pull-cord or a button on the case. If the cord is pulled or the button pressed, the last hour or quarter-hour are repeated.

A French gilt-metal mantel clock, the case surmounted by a cavalier and a portrait bust of a lady, the eight-day movement striking on a bell, dial damaged, 19thC, 12in (30.5cm) high.
£200–240 Hal

A French gilt-bronze and porcelain-mounted mantel clock, by Bourdin, Paris, with anchor escapement and countwheel strike on a bell, 19thC, 15in (38cm) high.
£2,500–3,000 P

A French gilt-metal mantel clock, applied with a figure of a young boy, 19thC, 12in (30.5cm) high.
£200–240 RID

A French ormolu mounted boulle mantel clock, with eight-day movement, 19thC, 12in (30.5cm) high.
£170–200 TAM

A French four-glass mantel clock, the eight-day two-train movement with anchor escapement striking the hour and half hour on a bell, mercury compensated pendulum, 19thC, 13in (33cm) high.
£950–1,150 DN

A French ormolu mantel clock, by Cauzard, Paris, supported on a 'lion-skin' cradle, the eight-day countwheel movement striking on a bell on the hour and half-hour, c1850, 19in (48.5cm) high.
£5,000–6,000 JIL

A German Black Forest carved beech mantel cuckoo clock, the brass movement with twin going barrels, mid-19thC, 17½in (44.5cm) high.
£425–500 Bon

A Continental carved giltwood and ivory-painted portico clock, mid-19thC, 19¾in (50cm) high.
£1,000–1,200 NOA

▶ A French gilt-bronze and porcelain mantel clock, the dial flanked by cherubs, the case inset with painted panels, the movement striking on a bell, c1870, 20½in (52cm) high.
£4,500–5,500 S

A Continental mahogany mantel clock, the dial flanked by alabaster pillars, with round bell striking movement, the concentric sweep calendar hand missing, 19thC, 15½in (39.5cm) high.
£300–350 Bon

Continental Bracket, Mantel & Table Clocks • CLOCKS 381

A French green onyx and champlevé mantel clock, by Batty & Co, Paris, with gong striking movement, c1880, 16½in (42cm) high.
£800–1,000 Bon

A French gilt-bronze and painted porcelain mantel clock, the bell striking Japy movement with Brocot suspension, c1880, 17in (43cm) high.
£2,200–2,500 S(S)

◀ A French Empire-style solid brass mantel clock, with eight-day movement striking on a bell, c1890, 13in (33cm) high.
£425–475 PTh

A French satinwood mantel clock, by Vincenti, Paris, the eight-day movement striking the hour and half hour on a bell, c1880, 13in (33cm) high.
£2,500–2,850 PAO

A French neo-classical-style mantel clock, with striking movement, sphinx finial, spinach-green marble base and entablature, late 19thC, 18in (45.5cm) high.
£8,000–10,000 FBG

A Louis XV-style boulle mantel clock, the two-train spring-driven movement with half hour striking on two bells, door glass missing, finial damaged, late 19thC, 23in (58.5cm) high.
£200–240 PFK

▶ A German rosewood bracket clock, striking the four quarters on gongs, c1900, 15in (38cm) high.
£1,500–2,000 BL

A French spelter mantel clock, with Sèvres panels on the base, the eight-day movement striking on a gong, c1890, 13in (33cm) high.
£600–700 PTh

An ormolu mantel clock, the eight-day movement striking on a bell, on a wooden base, late 19thC, 14½in (37cm) high.
£800–1,000 DDM

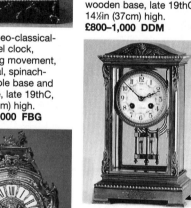

A French brass four-glass mantel clock, with gong striking movement, mercury compensated pendulum, 1900s, 12½in (32cm) high.
£400–500 Bon

CARRIAGE CLOCKS

A French carriage clock, with alarm, c1840, 6in (15cm) high.
£2,400–2,700 JeF

A French gilt-brass carriage clock, the repeating bell striking Japy movement with lever platform escapement, c1860, 6in (15cm) high.
£700–850 S(S)

A French carriage clock, by Henry Marc, Paris, with cylinder platform escapement, c1870, 7in (18cm) high.
£1,800–2,000 JeF

A French brass-cased carriage clock, with repeater mechanism, 19thC, 5in (12.5cm) high.
£400–450 RBB

Items in the Clock section have been arranged in date order.

A French gilt-brass carriage clock, with repeat button, c1880, 7in (18cm) high.
£900–1,000 S(Am)

A brass *grande sonnerie* carriage clock, the movement striking on two coiled gongs, with alarm, late 19thC, 6¾in (17cm) high.
£1,200–1,400 P(L)

A French carriage clock, with exposed movement, repeater mechanism and alarm, late 19thC, 6in (15cm) high.
£700–850 Bea(E)

A French eight-day brass carriage clock, with lever escapement, striking on a coiled gong, late 19thC, 8in (20.5cm) high.
£450–550 DN

An Edwardian brass carriage clock, with repeater mechanism, 6in (15cm) high.
£600–720 G(B)

◀ An ormolu carriage clock/ barometer, with thermometer and compass, inscribed 'J. & W. Mitchell, Glasgow', with leather travelling case, late 19thC, 6½in (16.5cm) high.
£650–750 GAK

A French eight-day carriage clock, with original leather carrying case, dated 1928, 5in (12.5cm) high.
£400–450 PTh

◀ A silver eight-day carriage clock, silver by Samuel & Ernest Drew, London 1910, 3¾in (9.5cm) high.
£900–1,100 BEX

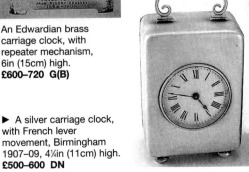

▶ A silver carriage clock, with French lever movement, Birmingham 1907–09, 4¼in (11cm) high.
£500–600 DN

CARTEL CLOCKS

A French gilt-bronze cartel clock, by Ferdinand Berthoud, Paris, with enamel dial and bell striking movement, 18thC, 18in (45.5cm) high.
£3,500–3,850 CGC

Ferdinand Berthoud (1727–1807) was an eminent clockmaker, who designed a spring detent escapement and was author of many important technical works.

A Louis XVI gilt-bronze cartel clock, signed Robin, Paris, decorated with acanthus leaves and ribbons, 18thC, 29in (73.5cm) high.
£6,500–8,000 S(Mon)

When sold at auction, clocks have sometimes had alterations to their movements or are in unrestored condition, which may be reflected in the prices realized.

A Swedish giltwood cartel clock, signed L. Sandgren, Stockholm, with painted Roman dial and twin barrelled movement, the rack striking on a gong, c1880, 33in (84cm) high.
£3,800–4,200 JIL

► A Louis XVI-style gilt-bronze cartel clock, with enamelled dial, the case hung with berried laurel garlands, late 19thC, 18in (45.5cm) high.
£1,800–2,200 S(NY)

A French eight-day gilt-bronze cartel clock, the twin barrelled movement striking on a bell, c1870, 21in (53.5cm) high.
£3,300–3,700 JIL

ELECTRIC CLOCKS

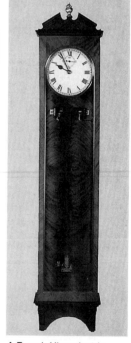

An electric mantel clock, by Eureka Clock Co, the movement with osculating balance wheel, 1906, 15in (38cm) high.
£900–1,100 P(NW)

A French Bulle Patent electric mantel clock, with silvered dial, the wooden base housing the battery, with a cut-glass dome, c1920, 15in (38cm) high.
£700–800 S

An electric mantel timepiece, by Thomas John Murday, the Reason Mfg Co, the brass movement mounted on twin turned columns supporting the three arm balance on a spring with three weights and timing screws, early 20thC, 12¼in (31cm) high.
£2,500–3,000 P

Thomas John Murday took out a series of patents concerning electrical horology between 1879 and 1921. The clock pictured above is an example of his most successful, of which only about 300 were made.

A French Hipp electric mahogany wall clock, with demi-regulator, the battery fitted to the top of the case, c1920, 67in (170cm) high.
£900–1,100 Mit

This timepiece is a copy of the system which was developed by Matthaus Hipp, Neuchâtel, in 1834.

Auction or Dealer?

All the pictures in our price guides originate from auction houses and dealers. When buying at auction, prices can be lower than those of a dealer, but a buyer's premium and VAT will be added to the hammer price. Equally, when selling at auction, commission, tax and photography charges must be taken into account. Dealers will often restore pieces before putting them back on the market.

Both dealers and auctioneers will provide professional advice, so it is worth researching both sources before buying or selling your antiques.

GARNITURES

A French ormolu and bronze-mounted white marble clock garniture, the countwheel eight-day movement striking on a bell, c1855, clock 18in (45.5cm) high.
£5,000–6,000 JIL

A French eight-day clock garniture, signed Howell and James, inset with blue jasperware medallions, late 19thC, clock 13¾in (35cm) high.
£650–800 AH

A matched French tortoiseshell and gilt-metal clock garniture, applied with a figure of Father Time, late 19thC, tallest 12⅝in (32cm) high.
£950–1,150 Bon

A French gilt-bronze and porcelain clock garniture, the porcelain painted and 'jewelled' with flowers on a pink ground, the bell striking Japy movement with Brocot suspension, with giltwood bases, faults, c1890, clock 12½in (32cm) high.
£1,500–1,650 S(S)

A French spelter and variegated green marble clock garniture, by Japy Frères, the eight-day movement striking on a bell, early 20thC, clock 24in (61cm) high.
£370–400 DN(H)

LANTERN CLOCKS

A Charles II brass lantern clock, by John Quelch, Oxford, with later anchor escapement, replaced bell, alarm work removed, c1665, 13in (33cm) high.
£3,200–3,500 S

▶ A French brass lantern clock, with pewter chapter ring, posted frame two-train movement and verge escapement with silk suspension, and internal rack striking on the top-mounted bell, c1770, 15¼in (38.5cm) high.
£1,000–1,100 S(S)

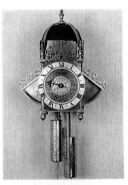

A wing lantern clock, by Nicholas Coxeter, London, with verge escapement, c1670, 15in (38cm) high.
£9,000–10,000 DRA

A brass thirty-hour lantern clock, by William Risbridge, the posted movement with a verge escapement, with a short bob pendulum, striking on a bell, bell replaced, early 18thC, 15in (38cm) high.
£2,000–2,400 Bon

▶ A brass lantern timepiece, with alarm, by Farmer, London, the movement with verge escapement, restored, 18thC, 9½in (24cm) high.
£1,600–1,750 P

A brass lantern clock, by Richard Rayment, Bury St Edmunds, with original anchor escapement and long pendulum, c1710, 15in (38cm) high.
£3,500–4,500 BL

LONGCASE CLOCKS

Weight-driven domestic clocks had been known since at least the 16th century. They had a variety of different escapements, which resulted in unreliable timekeeping and the need for daily checking. By the early 17th century, they had developed into the still inaccurate lantern clock, which needed winding and adjusting every day.

In 1658, the pendulum was introduced in London by Ahasuerus Fromanteel, allowing for greater accuracy and obviating the need for daily correction. It was now worthwhile to produce clocks of longer duration and as these needed two weights the case was introduced to counter the impracticality of placing them on a wall or shelf.

The longcase clock combines the work of several craftsmen – the clockmaker, whose name it bears, the case-maker, usually unidentified, and, in the case of painted dial clocks, the dial-maker, whose name is sometimes hidden behind the dial. In terms of value it is vital that a clock has not been altered from new, as many have been re-cased, had different movements fitted, or have been drastically changed over the years. Although a 'married' clock, as it is sometimes called,

or a 'composite' clock (meaning one made up from parts of others) may still look attractive and find buyers, its price will be nowhere near that of a similar unaltered one.

Prices of all longcase clocks have risen rapidly in the last year, but the greatest increase has been for completely original examples, and the price gap between the genuine clock and the suspect one grows ever wider. Another great influence on price is condition, as well as the size, proportion, colour, patina and style of the case. Some case styles are unpopular, and they may appear to be bargains. Great height can be a drawback for many buyers and can therefore hold the price down. On the other hand, a good example of a generally popular style in a size that is easily accommodated is off to a good start. Add outstanding condition, wonderful colour and patina, and such a clock will be at the top of its price range.

Variations in the values of clocks featured in *Miller's Antiques Price Guide* may baffle the beginner, and the reader should look closely in order to recognise these differences. It is easy to be tempted by an apparent 'bargain', but if the price seems low, there is usually a reason for it.

Brian Loomes

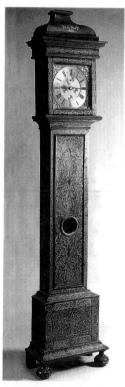

A William and Mary walnut and marquetry eight-day longcase clock, by Robert Page, Harwich, with inside countwheel strike and anchor escapement, 96in (244cm) high.
£3,500–4,200 DN

A Queen Anne chinoiserie-decorated eight-day longcase clock, by Samuel Stevens, London, with five-pillar movement, 99½in (252.5cm) high.
£3,500–4,200 WW

An oak eight-day longcase clock, by Jonas Barber, with twin-train movement, early 18thC, 84½in (214.5cm) high.
£1,400–1,700 P(E)

A walnut and marquetry longcase clock, by Draper, Chelmsford, the later twin-train movement with anchor escapement, altered, early 18thC, 85in (216cm) high.
£3,500–4,000 L&T

An ebonized pine longcase clock, by William Shortland, Stoney Stratford, with thirty-hour movement, single hand, plinth reduced, early 18thC, 76¾in (195cm) high.
£650–800 DN

A walnut eight-day longcase clock, by George Booth, Manchester, with countwheel striking, c1730, 80in (203cm) high.
£10,000–11,000 ALS

An oak eight-day longcase clock, by Freke, Chard, c1740, 82½in (209.5cm) high.
£4,250–4,750 ALS

A burr-walnut eight-day longcase clock, by George Booth, Manchester, c1730, 81in (205.5cm) high.
£7,500–8,500 BL

► A carved oak longcase clock, by Dicker, Silchester, with single hand, thirty-hour movement, c1745, 74in (188cm) high.
£2,000–2,200 ALS

Plates, birdcages and bedposts

The movements of most types of British clocks, and those of many other countries, fall into two distinct categories. The wheels are either held between two vertical brass plates front and back, or between straps which sit inside four corner posts. The majority of clocks (all eight-day and most thirty-hour examples) have plate movements, sometimes called plated movements or plate-framed movements. Since this is the normal method it is not usually felt necessary to mention this fact in descriptions.

Some thirty-hour clocks have posted movements, sometimes termed four-posted, bedpost or birdcage, because the construction resembles that of a four-poster bed or a birdcage as it has four corner posts. Thirty-hour clocks of such construction usually include one of these terms in the description.

Lantern clocks always have four corner posts and therefore this is not generally mentioned.

Items in the Clock section have been arranged in date order.

◄ An oak longcase clock, by Geo Wood, Nailsworth, with a single hand, thirty-hour birdcage movement, oak case restored, 18thC, 77in (195.5cm) high.
£600–700 WILL

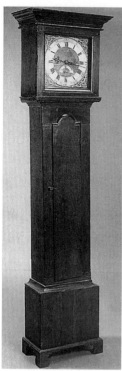

An oak and mahogany-crossbanded eight-day longcase clock, by Hampson, Chester, with boxwood-strung door, mid-18thC, 79in (200.5cm) high.
£1,600–2,000 Hal

An oak longcase clock, by James Bucknell, Crediton, with thirty-hour movement, the brass and silvered dial engraved with farm buildings, mid-18thC, 75½in (192cm) high.
£850–1,000 DN

An oak eight-day longcase clock, by George Goodall, Micklefield, c1760, 84in (213.5cm) high.
£4,000–4,500 BL

◄ An oak eight-day longcase clock, by Nathaniel Hedge, Colchester, the hood with detachable caddy, c1765, 81½in (207cm) high.
£6,500–7,250 PAO

A Scottish mahogany eight-day longcase clock, by James Niccoll, Edinburgh, c1765, 91in (231cm) high.
£8,500–9,500 JeF

A stained oak longcase clock, by Philip Avenell, Farnham, with five-pillar movement, c1770, 81in (205.5cm) high.
£750–900 Bon

A mahogany and line-inlaid eight-day longcase clock, by William Wasbrough, Bristol, with moonphase, mid-18thC, 88½in (225cm) high.
£2,000–2,400 Bri

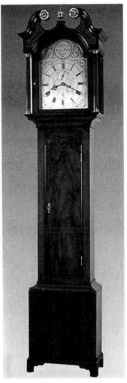

A George III mahogany longcase clock, by John Kirkwood, Redpath, the three-train movement striking on two bells, c1770, 85½in (217cm) high.
£3,500–4,200 B&L

A Dutch rococo walnut and floral marquetry longcase clock, signed David Le Feure, Amsterdam, with two-train chiming movement, c1770, 98in (249cm) high.
£9,500–10,500 SK

A Scottish mahogany and boxwood-inlaid longcase clock, by Andrew Scott, Edinburgh, with silvered brass dial, c1775, 87in (221cm) high.
£8,500–9,500 DRA

A George III oak eight-day longcase clock, by Thomas Lister, Halifax, with striking movement and moonphase, c1780, 79½in (202cm) high.
£1,600–1,800 Mit

Miller's Compares

I An oak and mahogany eight-day longcase clock, by Thomas Holmes of Cheadle, Staffordshire, the First Period dial by James Wilson, with rolling moon, 1780s, 90in (228.5cm) high.
£5,000–6,000 BL

II An oak eight-day longcase clock, by Edward Wilkins, Newport, Isle of Wight, 1820s, 80in (203cm) high.
£2,750–3,250 BL

Both clocks pictured here are genuine eight-day painted dial clocks, in their original oak cases and in good condition. Item I has a high quality First Period dial with rolling moon, and has additional features that explain its greater value, such as mahogany crossbanding and trim, dentil moulding below the hood, reeded quarter columns to the trunk and blind fret panels below the quarter columns. Item II has a later dial with no moon, although it has the desirable feature of being shorter.

A George III oak longcase clock, by Hugh Lough, Penrith, with thirty-hour movement and moonphase aperture, c1780, 84½in (214.5cm) high.
£1,300–1,500 PFK

A George III oak and mahogany eight-day longcase clock, by Beaumont, Howden, with crossbanded panel door and moonphase, 85in (216cm) high.
£1,000–1,200 AG

A George III figured mahogany eight-day longcase clock, by Tho. Bugden, Croydon, the movement with anchor escapement, 90in (228.5cm) high.
£4,700–5,500 JM

A mahogany eight-day longcase clock, signed Benson, W'Haven, the associated arch with a later painted country scene, associated twin-train striking movement, bracket feet reduced, late 18thC, 85¾in (218cm) high.
£1,250–1,500 P(L)

◄ A George III oak and mahogany-crossbanded longcase clock, by Burton, Ulverston, with boxwood and ebony-strung decoration, painted dial and thirty-hour movement, 82in (208.5cm) high.
£1,200–1,500 Mit

A George III mahogany longcase clock, signed John Clark, London, with arched silvered dial, restored, late 18thC, 97½in (247.5cm) high.
£2,500–3,000 P(S)

390 **CLOCKS • Longcase Clocks**

A flame-mahogany eight-day longcase clock, by John Price, Chichester, dated 1777, 83in (211cm) high.
£7,000–8,500 SoS

A mahogany longcase clock, by William Carter, Southwark, with strike/silent feature in the arch, c1780, 98in (249cm) high.
£11,000–12,500 JeF

An oak eight-day longcase clock, by Donisthorpe, Hinckley, c1780, 81in (205.5cm) high.
£3,750–4,250 BL

An oak and mahogany thirty-hour longcase clock, by Will Snow, Padside, c1780, 84in (213.5cm) high.
£2,750–3,250 BL

Will Snow (1736–95) made distinctive clock movements with 'skeleton' plates, whereby brass was cut out, jigsaw fashion, from areas that did not carry a load, thus saving costs. Clocks by Snow are sought after today by collectors.

An oak and mahogany thirty-hour longcase clock, by Edward Foster, Carlisle, with brass dial, c1780, 79in (200.5cm) high.
£1,100–1,300 PFK

A Scottish oak and mahogany-crossbanded eight-day longcase clock, by Jas Clarke, Kilmalcolm, c1780, 88in (223.5cm) high.
£1,800–2,200 HYD

◀ A George III Welsh oak eight-day longcase clock, by Watkin Owen, Llanrwst, with square brass dial, c1780, 80in (203cm) high.
£1,700–2,000 P(NW)

Types of striking

The number of hours struck by a clock are controlled by one of two ways:
- by the countwheel, or locking plate: a slotted wheel usually on the backplate.
- by the rack (or rack and snail): a form of mechanism that matches the striking with the movement of the hands. It was known by the 1690s but seldom used on longcase clocks until after 1720.

An oak eight-day longcase clock, by John Payne, Lenham, c1785, 80in (203cm) high.
£4,250–4,750 ALS

A Scottish oak eight-day longcase clock, by William Lunan, Aberdeen, with silvered brass dial, c1790, 86in (218.5cm) high.
£2,800–3,250 PAO

◀ A mahogany eight-day longcase clock, by S. Collier, Eccles, with painted dial, c1790, 89in (226cm) high.
£6,000–7,000 JeF

A George III mahogany eight-day longcase clock, by John Morse, Southampton, with anchor escapement, the hour strike on one bell and quarter strike on two bells, c1790, 91in (231cm) high.
£3,300–4,000 DN

A mahogany thirty-hour longcase clock, by John Harriman, Workington, late 18thC, 84in (213.5cm) high.
£1,200–1,400 PFK

An oak eight-day longcase clock, by James Crabb, Salisbury, with silvered dial, late 18thC, 80in (203cm) high.
£1,700–2,000 WW

◀ An oak and mahogany-crossbanded longcase clock, by John Pike, Wiveliscombe, c1780, 82in (208.5cm) high.
£900–1,100 P(E)

A George III silver basket, with mask and scroll handles, London 1791, 17¼in (44cm) wide.
£650–800 WL

A George III silver sugar basket, by John Emes, with original blue glass liner, London 1805, 7in (18cm) wide.
£650–800 CoHA

A German silver-gilt beaker cup, by Niclas Bille, Dresden, c1680, 3¼in (8.5cm) high, 4oz.
£2,500–3,000 HAM

A silver monteith, by W. & J. Barnard, with detachable rim, London 1893, 9¾in (25cm) diam, 48oz.
£1,350–1,500 P(L)

A George III silver brazier, by S. Herbert & Co for the American market, London 1765, 6¾in (17cm) diam, 17oz.
£2,000–2,400 S

A silver porringer, c1925, 9in (23cm) diam.
£450–500 BWA

◀ A George III silver cream pail, pierced with birds and scrolling foliage, London 1775, 2½in (6.5cm) high.
£450–550 Bea(E)

An Edwardian silver chamberstick, by Atkin Brothers, Sheffield 1907, 7in (18cm) wide.
£575–650 ASAA

A pair of Scottish silver candlesticks, by John Kincard, Edinburgh 1746, 6½in (16.5cm) high, 22¼oz.
£3,200–3,850 WW

A silver-gilt candlestick, London 1844, 8in (20.5cm) high.
£1,800–2,000 DIC

A George III silver coffee biggin, by Paul Storr, 11in (28cm) high, 53oz.
£5,000–6,000 G(L)

A set of three Dutch silver tea canisters, by Rudolph Sondag, in contemporary silver and mother-of-pearl-mounted case, damage to case, Rotterdam 1768, canister 4½in (11.5cm) wide.
£8,500–9,500 S

A Victorian silver owl caster, by George Unite, London 1867, 3½in (9cm) high.
£550–650 P(Ed)

A biggin is a form of coffee percolator invented c1799 by George Biggin.

A Regency silver coffee
pot, by Paul Storr, London
1815, 10in (25.5cm) high.
£4,000–4,750 WW

A silver four-piece tea and coffee service,
by Joseph Angell II, London 1857, 75oz.
£2,000–2,400 PFK

An American coin silver five-piece
tea service, by Shreve, Stanwood
& Co, Boston, c1860, the covers with
swan finials, urn 16in (40.5cm) high.
£2,500–3,000 NOA

A silver three-piece tea service and
biscuit barrel, by Robert Hennell,
London 1861, 84oz.
£3,000–3,500 PFK

A Russian parcel-gilt
standing cup and cover,
Moscow, c1760,
10¾in (27.5cm) high.
£1,650–2,000 S(Z)

An American silver vegetable dish and cover,
by Paulding Farnham for Tiffany & Co,
New York 1905, 15in (38cm) wide, 72oz.
£9,000–10,000 S(NY)

A silver seven-piece condiment set,
by Walker & Hall, Sheffield 1910,
in a fitted case, 12in (30.5cm) wide.
£625–700 CoHA

A Victorian silver-gilt and coral rattle, by Charles
Rawlings and William Summers, in a fitted
case, London 1838, 6¼in (16cm) long.
£800–1,000 GTH

A James I silver maidenhead spoon, by William
Frend, London 1613, 6in (15cm) long.
£17,000–20,000 S

**Ex-Roger Whittaker collection. It is rare to
find such a spoon in good condition.**

A George IV silver inkstand, by John
& Thomas Settle, Sheffield 1821,
12in (30.5cm) wide.
£3,000–3,500 P(L)

Three engraved trefid
spoons, and similar forks,
late 17thC, 4in (10cm) long.
£800–1,000 L

A William and Mary silver filigree nécessaire,
maker's mark 'HS', London 1694,
4¾in (12cm) long.
£3,250–3,750 S(Am)

A Victorian silver soup tureen and
cover, by Benjamin Smith III,
London 1840, 17¼in (44cm) wide.
£5,000–5,500 S

◄ A Victorian set of silver-gilt serving spoons
and sifter, in fitted case, by Thos. Smily,
London 1873–74, case 10in (25.5cm) wide.
£400–445 BEX

A tortoiseshell spring clock, by Humfry Adamson, London, with pull quarter repeat, c1680, 11¼in (29cm) high.
£24,000–27,000 DRA

A mahogany eight-day striking bracket clock, by B. J. Morse, Watford, with fusee movement, c1790, 22in (56cm) high.
£4,000–4,500 BED

A late Victorian walnut and ormolu-mounted striking bracket clock, by W. T. Strong, Barrow-in-Furness, with eight-day three-train fusee movement chiming on gongs, 29in (73.5cm) high.
£2,500–3,000 RBB

An ebonized bracket clock, by William Hill, St. Margaret's Hill, Southwark, the eight-day two-train movement with verge escapement, c1740, 19½in (49.5cm) high.
£3,000–3,500 CAG

A mahogany bracket clock, by Thomas Gray, London, with silvered brass dial, double fusee movement and verge escapement, c1790, 20in (51cm) high.
£3,000–3,500 BL

An ormolu mantel clock, by William Payne, London, c1840, 9in (23cm) high.
£2,750–3,000 JeF

◀ A chinoiserie lacquered mantel clock, by Aspreys, London, 1920s, 7in (18cm) high.
£250–300 PTh

A mahogany bracket clock, by Henry Faure, London, the movement with verge escapement, with floral engraved backplate, moonphases and alarm, c1760, 14in (35.5cm) high.
£15,000–16,500 DRA

▶ A brass and paste-set musical striking table clock, in the style of John Mottram, the musical three-train fusee and chain movement with verge escapement, playing one of two tunes at every hour or at will on eight bells, made for the Chinese market, c1790, 15in (38cm) high.
£30,000–35,000 HAM

A mahogany striking table/bracket clock, by Thomas Hampson, London, the eight-day five-pillar double fusee movement with anchor escapement, c1780, 17in (43cm) high.
£7,750–8,750 PAO

A gilt-bronze mantel clock, by Ragot, Paris, mounted with bronze figures, c1800, 22½in (57cm) high.
£28,000–32,000 HVH

A Polish gilt-metal quarter-striking table clock, by Antoni Barisch, Crackow, with single fusee verge escapement, in a fitted walnut box, early 18thC, 3in (7.5cm) high.
£6,000–7,000 Bon

An ormolu-mounted striking night clock, by Balthazar Blaser, Bern, c1760, 12½in (32cm) high.
£5,000–6,000 S(Z)

A French white marble and gilt-bronze ballooning clock, late 18thC, 20in (51cm) high.
£13,000–15,000 S(Mon)

A Louis XIV-style boulle *tête de poupée* mantel clock, with silk suspension striking on bell, c1820, 16in (40.5cm) high.
£5,500–6,200 JIL

◄ A Continental quarter-striking bracket clock, with two-train spring-barrel movement and matching painted and gilt wall bracket, late 18thC, 37in (94cm) high.
£850–1,000 TMA

An Austrian Biedermeier fruitwood musical portico clock, mid-19thC, 19in (48.5cm) high.
£2,400–2,700 NOA

A bronze ormolu striking mantel clock, by Raingo Frères, Paris, with eight-day movement, c1830, 12in (30.5cm) high.
£2,000–2,200 JIL

▶ A French gilt-metal mantel clock, by Japy Frères, with eight-day striking movement and giltwood stand, 19thC, 15in (38cm) high.
£450–500 CAG

A French ceramic and ormolu lyre clock, with paste set surround and calendar, c1860, 24in (61cm) high.
£5,000–6,000 Bon

A French boulle and ormolu-mounted bracket clock, with eight-day striking movement, 19thC, 19in (48.5cm) high.
£425–500 RBB

A French boulle mantel clock, with gilt mounts, late 19thC, 15¼in (39.5cm) high.
£600–700 E

▶ A French ormolu and alabaster mantel clock, with eight-day movement, late 19thC, 17in (43cm) high.
£550–650 DDM

▶ A German burr-walnut and brass-mounted bracket clock, with double fusee movement, c1900, 15in (38cm) high.
£2,250–2,750 BL

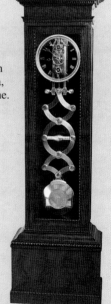

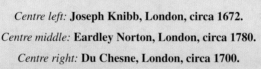

A lacquered brass chronometer carriage clock, signed Arnold & Dent, London, with spring detent escapement and maintaining power, mid-19thC, 8¾in (22cm) high.
£4,000–5,000 P

A French engraved and 'jewelled' porcelain-mounted *grande sonnerie* striking carriage clock, the movement with lever escapement, c1870, 7½in (19cm) high.
£4,500–5,500 Bon

A French carriage clock, by Margaine, Paris, retailed in Portsea, c1900, 3¾in (9.5cm) high.
£2,000–2,250 JeF

A French gilt-brass and porcelain-mounted striking and repeating carriage clock, attributed to Brunelot, c1880, 6in (16cm) high.
£5,500–6,500 JIL

A French cloisonné enamel carriage clock, with alarm, the repeating movement with lever platform escapement, c1900, 7in (18cm) high.
£2,700–3,000 S(S)

A French garniture, the ormolu clock case inset with Sèvres-style porcelain panels, 19thC, clock 14in (35.5cm) high.
£750–900 RBB

► A clock, set in a tortoiseshell, gold and mother-of-pearl-inlaid card case, c1870, 4in (10cm) wide.
£700–800 CHAP

An Italian wall clock, by Domenico Menetti, Campeggio, signed and dated '1786', 12¼in (31cm) high.
£1,700–1,900 S(Z)

A French gilt-bronze and porcelain clock, by Lepine, with revolving chapter rings and detachable cover, 19thC, 15½in (38cm) high.
£4,000–4,500 WW

A French ormolu and green marble clock, with revolving chapter rings, the bell striking movement with lever escapement, c1870, 20in (51cm) high.
£6,500–7,500 Bon

A Gothic revival gilt-bronze clock, with eight-day half-hour strike, probably French, 19thC, 21¼in (54cm) high.
£2,500–2,750 BB(L)

A Victorian brass skeleton clock, by Summersgill, Preston, with twin fusee movement, on a white marble and rosewood base with glass dome, c1860, 14in (36.5cm) high.
£1,500–1,800 TEN

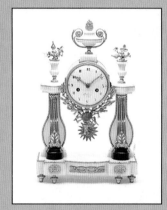

A walnut and marquetry eight-day longcase clock, by S. Bouquet, London, repaired and restored, late 17th/early 18thC, 78in (198cm) high.
£2,500–3,000 TRL

A walnut eight-day longcase clock, by John Andrews, London, with five latched pillars and countwheel, c1700, 73in (185.5cm) high.
£16,000–18,000 PAO

A walnut marquetry longcase clock, by Charles Gretton, with triple train movement chiming on eight bells and gong on the hour, c1690, with later chiming movement, c1880, 83in (211cm) high.
£5,500–6,500 Bon

A walnut and marquetry eight-day longcase clock, by Henry Mowtlow, London, the two-train movement with five ringed pillars, late 17thC, 82in (208.5cm) high.
£12,000–14,000 DN

A marquetry longcase clock, by Markwick, London, the month going movement with countwheel striking, c1705, 89in (226cm) high.
£22,000–25,000 ALS

◄ A walnut and marquetry eight-day longcase clock, by John Bottrill, Coventry, with associated and altered case, c1710, 93¼in (237cm) high.
£5,750–7,000 S(S)

A Virginia walnut eight-day longcase clock, by John Berry, Manchester, c1730, 96in (244cm) high.
£8,500–9,500 BL

A George II eight-day longcase clock, by Thos. Gardiner, London, decorated with red and gold lacquer, c1740, 100½in (255.5cm) high.
£9,000–11,000 WW

A George II walnut moon-phase longcase clock, signed Andrew Hewlett, Bristol, dated '1744', 91½in (232.5cm) high.
£5,000–6,000 HAM

An Irish inlaid mahogany longcase clock, signed Martin Kirkpatrick, Dublin, the door with later Adamesque inlay, 18thC, 87in (221cm) high.
£3,500–4,000 HOK

◄ A Dutch inlaid walnut longcase clock, with silvered chapter ring inscribed Jacob Fromanteel, Amsterdam, above a recessed mechanical scene of a girl in a swing, mid-18thC, 116in (294.5cm) high.
£12,500–15,000 BB(L)

An oak eight-day longcase clock, signed Phillip Avenell, Farnham, with automaton and five-pillar movement, c1750, 80in (203cm) high.
£7,000–8,000 PAO

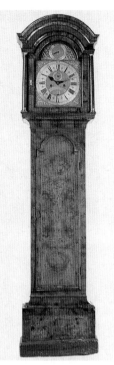

A walnut longcase clock, by Thomas Eastwick, London, base reduced, c1750, 84in (213.5cm) high.
£4,000–5,000 Bon

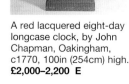

A red lacquered eight-day longcase clock, by John Chapman, Oakingham, c1770, 100in (254cm) high.
£2,000–2,200 E

An eight-day longcase clock, by Tho. Ansel, London, with arched brass dial with rocking bird, the case lacquered later with chinoiserie subjects on a red ground, c1755, 96½in (245cm) high.
£4,000–5,000 JM

◄ An oak eight-day longcase clock, by William Avenell, Alresford, with five-pillar movement, c1765, 84in (213.5cm) high.
£7,500–8,250 PAO

A blue japanned longcase clock, by Jn. De. Jersey, Westminster, late 18thC, 93in (236cm) high.
£9,000–10,000 BB(S)

An oak eight-day longcase clock, by Robert Watts, Stamford, c1770, 80in (203cm) high.
£2,000–2,400 BIG

A mahogany eight-day longcase clock, signed Percival, London, c1780, 89in (226cm) high.
£22,000–25,000 ALS

An oak longcase clock, by Roberts, Otley, with thirty-hour movement, c1770, 83in (211cm) high.
£2,000–2,400 AH

An oak and mahogany eight-day longcase clock, by John Wignall, Ormskirk, c1780, 87in (221cm) high.
£4,000–4,500 BL

An oak eight-day longcase clock, signed William Swaine, Ipswich, with five-pillar movement, c1780, 86in (218.5cm) high.
£6,500–7,250 PAO

An oak eight-day longcase clock, by James Rule, Portsmouth, with five pillar movement, the arch with strike/silent feature, c1775, 84in (213.5cm) high.
£6,000–6,750 PAO

An Irish mahogany longcase clock, signed Thos. Atkinson, Dublin, c1780, 92in (234cm) high.
£8,500–10,000 HOK

A mahogany eight-day longcase clock, by Joseph Gatward, Sevenoaks, with five-pillar movement, late 18thC, 87½in (222.5cm) high.
£6,000–7,000 CAG

An oak and mahogany eight-day musical longcase clock, signed Jno. Follit, Lichfield, with three-train movement striking on a bell and playing tunes on a nest of ten bells, c1780, 90¼in (229cm) high.
£10,000–12,000 S(S)

◄ A mahogany eight-day longcase clock, with later inlay, signed Band & Hine, Bridgewater, the arch with coat-of-arms of the Worshipful Company of Carpenters, c1780, 93in (236cm) high.
£8,250–9,250 PAO

A mahogany longcase clock, by Edward Courter, Ruthin, c1780, 88in (223.5cm) high.
£4,000–5,000 Bon

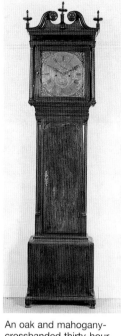

An oak and mahogany-crossbanded thirty-hour longcase clock, by Fearnly, Wigan, c1780, 92in (234cm) high.
£1,250–1,500 RBB

An Irish mahogany and crossbanded longcase clock, signed Bainbridge, Dublin, with painted dial and four-pillar movement with anchor escapement, 1780–90, 90in (228.5cm) high.
£3,200–3,500 P

A George III oak and mahogany eight-day longcase clock, signed Rathborn, Sandbach, with two-train movement, c1785, 87in (221cm) high.
£1,100–1,300 Gam

A mahogany eight-day longcase clock, signed Ephraim Moses, London, c1785, 87in (221cm) high.
£8,250–9,250 PAO

A mahogany eight-day longcase clock, by David Wyllie, Greenock, with brass face, c1790, 91¾in (233cm) high.
£2,000–2,400 TRM

◀ A walnut longcase clock, signed Traverse, Tournon, mid-18thC, 86¾in (220.5cm) high.
£2,000–2,400 S(Z)

An oak longcase clock, signed John Britless, Harborough, with thirty-hour striking movement, painted dial, the second dial with finger missing, c1790, 82in (208.5cm) high.
£1,200–1,400 WBH

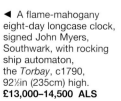

An inlaid flame-mahogany eight-day longcase clock, by John Buchanan, Ashton, c1790, 94in (239cm) high.
£7,000–8,000 BL

◀ A flame-mahogany eight-day longcase clock, signed John Myers, Southwark, with rocking ship automaton, the *Torbay*, c1790, 92½in (235cm) high.
£13,000–14,500 ALS

A French Louis XVI green-lacquered and chinoiserie-decorated longcase clock, signed Balthazar, the gilt-bronze dial with enamelled numerals, late 18thC, 91in (231cm) high.
£5,000–5,500 BB(S)

A George III elm and fruitwood-banded eight-day longcase clock, signed J. Cole, Stowey, plinth reduced, c1800, 71in (180.5cm) high.
£3,500–4,000 TAM

A mahogany eight-day longcase clock, signed Pearson, Halifax, with moonphase, c1810, 98in (249cm) high.
£7,000–7,800 PAO

A mahogany eight-day longcase clock, signed Thwaites & Reed, London, the movement with shaped plates and five pillars, c1812, 86in (218.5cm) high.
£10,000–11,250 PAO

An American Federal stained pine longcase clock, by Thomas Nawman, Mid-Atlantic States, with moonphase, early 19thC, 93in (236cm) high.
£1,850–2,200 BB(S)

An inlaid mahogany and oak eight-day longcase clock, signed Kent, Manchester, with two-train movement and moonphase, c1830, 92in (234cm) high.
£1,000–1,200 PFK

A Scottish mahogany eight-day longcase clock, by Wilkie, Cupar, Fife, c1830, 84in (213.5cm) high.
£3,250–3,750 BL

A mahogany eight-day longcase clock, signed Thomas Gibson, Berwick-on-Tweed, c1830, 84in (213.5cm) high.
£3,250–3,750 BL

A flame-mahogany eight-day longcase clock, signed John Thackwell, Cardiff, with rocking ship automaton, c1830, 81in (205.5cm) high.
£6,750–7,500 SOS

◄ An oak and mahogany-crossbanded eight-day longcase clock, signed C. H. Francis, Wem, with rolling moonphase, mid-19thC, 86in (218.5cm) high.
£2,000–2,400 HAL

A mahogany and
boxwood-inlaid eight-day
longcase clock, signed
John Cross, Trowbridge,
with moonphase, c1830,
92in (233.5cm) high.
£6,500–7,250 PAO

A mahogany eight-day
longcase clock, signed
Wickens, Rye, with
moonphase, faults, c1830,
83in (211cm) high.
£4,500–5,000 S(S)

An oak and mahogany
eight-day longcase clock,
with moonphase, c1830,
93in (236cm) high.
£1,500–1,800 S(S)

A flame-mahogany eight-
day longcase clock,
with painted dial, c1830,
81in (205.5cm) high.
£5,000–5,500 BL

◄ A mahogany and
rosewood-crossbanded
eight-day longcase clock,
signed Walter Leighton,
Montrose, c1850,
84in (213.5cm) high.
£4,750–5,250 PAO

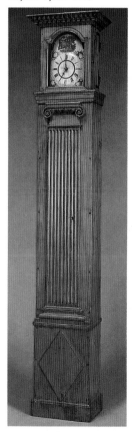

A French Provincial pine
longcase clock, mid-19thC,
98¼in (249.5cm) high.
£2,000–2,200 NOA

A mahogany eight-day
longcase clock, signed
C. Heizman, Canterbury,
with painted dial, c1830,
86in (218.5cm) high.
£2,300–2,750 CAG

► A Welsh mahogany
eight-day longcase clock,
signed W. Vaughan,
Newport, c1850,
90in (228.5cm) high.
£6,000–6,600 PAO

A French red shell and
brass-inlaid boulle longcase
clock, the brass dial with
enamel reserves, the
comtoise movement with a
pin wheel escapement, late
19thC, 84in (213.4cm) high.
£2,200–2,600 Bon

A Swiss Davos wooden wall clock, by Grisons, dated 1696, 13¾in (35cm) high.
£12,000–14,000 S(Z)

► A walnut and marquetry-inlaid eight-day wall clock, c1885, 32in (81.5cm) high.
£450–500 K&D

A black lacquered thirty-hour wall clock, signed William Andrews, London, with brass face, c1730, 32in (81.5cm) high.
£4,500–5,500 PHA

A mahogany eight-day wall clock, signed John Leroux, London, the fusee movement with anchor escapement, c1805, 27in (68.5cm) high.
£5,250–5,750 PAO

An American Federal mahogany *églomisé* mantel clock, by Aaron Willard, Boston, c1805, 36½in (92.5cm) high.
£15,000–18,000 S(NY)

◄ An American oak thirty-day Saturn wall clock, by Newhaven Clock Co, Connecticut, with double-wind spring run, c1880, 34in (86.5cm) wide.
£600–700 OT

A flame-mahogany eight-day longcase regulator, by John Minto, Newcastle, with deadbeat escapement and maintaining power, c1810, 81in (205.5cm) high.
£5,750–6,500 BL

A flame-mahogany thirty-day longcase regulator, signed Carter, Thornbury, with silvered dial, deadbeat anchor escapement and bolt and shutter maintaining power, c1820, 86in (218.5cm) high.
£5,700–6,400 PAO

A mahogany wall regulator, signed Melhuish & Parkin, with reversed fusee movement, deadbeat escapement and Harrison's maintaining power, c1850, 14½in (37cm) diam.
£5,000–5,500 S

An eight-day longcase regulator, signed James Murray, London, c1840, 75in (190.5cm) high.
£10,000–12,000 JeF

▶ A French mahogany longcase regulator, signed Breguet, with silvered dial, deadbeat escapement and maintaining power, late 19thC, 80in (203cm) high.
£20,000–22,000 P

A gilt and shagreen verge watch, signed Jno Bayley, London, c1710, 2in (5cm) diam.
£1,800–2,000 PT

A gold pair-cased verge watch, by Robt Allam, London, the cases by William Butcher, 1755, 2in (5cm) diam.
£850–1,000 TEN

A George III gold pair-cased verge watch, by Joseph Brookes, London, 1½in (4cm) diam.
£500–600 P(Ed)

A Swiss gold, enamel, diamond and pearl-set automaton verge watch, c1790, 2in (5cm) diam.
£9,000–11,000 S

A polychrome enamel-decorated gilt-metal chaise watch case, with later movement, signed Robt. Roskell, Liverpool and London, 18thC, 4¾in (12cm) diam.
£2,200–2,600 P

A silver-gilt and enamel watch, signed Dimier & Cie, Geneva, made for the Chinese market, c1840, 2¼in (5.5cm) diam.
£2,200–2,600 PT

A French gold full hunter fob watch, by Valogne, Paris, with enamelled decoration, inner plate dated '1854', 2in (5cm) diam.
£700–850 DDM

An 18ct gold half hunter lever watch, by Manoah Rhodes & Sons, Bradford, movement probably by Nicole Nielsen, 1900, 2in (5cm) diam.
£600–700 TEN

◀ A 14ct gold watch, signed International Watch Co, c1910, 2in (5cm) diam.
£800–900 TWD

▶ A silver Masonic watch, signed Golay Watch Co, marked, London Import 1935, 2in (5cm) wide.
£1,300–1,450 PT

A Swiss enamel and diamond-set gold keyless lever watch, late 19thC, 1¾in (4.5cm) diam.
£450–500 P

A Rolex gold and enamel bracelet watch, 1914, 25mm diam.
£900–1,100 S

A Harwood 18ct gold watch, c1930, 30mm diam.
£1,250–1,400 TWD

A Rolex 9ct gold chronometer watch, c1935.
£1,000–1,200 AG

A yellow and white precious metal cocktail watch, with diamond mounted bands, c1950.
£1,400–1,600 P

A Patek Philippe 18ct pink gold watch, c1946, 33mm diam.
£12,000–14,000 RM

A Universal, Aero-Compax rose precious metal chronograph watch, 1940s, 37mm diam.
£1,000–1,200 Bon

◄ A Universal 18ct pink gold military watch, 1940s, 37mm diam.
£2,000–2,400 RM

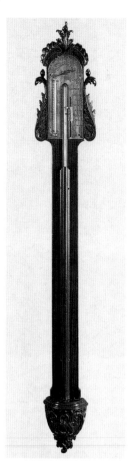

A George III mahogany stick barometer, by J. Hogben, Rye, with hygrometer, later cistern cover, 42in (106.5cm) high.
£8,000–10,000 S

J. Hogben appears to be an unrecorded maker.

A Scottish satinwood wheel barometer, by I. Tarra, Louth, with silvered brass scale, c1810, 8in (20.5cm) diam.
£2,200–2,450 PAO

▶ A balloonist's barometer, by Hottinger, Zurich, c1870, 3in (7.5cm) wide.
£1,400–1,600 JIL

A rosewood stick barometer, by T. Bennett, Cork, with vernier scale, adjuster missing, early 19thC, 39in (99cm) high.
£1,750–2,000 Bea(E)

A mahogany wheel barometer, by A. Poncal, Bedford, mid-19thC, 38in (96.5cm) high.
£650–800 NOA

A mahogany bowfront stick barometer, by J. Bassnett, Liverpool, mid-19thC, 39½in (100.5cm) high.
£3,500–4,000 DN

A rosewood and mother-of-pearl-inlaid wheel barometer, by J. Rabone, London, with hygrometer, c1840, 44in (112cm) high.
£700–850 Bon

▶ An oak aneroid wheel barometer, with porcelain dial, slight crack, c1914, 8in (20.5cm) diam.
£220–250 KB

An inlaid mahogany barometer, by P. Feranio, c1810, 8in (20.5cm) diam.
£850–950 ALS

A rosewood wheel barometer, signed Moritz Pillischer, with silvered dial, c1860, 10in (25.5cm) diam.
£950–1,100 KB

A carved oak longcase clock, by Josh. Dean, Birkenshaw, the associated twin-train movement with anchor escapement, case, dial and movement all associated, c1785, 88in (223.5cm) high.
£1,300–1,500 P

A late George III oak and mahogany-banded longcase clock, by Felton Jnr, Hansworth, with painted dial, c1785, 48in (122cm) high.
£1,000–1,100 P(O)

An oak and fruitwood longcase clock, signed Thos. Scott, Gainsborough, with painted dial, the arch with a painted tin automaton of a fully rigged sailing ship, c1785, 86¾in (220.5cm) high.
£1,700–2,000 HOK

A Scottish dark oak eight-day longcase clock, by Alex. Wilson, Kelso, with brass dial, c1790, 88in (223.5cm) high.
£1,000–1,200 PFK

A book-matched flame-mahogany eight-day longcase clock, by Lomax, Blackburn, c1790, 88in (223.5cm) high.
£4,500–5,000 BL

A George III eight-day longcase clock, by James Wilson, Hawick, with arched brass dial, c1790, 50½in (128.5cm) high.
£2,000–2,200 P(Ed)

A George III oak longcase clock, by Jas. Hinksman, Bridgnorth, with painted dial and thirty-hour movement, some case damage, feet missing, c1790, 77in (195.5cm) high.
£750–900 Hal

Parts of an eight-day longcase clock

The main components of a simple weight-driven eight-day clock, as shown, include:

A anchor escapement
B weight
C barrel
D main wheel
E centre wheel
F third wheel
G dial wheels
H front plate
I backplate
J dial feet
K pillars
L pendulum
M dial plate
N hands
O centre arbor
P pinions
Q winding arbor

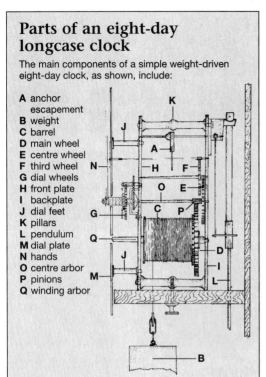

A George III eight-day mahogany longcase clock, with oval painted dial, the movement stamped SD for Samuel Deacon and dated, with typical Deacon baluster-turned pillars, the pinwheel countwheel on solid case barrels with internal clicks and with double-sized minute wheel, 1792, 100in (254cm) high.
£4,500–5,500 Mit

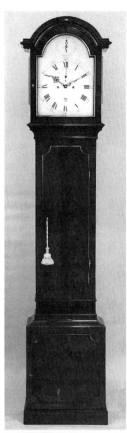

A flame-mahogany eight-day longcase clock, signed Walter Elliott, Plymouth, with silvered dial, the movement with dead beat escapement, c1800, 84in (213.5cm) high.
£7,500–8,250 ALS

A mahogany eight-day long-case clock, by Thomas Gatty, Bodmin, with silvered dial, the lower case with rope-twist columns, early 19thC, 85in (216cm) high.
£2,000–2,400 L

A Scottish flame-mahogany eight-day longcase clock, signed John Paterson, Leith, with painted dial, c1807, 88in (223.5cm) high.
£7,000–8,000 ALS

▶ A Welsh mahogany eight-day longcase clock, by W. Toleman, Caernarfon, with painted dial, early 19thC, 86in (218.5cm) high.
£900–1,100 JM

An oak and mahogany-crossbanded longcase clock, by T. Hadfield, Chapel-en-le-Frith, with painted dial, early 19thC, 85in (216cm) high.
£1,000–1,200 JM

A mahogany longcase clock, by James McCabe, London, with white dial, c1810, 83in (211cm) high.
£10,000–11,000 JeF

A mahogany and string-inlaid eight-day longcase clock, inscribed Geo. Stephenson, Warminster, with painted dial and moonphase, early 19thC, 86in (218.5cm) high.
£1,400–1,700 WW

A dark oak eight-day longcase clock, by J. Tucker, Tiverton, with painted dial, early 19thC, 81in (205.5cm) high.
£500–600 JM

A Scottish mahogany eight-day longcase clock, by Whytock, Dundee, with painted dial, early 19thC, 79in (200.5cm) high.
£1,250–1,500 P(Ed)

A mahogany eight-day longcase clock, with brass face, the trunk with inlaid door flanked by quarter columns, early 19thC, 85½in (217cm) high.
£1,650–2,000 TRM

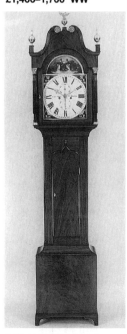

A Channel Islands mahogany eight-day longcase clock, signed F. G. Abel, St. Helier, the arched white dial painted with swans and rural landscapes, c1820, 90in (228.5cm) high.
£5,750–6,250 PAO

A Regency mahogany and boxwood-lined eight-day longcase clock, by Barwise, London, with painted dial, 80¼in (204cm) high.
£1,200–1,500 P(Ed)

A mahogany eight-day longcase clock, by Pearson, Halifax, the arched painted dial with moonphase, c1825, 96in (244cm) high.
£3,300–4,000 BIG

A George IV Irish inlaid mahogany longcase clock, by Edward Smith, Dublin, the case with ebony stringing, 80½in (204.5cm) high.
£2,750–3,250 JAd

▶ A Scottish oak longcase clock, by Robert Robertson, Perth, with painted dial, 1830, 80in (203cm) high.
£2,000–2,200 BLA

An inlaid and crossbanded flame-mahogany eight-day longcase clock, signed M. Symons, Hull, with rocking ship automaton above a painted dial, c1825, 93in (236cm) high.
£7,000–7,850 ALS

An oak and mahogany eight-day longcase clock, by J. Heitzman, March, the white dial with a landscape, the trunk with chamfered mahogany corners and inlaid with fruitwood, c1830, 85in (216cm) high.
£3,800–4,200 JIL

An oak longcase clock, signed James, Farnham, with thirty-hour movement, c1830, 77½in (197cm) high.
£1,000–1,100 HOA

◀ A William IV flame-mahogany eight-day longcase clock, inscribed Maggs, Wells, with enamelled dial and moonphase, 87¾in (223cm) high.
£2,200–2,600 HYD

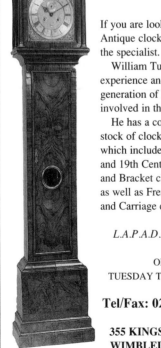

A William IV mahogany eight-day long-case clock, by Thomson, Alloa, the arch painted with a contemporary domestic scene, 86in (218.5cm) high.
£1,400–1,700 PFK

A Welsh faded mahogany and rosewood-banded eight-day longcase clock, by Jacob Morely, Neath, with painted dial, c1840, 89in (226cm) high.
£1,800–2,200 WW

An oak and mahogany eight-day longcase clock, by Unthank, Stokesley, c1840, 90in (228.5cm) high.
£2,750–3,250 BL

A mahogany and light oak eight-day longcase clock, by Charles Clay, Messingham, c1845, 90in (228.5cm) high.
£1,800–2,200 EH

An oak and mahogany-inlaid eight-day longcase clock, by Barkers, Easingwold, the dial painted with a view of Kirkstall Abbey, c1850, 88in (223.5cm) high.
£750–900 DD

A Scottish mahogany drumhead eight-day longcase clock, with painted dial above a spreading case, c1850, 83in (211cm) high.
£1,000–1,200 P(Ed)

VISIT THE ANTIQUE CLOCK SPECIALIST

The Essence of Time

A FINE SELECTION OF LONGCASE GRANDFATHER, VIENNA AND OTHER DESIRABLE WALL, MANTEL AND NOVELTY CLOCKS, ALWAYS IN STOCK

ALWAYS CONSULT AN ESTABLISHED DEALER FOR HELP AND ADVICE

TUDOR OF LICHFIELD ANTIQUES CENTRE, BORE STREET, LICHFIELD

Open Mon-Sat 10am to 5pm
(Use Main Bore Street Restaurant Entrance)

ONE OF THE BEST INVESTMENT DECISIONS YOU WILL EVER MAKE

**TEL: 01902 764900 Eves/Weekends
Days 01543 263951
Mobile 07944 245064**

Miller's Compares

I A mahogany, rose-wood-crossbanded and boxwood-strung eight-day longcase clock, by Lederer, Norwich, with painted dial, mid-19thC, 88¼in (224cm) high.
£1,450–1,750 DN

II A mahogany eight-day longcase clock, by W. Kirton, Newcastle, with painted dial, mid-19thC, 92in (233.5cm) high.
£900–1,100 DN

Both these clocks are examples of slightly eccentric local styles of design in the mid-19thC. Item I is more desirable because of its smaller dial and painted arch (hunting scenes are always popular). The case is also smaller and slimmer than that of Item II, in a better, dense-grained mahogany, with more stringing and crossbanding.

A Scottish mahogany drumhead longcase clock, with painted dial, mid-19thC, 77in (195.5cm) high.
£800–1,000 AG

▶ A mahogany and oak longcase clock, with painted dial, mid-19thC, 80¾in (205cm) high.
£1,400–1,600 DMC

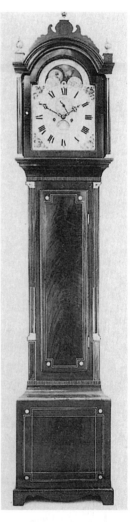

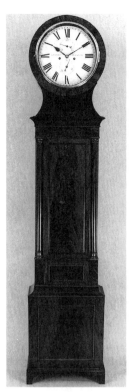

A Victorian mahogany eight-day longcase clock, the dial painted with a child with a dog, c1850, 93in (236cm) high.
£900–1,100 DDM

A Scottish flame-mahogany eight-day drumhead longcase clock, signed Greiner, Dalkeith, with white dial, c1850, 80in (203cm) high.
£3,750–4,200 PAO

A Scottish mahogany longcase clock, by Christie & Barries, Arbroath, with painted dial, 19thC, 82½in (209.5cm) high.
£2,000–2,200 P

A carved oak eight-day longcase clock, by Fiechter, Huddersfield, with twin-train movement, c1900, 81in (205.5cm) high.
£3,000–3,500 BL

A Viennese walnut eight-day longcase clock, late 19thC, 75in (190.5cm) high.
£1,700–2,000 AG

An Edwardian inlaid mahogany eight-day longcase clock, striking and chiming on eight tubular brass gongs, 106in (269cm) high.
£3,800–4,500 PFK

◄ An Edwardian inlaid mahogany eight-day long-case clock, with Westminster chime movement, 92in (233.5cm) high.
£1,000–1,200 BLH

MYSTERY & NOVELTY CLOCKS

A French bronzed ormolu fountain automaton clock, with bell striking movement and separately wound fountain mechanism, c1830, 18in (45.5cm) high.
£1,400–1,700 Bon

A French ormolu cathedral clock, by B & C, Paris, the pierced case now with coloured backing, the signed twin-train movement with countwheel strike, now striking on a gong, on an inlaid rosewood plinth, mid–late 19thC, 23in (58.5cm) high.
£800–900 P

◀ An illuminated globe desk timepiece, by Jaeger Le Coultre, the black marble base containing eight-day movement, with chrome surround, 1940s, 12in (30.5cm) diam.
£700–800 Bon

A Biedermeier quarter-striking picture clock, signed Karl Wahlrab, Birnbach, c1830, 32¼ x 39½in (82 x 100.5cm).
£4,250–4,750 S(Z)

A French musical picture clock, with activated automaton farrier's shop in foreground, choice of four airs, dial replaced, c1850, 27 x 31½in (68.5 x 80cm).
£5,500–6,000 S

A French ormolu mystery clock, with single arrow hand, the movement stamped Hy Marc, Paris, with indirect drive to a worm wheel mounted on the scrolled support, striking on a bell, late 19thC, 16in (40.5cm) high.
£4,000–4,500 P

A Continental picture clock, stamped Japy Frères, in chased gilt frame, the square twin-train movement striking on a gong, 1840–50, 22¾ x 28in (58 x 71cm).
£2,300–2,750 P

A Continental automaton clock, in the form of a pug, stamped Mayer, late 19thC, 5½in (14cm) long.
£400–500 P(L)

SKELETON CLOCKS

A French Directoire gilt-bronze skeleton clock, on a marble plinth, with ebonized wood stand and glass dome, early 19thC, 12½in (32cm) high.
£2,750–3,000 BB(S)

A brass skeleton clock, by Wright, Woolwich, the fusee movement with five-spoke hour wheel, the remainder with four spokes, anchor escapement striking on a circular section coiled gong, on a white marble base under a glass dome, mid-19thC, 22in (56cm) high.
£2,500–2,750 P

◄ A Victorian skeleton clock, with twin fusee movement, hour strike on a gong and half-hour strike on a bell, on marble base under a glass dome, c1870, 27in (68.5cm) high.
£3,750–4,250 ALS

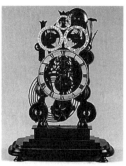

A chiming skeleton clock, with triple calendar, the triple fusee movement with a polished rafter-type frame, striking the quarters on eight bells, on an ebonized base under a glass dome, mid-19thC, 17½in (44.5cm) high.
£2,000–2,400 Bon

► A brass year-going skeleton timepiece, by Claude Reeve, the movement with massive spring barrel and high count train, with deadbeat escapement, on a mahogany base with glass cover, c1950, 15in (38cm) high.
£2,300–2,750 S(S)

A Victorian skeleton clock, with eight-day fusee movement and passing strike on the hour, 16in (40.5cm) high.
£1,800–2,000 PTh

WALL CLOCKS

A Swiss Neuchâtel ebonized wall timepiece, c1700, 13½in (34.5cm) high.
£1,300–1,500 S(Z)

Cross Reference
See Colour Review

A George I hooded wall clock, by Peter Godlyman, Hurley, in black painted pine case, the posted bell striking movement with reconversion to verge escapement, c1720, 17in (43cm) high.
£1,400–1,700 S

A Swiss ebonized thirty-hour pendulum wall clock, by Samuel Heinimann, striking the quarters on two bells, c1750, 24¾in (63cm) high.
£1,300–1,500 S(Z)

► A tavern clock, the trunk inscribed Wm Wasbrough, Bristol, the panel door decorated with figures beside an inn, late 18thC, 59in (150cm) high.
£5,000–6,000 P(B)

A George III mahogany clock, by William Nicoll, London, the fusee and chain movement with anchor escapement, in a wooden case, escapement and case altered, c1790, 14½in (37cm) diam.
£1,400–1,600 S

A mahogany non-striking drop-dial wall clock, the trunk inlaid with brass stringing, c1830, 22in (56cm) high.
£700–850 GAK

A mahogany non-striking wall clock, by J. Jordan, Manchester, with single train fusee movement, c1840, 17¼in (44cm) diam.
£600–700 DN

A mahogany non-striking wall clock, by Dilger, London, with single fusee movement, c1850, 12in (30.5cm) diam.
£1,000–1,200 Bon

A walnut wall clock, by H. Kempton, London & Ely, with eight-day double fusee bell striking movement, c1850, 20½in (52cm) high.
£800–1,000 BLH

A drop dial wall clock, by John Patrick, Maidenhead, the 8-day fusee movement with anchor escapement, the mahogany inlaid case with brass stringing, c1840, 18in (45.5cm) high.
£3,000–3,300 PAO

An Australian mahogany drop-dial wall clock, signed T. Gaunt, Melbourne, with fusee movement, 1840–50, 28in (71cm) high.
£850–1,000 TEN

An oak weight-driven wall longcase clock, by Bosworth, Nottingham, with painted dial, bell striking movement, mid-19thC, 51in (129.5cm) high.
£700–850 Bon

A mahogany wall clock, the painted 14in (35.5cm) dial signed Olivia, Buenos Aires, the crossbanded trunk with box stringing, with anchor escapement, five pillar bell striking and trip repeating fusee movement, c1830, 34in (86.5cm) high.
£1,750–2,000 S

▶ A Victorian rosewood and mother-of-pearl-inlaid drop-dial wall clock, signed Blundell, Liverpool, the twin fusee movement striking on a bell, c1850, 28¼in (72cm) high.
£500–600 P(NW)

A mahogany non-striking drop-dial wall clock, the trunk with inset brass stringing and rosettes, 1830–40, 23in (58.5cm) high.
£900–1,100 GAK

A mahogany non-striking drop-dial wall clock, by Dutton, Fleet Street, London, the four-pillar movement with anchor escapement, the dial engraved 'Board of Health VR 1852', 25in (63.5cm) high.
£3,200–3,600 P

A carved oak wall clock, the weight-driven movement with anchor escapement and maintaining power, repainted dial, late 19thC, 61in (155cm) high.
£1,800–2,200 P

◀ A walnut wall clock, with single-train movement, subsidiary thermometer and aneroid barometer to the base, crossed arrows mark of H. A. C., Württemberg, c1900, 27in (68.5cm) high.
£400–500 PFK

A French wall *comtoise* clock, with earlier eight-day horizontal verge movement, c1850, 15in (38cm) wide.
£450–500 K&D

A German Vienna-style walnut *grande sonnerie* wall clock, the three-train weight-driven movement chiming and striking on two gongs, faults, c1870, 53⅛in (136cm) high.
£2,300–2,600 S(S)

A mahogany wall clock, by Camerer Kuss & Co, London, the fusee movement with anchor escapement, c1860, 12in (30.5cm) diam.
£1,100–1,250 PAO

A mahogany wall clock, by Charles Frodsham, London, with a passing strike, the single fusee movement striking the hour on a bell, 19thC, 12in (30.5cm) diam.
£1,300–1,500 Bon

A French ormolu-mounted wall clock, by Balthazard, Paris, surmounted by a figure of Diana, the twin fusee movement striking on a gong, late 19thC, 48in (122cm) high.
£2,700–3,000 Bea(E)

A walnut and marquetry-inlaid wall clock, the eight-day movement striking the hour and half-hour on a gong, c1880, 41in (104cm) high.
£700–775 K&D

A German carved beech wall clock, the two doors opening to reveal a trumpeter, the case edges with applied carvings of dogs and foliage, the two-train spring-driven movement with carved pendulum and indicating the hour on three trumpets, c1890, 27¼in (69cm) high.
£900–1,100 S(S)

A mahogany wall clock, with single fusee movement, dial marked ERVII, early 20thC, 12in (30.5cm) diam.
£550–650 Bon

A Federal birch inlaid longcase clock, by Elisha Smith, Sanbornton, New Hampshire, the door with bird's-eye maple veneer and mahogany-crossbanded border flanked by reeded quarter columns, dial repainted, fretwork missing, early 19thC, 83in (211cm) high.
£2,000–2,400 SK(B)

A mahogany wagon-spring steeple clock, by Birge & Fuller, Bristol, Connecticut, the lower door with later etched geometric decoration, the dial with open centre showing the skeleton movement with inverted anchor escapement, striking on a gong, with eight-leaved accelerating lever spring fixed to the base, mid-19thC, 26in (66cm) high.
£2,000–2,400 P

A Federal mahogany and gilt gesso banjo clock, with eight-day weight-driven movement, probably Massachusetts, restored, c1820, 22½in (56cm) high.
£950–1,100 SK(B)

A mahogany longcase clock, retailed by Tiffany & Co, with option for three chimes, late 19thC, 98in (249cm) high.
£5,500–6,000 SK

► An Empire revival mahogany longcase clock, by the Royal Furniture Co, Grand Rapids, the brass works stamped 'B & D Limited, Elite, Germany', c1900, 103½in (263cm) high.
£2,200–2,600 NOA

A banjo clock, the door panel reverse-painted with Aurora in her chariot, dial repainted, New England, 19thC, 40½in (103cm) high.
£3,300–4,000 BB(L)

A carved walnut Parisian clock, by Ansonia Clock Co, Connecticut, with eight-day spring-operated movement and coil gong, 1895, 24in (61cm) high.
£340–380 OT

A Federal mahogany pillar and scroll clock, by Samuel Terry, Plymouth, Connecticut, with thirty-hour wooden weight-driven movement, restored, c1825, 31in (78.5cm) high.
£2,700–3,000 SK(B)

A carved mahogany non-striking Bagdad clock, by Ansonia Clock Co, Connecticut, with fifteen-day double wind movement, c1880, 51in (129.5cm) high.
£900–1,000 OT

A rosewood-veneered drop-dial wall clock, retailed by W. Horne & Sons, Leyburn, with eight-day bell striking movement, c1900, 29in (73.5cm) high.
£200–240 DA

REGULATORS

◀ A Scottish mahogany domestic regulator, by Reid & Auld, Edinburgh, No. 820, with rack and bell striking movement, maintaining power and wood rod pendulum, 1808, 80¾in (205cm) high.
£4,500–5,500 S

Thomas Reid, a celebrated Scottish clock maker, was born in 1746 and apprenticed to James Cowan. In 1806, he formed a partnership with his stepson, William Auld, which lasted until 1823 when they both retired. The numbering system introduced during their partnership can date an individual clock to a particular year, and also indicates where the clock comes in the sequence for that year.

A mahogany longcase regulator, signed Barker, Wigan, with crossbanding and boxwood inlay, the eight-day four-pillar movement with deadbeat escapement and maintaining power, the trunk possibly of later date, later plinth, early 19thC, 82in (208.5cm) high.
£1,100–1,300 P(NW)

A mahogany domestic longcase regulator, by Edwards, Godalming, the eight-day movement with deadbeat escapement and striking the hours on a bell, c1850, 80in (203cm) high.
£6,000–6,850 PAO

A mahogany regulator, by Alexander & Sons, Glasgow, with silvered dial, 19thC, 78¾in (200cm) high.
£2,400–2,650 P(Ed)

A mahogany longcase regulator, signed Alfred M. Jacobs & Co, London, with silvered dial, the eight-day movement with deadbeat escapement and maintaining power, faults, 19thC, 79½in (202cm) high.
£5,750–7,000 S(S)

◀ A German Vienna-style rosewood thirty-day wall regulator, the movement with high count train, deadbeat escapement and maintaining power, c1880, 78in (198cm) high.
£3,500–3,850 S(S)

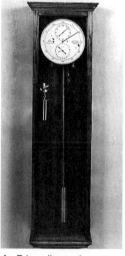

An Edwardian mahogany wall regulator, by Dent, London, the movement with deadbeat escapement and maintaining power, 48¾in (124cm) high.
£2,750–3,250 P

▶ A French silvered and gilt four-glass table regulator, by Jean-Baptiste Delettrez, with 4¾in (12cm) two-piece enamel dial and bell striking movement, c1875, 16in (40.5cm) high.
£2,000–2,200 S

A mahogany longcase regulator, by J. & T. Foster, Manchester, with silvered dial, the movement with deadbeat escapement, mid-19thC, 76¾in (195cm) high.
£7,000–8,000 P

Watches

POCKET WATCHES

A silver verge watch, signed Rensman, London, champlevé dial with date aperture, outer case missing, 17thC, 48mm diam.
£450–550 P

A verge watch, with silver champlevé sun and moon dial, signed Jon Williamson, the hours are indicated by a waxed champlevé silver and silver-gilt disc which rotates once every 24 hours, c1695, 56mm diam.
£3,000–3,300 PT

▶ A quarter-repeating verge watch, by Daniel Delander, London, the gold inner case pierced and engraved with arabesques and a landscape, marked 'P. R.', dated '1710', c1765, 57mm diam.
£1,500–1,800 TEN

A gold pair-cased verge watch, by Daniel Delander, marked 'London 1744', 50mm diam.
£800–900 P

A George III silver pair-cased pocket watch, the case by William Howard, London 1763, 50mm diam.
£350–420 DN

An 18ct gold open-faced verge watch, by Barraud, 1802, London mark, 52mm diam.
£350–420 Bon

An Irish silver pair-cased verge watch, signed Dav. Bigger, Belfast, the movement with round pillars, pierced and engraved masked cock, c1780, 50mm diam.
£750–850 PT

◀ A silver-gilt pedometer pocket watch, the movement signed Recordon, Spencer & Perkins, London, with white dial, the plain case marked 1807, 52mm diam.
£3,800–4,200 GH

A silver lever watch, by Frodsham, London, with white enamel dial, the three-train wheels under a single signed gilt cock, marked London 1825, 55mm diam.
£480–535 PT

An 18ct gold hunter pocket watch, signed Vulliamy, London, with duplex escapement and fusee movement, engraved balance and silvered regulation dial, London 1817, 2in (5cm) diam, with a mahogany travelling case.
£1,250–1,500 DN

A William IV 18ct gold lever watch, by Bramwell & Sons, Fishergate, Preston, the three-quarter plate movement with cut and compensated bi-metallic balance, marked for Chester 1836, 45mm diam.
£275–325 P

An 18ct gold hunter watch, by Dent, London, with resilient lever escapement and offset seconds, engraved with a motto, marked London 1872, 50mm diam.
£1,100–1,300 PT

A gold keyless lever hunter watch, by Picard Frères, Chaux de Fonds, for Edward Bralford, the double dial with day, month and date on one side, hours, minutes and seconds on the other, c1880, 55mm diam.
£1,100–1,200 TEN

A 17thC-style silver verge watch, by Jean Falise, the backplate with engraved decoration, the case pierced overall and engraved with hunting scenes, detached wheels, 19thC, 110mm long.
£700–800 S

A Swiss 14ct gold hunter chronograph, with keyless lever movement jewelled to the centre, and minute repeat train, late 19thC, 56mm diam.
£1,400–1,700 P

An 18ct gold engine-turned half hunter watch, by Le Roy & Son, London, the case with a blue enamel chapter on the front cover, c1890, 51mm diam.
£400–450 Bon

A steel Rolex pocket watch, c1915, 50mm diam.
£650–750 TWD

A 18ct gold Rolex pocket watch, 1910, 50mm diam.
£1,600–1,800 TWD

A silver eight-day Goliath lever watch, by Octava Watch Co, with three-quarter plate keyless movement with going barrel, marked London 1920, 67mm diam.
£375–425 PT

WRISTWATCHES

A Breitling stainless steel watch, c1940, 35mm diam.
£1,000–1,100 TWD

A Heuer 18ct rose gold manual wind chronograph, c1945.
£2,000–2,500 HARP

A Longines steel watch, c1920, 40mm diam.
£1,100–1,200 TWD

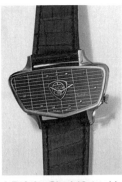

A Breitling Navitime gold-plated watch, c1950, 50mm diam.
£675–750 TWD

A Jaeger LeCoultre Futurmatic automatic steel watch, with power reserve indicator, the hands set from back of case, c1958.
£1,000–1,200 HARP

A Henry Moser 15ct pink gold watch, c1920, 30mm wide.
£1,600–1,800 TWD

◀ A Patek Philippe 18ct gold watch, with silvered dial, 18 jewel movement adjusted to five positions and temperature, 1940s, 25mm wide.
£2,500–3,000 Bon

A Bouche-Girod 18ct gold watch, in the shape of a Lancia radiator grille, 1960s, 39mm wide.
£1,650–1,800 RM

The firm of Bouche-Girod was founded by A. Bouche in 1937 and specialized in making wristwatches representing car grilles, especially Mercedes and Lancia.

▶ A Juvenia Arithmo Automatic 18ct pink gold mathematician's watch, with slide rule, self-winding and with centre seconds, 1950s, 36mm diam.
£950–1,150 RM

A Harwood silver-cased automatic watch, with silvered dial, 1929, 30mm diam.
£300–350 Bon

A Rolex silver half hunter watch, c1920, 30mm diam.
£1,600–1,800 TWD

A Rolex Oyster octagonal-cased chrome watch, with silvered dial, 1930s, 33mm diam.
£400–500 Bon

A Universal Genève Tri-Compax stainless steel astronomic watch, c1945, 34mm diam.
£1,200–1,400 RM

A Rolex diamond-set bracelet watch, with silvered dial, signed for C. Bucherles, 1920s, 15mm wide.
£600–700 Bon

A Rolex Oyster Perpetual stainless steel watch, with nineteen jewels, lever escapement, self-winding, water-resistant, 1950s, 32mm diam.
£1,100–1,200 RM

An Edwardian single and rose-cut diamond openwork watch, with a hinged openwork bangle, 57mm inner diam.
£400–500 Bon

A Rolex sterling silver watch, with hinged lugs, enamelled porcelain dial, the movement signed 'Rolex Breguet hairspring', case marked 'W. & D. ' and 'Rolex 7 world records gold medal Geneva-Suisse', marked for 1924, 27mm wide.
£1,000–1,200 HARP

A Rolex Precision 9ct gold watch, with silvered hobnail finish dial and centre seconds, 1956, 33mm diam.
£450–550 Bon

A diamond and platinum watch, 1920, 25mm wide.
£350–400 AnS

A Rolex 9ct gold watch, with silvered dial, 1934, 24mm wide.
£650–700 Bon

A Universal Genève Uni-Compax 18ct gold watch, with square button chronograph, register, tachometer and telemeter, c1942, 34mm diam.
£1,200–1,400 RM

A Swiss rolled gold automatic lever watch, the oscillating weight pivoted at the centre, stopped by spring buffers, and winding the watch in one direction only, c1930, 28mm wide.
£550–600 PT

This is an early example of an automatic wrist-watch using a similar mechanism to that patented by Harwood in 1926.

◄ A 14ct diamond bracelet watch, c1960, 155mm long.
£700–800 S

Barometers

STICK BAROMETERS

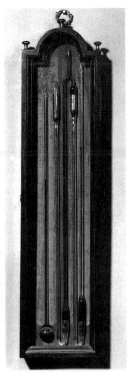

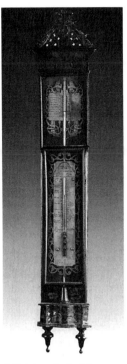

A George III mahogany double barometer, attributed to Baptista Roncheti, Manchester, the paper scales printed with Fahrenheit temperature scale and 0–50 barometric scale, the exposed W-shaped barometer tube filled alternately with mercury and oil alongside oil-filled thermometer tube, wire slide lacking pointer, c1785, 23½in (59.5cm) high.
£2,700–3,000 S

Mercury is the best liquid to ascertain barometric pressure. However, it has the disadvantage of a relatively compact scale. To expand this, thus permitting smaller barometric changes to be discernable whilst still leaving the instrument portable, Robert Hooke (1635–1703) mixed another liquid with mercury and produced the first double barometer which he demonstrated to the Royal Society in 1688.

▶ A George III inlaid mahogany stick barometer, by H. Dallaway, Bath, the exposed tube with silvered plates, hand-set vernier, c1800, 37in (94cm) high.
£2,000–2,400 S

A Dutch walnut and marquetry stick barometer, the pewter plates with English and German scales, the alcohol thermometer with pewter plate with Fahrenheit and Florence scales and signed Primavesi, faults, late 18thC, 48½in (123cm) high.
£2,500–3,000 S(S)

A George III mahogany stick barometer, by Bate, London, with engraved silvered plates, 37½in (95.5cm) high.
£2,300–2,750 L

A mahogany stick barometer, by John Wisker, York, with silvered scale and thermometer, late 18th/early 19thC, 39in (99cm) high.
£1,800–2,200 TEN

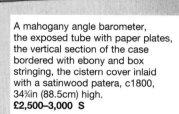

A mahogany angle barometer, the exposed tube with paper plates, the vertical section of the case bordered with ebony and box stringing, the cistern cover inlaid with a satinwood patera, c1800, 34¾in (88.5cm) high.
£2,500–3,000 S

A mahogany and ebony-inlaid bowfront stick barometer, by Troughton, London, with urn-shaped cistern cover and ivory float, cycle pointer and vernier, original cistern missing, early 19thC, 39in (99cm) high.
£5,500–6,000 P

The Troughton family had a high reputation as optical and mathematical instrument makers.

A mahogany and boxwood-strung stick barometer, by C. Jacopi, Shropshire, with silvered brass register scale, c1825, 37in (94cm) high.
£1,800–2,000 PAO

A mahogany stick barometer and thermometer, by Abraham & Co, Opticians, Liverpool, with engraved ivory scale and adjustable vernier, 19thC, 36in (901.5cm) high.
£1,000–1,200 CAG

Abraham & Co are recorded as having worked from 1817–60.

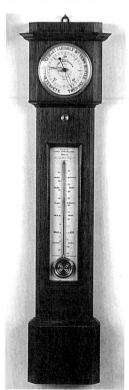

A Victorian mahogany stick barometer, by Johnson, London, with ivory scale and adjustment handles, with thermometer to the column, 37½in (95.5cm) high.
£800–1,000 P(S)

When sold at auction, barometers may have had alterations made to their mechanisms or be in unrestored condition, which may affect in the prices realized.

◀ A rosewood wall barometer, by Chevallier, Paris, with porcelain dial, the chamfered trunk with thermometer calibrated for Réamur and Centigrade, c1860, 37½in (95.5cm) high.
£800–1,000 Bon

▶ A burr-walnut and oak stick barometer, by J. Amadio, London, with silvered dial, 1860s, 40in (101.5cm) high.
£1,400–1,700 Bon

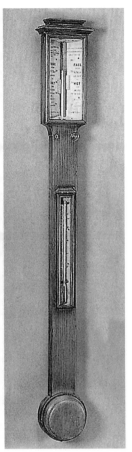

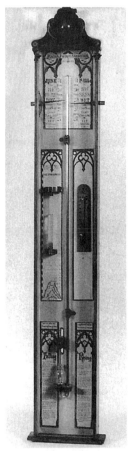

An oak stick barometer, the ivory face stamped Burrow, Malvern, mid-19thC, 37½in (95.5cm) high.
£600–700 DN(H)

A rosewood stick barometer, the ivory register inscribed George Wadham, Bath, 19thC, 37½in (95.5cm) high.
£550–650 AH

A Victorian oak Admiral Fitzroy's barometer, known as 'The Atmoscope Barometer', the 9½in (24cm) paper scale with twin adjustments, the lower part of the glazed case containing thermometer and hydrometer, 46in (117cm) high.
£500–600 CAG

An oak Admiral Fitzroy's barometer, with rise and fall and atmosphere dials, 19thC, 44½in (113cm) high.
£450–500 GAK

WHEEL BAROMETERS

A George III mahogany and paterae-inlaid wheel barometer and thermometer, by J. N. O. Corti, London, with silvered plates, 38in (96.5cm) high.
£900–1,100 L

A George III mahogany wheel barometer, by Loffler, Winslow, with dry/damp dial thermometer, the dial silvered above bone adjustment knob and spirit level, 38in (96.5cm) high.
£350–420 DN(H)

A mahogany wheel barometer inlaid with boxwood and ebony stringing, by P. Ramos, London, with silvered dial, early 19thC, 38in (96.5cm) high.
£550–650 DN

A mahogany wheel barometer and thermometer, by G. Arzoni, Canterbury, with silvered dial, early 19thC, 39in (99cm) high.
£500–600 CAG

A Regency mahogany, boxwood and ebony-inlaid wheel barometer, with silvered dial, 44in (112cm) high.
£550–650 HYD

A Louis XVI-style ebonized and giltwood wheel barometer, with framed thermometer case, early 19thC, 43in (109cm) high.
£1,000–1,200 NOA

An Irish rosewood wheel barometer, inlaid with brass and mother-of-pearl, signed Bennett, Cork, 19thC, 37½in (95.5cm) high.
£300–350 HOK

A mahogany wheel barometer, signed Braham, Optician, Bristol, the silvered dial with an engraved scale and central compass, c1830, 43½in (110.5cm) high.
£2,500–3,000 Bon

An inlaid mahogany wheel barometer, signed L. Gianna, with silvered dial, c1830, 37in (94cm) high.
£600–700 KB

A mahogany and boxwood-strung wheel barometer, signed J. Gilardi, Bristol, with silvered dial, c1840, 38in (96.5cm) high.
£700–770 KB

J. Gilardi is recorded as trading 1835–55.

◄ A mahogany wheel barometer, signed B. Cantoni, Horsham, with silvered dial, c1840, 48¾in (124cm) high.
£900–1,100 S(S)

A rosewood and mother-of-pearl-inlaid wheel barometer, with timepiece, the silvered dial signed J. & C. Corbetta, London, with hygrometer, mercury thermometer and level, the timepiece with white enamel dial, the fusee movement with in-line train and anchor escapement, c1835, 49½in (125.5cm) high.
£2,750–3,250 S(S)

A mahogany wheel barometer, by J. Ronchetti, Manchester, with silvered brass dial, c1830, 43in (109cm) high.
£1,700–1,875 PAO

A mahogany and boxwood-strung wheel barometer, signed Grassi & Fontana, Exeter, with silvered dial, c1840, 38in (96.5cm) high.
£700–800 KB

Grassi & Fontana are recorded as trading between 1815 and 1850.

A mahogany banjo barometer, by D. Fagioli & Son, London, some damage, c1845, 42in (106.5cm) high.
£450–500 RTw

A mahogany wheel barometer, by G. J. Bates, Catfield, with silvered dial, c1850, 38in (96.5cm) high.
£1,000–1,150 PAO

A mahogany wheel barometer, signed P. Pedrene, Bristol, with silvered dial, c1850, 38in (96.5cm) high.
£575–650 KB

A mahogany and boxwood-strung wheel barometer, with silvered dial, c1870, 44in (112cm) high.
£675–750 KB

▶ A Bakelite desktop baro-meter, by Short & Mason, London, with Cope's wording, c1930, 11in (28cm) wide.
£150–200 RTw

A carved and painted wheel clock barometer, the clock with thirty-hour movement, the thermometer with silvered scale over silvered vernier, damaged, marked 'JAs Pitkin Maker', late 19thC, 40½in (103cm) high.
£450–500 BLH

ANEROID BAROMETERS

A Victorian gilt-brass 'kettle drum' aneroid barometer, the silvered dial with foliate-engraved bezel overlaid with drum sticks, marked for 1873, 5½in (14cm) high.
£370–400 S

A walnut and ebony-strung slope-front table-top aneroid barometer, the silvered dial signed Callaghan, London, mid-19thC, 6¾in (17cm) wide.
£450–500 Hal

A carved oak aneroid barometer, by J. J. Hicks, London, the painted dial with intricate predictions, 19thC, 24in (61cm) diam.
£1,150–1,400 P

Further Reading
Miller's Clocks & Barometers Buyer's Guide, Miller's Publications, 1997

► A Victorian aneroid barometer, by W. Gerrard, with curved thermometer and weather indications, c1880, 5in (12.5cm) diam.
£400–440 JIL

A rope-carved oak aneroid barometer, signed Pastorelli & Rapkin, London, with porcelain dial, late 19thC, dial 5in (12.5cm) diam.
£180–200 KB

An Edwardian inlaid mahogany aneroid barometer, with opaque white glass dials and inscribed plaque, 35in (89cm) high.
£250–300 DA

A mahogany Harry Hall promotional aneroid barometer, by Short & Mason, c1935, 36in (91.5cm) high.
£250–300 RTw

BAROGRAPHS

An Edwardian oak-cased barograph, signed J. Lizars, Aberdeen, the chart drum driven by an eight-day movement with cylinder escapement, the pen controlled by a stack of eight vacuum flasks on brass bed plate, the plinth with drawer, c1905, 15in (33cm) wide.
£700–800 S

A mahogany-cased barograph, with chart roll and single bellow, c1910, 15in (38cm) wide.
£430–500 BLH

A Dines self-recording barometer, by J. Hicks, London, the ebonized case with solid mahogany backboard, early 20thC, 39½in (100.5cm) high.
£3,500–4,200 P

Miller's Compares

A mahogany-cased barograph, with open-faced dial and thermometer scale, chart drawer and bevelled glass, c1910, 15in (38cm) wide.
£1,400–1,600 RTw

An oak-cased barograph, by Short & Mason, with chart drawer and bevelled glass, c1935, 14in (35.5cm) wide.
£850–950 RTw

These barographs were made during the first half of the 20thC, and are desirable because they both have an additional barometer dial. However, Item I has a stack of eight individual diaphragms as opposed to the later style of a single 'concertina' bellow, often used from the mid-1930s, shown in the movement in Item II. The earlier barograph also has an open chapter displaying the lacquered brass mechanism behind and, in addition, there is a mercury thermometer attached which follows the radius of the dial. The mahogany case of Item I is more popular today than the oak of Item II.

▶ A mahogany-cased barograph, by Sewills, Liverpool, 'Makers to the Royal Navy', c1920, 14in (35.5cm) wide.
£900–1,000 ETO

A mahogany-cased barograph, by F. Darton & Co, Watford, with 16 aneroid bellows and chart drawer, c1930, 14in (35.5cm) wide.
£700–800 KB

A mahogany-cased barograph, by Richard Frères, complete with thermometer, c1935, 11in (28cm) wide.
£375–425 RTw

◀ A Russian Bakelite-cased meteorological office barograph, c1950, 9in (23cm) wide.
£350–400 RTw

Decorative Arts

AESTHETIC MOVEMENT FURNITURE

A Japanese-style bird's-eye maple bedstead, with 'bamboo' legs, late 19thC, 42½in (108cm) wide.
£450–550 SLN

A Victorian oak and pollard oak bookcase, the lower section enclosed by two marquetry-inlaid panel doors with ebonized background, with two shallow frieze drawers, 51in (129.5cm) wide.
£2,250–2,750 DD

An ebonized and painted bay-wood hanging wall cabinet, in the style of E. W. Godwin, decorated with white lines forming panels, scrolls and borders, c1870, 24in (61cm) wide.
£400–500 S

The incised Greek-style decoration is characteristic of some of the work of the pioneering designer Edward William Godwin (1833–86).

The Aesthetic Movement

The Aesthetic, or Art, Movement of the mid–late Victorian period is one of the hardest to define because it encompassed so many different influences. The world was beginning to be a much smaller place as more people travelled abroad and travellers and collectors shared the finds in private and in public museums.

For those with money and leisure time, there was plenty of opportunity to indulge and express oneself. The home, be it the building or the interior, was a classic way of displaying both your taste and your wealth. The word 'aesthetic' came into popular use in the last quarter of the 19th century and meant that something was artistic and pleasing to the eye and the soul. The 'aesthete', the individual who appreciated art, became a recognisable character sufficiently distinct to be made fun of in the newspapers at the time and even pilloried in the operetta *Patience* by Gilbert and Sullivan.

Stylistically, the Aesthetic Movement encompassed a diverse array of influences and styles. These included Queen Anne, Gothic, Japanese, Egyptian and Moorish, and it brought together artists, architects and painters such as William Burges, E. W. Godwin, Burne-Jones, Rossetti, William Morris and Christopher Dresser. For example, Godwin's work clearly shows the influence of Japan, and Dresser's work includes both Japanese and Peruvian influences.

From a more popular and commercial point of view, many of these influences became diluted or were combined. At this level it may be characterized with ebonizing, turned spindles and finials, painted panels and gilt highlights, sunflowers and stylized plant motifs, which again may be highlighted with gilt. A Gothic influence may be evident but in a much weaker way, and Japanism was often diluted to a level of twee daintiness.

◀ A walnut breakfront display cabinet, by Collinson & Lock, with astragal-glazed doors enclosing a velvet-lined interior, c1880, 64in (162.5cm) wide.
£1,500–1,800 S

The firm of Collinson & Lock was established in London in the third quarter of the 19thC, and quickly achieved both commercial success and a leading position in the field of design. In 1871, the firm issued an impressive illustrated catalogue of 'artistic furniture', with plates by J. Moyr Smith, and by 1873 was trading from extensive newly-built premises in St Bride Street. In 1897, the firm was taken over by Gillows but continued to produce furniture of this type for several years.

An American rosewood side cabinet, attributed to Herter Brothers, New York, the cupboard doors with figural and floral inlaid *pietra dura* plaques, late 19thC, 62in (157.5cm) wide.
£5,000–5,500 S(NY)

▶ A carved walnut low chair, the pierced and scrolled splat flanked by turned and fluted uprights, c1875.
£270–300 S

An American walnut and parcel-gilt rocking chair, by Schrenkeisen, carved throughout with incised geometric decoration and applied with carved paterae, requires restoration, c1875.
£650–750 S

A French brass and onyx pedestal, late 19thC, 41in (104cm) high.
£1,400–1,600 SK

A painted five-fold screen, each panel decorated with birds, flowering blossoms and lilies above Japanese-style panels of bamboo, prunus and other flowers, c1875, each panel 22¼in (56.5cm) wide.
£800–1,000 S

An ebonized and painted sideboard, with mirrored top and side doors, c1875, 59¾in (152cm) wide.
£2,000–2,300 OOLA

◀ A mahogany centre table, in the style of E. W. Godwin, late 19thC, 38¼in (97cm) diam.
£1,200–1,400 SK

▶ A macassar ebony and ebonized centre table, in the style of Collinson & Lock, the top with frieze drawer and serpentine ends with boxwood and ebony stringing, c1875, 39in (99cm) wide.
£2,000–2,200 S

AESTHETIC MOVEMENT METALWARE

◀ A silver four-piece tea and coffee service, by Frederick Elkington, with lozenge and floral borders, chased and engraved with a monogram, with bamboo moulded handles, in a burr-walnut and ebony box, 1880, box 29in (73.5cm) wide.
£1,250–1,500 P(EA)

A set of four silver and parcel-gilt seafood forks, by Martin & Hall, each finely engraved with fish and water weeds, the finials formed as scallop shells, Sheffield 1888, 6¼in (16cm) long.
£200–225 DAD

A Victorian silver picnic tea service, by Hukin & Heath, London, designed by Christopher Dresser, comprising 11 silver pieces and four porcelain pieces, in a fitted leather case, Sheffield 1894, 38oz.
£5,000–5,500 S

The designer of this service, Christopher Dresser, became Art Advisor to Hukin & Heath around 1877. The Furniture Gazette noted in 1879 that 'the firm have secured the services of [Dr Dresser] in order to be reliable in point of design'.

A silver sugar bowl and sifter ladle, by Heath & Middleton, the bowl formed as a fluted flowerhead resting on an openwork leafy tendril base, the interior chased to simulate petals, the sifter ladle with budding sprig stem, stamped marks, London 1887, 4½in (11.5cm) diam.
£450–500 DAD

▶ A Gorham silver covered jar, the hammered surface applied with gold-washed Japanese-style prunus blossoms on engraved branches, late 19thC, 4¼in (11cm) high, 6oz.
£600–700 SK

THE ARTS AND CRAFTS MOVEMENT

The Arts and Crafts Movement was arguably one of England's major contributions to design history. It was a noble movement, having a social conscience as well as promoting artistic integrity.

The Great Exhibition of 1851, held in Hyde Park beneath a huge canopy of glass, was hailed by many as displaying all the ingenuity, skill and beauty that man was now capable of producing. Half of the pieces exhibited came from Britain and her Colonies and the other half from the rest of the world, and over six million people visited the exhibition in five months. However, to some the Exhibition bore witness to the lack of taste and design consciousness of many of the nation's manufacturers, who seemed content to reproduce profusely-decorated derivative designs. To many, such excesses were proof of wealth and prosperity, to others it showed lack of originality and aesthetic appreciation.

Designers such as William Morris and John Ruskin played a major role in focusing attention on the need for design integrity. The term 'Arts & Crafts' originates from a letter written by Ruskin to Morris suggesting the staging of an exhibition of like-minded craftsmen and artists. Arts and Crafts design is characterized by an understanding of the purpose of the object to be designed and the various functions it may have to meet: this is more succinctly known as 'fitness for purpose'. Added to this was an appreciation of the materials used, an artistic eye and the skill to craft it. It is not coincidence that many of the best designers of the movement were either architects or artists. The Arts and Crafts Movement was not against decoration as such, only that it should be used appropriately and in keeping with the object's function. This often led, as in the case of furniture, to the construction methods (for example, mortise and tenon, butterfly or dovetail joints) being left exposed for decorative purposes and to show the integrity of the work.

Some examples of the greatest designers' and craftsmen's work may be found on the pages of this and previous editions of *Miller's Antiques Price Guide*. Look out for work by William Morris, C. R. Ashbee, C. F. A. Voysey, Ernest Gimson, Sydney Barnsley and William de Morgan, to name but a few, whose work, in whatever medium, will command high prices. This is because they were some of the best in their field, and among the originators of the style that we now know as Arts and Crafts.

Fiona Baker

ARTS & CRAFTS CERAMICS

A C. H. Brannam pottery mug, by Frederick Braddon, sgraffito-decorated beneath a green glaze, rim chip, marked, 1898, 5in (12.5cm) high.
£220–260 SK

A Burmantofts yellow-glazed pottery jardinière, 1900, 39in (99cm) high.
£500–600 PAC

A Burmantofts pottery vase, the neck applied with a dragon glazed in silver flake, turquoise, olive and brown above a streaked green body, early 20thC, 12¼in (31cm) high.
£700–800 DN(H)

A William de Morgan ruby and pink lustre pottery dish, painted by Charles Passenger, minor scratches, marked 'C. P.', 1888–98, 12in (30.5cm) diam.
£1,600–2,000 S

A William de Morgan Isnik pottery jug, painted by Fred Passenger in blue, turquoise, manganese and black with a band of eagles each clutching a lizard, small chip, impressed and incised marks, 1888–97, 11¼in (28.5cm) high.
£3,200–3,800 S

◀ An Ault pottery vase, by Christopher Dresser, with turquoise and brown glaze, signed and marked, c1890, 20in (51cm) high.
£1,300–1,500 SK

A Dunmore two-handled pottery vase, with green, black, brown and ochre glaze, impressed mark, 1870–1900, 5½in (14cm) high.
£100–130 SQA

A Leeds Fireclay Co jardinière and stand, for Liberty & Co, moulded with stylized bands of foliage enclosing foliate roundels, c1900, 37in (94cm) high.
£650–750 P

An American Merrimac Pottery green-glazed vase, 1900–08, 8¾in (22cm) high.
£2,500–2,800 JMW

A Dutch Rozenburg Pottery wall plate, painted by Theodorus Verstraaten, decorated in yellow, brown and green, with a black and gilt border, completed 8th May 1896, 22½in (57cm) diam.
£5,000–6,000 OO

An earthenware tile, by Grueby Faïence Co, Boston, Massachusetts, decorated in relief in green, brown and dark blue against a tan ground, impressed marks, early 20thC, 6in (15cm) square.
£475–525 SK

A Minton Art Pottery charger, painted by William Coleman with a young girl beside a dark blue sea, impressed and printed marks, 1871–73, 16½in (42cm) diam, in an ebony and gilt frame.
£4,750–5,500 JNic

William Coleman (1829–1904) trained as a surgeon, but achieved fame as an artist, applying his skills to ceramics. He was appointed Art Director at Minton's Art Pottery Studio in South Kensington in 1871 where he specialized in large plaques depicting maidens and cupids, which commanded between £30–50 each. Coleman gave up his position as Art Director in 1873 but continued to paint on Minton 'blanks', and used the Studio facilities until 1875. His designs were reproduced into the 1890s by Minton and in print form by Pears. De La Rue also adapted them for greetings cards.

William Grueby (1867–1925)

Grueby trained at the Low Art Tile Works in Boston, Massachusetts. After he founded his own firm in East Boston he continued to use processes learned at Low Art, such as the application of thick opaque glazes. He produced mainly architectural faïence, tiles and sanitary wares, many of which were designed to reflect and complement the Arts and Crafts furniture and furnishings popular at the time.

A Linthorpe Pottery moulded vase, designed by Christopher Dresser, decorated in green, brown and white, 1879–80, 10¾in (27.5cm) high.
£1,000–1,100 NCA

A Linthorpe Pottery ewer, designed by Christopher Dresser, c1880, 9in (23cm) high.
£600–700 G(L)

◄ A green vase, by Grueby Faïence Co, Boston, Massachusetts, with applied leaf and flower decoration, 1900–08, 21¾in (55.5cm) high.
£13,000–15,000 JMW

Impressively large examples of Grueby wares are most collectable, as are pieces made before 1910.

An American pottery jardinière, possibly by Peters & Reed, decorated in red and green, early 20thC, 15½in (39.5cm) high.
£150–180 SK

A Pindar, Bourne & Co planter, with blue-painted panels within a moulded black 'bamboo' frame, 1862–82, 7in (18cm) square.
£250–300 DSG

Pindar, Bourne & Co of Burslem, Staffordshire were taken over by Doulton & Co in 1882.

An oak bookcase, with three open compartments, one with mirrored panel, the lower section with leaded clear and blue glass doors, c1905, 56in (142cm) wide.
£2,500–3,000 M

An American Lifetime Furniture oak bookcase, with caned panels on lower front and sides, damaged, early 20thC, 46½in (118cm) wide.
£1,250–1,500 SK

An American oak bookcase, by L. & J. G. Stickley, New York, with hammered copper pull handles, labelled, c1912, 36½in (92.5cm) wide.
£4,500–5,500 SK

Leopold & J. George Stickley, elder brothers of the more famous Gustav Stickley, made simple, solid home and office furniture, including bookcases and tables. Their more progressive designs are very popular today. Many bear a branded signature or brass plate.

A German plane and maple veneered pearwood music cabinet, by Joseph Maria Olbrich, black-stained and inlaid with various woods and mother-of-pearl, with brass mountings, c1905, 55in (139.5cm) wide.
£15,000–18,000 DORO

An oak display cabinet, glazed to front and sides and with central door, early 20thC, 46in (117cm) wide.
£1,600–2,000 BB(L)

An oak coal box, with shovel, c1895, 17in (43cm) high.
£80–100 NAW

A pair of elm high back chairs, by George Walton, designed for The Ladies' Tea Room, Miss Cranston's Buchanan Street Tea Rooms, c1896.
£700–850 L&T

An oak chair, with 'spade' piercing to top rail, c1895.
£220–260 PFK

A pair of oak ladder-back chairs, c1895.
£480–530 NAW

▶ An open armchair, by Arthur Simpson of Kendal, with original studded hide panels to the back and seat, c1906.
£600–700 M

An American mahogany chest of drawers, by Roycroft, New York, with hammered copper drawer pulls, brand mark on lower drawer, early 20thC, 41in (104cm) wide.
£2,400–2,800 SK

The Roycrofters (1895–1938) was an American community founded at the end of the 19thC in East Aurora, New York by Elbert Hubbard, who named it after two 17thC English bookbinders. They originally produced lavish, leather-bound books, but by 1901 were manufacturing simple, well-made mahogany and fumed oak furniture in the Mission style, as well as textiles, hammered metalwork and lighting.

Cross Reference
See Colour Review

An oak nursery chest, designed by Ambrose Heal for Heal's of London, with turned handles, on stile feet, c1905, 44¾in (113.5cm) wide.
£2,200–2,600 M

A Gothic revival oak dresser, with chevron back and doors, the shelves with shaped pierced ends and ring-turned column supports, 19thC, 84in (213.5cm) wide.
£1,000–1,200 LAY

An oak dresser, by Gustav Stickley, New York, with swivel mirror and hammered brass handles, c1912, 48in (122cm) wide.
£6,000–7,000 SK

An oak plant stand, with studded metal bands, c1900, 36in (91.5cm) high.
£235–260 NAW

An oak double chair-back settee, by William Birch, with plank top rail and slip-in rush seats, c1910, 45in (114.5cm) wide.
£1,400–1,700 P

A walnut upright piano, by C. Bechstein, designed by Walter Cave, with a pierced panel frieze flanked by tapered candle sconces, faults, c1910, 61½in (156cm) wide.
£2,000–2,400 S(S)

An oak sideboard, by George Walton, Glasgow, the top with two plate rails above two panelled doors flanked by open shelves, c1890, 60in (152.5cm) wide.
£3,500–4,000 L&T

An oak sideboard, with mirrored back, copper and brass fittings and applied copper repoussé decoration, early 20thC, 60in (152.5cm) wide.
£1,600–2,000 SK

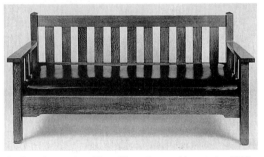

An American oak settle, with spring cushion seat, c1912, 81in (205.5cm) wide.
£700–800 SK

An oak sideboard, the back with inset enamel plaques, with open shelves above a pair of embossed lacquered brass panelled doors, c1910, 67in (170cm) wide.
£1,150–1,350 Bri

An oak stick stand, c1880,
28in (71cm) wide.
£300–350 OOLA

A mahogany Thebes saddle seat stool,
by Liberty & Co, maker's ivory plaque,
1884–1900, 17in (43cm) square.
£675–750 DAD

An oak dressing table and a
pair of pot cupboards, late 19thC,
dressing table 61in (155cm) wide.
£950–1,150 GAK

A Dutch carved oak extending table
and ten chairs, two with arms,
designed by Jac. van den Bosch
for 't Binnenhuis, Amsterdam,
branded monogram and metal label,
1907–10, table 94in (239cm) long.
£7,000–8,500 S(Am)

An oak settle and two armchairs, one with rockers,
c1919, settle 68in (173cm) long.
£2,000–2,200 SK

A Dutch oak occasional
table, designed by Jac.
van den Bosch for
't Binnenhuis, Amsterdam,
inlaid with a geometric motif
in ebony, with branded
monogram, 1907–10,
31in (78.5cm) diam.
£450–550 S(Am)

Carlo Bugatti
(Italy, 1855–1940)

Bugatti came to public
attention when he designed
the Moorish interior for the
Italian section at the Turin
International Exhibition of 1902.
His individual style was based
on extravagant ornamentation,
geometric shapes and Moorish
themes. His designs, as much
works of art as pieces of
furniture, earned him a
reputation as Italy's leading
furniture designer.

An Italian walnut, ebonized and
vellum covered centre table, by Carlo
Bugatti, the top with a pewter-inlaid
tablet within a stella-inlaid and vellum
frieze above a border of hammered
brass roundels, with pierced gallery
below, lacking spindles, c1905,
34½in (87.5cm) wide.
£4,500–5,500 P

▶ An oak library table, in the
style of Gustav Stickley, with central
drawer and hammered copper
handles, c1912, 48in (122cm) wide.
£330–400 SK

◀ An oak
dining table, with
segmented top,
early 20thC,
72in (183cm) diam.
£1,200–1,400 S(S)

An oak occasional table,
c1910, 27in (68.5cm) high.
£80–100 NAW

MILLER'S

Essential Guides for the Collector

If you have a passion for collecting, then take a look at the Miller's range of guides to antiques and collectables. From porcelain to paperweights and mahogony to motorbikes a Miller's guide will help you identify, authenticate and value your favourite antiques. Compiled with the help of a nationwide team of experts from every area of the market, our books provide thousands of photographs, independently assessed price ranges, insider collecting tips and essential background information. At auction or boot sale, antiques shop or fair, take a Miller's book with you for invaluable on the spot reference.

Miller's Price Guides

As well as the hugely successful *Miller's Antiques Price Guide*, Miller's also produce three other price guides, which provide the ultimate in useful reference books. Packed with thousands of new pictures every year, the guides give price bands and invaluable collecting information.

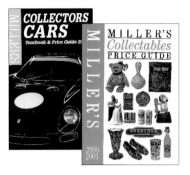

Miller's Collectables Price Guide   **Price £17.99**

**Miller's Collectors Cars
Yearbook & Price Guide**   **Price £19.99**

**Miller's Classic Motorcycles
Yearbook & Price Guide**   **Price £14.99**

Miller's Buyer's Guides   Price £19.99

Each of these invaluable reference guides concentrates on a popular area of collecting and features thousands of examples which are illustrated, authenticated and given an up-to-date price range by a team of top dealers and auction house specialists.

Titles available:

Art Nouveau & Art Deco

Ceramics

Chinese & Japanese Antiques

Clocks & Barometers

Late Georgian to Edwardian Furniture

Pine & Country Furniture

Miller's Facts at your Fingertips series   Price £12.99

These best-selling guides to popular collecting subjects combine historical background with practical advice for the collector by focusing on items that are available and affordable. They also look at identifying and dating pieces, assessing condition and recognising maker's marks. Each item is given a realistic price range while Fact Boxes highlight key collecting areas.

Titles available:

Antiques & Collectables

Furniture

Glass

Pottery & Porcelain

Silver

Teddy Bears & Dolls

Free Postage & Packing   credit card hotline 01933 443863   www.millers.uk.com

Miller's Collector's Guides

Price £5.99

These practical and accessible guides provide all the essential information you need to become a confident collector. The guides are packed with a wide range of items readily available at auctions, antiques shops, markets and car-boot sales. Each piece is accompanied by a detailed caption and a realistic price range.

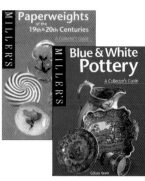

Titles available:

Advertising Tins

Blue & White Pottery

Ceramics of the '20s & '30s

Glass of the '20s & '30s

Paperweights of the 19th & 20th Centuries

Pens & Writing Equipment

Perfume Bottles

Popular Glass of the 19th & 20th Centuries

Postcards

Powder Compacts

Smoking Accessories

Soft Toys

Staffordshire Figures of the 19th & 20th Centuries

Watches

Miller's Pocket Factfiles

Price £7.99

These compact reference guides are ideal for the specialist collector and enthusiast. Packed with lists of key manufacturers, designers, patterns and marks and supported by detailed glossaries, they are invaluable sources of reference. Additional line drawings also provide excellent identification and dating information.

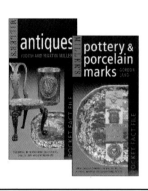

Titles available:

Antiques

Silver & Sheffield Plate Marks

Pottery & Porcelain Marks

Price £9.99

Miller's Antiques Checklists

Price £9.99

This popular series has been completely up-dated with new prices to reflect recent market trends. Fully illustrated, each guide provides a simple question-and-answer checklist, telling you what to look for and how to distinguish between the genuine article and a fake.

Titles available:

Art Deco

Art Nouveau

Clocks

Furniture

Glass

Jewellery

Pottery

Porcelain

Silver & Plate

Toys & Games

Victorian

Free Postage & Packing   credit card hotline 01933 443863   www.millers.uk.com

Miller's Antiques Encyclopedia   Price £40.00

Compiled by an international team of over 40 distinguished consultants
and writers, this ground breaking book explains materials, techniques and marks,
provides clues to identification, and offers hints as to what to consider when
buying an antique or examining one at home.

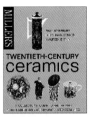

Miller's Twentieth-Century Ceramics   Price £25.00

This guide covers over 200 20th-century British and North American ceramics
factories. It includes the pre-war designers, the innovative designs of the 1950s
and 1960s and collectables of the future. Each item featured is given an
up-to-date price range.

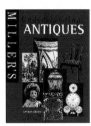

Miller's Understanding Antiques   Price £17.99

This is a practical reference book to the major collecting areas. It teaches readers
how to look at antiques, what questions to ask and why. It has sold over 190,000
copies and has established itself as an authoritative guide for the collector.

Miller's Collecting Textiles   Price £19.99

A new addition to the collecting series, this book covers all the key collecting
areas from embroidery and beadwork to Arts & Craft textiles, lace and quilts.
Packed with over 360 full-colour photographs, items are put into their historical
context and given an up-to-date price range.

Miller's Collecting Fashion and Accessories   Price £15.99

A great new addition to the collecting series, this book covers styles from the
beginning of the century to the present day. It includes illustrations for each
decade, and covers key designers and trends.

These titles are just a selection from the complete Miller's list,
which are available from all good bookshops.

In case of difficulty you may order direct from the publisher
on our *credit card hotline 01933 443863* quoting order
reference W413

Alternatively, you can send your order through to

Miller's Direct, Collets House, Denington Road,
Wellingborough, Northants. NN8 2QT.

We accept payment by cheque (payable to Octopus Publishing Group) or
the following credit cards: Visa, Access, American Express and Diner's Club.

Postage and packing is free in the UK, but please add £3.50 if you are
ordering from overseas.

ARTS & CRAFTS JEWELLERY

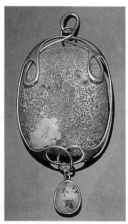

A silver-gilt floral spray brooch, by Dorrie Nossiter, set with sapphires, kunzite, emeralds, amethyst and seed pearls, c1900.
£1,750–2,000 SK

A gold and silver ring, by Bernard Instone, set with moonstone, garnets and pearls, 1920–30.
£900–1,000 DID

A gold pendant, by Murrle Bennett, with turquoise set in scroll gold mount suspending an oval-cut turquoise stone in collet mount, maker's mark, c1900.
£400–500 P(Ba)

A silver pendant necklace, by Ramsden & Carr, with interwoven tendrils surrounding a central green enamelled panel, maker's marks, London 1905, 3in (7.5cm) overall.
£1,700–2,000 S

▶ A 14ct yellow gold ring, attributed to Edward Oakes, set with a diamond, surrounded by twelve sapphires and a pierced foliate design, c1900.
£1,700–2,000 SK

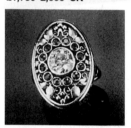

ARTS & CRAFTS LIGHTING

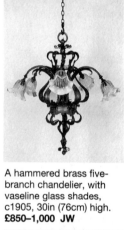

A hammered brass five-branch chandelier, with vaseline glass shades, c1905, 30in (76cm) high.
£850–1,000 JW

A pair of brass and copper wall lights, by W. A. S. Benson and James Powell & Sons, the green glass shades decorated with stylized flowers, 1880s, 18⅛in (47cm) high.
£5,500–6,000 S

Auction or Dealer?

All the pictures in our price guides originate from auction houses and dealers. When buying at auction, prices can be lower than those of a dealer, but a buyer's premium and VAT will be added to the hammer price. Equally, when selling at auction, commission, tax and photography charges must be taken into account. Dealers will often restore pieces before putting them back on the market.

Both dealers and auctioneers will provide professional advice, so it is worth researching both sources before buying or selling your antiques.

A hammered iron lantern, with vaseline glass shade, c1890, 28in (71cm) high.
£300–350 JW

▶ An oak table lamp, the shade with caramel and green glass panel inserts, glass replaced, early 20thC, 22in (56cm) high.
£200–240 SK

A ceiling light, by Koloman Moser, Vienna, with spherical glass shades, c1902, 47¼in (120cm) high.
£17,000–20,000 DORO

ARTS & CRAFTS METALWARE

A silver box and cover, by Josef Hoffmann for the Wiener Werkstätte, initialled and marked, c1910, 2¾in (7cm) diam.
£1,400–1,600 DORO

A pair of brass candlesticks, stamped with 'A' in a triangle, early 20thC, 14¼in (36cm) high.
£750–900 FBG

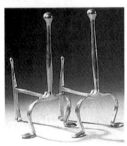

A pair of brass andirons, in the style of C. F. A. Voysey, c1905, 12in (30.5cm) high.
£1,600–1,750 S

Although an architect by training, and the designer of several landmark buildings, Charles Francis Annesley Voysey (1857–1941) excelled in all branches of the applied arts. He collaborated with leading manufacturers in the production of metalwork, furniture, carpets, textiles, ceramic tiles, wallpapers, even cutlery and tableware. He was closely associated with the Arts and Crafts Movement, and developed an original and idiosyncratic style.

A silver caddy spoon, by George Payne & Son, the stem terminating in four scrolls supporting a ball finial, Birmingham 1914.
£300–350 P

A. E. Jones and Omar Ramsden both made articles for Payne and Son, jewellers and silversmiths of Oxford and Tunbridge Wells.

A pair of silver candlesticks, by A. E. Jones, with oak barley-twist columns, the drip pans and bases with hammered decoration, Birmingham 1919, 6in (15cm) high.
£600–700 RTo

A silver cream jug, with hammered decoration and snake design handle, maker LW, Sheffield 1906, 3in (7.5cm) high.
£135–160 GAK

▶ A silver-plated fish knife and fork, designed by Charles Rennie Mackintosh for the Tea Rooms of Miss Cranston in Glasgow, with stylized trefid end pattern, the knife with rat-tail reverse, 1905, knife 8¼in (21cm) long.
£1,100–1,200 DAD

◀ A gilt-metal-mounted tortoise-shell hair comb, by the Wiener Werkstätte, one tooth broken, c1905, 4¼in (11cm) wide.
£575–700 S

A pair of American wrought-iron and brass fire dogs, early 20thC, 27in (68.5cm) high.
£1,250–1,500 SK

A claret jug, designed by Christopher Dresser, with silver-plated mounts and ebony handle, c1880, 8in (20.5cm) high.
£850–1,000 DORO

A set of four silver goblets, made by the Artificers' Guild, the bodies with ropework girdles and a frieze of fish in low relief, marked for 1923, 3in (7.5cm) diam, 19oz.
£2,000–2,200 P

A silver napkin ring, designed by Josef Hoffmann for the Wiener Werkstätte, initialled, marked, 1908–10, 2in (5cm) diam.
£700–850 DORO

A silver pepperette, by Charles Robert Ashbee, inlaid with five moonstones, London 1900, 3in (7.5cm) high.
£950–1,150 RID

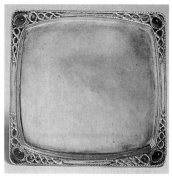

A silver salver, by Ramsden & Carr, with ropework edges, each corner set with chrysoprase, on four scroll and stump feet, base inscribed, 1913, 7in (17.5cm) square, 9¼oz.
£1,800–2,000 P

A hammered copper three-piece tea service and tray, by Joseph Heinrich, with silver bands at upper and lower edges, impressed marks, 1900–15, 20⅝in (52.5cm) wide.
£750–900 SK

A silver-coloured metal toothpick holder, by Alfred Mayer, designed by Josef Hoffmann for the Wiener Werkstätte, stamped and marked, c1905, 4in (10cm) wide.
£5,000–6,000 S

A silver bowl, by A. E. Jones, the body with a stud-work border and wirework tentril handles, Birmingham 1908, 8in (20.5cm) wide, 4oz.
£400–450 S(S)

A copper ashtray, 1900–10, 4½in (11.5cm) square.
£20–25 SAA

A silver-plated brass basket, by the Wiener Werkstätte, with square perforations, impressed marks, c1905, 10½in (26.5cm) high.
£2,800–3,200 DORO

A pewter bowl and spoon, by Hugh Wallis, c1910, 4¼in (11cm) diam.
£150–165 ANO

▶ A pair of silver spoons, by Omar Ramsden, with decorated finials, 1931, 6¼in (16cm) long.
£500–600 P(B)

A silver rose bowl, the hammered sides decorated in relief with four female mask cartouches on a leaf frieze, supported by four winged female figures, stamped and scratched 'Lydia Cooper Lon. 1911', 11¼in (28.5cm) diam, 70oz.
£2,400–2,650 P

▶ A silver caddy spoon, with stylized pierced scroll handle, marked, Birmingham 1924, 2¾in (7cm) long.
£200–240 Bon

DOULTON

A Doulton Lambeth stoneware biscuit barrel, with a silver-plated cover, decorated by Hannah B. Barlow, with a frieze of incised deer, impressed marks, artist's monogram, 1879, 8¾in (22cm) high.
£575–700 S(S)

A Doulton Burslem centrepiece, modelled as a maiden and child seated on the rim of a seashell, with costumes of beading, flora and shells, the faces framed by pink flora, c1890, 22in (56cm) high.
£1,500–1,800 P

A Doulton Lambeth stoneware jardinière, by Hannah B. Barlow, with brown ground and black rim, c1895, 11½in (29cm) high.
£2,000–2,400 JE

A Doulton Lambeth stoneware vase, incised with a frieze of horses by Hannah B. Barlow, the floral borders by Eliza Simmance, c1895, 15in (38cm) high.
£1,200–1,400 JE

A Doulton Lambeth stoneware jug, by Mark V. Marshall, decorated with brown and green glazes, c1895, 3¾in (9.5cm) high.
£500–600 JE

A Doulton Lambeth stoneware sauce boat, by Mark V. Marshall, with brown and green glaze, 1890s, 9in (23cm) wide.
£1,200–1,300 JE

A pair of Royal Doulton stoneware vases, by Hannah B. Barlow, decorated in earth tones, with incisions depicting sheep between floral borders, artist's monogram, numbered, c1905, 10¾in (27.5cm) high.
£950–1,150 FBG

A Doulton Lambeth stoneware three-handled mug, with silver-plated mount and cover, designed by John Broad, applied with a shot putter, long jumper and sprinter, each within a cartouche of foliage and blue flowers, one handle damaged, c1900, 7½in (19cm) high.
£230–275 Bea(E)

A pair of Doulton Lambeth stoneware vases, decorated by Florence Barlow, with swirled bands of stylized tulips in brown and blue below a beaded frieze, impressed marks, incised number, c1900, 12½in (32cm) high.
£500–550 S(S)

▶ A Doulton Burslem porcelain vase, retailed by Tiffany & Co, painted with cattle before mountains, signed 'Kelsall', c1900, 11½in (29cm) high.
£700–850 SLM

A Royal Doulton Lambeth stoneware vase, by Mark V. Marshall, decorated with brown and green glazes, 1904, 10¾in (27.5cm) high.
£400–500 JE

A Royal Doulton Burslem porcelain jar, moulded as a green artichoke, c1910, 5in (12.5cm) high.
£200–240 DSG

◀ A Royal Doulton Lambeth stoneware jug, moulded with flowers in low relief in green, pink and brown glazes, 1910, 7½in (19cm) high.
£100–120 RBB

A Royal Doulton Titanian Ware porcelain vase, by Harry Allen, decorated with polar bears in blues and white, signed, c1915, 9in (23cm) high.
£1,200–1,500 JE

Titanian Ware (produced c1915–30) used titanium oxide in the glaze to give a blue colouration ranging in tone from pale grey to dark royal blue. As shown here, it was used to provide a background for fine porcelain pieces decorated by artists such as Harry Allen and F. Henri.

A Royal Doulton Series Ware earthenware Gaffers hot water jug, signed 'Noke', c1920, 8½in (21.5cm) high.
£220–260 AOT

A Royal Doulton porcelain figure, Polly Peachum, HN550, 1922–49, 6¼in (16cm) high.
£180–220 DDM

A Royal Doulton Sung vase, The Alchemist, by C. J. Noke, decorated in relief in deep red with cream and yellow, signed, c1925, 18¼in (46.5cm) high.
£3,800–4,200 P

C. J. Noke began experimenting in the late 19thC with the production of high-temperature glazes, resulting in the launch of flambé-glazed wares in the early 20thC. The range was later increased to include animals, landscapes etc, painted beneath the glaze, and from these wares developed the Sung range, introduced in 1920.

A Royal Doulton Reynard The Fox coffee service, comprising 15 pieces, the handles designed as riding crops and the bases as whips, c1930.
£340–400 HAM

MARTIN BROTHERS

A Martin Brothers
stoneware jug, c1880,
9½in (24cm) high.
£1,700–2,000 G(L)

◄ A Martin Brothers
stoneware jug, c1880,
8¾in (22cm) high.
£550–650 G(L)

Miller's is a price GUIDE
not a price LIST

► A Martin Brothers bird
jar and cover, the feathers
picked out in ochre,
blue and brown enamels,
on a wood base, marked,
1903, 9¼in (23.5cm) high.
£4,000–5,000 S

MOORCROFT

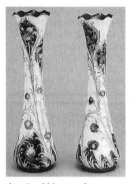

A pair of Moorcroft
MacIntyre Florian ware
vases, decorated with
trailing blue poppies,
slight damage, marked,
1898, 12in (30.5cm) high.
£1,800–2,200 EH

A Moorcroft MacIntyre
tankard, decorated with
the Hazledene landscape
pattern in blue and green
on a yellow ground,
marked, 1902–03,
5¼in (13.5cm) high.
£2,300–2,750 S

A Moorcroft stemmed
bowl, decorated with
Claremont toadstool
pattern on a sea-green
ground, marked, c1905,
8½in (21.5cm) high.
£1,200–1,400 S

A Moorcroft *sucrier* and
cover, decorated with
Liberty Hazledene pattern
in blue and green on a
cream ground, c1905,
4in (10cm) high.
£1,200–1,500 RUM

A pair of Moorcroft pottery vases, decorated
with Claremont toadstool pattern in peach and
cream on a green ground, marked, c1915,
3¼in (8.5cm) high.
£1,200–1,500 Bea(E)

A Moorcroft bowl, decorated with
Claremont toadstool pattern on a
shaded blue ground, marked,
1935–45, 9½in (24cm) high.
£700–850 GAK

A Moorcroft vase, decorated
with Wisteria pattern in
purple, mauve and yellow on
a blue ground, marked, mid-
20thC, 9¾in (25cm) high.
£275–325 SK

◄ A Moorcroft round pipe tray,
commemorating the coronation
of King Edward VIII, 1937,
5in (12.5cm) high.
£650–750 LT

► A Moorcroft plate, decorated with
Leaf and Fruit pattern in red, green
and cream on a blue ground, c1940,
7in (18cm) diam.
£200–240 AOT

ART NOUVEAU CERAMICS

A Bing & Grøndahl vase and cover, by Effie Hagerman-Lindencrone, with overall decoration of flowers and leaves in blue and cream, the cover with pierced decoration, marked, c1910, 21in (53.5cm) high.
£4,000–4,500 BUK

A Boch Frères Keramis handpainted vase, decorated with stylized flowers in lemon and sand on a cream ground, c1910, 40in (101.5cm) high.
£320–350 ANO

A pair of Gouda earthenware vases, painted with stylized flowers and foliage in green, blue and ochre, marked, early 20thC, 16½in (42cm) high.
£800–1,000 S(S)

A French pottery jardinière, by Delphine Massier, with lustre finish, c1900, 19in (48.5cm) wide.
£1,250–1,400 DSG

An Otto Eckmann earthenware two-handled vase, the exterior glazed with brown, green and yellow, the interior with red, the brown patinated-bronze mount modelled as stylized plant stems with the leaves converging to form the base, marked, c1900, 20½in (52cm) high.
£4,000–5,000 S

A Russian Imperial Porcelain Manufactory vase, in Japanese style, decorated with a band of beetles over stylized grass and blossom in blue, yellow and black, 1903, 16½in (42cm) high.
£5,000–5,500 S

A pair of Brantjes Purmerend earthenware vases, painted by Philippus Lagrand, decorated with violets in blue, green, yellow and brown, 1895–1904, 8in (20.5cm) high.
£1,000–1,100 S(Am)

Weduwe N. S. A. Brantjes & Co was a Dutch factory based in Purmerend and operated from 1895 to 1904. It concentrated on decorative earthenware, usually with strong forms and bright, floral decoration.

◀ A Gallé rabbit, blue tin-glaze on a biscuit base, marked, c1880, 14in (35.5cm) high.
£1,650–1,850 ANO

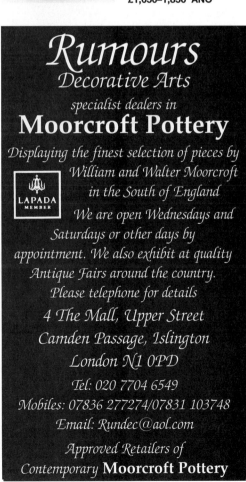

An American Marblehead Pottery, Massachusetts vase, decorated with dark green and yellow pattern on a mottled green ground, 1909–20, 3¼in (8.5cm) high.
£1,400–1,600 JMW

An American Newcomb College Pottery vase, by Joseph Meyer, decorated by Anna Frances Simpson with iris and foliage, cream and green on a blue ground, 1918, 6in (15cm) diam.
£3,000–3,500 NOA

A Riessner, Stellmacher & Kessel porcelain Amphora vase, decorated with cobwebs and fairies in cream, turquoise, grey and gilt, marked, c1900, 12¾in (32.5cm) high.
£1,200–1,400 DORO

Riessner, Stellmacher & Kessel (est. 1892) was a Bohemian ceramics firm whose main contribution to Art Nouveau was the Amphora range.

A Pfeiffer & Löwenstein/Schlackenwerth Modern porcelain tureen and cover, attributed to Joseph Maria Olbrich, white glazed decorated with gilt, marked 'PLS/Modern', c1901, 4¼in (11cm) high.
£2,000–2,200 DORO

An American Rookwood Pottery 'Iris' glazed vase, with moulded floral decoration in shades of grey and green, 1906, 7½in (19cm) high.
£2,000–2,200 JMW

An American Teco matt green-glazed pottery vase, designed by William Bryce Mundie, the rim moulded with buds, marked, 1910, 13¼in (33.5cm) high.
£1,800–2,200 BB(L)

An American Weller Pottery Tulips lamp base, by Lefter, decorated in yellow and green on a brown ground, 1895–1910, 11in (28cm) high.
£125–140 YAN

◄ A Swedish Rörstrand-style *pâte-sur-pâte* porcelain vase, decorated with a nymph seated on a rock with a gilt dragonfly, on a pale celadon ground, incised inscription 'Bergfee nach Diefenbach', marked, early 20thC, 11¾in (30cm) high.
£120–130 PFK

A Minton tile, moulded with a stylized flower in blue and lime on a dark green ground, c1900, in an oak frame, 7½in (19cm) square.
£40–50 DAD

An American Weller Pottery jardinière, moulded with tendrils and petals, glazed in brown and green, early 20thC, 8½in (21.5cm) high.
£120–130 DuM

An American Weller Pottery moulded Frurusset line vase, decorated in green and brown on a dark grey ground, c1910, 8¾in (22cm) high.
£1,150–1,275 JMW

An American pottery jardinière, with raised flowers motif in blue, green and brown, marked, early 20thC, 9in (23cm) diam.
£50–60 DuM

ART NOUVEAU CLOCKS & BAROMETERS

An oak mantel clock, inlaid with pewter and specimen woods, with entwined flower panel and two Yin and Yang roundel motifs, c1900, 9in (23cm) high.
£575-650 DAD

An Edwardian inlaid mahogany mantel timepiece, the case inlaid with a stylized flower, 9½in (24cm) high.
£250-300 P(L)

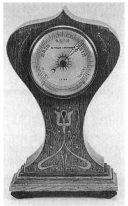

An Edwardian boxwood-strung and pewter-inlaid oak aneroid barometer, by Reynolds & Branson Ltd, Leeds, 10¼in (26cm) high.
£250-300 P(L)

A Liberty clock, with copper face and blue panel below, c1905, 6½in (16.5cm) high.
£3,200-4,000 ASA

A Liberty pewter timepiece, the copper and enamel face enclosed by raised stems of foliage, c1910, 8in (20.5cm) high.
£1,300-1,500 P

LOCATE THE SOURCE
The source of each illustration in Miller's can be found by checking the code letters below each caption with the Key to Illustrations, pages 789–795.

► An Austrian patinated-bronze table clock, by Gustav Gurschner, decorated with a pair of lovers in Gothic attire, marked, c1913, 18in (45.5cm) high.
£2,000-2,400 DORO

A brass repoussé-decorated wall clock, by Ellis Nairne, the twin-train movement striking on a coiled gong, the dial with stylized numerals within a panel depicting female figures garlanded with stylized roses, the hanging weights and pendulum also decorated, c1910, 19¼in (49cm) wide.
£2,200-2,600 L&T

ART NOUVEAU FIGURES & BUSTS

A French patinated-bronze bust of a lady, by V. Bruynee, Paris, indistinctly signed, late 19thC, 15¾in (40cm) high.
£800-1,000 S(S)

A Betnem patinated-bronze figural lamp, modelled as a woman supporting a flowerhead, with brown marble base, marked, c1900, 16¼in (41.5cm) high.
£1,000-1,200 S

A patinated-bronze figure of Phoebe, the moon goddess, cast from a model by Maritou, c1900, 25in (63.5cm) high.
£2,000-2,200 ART

A bronze figure, Etoile de Mer, by Edouard Drouot, c1900, 28½in (72.5cm) high.
£3,500-4,000 G(L)

A patinated-bronze figure of a naked female, by Auguste Seysses, cast by C. Valsuani, Paris, with marbled green stone base, c1900, 9¾in (50cm) high.
£1,700–2,000 DORO

A gilt-bronze figural lamp, by Georges Flamand, marked, c1905, 23½in (59.5cm) high.
£5,500–6,000 S(NY)

► A gilt-bronze and ivory figure of a cymbal dancer, by Louis Sosson, on a green veined marble base, the right arm formerly holding a cymbal, damaged, c1920, 10½in (26.5cm) high.
£650–750 CAG

A patinated-metal figural lamp, depicting Eros seated on a column amongst leafy branches, early 20thC, 28in (71cm) high.
£700–800 FBG

An ormolu and ivory figure of a dancer, by Henri Louis Levasseur, with marbled stone base, some defects, c1905, 15½in (39.5cm) high.
£2,500–3,000 DORO

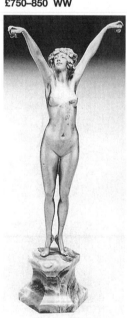

A bronze figure of a maiden dancing and playing a pipe, inscribed 'Matto Sc and Susse Frères', marked, early 20thC, 17in (43cm) high.
£750–850 WW

A patinated-bronze figure of a naked girl, by Claire J. R. Colinet, with arms outstretched, holding castinets, on an onyx base, signed, c1910, 13in (33cm) high.
£650–750 L&T

A gilt-metal and porcelain bust of a maiden, by Napoleon Alliot, with carved ivory face, dressed in northern European Renaissance costume, impressed mark, early 20thC, 21½in (54.5cm) high.
£1,650–2,000 BB(L)

A gilt-bronze figure, entitled 'Sword Dancer', by F. Ouillon Carrère, on a red marble plinth, marked, c1919, 14in (35.5cm) high.
£900–1,100 CAG

Condition

The condition is absolutely vital when assessing the value of an antique. Damaged pieces on the whole appreciate much less than perfect examples. However a rare desirable piece may command a high price even when damaged.

ART NOUVEAU FURNITURE

A pair of Austrian beech beds, probably by J. & J. Kohn, with brass feet, restained and polished, repaired, c1900, 78¼in (199cm) long.
£3,500–4,000 DORO

A pair of white-painted cast-iron bench ends, by Hector Guimard, one marked, c1905, 36¼in (92cm) wide.
£4,500–5,500 S

An inlaid mahogany display cabinet, c1910, 70in (178cm) high.
£1,200–1,350 NAW

An Edwardian mahogany and marquetry-inlaid display cabinet, the bowed astragal-glazed doors enclosing a lined and shelved interior, flanked by ribbon-tied trailing bellflower and paterae panels, with two small drawers below, c1910, 40¼in (102cm) wide.
£3,000–3,500 S(S)

An inlaid mahogany corner display cabinet, the leaded mirrored doors with mother-of-pearl handles, with doors below, early 20thC, 81in (205.5cm) high.
£1,100–1,300 JNic

◄ A mahogany coal box, with brass-covered copper fittings, c1910, 13in (33cm) wide.
£100–125 NAW

A set of four beech chairs, by Thonet or Kohn, with embossed seats, in need of restoration, c1890–95.
£800–1,000 DORO

◄ A pair of Swedish inlaid walnut chairs, by C. H. Benckert, with original leather seats, c1900.
£450–500 AnSh

► A Koloman Moser beechwood and plywood armchair, produced by J. & J. Kohn, model No. 413F, c1904.
£3,300–4,000 S(NY)

An Austrian black-stained elm armchair, designed by Anton Pospischil Jnr, c1900.
£1,200–1,400 DORO

◄ A pair of ebonized side chairs, by Thonet, with caned seats, late 19thC.
£370–450 SK

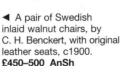

A beechwood Sitzmachine, by Josef Hoffman, designed c1906.
£6,500–7,500 S(NY)

A Dutch mahogany
armchair, design attributed
to K. P. C. de Bazel,
with ebony, fruitwood
and mother-of-pearl
inlay and carved detail,
with contemporary velvet
upholstery, c1910.
£600–700 S(Am)

A bentwood canterbury/
étagère, by Thonet, c1900,
48in (122cm) high.
£600–685 GBr

A beech étagère, designed
before 1904, produced
by Thonet after 1922,
stained light brown,
marked, 45in (114.5cm) high.
£850–950 DORO

A steel and copper
fireplace surround,
the grate surmounted by
a panel of stylized tulips
and a shelf with songbirds,
the mirror in a copper
surround flanked by
shelves with conforming
bird brackets, c1900,
79in (200.5cm) high.
£800–1,000 S(S)

◄ A Continental
giltwood mirror,
the lower half
decorated with
carved scrolls,
silvered and gilt
reeded border,
with curved
reeded flowers,
early 20thC,
22in (56cm) wide.
£370–450 SK

◄ A pair of French carved
mahogany, rosewood
and marble night tables,
possibly by Louis Majorelle,
one with a lower door,
c1900, 15in (38cm) wide.
£5,000–6,000 S(NY)

An inlaid mahogany
sideboard, with mirrored top,
c1910, 59in (150cm) wide.
£2,000–2,200 BLA

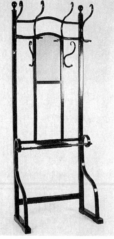

A bent beechwood and
bronze stand, by Thonet,
model No. 9641, c1904,
53in (134.5cm) high.
£6,000–7,000 S(NY)

A beech hall stand,
probably by J. & J. Kohn,
restored, c1900,
80¾in (205cm) high.
£1,300–1,500 DORO

A mahogany-coloured
beech plant stand, by
Thonet, model No. 9537,
1905–10, 22in (55cm) high.
£850–950 DORO

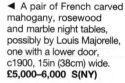

Further Reading

*Miller's Art Nouveau
& Art Deco Buyer's Guide*,
Miller's Publications, 1995

◄ A mahogany inlaid drawing room
suite, comprising nine pieces,
retailed by Liberty & Co, 1903.
£4,000–5,000 JNic

A German satin-walnut
and inlaid bowed
breakfront wardrobe, the
cupboards decorated with
stylized marquetry panels
heightened with mother-
of-pearl, enclosing
hanging space, c1905,
78¾in (200cm) wide.
£800–1,000 P

ART NOUVEAU GLASS

A pair of green glass vases, by Leopold Bauer, moulded in relief with a net-like decoration, c1905, 15½in (39.5cm) high.
£3,000–3,500 S

A Buchenau Glashüttenwerke glass vase, designed by Ferdinand von Poschinger, the grey glass internally decorated in pink, white, green and yellow, c1902, 14in (35.5cm) high.
£2,000–2,400 S

◀ A Daum Nancy cameo glass vase, overlaid in burnt sienna and cut with thorny stems, on a frosted mottled clear and yellow ground, signed, c1900, 19½in (49.5cm) high.
£3,200–3,800 BB(L)

A Burgun, Schverer & Co enamelled and wheel-carved cameo glass vase, decorated in pink, green and gilt, signed, c1900, 9¼in (23.5cm) high.
£6,000–7,000 S(NY)

The Lorraine glass-making company of Burgun, Schverer & Co was founded in 1711. Emile Gallé served a three-year apprenticeship at their factory in Meisenthal in the late 1860s, and in 1885 the company entered into a contract to produce glass for him. The designer Desiré Christian joined the company in the same year.

A Desiré Christian cameo glass vase, overlaid in olive green and rust and cut with poppies, the *martelé* ground shading to clear glass, incised mark, c1900, 12½in (32cm) high.
£1,500–1,800 BB(L)

A Gallé cameo and wheel-carved glass bowl and cover, the opaque ground etched and moulded with brown marine creatures, c1890, 5in (12.5cm) diam.
£6,200–6,800 ART

A Gallé cameo glass landscape vase, overlaid with coloured layers of glass and acid-etched with mountains and trees, c1900, 6in (15cm) high.
£2,000–2,300 ART

An American black glass vase, overlaid with silver flowers, c1900, 12in (30.5cm) high.
£2,200–2,500 ASA

◀ A Gallé cameo glass vase, with shaded yellow glass overlaid in pink and crimson, cut with roses, c1900, 6¼in (16cm) high.
£800–1,000 DuM

A Daum Nancy glass vase, the frosted body internally mottled in orange, white and raspberry red, the surface etched and enamelled with cowslips, signed, 1900–05, 13½in (34.5cm) high.
£2,500–2,750 DORO

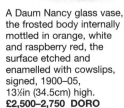

A Gallé gilt and enamelled *vase parlant*, with mottled green and white glass overlaid in white and enamelled in brown and green, with text by Em. Hinzelin, c1905, 15in (38cm) high.
£6,000–7,000 S(Am)

A Gallé cameo glass vase, the frosted body internally decorated in yellow and overlaid in cobalt and violet, signed, 1910–20, 12¼in (31cm) high.
£2,800–3,200 DORO

A Gallé cameo glass vase, the yellow glass overlaid in red and acid-etched in relief with leaves and flowers, c1910, 4in (10cm) high.
£1,400–1,600 ART

A Kosta glass bowl, by Gunnar Wennerberg, with cut and etched pink flowers on a matt white ground, signed, 1900–02, 11in (28cm) diam.
£1,750–2,000 BUK

A Loetz *marqueterie sur verre* vase, the clear glass overlaid and etched with turquoise, chocolate brown and green, 1885–90, 6¼in (16cm) high.
£2,800–3,200 S

A Loetz Phenomen iridescent glass vase, the interior and exterior covered in silver-yellow iridescence, c1900, 6in (15cm) high.
£1,500–1,650 DORO

A Loetz iridescent glass vase, applied with joined loops, c1900, 13½in (34.5cm) high.
£2,000–2,200 BB(L)

A Loetz iridescent glass vase, with silvery blue oil spots on a blood-red ground, c1900, 9½in (24cm) high.
£750–900 BB(L)

A Loetz Cytisus iridescent glass vase, internally decorated in opaque yellow, overlaid with blue threads and silver-yellow oil spots, c1902, 4¾in (12cm) high.
£1,400–1,600 DORO

A Stuart & Sons glass posy vase, with applied stylized clear and amethyst decoration, 1900–10, 12½in (32cm) diam.
£380–400 RUSK

A Müller Frères triple-overlaid cameo glass landscape vase, decorated in chocolate, peach and blue, signed, c1900, 10in (25.5cm) high.
£2,500–3,000 BB(L)

► A Tiffany Favrile glass Feather vase, decorated with blue iridescent pulled feathers rising to red and gold lustre at the top, signed, paper label, damaged and restored, c1895, 20¼in (51.5cm) high.
£1,800–2,000 SK

A Bohemian glass vase, applied with green glass and a pierced brass collar, 1900–10, 8¾in (22cm) high.
£200–240 DORO

A pair of American leaded glass panels, each with a branch of wisteria reserved against a trellis ground, in purple, green and blue striated glass, c1900, 18½ x 19½in (45.5 x 49.5cm).
£1,800–2,200 SK

ART NOUVEAU JEWELLERY

A pearl, diamond and enamel brooch, the rose-cut diamond lobster and grey natural pearl on a pink and green enamelled oyster shell, c1900.
£2,500–2,750 P

A 15ct gold brooch, by Murrle Bennett, centred with a chrysoprase cabochon within a scrolling frame set with two half pearls, stamped and marked, c1900.
£425–500 DN

An insect brooch, by Masriera, the articulated wings and body decorated with polychrome *plique-à-jour* enamel and set with diamonds, supporting two pear-shaped pearl drops, detachable brooch fitting, pendant fitting removed, c1905.
£5,000–5,500 S

A Lalique silver, smoky quartz and citrine bracelet, impressed mark, c1908, 8¼in (21cm) long.
£12,000–13,000 S(NY)

Articulated bracelets by René Lalique are rare.

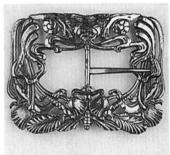

▶ A Schoonhoven silver buckle, designed by Gerrit Greup, stamped marks, c1900, 4in (10cm) wide.
£270–325 S(Am)

A silver belt buckle, designed by Kate Harris, the central section with a girl holding a bowl and surrounded by flowers, retailed by W. G. Connell, mark worn, London 1901, 5½in (14cm) wide, 2oz.
£200–240 Bon

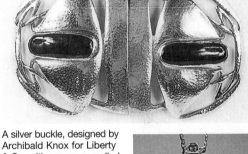

A silver buckle, designed by Archibald Knox for Liberty & Co, with green enamelled inserts, marked, London 1902, 3½in (9cm) wide.
£1,100–1,250 SHa

A hand-beaten silver belt buckle, by W. H. Haseler for Liberty & Co, with green and blue enamel inserts, stamped marks, Birmingham 1909, 3¼in (8.5cm) wide.
£280–325 DAD

▶ A pendant/mirror, the front modelled with a female, the reverse with engraved monogram, the swivel action revealing two mirrors, dated May 1902.
£80–100 P(Ba)

A gold pendant, by James Cromer Watt, decorated with foiled blue enamel and gilt tracery, with central opal and opal drops, marked, c1908.
£5,000–5,500 P

A gold pendant, by Philippe Wolfers, modelled as a crane, the wings decorated with pink *plique-à-jour* enamel and emeralds, with a baroque pearl pendant drop, c1909.
£7,000–8,000 S

A Gallé cameo glass and bronze Chinese butterfly lamp, base and shade signed, c1900, 10½in (26.5cm) high.
£10,000–12,000 S(NY)

A Handel stained glass and patinated brass desk lamp, the shade with mottled ivory and green overlaid panels, shade and base marked, early 20thC, 16¾in (42.5cm) high.
£1,800–2,200 NOA

A Handel bronze and leaded glass lily pad lamp, the shades in white and striated green glass, one petal loose, raised mark, early 20thC, 10¼in (26cm) high.
£2,000–2,400 SK

◀ A Handel reverse-painted glass and bronze lamp, the shade painted with palm trees against a sunset, the bronze base with green patina, signed, early 20thC, 24in (61cm) high.
£800–1,000 DuM

▶ A Jefferson reverse-painted glass table lamp, the shade with a continuous rural dawn landscape, on a patinated metal base, shade and base marked, c1920, 14in (35.5cm) high.
£1,200–1,400 DuM

A Daum Nancy chandelier, by Louis Majorelle, the grey glass shade mottled with salmon pink, with a brass band and patinated bronze frame, cut mark to shade, c1900, 21in (53.5cm) diam.
£2,800–3,200 S

An American gilt-bronze hanging lantern, the shade with violet, blue and white leaded glass, cracks to glass, inscribed 'J. La Farge', late 19thC, 36¾in (93.5cm) high.
£3,200–3,500 BB(L)

A Loetz table lamp, with pink, gold and green iridescent glass globe, supported on patinated bronze leaf and dragonfly shaped mount, 1902, 17in (43cm) high.
£1,500–1,800 S

A Loetz table lamp, designed by Koloman Moser, the white glass shade decorated with blue, the gilt-bronze base with abstract vegetation, c1905, 18½in (47cm) high.
£3,500–4,000 S

◀ A Pittsburgh reverse-painted glass and gilt-metal table lamp, the interior painted with russet and both sides with maple leaves, the base with red and black enamelled highlights, c1915, 25in (63.5cm) high.
£1,800–2,200 SK

A Suess leaded glass and bronze table lamp, with pink, yellow and green shade, c1906, 23½in (59.5cm) high.
£6,000–7,000 SK

Suess Ornamental Glass Company was located at 750–760 Throop Street, Chicago, Illinois.

A Suess leaded glass and bronze table lamp, with caramel, green and red shade, early 20thC, 21½in (54.5cm) high.
£2,000–2,200 SK

A Tiffany Favrile mottled green glass and bronze lamp shade, on an associated green patinated bronze base, impressed metal tag, early 20thC, 23¼in (59cm) high.
£4,750–5,250 BB(L)

◀ A Tiffany Favrile glass candle lamp, the swirled gold iridescent candlestick base with blue lustre and green leaves, with gold to blue iridescent shade, inscribed, c1900, 12¾in (32.5cm) high.
£800–1,000 SK

▶ A WMF silvered-metal figural lamp, the base in the form of a woman with flowing skirts, the shade with coloured glass, faceted inserts and black fringe, 1900–10, 21in (53.5cm) high.
£500–600 BB(L)

A spelter and art glass table lamp, the shade painted internally and externally, the base with raised foliate and heart decoration, early 20thC, 22in (56cm) high.
£650–750 FBG

ART NOUVEAU METALWARE

A pair of Kayserzinn pewter bowls, designed by Hugo Leven, c1900, 13in (33cm) wide.
£500–600 MoS

A Japanese silver-coloured metal bowl, decorated in relief with a band of irises on a textured ground, c1900, 4in (10cm) high.
£1,400–1,700 S

A miniature Prayer Book, with a silver cover by William Hutton & Sons, Birmingham 1904, 2in (5cm) high.
£220–250 SHa

Kayser & Sohn

Kayser & Sohn (1885–c1904), established at Krefeld-Bochum, near Düsseldorf, was one of the first German foundries to produce art pewter, manufactured under the name of Kayserzinn from 1896. Unlike WMF, Kayser did not electroplate their wares, and so they were more akin to ordinary pewter. A strong, malleable alloy of tin, copper and antimony was used which gave a silvery shine when polished.

▶ A W. H. Haseler silver box, for Liberty & Co, the detachable cover applied with a disc depicting a peacock on a blue and green enamel ground, with pale gilt interior, stamped marks, Birmingham 1906, 2in (5cm) diam.
£200–220 DAD

◄ A pewter chamberstick, 1905–10, 4in (10cm) high. **£80–100 AnSh**

A Gallia pewter dish, c1900, 14in (35.5cm) wide. **£350–400 ANO**

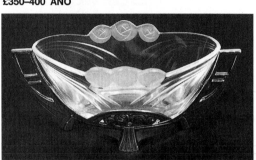

A pewter-mounted glass decanter, c1900, 10in (25.5cm) high. **£400–500 ASA**

A WMF decanter, with silver-plated pewter mounts, 1906, 17in (43cm) high. **£800–1,000 ANO**

◄ A WMF silver-plated pewter and glass bud dish, pierced and chased with rose-heads, the cut-glass liner etched with similar roses, stamped marks, c1905, 5¾in (14.5cm) wide. **£200–225 DAD**

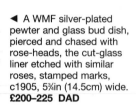

An Edwardian hammered silver bowl, by W. H. Haseler, with twin bifurcated loop handles, pierced with stylized flowerheads, Birmingham 1906, 5¼in (13.5cm) wide, 2½oz. **£200–220 S(S)**

An Edwardian silver double photograph frame, by William Hutton & Sons, the top with green and blue enamelled panels, 1903, 11in (28cm) wide. **£2,500–3,000 P(B)**

An Edwardian silver photograph frame, by Charles S. Green & Co, chased with a young woman picking apples, 1904, 6in (15cm) high. **£320–380 P**

A silver dressing table mirror, repoussé-decorated with flowering tendrils, London 1901, 23 x 16½in (58.5 x 42cm). **£500–600 HYD**

A Liberty & Co silver and enamel picture frame, Birmingham 1907, 7¼in (18.5cm) high. **£700–850 RTo**

A WMF silver-plated hot water kettle, cover, burner and stand, c1906, kettle 11½in (29cm) high. **£170–200 Hal**

◄ A German polished pewter jug with hinged cover, c1900, 13in (33cm) high. **£750–900 ASA**

A Liberty Cymric silver preserve spoon, by Archibald Knox, commemorating the coronation of Edward VII, the bowl inscribed AD1902 EVII, the stem with a ball spacer, stamped marks, Birmingham 1901, 4¼in (11cm) long.
£200–225 DAD

A set of six silver teaspoons, by William Comyns, with pierced and foliate terminals, London 1901, 4½in (11.5cm) long, 2oz.
£220–260 Bon

A pair of silver spoons, with scroll engraved and pierced handles and bowls, marked 'W. B. & S.', Sheffield 1905, in a fitted case.
£140–170 GTH

An Eduard Hueck patinated pewter card tray, designed by Josef Maria Olbrich, c1902, 14in (35.5cm) diam.
£1,600–2,000 MoS

Eduard Hueck was a German metalwork firm, established in 1864.

A silver vase, by Goldsmiths and Silversmiths Co, London 1901, 8in (20.5cm) high.
£270–300 ANO

A silver lily-shaped vase, with beadwork leaves, marked, Birmingham 1907, 13½in (34.5cm) high.
£575–650 SHa

A Tiffany & Co sterling silver vase, by John C. Moore, marked, c1910, 9in (23cm) high.
£1,100–1,250 SHa

A pair of Liberty Tudric silver tulip vases, the handles in the form of stems of foliage, c1910, 9¾in (25cm) high.
£700–850 P

An Augarten Mokka yellow porcelain coffee set, by Josef Hoffmann, comprising 17 pieces, marked, 1930s, pot 6¾in (17cm) high.
£3,000–3,300 S

A Beswick hand-decorated and glazed ceramic wall mask of a lady, 1930s, 12in (30.5cm) high.
£650–750 TF

A table lamp base, by Boch Frères, decorated with vines and fruits in yellow, brown and blue on an oatmeal ground, stamped, c1928, 24¼in (61.5cm) high.
£200–240 SK

A Crown Ducal Manchu pattern lamp base, by Charlotte Rhead, decorated with a gilt dragon on a green ground, 1930s, 8in (20.5cm) high.
£350–400 PAC

◄ A Crown Ducal Autumn Leaves pattern charger, by Charlotte Rhead, with tube-lined decoration in orange and green, c1935, 14¼in (36cm) diam.
£150–180 Mit

A Crown Ducal baluster vase, by Charlotte Rhead, decorated with blue and pale mauve stylized foliage on a mottled grey ground, marked, 1930s, 8½in (21.5cm) high.
£120–130 GAK

A Goldscheider ceramic model of a face mask, decorated in colours, on a black wood base, marked, 1933–34, 13in (33cm) high.
£380–420 DORO

A Crown Ducal Byzantine pattern vase, by Charlotte Rhead, decorated in blue, red, yellow, green and beige on a mottled beige ground, c1932, 10½in (26.5cm) high.
£350–380 CoCo

A Gouda Corona pattern vase, designed by W. P. Hartgring, painted by A. M. Rÿp in orange, beige, blue and green on a dark olive ground, 1920, 12in (30.5cm) high.
£450–500 OO

► An American Newcomb Pottery vase, by Joseph Meyers, decorated by Sadie Irvine, with green and pink flowers in relief on a deep blue ground, 1926, 8¼in (21cm) high.
£1,400–1,600 JMW

A Goldscheider ceramic double face mask, decorated in cream, orange and black, 1930s, 13½in (34.5cm) high.
£675–750 BEV

An American flambé vase, decorated in tones of brown and red, 1920–30, 10¼in (26cm) high.
£1,200–1,500 DSG

◄ An American Newcomb Pottery, vase, by Henrietta Bailey, decorated in relief with pink flowers and green foliage on a cobalt ground, 1926, 4¼in (11cm) high.
£900–1,000 JMW

A Poole Pottery oviform vase, decorated by Ruth Pavely, in blue and beige on a cream ground, 1928–34, 10in (25.5cm) high.
£575–650 ADE

A De Porceleyne Fles earthenware vase, designed by Jaap Gidding, decorated with a blue pattern on a white ground, marked, c1933, 7¾in (19.5cm) high.
£1,800–2,200 S(Am)

A Longwy Primavera faïence vase, moulded with a mythological ram and bird, with two nudes in a stylized landscape, decorated in ivory, turquoise, blue, purple and black, marked, c1925, 12½in (32cm) high.
£1,700–2,000 SK

An American Rookwood Pottery Yellow Vellum moulded vase, by Lenora Asbury, decorated with beige and green, Ohio, 1924, 6¼in (16cm) high.
£500–550 JMW

An American Roseville Pottery Vista vase, decorated with green trees on a light blue ground, faults, c1920, 17¾in (45cm) high.
£730–800 SK

▶ A Wedgwood Fairyland lustre plate, decorated with Roc Bird pattern, with crimson and violet imps on a bridge, blue sky and water, the gilt printed Twyford border on an orange lustre ground, c1925, 10½in (26.5cm) diam.
£1,300–1,500 TEN

The designs featured on Fairyland lustre wares were unusual for the 1920s and hark back more to 1900. However, the modern shapes and bright colours made them popular.

An American Rookwood Pottery moulded Wax Matte vase, by Katherine Jones, decorated with green and red stylized foliage on a terracotta ground, Ohio, 1923, 4¼in (11.5cm) high.
£500–550 JMW

An American Rookwood Pottery Vellum glaze vase, by Ed Diers, decorated with blue wisteria on a cream ground, marked, 1926, 13½in (34.5cm) high.
£2,800–3,200 JAA

▶ A pair of Wedgwood Fairyland lustre vases, designed by Daisy Makeig-Jones, decorated with Butterfly Women pattern in blue, green and gilt, marked, 1920s, 9½in (24cm) high.
£2,750–3,000 S

CLARICE CLIFF

A Clarice Cliff vase, decorated with Persian Inspiration pattern, c1929, 7½in (19cm) high.
£450–550 S

A Clarice Cliff Lotus jug, decorated with Football pattern, 1929–30, 10in (25.5cm) high.
£4,500–5,500 G(L)

A Clarice Cliff vase, shape no. 269, decorated with Applique Lugano Blue pattern in blue, orange, yellow, red and green, c1930, 6in (15cm) high.
£2,000–2,400 P

► A Clarice Cliff cigarette and match holder, Shape No. 463, decorated with Red Gardenia pattern, printed marks, slight damage, c1931, 2¾in (7cm) high.
£450–500 Bon

A Clarice Cliff cream jug, decorated with Football pattern, in orange, green, blue, black and yellow, 1929–30, 3¼in (8.5cm) high.
£440–480 CoCo

A Clarice Cliff Bizarre vase, decorated with Applique Lucerne pattern in blue, orange, red and green within black line edging, marked, No. 370, c1930, 6¼in (16cm) high.
£8,000–9,000 M

The Applique range was decorated in high-quality enamels, and was particularly desirable in its day. This example is in excellent condition.

A Clarice Cliff octagonal plate, decorated with Applique Idyll pattern, early 1930s, 7½in (19cm) diam.
£300–350 Hal

A Clarice Cliff conical coffee service, comprising 20 pieces, decorated with Pebbles pattern, with coloured ovals on an orange ground, marked, 1928.
£650–800 S(S)

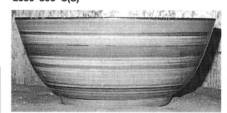

A Clarice Cliff Bizarre hand-painted bowl, with striped pattern, 1929–30, 7in (18cm) diam.
£75–100 MAR

A Clarice Cliff bowl, decorated with Orange Roof Cottage pattern in red, yellow, green and mauve, slight damage, 1932, 7in (18cm) diam.
£240–280 Hal(C)

A Clarice Cliff fruit bowl, decorated with pink, yellow and mauve flowers and green leaves on a cream ground, 1930s, 9in (23cm) diam.
£150–165 UNI

► A Clarice Cliff Bizarre vase, decorated with Persian pattern in blue, turquoise and purple, damaged, c1930, 8½in (21.5cm) high.
£160–200 JD

A Clarice Cliff Bizarre preserve pot and cover, decorated with Delecia Pansies pattern in mauve, red, yellow and green, marked, c1932, 5in (12.5cm) high.
£300–350 DD

A Clarice Cliff Newport Pottery sugar caster, decorated with My Garden pattern in grey, orange and brown, 1934–40, 5¾in (14.5cm) high.
£160–200 PFK

▶ A pair of Clarice Cliff Teddy Bear bookends, 1930s, 5¼in (13.5cm) high.
£1,500–1,800 G(L)

A Clarice Cliff Bon Jour sugar sifter, decorated with Coral Firs pattern in red, orange and brown, 1933–39, 12½in (32cm) high.
£550–600 TRM

▶ A Clarice Cliff Biarritz platter, decorated with Coral Firs pattern in orange, yellow and sand, 1933–39, 12¼in (31cm) diam.
£300–350 LJ

A Clarice Cliff Conical tea-for-two, comprising nine pieces, decorated with Honolulu pattern in orange, yellow and black with green rim, marked, 1933–35.
£5,500–6,000 S(S)

A Clarice Cliff jug, decorated with a variant of My Garden pattern, with embossed flowers to the handle in orange, green and brown on a light tan ground, marked, 1936–40, 9¼in (23.5cm) high.
£180–220 SK

A Clarice Cliff Bon Jour tea-for-two, comprising seven pieces, decorated with blue café-au-lait Cowslip pattern in blue, green, red and black, marked, c1933, teapot 5¼in (13.5cm) high.
£1,700–2,000 P

A Clarice Cliff Newport Pottery conical shaped coffee service, decorated with Moonflower pattern, 1933.
£1,500–1,800 LT

A Clarice Cliff Marilyn wall mask, with green beret and red hair, marked, 1930s, 9in (23cm) high.
£2,400–2,700 S(S)

A Clarice Cliff Lotus jug, decorated with Blue Chintz pattern in blue, green and pink, 1930s, 10in (25.5cm) high.
£1,000–1,200 G(L)

A Clarice Cliff bowl, decorated with Orange Capri pattern in orange, yellow, ochre and brown, marked, c1935, 7¼in (18.5cm) diam.
£80–100 MCA

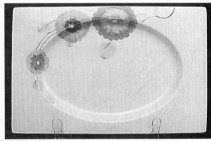

A Clarice Cliff Biarritz platter, decorated with Rhodanthe pattern in orange, yellow and brown, marked, c1935, 13¾in (35cm) wide.
£100–110 LJ

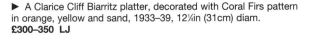

ART DECO CLOCKS

An Austrian brass wall clock, designed by Adolf Loos, c1920, 14¼in (36cm) diam.
£5,000–6,000 DORO

A rock crystal, diamond and enamel comet clock, the pale blue guilloche enamel dial with a diamond star indicating the hours and a smaller star indicating the minutes, within a white enamel and gold chapter ring and diamond border, on a rock crystal frame with matching stand, c1920, 2½in (6.5cm) diam.
£10,500–12,000 P

► A Roland mantel clock, the brown and black marble clock with bronze face and malachite panel, flanked by two 'invocation to the sun' cold-painted bronze and ivory figures, c1930, 12¼in (31cm) high.
£1,000–1,100 S

A Lalique opalescent glass clock, entitled 'Deux Colombes', moulded with two birds over a glass clock face, Waltham Watch Co electric movement, signed 'R. Lalique', c1926, 8¾in (22cm) high.
£3,000–3,500 BB(L)

A Zuid-Holland earthenware clock, designed by C. J. van der Hoef, 1929, 11¾in (30cm) high.
£1,000–1,200 S(Am)

A patent dated 1933 accompanying the clock explains the mechanism as a money-box. It runs for one week at the drop of a silver guilder.

A glass clock, attributed to René Lalique, with etched figures and flowers in frosted and colourless glass surrounding the clock, on a metal base, c1926, 13½in (34.5cm) wide.
£4,500–5,000 SK

ART DECO WATCHES

A Longines diamond wristwatch, marked, c1925, 6in (15cm) long.
£750–900 S

A Cartier 18ct gold concealed watch, by Movado Ermeto, the case with machine-finished closing covers, marked, c1928, 2in (5cm) wide.
£600–700 Bon

A cocktail watch, the dial set with diamonds and sapphire detail, with a seed pearl bracelet, c1925, 6¼in (16cm) long.
£1,500–1,800 Bon

► A Rolex 18ct white gold and diamond watch, c1930, 1¼in (3cm) long.
£2,000–2,400 TWD

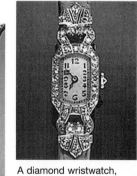

A diamond wristwatch, 1925–35.
£320–380 Bon

◄ A cocktail wristwatch, the bezel set with rubies and diamonds, with a similarly set stepped baton shoulder, c1940.
£650–750 P

ART DECO FIGURES

A brown-patinated bronze figure, entitled 'Amazon', by Marcel Bouraine, cast as a kneeling naked female holding a spear and shield, marked, c1925, 32in (81.5cm) wide.
£7,000–8,000 S

A Goldscheider ceramic group, designed by Stefan Dakon, decorated in colours, c1920, marked, 15in (38cm) high.
£2,750–3,250 DA

A bronze figure of a dancer, cast from a model by Lorenzl, marked, 1920–30, 13in (33cm) high.
£850–1,000 JD

◀ A cold-painted bronze and ivory figure, possibly by Lorenzl or Dakon, 1930s, 6¼in (16cm) high.
£850–1,000 ASA

▶ A cold-painted gilt spelter match striker, surmounted by a female figure, c1930, 9in (23cm) high.
£125–150 CARS

A Katzhütte figure of a female, with a blue drape, c1930, 12in (30.5cm) high.
£380–425 HarC

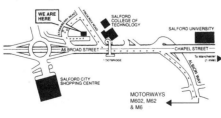
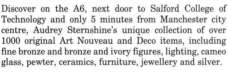

A burr-walnut dressing cabinet, with ivory handles, c1930, 31¼in (79.5cm) wide.
£1,500–1,650 S(S)

A French fruitwood drop-front secretaire, with mirrored top and fitted interior, c1940, 31½in (80cm) wide.
£5,500–6,000 S(NY)

An Austrian walnut cubist chair, c1925.
£575–650 DORO

A mahogany armchair, designed by Josef Frank, manufactured by Svenskt Tenn, model No. 695, with black hide upholstery and brass studs, renovated, 1935.
£850–1,000 BUK

A pair of rattan chairs, by Heywood Wakefield, with gold mock hide seats, one with an arm fitted for a newspaper, c1935, 30½in (77.5cm) high.
£500–550 SK

Shagreen or Galuchat

Shagreen, also known as Galuchat after the gentleman who brought it to prominence in 18thC France, is a material made from the skin of the spotted dogfish (a small member of the shark family) which is found around the coast of France. The skin has a distinct pattern to it, consisting of small dense circles lying closely packed together. When used to decorate furniture, the skin is soaked in a solution containing chlorine to bleach it, and then cut into equal sections and applied to the surface of the wood with glue, in much the same way as veneer may be used. It has a very exotic effect and can either be left bleached, varnished or tinted in pastel colours, most commonly green or pink.

Shagreen became popular again in the 1920s and '30s. It was used by a number of Art Deco designers on furniture and small items such as boxes.

A set of six pale blue shagreen side chairs, by Karl Springer, signed, mid-20thC.
£8,000–9,000 SK

A French macassar ebony desk and armchair, the frieze drawer covered with galuchat, the top with conforming galuchat central panel, the armchair upholstered in cream leather, c1930, desk 55in (139.5cm) wide.
£11,500–14,000 S

A mahogany chest of drawers, with three canted and zigzag drawers and sides, square patinated metal drawer pulls, the legs in a lighter shade of mahogany, c1935, 30½in (7.5cm) wide.
£1,200–1,300 SK

A French wrought-iron and marble console and mirror, c1930, 35¾in (91cm) high.
£8,000–9,000 S(NY)

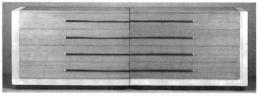

A pair of American walnut and maple chests of drawers, designed by Gilbert Rohde, manufactured by Herman Miller, with four long projecting drawers with black-painted metal rod pulls, late 1930s, 45in (114.5cm) wide.
£2,500–2,750 BB(L)

A bird's-eye maple and mahogany-crossbanded bedroom suite, comprising seven pieces, 1930s, dressing table 49in (124.5cm) wide.
£500–550 DD

A maple dining suite, with satinwood inlay, comprising table, six chairs with cream leather upholstered seats, and a sideboard, 1930s, table 72in (183cm) long.
£1,500–1,800 AH

A sycamore and ebonized lounge suite, by Maurice Adams, comprising four pieces, c1935.
£3,000–3,500 P

A maple card table, with reversible top, 1920–30, 26in (66cm) wide.
£900–1,000 OOLA

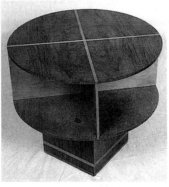

A walnut circular occasional table, with crossbanded inlay, the lower tier raised on a square base, c1930, 21in (53.5cm) diam.
£150–180 BTB

A Token Works rippled maple dressing table and stool, designed by Betty Joel, with graduated corner shelves opposing swivel-mounted drawers with ivory scallop shell handles and a central mirror, c1937, dressing table 68in (172.5cm) wide.
£2,000–2,200 S

A pair of bird's-eye maple tables, on oval fluted columns, 1930s, 29in (73.5cm) high.
£2,700–3,000 Hal

► An oak tiered geometric occasional table, retailed by Bowman, 1930s, 23in (58.5cm) high.
£180–200 BTB

A mahogany and boxwood-strung writing/dressing table, designed by Josef Frank for Svenskt Tenn, model No. 991, damaged, 1939, 55¼in (140.5cm) wide.
£1,000–1,200 BUK

A French *pâte-de-verre* vase, by Gabriel Argy-Rousseau, decorated with brown gazelles and yellow flowers, c1928, 3¾in (9.5cm) high.
£6,500–7,000 S(NY)

An etched and sand-blasted glass vase, by Aristede Colette, with a black glass base, inscribed, c1930, 15in (38cm) high.
£8,000–9,000 S(NY)

A Daum glass vase, acid-etched in relief and enamelled with a landscape scene, c1920, 3½in (9cm) high.
£1,500–1,700 ART

A Daum brown glass vase, acid-etched in bold relief, c1930, 13in (33cm) high.
£2,500–2,800 ART

A Degué cameo glass vase, the frosted baluster form overlaid with mottled orange glass and acid-etched with stylized sailing boats and waves, 1930s, 16¼in (41.5cm) high.
£1,500–1,650 S(S)

A Gray-Stan oviform bottle vase, with streaked yellow and brown internal decoration, c1930, 11in (28cm) high.
£550–620 RUSK

An American Fry Foval Art pearl glass tea set, comprising 16 pieces, each piece with a silver rim, c1920, teapot 6½in (16.5cm) high.
£550–600 SK

▶ A Gallé mould-blown cameo glass vase, the grey glass infused with lemon yellow, overlaid with lime green and deep amber and moulded in medium and low relief with branches and apples, signed, c1925, 11½in (29cm) high.
£6,000–7,000 S(NY)

A French opalescent moulded glass bowl, by Julien, 1930s, 12in (30.5cm) diam.
£65–75 PIL

A Lalique glass bowl, entitled 'Perruches', moulded with budgerigars, 1931–47, 9¼in (23.5cm) diam.
£1,500–1,800 GAK

A Lalique opalescent glass powder-box and cover, entitled 'Houppes', signed, 1920s, 5⅛in (14cm) diam.
£700–850 PSG

A Lalique opalescent glass dish, entitled 'Poissons No. 1', marked, 1931–47, 12in (30.5cm) diam.
£400–450 RUSK

A Lalique opalescent glass box and cover, entitled 'Cyprins', moulded with fish, 1921–47, 10in (25.5cm) diam.
£1,200–1,400 ART

A set of six Lalique moulded glass bowls, entitled 'Lotus', with black enamelled flowerhead centres, c1930, 5in (12.5cm) diam.
£320–360 DAC

A Monart pumice-effect glass vase, with off-white interior, pitted blue/green iridescent surface, c1930, 10in (25.5cm) high.
£1,000–1,200 RUSK

An Orrefors glass bowl, by Vicke Lindstrand, with facet-cut sides, raised on a black foot, marked, 1930s, 8in (20.5cm) diam.
£220–240 RUSK

A Schneider smoky glass stemmed bowl, with applied and acid-etched decoration, minor chips, signed, 1924–25, 11½in (29cm) high.
£600–700 BUK

A Steuben gold Aurene glass candlestick, No. 7613, the tulip-form with spiral leaf shaft, signed, c1920, 12in (30.5cm) high.
£1,750–2,000 DuM

A Fachschule Steinschönau covered glass jar, decorated with coloured enamels, c1920, 5in (12.5cm) high.
£475–550 DORO

A Stevens & Williams glass vase, designed by Keith Murray, wheel-carved with cactus, c1933, 15½in (39.5cm) high.
£2,200–2,800 ALiN

A Tiffany iridescent dimpled glass vase, No. T4013, engraved initials for Louis Comfort Tiffany, 1920s, 2in (5cm) high.
£120–140 Hal

A Vasart glass vase, internally decorated with splashes of colour against a white and pink fleck, cased in clear glass, c1930, 4in (10cm) high.
£45–55 BLA

► A James Powell, Whitefriars gold amber glass decanter, part of a wine service designed by Barnaby Powell, c1930, 15in (38cm) high.
£150–180 RUSK

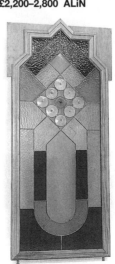

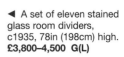

A Viennese purple glass beaker, 1910–15, 6¼in (16cm) high.
£600–700 DORO

◄ A set of eleven stained glass room dividers, c1935, 78in (198cm) high.
£3,800–4,500 G(L)

ART DECO LIGHTING

An Amsterdam School stained glass lamp, the panels decorated with an expressionist pattern in shades of brown, blue and purple, 1920s, 9½in (24cm) high.
£1,400–1,700 S(Am)

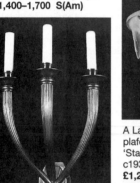

A pair of polished steel three-light sconces, designed by Paul Kiss, marked, c1930, 18¼in (46.5cm) high.
£3,500–4,000 BB(L)

► A wrought-iron and glass chandelier, the shade decorated with floral and geometric motifs, minor damage to glass, c1925, 37¾in (96cm) high.
£1,750–2,000 S

A chromed-metal six-light chandelier, each arm with an alabaster shade, 1930s, 32in (81.5cm) high.
£650–720 SK

A Daum acid-etched smoky glass lamp, marked, c1925, 16½in (42cm) high.
£2,500–3,000 BB(L)

A Lalique frosted glass plafonnier, entitled 'Stalactites', marked, c1930, 10⅜in (27.5cm) diam.
£1,200–1,400 P

A Daum acid-etched opaque glass lamp, signed, c1930, 14in (35.5cm) wide.
£7,000–7,800 ART

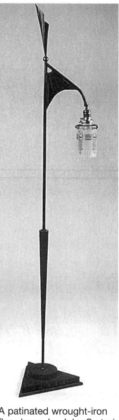

A patinated wrought-iron floor lamp, by John Sartori, with striated bronze finish, later frosted and colourless green glass shade of geometric design, c1930, 69¼in (176cm) high.
£500–600 SK

A set of four wall lights, each silvered-metal frame supporting a frosted glass shade moulded with flowers and abstract patterns, slight damage, 1930s, 15¾in (40cm) diam.
£2,750–3,000 S

An Editions Etling ceramic lamp, by Marcel Guillard, the ceramic base designed as a sphere within a cube, cream and grey crackle glaze, with a metal-framed ochre-coloured paper shade, marked, c1927, 16½in (42cm) high.
£450–500 SK

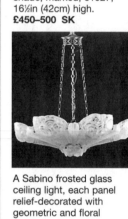

A Sabino frosted glass ceiling light, each panel relief-decorated with geometric and floral motif, marked, 1930s, 27¼in (69cm) diam.
£1,150–1,350 S

A spelter figural lamp, with a marble base and glass globe, rewired, c1930, 23in (58.5cm) high.
£450–500 BTB

A French silver-plated and green Bakelite bracelet, stamped 'Deposé', 1930s, 1¾in (4.5cm) high.
£220–250 LBe

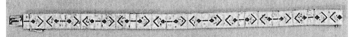

An American 14ct gold bracelet, by Carter, Gough & Co, with three carved jade plaques separated by openwork red and black enamel spacers, marked, 1932, 7in (18cm) long.
£1,500–1,650 SK

A geometric design diamond bracelet, consisting of nine panels, c1930, 6¾in (17cm) long.
£2,000–2,400 HYD

An onyx and diamond brooch, c1925.
£1,400–1,600 Bon

A silver and paste brooch, 1925–35, 1¾in (4.5cm) wide.
£200–240 DORO

A jadeite, diamond, coral and black enamel brooch, c1925.
£3,200–3,600 P

An emerald and diamond brooch, c1925.
£900–1,000 P(Ed)

A rock crystal and diamond clip brooch, c1925.
£2,200–2,600 Bon

A diamond double clip brooch, c1930.
£7,000–8,000 GTH

A French platinum, onyx, diamond and pearl brooch, 1930s, 3in (7.5cm) wide.
£600–700 JSM

A French silver marcasite plaque brooch, centred with synthetic blue spinel, 1930, 2in (5cm) wide.
£70–80 JSM

A pair of Art Deco gold-coloured cufflinks, each plaque centred with a raised diamond collet.
£1,000–1,100 P

A sapphire and diamond panel ring, c1930.
£850–1,000 DN

Insurance Values

Always insure your valuable antiques for the cost of replacing them with similar items, regardless of the original price paid. Both dealers and auctioneers will provide a valuation service for a fee.

ART DECO METALWARE

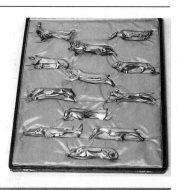

► A set of Cristofle Gallia silvered-metal knife rests, each modelled as a stylized animal, in a presentation case, c1920, box 11in (28cm) wide.
£850–950 ART

An Asprey's silver-plated cocktail shaker, 1930s, 8½in (21.5cm) high.
£450–550 ASA

A Wiener Werkstätte silver goblet, designed by Josef Hoffmann, c1920, 9in (23cm) high.
£4,300–4,800 ANO

A pair of Georg Jensen silver fish servers, each decorated with a dolphin, c1930, in a fitted case, 12in (30.5cm) long.
£900–1,000 S

A Charles Boyton silver sweetmeat stand, on a turned ivory stem, marked, London 1934, 4¾in (12cm) diam.
£500–600 F&C

A silvered-bronze tantalus, by Jacques Adnet, the glass bottles by Baccarat, c1935, 13in (33cm) wide.
£1,400–1,600 ART

A silver sugar caster, by Hamilton & Inches, with detachable pierced and moulded cover, Edinburgh 1937, 6in (15cm) high, 7oz.
£200–240 WW

► A Swedish faceted silver teapot, designed by Wiwen Nilsson, 1930s, manufactured 1947, 8½in (21.5cm) high.
£5,500–6,500 BUK

A Mappin & Webb silver toast rack, Sheffield 1938, 4in (10cm) wide.
£60–65 ASAA

Auction or Dealer?

All the pictures in our price guides originate from auction houses and dealers. When buying at auction, prices can be lower than those of a dealer, but a buyer's premium and VAT will be added to the hammer price. Equally, when selling at auction, commission, tax and photography charges must be taken into account. Dealers will often restore pieces before putting them back on the market.

Both dealers and auctioneers will provide professional advice, so it is worth researching both sources before buying or selling your antiques.

A silver tureen, by Evald Nielsen, with ivory handles, c1930, 11¼in (28.5cm) wide.
£3,400–3,750 SFL

DESIGN 1860-1945

A brass & beaten metal clock by Margaret & Frances MacDonald, circa 1895. Sold for £29,900.

'Les Amis de Toujours', A cold-painted & patinated bronze & ivory figural group by Dimitri Chiparus, circa 1920. Sold for £13,800.

Two William De Morgan lustre ware chargers, circa 1880's. Each sold for £2,300.

'Les Loups Dans La Neige', a pate-de-verre vase by Gabriel Argy-Rousseau, circa 1926. Sold for £13,800.

Items for inclusion in these sales are accepted throughout the year and we are happy to give free valuations, either in person or by means of an adequate photograph, with a view to selling through Phillips.

For further details please call Mark Oliver or Johanna Freidwall on (020) 7468 8367.

101 New Bond Street,
London W1Y 9LG
www.phillips-auctions.com

Phillips
INTERNATIONAL
AUCTIONEERS & VALUERS

FOUNDED 1796

An American Aesthetic Movement secretaire cabinet, probably by Herter Bros, New York, late 19thC, 42in (106.5cm) wide.
£3,700–4,000 NOA

An American Aesthetic Movement parcel-gilt, inlaid and ebonized cherrywood cabinet, by Herter Brothers, New York, altered, c1880, 38¼in (97cm) wide.
£4,000–4,500 BB(L)

An Aesthetic Movement ebonized and gilded side cabinet, c1875, 30in (76cm) wide.
£900–1,100 TF

A set of four American Aesthetic Movement brass-mounted oak side chairs, by Herter Brothers, New York, c1880.
£65,000–80,000 S(NY)

An Aesthetic Movement mahogany and painted screen, c1875, each panel 24in (61cm) wide.
£6,000–7,000 S

An Aesthetic Movement walnut, thuyawood, ebonized and parcel-gilt dressing table, by Henry Ogden & Sons, Manchester, c1880, 49¾in (126.5cm) wide.
£1,600–1,800 S

An Aesthetic Movement painted pine three-piece bedroom suite, c1880, dressing table 54in (137cm) wide.
£1,350–1,600 P(S)

An Aesthetic Movement burr-oak triple wardrobe, c1880, 72in (183cm) wide.
£1,000–1,200 WBH

An Arts and Crafts walnut and figured mahogany bookcase, in the style of John Ednie, probably by Wylie & Lockheed, c1900, 69in (175.5cm) wide.
£4,500–5,000 DAD

An Arts and Crafts oak display cabinet, 1890–1910, 36in (91.5cm) wide.
£320–400 AnSh

An Arts and Crafts walnut metamorphic library chair, with ceramic tile panel by J. Moyr Smith, c1878.
£1,300–1,500 S

◄ An Arts and Crafts oak firescreen, with original crewel work, c1890, 35in (89cm) high.
£275–300 GBr

A set of six Arts and Crafts dining chairs, with moulded splats, c1900.
£575–650 NAW

An Arts and Crafts oak settle, the panelled back inset with embossed copper roundels, c1900, 54in (137cm) wide.
£1,700–2,000 CRI

A Barum Ware terracotta vase, by C. H. Brannam for Liberty & Co, c1905, 11in (28cm) high.
£270–300 DAD

A Litchdon pottery vase, by C. H. Brannam, decorated by Frederick Braddon, 1909, 13¾in (35cm) high.
£400–450 HAM

A William de Morgan twelve-piece tile panel, forming a meandering river with fish and stylized flowers, 1888–97, each tile 6in (15cm) square.
£5,750–7,000 S(S)

◄ A Ruskin high-fired vase, dated '1908', 5¾in (14.5cm) high.
£1,500–1,650 S

A Dunmore crackle-glazed vase, c1900, 10½in (26.5cm) high.
£215–240 SQA

An American Arts and Crafts vase, by Hampshire Pottery, 1904–18, 9in (23cm) high.
£340–380 JMW

A silver-coloured metal beaker, with beaded edges, by Josef Hoffmann for the Wiener Werkstätte, 1905, 2½in (6.5cm) high.
£2,000–2,200 S

An Arts and Crafts copper-mounted oak book trough, c1905, 10in (25.5cm) wide.
£250–275 DAD

A wooden fruit bowl, decorated with pen and ink Celtic design and applied enamelled cabouchons, c1890, 11in (28cm) diam.
£375–425 ANO

An Arts and Crafts copper charger, c1890, 23in (58.5cm) diam.
£220–245 GBr

A Guild of Handicraft silver and enamel sugar bowl, cover and spoon, the design attributed to C. R. Ashbee, stamped maker's and London marks, bowl and cover 1906, spoon 1905, 5¾in (14.5cm) diam.
£1,800–2,200 S(NY)

An Arts and Crafts hammered copper lantern, c1900, 14in (35.5cm) high.
£220–250 JW

An American Arts and Crafts Handel bronze desk lamp, c1900, 16½in (42cm) high.
£750–900 DuM

A silver tea caddy, with blue and green inserts, early 20thC, 3¾in (9.5cm) high.
£1,200–1,500 ASA

A Gallé fruitwood marquetry cabinet, c1900, 25in (63.5cm) wide.
£8,000–10,000 S(NY)

A pair of mahogany chairs, inlaid with an Art Nouveau design to back splat, c1900.
£425–475 NAW

A Dutch Art Nouveau mahogany and fruitwood cupboard, attributed to K. P. C. de Bazel, c1905, 39¼in (99.5cm) wide.
£1,500–1,650 S(Am)

► A J. & J. Kohn stained beech three-piece salon suite, designed by Koloman Moser, c1901, sofa 49½in (125.5cm) wide.
£4,000–5,000 S

A Louis Majorelle ormolu-mounted mahogany and rosewood cabinet, c1900, 78in (198cm) wide.
£9,000–10,000 S(NY)

◄ An Edwardian inlaid mahogany music cabinet, the central door inlaid with an Art Nouveau tulip and enclosing folio shelves, 35¾in (91cm) wide.
£2,300–2,750 TEN

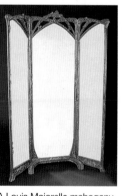

A Louis Majorelle mahogany-framed cheval mirror, c1900, 83in (211cm) high.
£1,500–1,800 TEN

A Glasgow school mahogany display cabinet, the central panel inlaid with abalone shell, boxwood and harewood, c1910, 39½in (100.5cm) wide.
£2,300–2,750 TRM

An Art Nouveau stained walnut firescreen, 40in (101.5cm) wide.
£240–280 PFK

An Art Nouveau mahogany and mother-of-pearl-inlaid display cupboard, c1900, 68in (172.5cm) wide.
£4,500–5,000 BB(L)

An oak armchair, designed by Henry van de Velde, restored, c1900.
£1,800–2,200 BUK

◄ A pair of Thonet armchairs, designed by Otto Prutscher, dark brown stained, reupholstered, c1910.
£3,300–4,000 DORO

A Gallé marquetry-inlaid side table, signed, c1900, 29½in (75cm) wide.
£900–1,000 ANO

A Gallé marquetry-inlaid writing table, c1900, 39½in (100.5cm) wide.
£2,750–3,000 BB(L)

An earthenware inkwell, designed by Adrien Dalpayrat, the gilt-bronze mount designed by Edward Colonna, 1898–1903, 6¼in (16cm) diam.
£900–1,100 S(Am)

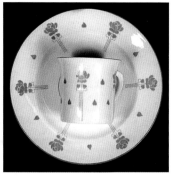

A Foley Peacock tea cup and side plate, designed by George Logan, c1900, plate 7in (18cm) diam.
£55–65 DAD

A Gouda Zuid-Holland ceramic plate, 1905–10, 6in (15cm) diam.
£130–145 ANO

A K. & Co Losol ware Tulip pattern soup tureen, cover and stand, designed by George Logan, c1910, stand 14½in (37cm) wide.
£500–550 DAD

▶ A Gouda Zuid-Holland vase, painted by Johannes Hartgring, c1910, 16¾in (42.5cm) high.
£1,000–1,250 OO

A Gouda Zuid-Holland twin-handled pottery vase, 1910, 16½in (42cm) high.
£2,200–2,500 OO

A Minton Secesssionist jardinière, two restored chips, printed and impressed factory marks to base, c1900, 10½in (26.5cm) high.
£350–420 BLH

A Linthorpe pottery vase, designed by Christopher Dresser, with incised decoration around the neck, 1879–82, 9in (23cm) high.
£750–850 NCA

An American Newcomb College Pottery high-glaze vase, decorated by Marie DeHoa LeBlanc, signed, 1903, 6½in (16.5cm) high.
£8,000–10,000 NOA

An American Newcomb College Pottery vase, by Joseph Fortune Meyer, decorated by Sarah Irvine, impressed marks, dated '1918', 6¼in (16cm) high.
£4,000–4,500 BB(L)

A Pilkington Lancastrian lustre vase, c1900, 3½in (9cm) high.
£280–350 ASA

A Pilkington Royal Lancastrian lustre bottle vase, 1920s, 6¾in (17cm) high.
£450–500 ASA

A Pilkington Lancastrian lustre bottle vase, c1910, 12in (30.5cm) high.
£800–1,000 ASA

A Rörstrand porcelain twin-handled vase, by Alf Wallander, moulded with swans, signed, c1900, 14¾in (37.5cm) high.
£6,500–8,000 BUK

A Rozenburg 'eggshell' porcelain coffee pot, painted by Rudolf Sterken, c1900, 10in (25.5cm) high.
£2,500–3,000 OO

A Rozenburg Juliana ware baluster vase and cover, 1911–12, 20in (51cm) high.
£2,000–2,250 OO

◄ A Zsolnay faïence jug, factory marks, c1895, 9¾in (25cm) high.
£600–700 DORO

A Rozenburg 'eggshell' porcelain vase, 1911–12, 4¾in (12cm) high.
£800–1,000 OO

A Zsolnay lustre vase, with all-over decoration of small birds perched amid foliage, applied seal to base, c1900, 14½in (37cm) high.
£1,800–2,200 P

A Doulton Lambeth Slaters patent stoneware vase, 1880–1900, 10in (25.5cm) high.
£280–325 BEV

A pair of Doulton figural ewers, by Mark Marshall, incised 'M.V.M', c1885, 32¼in (82cm) high.
£5,500–6,500 P

◀ A Martin Brothers saltglazed stoneware jug, 1893, 9¾in (25cm) high.
£1,200–1,400 Bon

▶ A William Moorcroft vase, for Liberty & Co, decorated with Eventide Landscape pattern, with Tudric pewter cover and base, stamped, c1925, 8¼in (21cm) high.
£3,500–4,000 DAD

A Royal Doulton Sung vase, c1920, 7½in (19cm) high.
£1,500–1,700 JE

A Royal Doulton 'Chinese Jade' model of a pair of cockatoos, c1935, 4⅓in (11.5cm) high.
£800–900 DSG

A pair of Moorcroft Florian ware vases, decorated with Japanese carp pattern, c1902, 11¾in (30cm) high.
£19,000–21,000 G(L)

A Daum internally-decorated acid-etched and enamelled glass vase, 1900–05, with relief signature, 13½in (34.5cm) high.
£2,000–2,400 DORO

A Gallé internally-coloured gourd bottle, engraved mark, c1900, 6in (15cm) high.
£3,200–3,800 S

A Moser Karlsbad glass, with cut, etched and gilded decoration, c1905, 10in (25.5cm) high.
£240–265 ANO

A Daum acid-etched and enamelled glass vase, with etched gilding around base, c1910, 9in (23cm) high.
£2,800–3,200 ART

A Loetz iridescent blue glass vase, c1900, 7½in (19cm) high.
£1,000–1,200 BB(L)

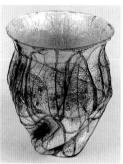

A Stevens & Williams Silveria vase, signed, c1900, 6in (15cm) high.
£5,000–6,000 ALiN

Silveria glass was developed by John Northwood II by enclosing silver foil between two layers of clear glass.

A Daum silver-mounted jug, c1910, 4in (10cm) high.
£1,200–1,350 ART

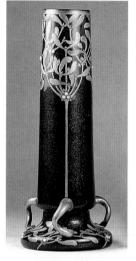

A Legras enamelled glass vase, painted with gilt mistletoe pattern and white dots, gilt signature 'Mont Joye', c1900, 17½in (44.5cm) high.
£1,800–2,200 DORO

A Pilkington Lancastrian mallet-shaped peach bloom lustre trial vase, c1908, 8½in (21.5cm) high.
£500–550 PGA

▶ An American leaded-glass window, depicting a neo-classical figure within a landscape of trees, late 19thC, 75½ x 54½in (192 x 135cm).
£3,200–3,800 BB(L)

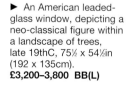

A Gallé cameo glass vase, acid-etched to leave clematis in relief, c1900, 8in (20.5cm) high.
£1,300–1,500 ASA

A Loetz iridescent blue baluster-shaped jug, c1910, 6¾in (17cm) high.
£430–470 RUSK

A Steuben Aurene blue glass vase, inscribed, early 20thC, 10¼in (26cm) high.
£950–1,100 BB(L)

A pair of champlevé enamel, opal and diamond pendant earrings, by René Lalique, c1900.
£9,000–10,500 S

▶ An Art Nouveau *plique-à-jour* enamel and gem-set pendant, by Philippe Wolfers, with *pâte-de-verre* female mask and with emerald and pearl detail, signed, c1902.
£50,000–55,000 Bon

A gold, *plique-à-jour* enamel and diamond bracelet, by Masriera, c1920, 7¼in (18.5cm) long.
£22,000–25,000 S

An Art Nouveau pewter box, inset with emerald-green stones, 1900–05, 3in (7.5cm) wide.
£350–400 ANO

A German silver rosebowl, by Friedrich Adler, c1902, 4½in (11.5cm) wide.
£800–900 SUC

A pair of Art Nouveau copper ice pails, with brass handles, c1910, 9in (23cm) high.
£400–450 ASA

An Art Nouveau embossed copper jug, with hinged cover and brass finial, stamped 'JS & S', c1900, 11in (28cm) high.
£100–125 DAD

▶ A cranberry glass vase, with silver overlay, by Alvin & Co, c1905, 10in (25.5cm) high.
£2,000–2,200 SFL

A pair of silver-plated chambersticks, by W. A. S. Benson, impressed marks, c1900, 10in (25.5cm) long.
£475–525 RUSK

A French Art Nouveau pewter thermometer, with standing cherub, c1900, 10½in (26.5cm) high.
£280–325 ANO

◀ A Swedish Art Nouveau silver and *plique-à-jour* enamel stemmed cup, by C. G. Hallberg, Stockholm, faults, stamped, 1899, 7in (18cm) high.
£2,750–3,250 S(Am)

A silver-coloured metal hand mirror, attributed to Josef Hoffmann, slight damage to glass, c1905, 9¾in (25cm) wide.
£21,000–23,000 S

▶ A Liberty & Co Tudric pewter jug, designed by Archibald Knox, with hinged lid and wicker-covered handle, c1900, 8in (20.5cm) high.
£500–600 ASA

A Liberty & Co set of six silver and enamel teaspoons, designed by Archibald Knox, stamped and hallmarked, 1926, 4¼in (11cm) long.
£675–750 DAD

A pair of French Art Nouveau candelabra, signed 'A. Perron', c1900, 21in (53.5cm) high.
£2,000–2,200 ANO

▶ A hammered copper vase, designed by Frans Zwollo Sr, set with turquoise stones, with original pewter liner, stamped mark, c1905, 5in (12.5cm) high.
£1,500–1,650 S(Am)

An 18ct gold bonbonnière, by Georg Jensen, designed by Johan Rohde, 1919, 5in (12.5cm) high.
£32,000–35,000 BUK

An American Art Nouveau silver-plated tyg, by E. G. Webster & Son, Brooklyn, c1900, 12in (30.5cm) high.
£500–550 NOA

A Bigelow & Kennard leaded glass and brass floor lamp, c1910, 69in (175.5cm) high.
£9,500–10,500 S(NY)

A Handel glass and patinated bronze Peacock Tail table lamp, early 20thC, 23in (58.5cm) high.
£750–900 NOA

A Gallé cameo glass table lamp, acid-etched and wheel-carved with morning glory, c1920, 12in (30.5cm) high.
£10,000–11,000 ART

▶ A French Art Deco gilt-bronze and onyx gazebo-form lamp, the figure cast after a model by Marcel Bouraine, shade possibly associated, c1925, 17¾in (45cm) high.
£1,500–1,800 BB(L)

A Gallé cameo glass lamp, c1900, signed, 21¼in (54cm) high.
£8,000–9,000 BB(L)

A Pairpoint interior-painted 'puffy' glass and metal Rose Bouquet lamp, impressed mark, early 20thC, 21in (53.3cm) high.
£12,000–14,000 BB(L)

A Tiffany Favrile glass poppy shade, with tags for Tiffany Studios, New York, 1898–1928, 17in (43cm) diam.
£40,000–45,000 BB(L)

A Hector Guimard gilt-bronze and glass hanging lamp, inset with four glass panels, c1912, 13in (33cm) square.
£8,000–9,000 S

A Tiffany Favrile glass and bronze acorn table lamp, stamped 'Tiffany Studios', c1900, 22¾in (58cm) high.
£10,000–12,000 DuM

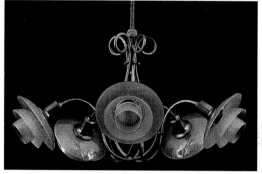

A patinated brass chandelier, by Paul Henningsen for Louis Poulsen, with amber-coloured glass shades, slightly chipped, 1930s.
£3,000–3,500 BUK

A Handel reverse-painted glass and bronze lamp, signed, early 20thC, 23½in (59.5cm) high.
£13,000–15,000 DuM

A Jugendstil bronze three-light table lamp, with inlaid glass stones, 1900–05, 26in (66cm) high.
£1,700–2,000 DORO

A reverse-painted glass table lamp, early 20thC, 20in (51cm) high.
£500–550 DuM

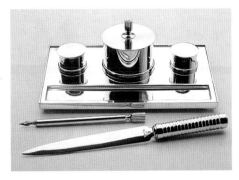
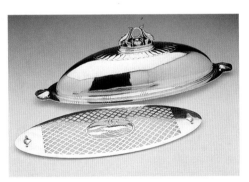

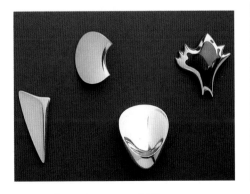

An Art Nouveau gilt-bronze figure, entitled 'Flore', after a model by Julien Caussé, repaired, marked, c1900, 20½in (52cm) high.
£1,300–1,500 BB(L)

A gilt-bronze and bone figure of a fisherwoman, by Fritz Heinemann, with marble base, slight damage, signed, c1900, 16in (40.5cm) high.
£1,400–1,600 BUK

A Demêtre H. Chiparus cold-painted bronze figure, entitled 'Cleopatra', marked, 1920s, 12¾in (32.5cm) wide.
£12,500–14,000 S

An Art Deco gilt-bronze and ivory figure, entitled 'Les Larmes', cast and carved after a model by Demêtre Chiparus, with a marble base, repaired, signed, c1925, 12in (30.5cm) high.
£2,200–2,500 BB(L)

A Goldscheider ceramic figure, designed by Josef Lorenzl, slight damage, marked, 1926–28, 10in (25.5cm) high.
£1,200–1,400 DORO

◄ A cold-painted bronze and ivory figure, entitled 'Cabaret Girl', cast and carved from a model by Ferdinand Preiss, 1920–30, 15¾in (40cm) high.
£12,000–15,000 ASA

An Art Deco patinated and gilt-bronze and ivory figure, entitled 'Danseuse d'Ankara', cast and carved after a model by Claire Jeanne Roberte Colinet, repaired, signed, c1925, 17in (43cm) high.
£15,000–18,000 BB(L)

A G. Argy-Rousseau *pâte-de-cristal* figure, entitled 'La Baigneuse', after a model by Marcel Bouraine, slight damage, c1928, 10in (25.5cm) high.
£4,500–5,000 BB(L)

A bronze figure, cast from a model by Henri Godet, replacement hands to the timepiece, c1900, 15in (38cm) high.
£1,800–2,000 ANO

A cold-painted bronze and ivory figure, entitled 'The Flute Player', cast and carved from a model by Ferdinand Preiss, 1920–30, 16½in (42cm) high.
£10,000–12,000 ASA

A Goldscheider polychrome pottery figure, from a model by Josef Lorenzl, black printed factory marks, c1930, 8¼in (21cm) high.
£550–600 Bon(C)

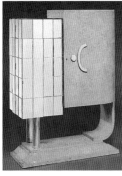

A burr-walnut and peach mirrored glass cocktail cabinet, by Ray Hille for Hille, c1935, 43¼in (101cm) wide.
£1,600–2,000 P

An Omega Workshop chest of drawers, painted by Roger Fry, c1919, 39in (99cm) wide.
£5,000–6,000 Bon

An Amsterdam School mahogany and rosewood sideboard, the design attributed to Piet Kramer, c1920, 43¼in (110cm) wide.
£5,500–6,000 S(Am)

An Art Deco amboyna and ivory-inlaid bedroom suite, by Jules Leleu, comprising bed, dressing table and two bedside cabinets, c1930, bedstead 59in (150cm) wide.
£6,250–7,000 BB(L)

A German Art Deco painted side cabinet, early 20thC, 55in (139.5cm) wide.
£2,200–2,500 L&E

An Art Deco palisander desk and chair, with sycamore detail, by Louis Sognot, marked, 1930s, desk 96½in (245cm) wide.
£14,000–17,000 S

An Art Deco amboyna bedroom suite, comprising double bed and two bedside cabinets, c1925, bed 63½in (160.5cm) wide.
£1,500–1,800 BB(L)

An Art Deco macassar ebony dining table and 12 armchairs, by Axel Einar Hjort, for Nordiska Kompaniet, 1934, table 98½in (250cm) long.
£14,000–16,000 BUK

An Art Deco rosewood draw-leaf dining table, inlaid with fruitwood marquetry and abalone, attributed to Jules Leleu, c1935, 78in (198cm) long.
£6,250–7,500 S(NY)

A pair of ebonized armchairs, re-upholstered, c1930, 32in (38.5cm) high.
£1,200–1,500 BTB

A Swedish Art Deco ash desk, by Alex Einar Hjort for Nordiska Kompaniet, renovated, 1935, 69¼in (176cm) wide.
£8,000–9,000 BUK

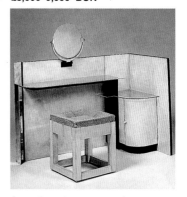

A parchment, macassar ebony and silvered-bronze dressing table, by Louis Sognot, marked, c1935, 50½in (128.5cm) wide.
£4,000–5,000 S(NY)

An Art Deco burr-walnut occasional table, 1930s, 26in (66cm) wide.
£180–200 BTB

A Boch Frères Keramis glazed stoneware vase, possibly designed by Charles Catteau, painted monogram 'C', c1925, 12in (30.5cm) high.
£200–240 AAV

A Susie Cooper, Grays Pottery, banded coffee can, 1930s, saucer 4½in (11.5cm) diam.
£80–100 CoCo

A Burleigh ware Budgie jug, 1930s, 8in (20.5cm) high.
£550–650 BEV

A Carlton Ware lustre vase, decorated with Heron and Magical Tree pattern, printed and impressed marks, 1930s, 9½in (24cm) high.
£1,600–2,000 RTO

A George Clews & Co Chameleon ware jug, printed and painted marks, c1935, 9in (23cm) high.
£100–120 DD

A Crown Devon vase, 1930s, 15in (38cm) high.
£450–550 CoCo

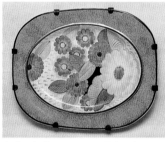

A Crown Ducal vase, decorated with floral pattern, 1930s, 9in (23cm) high.
£85–110 CoCo

A Gouda vase, by W. P. Hartgring, decorated with Marantha pattern, Arnhem, Holland, c1925, 11in (28cm) high.
£550–650 OO

A Gouda wall plate, painted by Henri Breetvelt, c1920, 14¼in (36cm) high.
£350–450 OO

A Gray's Pottery Paris milk jug, 1930s, 4in (10cm) high.
£140–180 CoCo

A Gray's Pottery meat dish, 1930s, 16in (40.5cm) wide.
£220–260 CoCo

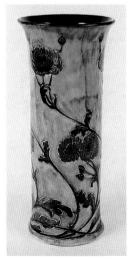

◄ A Morris Ware vase, by E. Hancock & Son, designed by Geo. Cartlidge, 1930s, 9¼in (23.5cm) high.
£320–400 ASA

An Art Pottery vase, by Jugtown Pottery, North Carolina, decorated with a 'Chinese Translation' glaze, c1930, 5¾in (14.5cm) high.
£440–480 JMW

A Longwy glazed earthenware charger, decorated with Printemps Fleur pattern, by M. P. Chevalier, stamped factory marks, c1925, 14½in (37cm) diam.
£600–700 BB(L)

A John Maddock & Son
hand-painted Ball vase,
c1930, 7in (18cm) high.
£150–165 BEV

A John Maddock & Son
Sunset Ware vase, 1930,
7in (18cm) high.
£150–165 BEV

A Melba Merrygo nursery service, 1930s,
teapot 5in (12.5cm) high.
£320–350 BEV

A Minton sugar shaker,
1930s, 5in (12.5cm) high.
£55–65 CoCo

A Myott Fan vase, 1930s,
8½in (21.5cm) high.
£180–220 CoCo

 ◀ A Myott Poppies jug,
1930s, 8¾in (22cm) high.
£140–180 CoCo

A Myott Pyramid vase,
1931–36, 8¾in (22cm) high.
£130–160 CoCo

A Poole Pottery vase,
by Mary Brown, c1930,
9¼in (23.5cm) high.
£700–800 DSG

A Quimper vase,
signed by M. Fouillon,
c1920–30, 6in (15cm) high.
£80–100 SER

A tube-lined vase, designed
by Charlotte Rhead, 1935,
7in (18cm) high.
£180–200 HEW

An American Rookwood
Pottery moulded vase,
1930, 9in (23cm) high.
£380–420 JMW

A Crown Ducal Byzantine plate,
designed by Charlotte Rhead, 1930,
14in (35.5cm) diam.
£250–300 BEV

▶ An American Roseville Pottery
Windsor moulded bowl, c1931,
7in (18cm) wide.
£340–380 JMW

▶ An American
Van Briggle
Pottery moulded
vase, covered
with a Persian
Rose glaze,
c1920, 9¾in
(25cm) high.
£475–525 JMW

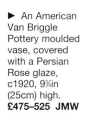

A Wedgwood Fairyland
lustre malfrey pot and
cover, designed by Daisy
Makeig-Jones, printed and
painted with the Ghostly
Wood pattern, 1920s,
13¾in (35cm) high.
£11,500–13,500 S(S)

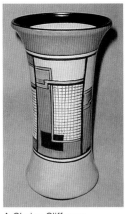

A Clarice Cliff vase,
decorated with Football
pattern, black Bizarre mark,
c1929, 11¼in (28.5cm) high.
£5,000–6,000 PFK

A Clarice Cliff Lotus jug,
decorated with Original
Bizarre pattern, printed
factory marks, faults,
c1930, 11½in (29cm) high.
£1,300–1,500 DD

A Clarice Cliff Fantasque Bizarre part tea service,
comprising 21 pieces, decorated with Berries pattern,
printed factory marks, some faults, c1930.
£4,000–5,000 RTo

A Clarice Cliff Fantasque bowl,
decorated with Farmhouse pattern,
moulded and printed marks and
facsimile signature, slight chips,
c1931, 6in (15cm) diam.
£450–550 Hal

A Clarice Cliff plate, decorated
with Red Roofs pattern, 1931,
9in (23cm) diam.
£220–260 CoCo

A Clarice Cliff bonbon basket and
six triangular dishes, decorated with
Delecia Citrus pattern, 'Bizarre' and
'Newport Pottery' marks, 1932,
basket 8¼in (21cm) wide.
£850–1,000 WW

A Clarice Cliff Dover flower holder,
painted with Canterbury Bells
pattern, c1932, 7in (18cm) diam.
£550–600 HEW

A Clarice Cliff Lynton coffee set,
comprising 15 pieces, decorated
with Blue Firs pattern, 'Bizarre' mark
and facsimile signature, c1933,
coffee pot 7½in (19cm) high.
£3,400–4,000 P

A Clarice Cliff Tankard coffee
set, comprising 15 pieces, decorated
with Alton pattern, 'Bizarre'
mark and facsimile signature,
c1933, coffee pot 7½in (19cm) high.
£2,600–3,200 P

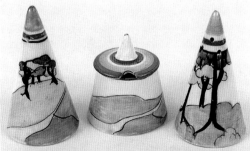

A Clarice Cliff Conical cruet set, decorated with Blue Firs
pattern, c1933, tallest 3¼in (8.5cm) high.
£1,000–1,200 ASA

A Clarice Cliff Isis jug,
decorated with Forest
Glen pattern, c1935,
10½in (26.5cm) high.
£2,700–3,200 LT

A Clarice Cliff vase,
moulded in relief with
budgerigar and foliate
stylized handle, 1930–40,
8¾in (22cm) high.
£280–320 G(B)

A *pâte-de-verre* vase, by Gabriel Argy-Rousseau, signed, c1925, 9in (23cm) high.
£9,000–10,000 ART

A Gallé cameo glass vase, decorated with daffodils, 1920–30, 10in (25.5cm) high.
£1,800–2,200 ASA

▶ A Legras glass bowl, enamelled with flowers on a frosted ground, relief signature, c1920, 8in (20.5cm) diam.
£475–575 DORO

A Steuben Pomona double-etched green glass vase, drilled for a lamp, c1920, 13in (33cm) high.
£2,500–3,000 DuM

A Maurice Marinot bottle and stopper, underside stamped 'marinot', c1925, 6in (15cm) high.
£11,000–12,000 S

A Lalique moulded and frosted glass vase, entitled 'Poivre', inscribed, 1921, 9½in (24cm) high.
£3,700–4,000 S(NY)

A Marcel Goupy enamelled glass vase, signed, c1925, 9in (23cm) high.
£2,000–2,200 BB(L)

◀ A James Powell Whitefriars wave ribbed lamp base, 1920s, 10in (25.5cm) high.
£300–340 RUSK

A Monart glass bowl, with everted rim, 1930s, 7in (18cm) diam.
£200–225 SAN

A Monart glass bowl, with flared sides, 1930s, 17in (43cm) diam.
£650–750 RUSK

A Gray-Stan ginger jar and cover, marked, c1930, 7in (18cm) high.
£280–320 RUSK

A Jobling Jazz pattern bowl, 1930s, 8in (20.5cm) diam.
£100–110 PIL

A James Powell Whitefriars threaded flared bowl, 1930s, 12½in (32cm) diam.
£230–260 RUSK

▶ A Daum glass vase, with acid-etched decoration, c1930, 6in (15cm) high.
£1,100–1,250 ART

An Art Deco gilt and patinated bronze figural clock, inscribed 'G. Prieur, Brest', c1925, 13¼in (33.5cm) high.
£1,300–1,500 BB(L)

A Lalique moulded and frosted glass clock, entitled 'Deux Figurines', on a patinated-bronze base, introduced 1926, 15¼in (38.5cm) high.
£10,000–12,000 S(NY)

An Art Deco diamond and blue jasperware brooch, c1930.
£2,000–2,400 P(L)

An Art Deco jade and diamond brooch, c1925.
£2,000–2,400 Bon

► A Georg Jensen silver centrepiece with cover, c1945, 15in (38cm) wide.
£18,000–20,000 SFL

A sapphire, emerald and diamond clip, c1930.
£4,500–5,500 S

A Jean Goulden silvered metal and enamelled cigarette case, c1929, 3¼in (8.5cm) wide.
£4,000–4,500 S

A Georg Jensen silver fish dish and cover, signed 'Johan Rhode', c1930, 30in (76cm) wide.
£40,000–45,000 SFL

► An Art Deco wrought-iron hall stand, c1925, 27½in (70cm) wide.
£1,650–2,000 BB(L)

An Art Deco silver five-piece tea and coffee set, by MM. Boulenger, Paris, with rosewood handles and finials, c1930, tray 23¼in (59cm) wide, 149oz in total.
£5,500–6,000 S

A Georg Jensen silver three-piece dressing table set, 1925–33, hairbrush 8¾in (22cm) long.
£450–550 BUK

A Georg Jensen silver stemmed bowl, 1930s, 4¼in (11cm) high.
£650–800 ASA

A Wiener Werkstätte postcard, autographed by Gustav Klimt and addressed to Emilie Flöge, 1909.
£1,700–1,850 S

An Art Deco carpet, some damage, c1930, 127 x 101in (322.5 x 256.5cm).
£7,500–9,000 S(NY)

A pair of Swedish birch armchairs, designed by
Alvar Aalto for Artek, 1935–6, manufactured 1945–55.
£4,500–5,500 BUK

A moulded plywood high
back chair, designed by
Gerald Summers,
manufactured by makers
of Simple Furniture, c1938.
£4,000–5,000 P(Ba)

A set of four Swedish dark
stained pine garden chairs,
designed by Alvar Aalto,
1938–39.
£5,000–5,500 S

A blonde wood cabinet supported on a palisander frame,
by Jean Royère, c1950, 70in (178cm) wide.
£6,000–6,750 S

▶ A mahogany coffee table and six stools, designed
by Frank Lloyd Wright, 2000 Series, c1956, coffee table
47in (119.5cm) wide.
£2,000–2,400 BB(L)

An Arflex four-piece suite,
by Marco Zanuso, designed in 1951.
£1,800–2,200 WBH

An American Coconut chair,
designed by George Nelson
for Herman Miller, the steel shell
supported on metal rod legs, 1955.
£2,500–3,000 P(Ba)

An Alu chromium-plated metal-framed
armchair and stool, by Herman
Miller, designed by Charles and
Ray Eames, 1958.
£900–1,100 S

◀ A pair of Danish theatre
armchairs, by Poul
Henningsen, with black
lacquered steel tube
frames and copper
back splats, 1957.
£600–700 BUK

An upholstered
beechwood armchair,
by Heal & Son, 1930s.
£250–300 BTB

A Danish cone chair,
designed by Verner
Panton, 1958, with fabric-
covered foam over
moulded sheet metal,
manufactured 1960s.
£700–800 PLB

◀ A set of six Danish cone
chairs, for Fritz Hansen, 1959.
£2,000–2,400 WBH

A plywood 'long chair', designed by Marcel Breuer for Isokon, 1936.
£3,000–3,500 RBB

A purple Tongue chair, by Pierre Paulin for Artifort, c1970.
£950–1,150 MARK

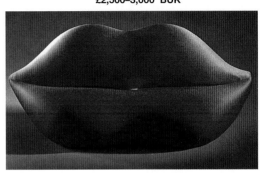

A Danish oak-framed Corona armchair, designed by Paul Volther for Eric Jörgensen, 1961.
£2,500–3,000 BUK

A bar stool, by Zoftig, Bude, Cornwall, 1960s.
£280–350 ZOOM

An Ultrafragola fibreglass-framed mirror, designed by Ettore Sottsass for Poltronova, c1970, 39¼in (99.5cm) wide.
£1,700–2,000 BUK

A Bocca sofa, designed by Studio 65 in 1970, for Gufram, Turin, 1986, 82¾in (210cm) wide.
£2,400–2,750 DORO

A stoneware plate, by Shoji Hamada, c1930, 10in (25.5cm) diam.
£4,500–5,500 Bon

A Dame Lucie Rie pottery vase, Vienna, c1930, 7in (18cm) high.
£5,250–6,000 S

A Form 2000 coffee service, comprising 21 pieces, designed by Heinrich Löffelhardt, made by Arzberg Porcelain Factory, Germany, three settings in red and three in blue, 1954–77, coffee pot 8in (20.5cm) high.
£2,500–3,000 DORO

A pottery bowl, by Elizabeth Fritsch, c1972, 9½in (24cm) diam.
£4,250–5,000 P

◄ A Kosta glass vase, 1970s, 5in (12.5cm) high.
£80–100 PIL

A Fili Policromi glass vase, by Seguso Vetri d'Arte, 1952, 11¾in (30cm) high.
£1,300–1,500 FF

A Pezzato glass bottle vase, by Fulvio Bianconi for Venini, Murano, etched signature, 1950s, 14½in (37cm) high.
£4,750–5,500 BUK

◄ An A. Toussaint tapestry, 1950s, 77 x 55in (195.5 x 139.5cm).
£2,500–3,000 S

An American Macchia blown glass bowl, by Dale Chihuly, signed, 1985, 22in (56cm) wide.
£8,000–9,000 S(NY)

An exhibition poster for Stuttgart 1968, celebrating 50 years of the Bauhaus, by Herbert Bayer, 23 x 12¼in (58.5 x 31cm).
£300–350 P(Ba)

An 18ct gold and tourmaline pendant and ring, set with diamonds, by Andrew Grima for the H. J. Co, 1966, pendant 3in (7.5cm) long.
£3,500–4,500 DID

◄ A two-branch desk lamp, designed by Carl Hagenauer, with revolving brass supports, the tinplate shades punched with designer's name, c1950, 21in (53.5cm) high.
£850–1,000 DORO

Twentieth-Century Design
CERAMICS

A stoneware jar, by William Staite Murray, the thick cream glaze with light blue and rust speckles, incised mark, 1922, 6¾in (17cm) high.
£850–1,000 P

An earthenware dish, by Michael Cardew, decorated with a yellow slip-trailed stag, impressed mark, c1930, 17½in (44.5cm) diam.
£5,500–6,500 Bon

A stoneware pot and cover, by Katharine Pleydell-Bouverie, shiny brown and with a carved frieze, impressed marks, c1930, 3½in (9cm) diam.
£700–850 Bon

A stoneware dish, by Bernard Leach, with speckled green and brown glaze, five unglazed areas in the well, impressed marks, c1932, 10¼in (26cm) diam.
£650–750 Bon

An American yellow glazed bowl, by Maija Grotell, Cranbrook Academy, Michigan, signed, 1934–46, 6¾in (17cm) diam.
£1,100–1,250 JMW

A German stoneware vase, by Otto Lindig, with beige and brown glaze, marked, c1935, 4¼in (11cm) high.
£900–1,100 P(Ba)

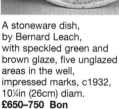

A stoneware flagon, by Helen Pincombe, the thick glossy light grey glaze covering an underglaze wavy design in brown and plum, incised mark, 1936, 9½in (24cm) high.
£250–300 Bon

A Corrida Verte series ceramic platter, by Pablo Picasso, painted in blue, green, red, white and black, stamped 'Madoura Pottery' and 'Empreinte Originale de Picasso', 1949, 14in (37cm) wide.
£1,800–2,200 FBG

A stoneware vase, by Charles Vyse, with celadon glaze, incised mark, 1936, 9¼in (23.5cm) high.
£700–850 Bon

◄ A Spode Velamour vase, with light brown glaze, 1940–50, 10¾in (27.5cm) high.
£50–60 DSG

► A Wedgwood stoneware vase, the brown body with glazed top and white spout, impressed mark for J. Dermer, mid-20thC, 11¼in (28.5cm) high.
£550–600 SK(B)

A stoneware vessel, by Hans Coper, the brown body with an incised white spiral, impressed mark, c1956, 14¾in (37.5cm) high.
£5,500–6,500 P

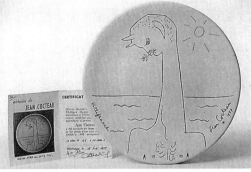

A limited edition ceramic plate, entitled 'Chèvre-Pied au Long Cou', by Jean Cocteau, decorated with ceramic crayons and highlighted with slip, signed, dated, marked '11/40', with certificate of origin, 1957, 12¼in (31cm) diam.
£800–1,000 P(Ba)

A Pearsons & Co cream-glazed ceramic vase, 1950s, 12in (30.5cm) high.
£65–75 DSG

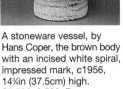

A Swedish Farstaware vase, by Wilhelm Kåge, Gustavsberg Studio, with vertical stripes in yellow, blue-green and brown glaze, signed, 1950s, 17½in (44.5cm) high.
£2,200–2,600 BUK

A blue and white tin-glazed bowl, by Alan Caiger-Smith, 1960, 10½in (26.5cm) diam.
£85–95 IW

A milk jug, cup and saucer, by Dame Lucie Rie, brown and white with sgraffito lines, impressed mark, c1960, jug 5in (12.5cm) high.
£550–650 P

A stoneware bottle vase, by Shoji Hamada, blue and brown-glazed, with panels of abstract motifs, 1963, 9½in (24cm) high.
£4,000–4,500 Bon

A stoneware pot, by Janet Leach, the grey-green glaze with vertical blue stripes, impressed marks, c1965, 5½in (14cm) high.
£350–420 Bon

A pottery bowl, by Dame Lucie Rie, with brown-speckled off-white glaze, impressed mark, c1982, 7in (18cm) wide.
£1,700–2,000 Bea(E)

◄ A Norwegian Stavangerflint plate, painted in green, yellow and black with a bird, 1960s, 8in (20.5cm) diam.
£25–30 MARK

A Swedish Höganäs pottery vase, by Yngve Blixt, with shiny green and beige glaze, 1966, 39in (99cm) high.
£1,250–1,500 BUK

A Danish Royal Porcelain Factory stoneware vase, by Gerd Bogelund, with diamond-shaped relief decoration in shades of green, brown and beige glaze, signed, 1967, 11in (28cm) high.
£380–450 BUK

A Troika pottery vase, with speckled brown glaze, 1970s, 7¾in (19.5cm) high.
£75–85 MARK

FURNITURE

A set of six ash ladderback chairs, by Gordon Russell, with leather lattice seats, five with metal labels, 1925.
£700–800 Bri

A limed oak part dining room suite, by Heals, London, comprising eight dining chairs, a sideboard and side table, early 20thC, side table 36in (91.5cm) wide.
£2,300–2,750 S(S)

A chromed tubular steel and plywood armchair, attributed to Mart Stam, designed 1928.
£400–500 P(Ba)

A set of six SP9 chromed tubular steel and red Rexine dining chairs, two with arms, by Rowland Wilton-Cox for Pel, stamped brass labels, 1932–34.
£700–800 P(Ba)

A Makers of Simple Furniture birch-veneered moulded plywood armchair, designed by Gerald Summers, with a drop-in sprung seat, designed 1933–34.
£4,000–4,500 Bon

A birch plywood sideboard, by Harry Mansell for Isokon, the four doors enclosing slides to one side and a shelf with bottle rack, c1937, 54in (137cm) wide.
£800–1,000

A laminated and bent birch-veneered low bookstand, by Egon Riss for Isokon, 1930s, 23½in (59.5cm) wide.
£1,100–1,300 Bri

The bookstand is known as the Penguin Donkey and was designed for storing Penguin paperbacks.

A Table B 10 chrome-plated steel-framed table, by Marcel Breuer for Thonet, with blue lacquered pine top, damaged, 1930s, 29in (73.5cm) wide.
£2,300–2,750 BUK

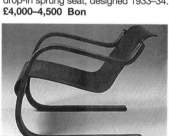

A plywood and laminated armchair, by Alvar Aalto, model No. 379, known as the Springleaf, 1932.
£1,600–2,000 Bon

A fruitwood two-tier table, by Gerald Summers, with black-painted edges, 1930s, 29in (73.5cm) diam.
£2,000–2,200 S

◀ A pair of armchairs with removable cushions, by Hans Wegner for Getama, designed 1951.
£600–700 Bon

An Artlight green anodised aluminium illuminated table, 1940s, 24in (61cm) diam.
£350–400 BTB

◀ A Noguchi table, designed in 1947 by Isamu Noguchi, probably for Herman Miller, USA, the three-sided glass top on a stained poplar base, 50¾in (129cm) wide.
£1,200–1,400 BUK

A Heywood Wakefield blonde wood corner table, model No. 311, marked, c1955, 44in (112cm) wide.
£300–350 SK

An American Dunbar oak desk, with cream-coloured laminated writing surface, the centre drawer flanked by shallow and deep drawers, mid-20thC, 50in (127cm) wide.
£300–350 SK

An asymmetrical chromium-plated table, model No. PK 61, by Poul Kjaerholm, with detachable grey and black veined alabaster top, marked, designed 1956, 31½in (80cm) square.
£1,400–1,600 S

A Form Group unit four-seat seating system, by Robin Day for Hille, each with ebonized plywood back with grey, cream and black striped tweed fabric, with a coffee table and pad seat, on black-enamelled squared steel frames, 1961, each frame 83in (211cm) wide.
£1,000–1,200 P(Ba)

► A Tandem Sling seating unit, by Charles and Ray Eames for Herman Miller, the two pairs of seats separated by a table, with cast aluminium steel frame and charcoal grey vinyl seats, designed 1962.
£1,000–1,200 Bon

A Johannes Hansen walnut valet chair, model No. PP250, the seat hinged to reveal a well, designed c1953.
£1,500–1,800 SK

A pair of steel-framed and leather chairs, by Poul Kjaerholm for E. Kold Christensen, model No. PK22, designed 1957.
£600–700 P(Ba)

A polished steel table and four chairs, with Lloyd Loom seats, 1950s.
£3,200–3,500 ZOOM

A red wool-covered chair, by Oswaldo Borsani for Tecno, model No. P40, with adjustable metal frame, elastic armrests and hinged footrest, designed 1956.
£850–1,000 Bon

A laminated plywood and black leather chair and ottoman, by Charles and Ray Eames for Herman Miller for Hille, model Nos. A670 and 671, some restoration, labelled, designed 1956.
£800–1,000 Bon

A pair of American bird chairs and a footstool, designed by Harry Bertoia, manufactured by Knoll Associates, model No. 423LU, manufacturer's label, c1958.
£600–700 SK

A desk, by Warren Platner, with a rust-coloured leather writing surface, leather-covered frieze drawer and conforming computer table, each with a chromium-plated metal base, c1960, desk 89¾in (228cm) wide.
£1,300–1,500 S

A black-painted wood credenza, by Florence Knoll for Knoll International, with white-veined black marble top, c1961, 74¾in (190cm) wide.
£2,500–2,750 S

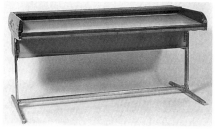

An Action office desk, designed by George Nelson for Herman Miller, with steel frame and a stained wood roll top, 1964, 65¾in (167cm) wide.
£850–1,000 DORO

A leather and matt chromed steel armchair, model No. PK31, designed in 1958 by Poul Kjaerholm for E. Kold Christensen, signed, 1960s.
£175–200 BUK

An American chrome and black child's chair, by Virco, Los Angeles, 1960s, 23½in (59.5cm) high.
£80–100 ZOOM

A Japanese sycamore nest of tables, 1960s, largest 23¾in (60.5cm) wide.
£180–220 P(Ba)

A set of four chrome and white plastic chairs, designed in 1969 by Giancarlo Piretti.
£350–400 OOLA

A pair of Jan lounge chairs, by Jan Ekselius for Stendig, with orange fabric on foam-upholstered metal frames, c1970.
£600–700 P(Ba)

A dining room suite, by Arkana of Bath, comprising a table with white plastic veneer, and six white plastic chairs with separate seat cushions, on steel pedestals, c1970, table 73in (185.5cm) long.
£400–475 L&T

A 3108 chair, designed in 1970 by Arne Jacobsen, manufactured by Fritz Hansen, with pale olive green lacquer finish on laminated plywood seat, on chrome tubular metal legs, the back legs extending upwards to support the elliptical armrests, moulded marks, 1971.
£1,200–1,400 P(Ba)

◀ A Papegojan armchair, designed by Ib Arberg, manufactured by Rocksjöverken, Sweden, with chromed steel frame, black lacquered metal support and upholstered in beige corduroy, c1970, 63¾in (162cm) high.
£650–720 BUK

A table, by Arkana of Bath, with white moulded top on white pedestal base, 1970s, 41½in (105.5cm) diam.
£400–450 ZOOM

▶ A pair of black-painted Seconda chairs, by Mario Botta for Alias, with mesh seats and ribbed drum backs, c1982.
£450–550 L&T

A pair of System 1–2–3 de luxe armchairs, designed in 1973 by Verner Panton for Fritz Hansen, upholstered in beige fabric and with aluminium bases, 1970s.
£800–900 BUK

GLASS

An Inciso sommerso glass vase, by Paulo Venini, in pale olive-green, pale amber and clear glass, paper label, stamped, designed c1955, 15¾in (40cm) high.
£950–1,150 P(Ba)

A Leerdam Unica glass vase, designed by A. D. Copier, 1950, 7in (18cm) diam.
£1,600–1,800 S(Am)

▶ A Vetreria Aureliano Toso glass vase, by Dino Martens, the clear glass decorated with white and pink diagonal threads, designed 1950–55, 10½in (26.5cm) high.
£380–450 DORO

An Orrefors Vattenlek glass vase, by Edvin Öhrström, with stylized decoration of figures on a blue ground, signed, 1953, 8¼in (21cm) high.
£1,400–1,600 BUK

A Barbarici glass vase, by Ecole Barovier, Barovier & Ioso, the surface covered with metal oxides, black base, 1950s, 13¾in (35cm) high.
£1,100–1,200 BUK

A Clessidre blue and red hourglass, designed by Paolo Venini, 1950s, 10¼in (26cm) high.
£280–320 TCG

▶ A clear glass vase, designed by Barbini for Venini, with incised sides, the centre with an aperture opening to a well, signed, 1960s, 7¼in (18.5cm) high.
£600–700 P(Ba)

A James Powell, Whitefriars smoked glass triangular Bark vase, designed by Geoffrey Baxter, 1966, 9½in (24cm) high.
£180–200 RUSK

A pair of Holmegaard glass bowls, one turquoise blue, one red, each with a white interior, 1970s, 6¼in (16cm) diam.
£60–75 each PLB

A James Powell, Whitefriars glass vase, designed by Geoffrey Baxter, applied with tangerine spots, 1969, 7½in (19cm) high.
£80–100 RUSK

An asymmetrical crystal bowl, entitled 'Reconciliation', by David Prytherch, engraved with figures, the rim carved with figures in relief, signed, titled and dated, 1985, 6in (15cm) wide.
£300–350 AH

▶ An American blown, cut, polished and electro-plated blue glass vase, by Michael Glancy, inscribed, 1980, 5in (13cm) high.
£3,300–3,800 S(NY)

A glass vase, by Gunnar Cyrén for Orrefors, with green stylized leaf decoration on a blue ground, signed, 1987, 10½in (26.5cm) high.
£1,200–1,300 BUK

LIGHTING

A double desk lamp, designed by Christian Dell, model No. 6580 Super, manufactured by Kaiser & Co, with black painted steel and chromed metal stem which adjusts in height and position, designed 1933–34, 21¼in (54cm) high.
£1,150–1,350 P(Ba)

A black and cream painted aluminium three-branch ceiling light, by Serge Mouille, designed 1953, 78in (198cm) wide.
£15,000–16,500 S

A pair of black and white lacquered aluminium wall lights, designed by Serge Mouille, lacquer renewed, c1950, 12in (30.5cm) high.
£1,400–1,700 DORO

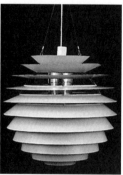

A PH Globe white-lacquered metal ceiling light, designed by Poul Henningsen for Louis Poulsen, 1958, 25½in (65cm) high.
£550–650 BUK

A wall light, designed by Gino Safartti for Arteluce, the red disk supported on a black rod arm, 1950s, 15in (38cm) high.
£250–300 P(Ba)

A white plastic table lamp, designed by Verner Panton, c1960, 27in (68.5cm) high.
£500–550 ZOOM

An Arco adjustable floor lamp, designed by Achille and Pier Castiglioni for Flos, Italy, with an aluminium shade and marble base, 1960s, 60in (152.5cm) high.
£650–750 BUK

A blue glass ceiling light, by Gino Vistosi for Murano, minor chips, 1960s, 17in (43cm) diam.
£270–325 BUK

A tablelamp, by Flos, designed by Achille Castiglioni, 1972, 10in (25.5cm) high.
£125–150 PLB

A chrome and glass bulb lamp, by E. Ironconi, designed by Achille Castiglioni, 1970s, 10in (25.5cm) high.
£140–160 PLB

◄ A smoked glass Sputnik lamp ceiling light, the glass shapes on metal spikes, c1970, 17¾in (45cm) diam.
£120–140 DORO

► A Wire Lamp, designed by Verner Panton for Lüber, with chromed steel tubes and orange plastic shade, 1969, 16in (40.5cm) high.
£120–140 BUK

A floor light, designed by Annig Sarian for Kartell, with a white plastic base and glass globe shade, 1970, 72¾in (185cm) high.
£180–220 BUK

JEWELLERY

◀ A 14ct gold brooch, designed by Bent Gabrielsen Pedersen for Hans Hansen, c1955, 2¾in (7cm) wide.
£450–500 DID

A silver-coloured metal necklace, No. 136, designed by Arno Malinowski for Georg Jensen, stamped marks, 1950s, 15½in (39.5cm) long.
£800–900 S

A black and clear crystal glass choker and bracelet set, signed by Kramer, 1960s.
£280–320 GLT

A sterling silver brooch, in the form of an abstract human figure, for J. Tostrup, c1970, 2¼in (5.5cm) high.
£350–400 DID

A silver bracelet, No. 188, by Georg Jensen, designed 1960s.
£300–330 DAC

A silver pendant, designed by Nanna Ditzel for Georg Jensen, 1963, 2¼in (5.5cm) diam.
£300–350 ASA

◀ A steel, gold and coral brooch, designed by Eva Dora Lamm for Anton Michelsen, c1980, 1½in (4cm) high.
£130–150 DID

METALWARE

A white metal tea strainer with stand, designed by Bernard Hötger for Franz Bolze, Bremen, c1930, stamped marks.
£1,200–1,400 P(Ba)

A silver bowl, designed by Georg Jensen after 1945, manufactured 1996, 15¾in (40cm) diam.
£8,500–10,000 BUK

A black-lacquered steel candlestick, designed by Marianne Brandt for Ruppelwerk GmbH, Gotha, marked, 1930–32, 11¾in (30cm) high.
£600–700 P(Ba)

> **Cross Reference**
> See Colour Review

A Campden stainless steel seven-piece breakfast set, designed by Robert Welch for Old Hall, 1956, coffee pot 8¾in (22cm) high.
£55–65 P(Ba)

▶ A pair of silver candlesticks, by Leslie G. Durbin, stamped marks for 1966, 8¼in (21cm) high.
£1,700–2,000 P(Ba)

Durbin created the centrepiece for the 1951 Festival of Britain exhibition in London, and is considered to be one of the greatest silversmiths of the post-WWII era.

Lamps & Lighting
CEILING & WALL LIGHTS

A horn and sheet-metal wagoner's lantern, c1800, 18in (45.5cm) high.
£300–350 AnSh

A French gilt-bronze basket-shaped hall lantern, late 19thC, 26½in (67.5cm) high.
£2,500–2,750 NOA

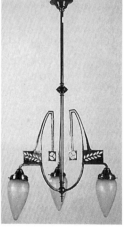

An Austrian three-branch ceiling light, with matt glass shades, restored, 1905–15, 40½in (10cm) high.
£650–750 DORO

▶ A chandelier, by Bagues, c1930, 78¾in (200cm) high.
£18,000–20,000 ART

This item was originally made for the Casino at Biarritz.

◀ A gilt-bronze chandelier, with two levels of six dished, scroll and leaf-cast reflectors, early 19thC, 20in (51cm) high.
£1,100–1,300 TMA

A brass hall lantern, 19thC, 31½in (80cm) high.
£1,200–1,400 AH

A six-branch electrolier, one branch damaged, c1900, 41¼in (105cm) high.
£1,100–1,300 Bea(E)

A Dutch black painted and gilt hall lantern, 19thC, 28in (71cm) high.
£450–550 E

A three-branch chandelier, with decorative pressed glass shades, c1910, 16in (40.5cm) high.
£320–360 LIB

A pair of George III-style giltwood three-branch wall appliques, with acanthus leaves and branches, surmounted by a winged dragon, mid-19thC, 58½in (148.5cm) high.
£4,500–5,500 Bon

A French gilded three-branch ceiling light, with etched glass shades, c1910, 27in (68.5cm) high.
£250–300 JW

A Swedish baroque-style pewter and brass ceiling light, 1920–30, 35½in (90cm) high.
£250–300 BUK

A gilt-brass hall lantern, with etched glass shade, 1920, 36in (91.5cm) high.
£1,500–1,650 ASH

TABLE & STANDARD LAMPS

A pair of French *faux marbre* brass and tole lamps, mid-19thC, 22in (56cm) high.
£2,200–2,500 NOA

A Victorian pink opaque glass oil lamp, the reservoir raised on a reeded brass column, 28in (71cm) high.
£170–200 DEN

A cranberry and white overlaid glass lamp, on a cast gilt-metal base decorated with swags of fruit, fitted for electricity, late 19thC, 26in (66cm) high.
£450–550 CGC

A Renaissance revival wrought-iron table lamp, with mica shade, late 19thC, 32½in (82.5cm) high.
£2,750–3,250 SK

A Chinese lamp, made from a bamboo tea caddy, with Laos silk shade, late 19thC, 20in (51cm) high.
£200–225 GHC

An oil lamp, by Taylor, Tunnicliffe & Co, with gilt-metal mounts modelled as elephant's heads, decorated in gilt with butterflies and foliage on a green lustrous ground, marked, 1875–98, 21in (53.5cm) high.
£450–550 CGC

A Victorian silver table lamp, by Elkington, Sheffield, with cut-glass reservoir, marked, 1900, 21in (53.5cm) high.
£800–900 L

◀ A pair of French bronzed-spelter table lamps, in the form of cherubs, entitled 'L'amour Vainqueur' and 'L'amour Vagabond', after Bruchon, on marble bases, damaged, early 20thC, 21¼in (54cm) high.
£550–650 Bea(E)

▶ A brass table lamp, the white glass shade decorated with peaches, 1920s, 19in (48.5cm) high.
£180–200 LIB

A Continental spelter figure of a putto holding a lamp, with wrythen cranberry glass shade, 19thC, 53in (134.5cm) high.
£1,000–1,200 AH

An Edwardian cast-brass desk lamp, with replacement shade, 1910, 22in (56cm) high.
£125–140 JW

Rugs & Carpets

A needlepoint carpet, the ivory field having an all-over design of polychrome floral sprays interspersed with foliate devices, framed by a charcoal border with further floral sprays, France, 1848–70, 145 x 108in (368.5 x 274.5cm).
£4,500–5,000 P

An Aubusson carpet, the green field with a central ivory medallion enclosing a crimson and gold stylized floral design, France, early 19thC, 108in (274.5cm) square.
£4,500–5,000 NOA

A rug, designed in 1929 by Märta Måås-Fjetterström, the field divided into rectangles of blue, red, yellow and brown, Sweden, produced before 1942, 122½ x 83¾in (311 x 212.5cm).
£5,000–6,000 BUK

The rugs in this section have been arranged in geographical sequence from west to east, in the following order: Europe, Turkey, Anatolia, Caucasus, Persia, Turkestan, India and China.

A hook stitch carpet, the madder field with an all-over design of large flowerheads, palmettes and vases with scrolling vines, enclosed by an indigo palmette border, Germany, 1920, 156 x 117in (396 x 297cm).
£1,200–1,400 P

A Bessarabian kelim, with a charcoal field and ivory border, Moldavian/Romanian border, 1820s, 117 x 89in (297 x 226cm).
£8,500–10,000 S

A Ushak carpet, the pale green field with all-over weeping willows and skeletal flowers and foliage, with pale brick main border of palmettes and ivory and pale gold striped guards, Turkey, 19thC, 105 x 78in (266.5 x 198cm).
£3,400–3,750 WW

An Anatolian rug, centred with an ivory medallion with stylized birds and foliage, enclosed by animal spandrels and an ice blue border containing rams' horn motifs, early 20thC, 83 x 47in (211 x 119.5cm).
£900–1,100 P

A Gendje long rug, the deep blue field containing stylized birds, west Caucasus, dated '1885', 109 x 40in (277 x 101.5cm).
£7,500–9,000 S

A Sewan Kazak rug, the madder field centred with a sky blue hooked cruciform medallion containing ivory mirrored fan-tailed motifs, enclosed by an ivory meandering vine border and reciprocal guard stripes, southwest Caucasus, c1900, 85 x 49in (216 x 124.5cm).
£1,100–1,200 P

A Kazak rug, with an elongated hexagonal medallion and matching spandrels in midnight and sky blue, ivory, gold and dark green on the dark red field, with sky blue border, damaged, southwest Caucasus, early 20thC, 68 x 48in (172.5 x 122cm).
£500–600 SK(B)

A Fachralo Kazak prayer rug, the madder field of polychrome S-motifs and rosettes centred by an ivory *mihrab* containing a six-pointed medallion in shades of madder, ivory and indigo, framed by a camel geometric motif border and mid-indigo guard stripes, southwest Caucasus, dated '1902', 52 x 45in (132 x 11.5cm).
£2,800–3,200 P

A Karabagh runner, Caucasus, late 19thC, 141 x 41in (358 x 104cm).
£1,750–2,000 SLN

A Talish rug, with brick-red field and charcoal border, east Caucasus, 19thC, 58 x 47¼in (147.5 x 120cm).
£4,000–4,500 SAM

A Konakend rug, the indigo field with an all-over angular lattice design, framed by a Kufic border and foliate guard stripes, east Caucasus, dated '1858', 61 x 48in (155 x 122cm).
£3,200–3,500 P

A Shirvan long rug, with a column of five stepped hexagonal medallions in red, royal blue, gold, ivory, light and medium blue-green on a midnight blue field, with red and blue reciprocal border, east Caucasus, late 19thC, 112 x 50in (284.5 x 127cm).
£2,000–2,200 SK(B)

A Shirvan rug, with rows of paired opposing triangles in royal blue, camel, ivory, gold and dark green on a midnight blue field, with an ivory border, east Caucasus, worn, late 19thC, 62 x 45in (157.5 x 114.5cm).
£400–500 SK(B)

A Bidjar carpet, with a brick-red field and yellow border, northwest Persia, 19thC, 96½ x 54¼in (244.5 x 137cm).
£3,200–3,500 SAM

A Heriz carpet, the deep rose field centred by an ivory medallion, with a deep red border, northwest Persia, late 19thC, 185 x 140in (470 x 355.5cm).
£9,000–10,000 S(NY)

A Bakshaish carpet, the pale brick field with a design in ivory, light blue, dark blue and sand, cut and reduced, northwest Persia, c1875, 140 x 96in (355.5 x 244cm).
£4,000–4,500 S(NY)

A Heriz carpet, the brick-red field with geometric motifs in blue, cream, black, and light blue, northwest Persia, c1930, 134 x 105in (340.5 x 266.5cm).
£1,350–1,500 Bon(C)

▶ A Tabriz carpet, the ivory field centred by a saffron palmette medallion, framed by similar spandrels and a rosette and leaf border, northwest Persia, c1900, 166 x 117in (421.5 x 297cm).
£2,000–2,200 P

A Tabriz carpet, the indigo field of scrolling vines centred by a madder medallion, framed by palmette spandrels and a rose pink flowerhead border, northwest Persia, c1920, 163 x 90in (414 x 228.5cm).
£1,750–2,000 P

A Sarab rug, northwest Persia, c1900, 77 x 52in (195.5 x 132cm).
£750–825 SLN

A Tabriz carpet, the ivory field with all-over arabesque flowers and palmettes in soft colours, with pale gold trailing floral main border and ivory floral guards, northwest Persia, 1930–40, 207 x 126in (526 x 320cm).
£3,000–3,500 WW

A Bidjar carpet, with brick red field and light blue border, west Persia, 19thC, 109 x 55in (277 x 140cm).
£4,000–4,500 SAM

A Sarouk Fereghan rug, the indigo field of angular floral vines centred by a pole medallion framed by ivory spandrels and meandering vine borders, with silk weft, west Persia, late 19thC, 87 x 53in (221 x 134.5cm).
£8,000–9,000 S(NY)

A Sarab runner, with brick-red field and borders, north-west Persia, 1890–1900, 118 x 38in (299.5 x 96.5cm).
£500–600 Bon(C)

◀ A Bakhtiyari vanity bag, the red field with a stylized animal in camel and black, west Persia, late 19thC, 14¼ x 17¾in (36 x 45cm).
£1,350–1,500 SAM

A Hamadan runner, the dark blue field with stylized red flowers, west Persia, c1920, 124 x 42½in (315 x 108cm).
£140–170 DN(H)

A Sarouk rug, the field with rows of large flowering plants enclosed by palmette borders, west Persia, c1920, 78 x 51in (198 x 129.5cm).
£1,300–1,500 SLN

A Bidjar rug, the over-all Herati design in blue, red, rust, gold, camel and light green on an ivory field, west Persia, mid-20thC, 78 x 48in (198 x 122cm).
£1,800–2,000 SK(B)

A Kashgai vanity bag, the ivory field decorated with stylized animals, southwest Persia, c1900, 8¾ x 12¼in (22 x 31cm).
£425–475 SAM

An Isfahan rug, the ivory ground with twining flower design in red, sand, blue and black, with crimson border, central Persia, c1930, 100 x 53in (254 x 134.5cm).
£5,000–6,000 S(NY)

A Kashan rug, the indigo floral field centred by a medallion framed by spandrels and palmette borders, central Persia, 1910–20, 76 x 52in (193 x 132cm).
£1,350–1,500 Bon(C)

A Kashan carpet, the madder field of floral vines with a pole medallion enclosed by spandrels and indigo borders, restored, central Persia, 1920–30, 173 x 126in (439.5 x 320cm).
£1,500–1,800 Bon(C)

▶ A Qum silk rug, the turquoise field depicting mounted huntsmen pursuing their quarry, within a salmon-pink cartouche and flowerhead border and three guards, central Persia, mid-20thC, 61½ x 43in (156 x 109cm).
£650–750 Bea(E)

A pair of Kashan rugs, each with an overall vine and palmette design within a conforming madder border of six guards, central Persia, 1940s, 59¾ x 41¼in (152 x 105cm).
£700–850 Bea(E)

A Yezd rug, the cream field with a scrolling flower and tree design in magenta, green and blue, south Persia, c1920, 87 x 56in (221 x 142cm).
£450–550 DN(H)

A Balouch prayer rug, the camel field with double *mihrabs* around a central flowerhead, with brick main border of flowerheads and latchhook tree motifs on a trailing vine, with dark brown and ivory running dog outer guard, northeast Persia, c1890, 57 x 33in (145 x 84cm).
£400–500 WW

A Balouch rug, the madder field with diagonal pattern of alternating blue and brick medallions, Persian/Afghan frontier, c1900, 57 x 32in (145 x 81.5cm).
£800–900 SAM

A Balouch saddle cover, the brown field with an indigo centre medallion, with brown main border and indigo inner border, northeast Persia, c1920, 44 x 33in (112 x 84cm).
£450–500 WW

A Balouch rug, the field with an all-over lattice design of hooked motifs enclosed by similar borders, with kilim ends, northeast Persia, c1900, 69 x 38in (175.5 x 96.5cm).
£450–550 SLN

An Afshar salt bag, with alternating panels of geometric designs on red and indigo fields, northeast Persia, 19thC, 22¾ x 13¾in (58 x 35cm).
£675–750 SAM

A pair of Kirman Ravar prayer rugs, the ivory *mihrabs* with all-over shawl design repeated in the indigo main border, with pale gold trailing floral guards, southeast Persia, c1930, 86 x 56in (218.5 x 142cm).
£3,500–4,200 WW

An Ersari Turkoman rug, the brick field with three rows of medallions in blue, ivory and camel, west Turkestan, late 19thC, 54in x 35in (137 x 35cm).
£1,800–2,000 SAM

An Arabachi Turkoman *ensi*, the brick field with four panels filled with rows of ram's horn motifs, the compartmented centre band repeated in the main border, each panel filled with a stylized tree motif, west Turkestan, late 19thC, 64 x 65in (162.5 x 165cm).
£500–600 WW

A silk saddle cover, the brick field with geometric border in ivory, gold and black, east Turkestan, 18thC, 68 x 36in (172.5 x 91.5cm).
£8,000–9,000 S

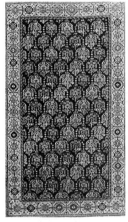

An Agra rug, the deep emerald field with an all-over design of floral *boteh*, framed by an ivory border of hooked octagons, north India, 82 x 49in (208.5 x 124.5cm).
£600–700 P

A Kansu rug, the brick field with all-over design in blue, cream, ivory and light blue, with yellow border, northwest China, late 18thC, 103 x 66in (261.5 x 167.5cm).
£7,000–8,000 S

A Khotan carpet, the brick field with three blue roundels enclosing stylized ivory flower design, with blue border, east Turkestan, early 19thC, 145 x 73in (368.5 x 185.5cm).
£1,800–2,200 S(NY)

An Indian carpet, the red field with all-over design of flowers and animals in blue, ivory, camel, pale blue and rose, late 19thC, 157 x 93in (399 x 236cm).
£11,000–12,500 S(NY)

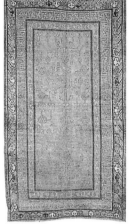

A Khotan silk carpet, the gold field with brick stylized flower motif, east Turkestan, 19thC, 98½ x 55in (250 x 139.5cm).
£6,500–7,500 S(Z)

A Mughal carpet, the pale green ground with red Lattice-and-Flower design, Lahore, north India, early 18thC, 276 x 103in (701 x 261.5cm).
£11,000–13,000 S

◄ A Ningshia rug, China, 19thC, 69 x 36in (175.5 x 91.5cm).
£700–800 SLN

A Yarkand silk *saph* fragment, with green *mihrabs* and repeating spandrels, east Turkestan, c1840, 44 x 109in (112 x 277cm).
£6,000–7,000 S

A Khotan carpet, the indigo field of stylized plants centred by a cloud roundel framed by an antique gold 'thunder and lightning' border, east Turkestan, c1890, 110 x 54in (279.5 x 137cm).
£5,000–5,500 P

> **Cross Reference**
> See Colour Review

A Tibetan rug, the indigo field with five-clawed dragons chasing flaming pearls, interspersed by mythical birds, clouds and swastikas, c1900, 68 x 36in (172.5 x 91.5cm).
£1,200–1,400 P

Textiles

EMBROIDERY & NEEDLEWORK

A needlework picture, worked in silk and metallic thread, depicting Abraham, Hagar and Ishmael, 17thC, 14¼ x 18in (36 x 45.5cm).
£2,800–3,200 TAM

A Charles II petit-point picture of The Judgement of Solomon, within a border of flowers, animals and insects, embellished with wirework, seed pearls and coral beads, 17thC, 14½ x 18¼in (37 x 46.5cm).
£6,500–7,500 Bea(E)

A Charles II stumpwork picture of two female figures representing Harvest and Plenty, in a border of flowers, birds, butterflies and dogs, on an ivory satin ground, 17thC, 12½ x 16½in (32 x 42cm), framed.
£6,000–7,000 Bea(E)

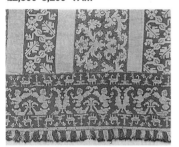

An Italian embroidered panel, worked in red silk on linen, 17thC, 16½ x 28¼in (42 x 72cm).
£800–900 P

A embroidered picture, worked in coloured wools highlighted with ivory silk, c1700, 11½ x 13½in (29 x 34.5cm).
£1,750–2,000 P

An embroidered picture, depicting Ceres and attendants by a fountain, with shades of blue, green and brown silk on an ivory ground, c1700, 8¼ x 6¼in (21 x 16cm), framed.
£750–825 P

A embroidered *aide-mémoire* case, depicting a trumpeter and dogs before a house, worked in silver wire and silk, c1710, 5in (13cm) wide.
£1,100–1,200 Bon

A needlework picture, depicting a pastoral scene, worked in silk and chenille threads and hand-painted watercolour on a silk ground, late 18thC, 20 x 19¼in (51 x 49cm), framed.
£1,700–2,000 SK(B)

◀ A George III silk embroidered picture, depicting a neo-classical female, her hands, head and the sky painted, 9¾ x 7½in (25 x 19cm), framed.
£130–150 PFK

▶ An embroidered panel, with Tree of Life pattern in red, yellow, green, blue and brown wools, repaired, c1720, 86½ x 43¼in (219.5 x 110cm).
£2,200–2,500 P

An embroidered picture, depicting a figural scene worked in pastel silks, c1790, 10¾in (27.5cm) diam.
£350–420 P

A silk and woolwork picture, depicting a child ascending steps towards a prophet, with painted faces, 18th/19thC, 12 x 14in (30.5 x 35.5cm).
£80–100 GAK

A needlework picture, entitled 'Rebecca at the Well', worked in crewel yarn and chenille threads and watercolour on silk, some damage, early 19thC, 14in (35.5cm) square.
£500–600 SK(B)

A Regency needlework picture, 18½ x 22½in (47 x 57cm), framed.
£1,600–2,000 M&K

▶ An embroidered and painted picture, wool on silk, some damage, early 19thC, 14 x 18½in (35.5 x 47cm).
£170–200 WW

A Spanish silk embroidery of the Holy Family, stitched in silver and gold threads, 18thC, 17 x 12½in (43 x 32cm), framed in a gold-painted wooden tabernacle-style door with keyhole.
£350–420 S(S)

A needlepoint and silk embroidery map of England, dated '1800', 18 x 20in (45.5 x 51cm).
£400–500 JPr

A needlework panel, depicting a partridge and pheasant on a stylized tree, worked in coloured silks on satin, early 19thC, 21½ x 16¼in (54.5 x 41.5cm), framed.
£400–500 RTo

An Italian altar frontal of four panels, the dark blue voided velvet applied and worked in coloured silks and metal thread, with gold braid edge, late 18thC, 30 x 102½in (76 x 260.5cm).
£1,600–1,800 P

A silkwork picture of a lion's head, early 19thC, 12½ x 10¼in (32 x 26cm).
£800–1,000 Bon(C)

An American silk needlework memorial, Rehobeth, Massachusetts, early 19thC, 18 x 21¼in (45.5 x 54cm), framed.
£2,200–2,500 SK(B)

A Regency embroidered silkwork picture, 14¼ x 11¼in (36 x 28.5cm).
£300–350 MCA

An embroidered map of Spain and Portugal, by Margaret Campbell Douglas, dated '1814', 22¼ x 25½in (56.5 x 65cm), framed.
£1,150–1,350 HAM

A pair of early Victorian petit-point canvaswork embroidered pictures, depicting game birds, worked in coloured wools, 16¾ x 13¾in (42.5 x 35cm), framed.
£500–600 DN(H)

An embroidered picture, depicting a woodcutter, worked in long stitch on silk, 19thC, 22 x 15in (56 x 38cm).
£90–100 GAK

A pair of Edwardian gros-point needlework pictures, worked in red, blue, yellow and brown on black grounds, 15¼ x 11½in (38.5 x 29cm), framed.
£200–240 PFK

An embroidered map of Ireland, by Susan Campbell Douglas, 1818, 22½ x 22in (57 x 53cm), framed.
£1,250–1,500 HAM

A needlework picture, with bouquets of flowers worked in coloured wools within beige medallions, c1860, 19¼ x 14½in (49 x 37cm), framed.
£250–300 WW

A late Victorian needlework picture, embroidered in coloured wools on a linen ground, some repairs, 19¾ x 18½in (50 x 47cm), framed.
£85–100 WW

A Nurata *susani*, embroidered in yellow, orange, crimson and blue-green silks on a cotton ground, Uzbekistan, mid-19thC, 82¾in x 60¾in (210 x 154.5cm).
£500–600 P

A Victorian bead embroidery picture of flowers and feathers, 11 x 9½in (28 x 24cm), framed.
£170–200 AAV

Miller's is a price GUIDE not a price LIST

A chinoiserie needlework panel, worked in gros- and petit-point, c1890, 31 x 26in (78.5 x 66cm).
£500–600 S(S)

◄ A Bochara *susani*, embroidered with crimson, blue, terracotta and fawn silks on a cotton ground, Uzbekistan, late 19thC, 58¼ x 43¼in (148 x 110cm).
£1,500–1,800 P

LACE

A panel of Venetian needlelace, c1670, 7¼ x 26¼in (18.5 x 66.5cm), mounted on black velvet.
£500–550 P

An Irish crochet flounce, with raised work, late 19thC, 121in (307.5cm) long.
£60–70 F&C

A matching pair of Brussels lace flounces, c1880, 165in (419cm) long.
£280–320 WW

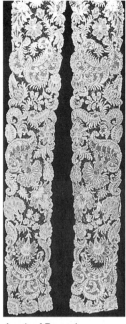

A pair of Brussels lace lappets, c1720, 47in (119.5cm) long.
£300–350 WW

Miller's is a price GUIDE not a price LIST

A Honiton bobbin lace collar, c1890, 16 x 14in (40.5 x 35.5cm).
£40–45 JuC

A lace collar, patterned with flower-heads and leaves, Bedfordshire, late 19thC, 9½in (24cm) deep.
£40–50 F&C

SAMPLERS

◄ A sampler, by Hannah Brown, worked in silks and depicting Adam and Eve, 1731, 16¾ x 11in (42.5 x 28cm), framed.
£6,000–7,000 CGC

► A George III sampler, by Ann Weston, worked in coloured silks on a linen ground, late 18thC, 16½ x 12in (42 x 30.5cm), framed.
£3,000–3,500 S(S)

A sampler, by Edith Cultredge, worked in coloured silks on a linen ground, 1716, 17¾ x 7in (45 x 18cm), framed.
£400–450 WW

► A needlework sampler, by Sarah Slade, 1778, 12¾ x 10½in (32.5 x 26.5cm).
£500–550 L

A needlework sampler, by Mary Hopkins, embroidered with silk on a linen ground, 1778, 10 x 11½in (25.5 x 29cm), framed.
£370–450 Mit

A sampler, embroidered with silk on an ivory linen ground, 1779, 13¼ x 9in (33.5 x 23cm), framed.
£500–550 S(S)

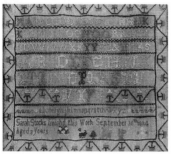

A sampler, by Sarah Stocks, worked in coloured silks on linen, 1804, 9¾ x 10¾in (25 x 27.5cm), framed.
£400–450 RTo

A George IV sampler, by Sarah Saddington, worked on linen, 1824, 11½ x 11in (29 x 28cm), framed.
£300–350 Mit

A sampler, by Mary Ann Lockwood, worked with a verse relating to slavery, some damage, 1798, 16½ x 12in (42 x 30.5cm).
£1,700–2,000 L

A sampler, by Mary Malsingham, worked in wool and silk on gauze, some damage, 1815, 14½ x 12in (37 x 30.5cm).
£200–240 GAK

◄ A sampler, by Eliza Wilson, worked in green, red and blue wools and silks on linen, early 19thC, 17 x 11¾in (43 x 30cm), framed.
£450–550 RTo

A George III sampler, by Hannah Nicholson, depicting Adam and Eve, worked in coloured wools on linen, 20½ x 16½in (52 x 42cm).
£500–600 DN(H)

► A sampler, by Sarah Stead, worked in coloured silks on gauze laid on linen, some damage, 1826, 21½ x 26½in (54.5 x 67.5cm), framed.
£1,350–1,500 WW

A sampler, by Louise Ann Redford, 1804, 18½ x 12½in (47 x 32cm), framed.
£650–800 JM

A sampler, by Mary Roswell, worked in coloured silks, 1818, 16½ x 12¼in (42 x 31cm), framed.
£500–550 CGC

A sampler, some damage, 1882, 22 x 17¼in (56 x 44cm), framed.
£550–600 SK(B)

A sampler, by Sarah Keal, worked in coloured silks on linen, damaged, 1827, 15½ x 11½in (39.5 x 29cm), mounted on mahogany pole screen.
£550–650 P(NW)

An American needlework family record, by Mary Vining, Essex County, Massachusetts, 1833, 17½in (44.5cm) square.
£1,250–1,400 SK(B)

A sampler, by Isabel Broomfield, worked in wool on a linen ground, 19thC, 17¼ x 16½in (44 x 42cm), framed.
£650–750 WW

An American sampler, by Mary H. Morrison, Nine Partners School, Dutchess County, New York, worked in blue, green and black silk on linen, 1827, 16 x 17in (40.5 x 43cm).
£2,000–2,200 S(NY)

A sampler, by Jane Shuffrey, worked in brown, pink, blue and cream silk on a linen ground, minor damage, 1833, 24in (61cm) square, framed.
£600–700 P(Ed)

A sampler, by Eliza Griffiths, embroidered with coloured silks on a linen ground, 1836, 17 x 12¼in (43 x 31cm), framed.
£500–550 WW

◄ A sampler, by Emily Clapp, with geometric and strawberry border, 1840, 13in (33cm) square.
£450–550 JPr

► A sampler, by Elizabeth Ellen Lindo, worked in coloured silks on linen, 1840, 16 x 12in (40.5 x 30.5cm).
£800–900 GAK

A needlework sampler, by Julia C. Hamilton, 1833, 21¼ x 25in (54 x 63.5cm), framed.
£500–550 SK(B)

A William IV sampler, by Mary Jane Martin, depicting Adam and Eve, worked in coloured wools, 1834, 16½ x 12½in (42 x 32cm).
£300–350 Hal

A sampler, by Ann Sanders, depicting Adam and Eve, worked in petit-point and silk stitch on an ivory linen ground, 1836, 14½ x 13in (37 x 33cm), framed.
£950–1,100 S(S)

A sampler, by Margeret Holmes, worked in coloured silks on a linen ground, 1841, 18in (45.5cm) square.
£750–900 P(Ed)

A sampler, by Mary Gerrard, depicting Adam and Eve, worked in coloured wools on a linen ground, '1845', 16½ x 16¾in (42 x 43cm), framed.
£500–600 WW

A black and brown silk mourning sampler, in original frame, 1844, 12 x 15in (30.5 x 38cm).
£320–400 JPr

A sampler, by Sarah Astill Marton, worked in coloured silks, 1848, 19 x 12in (48.5 x 30.5cm), framed.
£800–900 GH

A sampler, by Hannah Morter, worked in wool and silk on gauze, 1850, 16½ x 12in (42 x 30.5cm), framed.
£500–600 GAK

A sampler, by Jane Hughes, worked in coloured wools on an open weave linen ground, 1850, 16¾in (42.5cm) square, framed.
£400–500 WW

A temperance sampler, depicting a billiard table, beer barrel, glasses, beer mugs and verse, late 19thC, 11¼ x 12¼in (28.5 x 31cm).
£700–800 SWO

The British Association for the Promotion of Temperance was formed in 1835, and by 1900 it had been estimated that a tenth of the adult population were total abstainers from alcohol, which was deemed to be the curse of the community leading to vice and lunacy. Those that abstained needed somewhere to socialize and it is in one of these establishments mentioned in the verse that this sampler would have hung.

A sampler, by Mary Hooper, worked in brown wool, coloured silks and metal thread on a linen ground, 19thC, 22¾ x 12½in (58 x 32.5cm), framed.
£750–900 WW

▶ A commemorative sampler, celebrating the Festival of Britain, worked in wool depicting the changes between 1851 and 1951, 17¾ x 14¼in (45 x 36cm), framed.
£60–70 SAS

An American sampler, by Sara W. Cushing, worked in coloured silks on a linen ground, mid-19thC, 13½ x 17in (34.5 x 43cm), framed.
£950–1,100 SK(B)

TAPESTRIES

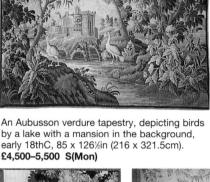

An Aubusson verdure tapestry, depicting birds by a lake with a mansion in the background, early 18thC, 85 x 126½in (216 x 321.5cm).
£4,500–5,500 S(Mon)

A set of four Aubusson tapestries within a four-fold screen, each depicting a lion mask urn at the base with cherubs frolicking among flowers and fruit above, woven in wool and silk on a red ground, 18thC, each panel 88 x 23in (223.5 x 58.5cm).
£10,000–12,000 WW

An Aubusson tapestry panel, depicting a general on horseback and a trumpeting angel, within a floral border interspersed with vases, 17thC, 111½ x 55in (282 x 139.5cm).
£3,200–3,500 S(NY)

► An Aubusson tapestry, depicting a maiden resting on a bank, woven in silk and wool, 19thC, 66 x 38in (167.5 x 96.5cm).
£1,200–1,400 WW

A pair of Flemish floral tapestry border cushions, with vases of fruit and flowers on an ivory ground, with silk tasseled fringe and backing, late 16thC, 18 x 14in (45.5 x 35.5cm).
£1,750–2,000 S

A pair of Aubusson tapestry hangings, each depicting a basket of flowers suspended by tendrils of honeysuckle, with fuchsias, roses, peonies, ferns and palms in green, red, pink and brown, late 19thC, 127 x 43in (322.5 x 109cm).
£2,000–2,400 DN(H)

A Flemish tapestry, depicting milkmaids and herdsmen in a wooded landscape, with a Palladian folly by a stream, early 18thC, 108 x 180in (274.5 x 457cm).
£6,000–7,000 SK

◄ A Franco-Flemish tapestry fragment, with a brown ground and pale gold border, depicting a hound, 16th/17thC, 29 x 21in (73.5 x 53.5cm).
£500–600 WW

A French *entre fenêtre* tapestry, decorated with flowers and leaves, 19thC, 104 x 44in (264 x 112cm).
£1,000–1,200 S(Z)

◄ A French tapestry panel, depicting figures by a building with steps, signed 'Braqueme & Cie', mid-19thC, 52½ x 29in (133.5 x 73.5cm).
£1,100–1,300 S(S)

COSTUME

A pair of lady's ivory kid shoes, covered with brocaded silk, woven in shades of pink, ivory and pale green, trimmed with metallic threads, c1730.
£2,000–2,400 Bon(C)

A Paisley shawl, the ivory ground worked with all-over floral motifs, with multi-coloured fringed ends and silk warp, 1840s, 64in (162.5cm) square.
£250–300 WW

A gentleman's waistcoat, the cream ground silk embroidered with flowers and leaves in shades of pink, blue and green, the borders and pocket flaps edged with lace, late 18thC.
£170–200 LAY

A light-brown and caramel cotton corset, c1860.
£650–750 P

◀ An American Bes Ben banana and leaf hat, with velvet and net head-piece, papier mâché bananas and green leaves, with gold leaf embellishment, Chicago, 1940s.
£350–400 SK

A Swiss or German beaded bonnet, c1820, 11in (28cm) high.
£160–180 JuC

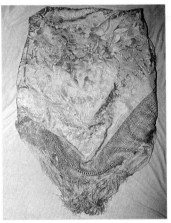

A cream embroidered silk shawl, c1860–80, 65in (165cm) square.
£900–1,000 JPr

A lady's lawn and lace peignoir, c1890.
£220–250 JuC

◀ A cream silk wedding dress, trimmed with silk chiffon and beadwork, 1906.
£150–200 CCO

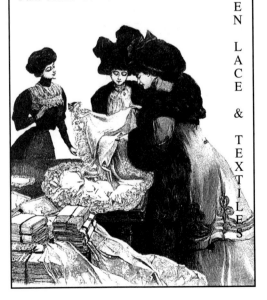

Fans

The word fan comes from the latin *vannus*, a fan-shaped implement used for separating chaff from grain, which served equally well to cool the brow of the hard-working field labourer. Later, the fan became bound up in Christian ritual as a *flabellum*, a type of fixed fly-whisk used to keep insects from dropping into the Eucharistic wine. It was the Portuguese, emerging as a formidable trading power in the 15th century, who introduced the fan to western Europe from China and Japan.

Fans were made in an infinite variety of styles and materials reflecting centuries of changing fashions. The height of production was the 18th century: being superbly hand-painted and of the finest workmanship, these fans are often the most sought-after and most expensive. In the 19th century, mass production rendered painted fans less important, and the trend was towards textile leaves of satin, silk, gauze and lace, with feathers becoming increasingly popular from the 1880s.

The size of fans tended to reflect the change in the circumference of women's skirts. At their smallest in the early 19th century, when women wore empire-line dresses, they were often pierced brisés of individual sticks, usually of horn, ivory or bone, frequently painted with vignettes or garlands of flowers. As the century progressed, skirts grew wider and by the 1890s, sticks were often more than twelve inches long.

Fans also serve as a form of social history. In the 18th century, printed fans were used to commemorate important events such as balloon ascents, and to illustrate items fleetingly in fashion such as the newest song, dance or riddle. Cheap and ephemeral, these fans were easily damaged and carelessly discarded, particularly the earliest examples, which were rather crude and garish. Consequently, they are now extremely rare and very collectable. Decorative chromolithographic fans, from the latter part of the 19th and early 20th century, were similarly used to commemorate events such as the opening of the Eiffel Tower in 1889, and for advertising hotels, perfumes and restaurants. These have survived in far greater numbers and are in better condition, and so are a more accessible area for collecting.

After WW1, a woman's role in society was changed irrevocably. With greater independence, they were less constrained by convention and were now more inclined to be holding a cigarette in one hand and a cocktail in the other. Something had to be discarded and, unfortunately, it was the fan. **Paula Raven**

A Chinese export brisé fan, the carved ivory sticks painted with phoenix and flowers in red, grey and gilt, early 18thC, 7½in (19cm) wide.
£1,000–1,200 P

A fan, the paper leaf painted with a river scene in grey, black and white, the stained wood guard sticks inlaid with mother-of-pearl, c1730, 11½in (29cm) wide.
£250–300 P

A fan, painted with Darius, his family and servants before Alexander, the carved and pierced ivory sticks painted with chinoiserie design, c1740, 15½in (39.5cm) wide.
£600–700 LDC

◀ A fan, painted with a classical scene of maidens and warriors, the mother-of-pearl sticks pierced and gilded with ladies and putti, c1740, 15in (38cm) wide.
£850–1,000 LDC

A fan, with a hand-coloured etching published by M. Gamble depicting the attack on Cartagena, with plain ivory sticks and gilded wooden guard sticks, 1740, 10in (25.5cm) wide.
£500–600 LDC

An Italian unmounted fan leaf, painted on chicken skin with Aurora in the style of Guido Reni, c1740, 22in (56cm) wide.
£500–600 LDC

◀ A fan, the paper leaf painted with the finding of Moses in the bulrushes, the ivory sticks carved and pierced with figures, possibly Dutch, c1740, 11½in (29cm) wide.
£230–275 P

A fan, the leaf hand-painted with a pastoral scene, with ivory sticks, c1740, 10in (25.5cm) wide.
£130–145 FAN

► A fan, the leaf painted with a battle scene of El Cid defeating the Moors, the ivory sticks carved, pierced and gilded with ladies, putti and the arms of Spain, c1750, 9½in (24cm) wide.
£750–950 LDC

A fan, the leaf painted with Venus and Adonis, with carved, pierced and silvered tortoiseshell sticks, possibly German, framed, c1750, 23in (58.5cm) wide.
£550–650 LDC

A fan, the leaf painted with a lady descending from her cabriolet, the ivory sticks carved, pierced and painted, c1760, 10½in (26.5cm) wide.
£450–550 LDC

A fan, the leaf painted with figures and cupid, with pierced ivory sticks, possibly a marriage fan, in original paper-covered box, c1760, 10½in (26.5cm) wide.
£150–180 WW

A French fan, the leaf painted with figures in a landscape, the carved and pierced ivory sticks with gilt figures and backed with mother-of-pearl, c1760, 10in (25.5cm) wide.
£650–750 LDC

A fan, the leaf painted with figures in a country scene, the ivory sticks carved and painted with figures and flowers, c1760, 22in (56cm) wide.
£500–600 LDC

A fan, the tarnished silvered paper leaf with insertions of tinsel-decorated net, with paper appliqué of figures and flowers, painted bone sticks, the guards with miniature portraits, c1770, 9¾in (25cm) wide.
£100–120 P

A French fan, the cream silk leaf painted with a central cartouche of a naval scene, the reverse with panels of ships and medallions of fruit, with gilt spangle decoration and gilt-painted ivory sticks, c1770, 10½in (26.5cm) wide, framed.
£700–800 P

A French fan, the paper leaf painted with the harvesting of reeds by a stream, the carved, pierced and painted ivory sticks designed with lovers and cupid in a pastoral scene, c1770, 11½in (29cm) wide, framed.
£550–600 P

A French fan, the silk leaf painted in black, grey and white, with gilt thread and sequin decoration, c1770, 11in (28cm) wide.
£500–550 P

A French fan, the silvered paper leaf painted with medallions of companions in country settings, with mother-of-pearl battoir sticks carved and silvered with cherubs, ribbons and vases, c1770, 9¾in (25cm) wide.
£400–450 P

A fan, the découpé paper leaf with chinoiserie decoration, with carved ivory sticks, c1780, 11½in (29cm) wide.
£400–450 P

A French fan, the silk leaf painted
with a couple in a fantasy garden,
the ivory sticks pierced and gilded
with figures, 14in (35.5cm) wide.
£700–900 LDC

A fan, the paper leaf painted with
Anthony and Cleopatra, a bust of
Caesar in the foreground, with
pierced ivory sticks, probably Italian,
c1790, 9¾in (25cm) wide.
£1,800–2,000 P

A Chinese Canton gilt-metal filigree
brisé fan, enamelled in blue, green
and gold with boats, birds and
figures by a pagoda, c1820,
7½in (19cm) wide.
£750–900 LDC

An Empire silk fan, decorated with
sequins and cut steel, the horn
sticks with piqué decoration, c1840,
8in (20.5cm) wide.
£130–145 FAN

A fan, painted with Neapolitan
dancers and vignettes of pixies
and Father Time and a fairy toasting
the New Year, decorated with
garlands of holly and mistletoe,
the bone sticks pierced and gilded,
1858–59, 11in (28cm) wide.
£500–600 LDC

A French fan, the silk leaf painted
with lovers and a female companion
in a garden, decorated with gold
thread embroidery and coloured
sequins, the mother-of-pearl sticks
carved and gilded with figures,
cherubs and symbols of love,
c1780, 15in (38cm) wide.
£550–650 LDC

▶ A Dutch fan,
the leaf painted
with Rinaldo
holding a mirror
for Armida, the
mother-of-pearl
sticks carved,
pierced and gilt,
the gilt guard
sticks carved
with musical
instruments, c1790,
15in (38cm) wide.
£550–650 LDC

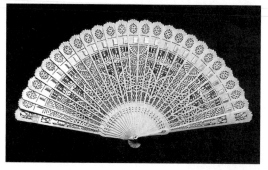

A French lithographic fan, depicting
Aphrodite reclining in a boat
surrounded by water nymphs,
dolphins and garlands, with gilded
mother-of-pearl sticks, c1840,
25in (63.5cm) wide.
£550–650 LDC

A Chinese export ivory brisé fan,
the finely carved sticks with birds
and flowers, the central panel
carved with 'A. Z.', c1790,
10¼in (26cm) wide.
£1,200–1,300 S

> **Cross Reference**
> See Colour Review

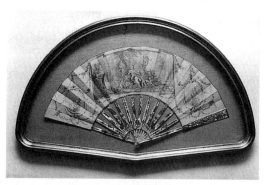

◀ A pierced
bone brisé
fan, in original
box, c1820,
6in (15cm) wide.
£80–100 FAN

A Chinese export tortoiseshell
brisé fan, the sticks pierced and
carved with figures, horses, trees
and boats, damaged, c1850,
7¼in (18.5cm) long.
£450–500 P

◀ A lithographic fan,
decorated with ladies
in a mythological scene,
the mother-of-pearl sticks
carved, pierced and
gilded with birds, fruit
and flowers, c1860,
9¼in (23.5cm) wide.
£400–500 LDC

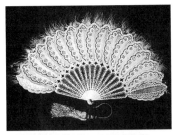

A fan, with sequinned cream silk moiré leaves, the pierced bone sticks heavily decorated with cut steel, c1860, 11in (28cm) wide.
£130–145 FAN

This type of fan is often called a Jenny Lind fan, after the singer.

A Japanese lacquered tortoiseshell brisé fan, one side inlaid with ivory figures in a garden before Mount Fuji, the other side with a frog procession, some damage, Meiji period, 1868–1911, 6in (15cm) wide.
£2,200–2,600 RTo

A French lithographic fan, decorated with a classical scene, the mother-of-pearl sticks carved, pierced and gilded with floral designs, c1860, 10½in (26.5cm) wide.
£220–250 LDC

◄ A silk fan, the leaf hand-painted with a Georgian lady, serpentine mother-of-pearl sticks, signed 'Vazle', c1880, 10in (25.5cm) wide.
£165–185 FAN

A Chinese export fan, the painted paper leaf with ivory and silk appliqué decoration of a court scene, the reverse with European-style figures, with black and gilt lacquer sticks, c1870, 11in (28cm) wide.
£600–650 P

An Austro-Hungarian brisé fan, with plain ivory sticks, the silver-gilt guards set with garnets, pearls and turquoise, one with a small enamel plaque of a shepherdess, late 19thC, 7¾in (19.5cm) wide.
£1,500–1,650 S

A late Victorian fan, the black lace hand-painted with cherubs, with decorated tortoiseshell sticks, c1880, 14in (35.5cm) wide.
£300–350 FAN

A fontange gauze fan, decorated with black sequins, with carved ebony sticks, c1900, 9in (23cm) wide.
£100–110 FAN

An Irish fan, the Carrickmacross lace leaf designed with tendrils and leaves, the pierced mother-of-pearl sticks with gilded decoration, c1900, 8¾in (22cm) wide.
£250–300 P

A fontange fan, the machine lace leaf painted with central panel of a cherub orchestra, with decorated bone sticks, signed 'Teomar', c1900, 10in (25.5cm) wide.
£100–110 FAN

An Edwardian ostrich feather fan, with mother-of-pearl sticks, 28in (71cm) long.
£70–80 FAN

A fan, with gilt gauze leaf appliquéd with a green silk eagle, the whole with gilt and coloured metal sequin decoration, the bone sticks carved and pierced, c1910, 9½in (24cm) long.
£300–330 P

► A French fontange fan, the black gauze leaf with gilt sequin appliqué in a shell design, signed 'Duvelleroy', c1900, 9in (23cm) wide.
£500–550 P

Jewellery

BANGLES & BRACELETS

A pair of Georgian 15ct gold bracelets, c1790, 3½in (9cm) diam.
£1,800–2,000 WIM

A Victorian gold cuff bracelet, applied with a two-colour gold rose spray between wirework and anthemia.
£500–600 P(Ed)

▶ A late Victorian diamond and gold bangle, set with eleven old mine-cut diamonds and interset with small rose diamonds, 1892.
£16,000–20,000 GTH

A Victorian gold bangle, set with a diamond.
£350–400 GAK

◀ A Victorian rose gold hinged bangle, set with nine rubies interspaced by eight pairs of diamonds.
£1,600–2,000 FHF

A Victorian 10ct rose gold bangle, the hardstone plaque inlaid with a *pietra dura* bouquet of flowers.
£375–450 SK

A Victorian 15ct gold bracelet, 8in (20.5cm) long.
£800–900 WIM

A cultured pearl bracelet, c1900, 2¼in (5.5cm) diam.
£575–700 S

A pearl and diamond hinged gold bangle, set with three pearls in old mine-cut diamond trefoil and scrollwork frames, c1900.
£1,200–1,400 WW

◀ A gold bangle, early 20thC.
£160–200 HCH

An Edwardian gold hinged bangle, set with a cluster of old-cut diamonds, with diamond-set shoulders.
£700–850 WL

A Russian silver and champlevé enamel bracelet, with a matching ring and pair of pendant earrings, Moscow 1899–1908, bracelet 2½in (6.5cm) diam.
£350–420 JAA

◀ A diamond cocktail bracelet, designed as a series of openwork scrolled ribbon links, c1930, 6¼in (16cm) long.
£3,200–3,800 Bon

BROOCHES

A George III diamond-set mourning brooch, with glazed locket compartments containing plaited hair.
£650–750 L

A gold, enamel, diamond and pearl mourning brooch, c1790, 2in (5cm) wide.
£320–350 JSM

A Regency gold and amethyst brooch/pendant, modelled as a guitar, with a glazed compartment to the reverse, c1830.
£900–1,100 Bon

Mourning jewellery

Mourning jewellery originated in the Middle Ages and until the 18thC generally consisted of rings made of gold and black enamel decorated with memento mori motifs such as skulls, skeletons and coffins. From the 1770s, forms became lighter and more graceful to reflect the fashion for neo-classicism. Glass or crystal-covered panels were painted with weeping willows, broken columns, Grecian urns, melancholy female figures in classical dress etc, and a lock of hair was often incorporated in the design.

The popularity of mourning jewellery increased dramatically in Victorian times due to the Queen's strict rules at court governing dress and social behaviour in times of mourning, becoming even more extreme after the death of Prince Albert.

The obsession with mourning was accompanied by a taste for sentimentality, with the result that by the 19thC motifs were less macabre and more romantic. Favourite symbols included forget-me-knots, hearts, crosses and ivy. The growing demand for mourning jewellery led to many styles becoming standardized – gold and black enamel rings and brooches bearing the inscription 'In Memory Of ...' in gold Gothic script were made in vast quantities. Jet jewellery was deemed particularly appropriate for mourning, and a large industry grew up in the Yorkshire seaside town of Whitby, where jet is found.

Because of the quantity of 19thC mourning jewellery still in existence, collectors should avoid poorly-made or damaged pieces.

A Victorian cruciform brooch, set with old-cut diamonds on a blue enamelled border, damaged.
£1,700–2,000 P(L)

A Victorian moonstone and diamond double-heart brooch, 1in (2.5cm) wide.
£1,600–1,750 WIM

A Victorian double-heart brooch, with a pink and a yellow topaz within a border of diamond brilliants, mounted in gold and silver.
£1,600–1,800 TEN

A Victorian 18ct gold brooch, the micro-mosaic floral design with flowers in relief, the frame decorated with vine tendrils and scrollwork, the reverse with locket compartment.
£1,100–1,200 SK

A Victorian gold filigree and mother-of-pearl butterfly brooch, with a heart-shaped pendant.
£250–300 AG

A Victorian gold knot brooch, set with five amethysts in foliage.
£180–220 LJ

◀ A Victorian 18ct gold and platinum brooch, set with a central ruby in a surround of smaller rubies and diamonds.
£500–600 WilP

A Victorian diamond star brooch, the central flowerhead surrounded by subsidiary diamonds.
£1,300–1,500 HYD

A Victorian 15ct gold brooch, c1875, 1½in (4cm) diam.
£775–875 WIM

A late Victorian crescent brooch, set with old-cut diamonds, the gold mount with silver setting, in original fitted box.
£1,250–1,500 WL

A French 18ct gold brooch, by Chaumet, c1890, 3in (7.5cm) long.
£2,500–3,000 WIM

A 9ct gold, red stone and seed pearl bar brooch, Birmingham 1900.
£55–65 PFK

A diamond, ruby and pearl brooch, modelled as a lyre, mounted in silver and gold, c1890.
£1,500–1,650 P

A gold brooch, with a ruby and diamond heart between Oriental pearls, c1895.
£400–500 WW

A Scottish silver-gilt penannular brooch, c1900, 2½in (6.5cm) diam.
£100–120 BWA

Celtic-inspired penannular brooches were very popular in Victorian times. The word penannular, meaning 'almost annular', relates to the shape, as it is a cleft ring. They were originally used to fasten cloaks.

An Edwardian 18ct white gold, diamond and natural pearl brooch.
£400–450 LJ

A 9ct gold bar brooch, set with three circular cut aquamarines in millegrain settings, c1910, 3in (7.5cm) wide.
£120–150 HofB

An Edwardian diamond, ruby and pearl clip, with central rubies and a pearl within a border of diamond-set flowers and leaves.
£1,400–1,700 GTH

A ruby and diamond brooch, c1915.
£1,700–2,000 Bon

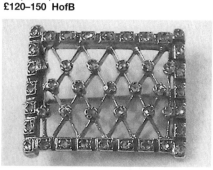

A diamond latticework brooch, 1930s, 1½in (4cm) wide.
£300–350 HCH

An Austrian agate and onyx plume brooch, c1925, 3in (7.5cm) high.
£1,800–2,200 Anth

CAMEOS

An Italian gold and shell cameo bracelet, c1810, 7in (18cm) long.
£1,300–1,500 S

A mid-Victorian shell cameo, depicting Medusa, within a surround of alternate pearls and filigree double scroll.
£700–800 P(Ba)

A cameo necklace, with nine graduated shell cameos set within a black enamel border, early 19thC.
£4,000–4,500 P

◄ A shell cameo brooch, by Saulini, c1850, 2¼in (5.5cm) wide.
£1,800–2,200 S

An agate cameo, by Nicolo Cerbara, the grey and white plaque carved with a head, possibly Alexander Pushkin, in a later mount with applied corded wire to the frame and shank, early 19thC.
£900–1,100 P

A hardstone three-cameo choker, carved with classical profiles, two signed 'Morelli', in chased yellow gold scalloped mounts, c1825.
£3,500–4,000 P

Nicolo Morelli (1771–1830) was an Italian gem-engraver, much favoured by Napoleon. In his work, he often used stones with a warmish pink tone.

A cornelian cameo brooch, with half-pearl fluted surround, c1860.
£900–1,100 P(Ba)

▶ A Victorian 14ct yellow gold, pearl and onyx cameo brooch, inscribed and dated '1866'.
£900–1,000 SK

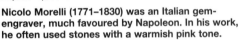

A Victorian gilt-metal cameo bracelet, 7½in (19cm) long.
£80–100 DA

A Victorian shell cameo brooch, mounted in a tubular gold filigree setting, c1880.
£350–400 LJ

A hardstone cameo brooch, depicting a bacchante in profile, with bead and wirework mount, c1880.
£2,000–2,200 Bon

A late Victorian agate cameo ring, carved with a standing lion in profile.
£400–450 P(NW)

Further Reading
Miller's Jewellery Antiques Checklist, Miller's Publications, 1997

CUFFLINKS

A pair of late Victorian turquoise, half-pearl, garnet and rose-cut diamond owl cufflinks, and a matching stud, ⅛in (1.2cm) diam.
£700–850 Bon

A pair of late Victorian 18ct gold cufflinks, set with diamonds, a sapphire and ruby.
£550–650 HCH

A pair of garnet cufflinks, with a central diamond within a textured gold serpent surround, c1890.
£1,500–1,800 P

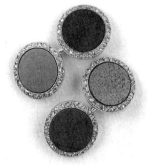

A pair of Cartier lapis lazuli and diamond cufflinks, signed and numbered, c1915, ½in (1.3mm) diam.
£2,200–2,500 S

A pair of Italian diamond cufflinks, by Orisa, c1935.
£450–550 S

A pair of Hermès gold-coloured cufflinks, each designed as a stirrup with a sprung lock, c1950, French control marks.
£700–800 P

EARRINGS

◄ A pair of Victorian 14ct yellow gold pendant earrings, with black enamel tracery, the circular tops suspending a shield-shape with tasselled drops, 2¾in (7cm) long.
£500–600 SK

A pair of Victorian pendant earrings, each with a garnet cabochon within a ropetwist and polished gold surround, with a tassel fringe.
£600–700 DN

A pair of 15ct gold earrings, c1880, ¾in (2cm) long.
£800–900 WIM

A pair of Russian gold earrings, set with demantoid garnets bordered by diamonds, in original fitted leather case, the interior stamped 'A. D. Ivanov, St. Petersburg', late 19thC.
£2,500–3,000 S(NY)

A pair of pendant earrings, the pink topaz set within a diamond border, c1910.
£1,750–2,000 P

A pair of pendant earrings, the diamond ribbon bow surmounts suspending detachable diamond tassels, c1930.
£1,800–2,200 Bon

NECKLACES

A necklace, pair of bracelets and pendant composed of a graduated line of garnets, each within a gold cannetille frame, c1830.
£3,700–4,000 P

A Victorian 15ct gold collar necklace and locket, in original box, necklace 19½in (49.5cm) long.
£4,250–4,750 WIM

A gold and micro-mosaic necklace, composed of three graduated plaques each depicting a classical architectural scene in a malachite border, within a gold ropework frame and suspended from a snake link chain, c1860.
£1,300–1,500 P

Micro-mosaic

- Tiny fragments, or *tesserae*, of coloured glass or stone are fitted together to form decorative plaques, usually backed by black glass.
- In the late 18thC Italian craftsmen in the Vatican workshops perfected a technique where opaque coloured glass was pulled into long strips and then cut into small *tesserae*, thereby greatly increasing the range of shades that could be produced for each colour, and enabling them to work on much smaller surface areas.
- Used throughout Italy in the 19thC to decorate souvenirs produced for the growing tourist trade.
- Most commonly found on jewellery and small decorative items such as boxes.
- Typical images depicted are ancient ruins, local landscapes or figures in national dress.

A gold necklace of pierced plaque links, 19thC.
£500–600 GTH

An amethyst necklace, with later clasp, 19thC, 13¾in (35cm) long.
£1,100–1,200 S

A Victorian 15ct gold serpent necklace, 17in (43cm) long.
£2,000–2,250 WIM

A French rococo-style silver and paste necklace, with *ésprit* pendant drop, 19thC.
£150–180 PFK

A late Victorian half-pearl floral necklet, suspended from a trace-link chain, 14½in (37cm) long.
£450–550 Bon

An Edwardian 15ct gold necklet, set with sapphires, diamonds and seed pearls.
£500–600 WL

▶ A cultured pearl necklace, with gold clasp, 1925, 18in (45.5cm) long.
£120–150 AnS

An Edwardian gold necklace, the centre set with seed pearls and garnet and glass doublets, 15½in (39.5cm) long.
£250–300 SK

PENDANTS

An Armenian image of Christ on copper, with a repoussé silver frame, 18thC, 3½in (9cm) long.
£600–650 ICO

A *pietra dura* cross, with a gold fitting, c1870, 2in (5cm) long.
£220–250 JSM

An Edwardian gold pendant, each segment set with seed pearls, around a central sapphire, hung with a teardrop sapphire, on an 18ct yellow gold chain.
£200–220 LJ

▶ An Edwardian diamond pendant/brooch, with pearl drop, in a case.
£2,300–2,750 GTH

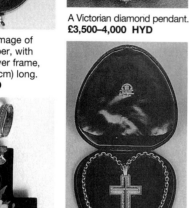

A Victorian diamond pendant.
£3,500–4,000 HYD

A late Victorian gold cross on a chain, with applied cross on a white enamel scroll ground, the reverse engraved '4th June 1890', in a heart-shaped leather-covered case.
£850–1,000 Bri

A Russian priest's silver cross and chain, the reverse with an inscription commemorating Tsar Paul I, late 19thC.
£450–500 ICO

A Victorian gold double drop pendant, with micro-mosaic panels of insects, with ropetwist chain.
£1,000–1,200 GAK

An Austro-Hungarian pendant, with emerald-set frame and scroll surmount, the locket containing a floral spray, 19thC.
£400–450 P(Ba)

A Russian gold pendant, set with diamonds and demantoid garnets, in original fitted leather case, stamped in Cyrillic 'I. V. Morozov, St. Petersburg', c1910, 2¾in (7cm) long.
£1,150–1,400 S(NY)

A Victorian gold locket pendant, centred with a turquoise beneath a ruby and diamond coronet, the glazed locket compartment containing a photograph, suspended from a gold bow brooch.
£800–1,000 L

A diamond-set scrollwork pendant, c1900.
£1,250–1,500 WW

A pendant of two carved and pierced jadeite plaques suspended from diamond and onyx connecting links, with later diamond and sapphire-set surmount, converted from a pair of pendant earrings, c1925.
£800–900 P

RINGS

A Tudor gold ring, set with a quartz stone, the faceted shank with reeded and leaf-cast shoulders, 16thC.
£2,500–3,000 HYD

A Victorian blue-enamelled 18ct gold ring, set with a solitaire diamond.
£650–750 WilP

An Edwardian platinum and diamond ring.
£1,300–1,500 LJ

A Georgian diamond flower ring, c1790.
£600–700 JSM

A late Victorian emerald and diamond cluster ring, stamped '18'.
£1,300–1,500 WL

A Georgian gold and silver ring, with carved shoulders, the central pale yellow citrine surrounded by nine diamonds.
£300–350 F&C

A Victorian 18ct gold memorial ring, set with a diamond.
£160–200 AG

◀ An Edwardian gold and platinum ring, with a trefoil of diamonds on a scroll of mixed cut stones.
£750–900 TEN

A memento ring, the grey and blue painted panel depicting a young woman kneeling before an altar inscribed 'Gratitude', within a border of seed pearls, the reverse inscribed 'A token of Friendship and Esteem, Y. A. E.', early 19thC.
£400–450 P(L)

An 18ct gold ring, the central sapphire flanked by diamonds, with two chip diamonds at opposite corners, two chips missing, Sheffield 1907.
£1,000–1,200 RBB

STICKPINS

A gold stickpin, by W. B. Ford, with an enamelled greyhound, 1867.
£320–380 TEN

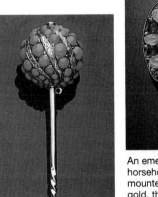

A gold running fox stickpin, c1880, 3in (7.5cm) high.
£700–850 Anth

◀ A gold and diamond set poodle stickpin, c1900, 2½in (6.5cm) long.
£650–800 Anth

▶ A gold horseshoe-shaped stickpin, set with rubies, sapphires and diamonds, French marks, in a case by Boucheron, 1912.
£1,200–1,300 S

This pin was a gift from Tsar Nicholas II.

A gold and turquoise stickpin, 19thC.
£220–260 Bea(E)

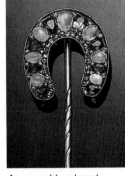

An emerald and opal horsehoe stickpin, mounted in silver and gold, the outer gallery inscribed 'J. A. C. from the Prince of Wales', in original fitted case, late 19thC.
£2,000–2,200 P

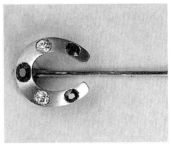

Enamel

A Bilston green enamel box, the lid decorated with a lady and a cherub in green, blue and beige, with gilt rim line, restored, c1770, 3in (7.5cm) wide.
£1,600–1,800 BHa

A Staffordshire enamel patch box, the cover painted in puce with a hydrogen balloon collapsing at sea, its pilot being rescued by a small boat, inscribed 'R. McGuire', late 18thC, 1½in (4cm) wide.
£1,800–2,200 Bon

In the summer of 1785 Richard McGuire, whose enthusiasm far outweighed his experience, attempted to cross the Irish Sea in a hydrogen balloon.

A dark amethyst enamelled patch box, the lid decorated with white and grey flowers, c1885, 2in (5cm) diam.
£70–80 GRI

A pair of Staffordshire white enamel candlesticks, with hand-painted floral decoration, restored, late 18thC, 9¾in (25cm) high.
£900–1,100 BLH

▶ A Russian cloisonné enamel box, the hinged cover painted in enamels with a groom unveiling his bride, within a green bead border, with a cabochon garnet thumbpiece, Moscow, 1908–17, 2¾in (7cm) diam.
£550–650 DN

A Russian gilded silver and enamel lidded jar, with scrolling foliage in blue, brown, yellow and turquoise and an onion-shaped finial, marked, Moscow 1899–1908, 3½in (9cm) high.
£1,400–1,600 JAA

A Swiss 18ct gold quizzing glass, decorated with dark blue and white enamel, c1830, 2½in (6.5cm) long.
£1,200–1,400 Anth

> **Cross Reference**
> See Colour Review

A French enamelled silver scent bottle, decorated in pastel shades with figures in a landscape, c1870, 4in (10cm) high.
£1,200–1,400 BHa

◀ A French silver-gilt and enamel vinaigrette, painted with figures in coloured enamels on a red ground, marked, late 19thC, ¾in (2cm) high.
£425–475 F&C

A cloisonné enamel and copper teapot, decorated in green, blue, purple and red, late 19thC, 5¼in (13.5cm) high.
£75–85 ELI

A pair of cloisonné enamel and copper vases, in red, blue, yellow and turquoise on a beige ground, c1890, 12in (30.5cm) high.
£200–250 AnS

Fabergé

A Fabergé gold and pink enamel button hook, with moonstone terminal, stamped mark, c1900, 3in (7.5cm) long.
£4,000–4,500 P

A Fabergé gold, ivory and diamond-set cigarette holder, workmaster H. Wigström, St. Petersburg, c1900, 3½in (9cm) long.
£1,100–1,250 SHa

A Fabergé silver comport stand, with cut-glass bowl, on four ribbed supports terminating in hoofed feet, damaged, Moscow, 1896, 10¾in (27.5cm) diam.
£4,000–4,500 P

A Fabergé silver cigarette case, the reeded ends chased with leaves, with cabochon sapphire thumbpiece, marked, Moscow, c1900, 3½in (9cm) high.
£2,000–2,200 S(NY)

A Fabergé blue enamel photograph frame, the backboard engraved, workmaster A. Nevalainen, St. Petersburg, 1908–17, 3½in (9cm) long.
£5,000–6,000 S

A Fabergé silver and blue enamel locket, decorated with a diamond-set flower, workmaster August Holmström, St. Petersburg, c1900, 1½in (4cm) long.
£2,800–3,200 S(NY)

◄ A Fabergé *kovsh*, the front panel with a man in a fur-trimmed mantle leaning on a staff, the sides and handle with cloisonné enamel in green, blue and orange on a pink ground, marked, 1908–17, 2½in (6.5cm) diam.
£5,000–5,500 P

A Fabergé gold, enamel and Siberian nephrite jade-set letter opener, workmaster Fedor Affanassiev, St. Petersburg, c1900, 5¼in (13.5cm) long.
£5,250–5,750 SHa

A Fabergé vase, the ceramic body glazed in *vieux rose*, mounted on a plain silver base with beaded rim and tasselled ribbons, workmaster Anders Nevalainen, St. Petersburg, c1880, 3¼in (8.5cm) high.
£5,000–5,500 S

A Fabergé silver vase, with glass liner, marked 'Moscow', 1908–17, 8½in (21.5cm) high.
£3,400–3,750 SHa

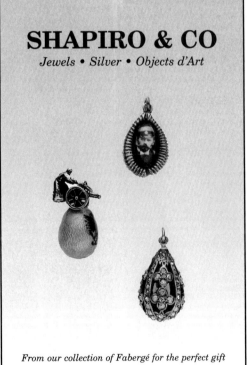

Gold

An ivory and rose gold patch box, with interior mirror and compartments, c1770, 2½in (6.5cm) wide.
£380–420 LBr

A Continental vari-coloured gold snuff box, set with paste stones and a dark blue enamel border, early 19thC, 3¼in (8.5cm) wide.
£3,000–3,500 Bon

A Swiss gold and enamel snuff box, with gold linear decoration on a pale blue ground, a horizontal band of latticework on a black ground, marked, Geneva, c1830, 3½in (9cm) wide.
£1,750–2,000 P

A gold and gilt-metal rococo-style chatelaine, with four panels of classical trophies emblematic of the Arts and Sciences, marked, c1750, 6in (15cm) high.
£350–420 TEN

A Cartier 9ct gold compact, in original fitted case, marked, London, 1947, 2¾in (7cm) square.
£1,300–1,450 SHa

A bloodstone needlecase, overlaid with gold rococo scrolling, English or German, c1760, 4½in (11.5cm) long.
£1,750–2,000 S(NY)

A gold cage-work scent bottle, with rococo-style scrolling, c1770, 2½in (6.5cm) long.
£800–900 LBr

A French gold needlecase, decorated with flowers and pineapples within leaf borders, Paris, 1809–19, 3in (7.5cm) long.
£370–420 S(S)

A French porcelain gold-mounted scent bottle, c1860, 3in (7.5cm) high.
£2,500–2,750 SHa

A gold and hardstone desk seal, with faceted smoky quartz handle, and heavy cast-gold scrolled shell mounts, damaged, early 19thC, 2⅛in (6.5cm) high.
£1,200–1,350 S

◄ A two-colour gold-mounted walking cane, possibly by James Graham, the handle engraved with floral garlands and raised foliate bands, with malacca shaft and steel tip, London, 1780, 42in (106.5cm) long.
£1,000–1,200 S(S)

A Regency gold vinaigrette, modelled as an acorn, engraved with trophies and floral garlands, with inscription on a white enamel band, ¾in (2cm) high.
£800–1,000 F&C

Asian Works of Art

CLOISONNE & ENAMEL

A Chinese cloisonné box and cover, the pale blue ground decorated with lotus flowers, with pierced gilt-metal double gourd-shaped finial, 18thC, 9in (23cm) high.
£1,500–1,650 P

A Chinese Canton enamel jardinière, decorated with ladies in terraced gardens, Qing Dynasty, c1860, 7in (18cm) wide.
£150–180 Hal

This piece would originally have had a stand.

A Chinese Peking enamel box, the sapphire ground with bats and floral scrolls surrounding 'wedded bliss' emblems, 19thC, 9in (23cm) diam.
£240–275 SK

A Chinese ormolu filigree work and enamelled cuspidor, decorated with four enamel floral cartouches within enamelled borders, incomplete, damaged, c1800, 5½in (14cm) diam.
£400–450 Hal

▶ A Japanese cloisonné enamel koro and cover, with panels of dragons and *ho-o* birds on an aventurine and turquoise ground reserved with lotus scrolls and flowers, Meiji period, 1868–1911, 8¼in (21cm) high.
£1,200–1,500 S(S)

A pair of Chinese cloisonné altar candlesticks, decorated all over with densely clustered flowers and leaves, 19thC, 21in (53.5cm) high.
£2,000–2,400 P

A Japanese cloisonné baluster vase, the lemon ground decorated with roses, early 20thC, 9½in (24cm) high.
£400–450 WW

Miller's Compares

I A Japanese cloisonné enamel vase and cover, by Hayashi Kodenji, decorated with gold and silver wire on a midnight blue ground with sparrows and reeds, the cover with assorted flowerheads, signed, Meiji period, 1868–1911, 4in (10cm) high.
£16,000–17,500 S

II A Japanese cloisonné enamel *koro* and cover, in the style of Hayashi Kodenji, decorated with gold and silver wire on a midnight blue ground with sparrows and foliage, the cover pierced with leaf-shaped apertures and decorated with flowerheads, Meiji period, 1868–1911, 4in (10cm) high.
£4,000–5,000 S

Item I is an example of excellent cloisonné work by a gifted maker. Item II is also very attractive but lacks the fine detail of Item I. The style of craftsmanship of Item II is similar to Item I but it is unsigned and therefore commands a lower price.

GLASS

◀ A Chinese Peking yellow glass vase, marked, Yongzheng period, 1723–35, 9in (23cm) high.
£6,000–7,000 S(HK)

▶ A Chinese Peking ruby glass bottle vase, the walls formed with a thin ruby layer covering the snow-flake core, minor damage, 18thC, 11in (28cm) high.
£1,650–1,800 BB(S)

A Chinese red glass covered jar, decorated in relief with a dragon chasing a flaming pearl, the cover with lotus petals, 19thC, 5in (12.5cm) high.
£2,500–2,750 S(NY)

JADE

A Chinese jade bowl, the pale celadon-coloured stone with lighter inclusions, the two handles in the form of mythical beasts, on a fitted carved wood stand, Qianlong period, 1736–95, 4in (10cm) diam.
£700–850 P

Ten Heavenly Stems

These are cyclical signs associated in pairs with the five elements, wood, fire, earth, metal, water. Originally used for naming days but later combined with the twelve branches to make the 60 day/60 year Chinese dating cycle.

A Chinese carved jade calendar disc, the green and white stone with a tab incised with the first of the Ten Heavenly Stems, both faces of the disc incised with a dial containing the characters of the Twelve Earthly Branches, with a wooden stand, Ming/Qing Dynasty, possibly 17thC, 6in (15cm) diam.
£2,500–3,000 S

A Chinese jade cylinder, the light celadon stone with black markings, the surface carved with a Taotie mask, the corner flanges with animal masks, 18thC, 3¼in (8.5cm) high.
£250–300 SK

▶ A Chinese Mughal-style white jade cup and saucer, the pale celadon stone with russet patches and veining, Qing Dynasty, 18thC, saucer 4¼in (11cm) diam.
£2,500–3,000 S(HK)

A Chinese jade ear-cup, the exterior carved in low relief with stylized archaistic designs, the handles carved with interlocking serpents, Ming Dynasty, 17thC, 6in (15cm) diam.
£4,500–5,000 S

◀ A Chinese pale green jade wine pot and cover, with apple green inclusions, carved in relief with lotus flowers, the cover in the form of a mother and child, 19thC, 4¼in (11cm) high.
£200–220 P

A Chinese jade snuff spoon, the pale apple-green stone carved with a phoenix among trailing foliate tendrils, later mounted as a brooch, 19thC, 2¾in (7cm) long.
£175–200 P

Twelve Earthly Branches

Used to divide the day into two hour periods. Also equated to the 12 signs of the Chinese zodiac and the twelve points of the Chinese compass.

LACQUER

A Japanese gold lacquer box with inner tray, decorated in gold, silver, *hiramakie* and *togadashi* with a Sumiyoshi river, the inner tray depicting a shrine, 19thC, 6¾in (17cm) wide.
£4,500–5,000 S(NY)

A Japanese gold lacquer box and cover, inside the cover decorated with lovers in a boat in a moonlit setting, 19thC, 5in (12.5cm) wide.
£5,800–6,500 KJ

A Japanese gilt lacquer box, the cover decorated in silver and gold *hiramakie* with a fishing village under a full moon, 19thC, 3½in (9cm) wide.
£2,800–3,200 BB(S)

A Japanese lacquer incense box, the wood surface decorated with a beetle in gold *hiramakie*, with *nashiji* interior, signed 'Shozan', late 19th/early 20thC, 3in (7.5cm) diam.
£1,100–1,200 S(NY)

A Japanese gold lacquer document box, decorated with eight panels in gold *takamakie*, *hiramakie* and *nashiji*, the inside of the lid with three further panels, late 19thC, 9½in (24cm) wide.
£450–550 HAM

A Japanese silver perfume cabinet, by Masayuki, with gold lacquer *Shibayama* panels inlaid with birds and flowers, the inside of the door and internal drawers decorated with butterflies and a dragonfly in gold *togidashi* and *hiramakie*, the edges of the cabinet and the feet simulating bamboo, damaged, signed, Meiji period, 1868–1911, 5in (12.5cm) wide.
£6,000–6,750 S

A Chinese export gilt-decorated lacquer sewing box, with fitted interior containing ivory sewing implements, above a compartmented drawer, 19thC, 14in (35.5cm) wide.
£1,000–1,200 SK(B)

A Japanese lacquer perfume cabinet, decorated in gold, silver and *hiramakie* with water landscapes, the interior fitted with three drawers, 19thC, 4in (10cm) wide.
£2,400–2,700 S(NY)

A Japanese lacquer box for tea ceremony utensils, decorated in *takamakie* with trees and rocks by a lakeside, the interior of *hirame*, gold-lacquered with pine trees, the rims mounted with pewter, c1700, 20in (51cm) wide.
£1,100–1,300 S

◄ A Japanese lacquered writing utensil box, the cover decorated with chrysanthemums and roses in gilt, red, green and yellow lacquer on a black ground, the fitted *nashiji* interior with writing implements, signed 'Minamoto', Taisho period, 1912–26, 10¾in (27.5cm) wide.
£600–675 P

► A pair of Japanese panels, inlaid in high relief with peacocks and prunus branches in bone, mother-of-pearl and ivory, within a hardwood frame carved with confronting dragons, Meiji period, 1868–1911, 25in (63.5cm) high.
£1,200–1,500 S(S)

METALWARE

A Chinese pewter box, the lid decorated in high relief with grapes inset with carnelian and jade, c1900, 11in (28cm) diam.
£250–300 DuM

A Chinese peach-shaped bronze incense burner, applied with a leafy branch, the tips and small fruit forming the feet, 17th/18thC, 7½in (19cm) wide, with fitted wooden stand.
£600–700 P

A Chinese silver presentation bowl, by Wang Hing, Hong Kong, decorated in relief with flowers, the handles in the form of dragons, c1900, 18½in (47cm) diam, 130oz.
£3,000–3,500 FBG

A Japanese bronze censer, the cover cast as a *shi-shi* fighting a dragon, the body cast with panels of birds, on an elaborately cast base with monkeys, peacocks and sparrows, late 19thC, 36in (91.5cm) high.
£1,600–2,000 Hal

▶ A Chinese silver mug, with dragon-form handle, c1860, 4¼in (11cm) high.
£700–800 ELI

A Chinese bronze *ding* tripod, Western Zhou Dynasty, 1100–771 BC, 9in (23cm) high.
£3,200–3,500 GLD

A Japanese gilt-bronze *keman*, each side with a knotted tassel and two Buddhist angels, above lotus flowers and leaves, c1700, 14½in (37cm) wide.
£4,500–5,500 S

Keman are a common decoration in Buddhist temples, and were probably introduced as a substitute for garlands of fresh flowers.

A pair of Japanese inlaid iron stirrups, by Murasawa Kunisada, decorated in silver with a repeated pattern of stylized roundels, the flange pierced with a stylized bird, the interior lacquered brown, signed, 18thC, 10¼in (26cm) long.
£2,000–2,400 S

A southeast Asian silver three-piece tea set, each piece with an anthropomorphic cover with antlers, the body worked in low relief with *shou* characters, 19thC, teapot 6in (15cm) high, total weight 41oz.
£250–300 P(E)

A Chinese silver tea canister, by Wang Hing, the sides embossed with panels of Oriental landscapes and figural scenes, marked, late 19thC, 4½in (11.5cm) wide, 10oz.
£700–800 Bon

A Chinese bronze 'garlic neck' vase, Han Dynasty, 206 BC–AD 220, 15in (38cm) high.
£1,000–1,200 GLD

▶ A Japanese bronze vase, mid-19thC, 13in (33cm) high.
£3,800–4,400 KJ

◀ A Japanese bronze flower vase, mid-19thC, 11¾in (30cm) high.
£4,500–5,000 KJ

◄ A pair of Japanese bronze vases, Meiji period, 1868–1911, 22in (56cm) high.
£1,350–1,500 MCN

A Japanese bronze vase, signed Yoshimitzu, Meiji period, 1868–1911, 10in (25.5cm) high.
£1,250–1,400 MCN

A Japanese bronze vase, in the style of Genryusai Seiya, cast and applied in high relief with a falcon on a perch and mother-of-pearl inlaid elephant, detailed in gilding and metallic oxides, Meiji period, 1868–1911, 26in (66cm) high, with hardwood stand.
£6,000–7,000 RTo

► A Japanese gilt-copper wine pot, engraved with autumn flowers, 18th/19thC, 10½in (26.5cm) high, in fitted labelled box.
£250–275 SK

A pair of Japanese bronze vases, the necks decorated in silver, copper and gilt with birds amid flowering branches, Meiji period, 1868–1911, 13in (33cm) high.
£1,500–1,800 WW

► A Japanese bronze vase, signed 'Ka-Do', c1900, 15in (38cm) high.
£1,500–1,700 BOW

WOOD

A Chinese carved wooden libation cup, carved in relief on the exterior with clusters of daisies among gnarled branches emerging from rocks beneath a craggy overhang, 19thC, 3in (7.5cm) high.
£550–650 P

► A Chinese *huanghuali* and burlwood medicine chest, the removable inset panel door opening to an interior fitted with four removable drawers, 17th/18thC, 9in (23cm) wide.
£4,000–5,000 S(NY)

A south Indian carved temple figure of the god Garuda, from a 17thC chariot, 19in (48.5cm) high.
£3,400–3,750 GRG

◄ A Japanese carved wood lion mask, with separate articulated jaw, decorated with red and black lacquer with gilt accents and a remnant of a horsehair crest, 19thC, 14in (35.5cm) high.
£400–450 SK

A Chinese bamboo finger citron, or Buddha's hand, 18thC, 2½in (6.5cm) high.
£1,600–2,000 KJ

A Japanese wood portable shrine, containing a seated court official, with gilt interior, dated 'Tempo 10', 1839, 5½in (14cm) high.
£1,300–1,500 S(NY)

ARMS & ARMOUR

A Japanese *Shiro-Ito-Odoshi-Do* cuirass, with white laced *do* on black lacquered plates, seven *kusazuri* ending with brown lacquered lower plates, Edo period, probably 18thC.
£750–900 WAL

An Indian gold-inlaid *khula khud*, 19thC, 15in (38cm) high.
£1,100–1,200 CCB

▶ An Indian powder-flask, formed from a nautilus shell, with embroidered pale orange silk suspension loop, 19thC, 6in (15cm) long.
£600–700 P

A Japanese suit of armour, with black lacquered iron plates and dark blue braiding, 19thC.
£2,400–3,000 SK

A Japanese *katana*, signed 'Bizen Nokuni Noju Osafune Sukesada Saku', 1554, blade 25in (63.5cm) long.
£1,000–1,200 WAL

A Japanese *shinshinto tanto*, blade early 19thC, ivory mounts Meiji period, 1868–1911, 10¾in (27.5cm) long.
£1,200–1,400 S

A Japanese officer's *katana*, c1940, 38in (96.5cm) long.
£550–650 GV

An Indian *shamshir*, the copper-gilt hilt chiselled with flowers and foliage, with a velvet-covered scabbard damascened in gold with birds and foliage, curved watered blade, early 19thC, blade 31½in (80cm) long.
£800–1,000 WAL

A Japanese lacquered sword stand for five swords, decorated in gold *hiramakie* and *nashiji*, 18th/19thC, 23in (58.5cm) wide.
£3,000–3,500 S

TSUBA

A Japanese Higo School iron *sukashi tsuba*, with an openwork design of scrolling clouds, 1700–50, 3in (7.5cm) wide.
£450–500 BB(S)

A Japanese Soten School iron and gold-inlaid *sukashi*-type *tsuba*, depicting a Samurai in battle with a giant demon, c1750, 3in (7.5cm) diam.
£800–900 KIE

A Japanese iron *tsuba*, made in the Chinese style and depicting dragons, c1760, 3in (7.5cm) diam.
£350–400 KIE

A Japanese gold lacquered *tsuba*, with *Shibayama*, ivory and mother-of-pearl inlay, with silver borders, Meiji period, 1868–1911, 4in (10cm) diam.
£5,250–5,750 S

CLOCKS

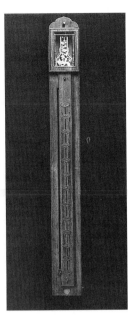

▶ A Japanese mahogany-cased eight-day wall clock, by Seikosica Clock Co, c1905, 15in (38cm) diam.
£330–365 K&D

A Japanese lantern clock, early 19thC, 38½in (98cm) high.
£6,500–7,200 S(Z)

◀ A Japanese hardwood thirty-hour stick clock, late 19thC, 37½in (95.5cm) high.
£2,200–2,500 BB(S)

FIGURES & MODELS

A Chinese beige-flecked green jade carving of two monkeys, carved as an infant resting across the shoulders of a parent, 18thC, 3in (7.5cm) high.
£650–750 P

A Chinese bronze Dog of Fo, Ming Dynasty, 17thC, 6in (15cm) long.
£750–850 GLD

A Chinese bronze and parcel-gilt censer, modelled as a *kirin*, with hinged head and open mouth, Ming Dynasty, 17thC, 6¾in (17cm) high.
£700–800 CGC

▶ A Japanese carved ivory model of a ram, signed 'Shuko', Meiji period, 1868–1911, 4in (10cm) long.
£1,100–1,200 LBO

A Chinese carved ivory group, depicting an old man holding a baby before a young warrior seated on a tree stump, 19thC, 6¼in (16cm) high.
£1,600–2,000 AH

A Japanese wood group of two puppies, signed 'Horitsune', 19thC, 5½in (14cm) high.
£2,000–2,400 KJ

◀ A Japanese carved ivory articulated lobster, Meiji period, 1868–1911, 12in (30.5cm) long.
£5,000–6,000 SK

A pair of Japanese rootwood geese,
19thC, largest 4in (10cm) high.
£1,800–2,200 KJ

A Japanese boxwood group,
carved as a rat-catcher kneeling
over his box, a club in one hand,
screaming in fury as the rodent
jumps onto his back, incised
signature, damaged, Meiji period,
1868–1911, 4¾in (12cm) long.
£600–700 P

A Japanese cast bronze model of a tiger,
with a golden-brown patina, signed 'Seikoku',
Meiji period, 1868–1911, 32in (81.5cm) long.
£2,500–3,000 BB(S)

A Japanese bronze model of a pheasant,
the body of a dark copper colour, with inlaid
glass eyes, signed 'Masatsune', Meiji period,
1868–1911, 23¼in (59cm) long.
£4,000–4,500 S

A pair of Chinese silver menu holders,
modelled as dragons, c1880, 5in (12.5cm) long.
£575–650 BEX

◄ A Japanese silvered-bronze model of a
hawk, on a gnarled branch of flowering prunus,
Meiji period, 1868–1911, 14½in (37cm) high.
£2,000–2,400 TEN

A Japanese ivory carving,
depicting Ashinaga and
Tanaka, signed 'Shogetsu',
c1870, 2¼in (5.5cm) high.
£2,200–2,500 KIE

**These carvings depict
characters from a legend
dating back to the 14thC,
in which Ashinaga was
born with long arms and
Tanaka was born with
long legs. They are often
depicted fishing in a
river, Ashinaga holding
a fish in each hand.**

► A Japanese
ivory model of a
fox in disguise,
by Tomokazu,
late 19thC,
5in (12.5cm) high.
£900–1,000 JaG

A Japanese carved ivory group,
late 19thC, 3¼in (8.5cm) wide.
£1,100–1,250 SHa

► A Japanese carved ivory group of
a fisherman with a cormorant on his
head, a basket of fish at his feet,
c1900, 12in (30.5cm) high.
£400–450 CAG

A Japanese carved ivory group of rats eating fruit,
stencilled in black, early 20thC, 4in (10cm) high.
£500–600 Hal

FURNITURE

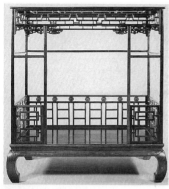

A Chinese *hongmu* canopy-bed, the ladder-pattern side struts surmounted by medallions carved with auspicious characters, Qing Dynasty, mid-19thC, 90½in (230cm) long.
£2,000–2,400 P

A Chinese Ningbo elm and blackwood single canopy bed, with bone inlay, 1850–70, 81in (205.5cm) wide.
£4,200–4,700 OE

A shell-inlaid gold lacquer travelling clothes chest, with a *nashiji* ground decorated in gold *hiramakie* and *takamakie* with shell and pewter inlay, gilt-copper mounts, c1900, 25in (63.5cm) wide.
£4,000–4,500 S

A Chinese lacquer cabinet, the doors decorated with geese and opening to reveal an arrangement of small drawers, on a European painted and parcel-gilt fretwork stand, c1800, 37¾in (96cm) wide.
£1,000–1,200 HOK

▶ A Chinese display cabinet, the carved door fronts with boxwood inlay and cloisonné handles, restored, c1900, 16in (40.5cm) wide.
£250–300 SK

A Chinese hardwood cabinet, with floral and leaf-pierced panels, sliding cupboards and drawers, 19thC, 41½in (105.5cm) wide.
£450–550 HYD

A Japanese display cabinet, decorated with *Shibiyama* panels depicting figures and birds within landscapes, with pierced and carved panels, late 19thC, 50in (127cm) wide.
£1,000–1,200 JAd

A Japanese lacquer table cabinet, decorated and gilded with birds in branches and figures in landscapes, the doors enclosing four drawers decorated with birds and flowers, painted coloured sides, 1920s, 14in (35.5cm) wide.
£270–300 Hal

A Chinese lacquered elm seal box, with interior drawers, mid-19thC, 12in (30.5cm) high.
£280–325 GHC

▶ A Chinese bamboo armchair, late 19thC, 29in (73.5cm) high.
£425–475 GHC

A Chinese black-lacquered elm coffer, Shaanxi Province, late 19thC, 38in (96.5cm) wide.
£800–1,000 K

A Korean hardwood chest, with ornate brass hinges, early 20thC, 26in (66cm) wide.
£300–350 SK

A Chinese red lacquer chest, with iron bail handles and pierced strap mounts, 19thC, 54in (137cm) wide.
£1,750–2,000 SLN

A Japanese miniature chest of drawers, c1900, 3in (7.5cm) wide.
£1,000–1,200 G(L)

A Japanese Kano School six-fold screen, decorated in ink and colour on a gold-leaf ground, 18thC, 59in (150cm) high.
£2,200–2,500 S

A Japanese two-panel paper screen, decorated in ink, colour and gold-leaf with cranes beside a tree, 19thC, 54½in)137cm) high.
£1,800–2,200 SLN

A Japanese ivory table screen, supported by two children, the screen framed with bats, Meiji period, 1868–1911, damaged, 8in (20.5cm) high.
£1,200–1,400 Bon(C)

A Japanese carved hardwood stool, by Arthur & Bond, the frieze carved with a border of scrolling foliage and stylized coloured swirls, and the apron carved with scrolling plants, c1920, 44½in (113cm) wide.
£650–750 S

The English-run firm of Arthur & Bond was established in Yokohama around 1870, and grew to become one of the leading furniture dealers in the area, also trading from premises in London.

◀ A Chinese *hongmu* table, 19thC, 38in (96.5cm) wide.
£850–950 OE

A Chinese gilt and black-lacquered wood sewing table, with fitted interior, the hinged top with an audience scene, Daoguang period, 1821–50, 25½in (65cm) wide.
£2,000–2,200 P

A Chinese hardwood centre table, with carved key design to the rim, the base carved as four *shishi*, late 19thC, 41½in (105.5cm) diam.
£900–1,100 M

A Chinese hardwood console table, the top with inset veined marble, 19thC, 57in (145cm) wide.
£2,500–3,000 L&T

▶ An Anglo-Indian padouk library table, with leaf and rosette carved frieze, 19thC, 53in (134.5cm) wide.
£850–1,000 DN

LOCATE THE SOURCE

The source of each illustration in Miller's can be found by checking the code letters below each caption with the Key to Illustrations, pages 789–795.

INRO

A Japanese red lacquer three-case *inro*, decorated with gold *hiramakie* and *takamakie* with carp among water weeds, 19thC, 3in (7.5cm) high.
£300–330 S(Am)

A Japanese four-case *inro*, decorated with a lakeside scene in gold and coloured *takamakie, hiramakie*, and *togidashi*, signed 'Kajikawa Yoshinobu', 18thC, 3¼in (8.5cm) wide.
£3,000–3,500 S

A Japanese lacquered *inro*, decorated and gilded with flying cranes, 19thC, 4in (10cm) high.
£700–800 KIE

A Japanese gilt and black lacquer four-case *inro*, decorated with a scene of foreigners in a ship, in red, black and gold *hiramakie* and *togidashi* on a black ground, 19thC, *inro* 2¾in (7cm) high, with an ebony *netsuke* carved as a temple, signed 'Tosei'.
£1,500–1,800 BB(S)

▶ A Japanese four-case gilt and black lacquer *inro*, with all-over autumn leaf decoration on a *nashiji* ground of wind-swept grasses, Meiji period, 1868–1911, *inro* 2¾in (7cm) high, with a carved ivory *netsuke*.
£750–900 P

NETSUKE

A Japanese carved ivory *manjua netsuke*, carved with Thousand Face pattern, 18thC, 1½in (4cm) diam.
£160–200 DuM

A Japanese Kyoto School carved ivory *netsuke*, in the form of a thief carrying a wine sack, damaged, late 18thC, 3in (7.5cm) high.
£150–180 PFK

◀ A Japanese carved ivory *netsuke*, by Tomochika, in the form of a geisha with a scroll, 19thC, 1¼in (3cm) high.
£1,000–1,100 HUR

▶ A Japanese carved ivory *netsuke*, in the form of a mother with children, signed 'Tononare', mid-19thC, 2½in (6.5cm) high.
£2,200–2,500 BOW

PRINTS & SCROLLS

A Japanese woodcut print, 'Furyu Nana Komachi', by Utamaro, depicting a girl combing the hair of a seated woman, c1900, 15 x 10in (38 x 25.5cm).
£1,500–1,800 JaG

◀ A Japanese woodcut print, by Eisen, depicting the courtesan Hana-murasaki, in shades of blue and black on an ivory ground, c1820, 14 x 9½in (35.5 x 24cm).
£600–675 JaG

A Japanese woodcut print from '100 views of the moon', by Yoshitoshi, in blue, red, green and black on a grey ground, with a poem by Mizuki Tatsunosuke, 1891, 14 x 9½in (35.5 x 24cm).
£150–165 JaG

▶ A Chinese hanging scroll, depicting the God of Wealth, signed 'Qian Hui'an', in ink and colour on paper, late 19thC, 51½ x 27in (131 x 68.5cm).
£650–800 S(Am)

◀ A Japanese hanging scroll, 'Cooling off on Summer Evening', depicting a girl in a kimono seated on a bench holding a fan, in ink and colour on paper, signed 'Ogata Gekko', early 20thC, 52¾ x 23¼in (134 x 59cm).
£800–1,000 S

ROBES & COSTUME

A Japanese Buddhist priest's silk brocade robe, decorated with flowers, the surround with dragons and phoenix woven in terracotta and sea-green silk and gold *kinrande*, 19thC, 45¾in (116cm) wide.
£300–350 P

A Chinese emperor's midnight blue silk surcoat, with four embroidered insignia worked in coloured silks and metal threads, 19thC.
£3,700–4,200 WW

A Chinese woman's robe, embroidered with figures in landscapes in various colours and gold threads on a midnight blue ground, 19thC.
£800–900 SK

▶ A Japanese red silk kimono, embroidered with various longevity emblems, late 19thC.
£370–400 SK

A Chinese export peach silk shawl, embroidered in pastel silks with figures in a landscape, early 20thC, 52in (132cm) square.
£250–275 P

A pair of Chinese sleeve panels, embroidered with birds on foliage in coloured silks, early 20thC, 20 x 3½in (51 x 9cm).
£160–175 PBr

SNUFF BOTTLES

A Chinese greenish-brown jade snuff bottle, carved as a double gourd, with coral stopper, c1900, 2¼in (5.5cm) high.
£2,200–2,500 P

Cross Reference
See Colour Review

► A Chinese amber snuff bottle, carved with a maiden on each side, with green glass stopper, 1820–1900, 2½in (6.5cm) high.
£2,250–2,500 JWA

A Chinese hair-crystal snuff bottle, the stone suffused throughout with fine black tourmaline needles, with jadeite stopper and garnet finial, 1780–1880, 3in (7.5cm) high.
£2,250–2,500 JWA

A Chinese rock crystal snuff bottle, inside-painted in muted wintery colours with a scene of a procession of figures on horseback, with carved ivory stopper, signed 'Tang Zi Chuan', late 19thC, 3¼in (8.5cm) high.
£500–550 P

◄ A Chinese rock crystal snuff bottle, inside-painted with deer and goats in a landscape, signed 'Liu Chao', dated '1935', 2¾in (7cm) high.
£320–350 S(Am)

TEXTILES

A Chinese temple hanging, the heavy brocade pennants with dragons on a blue ground, Qianlong period, 1736–95, 130 x 15in (330 x 38cm).
£750–900 SK

A Chinese terracotta damask silk panel, decorated in coloured silks and gold thread with figures in a garden, mid-19thC, 18½ x 71in (47 x 180.5cm).
£320–380 P

◄ A Chinese pale gold silk wall hanging, embroidered in coloured silks with peony blossoms, trailing floral vine and bats, lined with peach silk damask, early 19thC, 49 x 28in (124.5 x 71cm).
£400–450 WW

A set of four Japanese silk table screen panels, embroidered in coloured silks with cockerels on a black ground, framed and glazed, late 19thC, 19¼ x 9¾in (49 x 25cm).
£300–350 WW

A Chinese silk wall hanging, worked in coloured silks with scenes of a pagoda and animals on a dark blue ground, late 19thC, 32 x 152in (81.5 x 386cm).
£220–260 DN(H)

Islamic Works of Art

CERAMICS

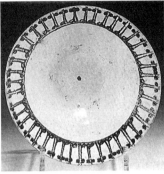

A Nishapur pottery bowl, slip-decorated with a band of Kufic around the rim, eastern Persia, 10thC, 7½in (19cm) diam.
£750–900 S

A Seljuk white-glazed pottery bowl, the sides with a frieze of vertical moulded ribs, Persia, early 13thC, 8in (20.5cm) diam.
£2,000–2,400 Bon

A Seljuk white-ware tankard, the exterior decorated with vertical streaks of underglaze cobalt blue, with a black band containing a cursive inscription on the rim, Kashan, early 13thC, 4½in (11.5cm) high.
£4,000–4,500 S(NY)

A Seljuk turquoise-glazed ewer, the shoulder moulded in relief with a frieze of stylized fish and scrolling tendrils, 13thC, Gurgan, 9½in (24cm) high.
£2,750–3,000 S(NY)

A Middle-Eastern blue and white charger, decorated with a stylized floret encircled by six flammiform leafy panels and stylized foliate designs, minor damage, 17thC, 14in (35.5cm) diam.
£700–800 P

A turquoise-glazed pottery model of a festive group, in the form of banqueting figures being entertained by musicians in the interior of a courtyard, with applied architectural details, Kashan, 13th/14thC, 6¾in (17cm) wide.
£320–350 P

A Safavid *cuerda seca* pottery tile, decorated in polychrome with a bird amid floral branches, on a yellow ground, Persia, 17th/18thC, 8¼in (21cm) square.
£1,200–1,400 Bon

A Safavid figural pottery tile, decorated in underglaze cobalt-blue, green, black and mustard with an elegant turbanned figure, surrounded by flowers, Persia, early 17thC, 6½in (16.5cm) square.
£1,600–2,000 Bon

Figural tiles such as this depicting either young men or women are painted in the style of 16thC Persian miniature painters.

A Kirman pottery vase, decorated in underglaze-blue and red slip with a Chinese landscape around lobed arabesques, Persia, 17thC, 5¾in (14.5cm) high.
£1,400–1,600 S

◀ A Qajar pottery tile, decorated in underglaze blue, yellow, green, brown, turquoise and purple with figures playing polo, foliage, courtiers and a rabbit, the border with inscriptions, 19thC, 12in (30.5cm) square.
£550–650 CGC

GLASS

A free-blown pale green glass ewer, with trailed handle, the body with four applied medallions, Persia, 9th century AD, 4½in (11.5cm) high.
£2,000–2,400 Bon

A free-blown amber glass bottle, the shoulder with a band of oval medallions above a honeycomb frieze, Persia, 11th/12thC, 9¾in (25cm) high.
£1,000–1,200 Bon

A gold filigree-mounted glass scent flask, with a hinged cover, Persia, 18thC, 4¼in (11cm) high.
£2,000–2,200 S

A Beykoz glass pitcher and ewer, decorated with a heart-shaped medallion enclosing a floral motif, the ewer with cut oval facets, each decorated in gilt with foliate sprays within a crescent, Turkey, early 19thC, tallest 9½in (24cm) high.
£1,400–1,600 S

METALWARE

A Khurasan silver and copper-inlaid bronze tray, the recess with incised and inlaid decoration, the rim with bands of cursive calligraphy, eastern Persia, c1200, 11¼in (28.5cm) wide.
£5,750–7,000 S

The purpose of these trays was possibly to serve sweetmeats or dried fruit. The use of sheet-metal may well have been a means by which craftsmen could imitate wares in gold and silver, although the status of this tray must have been raised by the lavish use of precious metal inlays.

A silver and copper-inlaid bronze inkwell, incised and inlaid with *mihrab*-shaped panels of vines, palmettes, Kufic and cursive inscriptions and rosettes, some handles missing, Persia, 12thC, 3¾in (9.5cm) high.
£3,000–3,500 Bon

A Khurasan bronze green-glazed bird-shaped oil lamp, the wick-holders extending from the chest and wings, eastern Persia, c1200, 5in (12.5cm) high.
£2,800–3,200 S

▶ A pair of silver candlesticks, the columns decorated with scrolls and simulated scales, the knops with leaf and scroll motifs, the base with shell, scroll and floral embossed bracket feet, Turkey, 1876–1909, 12½in (32cm) high.
£2,200–2,500 P

A Qajar bronze ewer, the hinged cover with tear-shaped finial, incised decoration of figural and calligraphic cartouches, Persia, 19thC, 15¾in (40cm) high.
£1,200–1,400 S

An Ottoman embossed silver mirror-back, with a continuous band of flowers and scrolls, encircling sixteen petal-shaped lappets radiating from a central floral boss, Tughra marks, 19thC, 12½in (32cm) diam.
£160–200 P

TEXTILES

Part of an Ottoman maroon silk satin panel, embroidered in coloured silks and metal thread with a repeating pattern, and decorated with woven braid, 18thC, 38½ x 23½in (98 x 60cm).
£500–600 ĐN(H)

A wall-hanging, the central lavender silk panel with pale gold panels, embroidered with gilt-metal threads, olive-green silk border, Turkey, 1850–60, 62 x 44in (157.5 x 112cm).
£600–700 WW

A *qalamkar* and printed wall-hanging, the cotton ground worked in red, blue and fawn with the Tree of Life pattern, Persia, mid-19thC, 71 x 47¼in (180.5 x 120cm).
£275–325 P

A portière, the pale gold silk ground embroidered with gilt-metal thread, a pale rose silk inner *mihrab* embroidered with flowers, the base with trellised flowers on a mid-gold ground, Turkey, c1860, 119 x 72in (302.5 x 183cm).
£1,000–1,200 WW

MISCELLANEOUS

A set of 16 ivory gaming pieces, with turned lines and dot and circle motif, Persia, 9th/10th century AD, largest 1½in (4cm) high.
£3,000–3,500 Bon

A Turkish Ottoman gilt-metal-mounted sword, the horn hilt with a red cabochon stone on either side of the pommel, the velvet-covered scabbard with gilt copper mounts, each end chased with a floral design on both sides, watered steel blade, late 18thC, 35in (89cm) long.
£5,500–6,500 Bon

An Islamic ebony powder flask, inlaid with horn and bone, with horn knop, 18thC, 6in (15cm) high.
£1,000–1,200 Herm

A Damascus mother-of-pearl-inlaid easel, the sides with floral motifs on a trailing palmette design, Syria, late 19thC, 67in (170cm) high.
£700–800 Bon

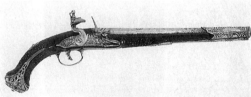

An Islamic/Balkan silver-mounted flintlock pistol, with walnut full stock, some restoration, mid-19thC, 20in (51cm) long.
£800–900 Herm

◄ A Seljuk gold ring, set with blue glass, the bezel decorated with raised foliate designs and panels, Persia, 12thC, 1¼in (3cm) wide.
£9,000–10,000 S

A Qajar etched steel *khula khud*, the front embossed with a devil's face, fitted with gold-damascened horns, central spike and adjustable nasal, Persia, 19thC, 11½in (29cm) high.
£300–350 Bon

Architectural Antiques

IRON

An American iron boot scraper, 19thC, 8in (20.5cm) high.
£80–90 Riv

A wrought-iron sign bracket, 1880s, 60in (152.5cm) wide.
£350–400 A&H

An American hand-made wrought-iron ornamental roof-top finial, 19thC, 34in (86.5cm) high.
£400–450 ASM

An American painted cast-iron fountain, attributed to J. W. Fiske, the base encircled by cranes, late 19thC, 46¾in (119cm) high.
£1,800–2,200 SK(B)

► A cast-iron pump, the body cast in high relief with scallop shells and stiff-leaf decoration, the handle cast with rococo scrolls and acanthus, late 19thC, 47in (119.5cm) high.
£575–700 S(S)

A selection of Victorian cast-iron hoppers, largest 17in (43cm) wide.
£14–30 each WEL

◄ A pair of decorative wrought-iron gates, with side supports, late 19thC, 69in (175.5cm) wide.
£700–775 NET

A Victorian red-painted cast-iron wall-mounted post box, 13in (33cm) wide.
£450–500 WEL

A Victorian cast-iron garden roller, 25in (63.5cm) wide.
£150–175 Recl

A Regency wrought-iron seat, with reeded triple-arcaded back and paw feet, 73in (185.5cm) wide.
£1,100–1,300 AH

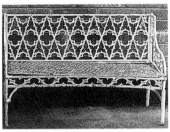

A Victorian white-painted cast-iron bench, 33in (84cm) wide.
£400–475 RAW

A Victorian Coalbrookdale white-painted cast-iron rustic garden seat, 51in (129.5cm) wide.
£1,000–1,200 JNic

A pair of Victorian cast-iron garden benches, with foliate and rope pattern scroll ends and teak slatted seats, 74in (188cm) wide.
£675–800 F&C

A Victorian Gothic-style three-piece suite of cast-iron garden furniture, with pierced backs and sides and honeycomb seats, bench 56in (142cm) wide.
£2,500–3,000 MEA

A green-painted wrought-iron garden bench, on later octagonal pad feet, 19thC, 48in (122cm) wide.
£450–550 CAG

◄ A pair of wrought-iron garden benches, with strapwork seats and backs and scroll arms, 19thC, 72in (183cm) wide.
£800–1,000 WBH

A cast-iron window/door surround, c1910, 55in (139.5cm) wide.
£140–175 A&H

A three-piece suite of cast-iron garden furniture, designed by Edward Bawden, with wooden slatted seats, early 20thC, bench 48in (122cm) wide.
£3,200–3,500 S(S)

Edward Bawden (b1903) painter, illustrator and graphic designer, studied at the Cambridge School of Art from 1919 and the Design School of the Royal College of Art from 1922–25 where Paul Nash was a tutor. He designed textiles for the Orient Steam Navigation Company and decorations for earthenware produced by Wedgwood.

► A cast-iron church window, c1890, 72in (183cm) wide.
£500–600 A&H

◄ A set of four Victorian green-painted cast-iron garden urns, with partly-reeded bodies and wide tongue pattern rims, and two conforming square pedestals, 16½in (42cm) high.
£800–900 CAG

► A pair of cast-iron campana-shaped garden urns on pedestals, with loop handles, mid-19thC, 53½in (135.9cm) high.
£3,000–3,500 BB(S)

A pair of cast-iron urns, slight damage, late 19thC, 15½in (39.5cm) high.
£200–240 SWN

MARBLE

A pair of white marble term figures, 18thC, 37in (94cm) high.
£6,300–7,000 S

A white marble group of Mercury and Argos, by John Graham Lough, 19thC, 38in (96.5cm) wide.
£12,000–14,000 Recl

A neo-classical-style marble garden fountain, the sides with frolicking putti, raised on three monopodia supports headed by sphinxes, late 19thC, 59in (150cm) high.
£7,000–8,000 BB(S)

An Italian white marble figure of a maiden, representing Winter, late 19thC, 62in (157.5cm) high.
£3,500–4,000 S(S)

A marble font, carved with scrolling acanthus brackets and bands of bellflowers, 19thC, 27½in (70cm) wide.
£1,500–1,800 LAY

> **Miller's is a price GUIDE not a price LIST**

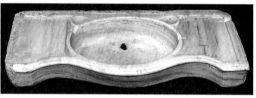

A Turkish marble sink, 18thC, 37in (94cm) wide.
£900–1,000 MIN

A pair of marble models of the Warwick Vase, each with a beaded and lamb's tongue rim, damaged, 19thC, 34in (86.5cm) wide.
£4,000–5,000 Bon(M)

A white marble sundial, on fruiting vine-carved baluster and rising circular foot, the bronze dial signed 'W. Carpenter, London', c1900, 49in (124.5cm) high.
£2,200–2,500 S(S)

A marble table, possibly Italian, 19thC, 76in (193cm) wide.
£2,750–3,000 BAB

STONE

A pair of stone models of eagles, 18thC, 40in (101.5cm) wide.
£4,500–5,000 DD

These items originated from Warter Priory, Yorkshire.

A pair of mid-Victorian composition stone models of recumbent lions, in the style of Canova, 28in (71cm) wide.
£1,700–2,000 Bon(M)

A stone figure of Ruth the Gleaner, stamped 'M. H. Blanchard', dated '1859', 78in (198cm) high.
£3,500–4,000 JBe

A pair of Victorian plaster statues, 48in (122cm) high.
£2,750–3,000 BAB

An American stone model of a soldier's head, late 19thC, 29in (73.5cm) high.
£550–600 Riv

A pair of limestone finials, late 19thC, 30in (76cm) high.
£1,600–1,800 Recl

A French limestone fountain, 19thC, 48in (122cm) wide.
£3,000–3,500 BB(S)

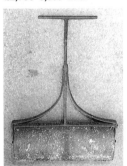

A stone and iron garden roller, 19thC, 33in (84cm) wide.
£140–170 WRe

◀ A Victorian millstone, 48in (122cm) diam.
£800–900 Recl

A staddle stone, 18thC, 29in (73.5cm) high.
£200–240 WRe

A Draycott stone trough, 18thC, 37in (94cm) wide.
£425–500 WEL

▶ A pair of composition stone urns, each with egg-and-dart moulded everted rim, late 19thC, 24in (61cm) high.
£5,500–6,000 S(S)

These urns originally formed part of the terrace at Hevingham Hall, Suffolk and were removed during the re-landscaping of the gardens. According to Pevsner, Hevingham is without doubt the grandest Georgian mansion in Suffolk. It was designed about 1778 by Sir Robert Taylor for Sir Gerard Vaneck, a merchant of Dutch descent. The interior was designed by James Wyatt, and the gardens were laid out in 1781–82 by Capability Brown.

A pair of Georgian stone urns, the rims showing signs of shamrock carving, the bowl carved with vertical leaves, dated '1813', 39in (99cm) high.
£950–1,100 DD

TERRACOTTA

A pair of Compton Pottery 'Four Seasons' terracotta planters, each with roundels of fruit and flowers emblematic of the Seasons flanked by ribbons, early 20thC, 22in (56cm) diam.
£2,300–2,750 S(S)

These jardinières were designed and made by Mary, wife of the artist G. F. Watts. Mary started the Compton Potters Art Guild in Compton, Surrey.

A Victorian terracotta ridge tile, modelled as a grinning dragon with webbed clawed feet and pointed tail, 23in (58.5cm) high.
£700–800 HYD

A pair of terracotta garden urns, each with an egg-and-dart rim and anthemion decoration, late 19thC, 23¾in (60.5cm) high.
£900–1,100 Bon(M)

WIREWORK

A pair of wirework jardinières, the Gothic arch form planters on wrought stands with scrolling spandrels, 19thC, 34¾in (88cm) wide.
£1,000–1,200 P

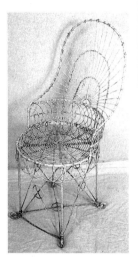

A double-sided wirework seat, on four scrolling legs joined by bowed stretchers, c1900, 48in (122cm) wide.
£1,150–1,350 S(S)

◄ A pair of Victorian wirework garden chairs, 17in (43cm) wide.
£500–550 SPU

WOOD

A pair of oak brackets, carved with stylized tulip design, 1580–1620, 5in (12.5cm) wide.
£100–110 AnSh

Two Italian walnut carvings of phoenixes, c1720, 12in (30.5cm) wide.
£350–400 HUM

A carved walnut swag, 17thC, 36in (91.5cm) high.
£80–100 OCH

► A Jacobean section of oak carving, depicting a bearded male surmounted by plumes, leaves and other motifs, and with scale pattern bracket beneath, 38in (96.5cm) high.
£775–900 MCA

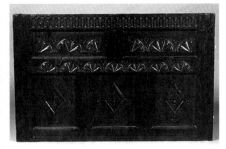

An oak overmantel, with carved panels, 17thC, 51¼in (130cm) wide.
£250–300 PFK

An oak wall panel, with diamond scroll pattern, 17thC, 55in (139.5cm) wide.
£1,250–1,400 SEA

A set of four pine columns, each with an Ionic capital, two painted, three capitals distressed, early 20thC, 129in (327.5cm) high.
£2,500–3,000 Bon(M)

▶ A teak garden seat, possibly by J. P. White, with slatted back and seat, the top rail carved in relief with a poem, early 20thC, 74in (188cm) wide.
£600–700 S(S)

MISCELLANEOUS

A selection of Victorian red corbel bricks, 10in (25.5cm) long.
£1–2 each WEL

An American copper floriform finial, 19thC, 48in (122cm) high.
£1,250–1,500 SK(B)

▶ A Victorian stoneware garden urn, the part-ribbed body with acanthus leaf decoration, stamped 'J. Stiff & Sons, Lambeth', 54in (137cm) high.
£2,700–3,000 WW

James Stiff & Sons, London Pottery, Lambeth, London operated c1863–1913 and were then taken over by Doultons.

An early Victorian square chimney pot, 30in (76cm) high.
£50–55 WEL

A terracotta chimney pot, 1930s, 26in (66cm) high.
£40–50 BYG

A Victorian vented chimney pot, 55in (139.5cm) high.
£100–120 Recl

A Scottish fireclay jardinière, the sides moulded with masks supporting swags of fruiting foliage, late 19thC, 28in (71cm) wide.
£450–550 S(S)

A salt-glazed trough, 1920s, 24in (61cm) wide.
£40–50 A&H

BATHROOM FITTINGS

A Victorian corner basin,
with a shell-shaped soap dish,
12in (30.5cm) wide.
£165–185 DOR

An Edwardian wash basin,
on a fluted pedestal, with original
brass taps, 33in (84cm) high.
£650–750 NOST

A toleware slipper bath,
with original paint, early 19thC,
17¾in (45cm) high.
£450–550 SPR

A French cast-iron roll-top bath, with lions' paw feet,
c1850, 63in (160cm) long.
£1,100–1,300 WEL

A vitreous enamel cast-iron bath, with lions' paw feet,
c1880, 63in (160cm) long.
£1,000–1,200 DOR

A blue and white floral-
painted lavatory pan, c1880.
£550–600 WEL

▶ A cast-iron bath,
with chromium-plated
shower attachment,
fully restored, c1920,
bath 74in (188cm) long.
£13,000–15,000 DRU

◀ A Triton
white embossed
lavatory pan,
by Morrison,
Ingram &
Son, c1890.
£900–1,000 WRe

A Victorian mahogany lavatory seat, with paper tray, 23in (58.5cm) wide.
£320–380 WRe

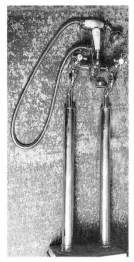

▶ A nickel shower mixer, on standpipes, 1930s, 37in (94cm) high.
£600–660 DOR

A brass-jointed copper towel rail, 1920–30, 60in (152.5cm) high.
£500–600 WRe

DOORS & DOOR FURNITURE

An oak boarded door, with oak nail-head ornaments, one iron strap hinge missing, 16th/17thC, 30in (76cm) wide.
£650–750 PFK

A studded oak plank door, 18thC, 32in (81.5cm) wide.
£200–225 WEL

An oak plank door, 18thC, 31in (78.5cm) wide.
£270–300 WEL

A Victorian pine four-panelled door, 32in (81.5cm) wide.
£60–70 WEL

A Victorian Gothic-style pine door, with red and blue stained glass panels, 30in (76cm) wide.
£600–700 WEL

A studded pine door, c1880, 60in (152.5cm) wide.
£1,800–2,000 WRe

Miller's is a price GUIDE
not a price LIST

▶ A brass Suffolk latch, c1880, 13in (33cm) high.
£12–15 HEM

A brass door handle, 1880, 15in (38cm) high.
£55–65 DRU

A brass door handle, c1930, 13½in (34.5cm) high.
£12–15 HEM

FIREPLACES

The rarity of good original items is one of the major issues when considering buying a chimneypiece or any fireplace accessory. It used to be possible to scour reclamation yards or keep an eye on property being redeveloped, where interior fittings were being removed to be replaced by more up-to-date versions. The early 1980s provided a glorious supply of good architectural fittings for the collector, trader, interior designer and the ever-hungry export market. Nowadays, however, the buoyant housing market and changing fashions have resulted in the fireplaces that were installed 20 years ago being replaced with the best that the client can afford, in keeping with the style of the property.

The best source of supply continues to be the fireplace specialists and, on occasions, the reclamation yards. Condition and quality are paramount as the restoration costs for marble and metalwork are expensive and it is often more cost-effective to buy an item fully restored.

The countless features in glossy magazines and on television encourage people to install original items whenever possible. While 18th-century chimneypieces continue to be popular, the majority of properties being restored today are 19th-century, thus increasing the demand for items from that period. Over the past 20 years prices have continued to escalate, particularly in respect of quality and rarer pieces with good provenance. Prices for 19th-century items such as simple corbelled marble and timber surrounds, as found in the secondary rooms and bedrooms of the Victorian red-brick properties built en-masse during the latter part of the 19th century, have levelled out due to the availability of cast-iron inserts and marble surrounds from the Far East. The quality of these imports is generally poor and may not be much cheaper than the original, but they have the benefit of being off-the-shelf. At the end of the day, however, you will only have a copy, whereas the real thing has so much more appeal.

Metalware, whether it is a set of fire irons, a brass fender, fire grate, scuttle or dog grate, is the finishing touch to any fireplace or chimneypiece. The survival rate of such is limited, due to the hard and virtually everyday use of these items during the first part of their lives. The few surviving pieces require expensive restoration. Dating metalware has always been difficult, as one can find exceptional copies of Georgian fire accessories which have been used and polished, giving them the appearance, after a while, of being the real thing. **Adrian Ager**

A French stone fire surround, centrally carved with a shell, c1760, 62in (157.5cm) wide.
£3,200–3,600 ASH

A pair of carved and painted pine and gesso fire surrounds, the central tablet decorated with a reclining figure of Diana, early 19thC, 66in (167.5cm) wide.
£2,500–3,000 P

These fire surrounds were removed in the 1960s from Park Crescent, London W1, which was designed and built by the architect John Nash in 1826.

A George III carved pine and gesso fire surround, the frieze decorated with scrolling foliage centred by a basket of fruit, 57½in (167cm) wide.
£850–1,000 P

An Adam-style pine fire surround, with an applied pewter urn-shaped motif draped with bellflower chains, late 18thC, 68in (172.5cm) wide.
£5,500–6,000 AG

A marble fire surround, with reeded frieze decoration and a cast-iron and brass insert, late 18thC, chimney piece 67in (170cm) wide.
Surround £3,500–4,000
Insert £2,000–2,500 NOST

A marble fire surround, with fluted jambs and frieze, cast-iron original insert, c1820, 52in (132cm) wide.
£2,200–2,650 ASH

Cross Reference
See Colour Review

A white and marble fire surround, the tablet carved in relief with a flaming urn flanked by foliage and with ribbon-tied festoons of flowers, with marble slips and hearth, mid-19thC, 79in (200.5cm) wide.
£8,000–10,000 S(S)

A carved and painted wood fire surround, the frieze decorated with a classical maiden flanked by floral swags, the jambs with a classical urn and scrolling foliage, 19thC, 19¾in (50cm) wide.
£1,200–1,400 P

A cast-iron fire insert, with brass trim, c1860, 44in (112cm) wide.
£1,100–1,250 DOR

A teak fire surround, with a secret compartment, and a cast-iron and bronze dog grate, late 19thC, fire surround 66in (167.5cm) wide.
Surround £2,000–2,200
Dog grate £1,100–1,200 NOST

A Victorian cast-iron fire surround, with tiled insert, 38in (96.5cm) wide.
£550–600 A&H

A Victorian walnut fire surround, with cast-iron and tiled insert, 69in (175.5cm) wide.
Surround £1,450–1,600
Insert £500–550 NOST

▶ A wood and composition fire surround, with reeded Ionic capital pilasters, c1900, 48in (12cm) wide.
£350–400 RTo

◀ A George III-style grey marble fire surround, with fluted panels and gilt-bronze mounts, c1910, 52in (132cm) wide.
£2,500–2,800 ASH

▶ An Edwardian pine fire surround, with a cast-iron dog grate, back-plate cracked, c1890, surround 48in (122cm) wide.
Surround £650–750
Grate £1,100–1,200 NOST

◀ A wrought-iron grate front, 1710–20, 24in (61cm) wide.
£250–300 AnSh

An iron grate, c1750,
19in (48.5cm) wide.
£450–500 SEA

A George III cast-iron hob grate,
with decorative front panels, 1810,
30in (76cm) wide.
£340–380 ASH

A Regency ormolu and cast-iron
register grate, the aperture plate
inlaid with an engraved running
pattern of anthemia and palmettes,
with anthemion mounts to the upper
corners, stamped 'Summers',
44in (112cm) wide.
£8,500–10,000 Bon(M)

A Regency cast-iron fire basket
with scrolling legs, decorated with
honeysuckle motifs, 33in (84cm) wide.
£2,250–2,750 AG

A Victorian cast-iron hob grate,
24in (61cm) wide.
£120–150 BYG

A Victorian cast-iron grate and
matching fire dogs, the backplate
cast in high relief with berried stems,
grate 35½in (90cm) wide.
£1,800–2,200 TEN

A neo-classical-style
brass fireplace insert,
with hand-painted central
plaque, c1880,
24in (61cm) wide.
£400–450 ASH

A steel and cast-iron fire
basket, with serpentine-
fronted grate, 19thC,
27in (68.5cm) wide.
£600–700 L&T

▶ A cast-iron
grate, flanked
by turned and
spirally-fluted
uprights topped
by orb finials,
19thC, 41¼in
(105cm) wide.
£500–600 P(Sc)

◀ A cast-iron and
bronze-mounted
grate, c1880,
34in (86.5cm) wide.
£1,500–1,650 ASH

FIREPLACE ACCESSORIES

A pair of wrought-iron andirons, 17thC, 28in (71cm) high.
£180–220 PFK

An American pair of brass andirons, New York, early 19thC, 22in (56cm) high.
£950–1,100 SK(B)

A pair of andirons, 19thC, 12in (30.5cm) high.
£140–155 SEA

A pair of wrought-iron and bronze andirons, late 19thC, 24in (61cm) high.
£220–240 ASH

A pair of cast-iron fire dogs, in the form of a lion and a unicorn, 19thC, 25in (63.5cm) wide.
£800–875 DOA

A set of mechanical fire bellows, with mahogany base, early 19thC, 27in (68.5cm) long.
£500–565 SEA

A Regency cast-iron Pontypool-style coal bin, the cover painted with flowers and leaves, 21in (53.5cm) high.
£600–700 BIG

A painted and decorated coal bin, c1840, 24in (61cm) wide.
£180–200 ASH

A pair of elm fire bellows, c1880, 22in (56cm) long.
£55–65 MIL

An early Victorian pierced and etched brass fender, 51in (129.5cm) wide.
£350–400 NOST

A mahogany-framed copper firescreen, c1910, 23in (58.5cm) wide.
£330–365 ANO

A brass and iron footman, with pierced frieze, the top platform incised with a forest scene, 19thC, 13¾in (35cm) high.
£450–550 P

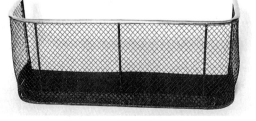

A brass-railed nursery spark guard, c1850, 48in (122cm) wide.
£180–200 ASH

A Georgian fire shovel, with brass and copper finial in the form of the bust of a child, 30in (76cm) long.
£120–140 RUL

◀ A pair of ember tongs, c1748, 45in (114.5cm) long.
£425–475 SEA

Sculpture

A Flemish polychrome-painted oak angel, c1460, 24½in (62cm) high.
£900–1,100 SPR

A carved alabaster fragment of St Christopher supporting the Christ child, with traces of original colour, Nottingham, late 15thC, 11in (28cm) high.
£2,800–3,200 DN(H)

A carved limewood figure of St Paul, damaged, 16thC, 34¾in (88cm) high.
£800–1,000 Bea(E)

An Italian terracotta head of a boy, some losses, 17thC, on a later base, 6¼in (16cm) high.
£1,650–1,850 S(NY)

A white marble bust of a classical youth, with associated marble plinth, late 17thC, 23¾in (60.5cm) high.
£700–850 HYD

A wooden carving of Flora, the goddess of flowers, early 18thC, 26in (66cm) high.
£435–485 OCH

A lead figure of John Locke, by John Cheere, the pedestal cast in relief with a figure of Britannia, c1749, 19¾in (50cm) high.
£8,500–10,000 S

A Tyrolean carved pine figure of a pedlar, 18thC, 17in (43cm) high.
£300–330 OCH

A French carved and painted pine figure of a girl, early 19thC, 13in (33cm) high.
£350–400 FOX

A pair of French ivory figures of Voltaire and Rousseau, on ivory plinths, early 19thC, 6in (15cm) high.
£3,500–4,000 LBO

An ebonized plaster figure of a classical maiden, by Humphrey Hopper, her right hand supporting a brass candle sconce, the base signed and dated '1806', 36in (91.5cm) high.
£2,500–3,000 WW

A French carved ivory figure of a lady, on an ebonized plinth, early 19thC, 5½in (14cm) high.
£700–850 TMA

A bronze group of archers, by F. Rudi, c1850, 16in (40.5cm) high.
£1,800–2,200 ART

A French bronze model of a cow, signed 'I. Bonheur', c1860, 5in (12.5cm) high.
£1,800–2,000 ChA

A bronze model of a pointer dog, signed 'Delabrièrre', c1870, 9½in (24cm) high.
£1,000–1,150 WeH

A bronze study of the Venus de Milo, c1870, 20in (51cm) high.
£1,000–1,200 ANT

An Italian bronze figure of a Roman general in armour, by A. Rohrich, on a fluted green marble column, damaged, 1870, 43in (109cm) high.
£2,800–3,200 RBB

An ivory group of a gentleman and lady in period costume, on a wooden plinth, c1880, 6in (15cm) high.
£1,000–1,200 LBO

A white marble bust of a young woman, 19thC, 20½in (52cm) high.
£1,750–2,000 AH

A French bronze figure of David and the head of Goliath, by Jean Antonin Mercie, signed and inscribed, 19thC, 18in (45.5cm) high.
£1,600–1,800 P

Mercie first exhibited this work at the 1872 Salon when he was at the French Academy in Rome, winning the Légion d'Honneur while still a student, which was unprecedented. In 1878, he sent a life-sized bronze version to the Exposition Universelle in Paris which was then acquired by the Musée du Luxembourg.
A marble version of this work was exhibited at the Exposition Universelle in 1889.

A Roman-style carved white marble bust of a gentleman, 19thC, 27in (68.5cm) high.
£1,800–2,200 JAd

A mottled black, pink and white marble bust, 'Jeanne d'Arc', signed 'Prof G. Besji', 19thC, 22in (56cm) high.
£1,200–1,400 DA

◀ An alabaster figure of a lady, some restoration, 19thC, 20in (51cm) high.
£300–350 SER

A French ivory figure of a cavalier blowing his trumpet, by E. Barillot, 19thC, 10in (25.5cm) high.
£2,400–2,700 LBO

An Italian bronze of Antonio, 19thC, 25in (63.5cm) high.
£2,200–2,500 DOA

A Continental cold-painted bronze model of a partridge, 19thC, 9¼in (23.5cm) high.
£2,000–2,400 AH

A Continental alabaster bust of a young woman, on a separate plinth, signed 'A. Gernai', 19thC, 14in (35.5cm) high.
£625–750 DD

An Austrian terracotta life-sized model of a dachshund, late 19thC, 10in (25.5cm) high.
£1,200–1,400 LT

A Continental white marble bust of a young lady, her hair tied with ribbons and flowers, 19thC, 20½in (52cm) high.
£2,700–3,200 JAd

A Continental bronze equestrian figure of Bartolommeo Colleone, in the style of Verrochio, on a black marble base, late 19thC, 13in (33cm) wide.
£1,200–1,300 SK

A Continental alabaster figure of the Kneeling Venus, damaged, 19thC, 35in (89cm) high.
£2,000–2,200 BB(S)

A patinated bronze group of Hercules and Antaeus wrestling, late 19thC, 23¾in (60.5cm) high.
£1,600–2,000 TEN

An Italian carved white marble group, Declaration d'Amour, signed 'E. Battiglia', late 19thC, 24¾in (63cm) high.
£2,000–2,200 BB(S)

◄ An Italian school carved marble group of Leda and the Swan, damaged, late 19thC, 51½in (131cm) high.
£6,000–7,000 Bon(C)

An Imperial Russian carved jade hen, set with ruby eyes, c1900, 2in (5cm) wide.
£2,500–2,750 SHa

A French bronze figure of Joan of Arc, signed 'H. Chapu', early 20thC, 12½in (32cm) high.
£700–850 CLE

Metalware

BRASS

A French shop display brass bed, c1900, 14in (35.5cm) wide.
£550–600 RUL

A Dutch brass and copper engraved tobacco box, 18thC, 6in (15cm) wide.
£275–300 AEF

◀ A pair of Huguenot-style brass candlesticks, 18thC, 6¾in (17cm) high.
£270–320 PFK

A pair of brass candlesticks, modelled as lions rampant, 1860, 9in (23cm) high.
£850–950 ARE

A Victorian brass chestnut roaster, 19in (48.5cm) long.
£180–200 CHAP

A gilt-brass humidor, the top engraved by L. Bottini with a scene in the style of Teniers, 'entitled The Prodigal Child', 19thC, 10in (25.5cm) wide.
£700–850 EH

A brass chafing dish, c1760, 5¾in (14.5cm) diam.
£340–380 SEA

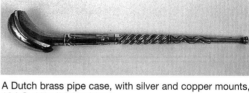

A Dutch brass pipe case, with silver and copper mounts, 18thC, 12in (30.5cm) long.
£675–750 AEF

◀ A brass kettle on a stand, c1820, 15in (38cm) high.
£350–400 SEA

A Dutch brass Hanukkah lamp, the embossed backplate decorated with a stylized vase of flowers, late 18thC, 12½in (32cm) high.
£650–800 P

A brass tinder box and candle holder, c1860, 9in (23cm) long.
£225–250 SEA

A Georgian brass and copper samovar, with gadrooned decoration to the edges and handles, 14in (35.5cm) wide.
£200–240 Mit

BRONZE

A pair of rococo cast gilt-bronze candlesticks, the stems decorated with scrolls, foliage and shells, early 19thC, 11¼in (28.5cm) high.
£350–400 WW

A pair of Regency bronze candlesticks, in the form of a dancing gallant and companion, on white marble columns, c1810, 12in (30.5cm) high.
£2,800–3,200 JIL

A Victorian bronze and ormolu ten-light candelabra, supported by a bronze figure of a dancing faun, 40in (101.5cm) high.
£2,000–2,400 JAd

A pair of French ormolu and bronze three-light candelabra, each on three bronze draped classical female figures, on white marble pedestals and bases, damaged, 19thC, 20¾in (52.5cm) high.
£600–700 MCA

A bronze censer, on a wooden platform base, c1850, 9in (23cm) high.
£1,100–1,200 ChA

A bronze inkstand, modelled as a scallop shell supported by a dolphin, the hinged cover opening to a fitted inkwell, pounce pot, vacant receiver and three quill holes, on a marble and bronze plinth, early 19thC, 6¼in (16cm) high.
£2,000–2,400 P

A bronze and gilded inkstand, the sides with applied floral swags, the top with three decorative covers and quill holders, inscribed, dated '1814', 11in (28cm) wide.
£1,150–1,350 WBH

▶ A French bronze pot and cover, in the form of three children sitting on a barrel, late 19thC, 4½in (11.5cm) high.
£350–400 SWO

A pair of bronze two-handled urns, decorated with a frieze of classical figures in relief, on black slate bases, 19thC, 10½in (26.5cm) high.
£400–500 RBB

A pair of bronze Gothic revival wall pockets, of architectural design, mid-19thC, 6in (15cm) high.
£700–800 NOA

An Italian gilt-bronze salt, centred on each face with an armorial cartouche, the cover cast with fruit, mid-17thC, 6in (15cm) high.
£1,400–1,600 S

▶ An early Georgian bronze shield-shaped wool weight, with a coat-of-arms, George I cypher, inscribed 'Richard Cressey 1742', 4in (10cm) wide.
£1,600–2,000 RBB

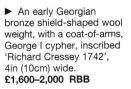

Bronze • METALWARE 577

COPPER

A copper jug and cover, 19thC, 10in (25.5cm) high.
£350–400 SEA

Cross Reference
See Colour Review

◀ A miniature copper longcase clock, by Pooles of Hayle, Cornwall, c1910, 14½in (37cm) high.
£240–280 RUSK

A Victorian copper tea kettle, with white opaque glass handle and finial, on a conforming stand, complete with heater, 14½in (37cm) high.
£100–120 PFK

▶ A copper ale jug, 19thC, 10in (25.5cm) high.
£175–200 NEW

A Victorian copper two-handled samovar, with brass tap, 17in (43cm) high.
£120–140 WilP

IRON

A cast-iron anvil and swage block, 1924, 28in (71cm) high.
£350–400 A&H

A Victorian Gothic revival painted cast-iron door stop, decorated with a geometric pattern in red, green and gold, c1860, 20½in (52cm) high.
£550–650 VOS

An iron Armada chest, the top, sides and front with painted floral decoration, the top with block plate enclosing a locking mechanism, 17thC, 28in (71cm) wide.
£1,100–1,300 L&T

A cast-iron bull's head, possibly from a butcher's shop, with original gilded paint, late 19thC, 4in (10cm) diam.
£90–100 NEW

A cast-iron door stop, Mr Punch, c1900, 14in (35.5cm) high.
£45–50 MIL

◀ A wrought-iron kettle tilter, 18thC, 17in (43cm) long.
£100–125 AnSh

A George III wrought-iron candlestick, probably Irish, 29½in (75cm) high.
£200–235 AnSh

A Welsh wrought-iron rushlight holder, on an oak base, 18thC, 11in (28cm) high.
£400–465 CoA

PEWTER

A pair of French pewter candlesticks, c1890, 6½in (16.5cm) high.
£340–375 SEA

A pewter quart ale jug, with double dome lid and gate thumbpiece, early 18thC, 8in (20.5cm) high.
£120–135 HEB

A pewter three-quart measure, 19thC, 9in (23cm) high.
£160–200 AnSh

A pewter spice or pepper pot, c1800, 4½in (11.5cm) high.
£50–60 AnSh

A Continental broad rim dish, engraved, 18thC, 17in (43cm) diam.
£380–440 AnSh

A Georgian set of pewter graduated measures, largest 6in (15cm) high.
£220–250 BLA

A pewter Passover plate, 18thC, with 19thC engraving of a nine-point star and nine circles containing Hebrew inscriptions, 12½in (32cm) diam.
£370–400 S(S)

An engraved pewter plate, c1860, 12in (30.5cm) diam.
£120–140 AnSh

▶ A pewter spoon, with acorn knop, maker's mark 'Flower' to bowl, 15th/16thC, 5in (12.5cm) long.
£240–300 P(NW)

A pewter lidded flagon, with shell thumb piece, Crown Rose quality touchmark of Franz Jos. Baeten, Turnhout, c1800, 8in (20.5cm) high.
£160–175 HEB

A French pewter lidded wine measure, with fleur-de-lys quality mark, Paris, 18thC, 7¼in (18.5cm) high.
£160–200 F&C

A pewter porringer, with bossed well, touchmark of Adam Bancks of Milngate, Chester, c1700, 4¾in (12cm) diam.
£750–900 P(NW)

Leather

A leather Gladstone bag, by Davis of Piccadilly, London, with brass fittings, c1900, 25in (63.5cm) wide.
£350–400 STS

A leather bucket-shaped hat box, with velvet lining, c1900, 14in (35.5cm) wide.
£120–150 STS

A leather peat bucket, c1780, 12in (30.5cm) high.
£320–350 SEA

An American painted leather fire bucket, inscribed in gilt 'City of Boston Ward No. 11 Fireman No. 3 1826', handle missing, early 19thC, 13¼in (33.5cm) high.
£950–1,100 SK(B)

A Victorian red leather fire bucket, painted with Royal arms, some damage, 11½in (29cm) high.
£280–320 WW

A pair of American painted leather fire buckets, both inscribed in gilt 'Semper Paratus L. T. Jackson' in a black cartouche on a red ground, 19thC, 15½in (39.5cm) high.
£5,000–5,500 SK(B)

A Liberty's leather elephant, stamped mark, early 20thC, 19in (48.5cm) high.
£350–400 SWG

An Army & Navy leather on oak cartridge case, with brass trim, c1910, 18in (45.5cm) wide.
£350–400 STS

A Victorian leather pouffe, 24in (61cm) diam.
£80–100 COLL

A leather tankard, or 'black jack', c1750, 10½in (26.5cm) high.
£225–250 SEA

A leather-bound and brass-studded elm travelling trunk, the lid decorated with two crowns above the letter 'R', early 18thC, 39¼in (99.5cm) wide.
£2,000–2,400 Bon(C)

▶ A leather trunk, with ribbed sides, the domed top with incised armorial and punched with initials, iron clasp, lacking handles, 18thC, 23½in (59.5cm) wide.
£500–600 DN

Papier Mâché

A papier mâché snuff box, by Stobwasser of Brunswick, the cover painted with a young woman, c1800, 3¾in (9.5cm) diam.
£400–450 Oli

A papier mâché snuff box, by Stobwasser, the cover painted with a coach and horses, the underside inscribed 'Le Relais', early 19thC, 3½in (9cm) wide.
£850–1,000 P

▶ A German papier mâché snuff box, the cover painted with a group of men, c1830, 3½in (9cm) wide.
£250–280 MB

A papier mâché snuff box, with hand-painted cover, c1820, 3½in (9cm) wide.
£200–220 MB

A papier mâché snuff box, possibly by Stobwasser, the cover painted with a portrait of Field Marshal Gebhard Leberecht Blücher, early 19thC, 3¾in (9.5cm) diam.
£220–260 P

A papier mâché snuff box, the cover painted with a post-hunting scene, c1830, 6in (15cm) diam.
£875–975 CHAP

A papier mâché cigar box, painted in the style of Landseer with scenes of 'Dignity and Impudence' and 'A Member of the Humane Society', the swivel front revealing a bowed fitted interior, c1860, 11in (28cm) wide.
£1,300–1,500 S(S)

A German papier mâché novelty sweet container, in the shape of a perch, c1880, 12½in (32cm) long.
£330–365 MSB

A George III papier mâché tea caddy, by Henry Clay, the hinged cover decorated with bands of berried leaves and anthemia, the body transfer-decorated with scenes of classical figures, Birmingham, c1780, 4¾in (12cm) high.
£6,000–6,750 S

A papier mâché tray, the border painted in gilt with butterflies, flowers and foliage, stamped 'Clay King St. Covt. Garden', mid-19thC, 29in (73.5cm) wide.
£320–380 DN

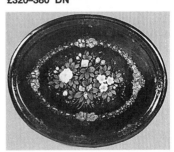

A Victorian papier mâché tray, painted with a chinoiserie scene of figures by a river, within a gilt scroll border, 32in (81.5cm) wide.
£900–1,000 DN

▶ A papier mâché tray, hand-painted with roses and foliage, the rim inlaid with mother-of-pearl and gilt, 19thC, 23in (58.5cm) wide.
£120–140 Mit

Tortoiseshell

A tortoiseshell snuff box/tobacco box, with an ornate silver hinge, 1730, 5in (12.5cm) wide.
£525–575 CHAP

A tortoiseshell snuff box, with a silver rim, 1750, 3in (7.5cm) diam.
£180–200 MB

A tortoiseshell and rose gold snuff box, with inset gold panel inscribed 'E. H. 1783', 4in (10cm) long.
£230–260 LBr

A tortoiseshell and gold-mounted snuff box, 1810, 3in (7.5cm) diam.
£125–150 MB

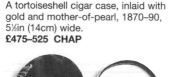

A tortoiseshell cigar case, inlaid with gold and mother-of-pearl, 1870–90, 5½in (14cm) wide.
£475–525 CHAP

A tortoiseshell pocket magnifying glass, with silver mounts, c1770, 3in (7.5cm) wide.
£120–140 HUM

A reading glass, in a tortoiseshell case with silver mounts and hinge, 19thC, 3½in (9cm) wide.
£220–260 P

A tortoiseshell and silver-mounted writing box, c1900, 11¼in (28.5cm) wide.
£1,350–1,500 GIO

A tortoiseshell purse, with gold inlay, c1860, 3in (7.5cm) wide.
£330–365 CHAP

A George III tortoiseshell and ivory-mounted tea caddy, the interior fitted with two lidded canisters, 6in (15cm) wide.
£600–700 WL

A Regency tortoiseshell bowfronted tea caddy, 7in (18cm) wide.
£1,600–2,000 G(L)

A tortoiseshell tea caddy, with shaped front, the interior fitted with two compartments, early 19thC, 8in (20.5cm) wide.
£1,200–1,400 CLE

An early Victorian tortoiseshell tea caddy, 8in (20.5cm) wide.
£900–1,100 LT

An early Victorian blonde tortoiseshell tea caddy, the hinged cover with central silver plaque and silver stringing, the interior fitted with two compartments, 5¼in (13.5cm) wide.
£750–850 DD

Treen

The vast range of objects that fall under the general heading of 'treen' often leads to confusion about its exact meaning, and it may be helpful to clear this up by saying that the word, as defined by the Oxford Dictionary, means 'made of tree, wooden, obtained from or made from a tree'. In other words, 'treen' usually describes the large number of small wooden objects in domestic, trade and professional use. This means that we are dealing with anything wooden, from a needlecase to a spinning wheel.

Treen collecting began in the 1930s with the publication of a book entitled *Domestic Utensils in Wood* by Owen Evan-Thomas, a collector and dealer specializing in treen. This was followed by the formation of the Pinto Collection which by 1964 was attracting 24,000 visitors a year to the Pinto home in Northwood, Middlesex. It was in that year that the collection was sold to Birmingham Museum and Art Gallery where it remains today as the Mecca for the enthusiastic treen collector.

In 1969, Edward Pinto published the treen collectors' 'bible', *Treen and other Wooden Bygones*, which firmly established the subject as a collecting field. The first book to be produced in colour was the excellent *Treen for the Table* by Jonathan Levi, published in 1998, which deals with wooden items used for eating and drinking.

Collectors also place objects made from nutshell under the general heading of treen. These include coconut cups and a wide range of boxes and other pieces such as spice containers made from coquilla nuts which were particularly popular during the Napoleonic period. Many of these were very finely carved and are minor works of art, such as the casket illustrated on page 584 which is made from an assembly of 16 nuts.

One of the joys of treen collecting is that the field encompasses such a wide variety of objects that will suit all tastes and pockets from simple kitchenware, such as the lemon squeezer on page 585, to finely carved pieces of great value and beauty. The beginner will find that items from the 19th and early 20th centuries are readily available and the experienced collector will know that pieces from earlier periods are now difficult to find. Recent years have seen 17th-century treen becoming more and more rare. However, for 19th- or 17th-century examples the criteria should remain the same – good quality, good colour and good condition.

Tony Foster

A metal-banded wooden harvest barrel or costrel, 19thC, 12in (30.5cm) long.
£270–300 SEA

A fruitwood *bilbouquet*, or cup and ball game, c1850, 10in (25.5cm) long.
£80–100 ALA

A wooden bowl, used for collecting reindeer milk, with incised decoration to handle and rim, Lapland, mid-19thC, 7in (18cm) diam.
£170–200 NEW

A fruitwood book press, 18thC, 14in (35.5cm) wide.
£350–400 DOA

▶ A lignum vitae wassail bowl, the central acorn spice box missing, 17thC, 13½in (34.5cm) high.
£1,800–2,200 P

A mahogany boot jack, early 19thC, 30½in (76cm) high.
£400–450 AH

A mahogany bread trolley, with horse-head handle, on turned wheels, 19thC, 19in (48.5cm) long.
£3,300–3,650 S(NY)

◀ A pair of Italian carved wood and silver-gilt candle-sticks, early 18thC, 26½in (67.5cm) high.
£2,200–2,500 DBA

A carved coquilla nut casket, c1790, 5in (12.5cm) wide.
£1,100–1,250 AEF

A wooden cribbage board, c1820, 14¾in (37.5cm) long.
£160–175 SEA

A wooden box for oats, decorated with equestrian scenes, 19thC, 15in (38cm) high.
£300–350 DOA

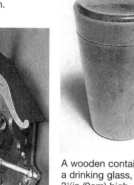

A wooden container for a drinking glass, 19thC, 3½in (9cm) high.
£25–28 ChA

An olive-wood barrel-shaped container, inscribed 'Jerusalem', 19thC, 3½in (9cm) high.
£16–18 ChA

A Russian painted wood processional cross, 18thC, 19in (48.5cm) high.
£750–850 ICO

An oak, carved wood and brass coat rack, modelled as a hound's head, with glass eyes, the open mouth holding a brass rail with coat hooks, 19thC, 30¼in (77cm) wide.
£2,000–2,200 TEN

▶ A Scottish laburnum egg cup stand, by G. Watson of Broughty Ferry, Dundee, holding six egg cups, the upper tier supporting six carved bone spoons, 19thC, 13½in (34.5cm) high.
£950–1,100 S(S)

◀ A Norwegian chip-carved wooden dipper cup, c1800, 3in (7.5cm) wide.
£270–300 AEF

Cross Reference
See Colour Review

A boxwood embroidery frame, c1850, 3in (7.5cm) diam.
£40–50 ALA

A sycamore funnel, c1820, 10in (25.5cm) high.
£160–175 SEA

A wooden inkwell, carved as an owl, the head hinged to reveal a glass and metal-lined interior, c1800, 6¼in (16cm) high.
£800–900 Mit

◀ A wooden knitting sheath, dated '1785', 8in (20.5cm) long.
£180–200 AEF

A north European wooden brass-bound beer jug, in the form of a barrel, with carved spout, lid and handle, mid-19thC, 11in (28cm) high.
£2,000–2,500 PdC

A mulberry-wood ladle, early 19thC, 10in (25.5cm) long.
£60–70 ALA

A fruitwood lemon squeezer, c1820, 5in (12.5cm) diam.
£700–800 AEF

A Scottish sycamore and alder-wood luggie, c1800, 7in (18cm) high.
£200–220 AEF

An Irish bog oak napkin ring, decorated with shamrocks, 19thC, 2in (5cm) diam.
£27–30 STA

A Greek penknife, with carved wood handle, 19thC, 4in (10cm) long.
£450–500 AEF

An American Shaker wood and fabric pincushion and spoolholder, c1880, 5½in (14cm) high.
£200–220 YAG

A silver-mounted carved boxwood pipe tamper, modelled as a greyhound, 18thC, 4in (10cm) long.
£625–700 AEF

An engine-turned wooden cosmetic pot, early 18thC, 2in (5cm) diam.
£300–350 PdC

A carved fruitwood rule, the pierced central panel decorated with roses, 18thC, 15½in (39.5cm) long.
£250–300 P

An oak post box, with brass fittings and glass front, 19thC, 12in (30.5cm) high.
£800–880 CAT

A wooden salt, 18thC, 5in (12.5cm) high.
£500–550 AEF

◄ A painted Brighton Pavillion ribbon tower, early 19thC, 5½in (14cm) high.
£800–1,000 Bon(C)

A French carved and silver-mounted boxwood snuff box, 17thC, 3½in (9cm) high.
£2,500–3,000 PdC

A yew-wood snuff box, carved in the form of a hand, 18thC, 2¾in (7cm) high.
£500–600 P

A mulberry and ebony-inlaid snuff box, with horn lining, c1815, 3in (7.5cm) wide.
£120–140 MB

A Scandinavian wooden snuff box, one end in the form of a fish, the other a duck's head, 19thC, 5¼in (13.5cm) long.
£400–450 WW

A Continental carved fruitwood snuff box, in the form of a bulldog's head, with glass eyes and carved bone teeth, late 19thC, 2½in (6.5cm) high.
£850–1,000 P

A Swedish hook-back wooden spoon, the handle in the form of a cage with three trapped balls, dated '1786', 13in (33cm) long.
£130–145 NEW

A Scottish oak spinning wheel, c1860, 37in (94cm) high.
£300–350 BLA

A carved wood spoon, 1880, 7in (18cm) long.
£75–85 WeA

A carved wood porridge spoon, 19thC, 12½in (32cm) long.
£18–20 OCH

A Welsh carved fruitwood love-spoon, early 19thC, 11in (28cm) long.
£1,250–1,500 PdC

A wooden tape measure, c1880, ½in (1.25cm) high.
£30–35 VB

An inlaid mahogany drinks tray, 1850–70, 15in (38cm) diam.
£140–180 MRW

A wooden wallpaper print roller, c1900, 24in (61cm) long.
£100–120 RUL

A Norwegian burr-birch pegged tankard, the lid, handle and feet with lion carvings, c1800, 10in (25.5cm) high.
£1,200–1,350 NEW

A painted wood washing dolly love-token, late 19thC, 21in (53.5cm) high.
£250–300 S(S)

A painted lime-wood and pine watch stand, in the form of a portcullis, c1810, 18in (45.5cm) high.
£1,350–1,500 RYA

Further Reading
Miller's Collectables Price Guide, Miller's Publications, 2000

Tunbridge Ware

A Victorian Tunbridge ware rosewood work box, inlaid with a picture of Penshurst Place, probably by Henry Hollamby, 8in (20.5cm) wide.
£250–300 CAG

A Tunbridge ware walnut jewellery box, the lid inlaid with a spray of roses, 19thC, 9in (23cm) wide.
£250–300 Mit

A Tunbridge ware box, 1870–90, 3½in (9cm) wide.
£170–200 VB

A Tunbridge ware rosewood glove box, with plush-lined interior, labelled 'Edmund Nye, Mount Ephraim and Parade, Tunbridge Wells', c1845, 9½in (24cm) wide.
£180–220 GAK

A Tunbridge ware rosewood glove box, the lid inlaid with a picture of Eridge Castle, the interior fitted with later silk lining for use as a needlework box, 19thC, 9½in (24cm) wide.
£160–200 DN

A Tunbridge ware rosewood deskstand, with hobnail cut-glass bottle, the sloping sides with tesserae mosaic flowers, mid-19thC, 6in (15cm) wide.
£320–380 BR

A Tunbridge ware letter opener, with inlaid handle, c1860, 10in (25.5cm) long.
£40–50 ALA

A Victorian Tunbridge ware walnut writing box, inlaid with geometric bands, 13in (33cm) wide.
£275–300 MB

A Tunbridge ware walnut table-top, inlaid with a picture of Battle Abbey, mid-19thC, 19in (48.5cm) wide.
£180–220 BR

A Tunbridge ware desk thermometer and compass, by Barton, thermometer broken, c1880, 5in (12.5cm) high.
£300–350 M

An early Victorian Tunbridge ware writing box, the slope inlaid with a picture of two deer in a landscape within a floral border, 11¾in (30cm) wide.
£700–850 CGC

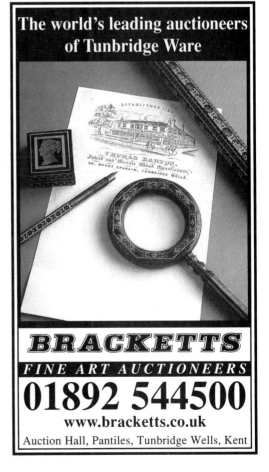

Boxes

A walnut lace box, 1720–40, 12in (30.5cm) wide.
£550–600 CAT

An American Queen Anne walnut table-top desk, the interior with compartments above two drawers and a well, restored, 1740–60, 23½in (60cm) wide.
£1,600–1,800 SK(B)

A George III walnut tea chest, with chequer stringing, the interior fittings and slides missing, 10¼in (26cm) wide.
£125–150 BIG

A George III ivory and tortoiseshell tea caddy, the hinged lid with silver handle and inlaid with mother-of-pearl, the front with shield and swag decoration, 4in (10cm) wide.
£1,250–1,500 L&T

A George III inlaid mahogany jewellery box, with gilt-metal lion's head and ring handles, 12in (30.5cm) wide.
£200–240 JBe

A Russian walrus ivory engraved casket, the lid and sides with fretted panels and green and red stylized floral motifs, Archangel, late 18thC, 8½in (21.5cm) wide.
£700–800 CORO

A coromandel writing slope, inlaid with brass foliate designs and mother-of-pearl detail, the interior with letter rack and compartments, c1800, 15in (38cm) wide.
£550–650 GAK

A carved ivory snuff box, early 19thC, 3in (7.5cm) wide.
£450–500 HUM

A Regency satinwood and rosewood-crossbanded tea caddy, with brass ball feet, 12in (30.5cm) wide.
£675–750 CRU

A rosewood tea caddy, bowl missing, c1835, 15in (38cm) wide.
£220–250 NAW

A mahogany scent box, with six paper-labelled bottles, satin lining, 19thC, 4in (10cm) wide.
£420–470 LBr

◄ A mahogany and bird's-eye maple writing slope, with foliate scroll marquetry, the interior with a hinged mirror section, fitted as a toilet box and for writing, with velvet lining, 19thC, 18in (45.5cm) wide.
£450–550 TRM

A gilt-metal jewellery casket, the lid inlaid with micro-mosaic classical ruins, the body inlaid with a polychrome champlevé enamel frieze, 19thC, 3½in (9cm) wide.
£450–550 EH

A Victorian brass-bound coromandel tea caddy, 9in (23cm) wide.
£320–350 MB

A Victorian cedar-lined rosewood table-top secretaire, fitted with satinwood and ebony-inlaid compartments, drawers and pigeonholes, 22in (56cm) wide.
£500–600 PFK

A Victorian burr-walnut cigar box, with ivory and gilt-metal mounts and fitted interior, 6¼in (16cm) wide.
£350–420 AH

A set of carved oak drawers, c1880, 20in (51cm) wide.
£150–165 AL

A Victorian oak and brass-bound desk stand, the raised back with enclosed stationery divisions, fitted with two glass inkwells and a secret drawer, 11¾in (30cm) wide.
£200–240 WL

A Bengal Cavalry oak box, the interior fitted for silver, c1870, 21in (53.5cm) wide.
£320–350 GBr

◄ A Chinese carved ivory jewellery casket, 19thC, 6¾in (17cm) wide.
£1,100–1,300 G(L)

► An Anglo-Indian Vizagapatam ivory and metal-inlaid wood stationery box, with fitted interior, 19thC, 5½in (14cm) wide.
£400–450 RTo

◄ An Anglo-Indian ivory and sandalwood games box, 19thC, 6in (15cm) wide.
£100–120 TMi

► A brass-mounted coromandel smoker's box, 1906, 11in (28cm) wide.
£450–500 GIO

Music

CYLINDER MUSICAL BOXES

A Swiss cylinder musical box, by Lecoultre, the 12¾in (32.5cm) cylinder playing eight airs, with tune sheet, contained in a rosewood case, 1860, 20in (51cm) wide.
£1,200–1,400 S

A Swiss musical box, the 22½in (57cm) cylinder playing numerous airs, contained in a rosewood and marquetry-inlaid box, 19thC, 22½in (57cm) wide.
£550–650 HYD

A Swiss musical box on a stand, the 13in (33cm) cylinder playing 12 airs, contained in a walnut and ebonized case with feather-banding and stringing, 19thC, 29in (73.5cm) wide.
£1,400–1,600 AH

◄ A Swiss musical box, the 13in (33cm) cylinder playing 36 airs, contained in a satinwood box banded and inlaid with leaf and floral scrolls, 19thC, 20in (51cm) wide.
£800–1,000 AAV

► A Swiss musical box, the 15in (38cm) cylinder playing eight airs, contained in a walnut twin-panel door cabinet on ebonized bun supports, c1880, 27¼in (69cm) wide.
£2,300–2,750 Bri

A Swiss musical box, the 8in (20.5cm) cylinder playing six airs, contained in a rosewood ebonized case inlaid with a flower spray, 19thC, 16½in (42cm) wide.
£600–700 RTo

A Swiss Quatuor Accord Parfait musical box, by Paillard Vaucher & Fils, with 19in (48.5cm) cylinder, contained in an inlaid and crossbanded case with handles, 1890s, 36½in (92.5cm) wide.
£3,000–3,500 Bon

A Swiss Ideal Sublime Harmonie Piccolo interchangeable cylinder musical box, the 18in (45.5cm) cylinders each playing six airs, with zither attachment, three additional cylinders, contained in a walnut case with two fitted drawers, late 19thC, 15in (38cm) wide.
£4,250–5,000 S(NY)

A Swiss musical box, the 16in (40.5cm) cylinder playing 12 airs, with tune sheet, contained in an inlaid rosewood case, late 19thC, 24¼in (62cm) wide.
£650–800 Bri

◄ A Swiss musical box, the 13in (33cm) cylinder playing ten airs, contained in a rosewood marquetry case with lock, stamped 'MM & Co', c1900, 28in (71cm) wide.
£600–700 Bea(E)

► A Swiss interchangeable cylinder musical box, the six cylinders playing 36 airs, contained in a simulated burr-walnut and marquetry case, early 20thC, 20½in (52cm) wide.
£1,100–1,300 Bea(E)

DISC MUSICAL BOXES

A Polyphon disc musical box, by Nicole Frères, with coin-operated mechanism, in a walnut case with moulded cornice and turned columns, 19thC, 27in (68.5cm) high.
£3,500–4,200 AH

An American Regina disc musical box, contained in a folding top mahogany case, c1896, 32½in (82.5cm) wide.
£6,000–7,000 S(NY)

The folding top style of the Regina musical box was developed for those situations where a large diameter disc was required but space was at a premium. When not in use the top can be folded down.

► A Symphonion disc musical box, fitted with coin-operated mechanism, with 31 discs, in a walnut case, late 19thC, 54in (137cm) high.
£2,500–3,000 RBB

◄ A Swiss Symphonion monkey-cyclist automaton 13in (33cm) disc musical box, monkey missing, the mechanism incorporating a 40-note musical box playing No. 28 discs, together with eleven discs, c1904, 21in (53.5cm) wide.
£1,300–1,500 S

An American Mira 9in (23cm) disc musical box, contained in a mahogany case, c1900, 16in (40.5cm) wide.
£900–1,000 S(NY)

A German Symphonion Sublime Harmony 19in (48.5cm) disc musical box, with 10 discs, coin-operated mechanism and winding handle, in an upright wooden case with glazed wooden door, c1900, 25¼in (64cm) wide.
£1,000–1,200 Bon

MECHANICAL MUSIC

A table-top bird organ, playing eight airs, in a mahogany case inlaid with chequered banding and simulated organ pipes to the fascia, c1800, 12in (30.5cm) high.
£1,000–1,200 DD

Cross Reference
See Colour Review

A musical automaton picture, the painting signed 'Ch. Rivière', depicting a dental surgeon with tooth key in his hand performing surgery on a seated young lady, both figures with moving arms and heads, probably French, c1845, framed, 17¾ x 14½in (45 x 37cm).
£3,700–4,000 S

► A Pasquali & Co wooden barrel organ, with moving central panels, labelled, early 20thC, 59in (150cm) high.
£1,300–1,500 Bon

A Victorian silver singing bird box, by John Manger, the lid inlaid with an oval Swiss enamel landscape, the interior with two birds, 1887, 4in (10cm) wide.
£8,500–10,000 P(B)

PHONOGRAPHS

A Columbia Graphophone Domestic B-type phonograph, c1900, 12in (30.5cm) wide.
£250–300 HHO

An Edison Model B Fireside phonograph, in an oak case, with blue-painted tin horn, early 20thC, 11½in (29cm) wide.
£350–400 DuM

An Edison Standard Model A phonograph, 1900–05, 11¾in (30cm) wide.
£300–350 HHO

A Puck phonograph, 1902–3, 13in (33cm) long.
£300–350 ET

▶ An Edison Diamond Disc table-top phonograph, 1920s, 24in (61cm) wide.
£450–500 ET

A German Excelsior Pearl oak phonograph, with original red 'flower' horn, c1905, 10in (25.5cm) wide.
£300–350 HHO

GRAMOPHONES

A Columbia Disc Graphophone, type AH, with brass belled steel horn, c1904, 13in (33cm) square.
£1,200–1,500 HHO

An HMV 'Baby' Monarch gramophone, with original green horn and oak case, c1908, 11in (28cm) square.
£600–750 HHO

A Neophone horn gramophone, with Neophone soundbox, 1905–06, 18in (45.5cm) wide.
£600–700 ET

An HMV Intermediate Monarch horn gramophone, with a light oak case and horn, 1910–20, 18in (45.5cm) wide.
£1,200–1,400 P(WM)

An EMG Mark IX electric gramophone, with oak case, 1930s, 21in (53.5cm) wide.
£1,000–1,200 HHO

An RCA Victor Victrola, the oak case with two pairs of cabinet doors, c1910, 22in (56cm) wide.
£200–240 DuM

MUSICAL INSTRUMENTS

A Cavaquinho, by Rufino Felix d'Athouguia, the body of exotic wood, the table of pine with oakleaf and marginal inlay decoration, Madeira, 1850, length of back 9in (22.5cm).
£550–600 P

A cello, by Robert Cuthbert, London, c1700, length of back 28¾in (73cm).
£7,500–8,250 P

A cello, Kennedy School, c1810, length of back 29in (73.5cm).
£11,500–13,500 P

◀ A cello, possibly by Marcucci Custode, labelled 'Marcucci Custode fece in S. Agata sut Santerno l'anno 19..' c1900, length of back 29½in (75cm).
£5,000–6,000 Bon

A Scottish cello, by Matthew Hardie, Edinburgh, 1818, length of back 29½in (75cm), with a bow.
£11,500–14,000 P

A cello, by Neuner & Hornsteiner, with trade label, 19thC, length of back 29½in (75cm).
£900–1,100 Mit

▶ A cithern, probably by Henry Lockey Hill, branded 'Thomsons Makers London', with tortoiseshell finger-board and decorated soundhole, c1770, 36in (91.5cm) long.
£950–1,100 Bon

A guitar, by Lacote, Paris, 1821, length of back 17½in (44.5cm).
£2,200–2,500 P

▶ An American arch-top guitar, by John d'Angelico, New York, with bound ebony fingerboard with block mother-of-pearl inlay, marked, 1935, length of back 20½in (52cm).
£5,000–6,000 SK

A guitar, French School, c1850, length of back 17½in (44.5cm).
£450–550 P

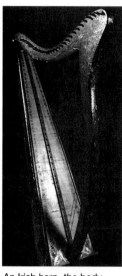

An Irish harp, the body painted green and decorated with hand-painted shamrocks and gilt griffins, early 19thC, 66½in (169cm) high.
£1,400–1,700 JAd

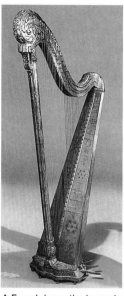

A French harp, the bowed soundboard with floral and foliate-painted decoration, c1890, 64in (162.5cm) high.
£1,300–1,500 P

A parcel-gilt Gothic-style harp, by Erard, the shaped base with two winged dragon feet, restored, inscribed, early 19thC, 69in (175.5cm) high.
£1,400–1,600 PF

An American mandolin, by The Gibson Mandolin-Guitar Co, Style A-1, the bound ebony fingerboard with mother-of-pearl dot inlay, labelled, 1917, length of back 13¾in (35cm).
£475–525 SK

A Swanen mahogany square piano, with ebony and boxwood inlay, restored, Paris, 1792, 46in (117cm) wide.
£8,000–9,000 PPC

A rosewood cabinet piano, by Richard Russell, London, c1830, 48in (122cm) wide.
£2,000–2,500 PEx

A mahogany square piano, by Clementi, with two drawers and applied brass paterae, early 19thC, 62in (157.5cm) wide.
£2,000–2,400 DN(H)

A Cuban mahogany square piano, by Bernhardt, Paris, restored, 1828, 69in (175.5cm) wide.
£9,000–11,000 PPC

◄ An American mahogany piano, by Thomas Gibson, with rosewood crossbanding and gilt fruit and flower stencilling on the case front, labelled, 1825–35, 67½in (170cm) wide.
£900–1,000 SK(B)

Auction or Dealer?

All the pictures in our price guides originate from auction houses and dealers. When buying at auction, prices can be lower than those of a dealer, but a buyer's premium and VAT will be added to the hammer price. Equally, when selling at auction, commission, tax and photography charges must be taken into account. Dealers will often restore pieces before putting them back on the market.

Both dealers and auctioneers will provide professional advice, so it is worth researching both sources before buying or selling your antiques.

A mahogany grand piano, by Collard & Collard, London, restored, c1850, 84in (213.5cm) wide.
£8,000–9,000 PPC

A Victorian burr-walnut grand piano, by Ernst Kaps, overstrung, 72in (183cm) long.
£2,500–3,000 PEx

A rosewood grand piano, by Erard, restored, 1851, 99in (251.5cm) wide.
£11,000–13,000 PPC

A figured-walnut grand piano, by John Broadwood & Sons, mid-19thC, 93in (236cm) long.
£1,100–1,300 L

A Napoleon III-style grand piano, by Pleyel, Paris, with gilt mouldings and ormolu mountings, restored, 1854, 84in (213.5cm) wide.
£17,000–19,000 PPC

▶ A rosewood grand piano, by Bechstein, restored, 1865, 75in (190.5cm) wide.
£11,500–13,500 PPC

An American Renaissance-revival carved rosewood, walnut and brass-mounted upright piano, by Chickering Piano Company, the case attributed to Pottier and Stymus, 1870–80, 76in (193cm) wide.
£12,000–14,000 BB(S)

◀ A rosewood grand piano, by Steinway & Sons model B, with original floral-carved pedal harp, c1885, 54in (137cm) wide, with a mahogany bench.
£5,500–6,500 NOA

An oak grand piano, by Broadwood, London, restored, 1889, 99in (251.5cm) wide.
£10,000–12,000 PPC

A rosewood grand piano, by Kirkman, London, late 19thC, 56in (142cm) wide, and a mahogany bench.
£1,500–1,800 NOA

A mahogany grand piano, by Bechstein, c1900, 56½in (143.5cm) wide.
£6,500–8,000 PEx

A burr-walnut grand piano, by Bechstein, c1900, 56in (142cm) wide.
£7,500–9,000 PEx

A mahogany grand piano, by Bechstein, with walnut banding, gilt-metal mounts and classical embossed plaques, c1901, 57in (145cm) wide.
£8,000–9,500 P(Ba)

A satinwood grand piano, by Steinway, with boxwood stringing and oval parquetry panels, c1903, 57in (145cm) wide.
£23,000–25,000 P(Ba)

A rosewood grand piano, by Erard, London, with dual legs, c1905, 56½in (143.5cm) wide.
£2,300–2,750 PEx

An inlaid satinwood grand piano, by Broadwood, restored, 1906, 66in (167.5cm) wide.
£13,000–15,000 PPC

An upright player piano, by Steck, in a mahogany geometrically-inlaid, boxwood-strung and crossbanded case, together with a small collection of rolls, c1910, 52in (132cm) wide.
£1,300–1,500 P(Ba)

A bird's-eye maple baby grand piano, 1920s, 54in (137cm) long, with a matching stool.
£3,500–4,000 PEx

A mahogany boudoir grand piano, by George Rogers & Sons, London, c1920, 54in (137cm) wide.
£900–1,100 LF

▶ A grand piano, by Schiedmayer & Söhne, the green case decorated with gold chinoiserie, c1911, 58in (147.5cm) wide.
£2,000–2,400 P(Ba)

A Louis XV-style carved walnut grand piano, by Steinway & Sons, 1929, 54in (137cm) wide.
£9,000–10,000 DuM

A mahogany baby grand piano, by George Rogers, London, c1930, 54in (137cm) wide.
£750–900 WBH

An Art Deco chrome and black lacquer grand piano, marked, 1930s, 54½in (138.5cm) wide, with a matching stool.
£4,500–5,000 S

A cream lacquer piano and stool, by Strohmenger, the D-shaped body supported on straight legs, marked, faults, c1935, 55in (139.5cm) wide.
£650–800 S

An Art Deco walnut upright piano, Bongolo Grand, by Bentleys, 1930s, 53in (134.5cm) wide.
£650–750 OOLA

A Danish upright piano, by Andreas Christensen, 1943, 53¼in (135.5cm) wide.
£1,600–2,000 BRH

An ebonized grand piano, by C. Bechstein, model B, 1985, 53in (134.5cm) wide.
£12,000–14,000 BB(L)

LOCATE THE SOURCE

The source of each illustration in Miller's can be found by checking the code letters below each caption with the Key to Illustrations, pages 789–795.

▶ A Tyrolian pochette, by Matthias Worle, the five-staved back veneered in tortoiseshell, the top with inlaid floral motif, 18thC, length of body 10½in (26.5cm).
£5,500–6,000 SK

A German viola, by A. Kloz, 1772, length of back 15½in (39.5cm).
£3,000–3,500 Bon

An American mahogany ukulele, by C. F. Martin & Co, the back and top of koa with decorative binding, stamped, c1920, length of back 9½in (24cm).
£700–800 SK

A viola, by James and
Henry Banks, labelled and
stamped, c1803, length of
back 15½in (39.5cm).
£7,000–8,500 Bon

A viola, probably
by Thomas Dodd,
1820, length of back
15½in (39.5cm).
£7,500–9,000 Bon

A French viola, by Charles
Gaillard, Paris, c1860,
length of back 16in
(40.5cm), in a lined and
fitted carrying case.
£8,500–10,000 P

A French viola, by Charles
Gaillard, Paris, labelled,
signed and branded, 1861,
length of back 16in (40.5cm).
£4,000–4,500 P

► A violin, from the
workshop of Richard Duke,
London, stamped, c1800,
length of back 14in (35.5cm).
£2,000–2,200 SK

A Continental violin,
with lion's-head finial,
early 18thC, length of
back 14in (35.5cm).
£150–180 Wilp

A violin, probably Italian,
labelled 'Julius Caesar
Gigli Romanus fecit
Romae Anno 1757', length
of back 13¾in (35cm).
£9,000–11,000 Bon

◄ A Czechoslovakian violin,
by Joh. Kulik, Prague,
labelled, 1835, restored,
length of back 14in (35.5cm).
£2,200–2,600 P

A violin, probably Dutch,
labelled, c1790, length of
back 14in (35.5cm).
£2,200–2,600 Bon

► A French violin,
Vuillaume School, labelled
'Jean Baptiste Vuillaume
à Paris', c1850, length
of back 14¼in (36cm).
£2,800–3,200 P

A violin, in the style of Del Gesu, c1870, length of back 14in (35.5cm).
£2,000–2,400 Bon

A French violin, by M. Mermillot, Paris, after Francesco Guadagnini, labelled, 1884, length of back 14¼in (36cm).
£5,000–6,000 Bon

◀ A French violin, by Paul Bailly, Paris, 1886, length of back 14in (35.5cm).
£4,500–5,000 SK

A violin, by William E. Hill & Sons, London, labelled, 1885, length of back 14in (35.5cm).
£5,000–6,000 P

A violin, by Szepessy Bela, London, 1885, length of back 14in (35.5cm).
£5,750–7,000 P

An Italian violin, by Eugenio Degani, Venice, labelled, 1893, length of back 14½in (37cm).
£13,000–15,000 P

◀ A French violin, by Ch. J. B. Collin-Mezin, Paris, labelled and signed, 1892, length of back 14¼in (36cm).
£2,500–3,000 P

A French violin, labelled
'Ludivicus Piatti Violins
Anno 17..', late 19thC,
length of back 14¼in (36cm).
£200–240 BLH

An Italian violin,
attributed to Stefano
Scarampella, Mantua,
labelled, 1899, length
of back 14in (35.5cm).
£2,500–3,000 P

A German violin,
by M. Kuntze-Fechner,
Brussels, 1910, length
of back 14in (35.5cm).
£4,000–5,000 Bon

An Italian violin,
by Romeo Antoniazzi,
Cremona, signed, 1911,
length of back 14¼in (36cm).
£10,000–12,000 Bon

A French violin,
by Paul Blanchard, Lyon,
branded, 1912, length
of back 14in (35.5cm).
£10,000–11,000 P

A violin, by A. Richardson,
labelled, 1919, length of
back 14in (35.5cm).
£3,500–4,200 Bon

◄ A violin, by Vincent,
London, labelled,
1929, length of back
14¼in (36cm).
£1,800–2,200 BLH

A violin, by William
Robinson, labelled and
branded, 1920, length
of back 14in (35.5cm).
£1,500–1,800 Bon

▶ A French violin, by Paul
Kaul, Paris, 1933, length
of back 14in (35.5cm).
£5,000–5,500 P

An American violin,
by Giovanni Longiaru,
New York, 1925, length
of back 14in (35.5cm).
£1,700–2,000 SK

A French silver-mounted bass bow, by J. Thibouville
Lamy, the ebony frog with pearl eye and rounded heel,
the adjuster of silver, ebony and mother-of-pearl,
stamped, c1930.
£1,400–1,600 P

A south German polychrome and giltwood 'Little Woman' wall sconce, modelled as a mermaid archeress, bow missing, fitted for electricity, 18th/19thC, 24½in (62cm) high.
£3,500–4,000 S(Am)

◄ An Italian Murano glass chandelier, 19thC, 47¼in (120cm) high.
£3,000–3,300 S(Z)

An Austrian ormolu and bronze eight-light chandelier, 19thC, 27¼in (69cm) high.
£12,500–15,000 HAM

◄ A pair of French brass oil lamps, with painted glass shades and founts, 19thC, 19in (48.5cm) high.
£180–220 LIB

A cut and pierced brass hall lantern, with bevelled and coloured glass panels, c1880, 36in (91.5cm) high.
£400–450 ASH

A vestibule lamp, with amber glass bowl, fitted for a single candle, c1890, 30in (76cm) high.
£200–240 JW

A brass oil lamp, with cranberry glass shade, c1870, 26in (66cm) high.
£300–350 JW

An enamel and champlevé oil lamp, by F. Barbedienne, fitted for electricity, late 19thC, 28in (71cm) high.
£1,400–1,600 Bon

A wrought-iron lamp, with amber glass shade, c1900, 27in (68.5cm) high.
£700–800 RUL

◄ An Erhard & Söhne brass and rootwood table lamp, 1910–15, 17¾in (45cm) high.
£650–750 DORO

A glass paraffin lamp, c1900, 28½in (72.5cm) high.
£500–600 PFK

A Continental crystal-beaded and rose prism-hung six-light chandelier, early 20thC, 30in (76cm) high.
£2,000–2,200 NOA

A Cuenca carpet, reduced in size, Spain, c1950, 156 x 132in (396 x 335.5cm).
£1,750–2,000 P

An Axminster carpet, England, c1830, 432 x 252in (1,097 x 667cm).
£37,000–40,000 S

A needlepoint carpet, repaired, England, c1880, 211 x 108in (536 x 274.5cm).
£16,000–20,000 S(NY)

An Aubusson carpet, France, early 19thC, 98 x 110in (249 x 279.5cm).
£4,500–5,500 NOA

A Swedish carpet, designed before 1918 by Märta Måås-Fjetterström, with design of stylized horses, produced before 1942, 121½ x 79½in (308.5 x 202cm).
£10,000–12,000 BUK

A needlepoint carpet, Russia, c1850, repaired, 113 x 86in (287 x 218.5cm).
£9,500–11,000 S(NY)

A pile and flatwoven rug, repaired, Ukraine, early 19thC, 97 x 92in (246.5 x 233.5cm).
£17,000–20,000 S(NY)

A Karabagh rug, woven with two hexagonal motifs filled with cloud band motifs, within conforming borders, south Caucasus, c1860, 79 x 53in (200.5 x 134.5cm).
£800–1,000 CAG

◄ A Konya prayer rug, central Anatolia, repaired, mid-19thC, 61 x 41in (155 x 104cm).
£2,200–2,500 S(NY)

A Karabagh rug, south Caucasus, dated '1894', 100 x 46in (254 x 117cm).
£600–700 P

A Karabagh rug, one end trimmed, restored, south Caucasus, c1900, 95¾in x 50¼in (243 x 128cm).
£700–800 P(S)

A Shirvan Bidjov design rug, east Caucasus, early 20thC, 38 x 28½in (96.5 x 72.5cm).
£850–1,000 WW

A Talish prayer rug, east Caucasus, mid-19thC, 61 x 43in (155 x 109cm).
£5,000–5,500 SAM

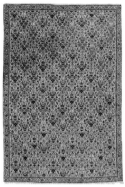

A Zili Sultan rug,
with original flatwoven end
finishes, northwest Persia,
early 20thC, 77 x 51in
(195.5 x 129.5cm).
£6,000–7,000 S(NY)

A Mahal carpet, with all-
over floral lattice design,
enclosed by indigo rosette
borders, west Persia,
early 20thC, 111 x 79in
(282 x 200.5cm).
£1,600–2,000 Bon(C)

A Kalardasht rug,
Azerbaijan, northwest
Persia, c1900, 84 x 44in
(213.5 x 112cm).
£1,600–1,800 SAM

A Bidjar rug, Persian
Kurdistan, c1940,
111 x 52in (282 x 132cm).
£1,000–1,200 Bon(C)

A silk Tabriz prayer rug,
northwest Persia, c1875,
64 x 50in (162.5 x 127cm).
£9,000–10,000 S(NY)

An Isfahan rug, central
Persia, c1950, 86 x 61in
(218.5 x 155cm).
£1,100–1,200 P

A Kashgai rug, southwest
Persia, late 19thC,
76 x 42in (193 x 106.5cm).
£3,200–3,500 SAM

A Baluch prayer rug,
northeast Persia, mid-19thC,
51¼ x 30in (130 x 76cm).
£1,600–1,750 SAM

A pair of Kurdish
saddlebags, northeast
Persia, late 19thC,
41 x 22in (104 x 22cm).
£2,200–2,500 SAM

A Yomud Turkoman
flatweave prayer rug,
northwest Turkestan, c1900,
51¼ x 35⅜in (130 x 91cm).
£2,200–2,500 SAM

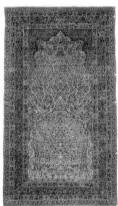

A Kirman millefleurs
prayer rug, southeast
Persia, dated '1892–93',
96 x 55in (244 x 139.5cm).
£12,000–14,000 S

An Agra carpet, with an
overall Herati design,
India, c1900, 216 x 155in
(549 x 393.5cm).
£7,500–9,000 Bea(E)

An Afghan Ersari juval, west Turkestan, 1900–10,
78 x 40in (198 x 101.5cm).
£550–650 WW

▶ A yellow silk carpet,
woven with a five-character
inscription 'For use in the
Palace of Heavenly Purity',
China, c1900, 97 x 61¾in
(246.5 x 157cm).
£4,000–5,000 S(NY)

An oak box, the lid inset with an embroidered panel with silver threadwork borders, some losses, c1630, 11½in (29cm) wide.
£3,700–4,500 HAM

A stumpwork cushion cover, embroidered in coloured silks and metal threads, 1650–80, 10¼ x 13¼in (26 x 33.5cm), framed and glazed.
£3,700–4,000 S(S)

A Charles II beadwork and stumpwork basket, c1670, exterior sides now mounted with late Regency geometric needlework, handles missing, 19in (48.5cm) wide.
£9,500–11,000 S(NY)

A set of four needlework panels, late 17thC, each panel 35 x 14in (89 x 36cm).
£2,200–2,500 SWO

A needlework picture, worked in coloured silks depicting King Solomon and the Queen of Sheba, early 18thC, 18 x 20in (45.5 x 51cm).
£2,800–3,200 L

◄ A needlework picture, worked in coloured silks and wool depicting a shepherdess with her dog and lambs, initialled and dated, in a gilt-painted frame, 18thC, 11¾ x 18¼in (30 x 46.5cm).
£3,200–3,800 WW

A French needlework picture, c1760, 12 x 16in (30.5 x 40.5cm).
£1,200–1,350 CAT

A needlework picture, in original gilt-decorated carved wood frame, c1790, 17in (43cm) wide.
£5,000–5,500 CAT

◄ A Kaitag embroidery, northeast Caucasus, 18thC, 42 x 22in (106.5 x 56cm).
£4,000–4,500 S(NY)

A pair of Georgian silkwork pictures of children, in gilt frames, 6 x 5in (15 x 12.5cm).
£900–1,100 RBB

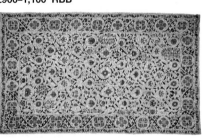

A Bochara *susani*, the cotton ground embroidered in chain stitch, Uzbekistan, mid-19thC, 91¼ x 56¾in (232 x 144cm).
£1,100–1,300 P

► A needlework panel, embroidered and appliquéd with coloured wools and silks on satin, in a gilt and black-painted glass mount and a gilt frame, early 19thC, 15¼ x 12½in (38.5 x 32cm).
£280–320 RTo

A needlepoint panel, depicting Bacchus attended by putti, probably French, 18thC, 34⅜ x 26½in (88.5 x 67.5cm).
£2,000–2,200 BB(S)

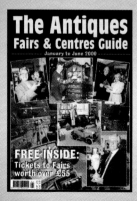

A needlework sampler, by Sarah Daveney, embroidered in petit point stitch, in a glazed frame, 1774, 15 x 13in (38 x 33cm).
£1,800–2,200 S(S)

A needlework sampler, by Alice Bradburn Preston, 1802, 21½ x 17½in (54.5 x 44.5cm).
£750–900 JM

A needlework sampler, by Mary Ann Wells, 1823, 19¾ x 18½in (50 x 47cm).
£580–650 OCH

A needlework sampler, by Eliza Brown, worked in coloured silks on a linen ground, 1828, 16¼ x 12¼in (41.5 x 31cm).
£250–300 BIG

A silk and linen needlework sampler, by Mary Pennington, 1830, 25 x 23in (63.5 x 58.5cm).
£5,500–6,000 BB(S)

A needlework sampler, by Martha Chadwick, 1848, 26in (66cm) square, in a rosewood frame.
£800–1,000 GH

A needlework sampler, by Mary L. Sisson, worked with Castle Howe, Tebay, Westmorland, 1878, 22½ x 25in (57 x 63.5cm), framed.
£200–240 PFK

◀ An Aubusson tapestry, damaged, 18thC, 90 x 84in (228.5 x 213.4cm).
£1,800–2,200 RBB

A Flemish border panel, late 16thC, 25½ x 55½in (65 x 141cm).
£2,500–2,750 S(Z)

A Flemish verdure tapestry, mid-18thC, within a 19thC stylized border, 92 x 53in (233.5 x 134.5cm).
£2,500–3,000 SWO

A Flemish tapestry, depicting the Judgement of Paris, Oudenaarde, 17thC, 102¼ x 127½in (259.5 x 324cm).
£6,500–8,000 HVH

A Flemish pictorial tapestry panel, with silk highlights, early 18thC, 40 x 60½in (101.5 x 153.5cm).
£4,750–5,250 NOA

◀ A French allegorical tapestry, depicting shepherds fleeing from Father Time, 17thC, 74 x 107½in (188 x 273cm).
£4,250–4,750 S(Z)

A French baroque verdure tapestry, early 18thC, 79 x 84in (200.5 x 213.5cm).
£6,000–7,000 BB(S)

A dismounted fan leaf, depicting Diogenes searching for an honest man at a carnival, framed, c1680, 20 x 11½in (51 x 29cm).
£2,500–3,000 LDC

An Italian fan leaf, painted with Satyr musicians and Jupiter, framed, c1720, 24 x 13½in (61 x 34.5cm).
£3,500–4,000 LDC

A Georgian carved ivory and hand-painted fan, c1760, 11in (28cm) wide.
£320–350 FAN

An Italian ivory Grand Tour fan, the chicken-skin leaf painted with St. Peter's, Rome and other classical ruins, c1790, 11in (28cm) wide.
£1,000–1,200 LDC

A French cut-steel fan, the paper leaf printed and painted with figures in a landscape, c1815, 8½in (21.5cm) wide.
£350–420 P

▶ A fan, the leaf hand-coloured, the ormolu guard sticks set with red paste stones, probably French, dated '1821', 9in (23cm) wide.
£250–300 LDC

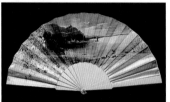

A Victorian bone fan, the cream silk painted with a seascape, c1880, 14in (35.5cm) wide.
£130–145 FAN

▶ A Japanese painted wood court fan, the upper guards with gilt-metal chrysanthemums and applied silk tassel fringing, c1850, 13¾in (35cm) wide.
£700–800 P

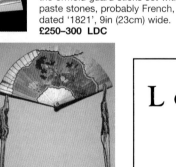

A Chinese Canton tortoiseshell cabriolet fan, painted with Chinese landscapes and figures, c1860, 8½in (21.5cm) wide.
£600–700 LDC

▶ A wooden fan, the paper hand-painted with a butterfly motif, c1900, 11in (28cm) wide.
£80–100 FAN

An enamel, pearl and diamond hinged bangle, c1860.
£1,000–1,200 P

A Victorian gold, garnet and seed-pearl bracelet.
£700–850 Bea(E)

A gold and turquoise bangle, with locket back compartment, c1865.
£1,000–1,100 P

A Victorian 15ct gold cuff bracelet, 3½in (9cm) diam.
£2,000–2,250 WIM

A diamond and sapphire bangle, c1880, 2¼in (5.5cm) diam.
£2,500–3,000 Bon

A late Victorian ruby and diamond bangle/brooch.
£7,000–8,000 P

A gold bracelet, set with opals, c1840.
£1,300–1,500 P

A citrine, amethyst and smoky quartz bracelet, c1860.
£750–900 P(Ed)

▶ A gold flexible bracelet, centred by a diamond-set star, with locket back compartment, in a Hunt & Roskell fitted case, c1860.
£1,750–2,000 TEN

A Florentine gold and *pietra dura* bracelet, c1870.
£2,500–2,750 P

◀ A late Victorian diamond bracelet, in original box.
£6,000–7,000 AG

An Italian suite of micro-mosaic jewellery, Italian control marks, c1880, bracelet 7in (18cm) long.
£2,000–2,400 Bon

A gold, ruby and diamond hinged bangle, c1890, 2¼in (5.5cm) diam.
£2,500–2,750 S

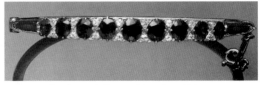

A ruby and diamond bangle, c1895.
£2,500–2,750 P

◀ A Russian charm bracelet, including a gold elephant, a medallion set with diamonds and a gold and red enamel egg pendant, c1910.
£2,200–2,500 P

A 15ct gold brooch, with multi-gem pendants, c1810, 3in (7.5cm) high.
£1,800–2,000 WIM

A micro-mosaic brooch, depicting the Spanish Steps in Rome, c1840.
£2,200–2,500 Bon

A gold, garnet and chrysoberyl brooch, c1840.
£1,150–1,350 P(Ba)

A Victorian brooch/pendant, with a central sapphire surrounded by 24 diamonds.
£2,000–2,400 RBB

A Victorian gold foil brooch, the central citrine surrounded by four green tourmalines.
£160–200 P(L)

▶ A Victorian gold and silver brooch, with a coral bud on a diamond-set stem.
£1,700–2,000 TEN

A Victorian gold and opal brooch/pendant, 1½in (4cm) diam.
£900–1,000 WIM

A Victorian diamond, pearl, blue enamel and gold brooch.
£400–450 AG

A Victorian gold and enamel brooch, decorated with a lake scene, 19thC, 1¼in (3cm) wide.
£450–550 L

A Swiss gold and enamel brooch, decorated with a lake scene, 19thC, 1¼in (3cm) wide.
£450–550 L

◀ A late Victorian amethyst and gold brooch, 2½in (6.5cm) wide.
£320–380 HCH

A dragonfly *en tremblant* brooch, the opal wings set with diamonds, with ruby cabochon eyes and diamond set body, c1900.
£8,000–9,000 DN

A diamond and ruby brooch, c1935.
£850–1,000 WW

A bee brooch, with white opal body and seed pearl and demantoid garnet set wings, c1910.
£400–500 LJ

A gold bracelet, comprising six shell cameos each depicting a classical female figure, c1870.
£2,000–2,200 P

A Victorian gold-mounted buckle, with three shell cameos.
£700–850 TEN

A French hardstone cameo bracelet/brooch, with green and white enamelled gold frame, 19thC.
£800–1,000 P(L)

A French hardstone cameo brooch/pendant, the gold mount set with rose diamonds and a pearl, French control marks, c1870.
£1,350–1,500 TEN

A Victorian shell cameo necklace.
£1,000–1,200 P(L)

A pair of Georgian 15ct gold pendant earrings, set with turquoise, 3in (7.5cm) long.
£2,500–2,750 WIM

◀ A pair of Victorian gold, ruby and pearl earrings.
£525–585 WIM

A pair of gold and amethyst pendant earrings, c1840.
£900–1,100 P

A pair of Russian emerald and diamond cluster earrings, marked, late 19thC.
£8,000–9,000 S

◀ A pair of Victorian gold earrings, each with a coral bead and diamond drop suspended from green enamel and rose diamond leaves.
£800–1,000 P(L)

A pair of Victorian 15ct gold and amadine garnet earrings.
£1,000–1,175 WIM

A Victorian gold, ruby and diamond ring.
£1,000–1,100 MJB

An emerald and diamond ring, c1910.
£2,750–3,250 S

A Victorian gold, amethyst and citrine ring.
£1,650–1,850 WIM

A ruby and diamond ring, c1905.
£1,000–1,200 S

A Russian priest's cross and chain, in silver and multi-coloured cloisonné enamel, 18thC, chain 34in (86.5cm) long.
£2,000–2,250 ICO

A chantille work gold necklace, set with pink topaz, emeralds and pearls, c1820.
£1,350–1,500 JSM

A gold and coloured stone necklace, c1840.
£5,000–6,000 P

◄ A Chinese silver filigree and rose quartz necklace, c1890, 6in (15cm) long.
£400–450 JSM

An Austrian Renaissance revival pendant, enamelled and set with a natural pearl and precious stones, c1860, 2½in (6.5cm) long.
£6,750–7,500 SHa

A Victorian 18ct gold, amethyst, diamond and pearl pendant.
£550–650 P(L)

A late Victorian gold necklace, with turquoise and half pearl flowerheads and pearl-set chain, in original fitted case.
£900–1,100 WW

An Edwardian amethyst, peridot and diamond pendant.
£700–800 P(Ba)

An Edwardian enamelled pendant, on a filigree silver chain.
£170–200 LJ

◄ An aquamarine and diamond pendant, the chain set at intervals with seed pearls, later rhodium-plated, c1910.
£3,000–3,300 S

A Russian gold pendant, with demantoid garnets, diamonds and a ruby, in original fitted leather case, Moscow, c1910, 2¾in (7cm) high.
£1,500–1,800 S(NY)

An Edwardian peridot and half pearl pendant.
£300–350 P(Ba)

An Edwardian gold and amethyst necklace.
£350–420 GTH

A George III enamelled tea caddy, painted with a portrait of the King, the reverse with a portrait of Queen Charlotte, south Staffordshire, c1760–61, 4¼in (11cm) high.
£16,000–18,000 Bon

The exceptional painting on this piece suggests that it may have been made as a presentation item.

A Bilston enamel box, c1780, 2½in (6.5cm) wide.
£550–600 BHa

A pair of green enamelled candlesticks, 18thC, 10¼in (26cm) high.
£1,600–1,800 P(B)

◄ An enamelled patch box, the cover painted with a portrait of Admiral Lord Nelson, marked 'Trafalgar 21st October 1805', early 19thC, 2in (5cm) wide.
£900–1,000 TMA

A French chatelaine, set with gold, enamel and diamonds, inset with miniatures on ivory, c1800, 6in (15cm) long.
£4,000–4,500 SHa

A Limoges enamel-on-copper plaque of a falconer, with a red velvet frame, signed 'T. Soyer', 19thC, 20½ x 12in (52 x 30.5cm).
£3,000–3,500 SK

A silver-gilt *guilloche* enamelled cigarette case, the interior marked 'St. Petersburg 1908', initialled for Andrei Gorianov, 4in (10cm) wide.
£3,500–4,200 JAA

A Fabergé enamelled dish, by August Hollming, St. Petersburg, c1895, 4½in (11.5cm) wide.
£4,000–4,500 SHa

A Fabergé Art Nouveau silver and enamel cigarette case, Moscow, c1890, 4in (10cm) wide.
£6,500–7,500 S(NY)

A French gold viniagrette, c1800, 1in (2.5cm) diam.
£1,100–1,250 BEX

A pair of French enamelled opaline vases, 19thC, 11in (30cm) high.
£250–300 GSP

◄ A pair of late Victorian 18ct gold-mounted scent bottles, by William Comyns, London 1895, 5½in (14cm) high.
£7,000–8,500 P(L)

An 18ct gold bottle, with flip cap and glass stopper, French marks, 19thC, 2½in (6.5cm) long.
£700–800 LBr

A Chinese cloisonné bowl, Qianlong period, 1736–95, 17in (43cm) diam.
£1,000–1,100 S(Am)

A Japanese silver and enamel bowl, signed 'Hiratsuka Sei', Meiji period, 1868–1911, 8½in (21.5cm) wide, with conforming wood stand.
£6,000–7,000 P

A Chinese Peking six-colour glass jar and cover, Qing Dynasty, late 18thC, 5¾in (14.5cm) high.
£3,500–4,200 S

A Japanese cloisonné vase, signed 'Kumeno Teitaro', c1900, 9½in (24cm) high.
£2,200–2,500 S(NY)

A Japanese cloisonné enamel vase, by Hayashi Kodenji, Meiji period, 1868–1911, 6in (15cm) high.
£7,000–8,000 S

A pair of Chinese Canton enamel wine cups and cup stands, Qianlong period, 1736–95, stands 4¾in (12cm) diam.
£2,200–2,600 S(HK)

A Chinese reverse glass painting, late 18thC, 22in (56cm) wide.
£2,800–3,200 P

A pair of Chinese yellow glass vases, 19thC, 12½in (32cm) high.
£7,000–8,000
A Chinese yellow glass beaker vase, carved in three sections, 18thC, 8¼in (21cm) high.
£6,000–7,000 S(NY)

A Chinese carved red lacquer vase, 19thC, 10in (25.5cm) high.
£300–350 DuM

► A north Indian stone sculpture of Vaikuntha, 11thC.
£10,000–12,000 GRG

◄ A Japanese mixed metal figure of a cockerel on a drum, signed 'Kyukando-Sei', Meiji period, 1868–1911, 12½in (32cm) high.
£10,000–11,000 MCN

A pair of Japanese bronze vases, 19thC, 12in (30.5cm) high.
£1,000–1,200 WBH

A Japanese silver and enamel vase, mounted with six *Shibayama* plaques, c1880, 9½in (24cm) high.
£2,500–3,000 SFL

A Japanese gilt lacquer four-case *inro*, 19thC, 3½in (9cm) high.
£9,000–10,000 BB(S)

A Japanese gold lacquer three-case *inro*, with *Shibayama* inlay, 19thC, 2¼in (5.5cm) high.
£1,750–2,000 S

A Japanese four-case *inro*, 19thC, 3in (7.5cm) high.
£650–800 TMA

A Japanese four-case *inro*, with a Chinese motif, 19thC, 2in (5cm) high.
£800–900 KIE

A Japanese woodcut print, by Yoshitoshi, entitled 'The Cry of the Fox', published 1886, 9½in (24cm) wide.
£500–550 JaG

A Japanese woodcut print of Shiraishi-jima, signed 'Hiroshi Yoshida', published 1930, 16in (40.5cm) wide.
£500–550 JaG

A Japanese woodcut print, by Hiroshige, entitled 'Takuhi shrine in Oki province', published 1853, 9½in (24cm) wide.
£800–885 JaG

A Chinese crimson silk damask robe, late 19thC.
£550–600 P

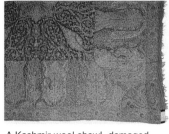

A Kashmir wool shawl, damaged, c1840, 78¾in (200cm) square.
£1,800–2,200 P

A Chinese ceremonial armour costume, in silk applied with gilt-metal studs, late 19thC.
£3,200–3,500 P

A Chinese Canton enamel snuff bottle, with silvered bronze stopper, 1850–1900, 3in (7.5cm) high.
£5,000–5,500 JWA

A Chinese glass overlay snuff bottle, attributed to the Beijing Palace Workshops, Qianlong period, 1736–95, 3in (7.5cm) high.
£6,750–7,500 JWA

A Chinese agate snuff bottle, 19thC, 2¾in (7cm) high.
£1,000–1,200 BOW

► A Japanese *sake* gourd in the shape of a duck, 19thC, 9in (23cm) long.
£850–1,000 KJ

A Chinese lacquered-bronze figure of a seated Guanyin, base possibly reduced, Ming Dynasty, 14th–17thC, 32½in (82.5cm) high.
£10,000–11,000 BB(S)

A Chinese carved and gilded wood figure of Wei Tuo, Ming Dynasty, 17thC, 42in (106.5cm) high.
£5,000–6,000 S

A Tibetan gilt-bronze figure of Buddha, 18th/19thC, 8¼in (21cm) high.
£450–550 SK

A Japanese ivory group, late 19thC, 3¼in (8.5cm) high.
£1,100–1,250 SHa

A Chinese gilt-bronze figure of Buddha, 16th/17thC, 8¼in (21cm) high.
£2,600–3,000 Wai

A Chinese carved celadon crab-shaped box, 18thC, 4¼in (11cm) wide.
£6,500–7,500 S(NY)

A Japanese carved wood and ivory group of street entertainers, signed 'Seïko', Meiji period, 1868–1911, 9in (23cm) wide.
£3,200–3,500 LBo

A Japanese ivory netsuke, carved in the form of Benkie killing a giant carp, inlaid with gold, silver, horn and various gemstones, late 19thC, 2¼in (5.5cm) high.
£4,000–4,500 KIE

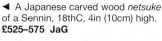 A Japanese carved wood netsuke of a Sennin, 18thC, 4in (10cm) high.
£525–575 JaG

A Chinese pair of cloisonné deer holding candlesticks, c1800, 13¾in (35cm) high.
£5,000–6,000 S(NY)

A Japanese ivory okimono, in the form of a group of rats, signed 'Tomomasa', mid-19thC, 2in (5cm) high.
£1,200–1,400 BOW

A Chinese jade carving of a recumbent beast, 17thC, 4½in (11.5cm) wide.
£4,000–4,500 P

A Japanese ivory and lacquered figure of a Chinese beauty, signed 'Kiyonori', Meiji period, c1900, 25¼in (64cm) high.
£5,800–6,500 BB(S)

◄ A Japanese ivory figure, signed 'Chikamichi', c1900, 5¼in (13.5cm) high.
£1,450–1,600 MCN

A Dutch Colonial oak four-
poster bed, early 19thC,
60in (152.5cm) wide.
£1,100–1,300 NOA

An Anglo-Indian carved
and ebonized four-
poster bed, c1880,
70¾in (179.5cm) wide.
£7,500–8,250 S

A Chinese bamboo and *ju* wood daybed,
76in (193cm) long.
£800–900 K

A Japanese carved
bamboo, oak and bronze
revolving bookcase,
c1900, 35½in (90cm) wide.
£28,000–32,000 S

An Anglo-Singhalese box,
on cabriole legs, c1820,
18in (45.5cm) wide.
£5,500–6,000 CAT

A Chinese export cabinet,
on a European silvered
stand, late 17thC,
38¼in (97cm) wide.
£50,000–60,000 P

An Anglo-Indian rosewood
cabinet, on a cupboard
base, early 19thC,
45in (114.5cm) wide.
£800–1,000 TMA

A Singhalese satinwood
and ebony cabinet-
on-stand, 19thC,
54⅛in (138.5cm) wide.
£5,500–6,000 S(NY)

A Chinese bamboo cabinet,
c1900, 35in (89cm) wide.
£575–650 NET

A Regency Anglo-Indian
hardwood clothes
press, early 19thC,
49½in (125.5cm) wide.
£7,500–8,250 NOA

A Chinese elm bedroom
cabinet, with original
lacquer and finely etched
brassware, 19thC,
23in (58.5cm) wide.
£550–620 OE

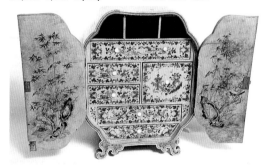

A Japanese silver lacquer
table-top cabinet, Meiji
period, 1868–1911,
19in (48.5cm) wide.
£5,000–5,500 NAW

A Japanese lacquer miniature
cabinet, signed 'Senpo',
19thC, 6in (15cm) wide.
£4,750–5,250 BB(S)

A north Chinese folding
chair, late 19thC.
£475–525 GHC

◀ A Tibetan painted
cabinet, 19thC,
28in (71cm) wide.
£850–950 OE

A pair of Chinese elm armchairs, with cane seats, mid-19thC.
£1,500–1,700 HGh

A Tibetan painted wood ceremonial chest, restored and repainted, 19thC, 56¼in (143cm) wide.
£800–900 BB(S)

◄ A Chinese elm scholar's chair, with yoke back, Beijing, c1860.
£350–400 SOO

A Chinese fruitwood chest, Henan Province, late 19thC, 40in (101.5cm) wide.
£700–800 K

A Japanese hardwood chest, with iron fittings, 19thC, 18¼in (46.5cm) wide.
£1,750–2,000 TMA

An elm cupboard stool, late 19thC, 24in (61cm) wide.
£425–475 GHC

A north Chinese elm low coffer, with carved side panels, late 19thC, 50in (127cm) wide.
£375–425 OE

A south Chinese red lacquer cupboard, with decorated panels, 20thC, 35in (89cm) wide.
£1,100–1,200 OE

A pair of Chinese elm doors, Beijing, 19thC, 90in (228.5cm) high.
£1,600–2,000 K

An Indian padouk and ivory-inlaid toilet mirror, Vizagapatam, 18thC, 20in (51cm) wide.
£11,000–12,000 P

A pair of cinnabar lacquer porcelain-mounted stands, repaired, late Qing Dynasty, 17¾in (45cm) wide.
£4,500–5,000 BB(S)

▶ A pair of Chinese carved and incised red lacquer low tables, reduced in height, losses, 17thC, 48¾in (124cm) wide.
£13,000–15,000 S(NY)

A north Chinese elm table, with traces of original lacquer, late 19thC, 25½in (65cm) high.
£425–475 GHC

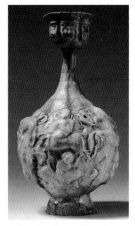

A Turkish Iznik pottery border tile, c1590,
11¼in (28.5cm) wide, framed.
£3,700–4,000 S

A Persian Ilkhanid lustre-
ware pottery ewer, spout
tip restored, late 13thC,
13in (33cm) high.
£6,000–7,000 S(NY)

A Persian Ilkhanid white-
glazed pottery vase, late
13thC, 13¾in (35cm) high.
£18,000–20,000 S(NY)

▶ A Persian
Qajar moulded
pottery tile, 19thC,
20¼in (51.5cm)
wide, framed.
£2,200–2,500 Bon

A Turkish Iznik pottery tile, 1530–40,
10¾in (27.5cm) diam.
£5,500–6,000 S

A Persian glass bowl, AD 8th–10th
century, 6½in (16.5cm) diam.
£22,000–24,000 S

A Turkish Iznik pottery dish, c1560,
12¼in (31cm) diam.
£7,000–8,000 Bon

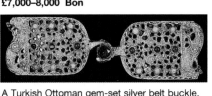

A Turkish Ottoman gem-set silver belt buckle,
16thC, 7in (18cm) wide.
£3,000–3,300 Bon

A Persian Khorasan silver-inlaid bronze
bucket, c1200, 8½in (21.5cm) diam.
£15,000–18,000 Bon

A Persian lacquered papier
mâché mirror-case, with
portraits of the Shah of Persia
and his Prime Minister, dated
'1854', 6½in (16.5cm) wide.
£4,500–5,000 S

A pair of Turkish
Ottoman flint-
lock pistols,
early 19thC,
19¾in (50cm) long.
**£2,500–3,000
Herm**

▶ A Turkish
polychrome and
gilt-decorated
wood turban
stand, c1800,
51½in (131cm) high.
£5,750–7,000 S

A Persian Safavid gold damascened
steel helmet and arm guard,
late 17thC.
£4,000–5,000 Bon

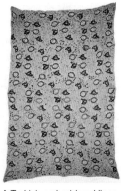

A Turkish embroidered linen
quilt facing, mid-18thC,
88¼ x 54¼in (224 x 138cm).
£4,250–4,750 P

A Viennese School cold-painted and patinated bronze birdbath, c1900, 11in (28cm) high.
£1,300–1,500 S(Am)

A cast-iron Royal coat-of-arms, late 19thC, 49in (124.5cm) wide.
£1,500–1,800 Bon(M)

◀ An Italian cast-bronze figure of Pan, probably Naples, late 19th/early 20thC, 47¼in (120cm) high, with associated concrete base.
£1,500–1,800 RTo

A Victorian cast-iron garden planter, 48in (122cm) high.
£1,000–1,100 JAA

A marble cistern and cover, probably late 16th/early 17thC, 17½in (44.5cm) wide.
£1,200–1,400 HYD

A French terracotta pediment, c1900, 35in (89cm) wide.
£500–600 RUL

▶ A pair of Compton Pottery terracotta garden urns, early 20thC, 10in (25.5cm) diam.
£4,000–5,000 HAM

A mid-Victorian sandstone sundial, surmounted by a cast-iron plate and gnomon, 49in (124.5cm) high.
£3,000–3,500 Bon(M)

A pair of French terracotta angels, with traces of old gilt, 19thC, 48in (122cm) high.
£3,700–4,000 S(S)

A pair of French carved oak panels, 1580–1600, 22in (56cm) high.
£200–225 AnSh

A Flemish carved panel, 16thC, 20in (51cm) high.
£250–285 OCH

A cast-iron roll-top bath, with ball-and-claw feet, restored, 1920s, 66in (167.5cm) long.
£675–750 ACT

An oak corbel, 15thC, 18in (45.5cm) high.
£5,750–6,500 DBA

▶ A Brunswick floral-decorated lavatory pan, c1895, 18in (45.5cm) wide.
£1,100–1,300 WRe

◀ An Edwardian stained glass window, set with Victorian hand-painted roundels, 46 x 69in (117 x 175.5cm).
£1,100–1,300 DD

A Regency marble fire surround, with Doric capitals, c1820, 72in (183cm) wide.
£12,500–14,000 ASH

A carved marble Louis XVI-style fire surround, with ormolu decoration, the cast-iron interior with floral decoration, 19thC, 68in (172.5cm) wide.
£12,000–13,500 NOST

A Victorian red-veined yellow marble fire surround, in the Aesthetic style, 80in (203cm) wide.
£2,000–2,400 PFK

A marble fire surround, with deep moulding to the frieze jambs and mantel shelf, 1880, 48in (122cm) wide.
£2,300–2,600 ASH

A Louis XV-style marble fire surround, late 19thC, 52½in (133.5cm) wide.
£3,000–3,500 BB(S)

A Victorian cast-iron and tiled combination grate, 1884, 41in (104cm) wide.
£700–800 NOST

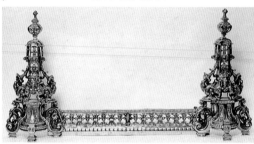

A pair of American Federal brass steeple andirons, by J. Davis, Boston, c1800, 20in (51cm) high, with similar brass and iron shovel and tongs.
£2,400–2,750 BB(S)

A cast-brass kerb, decorated with garlands of flowers and bearded male masks, c1870, 54in (137cm) wide.
£1,100–1,250 ASH

A hand-painted toleware coal bin, on paw feet, 19thC, 17in (43cm) wide.
£600–700 BG

A chinoiserie-decorated metal coal box, mid-19thC, 21in (53.5cm) wide.
£2,200–2,500 DOA

An Edwardian cut and pierced brass coal bin, c1900, 16in (40.5cm) diam.
£165–185 ASH

◄ A Regency steel and wrought-iron fireside plate warmer, with later decoration, c1830, 18in (45.5cm) wide.
£600–700 AnSh

► A copper coal scuttle, c1870, 17½in (44.5cm) wide.
£125–140 AL

A German carved oak group of King Louis IX of France and his wife Margaret, c1300, 54in (137cm) high.
£37,000–40,000 P

A carved limewood group of the Virgin and Child, probably French, late 15th/early 16thC, 35in (89cm) high.
£7,000–8,000 DBA

A south German carved limewood figure of St. Michael, early 16thC, 48in (122cm) high.
£16,000–18,000 WW

A Continental carved figure of a knight on horseback, 16thC, areas re-cut, 51½in (131cm) high.
£6,500–7,500 Bon(C)

A south German carved wood figure of Mary Magdalene, late 16th/early 17thC, 35½in (90cm) high.
£5,500–6,000 BB(S)

A pair of south German giltwood figures of angels, late 17thC, 15¾in (40cm) high.
£4,000–4,500 S(Am)

A Dutch wax bust, 17thC, 7½in (19cm) high.
£1,600–1,800 JHo

A Flemish carved wood figure of St. Luke, c1680, 25in (63.5cm) high.
£1,300–1,450 SEA

A pair of Continental carved wood, gilt and polychrome cherubs, late 17thC, 19in (48.5cm) high.
£3,200–3,500 NAW

A carved wood figure of the Virgin and Child, possibly Spanish or Italian, early 18thC, 14in (35.5cm) high.
£280–325 OCH

An Italian baroque gilded wood carving of a cherub, 18thC, 9in (23cm) high.
£180–200 OCH

A carved and painted wood figure of a lady, with composition and wood body, clad in brocaded silk and velvet, late 18thC, 30½in (77.5cm) high.
£2,000–2,200 S(S)

▶ A wax figure of Queen Charlotte, by Samuel Percy, seated on a carved giltwood settee, late 18thC, 12½in (32cm) wide.
£4,000–4,500 S(NY)

A German carved ivory figure of a young maiden, late 18thC, 10in (25.5cm) high.
£3,000–3,500 P

A pair of carved wood lions, probably originally newel post decorations, early 19thC, 22in (56cm) high.
£3,500–4,000 DBA

A pair of wax figures of grotesques, by T. Cooper, London, signed and dated '1840', 7½in (19cm) high, on later oval plinths.
£300–350 Hal

◄ A bronze group of Romulus and Remus with the she-wolf, after the original antique, on a marble socle, mid-19thC, 8¼in (21.5cm) wide.
£1,100–1,250 ANT

A French bronze group of a Native American mother and child, by Charles Cumberworth, mid-19thC, 21in (53.5cm) high.
£4,000–4,500 S

An American white marble bust, entitled 'Proserpine', by Hiram Powers, mid-19thC, 22½in (57cm) high.
£8,500–9,500 S

A bronze group of a partridge and chick, by Ferdinand Pautrot, c1860, 10¼in (26cm) high.
£2,000–2,200 CAG

A French terracotta figure of a gardener, signed 'J. Le Galuchs', c1880, 26in (66cm) high.
£1,200–1,400 HUM

A German group of ivory and fruitwood figures, 19thC, largest 7in (18cm) high.
£3,400–3,750 SHa

A French bronze model of a tiger, by T. Cartier, on a green marble plinth, signed, 19thC, 19in (48.5cm) wide.
£1,250–1,500 Mit

A pair of bronze figures of children, emblematic of Winter and Autumn, by Eugene Laurent, late 19thC, 13¾in (35cm) high.
£1,400–1,700 TEN

A bronze group entitled 'Watching Punch and Judy', signed 'Juan Clara', c1905, 4½in (11.5cm) high.
£1,650–1,850 ChA

A French pair of wood and ivory figures, Dieppe, c1880, 12in (30.5cm) high.
£7,500–8,500 LBo

◀ A pair of brass candle-sticks, 17thC, 6¾in (17cm) high. **£5,000–5,500 P(C)**

▶ A Russian brass and enamel crucifix, 18thC, 6¾in (16cm) high. **£340–380 RKa**

A pierced brass footman, with pendant tassels on cabriole front supports, 18thC, 15in (38cm) wide. **£250–300 RBB**

A brass baluster-shaped kettle, probably Dutch, c1820, 14in (35.5cm) high. **£425–475 SEA**

An early Victorian brass jardinière, 28in (71cm) wide. **£1,000–1,200 Bon**

A pair of Empire bronze and ormolu candlesticks, c1800, 10in (25.5cm) high. **£2,800–3,200 JIL**

An Austrian cold-painted bronze group of three Arab huntsmen, stamped, early 20thC, 14½in (37cm) high. **£2,200–2,500 S(S)**

A gilt-copper cockerel weather vane, on a later plinth base, late 18thC, 28¾in (73cm) high. **£900–1,100 Bon**

A tortoiseshell, silver and mother-of-pearl card case, 1860, 4⅛in (11cm) wide. **£340–375 CHAP**

◀ A Scottish copper brewery watering can, early 19thC, 14½in (37cm) high. **£425–475 OCH**

This can was used for watering barley in a brewery.

A pair of Regency bronze and ormolu candlesticks, c1810, 9in (23cm) high. **£2,200–2,500 HAM**

A pair of Louis XV ormolu candlesticks, mid-18thC, 10in (25.5cm) high. **£2,500–3,000 S(NY)**

A Regency papier mâché tray, on a later stand, 24in (61cm) wide. **£1,200–1,400 RBB**

A hand-painted papier mâché snuff box, c1820, 4in (10cm) diam. **£200–225 MB**

A French burr-birch table snuff box, 1790, 3in (7.5cm) diam.
£150–175 MB

A Georgian mahogany and holly box, c1820, 9in (23cm) high.
£550–600 SEA

A Norwegian carved and painted pine box, c1830, 12in (30.5cm) diam.
£1,500–1,800 RYA

A Dutch carved pen box, 18thC, 22in (56cm) wide.
£1,100–1,250 AEF

A wooden lemon squeezer, c1870, 6in (15cm) long.
£80–100 WeA

A Scottish bucket, with alternate staves of alder and sycamore, 1860, 16in (40.5cm) high.
£500–600 TMi

A lignum vitae tobacco jar, c1820, 9in (23cm) high.
£1,450–1,600 AEF

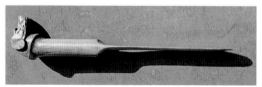

A walnut letter opener, the top carved as a dog's head with inset glass eyes, 19thC, 14in (35.5cm) long.
£170–200 OAS

A French boxwood nutcracker, modelled as the head of a bearded man, c1700, 8in (20.5cm) long.
£1,450–1,600 AEF

A sycamore nutcracker, carved as a hare, with glass eyes, late 19thC, 9in (23cm) long.
£200–240 TMA

A boxwood muffineer, 19thC, 6in (20.5cm) high.
£100–120 ALA

A pair of carved coquilla nut nutmeg graters, 1860, 3in (7.5cm) high.
£130–150 WeA

► A Hungarian brass-mounted fruitwood pipe, late 17thC, 7in (18cm) high.
£2,500–3,000 PdC

A lignum pestle and mortar, 1750–1800, 6in (15cm) high.
£500–550 NEW

Icons

Icons (the word means 'image' in the sense that the reflection in a mirror is an image) are the paintings through which Orthodox Christianity has always focused inspiration and prayer. They are first known from 6th-century Byzantium and Egypt, then Greece, and spread with Orthodoxy through the Balkans to Russia over a thousand years ago. The private collector's interest is effectively limited to the period since the 15th century but, with some dozen countries of origin, that is scope enough as only a handful of the painters are known by name, and there are few books giving any attention to work from this period.

Icons are executed in egg tempera on gesso laid on a wooden panel, often with the liberal use of gold leaf. Until the 10th century, even the poorest Orthodox family had at least one icon, and the majority of those on the market have come from homes rather than churches. Virtually all the countries where they were painted have, for many years, prohibited their export. The subjects include Christ, the Mother of God (the Virgin Mary who is almost always depicted holding Christ), the saints and prophets (sometimes with scenes from their lives and miracles), the principal Feasts of the Church and, less commonly, allegories of theological concepts. Although the same composition is often repeated, these are not copies of an original any more than a musician performing the work of a great composer is copying him. The icon painter remains faithful to the 'score', but his interpretation reflects the time and place where he worked and it is these changes which provide the main basis for dating icons.

Early Russian icons (among the most sought-after) have the laconic simplicity of children's book illustrations. After the 16th century, Russian work is characterized by fine detail and impeccable execution and, from the middle of the 18th century, a separate type emerges in which a pierced metal cover (riza, oklad or basma) becomes the dominant element. Icons from mainland Greece, and those from the Balkans and Middle East, follow Byzantine tradition but the poverty which resulted from occupation by the Ottoman Turks is evident – with these, brilliant colours and the fire of faith predominate over technical skill. Greek island work, particularly from Crete, reflects Venetian rule and influence through a progressive trend towards 'westernized' interpretation, while traditional skills were maintained at the highest level. **Christopher Richardson**

A Russian icon of the Mother of God of Tikhvin, Novgorod school, 16thC, 11¼ x 9in (28.5 x 23cm).
£2,500–3,000 SLN

A Greek icon of St Nicholas, originally the centre panel of a tryptych, Macedonia, c1600, 8¾ x 5¼in (22 x 13.5cm).
£2,500–3,000 RKa

◄ A Russian icon of the Dormition of the Virgin, 17thC, 14¼ x 12¼in (36 x 31cm).
£6,000–7,000 S

A Russian pierced brass icon of the Saints Boris and Gleb, 18thC, 5 x 3½in (12.5 x 9cm).
£450–500 ICO

► A Greek icon of the Mother of God Portaetissa, Macedonia, 17thC, 9½ x 7¼in (24 x 18.5cm).
£3,200–3,500 RKa

A Russian icon of Christ in Majesty with Saints Sergius and Varlaam at his feet, c1700, 12 x 10in (30.5 x 25.5cm).
£1,200–1,500 ICO

A Greek icon of the Mother of God Hodegetria, 18thC, 11¾ x 9½in (30 x 24cm).
£300–350 S(NY)

A Russian triptych of St Nicholas, with Feasts of the Church on the wings, in copper alloy and enamel, 18thC, 4 x 6in (10 x 15cm).
£100–120 ICO

The lost wax copper alloy castings particularly associated with the Old Believers (a sect which broke away from Russian Orthodoxy around 1660) include the whole spectrum of iconographic subjects and are generally accepted as icons. These castings are finely detailed and, from the early 18thC, were frequently enamelled – at first in dark blue and white and later in a variety of colours. Originally always kept polished, it is a shame that copper alloy icons are now often passed off, in a tarnished state, as bronze, losing much of their sparkle and beauty.

A Russian icon of the Resurrection and Descent into Hell (Anastasis), with brass basma, c1700, 16¾in (42.5cm) square.
£2,000–2,200 S(NY)

A Russian icon of the Beheading of St John the Baptist, early 18thC, 14 x 11¾in (35.5 x 30cm).
£1,600–1,800 RKa

Continuous representation, in which a series of events is combined in a single composition, was a device adopted by Byzantine painting at least as early as the 11thC, and has been used ever since. Thus an icon may show St John the Baptist in prison, in the act of being beheaded, and his head being presented to Salome, simultaneously – or in another example the Archangel Gabriel can be seen receiving his message from God the Father, arriving on earth and greeting the Virgin all on the same icon of the Annunciation.

A Russian icon of St Nicholas, with scenes from his life and miracles, 18thC, 12¼ x 10½in (31 x 26.5cm).
£1,600–1,800 RKa

Icon painting

Icon painters knew that the flat panels on which they painted would warp over time into a gentle curve. They almost always positioned their work so it would be on the outside of the curve, where the gesso layer could stretch with the movement of the panel, and the axis of the curve would be vertical. Unfortunately, they also tried to prevent the panel curving by applying stiffeners across the back (in Russia, inset into slots in the wood) and it is these stiffeners fighting the natural tendency to warp that is the main cause of the cracks commonly found down the centre of icons.

A Greek icon of the Mother of God Vatopedi, Mount Athos, the central image of the Virgin and Child surrounded by 22 miniature representations of scenes of the life of the Virgin, dated '1718', 25 x 20in (63.5 x 51cm).
£3,500–4,000 S

A Russian icon of the Mother of God of Kazan, with an elaborate silver-gilt riza, dated '1787', 14¼ x 11in (36 x 28cm).
£3,200–3,500 SLN

Cross Reference
See Colour Review

A Russian copper alloy and enamel icon of Saints Zossima and Sabbati with a margin depicting the Deesis, archangels and saints, 18thC, 5¾ x 4¾in (14.5 x 12cm).
£400–450 RKa

A Russian icon of the Mother of God of Theodore, with patron saints on the margins, 19thC, 12½ x 10½in (32 x 26.5cm).
£320–400 P

A Greek icon of the Mother of God Enthroned, c1800, 14¼ x 9¼in (36 x 24cm).
£240–300 P

A Russian provincial icon of St George and the Dragon, 19thC, 17 x 15in (43 x 38cm).
£450–500 ICO

A Russian icon of St John the Evangelist, c1800, 17½ x 14¾in (44.5 x 37.5cm).
£1,600–1,800 S(NY)

A Greek triptych, Christ with the Mother of God and St John the Baptist (the Deesis) on the central panel, with various saints on the wings, c1800, 12½ x 17¾in (32 x 45cm).
£1,000–1,200 P

A Russian icon of St Nicholas, with patron saints on the margins, 19thC, 18 x 15in (45.5 x 38cm).
£320–350 ICO

The patron commissioning an icon could ask for particular saints important to him or the intended recipient (particularly the 'name day' saints of members of the family) to be included, although they were unrelated to the subject of the icon. In Russian icons, these 'patron saints' appear on the side margins, while the Greeks tended to show them in a separate section above the bottom margin.

A Russian icon of Christ with the Mother of God and St John the Baptist (the Deesis), surrounded by saints, prophets and angels, early 19thC, 19 x 14in (48.5 x 35.5cm).
£575–650 ICO

▶ A Russian quadrapartite icon of three versions of the Mother of God and St Nicholas centred on the Crucifixion and with patron saints on the margins, 19thC, 17 x 15in (43 x 38cm).
£170–200 MEA

A Russian icon of the Intercession of the Mother of God Pokrov, 19thC, 17¾ x 15¾in (45 x 40cm).
£3,200–3,500 RKa

A Russian icon of Saints Cosmas and Damian paying homage to the Mother of God of Smolensk, with silver-gilt riza, hallmarked, dated '1867', 9 x 7in (23 x 18cm).
£700–850 JAA

A Russian icon of the Mother of God of Tikhvin, 19thC, 14 x 12½in (35.5 x 32cm).
£350–400 JAA

A Russian icon of St John the Baptist, Angel of the Desert, 19thC, 17¾ x 15½in (45 x 39.5cm).
£1,100–1,300 P

A Russian icon of the Resurrection and Descent into Hell (Anastasis), surrounded by Feasts of the Church, 19thC, 14 x 12½in (35.5 x 32cm).
£2,300–2,600 RKa

The Russian passion for miniature painting found a splendid outlet when, from the middle of the 18thC, the idea of surrounding a central icon of the Resurrection and Descent into Hell with a frieze illustrating the Feasts of the Church was adopted. At first, this was limited to the 12 feasts that were considered the most important, but by the mid-19thC there could be two or three tiers of small 'icons' depicting a variety of saints and miracles, or the Stages of the Passion, surrounding the central subject.

A Russian icon of Christ Pantocrator, 19thC, 9¾ x 7¼in (25 x 18.5cm).
£800–900 RKa

A Greek icon of St Medosios, late 19thC, 19 x 13¾in (48.5 x 35cm).
£600–700 P

A Russian icon of The Annunciation, 19thC, 14 x 12¼in (35.5 x 31cm).
£400–500 JAA

A Russian icon of Christ Pantocrator, the silver riza indistinctly marked and dated '1881', 10¼ x 8¾in (26 x 22cm).
£500–600 P

A Russian icon of Christ Pantocrator Enthroned, 19thC, 12½ x 10½in (32 x 26.5cm).
£1,800–2,000 RKa

A Russian icon of the Mother of God Helper in Birth, the riza of stiffened and gilded cloth, 19thC, 11 x 8in (28 x 20.5cm).
£800–1,000 JAA

This icon was so comforting to expectant mothers that it was commonly found in hospital maternity wards prior to the 1917 Revolution.

A Russian icon the Mother of God 'Joy of All that Grieve', 19thC, 12¼ x 10¼in (31 x 26cm).
£200–220 P

A Russian icon of Christ Pantocrator Enthroned, 19thC, 20 x 17in (51 x 43cm).
£2,700–3,000 S(NY)

A Russian icon of St Andrew, with silver and champlevé enamel frame, in original glazed wooden case, late 19thC, 3 x 2in (7.5 x 5cm).
£1,500–1,650 ICO

A Russian copper alloy and enamel icon of St Nicholas, 19thC, 4¼ x 3¾in (11 x 9.5cm).
£350–400 RKa

Miller's is a price GUIDE not a price LIST

A Russian icon of Christ King of Kings with the Mother of God and St John the Baptist (the Deesis), late 19thC, 12¼ x 11in (31 x 28cm).
£850–1,000 JAA

A Russian icon of St Parasceva, late 19thC, 12 x 10in (30.5 x 25.5cm).
£320–350 ICO

A Russian icon of Christ Pantocrator, the silver-gilt riza and cloisonné enamel halo indistinctly marked and dated '1895', late 19thC, 9 x 7in (23 x 18cm).
£600–700 P

A Russian icon of the Mother of God Key to Wisdom, with patron saints on the margins, 19thC, 12 x 10in (30.5 x 25.5cm).
£1,300–1,500 S(NY)

▶ A Russian copper alloy and enamel quadratych of the Feasts of the Church Dodecaorton, and four miracle-working icons of the Mother of God, 19thC, 6¾ x 16in (17 x 40.5cm).
£500–550 RKa

Portrait Miniatures

A portrait miniature of a girl with brown hair and wearing a white dress, by Edith Alice Andrews, c1920, 2½in (6.5cm) high.
£140–170 Bon

Edith Alice Andrews (née Cubitt) flourished 1900–45 and exhibited at the Royal Academy.

A portrait miniature of a lady in a lace-trimmed black dress, by Julie Berthod, the gilded frame with vine leaf and berry border, signed and dated '1858', 7in (18cm) high.
£1,300–1,500 P

A portrait miniature of a gentleman wearing a grey coat and yellow waistcoat, by John Comerford, c1800, 3½in (9cm) high.
£800–950 MEA

A portrait miniature of a gentleman, probably Sir Richard Steele, wearing crimson, by Peter Cross, signed, c1700, 3¼in (8.5cm) high.
£4,500–5,000 S

A portrait miniature of a young man wearing armour and with a lace cravat, attributed to Catherine da Costa, c1720, 2¾in (7cm) high.
£600–700 Bon

Catherine da Costa (1712–30) was a pupil of Bernard Lens, both of whom were among the first miniaturists to work on ivory.

A late Victorian portrait miniature on ivory of a young boy, wearing a lace-trimmed white shirt with a blue bow, signed 'L. Fowler', 3in (7.5cm) high.
£320–380 FHF

A portrait miniature of a young woman, wearing a white dress with a blue wrap, by Alexander Gallaway, c1795, 4in (10cm) high.
£1,800–2,000 BHa

A portrait miniature of a lady, wearing a white dress, by Peter Paillou Jnr, c1790, 3in (7.5cm) high.
£1,100–1,300 BHa

A portrait miniature of a lady, wearing a buff-coloured dress, by Mlle Elizabeth Pfenninger, the gilt-metal frame with applied flowers, signed and dated '1834', 5¾in (14.5cm) high.
£1,100–1,300 P

Elizabeth Pfenninger was born in Zurich. She was the pupil of Heinrich Pfenninger, her uncle, P. L. Bouvier, J. B. Regnault and J. B. J. Augustin in Paris. She exhibited at the Salon from 1810–37.

A pair of portrait miniatures of a husband and wife, by Andrew Robertson, c1820, 4in (10cm) high.
£7,250–8,000 BHa

A late Victorian portrait miniature of a young boy, wearing a sailor suit, possibly by Royal, in a gold-plated frame, 2½in (6.5cm) high.
£160–200 MRW

◄ A portrait miniature of a lady, attributed to R. Thorburn, c1835, 2¼in (5.5cm) high.
£1,200–1,400 BHa

Cross Reference
See Colour Review

A portrait miniature on ivory of a gentleman, wearing a black cloak, by Rochard, signed and inscribed '1815 Auxelles', cracked and over-painted, 3¼in (8.5cm) high.
£700–850 MJB

▶ A German carved ivory portrait miniature of Martin Luther, c1820, 4in (10cm) high.
£350–400 HUM

A pair of portrait miniatures on ivory of a lady and a gentleman, by Wingate, 19thC, 5¼in (13.5cm) high.
£150–180 TRM

A portrait miniature of Colonel Taylor, c1780, 3in (7.5cm) high.
£320–380 L

A portrait miniature of Sarah Elizabeth Hambly, wearing a pink dress, late 18thC, 11in (28cm) high.
£1,000–1,200 Oli

◄ An American portrait miniature on ivory of William Henry Harrison, in an embossed and gilt-decorated leather case, 19thC, 4¼in (11cm) high.
£600–700 S(NY)

Silhouettes

A silhouette of a gentleman, wearing a brown coat, blue trousers and red-patterned cravat, on a monochrome watercolour ground, by John Dempsey, c1840, 11¾in (30cm) high.
£450–550 Bon

A silhouette of the Compte de Bouille, by Augustin Edouart, signed and dated '1831', 10½in (26.5cm) high.
£350–400 L

The sitter was one of the members of the Court and entourage of the exiled Charles X.

A silhouette of a lady sewing, inscribed 'Emily Cuppage', in a rosewood frame, signed 'L. L Kerr', 1847, 11in (28cm) high.
£280–340 WilP

A pair of silhouettes of Samuel Allenby and his wife Harriet, both mounted on horses, he painted in colour, she cut out and mounted on card, in the style of Richard Dighton, mid-19thC, 9¼in (23.5cm) high.
£600–700 P

A silhouette of Charles Burrall Hoffman, on a lithographed ground, by Augustin Edouart, 1837, 11in (28cm) high.
£800–900 SK(B)

A silhouette of Mrs Walker of Tiverton, painted on card, with hammered brass frame, attributed to Mrs. L. M. Lane Kelfe, c1785, 4in (10cm) high.
£160–200 Bon

Mrs Kelfe was predominantly based in the West Country and is known to have worked in Cornwall, making it very likely that she would also have worked in Devon and hence Tiverton.

A pen and ink silhouette of a woman, by Augustin Edouart, signed and dated '1830', 11in (28cm) high.
£300–350 L&T

A silhouette of Sir Gilbert Elliott, painted on laid paper, the watercolour surround painted in blue, white and reddish-brown, the reverse with accolade, with patterned frame, attributed to Mrs Sarah Harrington, mid-18thC, 3½in (9cm) high.
£320–380 P

Harrington occasionally produced silhouettes painted on paper, as opposed to her usual hollow-cut technique.

A silhouette of Mr Matthew Simpson, by Joshua Trewinnard, 1813, with gilt-mounted papier mâché frame, 3½in (9cm) high.
£250–300 Bon

Antiquities

An Egyptian green schist cosmetic palette, in the form of a fish, with traces of red pigment, Predynastic Period, late Nagada II/III, circa 3300–3000 BC, 6¾in (17cm) long.
£5,000–5,500 S(NY)

The items in this section have been arranged chronologically in sequence of civilizations, namely Egyptian, Near Eastern, Greek, Roman, Byzantine, western European, British, Anglo-Saxon and medieval European.

An Egyptian alabaster vessel, circa 18th–19th Dynasty, 1450–1250 BC, 7in (18cm) high.
£1,700–2,000 P

This item was collected in Egypt in 1882.

An Egyptian polychrome painted wood stele, the central register showing the figure of the deceased standing before Osiris and Re-Herakhty, the surface painted in red, green, blue and black, Third Intermediate Period, circa 1085–709 BC, 12¼in (31cm) high.
£700–850 P

An Egyptian carved wood figure of an ibis, the beak probably restored, remains of pigment, Late Period, 716–30 BC, 10¼in (26cm) high.
£1,800–2,200 S(NY)

An Egyptian bright blue glazed composition ushabti, inscribed for 'The Sehedj, the Osiris Tent-shed-Khonsu justified', 21st Dynasty, 1070–945 BC, 5in (12.5cm) high.
£1,400–1,600 Bon

An Egyptian bronze ushabti, with a frontal column of hieroglyphs inscribed for the General Wendjebauendjet, 21st Dynasty, 1040–992 BC, 3¼in (8.5cm) high.
£1,200–1,400 Bon

An Egyptian inscribed and green-glazed ushabti, circa 6th century BC, 6½in (16.5cm) high.
£400–500 P

A Sumerian carved white stone recumbent bull, 3rd millennium BC, 1½in (4cm) high.
£700–850 Bon

An Egyptian carved limestone head of a priest, damaged, 7th–6th century BC, 4½in (11.5cm) high.
£2,000–2,400 HEL

An Egyptian hollow cast-bronze head of a cat, with pierced ears and incised whiskers, Late Period, circa 600 BC, 1¾in (4.5cm) high.
£3,000–3,500 P

A Trans-Jordan Bronze Age pottery bowl, with continuous notched decoration around the exterior upper body, circa 3000–2500 BC, 12½in (32cm) diam.
£200–240 Bon

A Babylonian pottery plaque, moulded with a bearded deity, 1500–1200 BC, 4¼in (11cm) high.
£400–500 HEL

An Achaemenid silver lotus bowl, damaged, circa 3rd–1st century BC, 8in (20.5cm) diam.
£3,200–3,800 Bon

A Mycenaean buff pottery storage jar, decorated in umber with encircling bands and a line of vertical strokes around the shoulder, circa 1100–1000 BC, 15½in (39.5cm) high.
£1,600–1,800 Bon

A south Arabian alabaster head of a male, the eyes and eyebrows recessed for inlay, now missing, the top and back unmodelled, circa 1st century BC, 10in (25.5cm) high.
£4,500–5,500 Bon

A Cypriot lime-stone votive figure of a goddess, restored, circa 5th century BC, 9½in (24cm) high.
£1,300–1,600 HEL

An Attic Black Figure band cup, decorated in the band on both sides with Herakles fighting the Nemean lion, with a standing male figure on either side, handles re-attached, circa 525 BC, 9in (23cm) diam.
£1,300–1,500 Bon

A Parthian turquoise-glazed amphora, the shoulder decorated in relief beneath the glaze, with applied roundels and heads, a bearded head beneath each handle, circa 2nd–3rd century AD, 12in (30.5cm) high.
£2,200–2,600 S(NY)

An Attic black-glazed mug, the body and mouth incised with lotus-bud decoration, late 5th century BC, 3½in (9cm) high.
£1,500–1,800 S(NY)

A Greek black-glazed askos, in the form of a wild boar, with pouring hole in the mouth and large eyes with white painted detail, the bristles on the forehead and back indicated by cross-hatching, mid-4th century BC, 7¾in (19.5cm) long.
£4,000–5,000 S(NY)

An Attic black-glazed hydria, with ribbed body, the neck and shoulder decorated with a chain of interlinked lotus buds in added yellow/cream slip, 5th–4th century BC, 20½in (52cm) high.
£5,000–6,000 Bon

A Greek terracotta head of Athena, wearing disk earrings and helmet with fragmentary crest, 4th–3rd century BC, 2½in (6.5cm) high.
£475–550 S(NY)

◄ A Campanian Red Figure bail amphora, decorated with added white to show on both sides a draped figure standing in profile, palmettes between them, late 4th century BC, 10in (25.5cm) high.
£500–600 Bon

An Etruscan bronze torch holder or sacrificial meat hook, with incised twisted decoration along the upper shaft of the handle, damaged and repaired, circa 450–400 BC, 11½in (29cm) high.
£650–750 Bon

A South Italian Greek black-glazed pottery guttus, with moulded discus, repaired, 4th century BC, 4in (10cm) high.
£250–300 HEL

A Roman pillar-moulded bowl, eastern Mediterranean, 1st century AD, 6in (15cm) diam.
£900–1,000 PARS

A South Italian Greek Daunian buff pottery double askos, decorated in umber, pink and red with undulating bands of scrolling, hatching and a chain-pattern, circa 300–250 BC, 9in (23cm) high.
£400–500 Bon

A Hellenistic glass beaker, with wheel-cut encircling grooves and surface iridescence, circa 1st century BC, 3¼in (8.5cm) high.
£675–750 PARS

A Roman silver bowl, the interior with incised central ring, on a shallow foot with incised dot and circle centre, 1st–2nd century AD, 8¼in (21cm) diam.
£3,400–3,750 P

This bowl was discovered in the ceiling cavity of an Elizabethan and Georgian house in a Norfolk village.

A necklace, composed of spherical blue and white glass beads, re-strung, mainly Roman, 1st–3rd century AD, 20in (51cm) long.
£320–350 PARS

A Roman Imperial bronze figure of Aphrodite, a mirror probably once held in the left hand, circa 2nd century AD, 9in (23cm) high.
£6,000–7,000 S(NY)

A Roman Imperial marble figure of an eagle, sacred to Zeus, the freely-carved feathers with drilled detail, head restored, circa 2nd–3rd century AD, 15½in (39.5cm) high.
£7,000–8,000 S(NY)

A twin-handled storage vessel, with dimpled body, eastern Mediterranean, probably Syria, 4th century AD, 5½in (14cm) high.
£850–950 PARS

A late Roman pale green glass lamp, with a row of applied blue glass circles around the shoulder and wheel-cut lines around the body, 4th–5th century AD, 5in (12.5cm) diam.
£1,800–2,200 Bon

LOCATE THE SOURCE

The source of each illustration in Miller's can be found by checking the code letters below each caption with the Key to Illustrations, pages 789–795.

A Byzantine stone relief of a figure and a leaf, 6th–8th century AD, 6in (15cm) high.
£250–300 HEL

A necklace, composed of spherical and faceted beads, re-strung, probably Roman/Byzantine Periods, 7th century AD, 16in (40.5cm) long.
£225–250 PARS

A Celtic iron sword, with applied bronze spiral bosses to the hilt, 6th–5th century BC, 23¾in (60.5cm) long.
£1,700–2,000 Herm

A bronze neck ring with spiral discs, Bronze Age, Urnfield Period, circa 900 BC, 7in (18cm) diam.
£2,700–3,000 Herm

A Romano-Celtic horse brooch, with spring and part pin, Carnuntum, Austria, 2nd century AD, 1¼in (3cm) wide.
£80–100 ANG

A Roman duck brooch, with some red and blue enamelling, with spring, catchplate and chain loop, pin missing, 1st–2nd century AD, 1¼in (3cm) wide.
£80–100 ANG

A Roman prancing horse brooch, with hinge lugs and catchplate, pin missing, Bulgaria, 2nd century AD, 1½in (4cm) wide.
£100–125 ANG

A Romano-Celtic rabbit brooch, decorated with punched zigzags, with spring and catchplate, pin missing, 2nd century AD, 1in (2.5cm) wide.
£65–75 ANG

A Roman peacock brooch, with incised feather decoration, with pin, spring and catchplate, Rhineland, 1st–2nd century AD, 1¼in (3cm) wide.
£80–100 ANG

Tribal Art

A Cheyenne beaded tobacco bag, the main panel worked in stripes of contrasting colours, Native American, 24½in (62cm) long.
£5,500–6,000 BB(S)

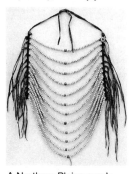

A Northern Plains man's dance necklace, possibly Blackfoot, composed of 12 white-beaded strings, each with central blue bead, Native American, 15in (38cm) long.
£400–500 Bon(C)

A Navajo eye dazzler rug, Native American, c1930, 69 x 42in (175.5 x 106.5cm).
£500–600 SLN

An Apache polychrome twined burden basket, with red and green paint on the exterior, Native American, early 20thC, 15in (38cm) diam.
£700–800 SK

▶ A Woodlands turtle shell rattle, painted in red, white, yellow and black, possibly Cayuga, Native American, mid-19thC, 17in (43cm) long.
£140–170 F&C

◀ A wooden bowl, in the form of a frog, the eyes set with abalone shell, Native American, northwest coast, 6in (15cm) long.
£1,300–1,500 P

An Inuit carved caribou ivory needle case, 1000–1200 AD, 2¾in (7cm) long.
£1,600–1,800 HUR

An Aleut wood mask, with pierced almond eyes, enormous up-turned nose and frowning mouth, black pigment colouring the nostrils, Inuit People, 8½in (21.5cm) high.
£6,000–7,000 BB(S)

This item was purchased in 1947, and is said to have been obtained originally in the 1920s.

A hardwood gameboard, the sides incised with geometric linear motifs, Africa, 24¾in (63cm) long.
£3,300–3,800 S(NY)

The sides of gameboards are often highly decorated with an incised pattern, never the same on each side of the board. The game is a complicated exercise for the mind, and is played throughout Africa. This example was obviously highly used as each hole is indented at the bottom where the players' fingers, picking up the pieces out of the hole, have created a depression.

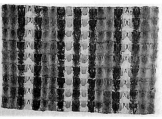

A Greenland Inuit duck down blanket, the patchwork construction arranged in stripes of pale and dark brown feathers interspersed with squares of grey, green and white feathers, 63¾ x 40½in (162 x 103cm).
£800–900 P

▶ A hardwood maternity figure with children, with cloth decoration, possibly Yuruba, Nigeria, West Africa, 19½in (49.5cm) high.
£40–50 GAK

A Baule pulley, the frame with incised herringbone decoration, cracks and chip to nose, Ivory Coast, West Africa, 6¾in (17c) high.
£1,700–2,000 Bon(C)

A pair of Yoruba brass staffs, cast as a male and female with conical headdresses and slender limbs, Nigeria, West Africa, larger 14¼in (36cm) high.
£400–450 P

The male and female castings represent the first members of the Ogboni society and also emphasize the importance of male/female cooperation. The staffs serve as signs of office for members of the Ogboni society who, as community elders, sit in judgement for serious issues of law and punishment.

◄ A Bamana carved wood tribal mask, with incised decoration, Mali, West Africa, 11in (28cm) high.
£320–380 FBG

A Nunuma hardwood face mask, painted with kaolin, Burkino Faso, West Africa, 19thC, 10¼in (26cm) high.
£1,800–2,200 GRG

A pair of seated male and female carved hardwood figures, probably used to ensure good harvesting or guard crops from pests, Nigeria, West Africa, 24in (61cm) high.
£145–175 GAK

A Mangbetu chief's stool, northeast Zaire, Central Africa, 23½in (59.5cm).
£4,500–5,000 S(NY)

Carved from a single piece of wood, these stools served as symbols of the chief's power. The women of the chief's household had smaller versions of this stool which they used in a particular dance. The chief's taller version of the stool allowed him to remain taller than his female attendants.

A Baule carved wood standing female figure, with decorated anklets, cicatrisation marks to face, neck and back, splits and with old repairs to base, Ivory Coast, West Africa, probably late 19thC, 15in (38cm) high.
£250–300 F&C

A Yoruba wood carving of a colonial couple, by Thomas Ona, each wearing a removable hat, the details painted in red and black, Nigeria, West Africa, 9in (23cm) high.
£1,000–1,100 P

The Yoruba carver Thomas Ona Odulate worked in Lagos in the 1940s, producing distinctive figurative carvings inspired by British colonial characters. The figures are characterized by large eyes and pointed noses, with details coloured in red and black ink as well as white shoe polish.

A carved wood stool, supported by a central figure of a leopard with cub, the frieze with seven native figures in European dress, decorated in coloured pigments, West Africa, early 20thC, 14in (35.5cm) diam.
£140–170 F&C

A Sepik River wooden shield, carved in shallow relief with a series of six stylized faces, New Guinea, 73¾in (187.5cm) high.
£500–600 P

A Kuba wood cup, incised with bands of geometric ornament, Zaire, Central Africa, probably mid-19thC, 5¾in (14.5cm) high.
£300–350 F&C

A Kuba wood and fibre mask, the face painted with triangular motifs in black, white, red and yellow, a band of cowrie shells traversing the mouth and nose, Nady Amwash, Democratic Republic of Congo, collected c1920, 12½in (32cm) high.
£800–1,000 P

A Zulu club, carved with a raised gridwork surface, South Africa, 18in (45.5cm) long.
£1,150–1,350 P

A Zulu neckrest, South Africa, 17in (43cm) wide.
£4,000–4,500 S(NY)

Purchased in the 1870s by an Englishman who moved from England to South Africa in 1870. He ran a successful farm and store which supplied local farmers with essential supplies.

A set of wooden lime and betel nut crushers, with carved heads, Indonesian islands, 4in (10cm) high.
£100–120 LHAr

The betel nut is put into a cylindrical container and chopped up with the chisel end of this implement. Lime is added and then the whole is chewed to get a 'high' – a mild narcotic.

A Maori green basalt patu, with a long symmetrical blade, small chips, New Zealand, 19thC, 17¼in (44cm) long.
£1,500–1,800 Bea(E)

An aboriginal pearl-shell, the face engraved with interlocking square key patterns and dots, north Australia, 6in (15cm) high.
£420–500 Bon(C)

These shells are collected by Dampier Peninsula aborigines of the far northwest of Australia, and worn by partly-initiated youths. After initiation, they are traded away from source to become love charms, initiation ritual objects or rain-making shells.

▶ An Admiralty Islands ladle, the handle in the form of a crocodile, the torso incised with alternating zigzag and plain bands encircling the top, Melanesia, 20in (51cm) long.
£750–900 S(NY)

The patterns on the handles of ornamental ladles are associated with rites. They were used for special occasions in the Admiralty Islands, and were kept in the men's house.

A Manam Islands carved wood mask, with traces of white and dark red colouring, Oceania, possibly 19thC, 16in (40.5cm) high.
£1,200–1,400 PFK

A patinated face mask of the demi-God Garuda, Bhutan, Himalayas, 19thC.
£350–380 GRG

A Maori lure hook, with a shell panel applied to the wood shank, probably North Island, New Zealand, early 19thC, 4½in (11.5cm) long.
£130–150 F&C

An Easter Island ancestral figure, the face marked by bushy eyebrows and inset bone and black stone eyes, labelled 'Easter Island Household God', said to be 200 years old', Oceania, 23in (58.5cm) high.
£2,800–3,200 BB(S)

Books & Book Illustrations

William Harrison Ainsworth, *The Tower of London*, 1853, 9 x 6in (23 x 15cm).
£40–45 CBO

Anstey's New Bath Guide, 1832, 8 x 5in (20.5 x 12.5cm).
£70–80 CBO

Cross Reference
See Colour Review

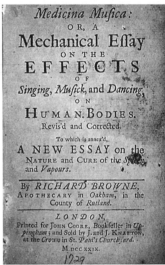

Roger Ascham, *The Scholemaster*, printed by John Daye, lacking final leaf, 1579, 4°.
£900–1,000 S

John James Audubon, *Pigeon Hawk*, engraved and hand-coloured by Robert Havell, c1830, 28 x 23in (71 x 58.5cm).
£300–350 SK

The Holie Bible, conteyning the olde Testament and the newe, 1568, 2°, calf over wooden boards, 4 (of 8) original brass corners.
£5,000–6,000 DW

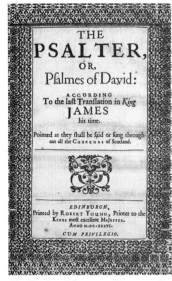

The Booke of Common Prayer, and Administration of the Sacraments. And other parts of divine service for the use of the Church of Scotland..., with *The Psalter*, edited by Archbishop William Laud, first edition for the Episcopal Church of Scotland, 1637, 2°, late 19thC polished morocco and gilt, slight rubbing.
£1,100–1,200 BBA

The imposition of this prayer book by Charles I led to rioting in Edinburgh, and war beween the King and his Scottish subjects.

The Distiller of London: With the Clavis to unlock the deepest Secrets of that Mysterious Art...

Richard Browne, *Medicina Musica: or, a Mechanical Essay on the Effects of Singing, Musick and Dancing on Human Bodies*, London 1729, 8°, later calf.
£370–400 SK

◀ Thomas Cademan, *The Distiller of London: With the Clavis to unlock the deepest Secrets of the Mysterious Art*, London, printed for Tho. Huntington and Wil. Nealand, 1652, 12°.
£600–700 RTo

Book Sizes

The size or format of a book is expressed by the number of times a single sheet of paper is folded into the sections which, when gathered and sewn, make up the finished volume.
Shown below are some of the usual descriptions of sizes:

Folio:	1 fold	2 leaves	Fo or 2°
Quarto:	2 folds	4 leaves	4to or 4°
Octavo:	3 folds	8 leaves	8vo or 8°
Duodecimo:	4 folds	12 leaves	12mo or 12°
Sextodecimo:	5 folds	16 leaves	16mo or 16°
Vicesimo-quarto:	6 folds	24 leaves	24mo or 24°
Tricesimo-secundo:	7 folds	32 leaves	32mo or 32°

Marc Chagall, *Illustrations for the Bible*, New York, 1956, 2°, first American edition, 2°, boards with 28 lithographs by Chagall, 16 in colour.
£2,000–2,400 SK

Agatha Christie, *The Mysterious Affair at Styles*, first English edition of the author's first book, published by John Lane, 1921, 8°.
£2,500–2,750 S

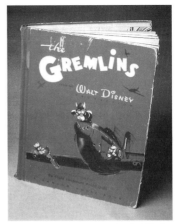

Flight Lieutenant Roald Dahl, *The Gremlins*, inscribed 'To Freda Cox with best wishes from Roald Dahl, 10/5/43, New York, 1943', cloth-backed picture board, 12 x 10in (30.5 x 25.5cm).
£1,600–2,000 HAM

Freda Cox worked with Dahl in the Secretary of War's Department, and assisted in typing the manuscript.

Alexandre Dumas, *Les Trois Mousquetaires*, one of two volumes, illustrated by Maurice Leloir, 1894, 12 x 8in (30.5 x 20.5cm).
£45–50 CBO

Robert Furber, *The Flower-Garden Display'd*, first edition, published by Hazard et al, London, 1732, 4°, with 12 hand-coloured plates and frontispiece, bound in contemporary full calf with raised bands to spine, bookplate of Westport House to inside front cover.
£3,000–3,500 BLH

Robert Gibbings, *Fourteen Engravings on Wood*, published by Golden Cockerel Press, London, c1933, 2°, two vignettes, 14 plates, original wrappers.
£300–350 RTo

Roger Fry, 12 original woodcut prints, published by Richmond, Hogarth Press, 1921, 4°, original marbled wraps.
£1,250–1,500 L

John Gay, *Trivia: or, the Art of Walking the Streets of London*, first edition, 1716, 8°, later red crushed half morocco, engraved frontispiece.
£275–325 SK

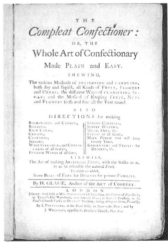

R. Fulton, *The Illustrated Book of Pigeons*, c1880, 4°, 50 full colour lithographic plates, in the style of J. W. Ludlow, other lithographic plates and woodcut illustrations, full embossed publishers' cloth.
£400–500 HAM

Hannah Glasse, *The Compleat Confectioner: or, the Whole Art of Confectionary made Plain and Easy*, printed by I. Pottinger and J. Williams, c1762, 304pp, tall 8°, original boards, leaves untrimmed, in a clamshell box.
£500–600 SLN

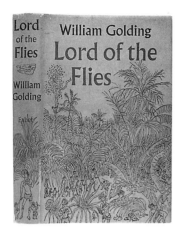

William Golding, *Lord of the Flies*,
first edition of author's first novel,
signed, published by Faber & Faber,
1954, 8°, original red cloth lettered in
white, dust-jacket.
£900–1,100 S

Graham Greene, *The Man Within*,
first edition of author's first book,
1929, 8°, adverts on back of
dust-jacket.
£2,200–2,600 HAM

Graham Greene, *Stamboul Train*,
first edition, author's inscribed
presentation copy, published by
William Heinemann, 1932, 8°,
original black cloth lettered in gilt.
£2,300–2,750 S

Rev. William Hanbury, *The Complete
Body of Planting and Gardening*,
two volumes, first edition, 1770–71,
2°, engraved frontispieces, 20 plates,
pressed flower and leaf specimens
throughout, contemporary calf.
£1,100–1,200 BBA

Joseph Harrison, *The Floricultural
Cabinet, and Florist's Magazine*,
Vols 1–11, Vol. 1 second edition,
1833–43, 8°, half green stained
calf, spines with gilt, six engraved
titles and 146 hand-coloured
engraved plates.
£400–450 L

George Heriot, *Travels Through the
Canadas*, first edition, 1807, 4°,
26 aqua-tinted plates, including five
folding, contemporary polished calf.
£750–850 DW

James Hilton, *Goodbye Mr Chips*,
first edition, 1934, 8°, four black and
white illustrations, original blue cloth
with gilt.
£220–260 DW

David Hockney and Stephen
Spender, *China Diary*, first edition,
published by Thames & Hudson,
signed limited edition 301/1000,
1982, small 4°, numerous colour and
black and white illustrations, original
cloth with gilt, boxed.
£500–600 DW

Constance Howard, the *Ameliaranne*
series, illustrated by S. B. Pearse,
six volumes, first editions, original
cloth-backed pictorial boards,
1930s, 8 x 5in (20.5 x 12.5cm).
£500–600 F&C

LOCATE THE SOURCE
The source of each illustration in
Miller's can be found by checking
the code letters below each
caption with the Key to
Illustrations, pages 789–795.

Gertrude Jekyll and Christopher Hussey, *Garden Ornament*, second edition (revised), 1927, 2°, numerous black and white illustrations from photographs, original cloth with gilt.
£250–300 DW

This signed edition is limited to four hundred and twenty-five numbered copies of which one hundred and twenty-five copies are for sale in Great Britain and three hundred copies in the United States of America

This copy is number
74

The Infant's Library, a miniature cedarwood bookcase containing 16 miniature books for the teaching of infants, numbered 1–15 plus one not numbered, most containing engravings, published by John Marshall, early 19thC, case 5½ x 3½in (14 x 9cm).
£4,500–5,000 BLH

Edward Lear, *Illustrated Excursions in Italy, First and Second series,* two volumes, 1846, 2°, original cloth with gilt, engraved maps and 55 lithographic plates.
£2,500–3,000 L

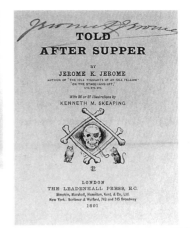

Jerome K. Jerome, *Told After Supper*, first edition, signed by author, published by The Leadenhall Press, 1891, 8°, original pictorial red cloth, unopened.
£280–320 L

Edward Lear, *Views in the Seven Ionian Islands*, first edition, 1863, 2°, 21 plates, original cloth with gilt.
£2,000–2,400 DW

James Joyce, *Finnegans Wake*, limited edition, 74 of 425, signed by author, published by Faber & Faber and The Viking Press, 1939, 4°, cloth with gilt.
£3,000–3,500 SLN

The History and Adventures of Little Henry, printed by D. N. Shury for S. and J. Fuller, 1810, with paper doll and seven outfits, in slip case.
£500–600 Bon(C)

William Lewin, *The Birds of Great Britain, Systematically Arranged, Accurately Engraved and Painted from Nature*, eight volumes, 1795–1801, 2°, 278 plates of birds and 57 of eggs, all hand-coloured.
£2,700–3,000 L

▶ A set of 14 *Lytton's Novels*, published by George Routledge & Sons, 1845, 9 x 5in (23 x 12.5cm).
£380–420 CBO

Rambles among our Industries: Iron and the Iron Worker and *Rambles in Science: Telephones and Gramophones*, designed by Charles Rennie Mackintosh, published by Blackie & Son, 1922, 7 x 5in (18 x 12.5cm).
£75–85 RUSK

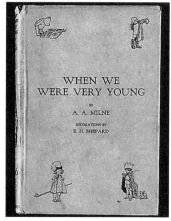

A. A. Milne, *When We Were Very Young*, first edition, illustrations by E. H. Shepard, 1924, 8°, original pictorial cloth with gilt, dust jacket.
£2,200–2,500 BBA

James Newton, *Newton's Complete Herbal*, 1805, 8 x 5in (20.5 x 12.5cm).
£200–225 CBO

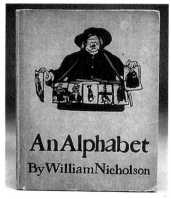

William Nicholson, *An Alphabet*, New York, 1898, 4°, with 26 full-page lithographed plates, original boards.
£450–500 SK

Rev. Owen Manning and William Bray, *The History and Antiquities of .... Surrey*, three volumes, 1804–14, 2°, engraved maps, views, portraits, pedigrees and text illustrations, old half maroon morocco gilt.
£600–700 L

A Chinese Man with Puppies and Rats to sell for pies.

A. Mills, *Costume of Different Nations*, in miniature, from drawings by Alfred Mills, with descriptions, 1814, small 4°, 47 engraved plates, publisher's full morocco binding.
£130–150 WW

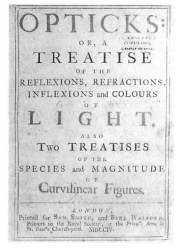

Isaac Newton, *Opticks*, 1704, 4°, with 19 fold-out engravings, library cloth.
£3,200–3,800 AG

Mrs Agnes B. Marshall, *Fancy Ices*, first edition, c1888, 8°, 86 woodcut illustrations, original silver decoration on blue cloth.
£350–420 HAM

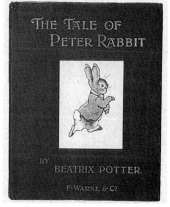

Robert Rait, *The Scottish Parliament*, published by Blackie & Son Ltd, 1865–1911, 9 x 6in (23 x 15cm), dark blue cloth with gilt.
£90–100 DAD

Beatrix Potter, *The Tale of Peter Rabbit*, first trade edition, published by F. Warne & Co, 1902, 8°, with 30 colour illustrations and colour frontispiece.
£850–1,000 DW

◄ Mary Wollstonecraft Shelley, *Frankenstein or The Modern Prometheus*, second edition in two volumes, 1823, 8°, rebound in half blue calf with gilt.
£9,500–11,500 HAM

William Stukeley, *Stonehenge & Abury Temple*, two volumes in one, 1740 and 1743, 2°, illustrated with fold-out engravings, library cloth.
£450–500 AG

Virtue's Picturesque Beauties of Great Britain, series of views, 1832, 11 x 9in (28 x 23cm).
£320–350 CBO

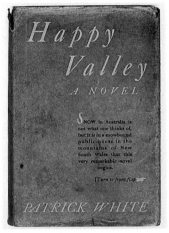

Patrick White, *Happy Valley*, first edition of author's first novel, 1939, 8°, original cloth.
£1,300–1,500 DW

P. G. Wodehouse, *Psmith in the City*, first edition, illustrations by T. M. R. Whitwell, 1910, 8°, original pictorial cloth.
£320–380 L

Edmund Spenser, *The Faerie Queene*, illustrated by Walter Crane, edited by Thomas J. Wise, 1896–97, 4°, plates and decorations throughout.
£250–300 F&C

Louis Wain, *Pa Cats and Ma Cats and their Kittens*, printed in Germany for R. Tuck, c1898, 2°, with ten full-page colour lithographic plates, double-page centre colour lithographic plate, illustrated title page and tinted illustrations throughout, printed decorative paper boards.
£500–600 HAM

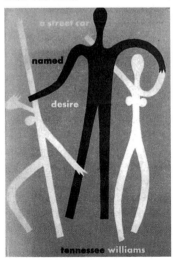

Tennessee Williams, *A Streetcar Named Desire*, first edition, published by New Directions, New York, 1947, 8°, original pink pictorial boards.
£200–220 BBA

Archibald Thorburn, *Game Birds and Wild-fowl of Great Britain and Ireland*, No. 122 of 155 copies, published by Longmans Green & Co, 1923, large 2°, gilt-tooled full green morocco, slip case.
£1,600–1,800 MCA

George Walker, *The Costume of Yorkshire*, titles and text in English and French, illustrated by R. and D. Havell in the style of Walker, published by Longman & Co, London, 1814, 2°, 41 hand-coloured aquatint plates, modern half morocco.
£1,750–2,000 S

P. G. Wodehouse, *Mike, A Public School Story*, first edition, illustrations by T. M. R. Whitwell, published by A. & C. Black, 1909, 8°, 12 plates, original pictorial cloth.
£1,150–1,350 BBA

Maps & Atlases

WORLD

Abraham Ortelius, *Typus Orbis Terrarum*, double-page hand-painted engraved map on an oval projection enclosed within a cloud border, Antwerp, c1579, 13¼ x 19¼in (33.5 x 49cm).
£2,500–2,750 S

This was the first of Ortelius' atlas world maps.

> **Miller's is a price GUIDE not a price LIST**

Philippus Cluverius, *Introductio in Universam Geographiam*, 61 maps and plates, London, 1711, small 4°.
£900–1,100 DW

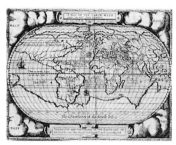

Jodocus Hondius, *A Map of the Earth with Names (The Most) from Scriptures*, based on Ortelius, c1590, 63 x 82¾in (160 x 210cm).
£750–825 BBA

Edward Wells, *A New Map of the Terraqueous Globe according to the latest Discoveries and most general Divisions of it into Continent and Oceans*, a pair of hand-coloured twin-hemisphere world maps, c1700, 14½ x 20in (37 x 51cm).
£700–800 DW

John Speed, *A New and Accurat Map of the World*, hand-coloured, framed and double-glazed, 1626, 15½ x 20½in (39.5 x 52cm).
£5,750–7,000 S

This is the first map from an English atlas to show California as an island.

J. B. Nolin, *Mappe-Monde, Carte Universelle de la Terre*, original outline hand-colouring, with title cartouche, the corners with allegorical figures and landscapes of the continents, 1817, 19 x 25½in (48.5 x 65cm).
£1,150–1,350 BBA

AFRICA, ARABIA & EUROPE

Robert Walton, *A New, Plaine, & Exact Map of Africa*, double-page engraved general map enclosed within figured borders, London, c1660, 16½ x 20¾in (42 x 52.5cm).
£2,750–3,250 S

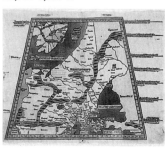

Abraham Ortelius, *Presbiteri Johannis, Sive, Abissinorum Imperii Descriptio*, engraved map of central and northeast Africa south to Mozambique, Antwerp, c1570, 14¾ x 17¼in (37.5 x 44cm).
£300–350 BBA

◀ Claudius Ptolemaeus, *Octava Europe tabula*, double-page woodcut from Scandinavia to the Crimea, Ulm, 1486, 15½ x 22¼in (39.5 x 56.5cm).
£2,500–2,750 S

▶ Abraham Ortelius, *Islandia*, double-page engraved map, with Latin text and contemporary hand colour, Antwerp, 1592, 13¼ x 19¼in (33.5 x 49cm).
£2,000–2,200 S

Jacques Nicolas Bellin, *Le Portugal*, Paris, 1762, 44 x 31in (112 x 78.5cm).
£500–575 CBO

AMERICAS

Joannes Blaeu, *Nova Virginia Tabula*, hand-coloured engraved map, c1640, 15 x 19in (38 x 48.5cm).
£600–700 SLN

Herman Moll, *A New & Exact Map of the Coast, Countries and Islands within ye limits of ye South Sea Company, from...Terra del Fuego... to...California*, c1720, 17¼ x 19¼in (44 x 49cm).
£450–550 DW

Herman Moll, *A Map of the West-Indies or the Islands of America*, engraved map on two sheets, with inset view of Mexico City and larger scale harbour plans, c1710, 23¼ x 40in (59 x 101.5cm).
£650–750 BBA

G. Delisle, *Carte d'Amerique*, hand-coloured engraving, printed by Covens & Mortimer, Amsterdam, 1774, 21 x 24¼in (53.5 x 61.5cm).
£1,200–1,350 NOA

▶ Louis Brion de la Tour, *Carte du theatre de la guerre entre les Anglais et les Americains*, double-page engraved map extending from Cape May, New Jersey, to Kennebunk, Maine, with original outline colour, Paris, 1779, 29 x 20in (73.5 x 51cm).
£4,000–5,000 S

This general map of the northern American colonies is one of the earliest published continental maps relating to the American Revolution.

ASIA & AUSTRALIA

Jodocus Hondius, *Insulae Indiae Orientalis,* hand-coloured engraved map, with Latin text on verso, c1620, 5½ x 7¾in (14 x 20cm).
£160–200 DW

John Speed, *The Kingdome of China*, double-page hand-coloured engraved general map, with side borders of costumed figures and top frieze of town plans, London, 1627, 15½ x 20in (39.5 x 51cm).
£1,250–1,500 S

Gerard Mercator and Jodocus Hondius, *Japoniae Nova Descriptio*, engraved map with English text to verso, 1636, 14¼ x 18½in (36 x 47cm).
£500–600 DW

Matthaeus Seutter, *Opulentissimum Sinarum Imperium*, original hand-coloured map of China, with decorative cartouche, Augsburg, c1740, 19¼ x 22¾in (49 x 58cm).
£400–450 BBA

Emanuel Bowen, *A New and Accurate Map of the Empire of Japan*, hand-coloured engraved map, 1747, 14¾ x 19½in (37.5 x 49.5cm).
£400–450 SLN

J. Tallis, *Western Australia, Swan River*, steel-engraved map with original outline colour, 1850, 13½ x 9½in (34.5 x 24cm).
£150–170 MAG

Christopher Saxton, *Westmorlandiae et Cumberlandiae*, double-page hand-coloured contemporary county map engraved by Augustine Ryther, London, 1576–79, 15 x 19in (38 x 48.5cm).
£3,200–3,500 S

This was the first printed map of Westmorland and Cumberland, issued as part of Christopher Saxton's *Atlas of England and Wales*.

Jan Baptiste Vrients, *Angliae et Hiberniae accurata descriptio*, double-page engraved map, with Italian text, Antwerp, 1608, 17 x 22½in (43 x 57cm).
£1,800–2,200 S

John Speed, *Britain as it was Devided in the Tyme of the Englishe-Saxons Especially During Their Heptarchy*, hand-coloured engraved map, 1611–76, 15½ x 20¼in (39.5 x 51.5cm).
£600–700 SLN

Christopher Saxton, *Dorcestrie*, county map of Dorsetshire, late 17thC, 14½ x 21in (37 x 53.5cm).
£800–950 BR

Giovanni Camocio, *Irlanda*, engraved general map, Venice, c1575, 5¼ x 7¼in (13.5 x 18.5cm).
£700–800 S

Coignet Ortelius, *Anglia*, miniature engraved map, probably 1609, 3 x 4in (7.5 x 10cm).
£100–120 DW

John Speed, *Stafford Countie and Towne*, original hand-coloured map, with inset plans of Stafford and Lichfield, Latin text on verso, 1616, 15¼ x 20in (38.5 x 51cm).
£270–300 BBA

John Speed, *Somerset-shire described*, double-page hand-coloured engraved general county map, with inset plan of Bath, London, 1646, 14½ x 19½in (37 x 49.5cm).
£400–450 S

▶ Robert Morden, *The Smaller Islands in the British Ocean*, original two-page hand-coloured map, c1695, 22 x 20in (56 x 51cm).
£285–325 CBO

Gerard de Jode, *Angliae Scotiae et Hibernie nova descriptio*, double-page engraved general map, with Latin text, Antwerp, 1593, 13½ x 19½in (34.5 x 49.5cm).
£900–1,100 S

John Speed, *The Countie of Leinster with the Citie Dublin Described*, hand-coloured engraved map, 1610, 15 x 20¼in (38 x 51.5cm).
£275–300 SLN

Christopher Saxton, *Monmouthshire*, copper-engraved by Hole, with later colouring, 1637, 11 x 13½in (28 x 34.5cm).
£135–150 MAG

Vincenzo Maria Coronelli, *Irlanda*, engraved map on two sheets, with ornate title cartouche, Venice, c1690, 18½ x 24½in (47 x 62cm).
£280–320 DW

John Senex, *Ireland*, hand-coloured engraved map, London, 1712, 37¾ x 26in (96 x 66cm).
£350–420 CGC

Eugene Henry Frier, *Cartes des Provinces des Pays Bas*, map of East Kent with ornate cartouche, Paris, 1744, 19¼ x 27¾in (49 x 70.5cm).
£180–220 CAG

◄ Henry Overton, *A New and Accurate Mapp of Great Britain and Ireland*, double-page hand-coloured engraved map, with decorative cartouche, the side borders with 12 views of cities and ports, 1760, 22½ x 38¼in (57 x 97cm).
£1,000–1,100 P

E. Bowen, *Buckinghamshire*, copper-engraved, with later colouring, c1720, 7 x 5in (18 x 12.5cm).
£45–50 MAG

T. Osborne, *Geographia Magnae Britanniae*, with double-page engraved decorative title, 60 double-page engraved maps, old calf-backed boards, worn, 1748, 8°.
£750–900 BBA

Thomas Badeslade and William Henry Toms, *A Set of Maps of all the Counties in England and Wales*, first edition, with 46 engraved maps, contemporary sprinkled calf gilt, 1742, 8°.
£550–650 DW

Norden, *County map of Hampshire*, hand-coloured, late 18thC, 15¾ x 17in (40 x 43cm).
£450–500 BR

C. and J. Greenwood, *Map of the County of Kent, Made in the Years 1819–1820*, inset with a view of Canterbury Cathedral, 39 x 34in (99 x 86.5cm).
£300–345 CBO

TOWN & CITY PLANS

Georg Braun and Frans Hogenberg, *Moscauw*, engraved bird's-eye plan with early hand-colouring, Cologne, c1580, 13½ x 19¼in (34.5 x 49cm).
£400–450 BBA

Valletta, Renvoy & Explication des Chiffres compris au Plan General des Villes, Forts & Chateaux de Malthe, a manuscript map in ink and colours with key listing the fortifications of Malta, mid-17thC, 20¾ x 29¾in (52.5 x 75.5cm).
£2,300–2,500 S

T. Moule, *City and University of Oxford*, steel-engraved plan with later colouring, 1840, 9½ x 7½in (24 x 19cm).
£70–80 MAG

Dolls

SELECTED MAKERS

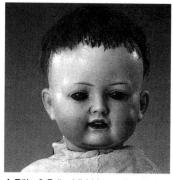

A Bähr & Pröschild bisque-headed doll, with weighted blue eyes, two moulded teeth, jointed composition body, impressed '604 4', c1920, 13½in (34.5cm) high.
£500–600 S(S)

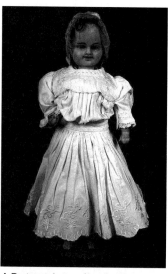

A Bartenstein two-faced wax-headed doll, with inoperative voice box, 1879–87, 16in (40.5cm) high.
£250–300 BGC

A shoulder-headed doll, with cloth body and poured wax lower limbs, fixed blue glass eyes, repaired, stamped on chest 'D. Bowden, late Moody, Doll Counter, Soho', c1880, 18½in (47cm) high.
£750–825 S(S)

A Bucherer character doll, with composition head and metal jointed body, from the American comic series *Katzenjammer Kids*, c1920, 7½in (19cm) high.
£500–600 KOLN

A Chad Valley fabric doll, with moulded face, velvet body and glass eyes, 'Hygienic Toys' label on foot, c1930, 20¾in (52.5cm) high.
£250–300 WA

Two Chad Valley Mabel Lucy Atwell fabric dolls, each with velvet body, 'Bambina' label to foot, c1935, tallest 17¾in (45cm) high.
£350–400 each S(S)

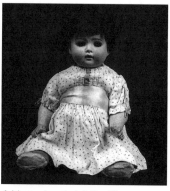

A bisque-headed doll, with composition body, probably by Crämer & Heron, marked, c1915, 14in (35.5cm) high.
£140–180 BGC

A bisque-headed doll, probably by Danel & Cie, with SFBJ-type turned wood and composition body, replacement wig, c1892, 14½in (37cm) high.
£1,250–1,400 S

A British National Dolls composition doll, c1930, 17in (43cm) high.
£100–120 DOL

An EFFanBEE Sweetie Pie composition doll, c1942, 19in (48.5cm) high.
£200–250 DOL

A Japanese Gotcho Ninyo doll, 1920s, 19½in (49.5cm) high.
£130–150 BGC

A François Gaultier bisque-headed fashion doll, with kid leather body, c1880, 14in (35.5cm) high.
£2,000–2,500 EW

A François Gaultier bisque-headed doll, with composition body, impressed mark, 1879–87, 16in (40.5cm) high.
£1,800–2,000 BGC

A Heinrich Handwerck bisque-headed doll, the head by Simon & Halbig, with jointed wood and composition body, c1910, 30in (76cm) high.
£675–750 EW

Marriages

Before purchasing, always examine a doll without its clothes. If the head appears out of proportion to the body it is likely to be a marriage. Check that the joints fit comfortably into the sockets, and inspect closely for replaced limbs, as these will adversely affect the value.

An Adolph Heller bisque-headed doll, with weighted brown eyes, ball-jointed wood and composition body, impressed 'A6H', c1910, 22½in (57cm) high.
£400–450 S(S)

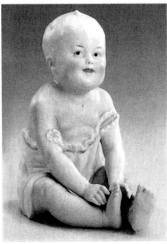

A Gebrüder Heubach piano baby, printed and impressed mark, early 20thC, 8in (20.5cm) high.
£370–400 S(S)

▶ A Heubach bisque-headed doll, with weighted brown eyes, ball-jointed composition body, one arm repaired, c1914, 27¼in (69cm) high.
£350–400 KOLN

A Heubach bisque-headed doll, with composition body, c1915, 24in (61cm) high.
£500–550 AnS

A Jumeau bisque-headed portrait doll, with fixed blue paperweight eyes, gusseted kid leather body, c1870, 29in (73.5cm) high.
£3,700–4,000 S

A Jumeau pressed bisque swivel-headed doll, with gusseted kid leather body, original costume, impressed '5', c1870, 16in (40.5cm) high.
£2,000–2,200 EW

A Jumeau bisque-headed portrait doll, with wooden ball-jointed body, original mohair wig, 1880, 15in (38cm) high.
£5,500–6,000 EW

A Tête Jumeau bisque-headed *bébé* doll, with jointed composition body, blonde mohair wig, marked 'Medaille d'Or', c1880, 15in (38cm) high.
£650–800 P(WM)

A Jumeau bisque-headed *bébé* doll, with spiral-spring neck attachment, ball-jointed composition body, original clothes, c1883, 18in (45.5cm) high.
£5,750–6,500 EW

A Jumeau bisque-headed doll, with fully jointed body, original clothes, marked, 19thC, 14in (35.5cm) high.
£1,300–1,600 DuM

A Jumeau bisque-headed *bébé* doll, with jointed composition body, brown paperweight eyes, marked 'Déposé Tête', 1886, 17in (43cm) high.
£4,000–4,500 EW

A Tête Jumeau bisque-headed doll, with jointed wood and composition body, marked, c1890, 22in (56cm) high.
£2,700–3,000 S

A Jumeau bisque-headed *bébé* doll, with jointed composition body, blue paperweight eyes, incised '11', late 19thC, 27in (68.5cm) high.
£800–1,000 S(NY)

A Jumeau moulded bisque-headed doll, with jointed wood and composition body, marked '11', c1900, 26in (66cm) high.
£900–1,000 S

A Jumeau bisque-headed *bébé* doll, with jointed composition body, late 19thC, 20in (51cm) high.
£1,500–1,800 S(NY)

l A Jumeau bisque-headed doll, with fully jointed wood and composition body, incised 'S.F.B.J.', c1900, 36in (91.5cm) high.
£600–700
r A Jumeau bisque-headed *bébé* doll, with fully jointed wood and composition body, paper label, incised 'DEP, 9', 1900, 21in (53.5cm) high.
£700–800 Bon(C)

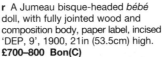

A Jumeau bisque-headed *bébé* doll, with jointed composition body, c1900, 14½in (37cm) high.
£900–1,100 AH

A German bisque-headed character doll, with ball-jointed composition body, brown glass eyes, incised 'K & H 169–4', late 19thC, 14in (35.5cm) high.
£1,200–1,400 S(NY)

A pair of Kamkins fabric dolls, both with painted fabric faces, jointed fabric bodies, in original clothes, heart-shaped label, c1930, each 18in (45.5cm) high.
£1,400–1,600 S

A Kämmer & Reinhardt Kaiser baby bisque-headed doll, with painted blue eyes, curved limb composition body, impressed marks '36 K&R 100', 1918–20, 14in (35.5cm) high.
£350–420 P(WM)

◄ A Kämmer & Reinhardt character bisque-headed Marie doll, No. 101, with wood and composition body, c1910, 8½in (21.5cm) high.
£1,200–1,500 EW

A Kestner bisque shoulder-headed doll, with gusseted kid body and bisque forearms, with silver-backed mirror and brush, arms re-attached, c1880, 16½in (42cm) high.
£650–720 S

A Kestner bisque-headed doll, with jointed wood and composition body, c1897, 29½in (75cm) high.
£650–720 KOLN

A Kestner bisque-headed Gibson Girl character doll, No. 172, c1910, 18in (45.5cm) high.
£2,700–3,000 EW

A J. D. Kestner bisque-headed googly-eyed character doll, with ball-jointed wood and composition body, minor damage, printed label, impressed mark, c1913, 13½in (34.5cm) high.
£3,500–3,850 S

A Lenci felt-headed scowling face doll, with fabric body, c1929, 18in (45.5cm) high.
£1,500–1,800 DOL

An Armand Marseille bisque-headed doll, with jointed wood and composition body, c1900, 32¼in (82cm) high.
£320–350 KOLN

An Armand Marseille bisque-headed doll, with jointed body, c1910, 17in (43cm) high.
£450–500 AnS

An Armand Marseille bisque-headed Oriental doll, with composition body, marked, c1910, 13in (33cm) high.
£800–900 BGC

► An Armand Marseille bisque-headed doll, c1920, 8in (20.5cm) high.
£135–150 AnS

An Armand Marseille Oriental Dream Baby doll, with weighted brown glass eyes, curved limb composition body, impressed '5/0 Germany', 1920–30, 9½in (24cm) high.
£300–350 P(WM)

A Barbie doll, by Mattel, with a black 'Barbie and Midge' carrying case containing many outfits, 1964, 11in (28cm) high, in original box.
£450–500 Bon(C)

An Armand Marseille character doll, mould No. 362, c1925, 18in (45.5cm) high.
£450–500 DOL

A poured wax doll, probably by Montanari, with a replica cloth body and wax lower limbs, c1860, 19in (48.5cm) high.
£450–500 S

◄ A Grace Storey Putnam bisque-headed Bye-Lo baby doll, with composition body, maker's label, 1920s, 12in (30.5cm) high.
£850–950 DOL

A Reliable Toy Co composition Shirley Temple character doll, with jointed limbs, weighted green eyes and real lashes, label to dress, c1935, 16in (40.5cm) high.
£110–130 Bon(C)

◄ A Schmitt et Fils bisque-headed doll, with jointed wood and composition body, replaced brown wig, marked, c1880, 17¾in (45cm) high.
£3,200–3,500 S

An Armand Marseille Dream Baby bisque-headed doll, with composition body, c1926, 10½in (26.5cm) high.
£160–200 KOLN

A French bisque shoulder-headed fashion doll, with kid leather body, with 'Poupé de Paris' label, c1875, 12in (30.5cm) high, in original box.
£3,500–4,000 EW

A Schoenau & Hoffmeister bisque-headed marotte musical doll, with blonde hair and blue glass eyes, original costume, turned wooden handle, moulded mark 'SH' and 'PB' within a star, No. 14, c1900, 11in (28cm) high.
£250–300 Mit

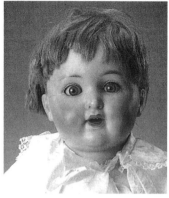

A Schutzmeister and Quendt bisque-headed character doll, with composition body, weighted blue eyes, impressed '201 9', with a metal folding cot with canopy bar, c1920, doll 16in (40.5cm) high.
£400–450 S(S)

A Simon & Halbig bisque-headed doll, with jointed wood and composition body, incised '247', c1900, 15in (38cm) high.
£1,200–1,500 EW

Cleaning dolls
• bisque heads can be cleaned by washing with cotton wool dipped in pure soap and water, but keep the water well away from the eyes as it can remove or loosen eyelashes and eyes.
• china and parian heads can be wiped with a damp cloth if necessary.
• do not attempt to clean composition bodies, as this will damage varnish and cause loss of colour and shine.

A Simon & Halbig bisque-headed character doll, with weighted blue glass eyes, two upper teeth and tongue, blonde mohair wig, five-piece toddler body, impressed 'K & R Simon & Halbig', 1905–10, 22in (56cm) high, together with box.
£300–350 P(WM)

An S.F.B.J. bisque-headed *bébé* character doll, with jointed composition body, painted hair, 1910, 20in (51cm) high.
£700–800 BGC

A Simon & Halbig bisque-headed Oriental doll, with jointed wood and composition body, impressed '1329 4', c1910, 13¼in (33.5cm) high.
£700–800 S(S)

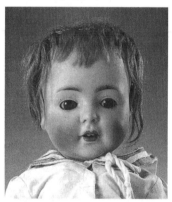

A Simon & Halbig bisque-headed character doll, with ball-jointed wood and composition body, impressed '1397 35', c1915, 14¼in (36cm) high.
£400–450 S(S)

► A Steiff felt dwarf doll, 1920s, 24in (61cm) high.
£450–500 CLE

A Jules Steiner bisque-headed mechanical kicking and crying *bébé* doll, with leather body, composition arms and lower legs, clockwork key-wind action operates cry, swivels head and moves arms and legs, c1900, 18in (45.5cm) high.
£1,100–1,200 AH

Cross Reference
See Colour Review

UNKNOWN MAKERS

A wooden doll, with enamelled eyes, brown hair wig, wooden body and cloth limbs, in original dress, early 19thC, 13½in (34.5cm) high.
£800–1,000 P(WM)

A French papier mâché shoulder-headed doll, with real hair wig, wooden arms, altered leather body, head restored, c1840, 31in (78.5cm) high.
£320–385 S

A Victorian papier mâché doll, 16in (40.5cm) high.
£275–300 AnS

The bisque swivel-head, shoulders and arms of a fashion doll, with fixed pale blue glass eyes, blonde wig, on made-up padded base, France, c1880, 16½in (42cm) high.
£500–600 S(S)

A bisque shoulder-headed doll, with fixed blue eyes, blonde wig over bald head, kid body, original costume, arms worn, impressed '5', Germany, c1885, 12½in (32cm) high.
£400–500 S(S)

A Victorian moulded-head doll, 13in (33cm) high.
£275–300 AnS

A French primitive carved black wooden doll, with glass eyes, painted mouth and teeth, body not original, late 19thC, 19in (48.5cm) high.
£400–475 Bon(C)

A German musical *poupard* doll, on turned wooden stick, 1890, 15in (38cm) high.
£400–450 AnS

A pair of Swiss metal-jointed dolls, c1930, 7in (18cm) high.
£160–180 AnS

Dolls' Houses & Furniture

DOLLS' HOUSES & SHOPS

A Moritz Gottschalk Blue Roof Victorian dolls' house, lithographed paper on wood, with turned wood exterior architectural details, glass windows, front-opening simple two-room interior with lithographed wallpaper and floors, c1870, 26½in (67.5cm) wide.
£2,750–3,250 SK(B)

A German Gothic-style carved oak dolls' house, on a stand, 19thC, 40in (101.5cm) high.
£350–400 HOB

A wooden dolls' house, 'Rose Cottage', with brown exterior, four windows with wooden Venetian blinds, green balcony and railings, lift-off grey roof revealing one room, together with three bisque dolls and a wire doll dressed in WRNS uniform, c1900, house 11¾in (30cm) wide.
£250–300 S(S)

A Lines Brothers No. 3 dolls' house, with gardens and garage with living quarters above, cream-painted façade and paper brick-effect sides, carved wooden fireplaces to each room, each room fully furnished, c1905, 40in (101.5cm) wide.
£1,200–1,400 Bon(C)

An early Victorian-style dolls' house, possibly by Lines Brothers, with double-opening front, 19 windows, central staircase, overpainted in white, partly sanded down, new hinges, c1905, 48in (122cm) high.
£1,800–2,200 HAM

A butcher's shop dolls' house, with contents and figures, 1920–30, 28in (71cm) high.
£550–600 NAW

> Miller's is a price GUIDE not a price LIST

◀ An open room setting of a dolls' shop, with approximately 150 dolls, c1900, 16in (40.5cm) wide.
£4,000–4,500 EW

A painted wood toy grocery shop, with six labelled transfer-printed drawers, matching counter, tinplate scales, parian grocer, lithographed wall panels, Germany, c1900, 15¼in (38.5cm) wide.
£550–600 S

▶ A German wooden toy grocery shop, with stained wood exterior, carved pediment, shelving drawers and counter, original paper to walls and floor, together with a wooden money box in the form of a golly, marked '27' to base, c1908, shop 16½in (42cm) wide.
£270–300 S(S)

DOLLS' HOUSE ITEMS

A Queen Anne-style chest-on-chest, with triple arch pediment, 1920s, 6½in (16.5cm) high.
£250–300 Bon(C)

A Waltershausen mantel clock, in the Biedermeier style, with shaped pediment, paper dial, supported by two turned white-painted pillars on a double drawer base, 1860–70, 3¾in (9.5cm) high.
£150–180 Bon(C)

A dressing table, with japanned mirror, pincushion and 15 japanned papier mâché boxes gilt-decorated with landscape scenes, mounted on a japanned box with concave sides on gilt paw feet, together with a letter of authenticity, 19thC, 5in (12.5cm) high, under glass dome.
£550–600 S

A papier mâché toy roast beef on a plate, Germany, 1900s, 3¼in (8.5cm) wide.
£70–80 MSB

A papier mâché toy roast on a plate, Germany, 1900s, 4in (10cm) wide.
£70–80 MSB

A papier mâché toy plate of eggs, Germany, 1900s, 4in (10cm) wide.
£70–80 MSB

A wooden-framed model greenhouse, with paper brick effect to lower section, hinged door, shelving and 15 ceramic pot plants, watering can, three parian baskets and two glazed ceramic vases, 1920s, 18in (45.5cm) long.
£550–600 Bon(C)

A papier mâché toy roast ham on a plate, Germany, 1900s, 4in (10cm) wide.
£70–80 MSB

A boxed set of Britains Miniature Kitchen Utensils No. 2, 1920s.
£160–200 WAL

A suite of wooden gold and blue transfer-decorated dolls' house furniture, comprising day bed, table and two chairs, single pillar support and display cabinet, France, late 19thC, day bed 9in (23cm) long.
£380–420 Bon(C)

A suite of Victorian-style machine-carved oak dolls' house furniture, comprising three dining chairs, armchair, settee, footstool and piano stool, all with blue damask upholstery, dining table, two sideboards and wall-hanging console, c1910, settee 5in (12.5cm) wide, in original box.
£275–300 S(S)

A Waltershausen dolls' writing table, the top lithographed in gilt with a view of the Exposition Universelle, 1867, surmounted by an eagle pediment, late 19thC, 12¼in (31cm) wide.
£400–450 S

Teddy Bears

A Chiltern mohair teddy bear, with glass eyes and velvet paws, 1950s, 17in (43cm) high.
£200–250 TED

A Richard Diem grey mohair teddy bear, with glass eyes, growler voice and cropped mohair paws and muzzle, 1950s, 14in (35.5cm) high.
£120–150 TED

A Hermann teddy bear, with brown and black eyes, pads re-covered, 1954, 20½in (52cm) high.
£80–100 KOLN

A Zotty mohair teddy bear, probably by Hermann, with open mouth, red ribbon bow, c1960, 20in (51cm) high.
£70–90 TED

Open-mouthed baby bears were more popular in their native Germany than in the UK. Zotty is from the German, *zottig*, meaning shaggy.

A Knickerbocker brown mohair teddy bear, with jointed head, floppy arms and legs, glass eyes, head and body stuffed with wood shavings, c1924, 13½in (34.5cm) high.
£40–50 TED

A Schuco lilac mohair teddy bear, in the neck is a lipstick container, in the body a manicure set, 1925–30, 3½in (7.5cm) high.
£650–800 TED

A Schuco Yes-No mohair teddy bear, with glass eyes, his tail moves his head up and down as well as from side to side, paws re-covered, 1925–30, 16½in (42cm) high.
£850–1,000 TED

A Steiff gold mohair teddy bear, with button eyes, jointed arms and legs, early 20thC, 20in (51cm) high.
£2,250–2,500 FBG

◄ A Schuco Yes-No mohair Dutch Girl Tricky teddy bear, original clothes frayed, label with 'made in US-zone Germany', c1952, 9in (23cm) high.
£600–700 TED

A Steiff mohair teddy bear, with button in ear, shoe button eyes, working squeaker voice, c1907, 12½in (32cm) high.
£2,000–2,500 TED

A Steiff white plush bear, with clipped snout, brown stitched nose, amber and black glass eyes, button in ear, hump back, c1910, 16in (41cm) high.
£800–900 P(WM)

A Steiff black and white mohair panda, with open mouth, brown and black glass eyes, fully jointed, c1955, 8¼in (21cm) high.
£200–240 KOLN

A golden teddy bear, 1920s, 14in (35.5cm) high.
£150–170 AnS

A golden yellow mohair teddy bear, with brown and black eyes, working growl, some wear, c1930, 12½in (32cm) high.
£60–70 KOLN

> **Cross Reference**
> See Colour Review

A golden teddy bear, 1950–60, 14in (35.5cm) high.
£90–100 AnS

A plush and plastic brown teddy bear, with glass eyes, c1950, 8in (20.5cm) high.
£60–70 AnS

▶ An American gold mohair miniature teddy bear, wearing original Pooh bib, c1960, 2½in (6.5cm) high.
£160–200 TED

This bear was specially commissioned for I. Magnin, a San Francisco store, in the 1960s.

A gold cotton plush teddy bear, probably English, with plastic eyes, 1955–60, 31in (78.5cm) high.
£65–80 TED

This bear was a fairground prize.

Soft Toys

A Chad Valley brushed wool long-haired terrier dog, with button eyes, moveable head, collar with black and green 'Chad Valley British Hygienic Toys' button, red and white label on left paw, c1930, 9½in (24cm) high.
£100–120 WA

A Merrythought black and white dog, c1950, 10in (25.5cm) high.
£50–60 AnS

A Steiff white dog, 'Rattler', with articulated head, the collar with two Steiff buttons and another in his ear, partially damaged Steiff paper label, c1910, 6in (15cm) high.
£370–420 Odi

A Steiff naturalistically coloured plush fox, eyes missing, early 20thC, 15in (38cm) long.
£300–350 PFK

A set of three Steiff ginger and black velvet cat skittles, on varnished wooden bases, c1910, tallest 8½in (21.5cm) high.
£1,200–1,400 S

A brown mohair rat, c1920, 14in (35.5cm) high.
£35–45 AnS

A gold and silver plush hare, with glass eyes and red stitched nose and mouth, early 20thC, 27in (68.5cm) high.
£350–400 CLE

A Steiff light brown wool plush deer, 1948–49, 8in (20.5cm) high.
£60–70 KOLN

A brown horse pyjama case, c1930, 21in (53.3cm) long.
£40–50 AnS

▶ A brown and white dog pyjama case, 1930s, 18in (45.5cm) long.
£40–50 AnS

A golly, wearing a red jacket and green trousers, 1940s, 18in (45.5cm) high.
£75–90 FHF

Toys

AEROPLANES

A Hubley cast-iron tri-motor aeroplane, painted in grey with red markings, featuring a pulley system that connects the propellers to the wheels, c1930, wingspan 17in (43cm).
£2,400–2,700 S(NY)

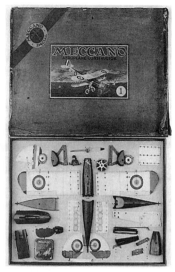

A Dinky No. 62t Armstrong Whitworth Whitley bomber, painted in dark brown and green camouflage colours, dated '12–38', with box.
£175–200 WAL

◀ A Meccano No. 1 aeroplane constructor set, the pieces finished in cream, blue and red, 1930s, in original box, 21in (53.5cm) wide.
£200–240 Bon(C)

SHIPS

A Bing clockwork gun boat, *Vlastny*, c1900, 15in (38cm) long.
£500–600 P(WM)

This model, like the similar *Kasuga*, was made by Bing to commemorate the Battle of Tishima during the Japanese-Russian war.

Further Reading

Miller's Toys & Games Antiques Checklist, Miller's Publications, 1995

A Welsotoys tinplate clockwork Speed-y-Launch, in red with yellow trim, 1950s, 10½in (26.5cm) long, with box.
£30–35 RAR

A Corgi gift set No. 31, comprising Buick Riviera, Dolphin 20 cabin cruiser, water skier and trailer, 1960s, with box.
£85–100 WAL

▶ A German tinplate battleship, probably by Carette, hand-painted in light grey on a brown hull with black lining, red deck and dark grey superstructure, c1910, 17¼in (44cm) long.
£2,000–2,200 SK(B)

A Hornby Limousine Boat No. 4, green and cream with an orange propeller and detail, 1930s, 16½in (42cm) long.
£200–240 Bon(C)

▶ A Hornby Minic Ships 1:1200 scale diecast model of HMS *Vanguard*, 1960, 12in (30.5cm) long, with box.
£30–40 FA

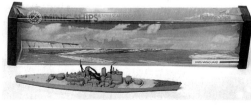

◀ A WWI wooden toy battleship, with moveable turrets and lead ballast, 1914–18, 18in (45.5cm) long.
£40–50 AnS

TRAINS

A painted wood four-piece toy floor train, finished in black with red and yellow details, the dark green baggage car with yellow and black detail, late 19thC, total length 54¾in (139cm).
£4,500–5,000 SK(B)

A Bassett-Lowke 4–4–0 LMS locomotive and tender, finished in red, c1940, 14in (35.5cm) long.
£300–350 AH

A Bing 4–4–0 live steam locomotive and six-wheel tender, pair of wheels missing, late 19thC, 23in (58.5cm) long.
£1,800–2,200 WAL

A Carette for Bassett-Lowke gauge II LNWR six-wheel coach for 1st/3rd class passengers, c1900, with original box base.
£200–400 P(WM)

◀ A French Dessin clockwork 2–2–0 floor locomotive, with articulated four-wheel tender, composition driver and two four-wheel coaches, c1890, in original coloured illustrated box.
£2,500–3,000 P(WM)

Bing/Bassett-Lowke

W. J. Bassett-Lowke & Co (1899–1969) was founded by Wenman Bassett-Lowke in Northampton to supply components for model steam trains and locomotives through his mail order business. Following a meeting in 1900 with Stefan Bing, director of the German toy train manufacturers Gebrüder Bing, the German firm supplied Bassett-Lowke with trains for sale both through its retail outfit in London and its mail order catalogues, until Bing was taken over in 1933. Bassett-Lowke set up a manufacturing branch with George Winteringham in 1908 and also collaborated with Carette & Cie of Nuremberg.

A Bing for Bassett-Lowke gauge I Adams clockwork 0–4–4 locomotive, in Southern livery, No. 109, 1930s, 14in (35.5cm) long.
£900–1,000 BKS

A Bassett-Lowke gauge 0 clockwork LMS locomotive, 1948, 14in (35.5cm) long.
£270–300 RAR

A Bing gauge II clockwork 4–6–2T Great Central locomotive, c1910, in original wooden box with part of lid.
£3,800–4,200 P(WM)

A Bing gauge 0 clockwork 4–4–0 'George the Fifth' locomotive and tender, in lined black LNWR livery, No. 2663, 1910–20, 14in (35.5cm) long.
£120–140 DN

An Exley GWR coach with side corridor, finished in brown and cream, 1936, 18in (45.5cm) long.
£250–300 HOB

A Hornby 1st series Shell Motor Spirit tank wagon, finished in red, with solid axle and bright wheels, 1925, 7in (18cm) long, with box.
£150–180 HOB

A Hornby No. 2 double electric yard lamp, finished in grey and white, c1930, 10in (25.5cm) high, in original red box.
£200–240 BKS

Cross Reference
See Colour Review

◀ A Hornby 1st series LNWR Gunpowder Van, with red with white lettering and roof, solid axle and bright wheels, c1927, 7in (18cm) long.
£200–240 HOB

▶ A Hornby No. 1 gauge 0 clockwork Great Western locomotive and tender, finished in GW livery, 1930, 12in (30.5cm) long, in original red boxes.
£500–600 HOB

A Hornby No. 3 electric LNER Flying Scotsman locomotive and tender, 1930s, 16in (40.5cm) long.
£180–220 BKS

A Hornby cement wagon, finished in red with cream lettering, 1935, 7in (18cm) long.
£60–70 HOB

A Hornby Wakefield Castrol Motor Oil tank wagon, finished in green with yellow and orange lettering, 1932, 7in (18cm) long.
£60–75 HOB

A Hornby gauge 0 platelayer's hut, 1930s, 4in (10cm) wide, with box.
£45–50 RAR

A Hornby gauge 0 Mitropa Schlafwagen, finished in red with white roof and yellow lettering, 1936, 13in (33cm) long.
£500–600 HOB

A Hornby LMS Princess Elizabeth locomotive, No. 6201, c1938, in original blue presentation case with green lining.
£1,000–1,100 S(S)

A Hornby gauge 0 clockwork 0–4–0 LNER Silver Link locomotive, No. 2509, with tender and two coaches, finished in silver and green-grey livery, with track, 1950s, with box, 24in (61cm) long.
£250–300 CGC

A Leeds Model Company GWR brake end coach, finished in chocolate and cream, 1930, 18in (45.5cm) long.
£100–120 HOB

A Märklin Central Bahnhof, hand-painted in orange and green, fitted with later electric lighting, with two cast lamp stands with later lamp fittings, c1902, 13in (33cm) long.
£4,000–5,000 P(WM)

A gauge 4¾ steam outline wooden 2–2–2 locomotive, c1850, 7in (18cm) long.
£250–300 P(WM)

▶ A gauge 5½ 4–4–0 North Eastern locomotive and tender, finished in green North Eastern livery, early 20thC, engine 30½in (77.5cm) long.
£2,200–2,500 Bon(C)

A 2½in Great Western bogie passenger corridor coach, finished in brown and yellow, 1930s, 34in (86.5cm) long.
£500–550 BKS

A Hornby gauge 0 'Trent' tinplate island platform, with red tiles and cream platform, c1957, 17in (43cm) long.
£80–90 WaH

A Lionel Set No. 269E gauge 0 electric freight locomotive and tender, with oil tank, box car, dump car and caboose, late 1930s, all with boxes except dump car.
£600–700 SK(B)

An LBG circus train, comprising 0–4–0T locomotive, low-sided wagon with truck load, low-sided wagon with animal cage load, truck fitted with speaker, a large wagon and a coach, 1950s.
£100–125 P(WM)

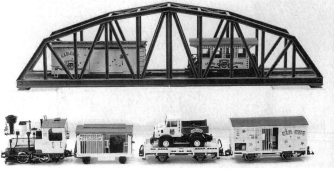

A Milbro gauge 0 Southern locomotive and tender, No. 901, finished in olive green and black with yellow lettering, 1936, 16½in (42cm) long.
£700–800 WaH

A hand-built 4–6–0 'St David' electric locomotive and tender, finished in black BR livery, 1970s, 17½in (44.5cm) long.
£400–450 WaH

667

VEHICLES

An Alps tinplate friction-powered Cadillac, finished in grey with red seats, Japan, 1952, 11¾in (30cm) long.
£1,150–1,300 KOLN

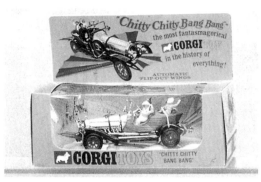

A Corgi Toys 'Chitty Chitty Bang Bang' car, with original figures, 1960s, in original yellow box.
£230–275 WAL

A Corgi Toys die-cast 'The Man From UNCLE Gun Firing Thrush-Buster' car, finished in dark blue with green interior, 1966, 6in (15cm) long, with box.
£110–120 DAC

A Günthermann tinplate limousine, finished in cream with red and orange lining, early 20thC, 12in (30.5cm) long.
£300–350 PFK

A Matchbox 'Models of YesterYears Gift Set' No. G7, comprising Tramcar, Morris Cowley, Fowler Showman's Engine, horse-drawn bus and Duke of Connaught locomotive, c1950s, in original box.
£250–300 DN

Miller's is a price GUIDE not a price LIST

▶ A Matchbox Removals Service van, finished in blue with gold trim, 1950s, with box.
£180–220 P(WM)

A model carriage or brougham, with two polychrome-decorated wooden horses with leather tack, 19thC, 48in (122cm) long.
£900–1,000 MEA

A tinplate clockwork Singer Saloon, with remote control, damaged, early 20thC, 9in (23cm) long.
£550–600 AH

SOLDIERS

A Britains for CFE, City Imperial Volunteers, comprising four-horse Army Supply Column Wagon, with two seated men, one arm missing, 1925–41, 2¼in (5.5cm) high.
£450–550 P(WM)

A Britains set No. 19, The West India Regiment, comprising eight marching troops, some repainting, 1925–36, 2¼in (5.5cm) high, in original box.
£60–70 Bon(C)

A Britains set No. 1722, Pipes and Drums of the Scots Guards, with 21 pieces, 1939–41, boxed, 18in (45.5cm) wide.
£300–350 S(S)

A Britains set No. 1527, The Band of the Royal Air Force, with 12 pieces, 1930s, boxed, 18in (45.5cm) wide.
£350–420 WAL

A Britains set No. 37, Coldstream Guards Band, with 21 figures, c1938, 2¼in (5.5cm) high.
£200–240 S(S)

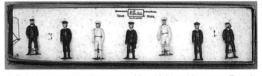

A Britains war-time issue set No. 1911, with seven Royal Navy Officers and Petty Officers in dark blue and white service uniforms, c1940, boxed, 20in (51cm) wide.
£180–220 WAL

A Britains set No. 145, RAMC grey-painted ambulance wagon, with two figures and four horses, 1950s, in original box, 12in (30.5cm) wide.
£230–275 WAL

A Britains set No. 9420, Royal Artillery, comprising 11 pieces, 1962–65, in original All Nations box, 10in (25.5cm) square.
£130–160 Bon(C)

A Britains set No. 2111, Colour Party of the Black Watch, comprising six pieces, 1956–60, 2¼in (5.5cm) high, in original All Nations box.
£230–275 Bon(C)

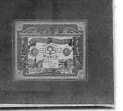

A Heyde Royal Artillery gun team, comprising six-horse team with limber, three mounted postilions, gun with tinplate shield and seats, a mounted officer and trumpeter, German, 1910–20.
£150–165 P(WM)

A CBG set of Marine Fusiliers, comprising nine men in winter overcoats, with officer, bugler and standard-bearer, France, 1950s, in original box.
£140–170 P(WM)

► A Heyde set No. 1388, The Triumph of Germanicus, solid-cast in 45mm scale, German, c1920, in original red box.
£750–900 S(S)

MECHANICAL TOYS

A bisque-headed young girl automaton, with moving arms which control a harlequin, 19thC, 18in (45.5cm) high.
£250–300 EH

A French Roullet and Decamps clockwork dark brown bear, holding chimes for playing two mounted bells, on a wooden base, c1910, 14½in (37cm) high.
£500–600 Bon(C)

◀ A German Schuco clockwork monkey violinist, dressed in red and blue felt, early 20thC, 4¾in (12cm) high.
£115–135 S(S)

A Japanese clockwork elephant, with red jacket and black boots, ringing a bell and holding a 'Welcome' sign, 1930s, 6in (15cm) high.
£150–180 AAV

A Lehmann mechanical toy, 'The Miller', red, green and white, with two flour sacks that allow the miller to climb rapidly up and down the pole, c1930, 19in (48.5cm) high.
£120–140 BKS

◀ A Japanese Nomura tinplate battery operated Robby the Robot, finished in black and red, 1955–60, 13in (33cm) high.
£750–900 Bon(C)

MONEY BOXES

A German metal dog money box, decorated in brown and black, c1910, 4in (10cm) high.
£120–150 HAL

An American cast-iron money bank, 'Tammany', by J. & E. Stevens, the politician depositing a coin into his pocket as he nods his head, in brown jacket, grey trousers and yellow waistcoat, patent date 1875, 5¾in (14.5cm) high.
£200–240 P(WM)

▶ A metal Robot money bank, decorated in red, green and blue, by Starkies Blarney, c1920, 9in (23cm) high.
£1,800–2,000 HAL

ROCKING HORSES

A wooden racer rocking horse, 1840, 78in (198cm) long.
£4,500–5,000 STE

A carved and painted wooden rocking horse, with glass eyes, hair mane and tail and leather straps, mid-19thC, 84¾in (215.5cm) long.
£1,150–1,350 Bri

A wooden rocking horse, with side-saddle, 1870–80, 88in (223.5cm) long.
£4,000–4,500 STE

The pommel of this saddle is designed to fit either side, so that the child did not damage the legs by using one side only.

A wooden rocking horse, painted dapple grey, with long mane, on a trestle base with turned supports, late 19thC, 42in (106.5cm) long.
£500–600 E

A wooden rocking horse, by F. H. Ayres, on a spring base, 1880–90, 64in (162.5cm) long.
£4,000–4,500 STE

A wooden rocking horse, with side saddle, original paintwork, on a trestle base, late 19thC, 58in (147.5cm) long.
£4,400–4,800 JuB

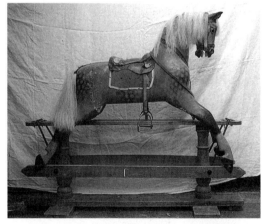

A wooden rocking horse, sold by Army & Navy Stores, London, on a trestle base with turned supports, c1900, 54in (137cm) long.
£3,200–3,500 STE

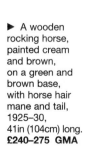

► A wooden rocking horse, painted cream and brown, on a green and brown base, with horse hair mane and tail, 1925–30, 41in (104cm) long.
£240–275 GMA

An Edwardian table croquet set, the boxwood mallets, markers and balls standing on a turned circular mahogany display stand, with hoops, boxed, 15in (38cm) high.
£600–700 L&T

An American black and yellow painted paper game board, the turquoise border decorated with flowers and butterflies, mid-19thC, 18 x 17in (45.5 x 43cm).
£900–1,000 BB(S)

◀ A boxwood diabolo game, with playing sticks, mid-19thC, 4in (10cm) wide.
£65–80 ALA

A Victorian coromandel and brass-mounted games compendium, with two lift-out trays and shelved compartments containing a Staunton pattern ivory and stained red chess set, similar draughts pieces, painted lead racehorses and fences, treen dice tumblers, gaming counters, marker boards, brass cribbage board, packs of playing cards, a fold-out chess/backgammon/racehorse board to the lid, 14¼in (36cm) wide.
£1,500–1,800 P(E)

An Elastolin Noah's Ark, containing 41 various composition figures and animals, with Hausser label and gold sticker, c1930, 17in (43cm) long.
£700–800 P(WM)

A Chinese bone and bamboo mahjong set, in a brass-bound hardwood box, 1920, 8in (20.5cm) wide.
£170–200 TMi

A Meccano steam engine, in original yellow and blue box, c1929, 7in (18cm) wide.
£380–420 RAR

A puzzle, Lyin' Quiet, by Jean David, about 775 pieces, mid-20thC, 19¼in (49cm) wide, in original box.
£620–680 SK(B)

A wooden quoits board, with original hoops, late 19thC, 14in (35.5cm) square.
£120–150 SEA

▶ A Subbuteo Table Soccer game, with goals, players, baize cloth and original literature, c1950, in original box.
£70–85 MUL

A French oak, steel and gilt-metal table-top spinning game, mounted with three moveable gilt-metal figures and suspended bell, two string-pull spinners, late 19thC, 61in (155cm) long.
£800–950 Bon(C)

Ephemera

ANNUALS, BOOKS & COMICS

The Rosebud Annual, front board and interior illustrations by Louis Wain, published by James Clarke & Co, 1903.
£130–150 CBP

The Hotspur, issue No. 1, slight damage, 1933.
£120–140 CBP

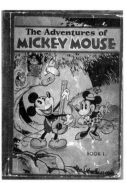

The Adventures of Mickey Mouse Book 1, Walt Disney, published by David McKay Co, Philadelphia, 1931, 4°.
£300–350 DW

This is the first Mickey Mouse annual.

◀ Batman, issue No. 11, National Periodical Publications, June/July 1942.
£2,200–2,500 S(NY)

▶ The Magic-Beano Book, 1945.
£425–475 CBP

The Hotspur Book for Boys, published by D. C. Thomson & Co, 1935.
£30–35 WW

Detective Comics, issue No. 20, National Periodical Publications, October 1938.
£900–1,000 S(NY)

Dan Dare, original monochrome artwork for Eagle comics, 11½ x 15in (29 x 38cm) with five smaller full-colour illustrations, 1950s.
£250–300 DW

Jimmy Olsen, Superman's Pal, issue No. 2, 1954.
£70–85 CBP

My Greatest Adventure, Issue No. 1, 1955.
£70–85 CBP

The Amazing Spider-Man, issue No. 14, published by Marvel Comics Group, July 1964.
£1,800–2,200 S(NY)

AUTOGRAPHS

Ulysses Grant, an autographed letter signed as Major General, Headquarters Dept of Tennessee, to Rear Admiral Daniel G. Farragut, dated 'June 5th, 1863', 4°.
£2,000–2,200 SK

Edward Elgar, a signed sepia carte de visite, c1900, 6 x 4in (15 x 10cm).
£450–550 HAM

G. Puccini, a signed programme for *Tosca* in Rome, dedicated to Alfredo Campoli's father, 1900, 8 x 5½in (20.5 x 14cm).
£850–1,000 P

An Athenaeum menu card, signed by members of the Antarctic expedition prior to their departure to the South Pole, Edward A. Wilson, R. F. Scott, D. H. Shackleton and others, dated '23rd July 1901'.
£1,100–1,300 E

William Booth, wearing Salvation Army uniform, a signed photograph with additional words in his hand 'with thanks for kindly arrangements for my comfort on the Campania', dated '14th March 1903', 8 x 6in (20.5 x 15cm).
£100–120 VS

Enrico Caruso, a signed postcard, inscribed 'London 1904'.
£220–250 VS

Theodore Roosevelt, a signed letter to President Thwing declining an invitation to speak at an engagement but inviting recipient to the White House, dated 'January 21, 1904'.
£350–380 SK

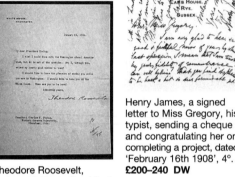

Henry James, a signed letter to Miss Gregory, his typist, sending a cheque and congratulating her on completing a project, dated 'February 16th 1908', 4°.
£200–240 DW

Queen Elizabeth II, a black and white family wedding photograph, signed on the mount 'Elizabeth R', framed and glazed, 1949, 14 x 11in (35.5 x 28cm).
£300–350 Bon(C)

WIMBLEDON THEATRE

Laurel & Hardy, a programme for a performance at the Wimbledon Theatre, signed and inscribed by Stan Laurel and Oliver Hardy, 1950s.
£200–240 VS

Charlie Chaplin, a signed letter enclosing a photograph and thanking the recipient for his New Year greetings and the interest taken in Chaplin's work, dated '5th January 1915'.
£500–550 S(NY)

▶ Betty Grable, a signed and inscribed photograph, 1972, 7 x 5in (18 x 12.5cm).
£50–60 VS

Charlie Chaplin, a signed photogravure portrait of Chaplin as The Little Tramp, 1920s, 10 x 8in (25.5 x 20.5cm).
£550–650 DW

▶ Mother Teresa, a photograph inscribed 'Love others as God loves you, God bless you, M. Teresa M. C.', dated '20th Aug 1984'.
£250–300 VS

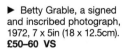

CIGARETTE CARDS

E. & W. Anstie, Scout Series, set of 50, 1923.
£40–50 VS

W. A. & A. C. Churchman, Men of the Moment in Sport, set of 50, 1928.
£130–150 WL

◄ John Player & Sons, Curious Beaks, set of 50, 1932.
£35–40 JMC

► W. D. & H. O. Wills, Cricketers, set of 50, plus five duplicates, 1908.
£130–150 WL

Cope Brothers & Co Ltd, The World's Police, set of 25, 1937.
£55–65 VS

Lambert & Butler, Motor Cars Radiators, set of 25, 1928.
£80–100 VS

W. D. & H. O. Wills, Butterflies, set of 50, 1927.
£35–40 JMC

POSTCARDS

◄ A postcard showing Racer, printed by Harry Paine, c1910.
£22–25 JMC

A postcard, MacFarlane Lang & Co advertising series, c1910.
£27–30 JMC

A suffragettes postcard, of Levetleich, St Leonards, Sussex, destroyed by fire, 15th April, 1913.
£110–130 VS

POSTERS

A poster, by Leonetto Cappiello, advertising Cognac Albert Robin, printed in brown, red and green on black, published by Vercasson, Paris, 1906, 63 x 46in (160 x 117cm).
£500–600 BB(L)

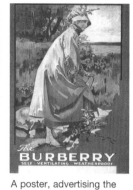

A poster, advertising the Burberry self-ventilating weatherproof, printed by David Allen, in brown, green and blue, indistinct artist's signature, c1910, 60 x 40in (152.5 x 101.5cm).
£1,100–1,300 ONS

A Sauvion's Brandy poster, featuring a clown dressed in red, published by Joseph Charles, Paris 1925.
£250–300 MUL

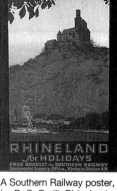

A Southern Railway poster, by R. G. Praill, Rhineland for Holidays, printed by Avenue Press, 1929, 25¼ x 40¼in (64 x 102cm).
£200–220 ONS

A Southern Railway poster, by Leslie Carr, Canterbury, printed by McCorquodale, 1929, 25¼ x 50in (64 x 127cm).
£800–950 ONS

A Southern Electric poster, by Shields, Spring Radiance, Go As You Please Tickets, printed by Waterlow, 1932, 40¼ x 25¼in (102 x 64cm).
£320–380 ONS

A Great Southern Railways poster, Blarney Castle, Co. Cork Ireland, 1930s.
£180–220 WA

A London Transport poster, by Clive Gardner, At London's Service, printed by Vincent Brooks-Day, 1934, 40¼ x 25¼in (102 x 64cm).
£200–240 ONS

A Warner Bros. poster, *The Woman in Red*, 1935, 41 x 27in (104 x 68.5cm).
£1,650–1,800 S(NY)

An LMS poster, by Fred Taylor, for the Empire Exhibition, Glasgow, 1938, 40¼ x 25¼in (102 x 64cm).
£450–500 ONS

A Warner Bros. poster, James Cagney, c1935, 28 x 22in (71 x 56cm).
£950–1,100 S(NY)

A Gaumont-British poster, advertising *The 39 Steps*, three-sheet lithograph, 1935, 81 x 41in (205.5 x 104cm).
£5,000–5,500 S(NY)

◄ A Warner Bros. poster, advertising *Jezebel*, 1938, 41 x 27in (104 x 68.5cm).
£6,250–7,000 S(NY)

▶ A poster, advertising Vins Camp Romain, by L. Gadoud, published by Affiches Camis, Paris, 1930s, 63 x 47¼in (160 x 120cm), framed.
£620–680 BB(L)

A CDI poster, advertising *La Posada Maldita*, (*Jamaica Inn*), 1939, 41 x 27in (104 x 68.5cm). **£130–150 Bon(C)**

An LMS poster, by Paul Henry, Connemara, 1930–40, 43¼ x 25¼in (110 x 64cm). **£1,000–1,200 WA**

A Warner Bros. poster, advertising *To Have and Have Not*, 1944, 41 x 27in (104 x 68.5cm). **£1,200–1,500 S(NY)**

A Rank poster, advertising *Brief Encounter*, 1946, 41 x 27in (104 x 68.5cm). **£650–800 S(NY)**

A British Railways poster, by Paul Henry, Lough Derg, Ireland, for Holidays, printed by Jordison, London, 1940s, 43¼ x 25¼in (110 x 64cm). **£800–1,000 WA**

A British Railways poster, by Paul Henry, showing Dingle Peninsula, Kerry, Nottingham, 1940s, 41 x 27in (104 x 68.5cm). **£1,400–1,700 WA**

A Universal poster, advertising *Creature from the Black Lagoon*, by Wm. Reynold Brown, 1954, 22 x 28in (56 x 71cm). **£3,000–3,500 S(NY)**

◄ A poster by Norman Wilkinson, Come to Britain for Fishing, c1948, 41 x 27in (104 x 68.5cm). **£450–550 ONS**

A 20th Century-Fox poster, advertising *Viva Zapata*, 1952, 41 x 27in (104 x 68.5cm). **£650–800 S(NY)**

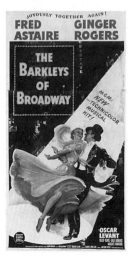

◄ An MGM poster, advertising *The Barkleys of Broadway*, 1949, 81 x 41in (205.5 x 104cm). **£600–700 S(NY)**

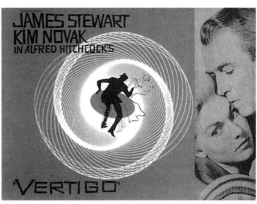

An Irish International Airlines poster, showing the Constellation airliner over an ancient church with twin towers, signed by Adolph Treidler, 1950s, 39½ x 25¼in (100 x 64cm).
£350–420 WA

A Chipperfields Circus colour litho poster, depicting 'The Raluy's Human Canonballs', 1950s, 30 x 20in (76 x 51cm).
£150–180 LAY

A Paramount poster, by Saul Bass, advertising *Vertigo*, 1958, 22 x 28in (56 x 71cm).
£1,200–1,350 S(NY)

◀ A British Railways poster, by Terence Cuneo, Royal Albert Bridge, Saltash Centenary, printed by Waterlow, 1959, 40¼ x 50in (102 x 127cm).
£800–950 ONS

An MGM poster, advertising *Forbidden Planet*, 1956, 41 x 27in (104 x 68.5cm).
£3,500–3,850 S(NY)

A 20th Century-Fox poster, advertising *Bus Stop*, 1956, 81 x 41in (206 x 104cm).
£1,000–1,200 S(NY)

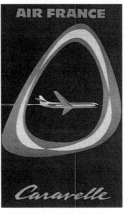

An Air France Caravelle poster, by Jean Colin, published by Perceval, 1959, 39½ x 24in (100 x 61cm).
£220–265 ONS

A Billy Smart's Circus colour lithographic poster depicting 'Tagora, The Human Volcano', 1950s, 30 x 20in (76 x 51cm).
£160–200 LAY

A United Artists poster, advertising *From Russia with Love*, 1964, 41 x 27in (104 x 68.5cm).
£180–220 Bon(C)

A Columbia poster, by Howard A. Terpning, advertising *Lawrence of Arabia*, 1962, 41 x 27in (104 x 68.5cm).
£5,000–5,500 S(NY)

▶ A Columbia poster, advertising *A Man for All Seasons*, 1966, 41 x 27in (104 x 68.5cm).
£800–900 S(NY)

A United Artists poster, advertising *Goldfinger/ Dr No*, 1966, 41 x 27in (104 x 68.5cm).
£70–85 Bon(C)

A United Artists poster, advertising *Diamonds Are Forever*, 1971, 41 x 27in (104 x 68.5cm).
£250–300 Bon(C)

Rock & Pop

A Columbia *Rock Around the Clock* poster, 1956, 81in (205.5cm) square.
£900–1,000 S(NY)

The Beatles Book Monthly, No. 5, Xmas Edition, signed in ink by each band member and 'To Sue love from THE BEATLES', December 1963.
£300–350 Bri

A Rolling Stones black and white publicity photograph, signed in blue ballpoint pen, c1963, 10 x 8in (25.5 x 20.5cm).
£250–300 Bon(C)

◄ A Corgi prototype of the unissued The Beatles Cadillac, painted cream, the roof section open with a false floor to support two pairs of hand-painted white metal figures in blue fitted suits, instruments held aloft, hand-painted logo to bonnet over an image of a guitar, 1965–66, 4½in (11.5cm) long.
£3,200–3,500 S

A Beatles programme for the band's 1964 British Tour, signed on an interior portrait in blue ballpoint pen, John Lennon's signature is signed by George Harrison, 10 x 8in (25.5 x 20.5cm).
£800–950 Bon(C)

A Hard Day's Night, the paperback book of the film signed by each of the Beatles and co-star Wilfred Bramble, John has inscribed 'to Phyllis from John Lennon' with doodle character, c1964.
£500–600 HAM

An Aquascutum navy blue cashmere coat, inscribed 'John Winston Lennon, His Coat' within a pair spectacles, 1964–65.
£3,500–4,000 Bri

► A Jimi Hendrix signed single record, 'Purple Haze', 1967.
£350–420 VS

Autographs of The Rolling Stones, Mick Jagger, Brian Jones, Keith Richards, Bill Wyman and Charlie Watts, in blue ballpoint pen, late 1960s, framed, 7 x 5in (18 x 12.5cm).
£250–300 Bon(C)

A Squier Fender Stratocaster electric guitar, signed by Eric Clapton, 1990s, 39in (99cm) long.
£500–600 DuM

An LP album cover for 'Imagine', autographed in blue ballpoint pen by John Lennon, with a self portrait caricature of Lennon's smiling face, additionally annotated with a doodle of a couple looking up at a four-legged animal standing on a cloud, 1976.
£5,000–6,000 S(NY)

◄ A concert poster by D. W. Beeghly, for Jimi Hendrix Experience, 16th August, 1968, 28 x 22¼in (71 x 56.5cm).
£1,500–1,800 S(NY)

A waistcoat worn by Jimi Hendrix at Memorial Auditorium, Dallas, black faux fur with multi-coloured beaded trim and black fringe, 20th April, 1969.
£4,000–4,500 S(NY)

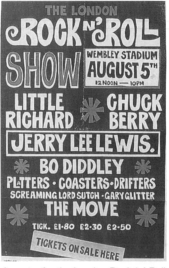

A poster for the London Rock 'n' Roll Show at Wembley 5th August 1972, featuring Little Richard, Chuck Berry, Jerry Lee Lewis, Bo Diddley, The Move and others, 29 x 20in (73.5 x 51cm).
£200–240 Bon(C)

A Syd Barrett watercolour in two segments of joined white paper, comprising a triangular design in white, black, blue and orange, titled 'Design For a Mural for the Blue Trailer', signed 'Roger Barrett 11.9.79', mounted, framed and glazed, 15 x 30in (38 x 76cm).
£950–1,100 Bon(C)

A copy of Rolling Stone magazine, autographed on the front cover in black ballpoint pen by Janis Joplin, 15th March, 1969.
£1,200–1,400 S(NY)

A black and white photograph of Deborah Harry, taken by Chris Stein, signed by the photographer and by Harry, early 1980s, 17¼ x 11¾in (44 x 30cm).
£650–800 S(NY)

A Kay six-string lead guitar, with hardwood body, formerly owned and played by Nicky Wire (Jones), bassist from The Manic Street Preachers, with a Fuzz Box/Wah Wah pedal and a Linear Linnet Five amplifier, all used by Wire pre-1988.
£400–500 Bon(C)

Scientific Instruments

CALCULATING MACHINES

An Odhner No. 1 arithmometer,
by Willgodt T. Odhner, with nine-digit
input, thirteen-digit results and eight-digit
revolutions, 1886.
£3,400–3,750 KOLN

A T. I. M. calculating machine, by
Ludwig Spitz & Co, with eight sliding
indices, in a wooden case with tables,
late 19thC, 17¾in (45cm) wide.
£220–260 Bon

A Fowler's long-scale
calculator, c1920,
5in (12.5cm) diam.
£160–180 ETO

► A Fowler's
textile calculator,
in original
case, c1920,
3in (7.5cm) diam.
£175–200 ETO

A step-drum arithmometer, by Seidel
& Naumann, Dresden, 1906.
£3,000–3,500 KOLN

An Otis King's calculator, by Carbic Ltd, c1920,
10in (25.5cm) long, with instructions and original box.
£120–150 ETO

A Curta Type 1 calculator,
Liechtenstein, 1960s,
4¾in (12cm) high.
£400–450 Bon

A Fuller's patent calculator,
with original mahogany
box and mounting bracket,
1930, 18in (45.5cm) long.
£400–450 ETO

COMPASSES & DIALS

◄ An ivory diptych dial, by Hans
Tröschel, inscribed on all four faces
in red and black, with wind rose,
latitude table for 16 European
countries and cities, standard
German lunar volvelle, horizontal
compass bowl missing glass and
needle, c1600, 2¼in (5.5cm) wide.
£2,500–3,000 S

**A vovelle is a device consisting of
moveable concentric circular scales.**

A silver perpetual calendar, engraved
with stylized foliate decoration on
both sides, German, early 18thC,
1¾in (4.5cm) diam.
£750–900 S

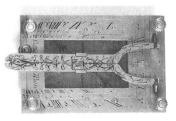

◄ A Le Maire brass horizontal
string-gnomon dial, with inset
compass well with engraved rose,
signed, mid-18thC, 3½in (9cm) long.
£1,000–1,200 S

A Godfried Weiss brass horizontal dial, the shaped plate calibrated 4–12–8 and IIII–XII–VIII with five-minute divisions between the two scales, with inset compass, signed, 18thC, 8¾in (22cm) long.
£2,200–2,500 Bon

A G. Adams lacquered brass inclining dial, with folding gnomon and sprung folding latitude arc, in a mahogany case, late 18thC, 3½in (9cm) square.
£550–600 P

A Johan Schrettegger octagonal universal equinoctial dial, Augsburg, late 18thC, 2in (5cm) wide.
£400–450 Bon

A silver pocket compass, London 1806, 2in (5cm) diam.
£400–500 GAK

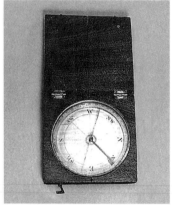

A compass, with silvered dial engraved with compass points, in a mahogany case, early 19thC, 6in (15cm) square.
£250–300 DN

A Dollond bronze horizontal sundial, early 19thC, 13½in (34.5cm) diam.
£850–950 JeF

A W. & S. Jones equinoctial ring dial, early 19thC, 4in (10cm) diam.
£1,650–1,850 JeF

A W. & S. Jones brass inclining dial, signed, mid-19thC, 2½in (6.5cm) diam, in a red morocco fitted case.
£700–800 S

◄ A French noon cannon, the marble base engraved VIII–IIX–IIII, the brass gnomon set for 46° 30, brass twin calendar arcs and brass cannon, mid-19thC, 10¾in (27.5cm) diam.
£1,800–2,000 S

A Continental brass dip circle, c1890, 14in (35.5cm) high.
£325–360 ETO

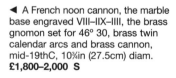

► A pocket compass, in a wooden case, 1918, 3in (7.5cm) square.
£180–200 REG

GLOBES, ORRERIES & ARMILLARY SPHERES

A John Senex pocket globe, in a black fishskin case with coloured celestial map to the interior, c1728, globe 3in (7.5cm) diam.
£7,000–8,000 S

John Senex (1690–1740) is noted as being an early 18thC English globe-maker, following after Joseph Moxon. He began his working life as a stationer and then moved into map-making and publishing globes. In 1728 he was elected a Fellow of the Royal Society.

A W. & S. Jones New Portable orrery, with terrestrial globe, three ivory planetary spheres and a central brass sphere representing the moon, contained in a wooden case with a booklet, dated '1794', 13in (33cm) diam.
£9,000–10,000 S

Cross Reference
See Colour Review

A New and Improved celestial globe, by Newton, on a turned wood stand, mid-19thC, globe 15in (38cm) diam.
£3,000–3,500 TMA

◀ A French Ptolemaic armillary sphere, by Delamarche, with central terrestrial globe with engraved paper sun and moon discs on brass revolving arms, on an ebonized baluster column and base, late 18thC, 21in (53.5cm) high.
£5,000–5,500 S

An armillary sphere is a representation of the heavens, but not as a celestial globe. First made in the Middle Ages, they proliferated in the Renaissance as demonstrational or teaching aids. Nearly all those seen today are French and made between mid-18th and mid-19thC. They should not be confused with the *planétaire*, the French version of the English orrery, both of which show the planets orbiting the sun, and which may also be called heliocentric or Copernican. If they show the old notation, with the Earth at the centre of the universe, they are called Ptolemaic.

Buying globes

Avoid buying globes that need extensive restoration. If the work is carried out professionally to a high standard this can often cost more than the original price of the globe, and the result is still a much-restored article that has little or no appreciation value. Avoid floor-standing (library) globes that are missing the compasses and stretchers. Never buy a globe without first looking at it very carefully – this makes a special trip to view an auction worthwhile. A general guide is to buy the best example you can afford from a specialist who can provide full information about it, since globes are physical records of not only the geography and exploration, but also the history and politics of the 18th, 19th and early 20thC. Early globes, that is those made before 1800, increase in value more quickly than later examples.

19thC globes made in European countries such as Sweden, Poland, Germany, Italy and Spain are acceptable but do not appreciate as quickly as those made in Britain, France or the USA. Buyers should be aware of recent English-made replicas that appear to the untrained eye to be the real thing. Also avoid miniature ivory globes which are made for unwary tourists and carved from old billiard balls – some versions are cut in half and hinged, opening to reveal a sundial and gnomon. All these turn up at country auction sales, fairs and flea-markets in the UK and Europe, and have even been spotted in the USA. Always ask a dealer for a receipt on his headed notepaper giving a brief description and date of the item. If he refuses, either go elsewhere or be prepared to stand the loss if the item turns out to be not quite what it seems.

◀ A celestial globe and stand, by J. & W. Cary, with calibrated brass meridian ring, 1816, globe 18in (45.5cm) diam.
£3,300–4,000 BB(L)

A pair of table globes, by G. & J. Cary, with brass equinoctial and printed horizon charts for the signs of the zodiac and months, the early celestial globe with label dated '1800', pole missing, on replaced oak legs, 1833, globes 12in (30.5cm) diam.
£4,500–5,000 WW

◀ A terrestrial globe, by G. & J. Cary, with engraved brass meridian ring, early 19thC, on a later turned mahogany stand, globe 18in (45.5cm) diam.
£2,700–3,000 DN

A pocket terrestrial globe, by Abel/
Klinger, 1852, globe 3in (7.5cm) diam.
£1,400–1,600 S

A Felkl table terrestrial globe, brass
meridian and horizontal rings restored,
on an oak tripod stand, Prague,
late 19thC, globe 6in (15cm) diam.
£1,800–2,200 S

A French terrestrial globe, lacquered
brass latitude arc, on a cast-iron
stand, c1900, globe 7½in (19cm) diam.
£550–600 P

◄ A Dutch globe, on an ebonized wood stand, 19thC, 9½in (24cm) high.
£750–850 S(Am)

MEDICAL & DENTAL

A mahogany domestic
medicine chest, with a frieze
drawer over two cupboard
doors enclosing drawers,
19thC, 51in (129.5cm) wide.
£1,000–1,100 GAK

An American mahogany
apothecary cabinet, the
upper section with a pair
of glazed doors opening to
shelves, the lower section
with two frieze drawers over
a pair of panelled doors
opening to shelves, late
19thC, 32in (81.5cm) wide.
£1,000–1,100 SLN

A Victorian walnut medical
cabinet, with a roll-top
shutter and an arrangement
of 12 drawers, the base
fitted with a brushing slide
and single drawer above
a pair of panelled doors,
65¾in (167cm) high.
£1,500–1,800 RTo

A silver ear wax spoon and tweezers, from an *etui*,
c1750, 3in (7.5cm) long.
£150–165 BEX

A mahogany domestic
medicine chest, containing
17 glass bottles mostly
with square glass stoppers
and leatherette covers, the
drawer below containing a
large quantity of medical
apparatus and equipment,
19thC, 12¾in (32.5cm) wide.
£800–900 S

A silver-plated ear trumpet,
by R. C. Rein & Son,
London, with engraved
foliate decoration and
ivory earpiece, c1865,
4½in (11.5cm) high.
£800–1,000 Bon

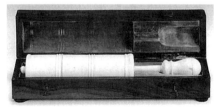

An ivory enema, in a plush lined fitted
mahogany case, 19thC, 15¼in (38.5cm) wide.
£875–1,000 S

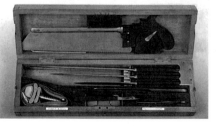

◄ A surgeon's
set, by Arnold
& Sons, with
ebony-handled
instruments,
in a fitted
mahogany case,
late 19thC, 16in
(40.5cm) wide.
£650–750 Bon

A set of chromed plated dental instruments, with chequered handles, by Maw, Weiss, J. Wood, O. Ash & Sons, in an oak box with ebony and boxwood stringing, late 19th/early 20thC, box 18in (45.5cm) wide.
£60–70 AP

A Victorian mahogany-cased 'Newly Invented Improved Magneto-Electric Machine for nervous diseases', 10in (25.5cm) wide.
£50–60 PFK

Miller's is a price GUIDE not a price LIST

A carved ivory phrenology head, with 37 numbered divisions showing localization of medical faculties, the key given below, base missing, mid-19thC, 3¼in (8.5cm) high.
£450–550 Bon

A pair of medical ceramic jars, decorated in pink and white and with transfer labels, minor damage, late 19thC, 11½in (29cm) high.
£230–275 S

A pair of German leather-framed eye glasses, contained in a later carved wood case, Nuremberg, 16thC, 3in (7.5cm) wide.
£3,700–4,200 S

▶ An 'Illustrated Physiological Manikin', by John Trigg, the wax-finished printed coloured card opening to reveal various parts of the human anatomy, depicting the muscle network, veins, arteries and the major organs, the inner pages unfold to reveal black and white numbered illustrations of parts of the anatomy, early 20thC, length of body 60½in (153.5cm).
£230–275 S

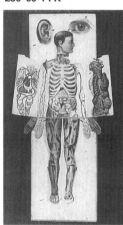

A pair of silver sun spectacles, in leather case, Birmingham 1822, 5in (12.5cm) wide.
£350–400 CHAP

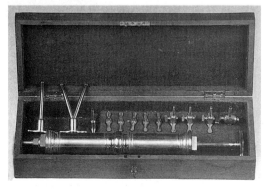

A lacquered brass mortician's syringe, by Laundy, with 12 graduated nozzle attachments, signed, c1810, in a mahogany case, 17in (43cm) wide.
£140–170 Bon

METEOROLOGICAL

A brass air meter, with aluminium vanes, main and subsidiary dials, c1900, 6in (15cm) diam, in a leather case.
£340–375 PHo

This was used for measuring the air-flow in a flue or ventilation shaft for a factory or mine. They were first issued to inspectors following the Factory Acts from 1842 which, among other things, regulated the amount of fresh air needed in mines or factories.

A Customs and Excise hydrometer, by Dring & Fage, c1890, in a fitted wooden case, 6in (15cm) wide.
£140–175 ETO

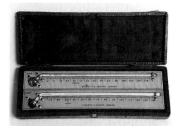

A pair of maximum and minimum boxwood thermometers, by Negretti & Zambra, c1880, in fitted case, 8in (20.5cm) wide.
£225–250 ETO

Insurance Values
Always insure your valuable antiques for the cost of replacing them with similar items, regardless of the original price paid. Both dealers and auctioneers will provide a valuation service for a fee.

MICROSCOPES

Buying optical instruments
Before buying a microscope or telescope, check that it is working properly. Ask the vendor to demonstrate it for you – if he is unable or unwilling to do so, think carefully before purchasing.

A Cuff-type microscope, by George Adams, with Ayscough stage, rack and pinion focusing, accessories including condenser lens, Lieberkühn, fish-plate, livecage, stage forceps, five objectives and five sliders, in mahogany case, c1780, 16¼in (41.5cm) high.
£2,750–3,000 KOLN

A lacquered brass microscope, by A. Ross, with rack focus, long-lever fine focus, square mechanical stage and mirror with many accessories, c1850, 18in (45.5cm) high, in a brass-bound mahogany case.
£2,500–3,000 Bon

A brass botanical microscope, by Cary, London, 19thC, 14in (35.5cm) high.
£500–600 Mit

A brass compound binocular microscope, by R. & J. Beck, with circular stage, rack and pinion focusing and micrometer screw, c1880, 13in (33in) high, in a wooden case with accessories.
£450–500 S

A brass and mahogany dissecting microscope, 1885, in mahogany box, 5½in (14cm) wide.
£350–380 PHo

A Victorian compound monocular microscope, slide drawer and slides, 14in (35.5cm) high, with original box.
£375–425 JeF

A binocular microscope, by Swift & Son, the brass binocular tubes with rackwork to adjust interocular distance and rack and pinion focusing, signed, late 19thC, 16½in (42cm) high.
£1,800–2,200 S

SURVEYING & DRAWING INSTRUMENTS

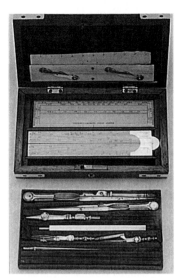

A presentation set of silver, steel and ivory drawing instruments, marked 'Watkins, Charing Cross, London', late 18thC, in a silver-mounted fruitwood box, 7½in (19cm) wide.
£600–675 P

Beware

Always check that all the items in a set of drawing instruments, especially the ivory rules, are original to the set. Later replacements can seriously affect the price.

A set of drawing instruments, in a rosewood case with brass and nickel inlay, comprising two tiers of instruments over a base tray containing four wooden rules, mid-19thC, 14¼in (36cm) wide.
£1,200–1,350 S

A folding boxwood inclinometer, with compass, 1880, 6in (15cm) long, in a fitted case.
£140–160 TOM

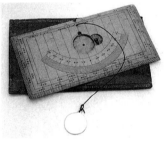

A 'Sandhurst' boxwood protractor, by Stanley, London, with brass plumb, c1900, 5½in (14cm) wide.
£120–150 TOM

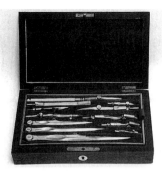

A drawing set, in a fitted wooden case, 1890, 8½in (21.5cm) wide.
£250–285 REG

A Customs and Excise brass-mounted boxwood six-fold measure, by Dring & Fage, engraved with 'Hogsheads, Barrels, Firkins, Pins and Gallons', 1883–1902, 48in (122cm) long.
£225–275 ETO

A late Victorian set of Marquois scales, by Stanford, London, 12in (30.5cm) long, in original mahogany box.
£80–90 JeF

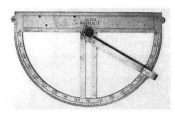

A Wilson brass protractor, with revolving radius arm, signed, 18thC, 9½in (24cm) wide.
£450–550 S

A brass rule, by Coggs, signed, mid-18thC, 24in (61cm) extended.
£450–550 S

► A brass theodolite, by Dollond, the telescope with rack and pinion focusing, vertical circle of degrees with vernier, in a mahogany case, 19thC, 5in (12.5cm) diam.
£1,750–2,000 Oli

A French brass Lenoir theodolite, with underslung trough compass and bubble level, centrally mounted telescope with vernier for inclined and declined readings, Paris, c1825, 8in (20.5cm) diam.
£2,000–2,400 S

◄ A French lacquered brass theodolite, with silvered compass rose and scales, telescope with rackwork focus, c1890, 12½in (32cm) high.
£550–600 PHo

TELESCOPES

An Italian hand-held rayskin horn and brass-mounted two-draw refracting telescope, late 18thC, 9in (23cm) extended.
£750–900 S

A mahogany and brass single draw five-lens telescope, by Dollond, c1760, 17½in (44.5cm) extended.
£270–300 TOM

A mahogany and brass hexagonal telescope, c1770, 31in (79cm) extended.
£500–550 PHo

A 4in (10cm) lacquered-brass reflecting telescope, by J. Dollond & Son, the 24in (61cm) long body tube with 10½in (26.5cm) finder, with two eyepiece tubes, a further eye lens, eyepiece caps, etc, mid-18thC, in a fitted felt-lined mahogany box.
£1,800–2,200 P

An Italian three-draw telescope, each of the inner tubes with paper covering, the outer tube with parchment cover stamped with a foliate design and maker's name 'Olivo, Venezia', late 18thC, 13in (33cm) long.
£1,000–1,200 S

A 3in (7.6cm) refracting telescope, by Dollond, with additional eye-piece and eye tube, rack and pinion focusing and lens cap, lens cracked, early 19thC, 43¾in (111cm) long.
£450–550 S

▶ A leather and brass telescope, early 20thC, 32in (81.5cm) extended.
£200–250 NC

WEIGHTS & MEASURES

A George III mahogany way-wiser, or hodometer, by F. Watkins, the engraved brass dial with Roman and Arabic numerals, measuring poles, furlongs and miles, 53in (134.5cm) high.
£900–1,100 HYD

A brass letter balance, mid-19thC, 5in (12.5cm) high.
£300–350 Bon

A French set of brass metric weights, 1890s, in a wooden case, 8in (20.5cm) wide.
£100–125 MSB

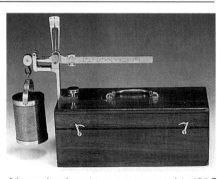

A brass chondrometer or corn measure, late 19thC, in fitted mahogany case, 12½in (32cm) long.
£350–400 S

In the United Kingdom the cereal crop was harvested by the bushel, a volumetric measure, but purchased by the grain dealers by weight. This apparatus, by taking random samples, converted the volume to weight.

A brass County of Kent yardstick, with original certification stamps for Queen Victoria, 1892, in original oak case.
£350–400 ETO

A Greek wooden reliquary casket, decorated in egg tempera and gold leaf, c1700, 8¾in (22cm) wide.
£6,750–7,500 RKa

A George III curled paper tea caddy, c1785, 7in (18cm) wide.
£2,300–2,750 S

A George III inlaid walnut box, opening to reveal a folding mirror, with one drawer under, 13½in (34.5cm) wide.
£170–200 E

A George III burr-yew, sycamore and tulipwood tea caddy, the front with an inlaid architectural view of a house façade, c1790, 8½in (21.5cm) wide.
£28,000–32,000 S

A George III satinwood tea caddy, with later cut-glass mixing bowl, c1790, 13¾in (35cm) wide.
£3,200–3,800 HAM

A French lacquer, tortoiseshell and cut-steel box, c1790, 3in (7.5cm) diam.
£2,500–2,750 SHa

▶ A Regency japanned sewing box, with fitted interior, on foliate-cast paw feet, 15in (38cm) wide.
£850–1,000 P

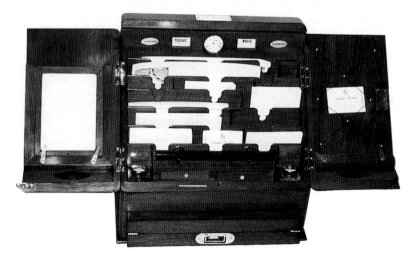

A Regency painted tea caddy,
c1817, 11½in (29cm) wide.
£5,500–6,000 S

A burr-maple and rosewood marquetry
box, c1830, 10in (25.5cm) wide.
£170–200 MB

A Regency inlaid rosewood and
mahogany four-division tea caddy,
10in (25.5cm) wide.
£2,500–2,750 OAS

A brass-inlaid rosewood tea caddy,
mixing bowl missing, mid-19thC,
12½in (32cm) wide.
£1,100–1,300 NOA

◀ A Victorian walnut writing box,
with brass and ebony banding,
secret drawers and writing slope,
c1850, 16in (40.5cm) wide.
£450–500 MB

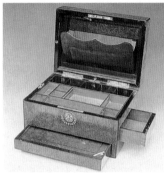

An inlaid yew-wood workbox, with
leather writing slope, the divided
interior with two yew-wood boxes,
above a drawer with two inkwells,
c1820, 12in (30.5cm) wide.
£575–700 S(S)

An early Victorian burr-walnut
combination needlework and writing
box, inlaid with mother-of-pearl,
sprung side drawer and base
drawer, 12¼in (31cm) wide.
£250–300 TMA

A walnut inkstand and copying press, by S. Mordan & Co, registered 1856, 11in (28cm) high.
£1,100–1,250 GeM

A porcupine quill and ebony box, 19thC, 11in (28cm) wide.
£220–250 TMi

A mother-of-pearl tea caddy, c1860, 8in (20.5cm) wide.
£850–950 CRU

A French boulle and brass-inlaid perfume box, the satin-lined interior with two bottles, 19thC, 4in (10cm) high.
£400–450 LBr

◄ An Edwardian oak smoker's box, with brass fittings, 12in (30.5cm) wide.
£200–235 MB

A Winsor & Newton mahogany artist's box, with lift-out trays and brass fittings, 19thC, 16in (40.5cm) wide.
£4,000–4,500 RBB

A Victorian lady's gilt-brass-mounted coromandel dressing case, fitted with silver-gilt topped jars, tools and fold-out trays, 15¼in (38.5cm) wide.
£3,500–4,200 CAG

An Italo-Cretan icon of the Mother of God, late 15thC, 11 x 9in (28 x 23cm).
£13,500–15,000 RKa

An eastern Mediterranean icon of The Presentation of Christ in the Temple, 16thC, 9 x 7¼in (23 x 18.5cm).
£9,000–11,000 S

An Italo-Cretan icon of the Virgin and Child, 16thC, 18½ x 21½in (47 x 54.5cm).
£9,000–10,000 S

A Russian icon of the Mother of God, with a silver riza, 18thC, 14 x 11¼in (35.5 x 28.5cm).
£2,400–2,700 RKa

A Russian icon of the Virgin and Child, the brass cover decorated with seed pearls and semi-precious stones, late 18thC, 12 x 10in (30.5 x 25.5cm).
£600–700 ICO

A Russian icon of St John the Evangelist, the gilded cover and body of the saint covered with padded textile decorated with glass beads, 19thC, 14 x 12¼in (35.5 x 31cm).
£2,200–2,500 JAA

A Russian icon of the Kazan Mother of God, 19thC, 10¾ x 9in (27.5 x 23cm).
£800–900 JAA

A shaped Russian icon of the Evangelist Mark, from an iconostasis panel, c1830, 22 x 13in (56 x 33cm).
£1,100–1,250 ICO

◀ A Russian icon of the All Seeing Eye of God, c1890, 12¼ x 10½in (31 x 26.5cm).
£1,100–1,300 JAA

▶ A Russian miniature icon of Christ Pantocrator, with silver and cloisonné enamel riza by Ovchinnikov, c1900, 4 x 3½in (10 x 9cm).
£1,500–1,650 ICO

A Greek icon of St Demetrius, 19thC, 14 x 9½in (35.5 x 24cm).
£1,400–1,600 RKa

A gilt-brass and enamel singing bird box, decorated with landscape scenes, c1925, 4in (10cm) wide.
£1,250–1,500 CAG

A Columbia oak coin-operated phonograph, type BS, with original backboard, c1900, 15in (38m) wide.
£1,200–1,500 HHO

A Capitol Mod. EA phonolamp, c1919, 18in (45.5cm) wide.
£2,500–3,000 KOLN

◄ A violin, by Hendrik Jacobs, Amsterdam, restored, late 17thC, 14in (35.5cm) long.
£8,000–9,000 P

An Italian harpsichord, in a painted wooden case, probably by Leopoldo Franciolini, late 19thC, 25¼in (64cm) wide.
£2,500–3,000 AH

An Erard Cuban mahogany square piano, with brass mouldings, restored, Paris, 1798, 68in (172.5cm) wide.
£11,200–12,500 PPC

A George III black lacquer and parcel-gilt piano, in Thomas Chippendale style, lacquer restored, late 18thC, 75¾in (192.5cm) wide.
£80,000–90,000 S(NY)

A Victorian burr-walnut upright piano, with fretted front and carved supports, c1860, 54in (137cm) wide.
£230–275 PEX

A Bechstein inlaid rosewood grand piano, c1897, 80in (203cm) wide.
£9,000–10,000 P(Ba)

An Ibach rosewood grand piano, Germany, 1906, 70in (178cm) wide.
£11,000–12,500 PPC

An Irish mahogany upright piano, by John Robert Woffington, with boxwood-strung and crossbanded case, 18thC, 37in (94cm) wide.
£6,500–7,500 P(Ba)

A Preiss Napoleon III-style ebonized and gilt upright piano, Paris, c1880, 53in (134.5cm) wide.
£14,500–16,000 PPC

A Steinway satinwood overstrung upright piano, the painted landscape panels signed by A. Blackmore, c1902, 56in (142cm) wide.
£8,500–10,000 P(Ba)

A Schiedmayer flame walnut square piano, with iron frame, restored, Stuttgart, c1850, 74in (188cm) wide.
£10,000–11,000 PPC

A Steinway painted satinwood grand piano, 1890s, 72in (183cm) wide.
£20,000–25,000 PEX

A Brinsmead grand piano, with floral-decorated case, c1905, 72in (183cm) wide.
£4,500–5,000 PEX

A mahogany-cased spinet, inscribed 'Wilson Whitby Fecit', mid-18thC, 48½in (123cm) wide.
£7,000–8,500 TEN

◄ A Steinway Model O satinwood, kingwood, marquetry and gilt-bronze-mounted grand piano, signed, c1908, 73in (185.5cm) wide.
£80,000–90,000 BB(S)

A portrait miniature of a young girl, by P. Benazzi, signed, 19thC, 2in (5cm) wide.
£700–800 RBB

An Irish portrait miniature of an officer, by Frederick Buck, Cork, c1800, 2¾in (7cm) high.
£700–850 SIL

A portrait miniature of Robert Bloomfield, by Henry Bone, the frame set with split pearls, the reverse glazed to reveal a lock of hair, signed, c1800, 2¾in (7cm) high, in original red leather travelling case.
£3,700–4,200 Bon

Robert Bloomfield (1766–1823), a shoemaker's apprentice and poet, was born in Suffolk. His works include *The Farmer's Boy*, *Rural Tales* and *Wild Flowers*.

A portrait miniature of a lady, by E. Corbould-Ellis, signed, early 20thC, 4¾in (12cm) high.
£500–600 P

A portrait miniature of Colonel Otto William Offeney, by George Engleheart, 1807, 3¾in (9.5cm) wide.
£8,000–9,500 S

A portrait miniature on ivory of a young lady, 19thC, 3in (7.5cm) high, in an ebonized frame.
£320–380 HYD

A French portrait miniature of the Comtesse d'Artois, by Pasquier, signed and dated '1778', 2½in (5cm) high.
£3,500–4,000 BHa

A portrait miniature of a gentleman, c1790, 3in (7.5cm) high.
£300–350 BLA

◄ A set of six watercolour silhouettes of a family, comprising two gentlemen, three ladies and a girl, 19thC, each 10 x 8in (25.5 x 20.5cm).
£350–450 CLE

A silhouette of Captain Peyton, wearing Naval uniform, by William Wellings, painted on card, signed and dated '1782', 9¾in (25cm) high.
£1,700–2,000 Bon

◀ An Egyptian white-glazed composition ushabti, with painted details, 19th Dynasty, circa 1200 BC, 4½in (11.5cm) high.
£500–600 HEL

An Egyptian bronze figure of a cat, Late Period, 716–30 BC, 6in (15cm) high.
£5,000–6,000 S(NY)

An Egyptian bronze and alabaster figure of an ibis, Late Period, 716–30 BC, 8½in (21.5cm) high.
£9,000–10,000 S(NY)

◀ An Egyptian turquoise glazed composition statuette of Thoth, Late Period, circa 600 BC, 5in (12.5cm) high.
£6,000–7,000 Bon

An Assyrian faïence vase, 8th/7th century BC, 4½in (11.5cm) high.
£5,000–6,000 S(NY)

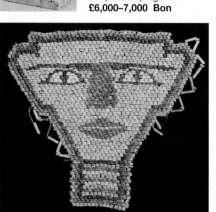

A Red Figure bell krater, Greek South Italy, circa 4th century BC, 11in (28cm) high.
£1,200–1,500 HEL

An Egyptian bead mummy mask, Late Period–Ptolemaic, circa 500–30 BC, 7½in (19cm) wide.
£1,800–2,200 Bon

An Italo-Corinthian oinochoe, with three registers of animals and birds, early 6th century BC, 14¾in (37.5cm) high.
£7,500–9,000 S(NY)

A Roman glass cup, with a loop handle, 1st/2nd century AD, 4¾in (12cm) high.
£4,500–5,500 S(NY)

An Apulian Red Figure volute krater, some restoration, Greek South Italy, circa 310–290 BC, 26¾in (68cm) high.
£2,000–2,400 Bon

A Cretan gold pectoral, decorated with mythological figures, circa 1500 BC, 7in (18cm) wide.
£1,800–2,200 Herm

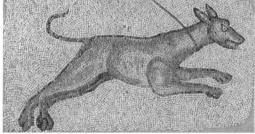

A Roman Imperial or Byzantine mosaic panel, 4th/5th century AD, 30 x 55½in (76 x 141cm).
£11,000–13,000 S(NY)

An Arapaho beaded cloth and hide papoose wrap, Native American, 32in (81.5cm) long.
£4,500–5,000 S(NY)

A Navajo Germantown fringed pictorial blanket, woven in commercial wool yarn, Native American, 36in (91.5cm) wide.
£6,000–7,000 S(NY)

An Idoma figure, Nigeria, West Africa, 31½in (80cm) high.
£7,000–8,000 Bon(C)

A Kwakiutl polychrome wood dance wand, attributed to Charlie James (1870–1938), Native American, 31in (78.5cm) high.
£5,000–6,000 S(NY)

A Northern Plains beaded octopus bag, Native American, late 19thC, 13in (33cm) long.
£1,400–1,600 SK

A Sarawak carved and polychrome mask, northern Borneo, 13½in (34.5cm) high.
£125–150 JAA

A Plains or Prairie Courting Flute, Native American, 25in (63.5cm) long.
£1,300–1,500 BB(S)

◄ A Navajo saddle blanket, Native American, 34in (86.5cm) wide.
£2,000–2,400 BB(S)

A twined spruce root basket, Native American, 19thC, 6½in (16.5cm) diam.
£350–400 HUR

► A Zulu figure, originally a staff top, South Africa, 9½in (24cm) high.
£750–900 Bon(C)

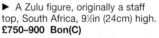

A Shona neckrest, stem repaired, southern Zimbabwe, Africa, 5¼in (13.5cm) high.
£950–1,100 Bon(C)

A Maprik hook figure, Abelam area, New Guinea, 47½in (120.5cm) high.
£1,800–2,200 S(NY)

◄ A Kula Valley painted face mask, northern India, late 19thC, 17¾in (45cm) high.
£1,400–1,600 GRG

Helen Allingham and M. B. Huish, *Happy England*, 1903, 4°, engraver's copy, inscribed by artist, one of 750 copies.
£700–800 HAM

A *Book of Hours,* Paris, c1510, 8°, printed on vellum, later brown morocco, gilt, some damage.
£4,750–5,250 BBA

Oscar Wilde, *The House of Pomegranates*, with 16 illustrations by Jessie M. King, published by Methuen and Co Ltd, 1915, 4°.
£250–300 DW

David Low, *The Breeds of the Domestic Animals of the British Isles*, 1842, 2 volumes, 2°.
£4,500–5,500 AG

Great blue Heron

John James Laforest Audubon, *Birds of America*, seven volumes, New York, 1856, 8°, half calf.
£3,300–4,000 AG

Robert Burns, *Poems*, 1781, first Edinburgh edition, chiefly in the Scottish dialect, 8°, for the author, specially bound in full violet levant morocco gilt, with miniature ivory portrait of Burns under glass.
£3,000–3,300 S

▶ A manuscript album, *The M.S. Annual MDCCCXLIX*, illustrated by N. J. Roosenboom and others, 1849, 4°, contemporary green morocco, gilt.
£900–1,100 RTo

I PLAY WITH THE TREES AND THE STARS AND THE SHADOWS AND THE MOONBEAMS

Marion, *Mummy's Bedtime Story Book*, with colour illustrations by Jessie M. King, 1929, 4°.
£1,750–2,000 BBA

▶ Elizabeth Twining, *Illustrations of the Natural Orders of Plants*, 1849–55, two volumes, 2°, half green morocco, gilt.
£16,000–18,000 L

An illuminated miniature on vellum, possibly from a *Book of Hours*, probably Italian, late 15thC, 5¾ x 4½in (14.5 x 11.5cm), mounted on paper.
£2,300–2,750 DW

William Morris, *The Defence of Guenevere and other Poems*, with illustrations by Jessie M. King, published by John Lane, 1904, 9½ x 8in (24 x 20.5cm).
£500–550 DAD

A wooden doll, in silk robe, replacement real hair wig, c1760, 16½in (42cm) high.
£9,000–11,000 S

A German flirty-eyed doll, c1910, 28in (71cm) high.
£700–775 AnS

A Fleischmann & Blaedel bisque-headed doll, with composition body, c1890, 23in (58.5cm) high.
£1,800–2,000 BGC

A Gaultier bisque-headed fashion doll, with shoulder plate and swivel head, 1880–85, 22in (56cm) high.
£1,500–1,650 BGC

A Hertel, Schwab & Co bisque-headed doll, with real hair wig, c1920, 20½in (52cm) high.
£220–250 KOLN

A Jumeau bisque swivel-headed portrait doll, on gusseted kid leather body, with bisque lower arms and fabric lower legs, 1870–75, 25in (63.5cm) high.
£4,000–4,500 S

A Jumeau bisque-headed doll, with open mouth and jointed composition body, c1890, 27in (68.5cm) high.
£900–1,000 BGC

A Kämmer & Reinhardt doll, with celluloid and kid leather body, 1925–30, 17in (43cm) high.
£300–350 DOL

A J. D. Kestner bisque-headed doll, with real hair wig, c1900, 33in (84cm) high.
£1,000–1,100 KOLN

An Armand Marseille 'Queen Louise' bisque-headed doll, with real hair wig, c1910, 24½in (62cm) high.
£200–240 KOLN

An Armand Marseille Oriental baby, with composition body, c1920, 12in (30.5cm) high.
£1,200–1,350 GrD

A Schoenau & Hoffmeister bisque-headed doll, with jointed wood and composition body, c1910, 24in (61cm) high.
£450–500 AnS

◄ An Armand Marseille bisque-headed doll, on a toddler body, incised 'A. M. 990', c1920, 19in (48.5cm) high.
£220–225 YC

◄ A Jules Nicholas Steiner porcelain-headed doll, with porcelain hands and jointed body, c1885, 21in (53.5cm) high.
£1,800–2,000 BGC

A Steiff mohair teddy bear, with button in ear, paws re-covered, c1907, 17in (43cm) high.
£3,000–3,500 TED

A Steiff mohair teddy bear, c1910, 30in (76cm) high.
£2,500–3,000 Bon(C)

A Merrythought teddy bear, 1940s, 23in (58.5cm) high.
£400–450 AnS

A Merrythought 'Cheeky' teddy bear, c1961, 26in (66cm) high.
£200–230 BOL

A Steiff plush teddy bear, with button in ear and growler box, early 20thC, 25in (63.5cm) high.
£8,000–9,000 CLE

A Steiff mohair teddy bear, c1950, 13¾in (35cm) high.
£250–300 KOLN

A Steiff teddy bear, with button in ear, 1920s, 18in (45.5cm) high.
£1,800–2,200 TED

A William J. Terry teddy bear, c1920, 19in (48.5cm) high.
£1,600–2,000 TED

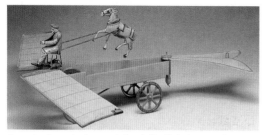

An aeroplane donkey cart, by J. Roullot, the wooden wagon drawn by a tinplate donkey, propelled by a pull-string mechanism, by releasing a latch on the wagon the cart is converted into a monoplane, c1911, 22in (56cm) long.
£3,700–4,000 S(NY)

A Chinese fruitwood boat, with two figures, both heads rise when wheels rotate, late 19thC, 9in (23cm) long.
£600–700 CRN

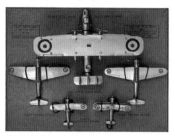

A Dinky Toys gift set No. 61, RAF Aeroplanes, in original box, 1937–41, box 7½in (19cm) wide.
£300–350 Bon(C)

A Bassett-Lowke gauge 0 spirit-fired 2⅛in scale Flying Scotsman locomotive, c1935, 20in (51cm) long, with tender.
£850–1,000 BKS

A Bassett-Lowke electric 4–6–2 Flying Scotsman locomotive and tender, c1952.
£1,000–1,100 S

A Bassett-Lowke clockwork gauge I Mogul 2–6–0 locomotive and tender, 1930s, 24in (61cm) long.
£680–750 BKS

A Bing clockwork gauge 0 LMS locomotive and tender, 1920, 14in (35.5cm) long.
£180–220 RAR

A Hornby coal wagon, 1930, 7in (18cm) long.
£120–150 HOB

A Hornby Eton locomotive and tender, with an electric motor, 1937–39, 15in (38cm) long.
£500–600 BKS

A Hornby closed axle goods wagon, c1938, 7in (18cm) long.
£1,000–1,200 HOB

A Hornby No. 4 Eton electric locomotive and tender, c1938, 13in (3cm) long.
£1,200–1,400 HOB

▶ A Hornby Dublo gauge 00 12v suburban loco-motive, and a trailing coach, 1962–64, each 9in (23cm) long, boxed.
£280–310 WaH

A Tipp & Co tinplate motorcycle with sidecar, c1935, 12in (30.5cm) long.
£10,000–11,000 KOLN

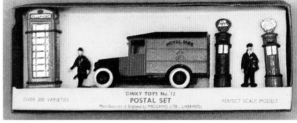

A Dinky Postal Set No. 12, pre-WWII.
£700–850 WAL

A Corgi Gift Set No. 23, Chipperfield's Circus, in orginal box, 1960s.
£380–420 WAL

A trade pack of six Dinky Motor Buses, pre-WWII, a in original box.
£1,800–2,200 WAL

A Gama tinplate tractor, No. 178, c1955, 8in (20.5cm) long.
£300–350 KOLN

A French automaton of a clown playing the violin, with papier mâché face and wooden torso, restored, c1890, 23in (58.5cm) high.
£2,000–2,400 Bon(C)

A Mickey Mouse clockwork organ grinder toy, probably by Distler, in original box, c1930, 7in (18cm) high.
£11,000–12,000 S

A G. & L. Lines wooden rocking horse, some restoration, late19th/early 20thC, 24in (106.5cm) long.
£1,600–1,750 CRU

A Scottish ivory chess set, c1870, king 3½in (9cm) high.
£2,500–3,000 TMi

A German painted wood Noah's Ark, containing 8 figures, 110 pairs and 36 single creatures, c1840, ark 22¾in (58cm) long.
£12,000–14,000 S

A Georgian-style doll's house, early 20thC, 38in (96.5cm) high.
£900–1,000 CLE

A boxwood and ebony chess set, c1900, king 4in (10cm) high.
£180–200 ALA

A French painted wood and metal child's tricycle, in the form of a galloping horse, with chain action powered by crank handles, 19thC, 25½in (65cm) high.
£700–850 CAG

EARLY TECHNOLOGY

Web: www.earlytech.com Email: michael.bennett-levy@virgin.net

Phone: 0131 665 5753 Fax: 0131 665 2839 Mobile: 0831 106768
Monkton House, Old Craighall, Musselburgh, Midlothian EH21 8SF
(Open any time day or night by appointment. 15 minutes from Edinburgh city centre)

WE BUY & SELL, EXPORT & IMPORT

Early Cameras, Cine Projectors and Photographs, Early Electricity Apparatus & Items, Early Television & Wireless, Early Items in Dentistry, Veterinary, Medical, Surgical, Radiology, Opticians & Pharmacy, Early Telephones & Telegraph, Barrel Organs & Mechanical Music, Gramophones, Phonographs, Early Juke Boxes & Rare "78s", Typewriters, Calculators & Early Office Equipment, Scientific Instruments & Nautical Items, Weights, Scales & Early Measuring Devices, Early Light Bulbs & Lighting, Physics & Chemistry Apparatus, Exceptional Tools & Drawing Instruments, Early Locks & Keys, Early Metalwork & Early Kitchen Items, Automata, Unusual Clocks & Barometers, Early Sewing Machines, Magic Lanterns & Optical Toys, Early Sporting Items, etc. + Early Books & Catalogues on Science & Technology . . . and of course "The Curious"

www.earlytech.com

Please visit our web site to see more of what we buy and sell. Please "Register your interest" on any category if you wish to be notified of new items on offer in a particular field. Then forget us!

Email: michael.bennett-levy@virgin.net

An American Adding Machine Company centigraph adding machine, patented by Arthur E. Shattuck, San Francisco, California, with five numbered finger keys and two-digit display, in original fruitwood carrying case, c1891, 8in (20.5cm) long.
£6,750–7,500 S

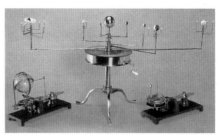

A George III lacquered brass drum-type orrery, with tellurium and lunarium attachments, by R. B. Bate, London, 18½in (47cm) high overall, in original mahogany box.
£35,000–40,000 DN

A French celestial globe, depicting stars and constellation figures, on an ebonized baluster column and base, polar ring missing, c1850, 22in (53cm) high.
£3,200–3,500 S

A set of French blue glass apothecary bottles, late 19thC, 8in (20.5cm) high.
£350–400 AL

A Sheraton-style flame-mahogany and inlaid dental cabinet, early 20thC, 72in (183cm) high.
£900–1,100 AAV

A brass binocular microscope, by Smith, Beck & Beck, London, 1866, 18in (45.5cm) high, in a Spanish mahogany case.
£1,400–1,600 TMA

A brass microscope, by Klönne & Müller, Berlin, holds eight different slides, with original wooden case, c1900.
£5,000–5,500 KOLN

A medical opium smoking set, by Gamble & Co, in a wooden box, c1880, 24in (61cm) long.
£400–450 HUM

A brass Society of Arts compound monocular microscope, by Apps, London, with all accessories, in a fitted mahogany case, c1880, 8in (20.5cm) wide.
£200–250 TOM

A brass theodolite, by W. & L. E. Gurley, Troys, New York, c1880, 15in (38cm) high.
£775–875 PHo

Beware!

Never attempt to polish an old scientific instrument without checking with an expert first, as the patina may be seriously damaged and the value reduced.

A shagreen-covered nécessaire, with a complete set of drawing instruments, 1810–20, 7in (18cm) long.
£1,200–1,350 CAT

◀ A brass protractor, fitted with clamp and slow motion screw, in original wooden case, late 19thC, 8in (20.5cm) wide.
£250–300 ETO

A rosewood and brass-mounted eight-day marine chronometer, by Barraud, London, early 19thC, dial 4½in (11.5cm) diam.
£7,000–8,500 DN

A shell-work valentine, the glazed case enclosing shells in geometrical patterns with a central star and flower form, probably West Indies, 19thC, 16in (40.5cm) wide.
£1,400–1,600 S

A Victorian sailor's woolwork picture, dated 'June 1859', in a mahogany frame, 27½in (70cm) wide.
£6,500–7,500 M&K

◀ A Danish 'telltale' compass, in the form of a crown, in a partially gilt and red-painted wood, marked 'Rasmus Koch', 1765, 18½in (47cm) high.
£2,500–3,000 BRH

▶ A ship's figurehead, carved in the form of a mermaid, painted in red, blue, navy and black, with a shield and coat of arms, dated '1877', 47¼in (120cm) high.
£2,500–3,000 BRH

A Chadburn's single lever ship's telegraph, 1920s, 42in (106.5cm) high.
£1,150–1,300 CRN

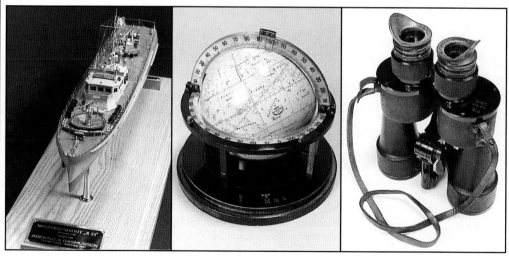

Scoops 1, science fiction, pre-publication promotional comic, 1934.
£280–320 CBP

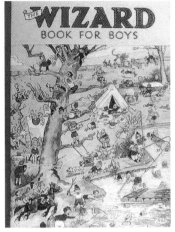

The Wizard Book For Boys, published by D. C. Thomson, 1935.
£35–40 WW

Marvel Comics No 1, published by Timely Publications, November 1939.
£12,500–15,000 S(NY)

Less than 50 copies of this comic are known to exist. This example has full margins for every page which is unusual, and is also in excellent condition.

W. D. & H. O. Wills, Cricketers, 35 of set of 50 cigarette cards, 1897.
£400–500 AAV

Daily Mail millennium newspaper, dated 'Jan 1st 2000', published for Ideal Home Exhibition, 1928.
£55–65 HAM

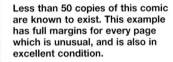

A poster, advertising *Les Magique Leons*, the Whirlwind Illusionist in the Palace of Mystery, c1910, 30 x 20in (76 x 51cm).
£70–85 DW

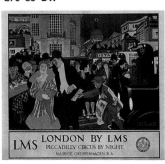

A lithograph, *Cachou Lajaunie*, printed in colours on woven paper, 1920, 58½ x 39in (148.5 x 99cm).
£800–950 BB(L)

◀ An LMS railway poster, 'Piccadilly Circus by Night', by Maurice Greffenhagen, 1926, 40¼ x 46in (102 x 117cm).
£5,000–6,000 ONS

An Irish film poster, *Willy Reilly and his Colleen Bawn*, 1920, 43¼ x 30in (110 x 76cm).
£600–700 WA

A poster, advertising Billy Smart's Circus, 1950s, 30¼ x 20¼in (77 x 54cm).
£50–60 DW

A north European cuirassier's armour, and a mortuary backsword, c1630.
Armour £13,000–15,000
Sword £2,250–2,500 WSA

A German partisan, with etched and gilt wrought-iron blade, dated '1718', 101½in (258cm) long.
£5,500–6,500 Herm

A Georgian midshipman's dirk, with double-edged blade, 11½in (29cm) long.
£250–275 GV

A William IV hunter's dirk, 17½in (44.5cm) long.
£2,500–3,000 CCB

A Scottish Gordon Highlanders silver-mounted officer's dirk, by Meyer & Mortimer, early 20thC, blade 12in (30.5cm), with *skean dhu*, and companion knife and fork.
£1,700–2,000 WAL

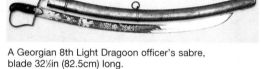

A Georgian 8th Light Dragoon officer's sabre, blade 32½in (82.5cm) long.
£1,600–1,800 WAL

A silver-hilted small-sword, mid-18thC, blade 32¼in (82cm) long.
£600–700 Bon

A brass-barrelled flintlock pistol, by Ralph Barass, c1720, 16in (40.5cm) long.
£2,000–2,250 WSA

A pair of German percussion pistols, converted from flintlocks, with walnut stocks and gilt-brass mounts, the triggers in the form of dolphins, c1830, 15¼in (38.5cm) long.
£1,300–1,500 Herm

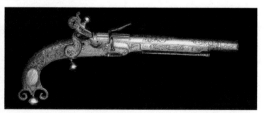

A pair of Scottish all-steel flintlock belt pistols, by Christy & Murdoch, c1770, 11½in (29cm) long.
£10,000–11,000 WAL

A pair of officer's flintlock pistols, by Cook, c1800, 15in (38cm) long.
£1,150–1,400 RBB

A pair of flintlock duelling pistols, by Henry Nock, London, in a fitted oak case, c1780, 17in (43cm) long.
£8,000–9,000 WSA

A 28-bore over-and-under tubelock pistol, by John Manton & Son, 1832, 11½in (29cm) long.
£15,000–17,000 Bon

A pair of percussion duelling/target pistols, by Joseph Lang, with original ramrods, 1821–74, 15in (38cm) long.
£2,300–2,650 GV

An Irish Duleek Volunteers officer's coatee, c1810.
£450–550 WAL

A moleskin top hat with original leather hatbox, c1835.
£15,000–18,000 Herm

By repute, this hat was given by the Duke of Wellington to the artist Andrew Morton, who painted at least four portraits of the Duke between 1835 and 1840.

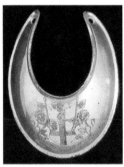

An Honourable East India Company officer's gilt-on-copper gorget, early 19thC, 6½in (16.5cm) wide.
£800–1,000 BOS

▶ A Royal Warwickshire officer's helmet plate, late 19thC.
£340–375 BOS

A Prince of Wales's Royal Lancers trooper's assembled full dress uniform, late 19thC.
£800–900 WAL

A Bavarian order of Military Merit, by Jacob Lesser of Munich, late 19thC.
£4,000–4,500 S

◀ A Victorian model brass cheese drum, 5in (12.5cm) diam.
£550–700 Q&C

◀ A Boer War DSO group of three medals, awarded to Major A. H. Tylden-Pattenson, East Kent Regiment.
£2,000–2,400 DNW

A group of five medals, awarded to Lieutenant Frederick Lord Wolverton, North Somerset Imperial Yeomanry, comprising Jubilee 1897, Delhi Durbar 1903, Coronation 1911, Queen's South Africa 1899–1902 and League of Mercy.
£650–750 DNW

A Qajar Order of the Lion and Sun silver neck badge, c1900.
£300–350 Bon

A German infantry officer's tombak gorget, 1760–80, 6¼in (16cm) wide.
£1,000–1,200 Herm

A Grenadier Guards officer's gilt rectangular shoulder belt plate, c1820.
£1,800–2,200 WAL

A 96th Foot officer's shoulder belt plate, pre-1855.
£650–750 BOS

A silver cigar lighter, in the form of a scale model of a nine-pounder field gun and limber, by W. Gibson & J. Langman, London 1893, 12in (30.5cm) long overall.
£24,000–27,000 B&L

An Allied Artists poster,
The Babe Ruth Story, 1948,
81 x 41in (205.5 x 104cm).
£750–900 S(NY)

A Columbia poster, *Safe At Home*,
1962, 22 x 28in (56 x 71cm).
£1,250–1,500 S(NY)

A Victorian mahogany snooker table, by
Thurston & Co London, 144in (366cm) long.
£1,450–1,750 TAM

A mahogany, rosewood, satinwood, ebony and ivory-
inlaid billiard table, by Brunswick, Balke-Collender
Company, c1900, 110in (279.5cm) long.
£22,000–25,000 BB(S)

A Staffordshire pottery
group of the pugilists John
Henan and Tom Sayers,
c1860, 9in (23cm) high.
£1,300–1,500 DN

**Ex-Rev. Harry
Bloomfield Collection.**

A pool scoreboard, by J. Ashcroft, Liverpool,
c1900, 38in (96.5cm) wide.
£900–1,000 CBC

A European ceramic figure
of a cricketer, c1900,
10in (25.5cm) high.
£270–300 BRT

A stuffed and mounted pike,
inscribed 'The Holywell Pike',
1876, 47½in (120.5cm) wide.
£1,450–1,750 CGC

A stuffed and mounted bream, inscribed
'August 1899', 29in (73.5cm) wide.
£750–900 CGC

An American green Bakelite
fishing-guide barometer, by
Taylor Instrument Company,
c1940, 3½in (9cm) diam.
£100–125 RTW

▶ A stuffed and
mounted jack
perch and jack
pike, early 20thC,
51in (129cm) wide.
£70–80 AXT

A Jardine's Improved Patent Pike Gag, with turning rosewood handle and brass jaws, c1895, 9½in (24cm) long.
£600–700 OTB

An Allcock Ariel 3¾in trotting reel, in fitted leather case,
with original outer card box and instructions, c1960.
£120–150 OTB

Two silvered-bronze figures of footballers, believed to be G. O. Smith and C. B. Fry, c1940, 9¾in (25cm) high.
£800–950 HAM

A framed lithograph, 'Famous English Football Players', issued with *Boys Own Magazine*, 1881, 10 x 15in (25.5 x 38cm).
£230–275 BKS

An official Football Association pennant, inscribed 'England v Uruguay Montevideo 1953', 13 x 18in (33 x 45.5cm).
£1,800–2,200 BKS

An autographed 1966 World Cup display, including the autographs of Sir Alf Ramsey and the eleven England finalists, 26 x 33in (66 x 84cm).
£3,000–3,500 S

◄ A colour lithograph poster, by Guillermo Laborde, the official poster of the 1930 World Cup, 31 x 15in (78.5 x 38cm).
£14,000–16,000 S

A Goudey Gum ice hockey card, depicting Eddie Shore, Sports King series, 1933.
£180–200 HALL

A single sculls rowing trophy, c1900, 7in (18cm) high.
£1,800–2,000 SMAM

A Northern Rugby Football League winner's gold and enamel medal, awarded to J. Sullivan of Wigan FC, 1925–26.
£750–900 S

A Prince Albert's steel and ivory deer-stalking knife, by Brown & Son, Newcastle-on-Tyne, 1850, 7in (18cm) long, in a red leather case.
£3,000–3,300 S

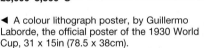

An Edwardian tennis racquet and ball letter-clip, on a wooden base, 8in (20.5cm) wide.
£125–150 TMA

A Staffordshire porcelain hunting/shooting tankard, 19thC, 4in (10cm) high.
£120–145 CoCo

► A pair of French bisque figures of tennis players, c1900, 17in (43cm) high.
£1,800–2,000 BRT

An *Eagle* and *Girl* table tennis set, 1950s.
£55–65 CBP

Marine

CANNONS

A late Victorian 1¾in (4.5cm) bore brass signalling cannon, with two-stage barrel, on a painted wooden carriage with brass mounts and wooden wheels, barrel 28¾in (73cm) long.
£1,600–1,800 WAL

This type of signalling cannon was much used by Victorian yacht clubs, especially after Queen Victoria and Prince Albert started visiting the Isle of Wight with their children in the 1850s.

A bronze multi-stage barrelled signal cannon, with ringed muzzle, the centre reinforced, engraved 'W. Pitt', mounted on an iron carriage, early 19thC, 17¾in (45cm) long.
£800–1,000 Gle

A 5in (12.5cm) bore bronze Royal mortar, the three-stage barrel with ringed muzzle, engraved with a crown over GR cypher and signed 'Cornelius King, 1822', on a later trunnion mounting.
£4,000–4,500 Gle

▶ A 1¼in (3cm) bore iron saluting cannon barrel, early 19thC, 20½in (51cm) long.
£370–420 WAL

CHRONOMETERS & TIMEKEEPERS

A brass-framed sandglass, probably French, mid-18thC, 7¼in (18.5cm) high.
£2,750–3,000 S

A Swiss lever 30-hour deck watch, by Zenith, with club foot lever escapement, in a circular brass deck case lined with dark blue velvet, c1920, 20in (51cm) diam.
£425–475 PT

A naval hourglass, supported on turned and lacquered brass pillars, with a leather disc stamped 'Sevastopol 1855' on each bulb, on a wooden base, 14¼in (36cm) high.
£5,000–6,000 Bon

During the Crimean War the city of Sebastopol was besieged by the Allies. When it finally fell in 1855 the Russians sued for peace. Ships of the Royal Navy assisted in the bombardment, and a Naval Brigade assisted the British Army. This hourglass would not have been used for serious timekeeping on board (the marine chronometer had long been introduced) and it was more likely a wardroom souvenir.

A two-day marine chronometer, by Cameron, Liverpool, the inside of the lid set with a signed ivory mercury thermometer, 19thC, in a rosewood box, 7in (18cm) wide.
£1,250–1,500 P

A chronometer, by Jno. Heron, Greenock, c1830, dial 4¼in (11cm) diam, in a brass-bound mahogany box.
£2,000–2,200 Mit

The design of this eight-day movement is unusual as it follows the standard two-day pattern with the addition of an extra wheel in the train. In order to achieve this, the train has a reverse fusee.

▶ A two-day marine chronometer, by Thomas Mercer, St Albans, the spotted movement with an Earnshaw spring detent escapement, c1945, bezel 4¾in (12cm) diam, in a mahogany box.
£500–600 Bon

MODEL SHIPS

A prisoner-of-war bone model of a three-masted 28-gun man-o'-war, damaged, early 19thC, 14in (35.5cm) long.
£750–900 RBB

A bone model of a 76-gun man-o'-war, with carved figurehead, on a chequer-inlaid wood plinth, 19thC, 9¾in (25cm) long.
£3,500–4,000 BB(S)

An American model of the schooner *Traviata*, c1875, 100½in (255.5cm) long.
£6,000–7,000 SK(B)

A builder's wooden half model of the paddle steamer *Cambra*, painted black with cream foliate decoration to the waterline, and copper below, on a mahogany backboard, mid-19thC, 82¾in (210cm) long.
£1,100–1,200 P

Half models of paddle-steamers are becoming increasingly rare.

A wooden diorama, depicting a merchant brig lying to anchor off a fort, the models carved from solid, the brig painted black to the waterline, with a painted backdrop and mirrored ends, in an ornate moulded frame, late 19thC, 26in (66cm) wide.
£650–750 P

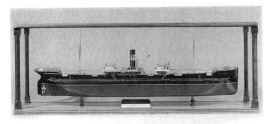

A builder's model of the turret deck ship *Dunbarmoor*, the hull of solid timber, painted dark red below the waterline and polished black above, early 20thC, in a glass case, 50½in (128.5cm) long.
£7,000–8,000 P

A model of the torpedo boat HMS *Maori*, c1910, 25in (63.5cm) long.
£1,500–1,800 G(L)

A carved pine pond yacht, finished in white, malachite underbody, with brass and nickel-plated fittings and silk sails, early 20thC, 71in (180cm) long.
£2,000–2,200 Bon

A scale model of a wooden pond yacht, with cream and white painted hull, dated '1954', 32in (81.5cm) long, on a wooden display stand with simulated sea.
£500–550 DN

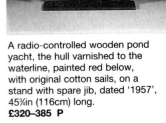

A radio-controlled wooden pond yacht, the hull varnished to the waterline, painted red below, with original cotton sails, on a stand with spare jib, dated '1957', 45¾in (116cm) long.
£320–385 P

NAUTICAL HANDICRAFTS

A sailor's woolwork picture of HMS *Northumberland*, worked with coloured wool, with Union flags and Cross of St. George in the background, 19thC, 15¾ x 24¾in (40 x 63cm).
£400–500 Bea(E)

A Victorian sailor's woolwork picture of the fully rigged ship *Sea Gull*, 18½ x 26¾in (47 x 68cm).
£850–1,000 M&K

A Victorian sailor's woolwork commemorative ship picture, depicting the Queen's Birthday Review of the Fleet off the Nore, the ships dressed with brightly coloured flags and detailed in bullion thread, incised on a crowned scarlet banner 'Majesty's birthday 1854', 26 x 34¾in (66 x 88.5cm).
£7,500–8,500 M&K

► A set of American scrimshaw whalebone busks or corset stays, c1880, 14in (35.5cm) long.
£1,200–1,400 LHAr

► A sailor's wool-work picture of the frigate *Star of India*, late 19thC, late 19thC, 17¾in x 23½in (45 x 59.5cm), framed and glazed.
£4,000–4,500 S(S)

A sailor's shell-work valentine, 'Home Again', 19thC, 9in (23cm) wide.
£2,000–2,200 SK(B)

A scrimshaw walrus tusk, decorated with two eagles, a lady, a native American and a vulture, age cracks, 19thC, 19in (48.5cm) long.
£1,200–1,400 SK(B)

NAVIGATIONAL INSTRUMENTS

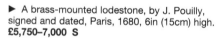

► A brass-mounted lodestone, by J. Pouilly, signed and dated, Paris, 1680, 6in (15cm) high.
£5,750–7,000 S

The lodestone is a piece of naturally-occurring magnetite, first discovered by the Ancient Chinese who used it to magnetize slivers of iron. These were then floated in a straw on a bowl of water and became the first mariner's compass. The idea was brought to Europe by the 10thC by Arabian sailors. The lodestone, used to 'refresh' the compass needle by stroking it, was therefore just as important as the compass itself, but few survive nowadays, unlike the compass.

A deviatometer, by Henry Hughes & Sons, the silvered compass marked for ship's head easterly and westerly deviation, c1890, 8¼in (21cm) diam, in a mahogany case.
£400–450 Bon

► A Danish gilt-metal telltale compass, rose marked 'Peder Nielsen Brenöe, Copenhagen', mid-18thC, 8¼in (21cm) high.
£1,800–2,200 BRH

This was known as a telltale compass because it hung in the captain's private quarters so that he could keep a discreet eye on the ship's course while he was not on the bridge.

► An octant, by Spencer, Barrett & Co, London, with 11in (28cm) radius, in original box, c1830.
£1,300–1,450 JeF

A Turkish wooden astrolabe-quadrant, signed by Ibrahim, painted in black, red and gilt, inscribed with operational instructions, 19thC, 5¾ x 6¼in (14.5 x 16cm).
£1,300–1,500 Bon

◄ An Edwardian nautical rolling ruler and dividers, by G. Lee & Son, Portsmouth, in a mahogany case, 19in (48.5cm) wide.
£165–185 GLO

A brass sector, by John Allen, each side engraved with scales with a logarithmic scale along one edge, signed, 1630–40, 7½in (19cm) wide closed.
£1,600–2,000 Bon

John Allen (fl. 1630–42) was apprenticed to his father Elias Allen, a pre-eminent instrument maker in London, and is recorded as working near the Savoy, London from 1630 to 1631.

A brass double frame sextant, by Troughton & Simms, London, signed, early 19thC, with 8¼in (21cm) radius index arm, in a mahogany case, with accesssories.
£900–1,100 Bon

► A lattice-framed brass sextant, by Elliott Brothers, London, with silver scales and rosewood handle, c1870, in a mahogany case, 13in (33cm) wide.
£675–750 ETO

SHIPS' FITTINGS

A bronze bell, from the Kriegsmarine Cruiser *Emden*, with cast laurel wreath detail around the rim, cracked, 1925, 17¾in (45cm) diam.
£2,000–2,400 P

A bronze bell from HMS *Echo*, clapper missing, 1934, 12½in (32cm) diam.
£850–1,000 M&K

A warship rum barrel, the stave construction with brass bands and brass motto 'The Queen God Bless Her', 19thC, 26in (66cm) high.
£750–850 DuM

A wooden ship's figurehead, in the form of a lady, with painted decoration, bearing an inscription plate inscribed 'The Figurehead of the Californian Clipper Emigrant Ship 'SAVANNAH', Built by Donald McCay of Boston, Sunk in Collision in Southampton Docks in 1849', unrestored, 65in (165cm) high.
£3,000–3,500 P

A brass-mounted oak ship's wheel, early 19thC, 48½in (123cm) diam.
£900–1,100 Bea(E)

LOCATE THE SOURCE

The source of each illustration in Miller's can be found by checking the code letters below each caption with the Key to Illustrations, pages 789–795.

◄ A copper 'Meteorite' ship's masthead light, Birmingham, c1890, 26in (66cm) high.
£275–350 CRN

MISCELLANEOUS

A fisherman's aneroid barometer, by Negretti & Zambra, London, issued by the Royal National Lifeboat Institution, in a cast-iron case, c1890, with 5in (12.5cm) enamel dial.
£120–150 KB

A Japanese silver cigarette box, the lid with a bronzed scene inlaid with gold and silver of a peacock and peahen, presented to Commander I. J. Hayes of HMS *Orvieto* by HIH Prince Yorohito of Hagashi Fushimi, together with ship's cap-band and itinerary, 1918, 7in (18cm) wide.
£8,000–9,500 BWe

A naval bicorn hat, a pair of epaulettes by Gieve & Sons, and two naval sword belts, early 20thC, in a red velvet-lined tin box.
£200–220 DN(H)

An oak launch casket, for HMS *Fidget*, comprising a carved oak mallet and bronze chisel with steel tip, the lid set with a glazed watercolour of the ship and an inscription, 1872, 13½in (34cm) wide.
£800–1,000 P

A silver-plated ship's dining room electric lamp, 1950s, 14in (35.5cm) high.
£180–200 CRN

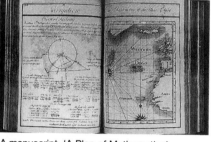

A manuscript, 'A Plan of Mathematical Learning Taught in the Royal Academy, Portsmouth, Performed by W. Hull', 555 pages, with full-page watercolour drawings, numerous maps and diagrams to text and one folding chart of the Atlantic Ocean, contemporary navy morocco gilt, rebacked, preserving original spine, 1807, 2°.
£2,800–3,200 DW

Insurance Values

Always insure your valuable antiques for the cost of replacing them with similar items, regardless of the original price paid. Both dealers and auctioneers will provide a valuation service for a fee.

A silver and leather presentation spy glass, with engraved inscription, dated 'November 1861', 24½in (62cm) long, in a fitted wooden case.
£1,300–1,500 SK(B)

A diver's torch, by Siebe Gorman, 1940s, 13in (33cm) long.
£80–90 CRN

► A gilt-bronze *Carpathia* and *Titanic* medal, with the *Carpathia* steaming between icebergs, reverse inscribed 'Presented to the Captain, Officers and Crew of RMS *Carpathia* in Recognition of Gallant and Heroic Services from the Survivors of the SS *Titanic* April 1912'.
£1,250–1,500 P

The 711 survivors were picked up by the *Carpathia*, whose officers and men were subsequently awarded this medal in gold, silver and bronze according to the rank of the recipient.

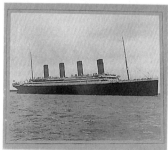

A framed photograph of SS *Titanic*, by Beken of Cowes, 1912, 15½ x 19½in (39.5 x 49.5cm).
£35–42 TRM

◄ A George III silver bosun's whistle, by Charles Rawlings, London 1818, 6in (15cm) long.
£1,100–1,250 BEX

Cameras

A British Ferrotype Co Telephot button tintype camera, with developing tank, c1910, 9¾in (25cm) long.
£500–600 APC

This 'Photo-while-you-wait' camera was popular with beach photographers.

An ERAC Selling Co Mercury 1 pistol camera, the black Bakelite body housing a 16mm miniature camera, with original box and instructions, c1938.
£220–280 APC

A Kodak stereo Hawkeye camera, with leather-covered wooden body, c1905.
£200–250 APC

A Leica I camera, with Leitz Elmar 3.5cm f3.5 lens, a Leitz Elmar 9cm f4 lens, a chrome VIDOM, a Leitz Elmar 5cm f3.5 lens, and a Leica screw-fit Taylor Hobson Anastigmat 2in f2 lens, c1931.
£900–1,000 S

An Ensign Focal Plane camera, with Carl Zeiss Jena Tessar 13.5cm f4.5 lens, c1914.
£300–350 JoW

An Ensign Midget Silver Jubilee camera, 1935, 2¾in (7cm) wide.
£100–120 APC

A special edition silver finish for the King and Queen's jubilee.

A KGB camera, with clockwork winding mechanism and a special grip release, built into a lady's evening bag, with lens opening cut into the side, c1960.
£16,000–18,000 RM

The photograph is taken by the carrier squeezing the bag and activating the shutter release.

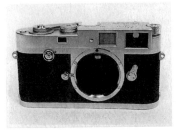

A Leica M2 camera body, c1958.
£450–500 VCL

An Ensign Cupid camera, with simple meniscus f11 lens, 1922.
£60–65 JoW

The first camera to take 16 exposures on 120 roll film.

An Ihagee Exakta B SLR camera, with waist-level viewfinder, with Exaktar 7.5cm f3.5 lens, 1935.
£200–220 JoW

A Kodak Petite vest-pocket camera, the enamelled body covered with fabric, original green bellows, c1930, 5in (12.5cm) long.
£140–160 APC

An Ernst Leitz Leica 111c 35mm camera, with Elmar 5cm f3.5 lens, c1941, with case.
£300–350 APC

A Moy & Bastie 35mm hand-crank motion-picture camera, with Ross 8x5 rapid symmetrical lens, in a mahogany and brass-bound case, c1909.
£900–1,000 DN

A W. W. Rouch full-plate mahogany and brass tailboard-style wet-plate camera, with Ross petzval lens, c1870.
£450–500 APC

▶ A Talbot & Eamer Talmer Detective or Hand camera, with mahogany body, canvas and wood bag changer and two metal plate holders, c1890.
£500–550 S

A Suzuki Camera-Lite, c1950.
£1,650–1,800 RM

The Camera-Lite combined a Zippo-style cigarette lighter with a 16mm subminiature camera and aimed primarily at the American GIs stationed in Tokyo. The popularity of the camera soared when it was seen being used in the 1950s comedy romance *Roman Holiday* starring Gregory Peck and Audrey Hepburn.

A Perken, Son & Rayment full-plate mahogany tailboard camera, with brass barrel Rapid Rectilinear 9x7 Optimius lens and a set of six Waterhouse stops from f8–f44, in a leather Optimus case, late 1880s.
£120–140 Bon

A Sanderson ¼-plate Tropical hand and stand camera, the polished teak body with brass fittings, with a Goertz Dagor f6.8 lens, 1890–1905.
£450–550 P(WM)

Further Reading
Miller's Collectables Price Guide, Miller's Publications, 2000–2001

A mahogany and brass ½-plate field camera, with Ross lens with Waterhouse stops, Thornton Pickard push-on shutter and three photographic plates, c1895.
£200–250 APC

A mahogany and brass Photo-Hall Folding Perfect camera, the polished wood body with brass fittings, with a Krauss AnastZeiss 136mm f8 lens, c1905.
£350–400 S

A Sanderson mahogany and brass ½-plate field camera, with Thornton Pickard shutter and Ross lens, c1910.
£250–300 APC

A Teddy Camera Co Model A metal box camera, painted red and gold, for 8x5 direct positive prints developed in the tank below the camera, tank missing, c1924.
£320–400 APC

A Zeiss Ikon Tropen Adoro Model 230/5 teak bodied camera, with Dominar lens, original plates and leather cases, c1931.
£350–400 APC

Optical Devices & Viewers

A Rowsells-style stereo graphoscope, c1875, 15¾in (40cm) long.
£300–360 APC

An Ernst Planck Standard child's gunmetal magic lantern, with slides, Germany, c1900, 10¼in (26cm) wide, with box.
£100–120 APC

A metal and brass magic lantern, professionally converted to electricity, with triple extension brass lens, chimney and slide carrier, c1910, 17¾in (45cm) long.
£160–200 APC

A French walnut table-top stereoscopic viewer, the box containing slides and cards of European scenes changed by turning the mahogany knobs, 19thC, 17¼in (44cm) high.
£800–1,000 S

A kaleidoscope, mid-19thC, 12¼in (31cm) high.
£400–450 Bon

An alabaster Peep Egg, with floral transfer decoration to the outside and three lithograph views on a rotating spindle inside, marked 'From the Crystal Palace', c1855, 6in (15cm) high.
£100–120 APC

A Smith, Beck & Beck Achromatic stereo viewer, with walnut veneer body and brass fittings, in a matching box which doubles as the base, c1865, 9¾in (25cm) wide.
£500–600 APC

A Bing child's gunmetal magic lantern, with slides, Germany, c1900, 13¾in (35cm) wide, with box.
£100–120 APC

A pair of Negretti & Zambra opera glasses with matching case, c1900, 5in (12.5cm) wide.
£240–270 JIL

A mahogany zograscope, used for viewing engravings and photographs, c1820, 28in (71cm) high.
£500–550 ETO

Arms & Armour

Collecting arms, armour and militaria can be approached from various starting points such as aesthetic, historic or romantic and provides a feast of interest for all pockets.

The aesthetic appeal lies in the appreciation of the skills employed in the manufacture of the items, particularly with finer pieces. A large variety of materials was used – wood, iron, non-ferrous and precious metals, even precious and semi-precious stones – all worked by craftsmen specializing in their particular field.

The historic aspect covers all items related to the military and the Navy, including weapons, armour, uniform, medals, badges and all the other accoutrements pertaining to the service-man. Many collectors choose to concentrate on a particular subject or date, the English Civil War and Napoleonic periods being especially popular. However, because of the increasing scarcity of good material from the early campaigns, late 19th- and early 20th-century items are now keenly sought after.

Under the heading romantic can be placed duelling pistols and coaching-related items. Most gentlemen in mid-Georgian times would have possessed a case of duelling pistols, and the idea of being 'called out' for something as trivial as treading on a lady's dress or to be thought to be holding her too closely while dancing, conjures up an evocative picture of the social morals of the period. A good pair of pistols in their original case, complete with the accessories required for loading and cleaning, is a very desirable item, and it was the development of such a specialized weapon by the great London gun-makers of the day – Wogdon, Twigg, Egg, Manton etc – that brought the flintlock mechanism to its ultimate perfection.

Coaching, as depicted in many prints and Christmas cards, reminds us that travelling in those days was a hazardous undertaking – highway robbery was rife and the coachman or postilion needed to be armed, usually with a blunderbuss and a brace of pistols. Arms carried by mail coaches were invariably marked with the route number and the words 'For His (Her) Majesty's Mail Coaches' in the thickness of the muzzles.

Collecting antique arms and militaria has grown strongly in recent years, creating a supply and demand situation that is relentlessly forcing prices upwards. Although there are still affordable items available, remember that quality, condition and authenticity are of paramount importance. **John Spooner**

ARMOUR

◀ A south German half suit of armour, c1580.
£6,000–7,000 Herm

A cabasset, formed in one piece and struck with crowned armourer's mark, brass rivets embossed with geometric ornament, c1600.
£300–350 WAL

A German heavy iron chainmail shirt, 16thC.
£3,700–4,000 Herm

A 15thC-style suit of armour, probably by Schmidt Workshops, 19thC.
£3,750–4,500 SK

A trooper's zischägge, German or Dutch, mid-17thC, 9½in (24cm) high.
£1,000–1,100 S(S)

A north Italian 'Spanish' Morion helmet, c1580, 11½in (29cm) high.
£4,500–5,000 CCB

A gorget, 17thC, 11½in (29cm) high.
£900–1,000 CCB

AXES & HALBERDS

A German halberd, with later shaft, c1500,
85in (216cm) long.
£1,600–2,000 Herm

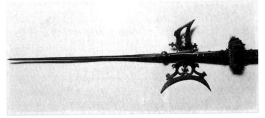

A Dutch parade halberd, c1580, 97in (246.5cm) long.
£900–1,000 WSA

▶ A German spontoon, richly engraved and with gilding,
the blade engraved with a saint, probably from Trier,
Mainz or Cologne, 18thC, 76¾in (195cm) long.
£850–1,000 Herm

An Indian Muslim steel
axe, with a cartouche of
Arabic above elephants,
19thC, 21¼in (54cm) long.
£140–170 WAL

Miller's is a price GUIDE
not a price LIST

EDGED WEAPONS

A Georgian 'figure of eight' pattern naval cutlass, 1804, 34in (86.5cm) long.
£450–500 WSA

A George III Scottish dirk, 19½in (49.5cm) long.
£2,700–3,000 CCB

A Scottish brass-mounted dirk, with a plain blade,
the pommel mounted with a cut crystal, the leather-
covered scabbard with companion knife and fork,
late 19thC, blade 13in (33cm) long.
£300–350 GV

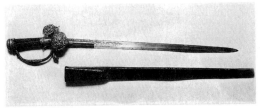

A German hunting hangar, with combined flintlock pistol,
c1730, 27in (68.5cm) long.
£2,750–3,000 WSA

A silver-mounted military
dirk, with tapering fullered
blade etched on one side
with the figure of Victory and
a garter star, the reverse with
a trophy of arms, the royal
arms and a cavalryman,
with reeded ivory grip,
marked for Birmingham
1798, 22½in (57cm) long.
£650–750 Bon

A bowie knife, the straight
single-edged blade
stamped 'Jackson & Co,
Sheaf Island Works,
Sheffield', with nickel-
mounted grip and leather
sheath, mid-19thC,
blade 8½in (21.5cm) long.
£1,200–1,400 S(S)

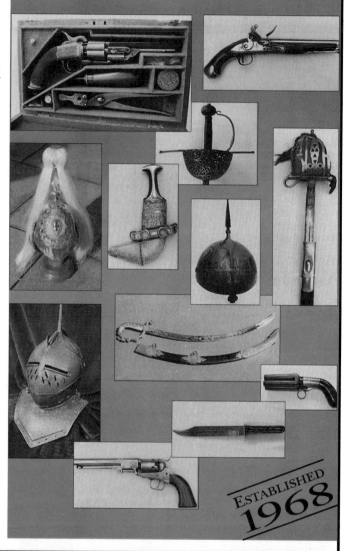

723

A Russian silver and niello *quama*, 19thC, 19½in (49.5cm) long.
£2,000–2,250 CCB

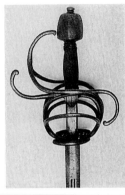

A skean dhu, c1880, 7½in (19cm) long.
£300–350 BLA

A Russian infantry hangar, with slightly curved single-edged blade and brass stirrup hilt, late 18th/early 19thC, blade 21¼in (54cm) long.
£125–150 S(S)

▶ A German swept hilt rapier, the blade with twin fullers for almost its entire length, the steel hilt with faceted pommel, wire-bound grip with 'Turks' heads', signed 'Fedrico Picinino', c1600, blade 46in (117cm) long.
£1,350–1,500 Gle

An infantry hangar, by Shotley Bridge Factory, with slightly curved single-edged blade, iron hilt and cast-brass grip in imitation bound wire and riband, marked with running fox and 'S. H.' inside, mid-18thC, blade 25¼in (64cm) long.
£400–450 S(S)

A rapier, the flattened diamond-section blade with short central fullers, steel hilt with traces of gilding, with spirally fluted wood grip, slight damage, c1630, blade 36½in (92.5cm) long.
£2,000–2,400 Gle

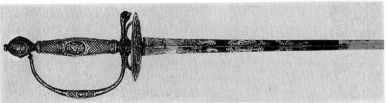

A cavalier's rapier, the blade gilded and etched with tendrils, trophies and a male bust, Paris inspection marks, 1781–89, blade 38½in (98cm) long.
£1,000–1,200 Herm

A Russian niello *shaska*, early 19thC, 42in (106.5cm) long.
£2,000–2,300 CCB

An officer's mameluke sabre, with clipped back blade, ivory grip secured by two brass rosettes, with steel scabbard, c1825, blade 32½in (82.5cm) long.
£400–450 WAL

A swept hilt rapier, probably Saxon, c1580, 38¼in (97cm) long.
£3,200–3,500 Herm

▶ A German sword, the pommel in the form of an open flower, early 16thC, 45in (114.5cm) long.
£2,750–3,000 Herm

◀ A late George III naval spadroon, by Cullum, the brass hilt with gilt ivory grip, with leather and gilt-brass-mounted scabbard with maker's name, 30½in (77.5cm) long.
£2,200–2,500 DN(H)

A south German cavalry sword, the blade grooved on both sides and incised with sun, moon and stars and the arm of God with a sabre, the associated pommel engraved with female busts and tendrils, mid-16thC, 45¼in (115cm) long.
£2,750–3,000 Herm

A silver-gilt hilted small-sword, with tapering blade of hollow triangular section inlaid with brass on one side, hilt cast and chased in relief with cherubs engaged in various forms of hunting, the wooden grip bound with twisted silver wire, marked for London 1737, maker's mark 'I. B.', blade 27½in (70cm) long.
£700–850 Bon

A Walloon hilted sword, the double-edged blade with a shallow centre fuller, with copper wire-bound grip, mid-17thC, blade 38¼in (97cm) long.
£575–650 GV

A silver-hilted hunting sword, with curved single-edged blade stamped 'Sahagum' within a narrow fuller and with date and double orb mark, silver hilt and stained horn grip, marked for London 1740, blade 25in (63.5cm) long.
£500–600 S(S)

A silver hunting sword, by Paul Bateman, c1743, 27½in (70cm) long.
£2,350–2,600 CCB

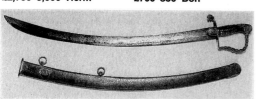

A Georgian presentation sword, the blade etched, engraved and gilded, with copper gilt stirrup hilt with lion's head pommel, wire and ribbon-bound ivory grip, contained in its engraved copper scabbard, signed on the reverse 'Hunter, Edinburgh', blade 32¾in (83cm) long.
£2,200–2,500 Gle

An 1821 pattern light cavalry officer's sword, with pipe back frost-edged blade, 38in (96.5cm) long.
£700–800 WSA

A late Victorian Scottish Highlanders' basket-hilted dress sword, with bi-fullered double-edged blade, regulation white metal hilt, wire-bound sharkskin grip, in steel scabbard within leather sword bag, marked 'R. & H. Nathan, London', blade 30½in (77.5cm) long.
£500–600 WAL

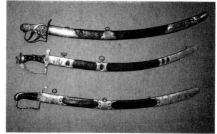

A blunderbuss, by James Freeman, London, c1715,
34in (86.5cm) long.
£2,750–3,000 WSA

A brass-barrelled flintlock blunderbuss, by W. Parker,
Holborn, with plain walnut full stock and brass mounts,
late 18thC, 31½in (80cm) long.
£800–1,000 WAL

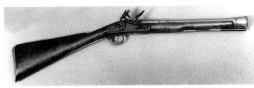

A blunderbuss, for the Southampton stagecoach,
the brass barrel inscribed 'Southampton',
with walnut stock, early 19thC, 12in (30.5cm) long.
£1,700–2,000 WW

A flintlock blunderbuss, by W. Ketland & Co, with brass
barrel formed in three stages, figured walnut full stock,
engraved brass mounts, Birmingham proof marks,
signed 'London', c1820, 14in (35.5cm) long.
£1,300–1,500 S(S)

A Scottish officer's .577 percussion 1861 pattern artillery
carbine, by Charles Ingram, Glasgow, with twist barrel,
walnut three-quarter stock, c1865, barrel 33in (84cm) long.
£550–650 Bon

An 1876 pattern Winchester 50–95 carbine,
with 56cm diam sighted half tube barrel, signed,
the pistol grip with horn inlay.
£6,500–7,500 Gle

A flintlock musket, with full-stocked brass barrel,
17thC and later, 53½in (136cm) long.
£1,100–1,300 PFK

A brass-barrelled flintlock blunderbuss, by John Collis,
Oxford, with three-stage barrel belled and turned at the
muzzle and fitted with spring bayonet above, with figured
walnut full stock, later brass-tipped ramrod, c1785,
14in (35.5cm) barrel.
£1,500–1,800 Bon

A flintlock blunderbuss, by William Andrew Beckwith,
with figured walnut full stock, brass mounts engraved
with martial trophies, London proof marks, early 19thC,
31in (78.5cm) long.
£1,000–1,200 Bon

**William Beckwith was appointed Master of the
Gunmakers' Company in 1808, 1814, 1825 and
again in 1840.**

A brass-barrelled persussion blunderbuss,
by Samuel Brummitt, Nottingham, converted from
flintlock, with walnut full stock, engraved brass mounts,
Birmingham private proof marks, barrel engraved
'Nottingham', early 19thC, 30in (76cm) long.
£750–900 Bon

An Irish flintlock blunderbuss, by John McDaniel,
Monaghan, with two-stage barrel flared at the muzzle,
signed octagonal breech stamped with Irish registration
number, walnut full stock, brass mounts, c1825,
17in (43cm) long.
£1,150–1,350 Bon

A double-barrelled 12 bore underlever hammer gun,
by George H. Daw, with walnut stock, in original oak
case with accessories, c1875, 47in (119.5cm) long.
£450–550 WAL

An Irish 11 bore percussion musket, by Kavanagh,
Dublin, with twist sighted barrel stamped with Irish
registration number, walnut three-quarter stock,
brass mounts of regulation type, original steel ramrod,
mid-19thC, barrel 32in (81.5cm) long.
£850–1,000 Bon

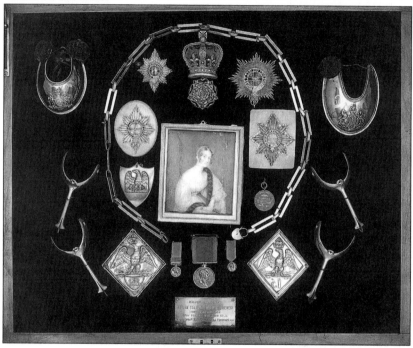

A composed 'English Lock' pocket pistol, the brass barrel engraved with flowerheads, rosettes and strapwork, wooden full stock, the iron parts heavily rusted, the stock with cracks and extensive worm damage, c1635, barrel 5½in (14cm) long.
£4,250–4,750 S(S)

**The shape and decoration of the barrel is Scottish and dates from the first quarter of the 17thC.
The style of the lock suggests a date of c1630 at the earliest. The crude workmanship of the stock implies that this pistol is a contemporary association of parts, using an earlier barrel and lock of c1630, assembled and stocked by a provincial craftsman c1635. It was found in the thatch of a medieval Devon hall house during renovation work.**

A pair of 34 bore flintlock pocket pistols, by Edward Newton, Grantham, with turn-off barrels formed in three stages, walnut butts carved with a scallop about the tangs, London proof and foreigners' mark, signed, c1750, each barrel 3in (7.5cm) long.
£500–600 S(S)

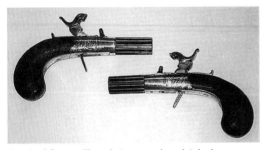

A pair of George III pocket percussion pistols, by Scudamore of London, marked Nos. 1 and 2, convertd from flintlock, Birmingham proof marks, 6¼in (16cm) long.
£550–650 TRM

A cavalry ordnance pistol, with beech stock with brass mounts, complete with ramrod, c1728, 21¼in (54cm) long.
£1,800–2,000 Herm

A pair of Queen Anne cannon-barrelled silver-mounted flintlock pistols, by Henry Delany, London, c1740, 12in (30.5cm) long.
£3,250–3,500 WSA

A Catalan Miquelet lock pistol, with walnut stock, pierced steel mounts, breech with maker's mark, with original ramrod and belt hook, mid-18thC, 15¼in (38.5cm) long.
£1,100–1,250 GV

◄ A Light Dragoons flintlock pistol, by Vernon, dated '1760', 15in (38cm) long.
£2,000–2,250 WSA

► A pair of steel flintlock muff pistols, with floral and scroll engraving, inscribed 'Richards, Strand, London', in original shagreen case, c1760, 6in (15cm) long.
£4,000–4,500 RBB

Components of a late 19thC flintlock pistol

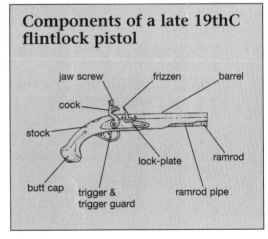

jaw screw · frizzen · barrel
cock
stock
butt cap
trigger & trigger guard
lock-plate
ramrod
ramrod pipe

◄ A pair of Irish silver-mounted flintlock holster pistols, by Alley, Dublin, with French barrels, c1775, 20in (51cm) long.
£5,500–6,000 WSA

Miller's Compares

I A Queen Anne-style cannon-barrelled flintlock travelling pistol, by Wogdon, London, with silver wire inlay in slab walnut butt, c1780, 11in (28cm) long.
£1,000–1,250 GV

II A Queen Anne-style cannon-barrelled flintlock travelling pistol, by John Lett, c1780, 10in (25.5cm) long.
£450–500 GV

Item I is a fine example of a pistol by one of the leading London gunmakers. The superiority of such pieces is to be seen in the finish, sharpness of line and attention to detail, such as the sliding safety catch behind the cock. Item II is a provincial piece made in imitation of examples made in the capital, but of lesser quality and in poorer condition.

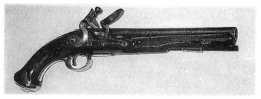

A flintlock Dragoon pistol, with walnut stock, brass trigger guard and butt, replaced ramrod, the butt dated '1786' and with London proof marks, 15½in (39.5cm) long.
£350–420 TRM

A French 12 bore military flintlock holster pistol, full stocked with regulation brass mounts, stock stamped 'A 1778' and fleur-de-lys, 18thC, barrel 16in (40.5cm) long.
£800–1,000 WAL

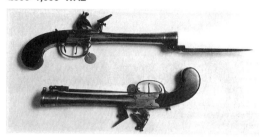

A pair of Waters patent blunderbuss pistols, with spring bayonets, c1790, 13in (33cm) long.
£4,000–4,500 WSA

► A pair of pocket pistols, by Baker, London, with walnut stocks and brass lock plates, 19thC, 6in (15cm) long.
£160–200 FHF

◄ A pair of flintlock pistols, by Henry Nock, with engraved chamber, walnut grip handles, inscribed 'London' and with proof marks, late 18thC, 8½in (21.5cm) long, in a fitted mahogany case.
£3,000–3,500 WW

Henry Nock was first recorded as a gun-maker of quality in 1771.

An over-and-under percussion pocket pistol, by Griffin & Tow, converted from flintlock, with 2¾in (7cm) rifled 50 bore cannon barrels, embossed grotesque mask butt cap, early 19thC, 8½in (21.5cm) long.
£400–475 AG

A pair of officer's 16 bore flintlock holster pistols, by Elston & Co, with octagonal barrels, plain walnut full stocks with silver escutcheons, marked, c1820, in a fitted mahogany case, 14½in (37cm) long.
£2,300–2,750 WAL

A pair of officer's 18 bore flintlock pistols, by James Stevens, London, with twist-sighted barrels, figured walnut full stocks, Birmingham proof marks, c1820, 11¼in (28.5cm) long, in original fitted oak case with accessories.
£2,000–2,400 Bon

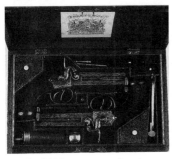

A pair of 40 bore over-and-under box-lock percussion pistols, by Forsyth & Co, London, 1833, 9in (23cm) long, in original mahogany case with accessories.
£8,500–10,000 Bon

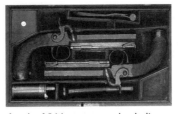

A pair of 34 bore percussion belt pistols, signed 'Manton, London', with octagonal sighted barrel engraved with foliage at each end and fitted with a stirrup ramrod beneath, chequered walnut butt, in a fitted mahogany case, Birmingham proof marks, signed, c1840, barrels 5in (12.5cm) long.
£1,200–1,400 S(S)

Restoration & repair of firearms

The most common restorations to antique firearms are replaced top jaws, screws (flintlocks), ramrod replacements, minor repairs to fore-end woodwork and rebrowned barrels. If carried out properly, none of these seriously affect the value. Major work such as replaced cocks or hammers, broken stocks and a degree of re-engraving can be acceptable, particularly if the piece is a rare example or of great age. Collectors should avoid re-converted or over-restored pieces.

A 32 bore all-metal percussion pistol, the brass full stock engraved with foliage including pommel with hinged butt-trap cover, ramrod missing, Birmingham proof marks, mid-19thC, 10¾in (27.5cm) long.
£425–500 Bon

A Tower percussion sea service pistol, full-stocked with regulation brass mounts, the lock engraved with crowned 'VR' and '1855 Tower', mid-19thC, 11½in (29cm) long.
£320–380 WAL

A 32 bore Caucasian Miquelet-lock holster pistol, with tapering reeded barrel etched in imitation of twist pattern, retained by three nielloed bands, with leather-covered wooden stock, mid-19thC, barrel 12¼in (31cm) long.
£450–550 S(S)

A Swedish 1850 model percussion pistol of musket bore, No. 386, with browned sighted barrel, walnut half stock, brass mounts, dated '1856', 18½in (47cm) long.
£350–420 Bon

► A pair of target pistols, by Charles & Henry Egg, with octagonal barrels, the diced grip handles inset with vacant silver shields, marked, c1850, 10½in (26.5cm) long, in an oak fitted case with accessories.
£3,000–3,500 WW

Charles & Henry Egg were of the family of gunsmiths started by Durs Egg in the 18thC and continued by Joseph Egg.

An 1856 pattern percussion rifled service pistol, with walnut full stock, regulation brass mounts and stirrup ramrod, Birmingham proof marks, dated '1865', barrel 10in (25.5cm) long.
£850–1,000 Bon

731

A steel pinfire pistol, with rim-fire action and mahogany stock, late 19thC, 11in (28cm) long.
£90–100 P(Ed)

A rim-fire knife-pistol, by Unwin & Rodgers, partly chequered dark horn side-plates, the butt with hinged trap cover for ammunition, two folding knife-blades (one incomplete), Birmingham proof marks, late 19thC, 6½in (16.5cm) long.
£500–600 Bon

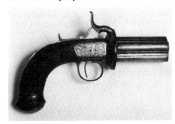

A percussion hand-rotated pepperbox revolver, by Osborne & Jackson, c1840, 8in (20.5cm) long.
£1,100–1,300 WSA

A 38 bore percussion cap revolver, by Adams, mid-19thC, in fitted case with accessories including reproduction powder flask, 15in (38cm) wide.
£700–800 CGC

> **Miller's is a price GUIDE not a price LIST**

A third model 54 bore Tranter percussion revolver, c1855, in fitted case with all accessories, 15in (38cm) wide.
£2,250–2,500 WSA

A German pump-up flintlock air rifle, with two stage sighted barrel, lightly carved half stock with horn fore-end cap, engraved brass mounts, the butt plate with hinged flap opened by steel sliding button for access to the reservoir concealed within the butt, mid-18thC, barrel 40½in (103cm) long.
£600–700 Gle

A Kentucky 10mm bore rifle, full-stocked in tiger-stripe maple and brass-mounted, ivory ramrod, the lock a drum and nipple percussion conversion and the plate engraved 'C. Bird & Co Philadelphia Warranted', c1800, 47¼in (120cm) long.
£1,100–1,250 GV

Bird & Co were gunsmiths in Philadelphia from 1790 to 1830.

▶ An American revolving percussion underhammer rifle, attributed to Elijah Jaquith, Brattleboro, Vermont, with 52 caliber six shot cylinder, part round/ part octagonal barrel, figured walnut stock, hammer possibly replaced, c1830, barrel 32in (81.5cm) long.
£4,500–5,500 SK(B)

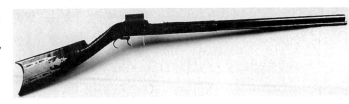

A 20 bore flintlock Baker rifle for an officer of a Volunteer Regiment, by Brander & Potts, London, with figured-walnut full stock, steel mounts engraved with martial trophies, original iron ramrod, London proof marks, early 19thC, 30in (76cm) long.
£4,500–5,000 Bon

Martin Brander and Thomas Potts were Contractors to Ordnance from 1815 to 1820.

A 'monkey tail' breech loading percussion rifle, by Westley Richards, with sighted barrel, full stock with regulation steel mounts and steel cleaning rod, signed and dated '1861', barrel 33in (84cm) long.
£700–850 Gle

▶ A German wheellock hunting rifle, by Hans Kattmann, Leipzig, with walnut half stock, trigger missing, signed and dated '1676', 96½in (245cm) long.
£2,800–3,200 Herm

Militaria

BADGES

A Victorian 3rd Middlesex Rifle Volunteers white metal glengarry badge.
£220–265 BOS

A Victorian Highland Light Infantry NCO's silver-plated glengarry badge.
£50–60 WAL

A West Kent Light Infantry Militia other ranks' white metal glengarry badge, 1874–81.
£100–120 DNW

COSTUME

A Renfrewshire Yeomanry officer's coatee, scarlet with yellow facings and gilt buttons, c1800.
£1,000–1,200 Gle

This was the only regiment on mainland Britain that used the apparently contradictory title of Yeomanry Infantry.

A Royal Artillery officer's 1864 pattern patrol tunic, the dark blue melton cloth with mohair cord, Austrian decoration, mid-19thC.
£300–350 BOS

A Madras Staff Corps captain's full dress scarlet tunic, c1875.
£550–650 WAL

A late Victorian Royal Irish Regiment captain's full dress scarlet tunic, with gilt lace, braid trim and silver-plated collar badges.
£270–320 WAL

A Royal Artillery officer's patrol uniform, the shoulder straps with bullion captain's rank stars and to the left breast Queen's South Africa Medal ribbon, late 19thC.
£170–200 BOS

A WWI Canadian Battalion officer's uniform, of khaki wool, with medal ribbons of Military Cross, Natal Medal, British War Medal and Victory Medal, 1918.
£500–600 BOS

A WWI Royal Artillery captain's khaki tunic, of heavy cavalry twill, with rank badge to cuffs.
£160–200 WAL

A WWI 11th Battalion East Yorkshire Regiment officer's tunic, with Battalion insignia, Regimental pattern buttons, collar badges and Major rank insignia, with medal ribbons of the Military Cross and 1914–15 Star.
£350–420 BOS

The service uniform of Air Chief Marshal Sir E. R. Ludlow-Hewitt, complete with pilot's wings, ribbons and sleeve rank insignia, tunic and trousers, 1944.
£575–650 S(S)

Cross Reference
See Colour Review

A WWII Territorial Army Nursing Service battledress uniform, comprising dress cap, battledress blouse, issue pattern skirt.
£130–150 BOS

A Victorian 26th Middlesex Rifle Volunteers (Customs) pouch belt, comprising a 2½in (6.5cm) black leather belt bearing silvered pouch belt plate, lion's head boss, two-strand chain, whistle and holder.
£140–170 BOS

A Queen's Own Staffordshire Yeomanry officer's pouch, the dark blue velvet flap with applied silver bullion Staffordshire knot surmounted by a bullion crown, with black morocco leather-covered metal pocket, early 19thC.
£220–260 BOS

A Brigade officer's frock coat and cap, with silver badge, and belt, 1950s.
Coat and belt   £350–400
Cap and badge £150–175
Q&C

◄ A Queen Elizabeth II State Trumpeter's dress, with hat and belt, 1952.
£1,000–1,200 Q&C

HELMETS & HEADDRESSES

A 1768 pattern Grenadier black fur mitre cap, with scarlet cloth top with tassel and hessian lining, 1867.
£2,500–3,000 WAL

A Gloucestershire Hussars trooper's shako, the dark blue cloth body with dished crown, a band of yellow mohair lace and three lines of scarlet, with yellow and scarlet plaited front cord, 1844–60.
£1,200–1,400 BOS

◄ An 1855 (French) pattern 22nd Cheshire Regiment officer's shako, with black beaver body, patent leather peaks, headband and top, with gilt shako plate and white over red ball-tuft plume, in a tin case.
£700–850 WAL

A Victorian South Salopian Yeomanry Albert-pattern OR helmet, with brass ornamentation and mounts, 1844.
£1,000–1,200 WAL

► A Victorian 20th Middlesex Rifles Volunteers green cloth helmet, c1860.
£375–450 Q&C

An 1847 pattern Hanoverian officer's helmet.
£2,300–2,500 Herm

A Hertfordshire Yeomanry officer's spiked helmet, the silvered skull mounted with gilt acanthus leaf decoration and gilt fluted spike, 1869–80.
£1,000–1,200 BOS

An 1871 pattern 5th Dragoon Guards officer's helmet, with gilded brass skull and fittings and silvered and gilded helmet plate, plume missing.
£950–1,100 S(S)

An 1867 pattern Prussian Bodyguard helmet, with original zinc parade eagle.
£2,700–3,000 Herm

A Royal Engineers officer's blue cloth helmet, with helmet plate, in original japanned iron box, early 20thC.
£500–600 PFK

A WWI Imperial Russian other ranks' cap, 1910-style, the khaki light weight material cloth body with green-painted leather peak.
£135–160 BOS

An Infantry Reserve officer's helmet, Württemberg, Germany, c1910.
£750–900 Herm

A Black Watch piper's ostrich-feather bonnet, c1911.
£180–220 Q&C

A 13th Hussars sealskin busby, with white horse-hair plume, pre-1922.
£350–400 Q&C

HELMET PLATES

A 14th Foot (Buckinghamshire) officer's gilt shako plate, 1855–61.
£200–240 BOS

A 4th Queen's Own Light Dragoons other ranks' brass shako plate, pre-1861.
£600–700 BOS

A Victorian Sherwood Foresters (Derbyshire Regiment) officer's gilt and silver-plated helmet plate.
£160–180 WAL

A 3rd Royal Jersey Light Infantry officer's all-gilt helmet plate, 1881–1901.
£250–300 DNW

LOG BOOKS

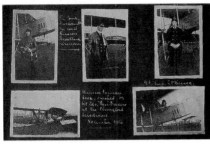

A pair of Royal Naval Air Service pilot's log books, covering the period 1915–18, containing photographs of pilots and aircraft, bound in red leather with gilt tooling, with family photograph album.
£550–650 BOS

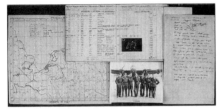

A WWII group of original bombing route maps and pilot's flying log book, relating to F/Lt E. Protheroe, DFC, comprising 54 maps with route drawn in, each annotated with target, bomb load and other details, covering the period July 1942–February 1945.
£1,800–2,200 S(S)

A Navigation Log from Winston Churchill's 1942 flight to Moscow via Arabia, bearing the signatures of the crew and Winston Churchill.
£1,700–2,000 Gle

At the top of the page are enquiries in pencil made by Churchill such as 'How far to go?' and 'What are those small dots below?', to which the Navigator answered 'camels'.

> Miller's is a price GUIDE not a price LIST

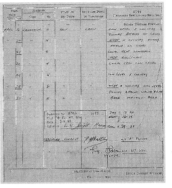

A page from the flying log book of P/O Les Knight, pilot of Lancaster AJ-N, ED912 which took part in the Dams Raid, May 1943, with seven entries, 16th–27th April 1943.
£2,800–3,200 S(S)

Knight, an Australian, was in the first wave of nine aircraft given the task of attacking the Möhne and Eder dams. After the breaching of the Möhne, Gibson led five Lancasters on to the Eder. Following attacks by Shannon and Maudslay, Knight (after a dummy run) dropped his mine, the last remaining, and it struck the dam, causing a large breach. For this, Knight was one of the five 617 aircrew to be awarded the DSO. Unfortunately, he was killed in action some four months later.

ORDERS & MEDALS

A pair of medals awarded to Pte B. Mitchell, 4th Foot, Military General Service 1793–1814 with four clasps, Waterloo 1815, renamed.
£700–800 Gle

A group of medals awarded to Admiral the Hon. S. T. Carnegie, Royal Navy, Order of the Bath (CB), Military Division, Companion's breast badge, Baltic Medal 1854, Crimea War Medal 1854, one clasp, Spain Order of St. Ferdinand, third class breast star and first class breast badge, Turkey Order of the Medjidie, fourth class breast badge, with set of related dress miniatures, in fitted glazed case.
£1,700–2,000 S

◄ A pair of medals awarded to J. Davey, New Zealand Medal 1861–66 and Long Service and Good Conduct Medal.
£280–320 FHF

► A China medal 1857 awarded to Jacob Cass 67th Regiment, with Pekin 1860 and Taku Forts 1860 clasps.
£170–200 WAL

A group of three medals awarded to Donald McKay, 71st Highlanders Light Infantry, Crimea one clasp, Indian Mutiny Medal and Army Long Service Good Conduct Medal.
£700–850 BOS

An Egypt medal awarded
to Major N. F. Way, RMLI,
with Suakin 1885 and Tofrek clasps.
£900–1,100 WAL

A group of five medals awarded to Colour
Sjt R. Davey, India Medal with two clasps,
1914–18 War Medal and Victory Medal, Meritorious
Service Medal and Long Service and Good
Conduct Medal, with a group of four miniatures.
£250–300 FHF

A Queen's South Africa
Medal with five clasps
awarded to Pte G. Curnow,
Grenadier Guards, c1900.
£80–100 BOS

A group of seven medals awarded to Armourer Quarter
Master Sgt J. H. Bird, Royal Army Ordnance Corps,
Ashanti 1900, Queen's South Africa 1899–1902 with
four clasps, 1914 Star, British War and Victory Medals,
India General Service 1908–35 with one clasp,
Army Long Service and Good Conduct, G.V.R., with
original commission document, Discharge and Character
Certificates, two identity discs and a group photograph.
£800–1,000 DNW

A group of five medals awarded to Bombardier Ketti,
Nigerian Artillery, West African Frontier Force D.C.M.,
1914–15 Star, British War and Victory Medal, West African
Frontier Forces Long Service and Good Conduct, G.V.R.
£900–1,100 Gle

◀ A collection of RAF
ephemera and medals
relating to Wing
Commander Ronald
William Jackson,
including Croix de Guerre,
Military OBE, Air Efficiency
Award, and standard
service medals, with eight
miniatures and two pilot's
flying log books, 1923–42
and 1942–48.
£700–850 CGC

A group of six medals awarded to
Major G. N. Kingsford, Royal Engineers,
Distinguished Service Order, Military Cross,
1914–15 Star, B.W.M., Victory Medal with
oak palm, War Medal 1939–45.
£700–850 DN

POWDER FLASKS & HORNS

A German turned wood and
inlaid powder flask, with wire
and bone dot-inlaid roundels,
17thC, 7½in (19cm) diam.
£500–550 TEN

An American powder horn, signed G. Swartnout,
engraved with a ship under full sail with the American
flag and inscription 'Success to the American eagle,
Who with an air of disdain, spit on the crown of
Great Britain', dated 'Sept 9th 1820', 9½in (24cm) long.
£800–1,000 S(NY)

◀ A German all-steel combined priming flask,
wheel-lock spanner and turnscrew, 17thC, 6in (15cm) long.
£1,100–1,300 Bon

A copper gun flask,
by Bartram, with embossed
scroll decoration, c1850,
7¾in (19.5cm) long.
£65–75 WSA

▶ A black pigskin-
covered powder flask
and matching shot flask,
by G. & J. W. Hawksley,
Sheffield, 19thC,
largest 9in (23cm) long.
£170–200 Bon

A Scottish cowhorn
dress powder flask,
with silver mounts and
set with pieces of faceted
foiled glass, 19thC,
13½in (34.5cm) long.
£550–650 Bon

A German antler and
ivory-inlaid powder flask,
carved in relief with a
huntsman overlooking
the kill of a boar by a
pack of hounds, with silver
metal mounts and nozzle,
19thC, 7¼in (18.5cm) long.
£1,150–1,350 TEN

SHOULDER BELT PLATES

A First North York Local
Militia officer's silver
shoulder belt plate,
by Peter and William
Bateman, London 1808.
£600–700 BOS

An East Kent Militia
officer's silver-plated
shoulder belt plate,
with silver mounts, 1840–55.
£350–420 DNW

An East Norfolk Militia
officer's burnished silver-
plated shoulder belt plate,
with a gilt Garter with red
translucent enamel Cross
of St. George mounted
on the star, pre-1855.
£600–700 BOS

A 1st Dumbarton Rifle
Volunteer Corps officer's
silver-plated shoulder belt
plate, overlaid with copper-
gilt mounts, at the centre
of the Cross a silver-plated
elephant with castle
howdah, 1887–1908.
£250–300 DNW

WAIST BELT CLASPS

▶ An Argyle
Highland Rifles
other ranks'
two-part white
metal waist belt
clasp, 1880–87.
£85–100 DNW

Miller's is a price GUIDE
not a price LIST

A Royal North British Fusiliers
officer's two-part silver and gilt plate
waist belt clasp, 1855–77.
£130–150 DNW

▶ An Essex Regiment officer's
silvered and gilt waist belt clasp,
with oak leaf ends and matching
numbers to both halves, the centre
with the arms of Essex on a red
translucent enamel ground, post-1881.
£150–180 BOS

A 3rd Royal Surrey Militia officer's
silvered waist belt clasp, with matching
numbers to both halves, pre-1881.
£130–150 BOS

MISCELLANEOUS

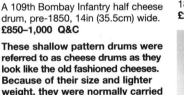

A Boer War Lancashire Fusiliers 'Relief of Ladysmith' pink silk armband, 1900.
£80–100 BOS

This would have been worn by a seller on flag days to raise funds for the Regiment.

An American silk artillery banner, with gold painted crossed cannons, '102' above and an 'S' below, on a red field, 19thC, 23½ x 37in (59.5 x 94cm) high.
£1,000–1,200 SK(B)

A Black Watch officer's silver plaid brooch, Edinburgh 1882.
£350–420 WAL

An American Civil War snare drum, listing 14 battles and engagements, including Petersburg, Vicksburg, and Fredericksburg, the interior with paper label inscribed 'Massachusetts Drum Manufactory, John C. Haynes & Co', c1862.
£2,800–3,200 SK(B)

An East India Company gunner's calipers, by C. Cummins, London, marked 'Inches, Guns, Shot,' 19thC, 7in (18cm) long.
£500–600 WAL

▶ A Victorian parcel-gilt and ebonized wood novelty inkstand, by E. H. Stockwell, modelled as a helmet of the Household Cavalry, flanked by a pair of spurs, 1870–71, 11in (28cm) long.
£2,800–3,200 P

A 109th Bombay Infantry half cheese drum, pre-1850, 14in (35.5cm) wide.
£850–1,000 Q&C

These shallow pattern drums were referred to as cheese drums as they look like the old fashioned cheeses. Because of their size and lighter weight, they were normally carried by the young boy soldiers in the band. The British Army still used these after WWI and the old British Indian Army and African Regiments of the Empire may have used them up to 1947.

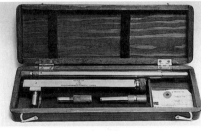

◀ A Canadian set of instruments for gun barrel inspection, by Hughes, Owen & Co, in a fitted wooden case, 1940, 12in (30.5cm) long.
£115–130 REG

A flintlock box-lock tinder lighter, by Bond, with engraved brass action, candle holder and flat-sided walnut butt, restored, defective, early 19thC, 7¾in (19.5cm) long.
£950–1,150 Bon

◀ A George III vinaigrette, by Mathew Linwood, the cover engraved with a vacant cartouche, opening to reveal a gilt grille cast and pierced with HMS *Victory* and text 'Victory, Trafalgar, Octr. 21, 1805', marked, 1¾in (4.5cm) high.
£1,700–2,000 P(Ed)

A terracotta tobacco jar and cover, the brown-glazed body moulded with four panels, inscribed 'In Action At The Second Battle of The Marne, Saint Mihiel Salient, Argonne Meuse Drive', c1918, 7in (18cm) high.
£60–70 SAS

Sport

BASEBALL

A baseball, inscribed in black ink 'With best Wishes/Honus Wagner/Sept. 11–26'.
£1,500–1,650 DuM

A Detroit Tigers metal button, depicting Ty Cobb, 1910.
£100–120 HALL

A Topps Gum baseball card, depicting Mickey Mantle, 1969.
£80–100 DuM

◄ A *Sporting News* baseball card, depicting Babe Ruth, c1915.
£2,800–3,200 HALL

George Herman 'Babe' Ruth was born in Baltimore in 1895. He joined the Baltimore Orioles, then a minor league team in 1914, hitting his first home run within a week. He was sold to the Boston Red Sox in July of the same year and was already a national celebrity by 1919 when he was bought by the New York Yankees because the Red Sox owner was desperate for cash.

An All Star Game ticket stub, for Fenway Park, Boston, Massachusetts, 1961.
£100–125 HALL

BILLIARDS

◄ A set of billiard balls, 1910, in a fitted wooden tray, 17in (43cm) wide.
£65–75 SPT

► A pair of oak billiard room benches, with red buttoned upholstery, late 19thC, 79½in (202cm) wide.
£6,000–7,000 HOK

A Victorian walnut snooker table, on six bulbous turned legs, 125½ x 66½in (319 x 169cm) wide.
£1,100–1,300 TAM

A French walnut and olive-wood billiard table, 1840s, 108in (274.5cm) long.
£35,000–40,000 WBB

A burr-walnut billiard table, by Ashcroft, c1878, 144 x 72in (366 x 183cm).
£32,000–35,000 WBB

A mahogany miniature billiard table, with ivory balls, c1860, 60 x 30in (152.5 x 76cm).
£1,200–1,400 GKe

A mahogany three-quarter size combination billiard/dining table, by G. Spencer & Sons, Bristol, c1900, 101 x 54½in (256 x 138cm).
£2,200–2,500 Bri

◄ An oak combination billiard/dining table, c1920, 72 x 36in (183 x 91.5cm) long.
£2,400–2,650 CBC

An engraved silver billiards trophy, by Thomas Slater, Walter Slater and Henry Holland, with presentation inscription, London 1895, 6¼in (16cm) high.
£250–300 Bon

An engraved silver two-handled billiards trophy, with lid, probably late Victorian, on an ebonized plinth, 8¾in (22cm) high.
£125–150 DW

A late Victorian frog diorama, in the form of a billiard room in a public house, within an ebonized and glazed case, restored, 69in (175.5cm) wide.
£2,000–2,400 P

BOXING

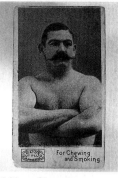

A silver boxing belt, by EBS, the central shield engraved with a scene of boxers in a ring, inscribed 'Cliff Anderson, uncrowned Featherweight Champion of the British Empire, presented by public subscription, 1947', linked to four medallions engraved with Anderson's career details, all attached to a leather-backed, red, white and blue cloth belt, 35¼in (90cm) long.
£400–500 S

A Mayo Cigarettes boxing card, depicting John L. Sullivan, 1st Heavyweight Champion of the World, 1895.
£600–675 HALL

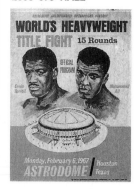

A pair of Spalding leather boxing gloves, 1940s, 11in (28cm) long.
£25–28 SPT

An unused boxing fight ticket, for Muhammad Ali v Henry Cooper, at Arsenal Stadium, 21st May 1966.
£140–170 VS

▶ A boxing programme, for Ali v Terrell at the Houston Astrodome, 1967.
£70–85 VS

CRICKET

A cricket ball, mounted with a silver plaque inscribed 'Ball used during 1st Innings, Gentlemen v Players, Lords July 18 1898, W. G. Grace's Jubilee Match', the leather carved 'WG'.
£850–1,000 S

A Victorian gold-coloured belt buckle, with central embossed figure of a cricketer, 1880s, 3½in (9cm) wide.
£100–120 VS

A black velvet cricket cap, the peak embroidered in yellow metal thread with '1924–26'.
£45–50 SPT

A photograph of RMS *Maloja* at Sydney, signed by 16 members of the MCC tour to Australia, in contemporary glazed frame, 1924–25, 9½ x 15in (24 x 38cm) overall.
£320–380 VS

An MCC official photograph of the Ashes Tour team, mounted on card, with fully autographed lower margin, framed and glazed, 1924–25, 11½ x 14¾in (29 x 37.5cm).
£500–550 S

A pair of Staffordshire pottery figures of cricketers, each with his jacket at his feet, picked out in coloured enamels, 1860–70, 14in (35.5cm) high.
£4,500–5,000 DN

Ex-Rev. Harry Bloomfield Collection.

A Doulton silver-mounted pitcher, decorated with applied cameo portraits of cricketers in green and white on a brown punch-decorated ground, the handle modelled with cricket bats, shoes and a ball surmounted by an umpire's hat, 1881, 9¾in (25cm) high, with a matching lemonade beaker.
Pitcher £1,600–2,000
Beaker £600–750 TAM

A London Transport billboard poster, advertising England v Australia Second Test Match at Lords, 1938, 10 x 12in (25.5 x 30.5cm).
£175–200 MUL

A leather cricketer's measuring tape, 1910, 5in (12.5cm) diam.
£40–45 SPT

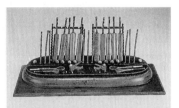

A Thorne's toffee tin, depicting the Australian cricketers to the side and the Oval to the lid, 1926, 5in (12.5cm) wide.
£85–100 VS

An American Whiting Manufacturing Co cricket players presentation silver tray, retailed by J. E. Caldwell & Co, etched to the front with a cricket bat and gear and laurel branches, inscribed 'Gentlemen of Philadelphia 1884 British Tour', 6½in (16.5cm) wide, 4oz.
£150–180 SK

A miniature cricket display trophy, comprising maple bats supported by barley-twist wooden gates, behind stumps, with balls and other sporting bats and rackets, mounted on a walnut base, late 19thC, 19¾in (50cm) long.
£3,200–3,500 S

CROQUET

R. Fellow, *The Game of Croquet: Its Appointment and Laws*, first edition, New York, 1866, 8°, new front endpaper, original cloth.
£100–120 DW

A table croquet set, comprising eight mallets with holly heads and ash handles, balls, two posts, metal hoops, markers, all supported on a beech stand, early 20thC, 16in (40.5cm) high.
£650–750 S

◄ A silver-plated desk croquet set, by Heath & Heath, c1880, 8in (20.5cm) wide.
£350–450 STS

CYCLING

J. Bottomley-Firth,
*The Velocipede. Its Past,
its Present & its Future*,
first edition, 1869, 8°,
lettered in gilt, original cloth.
£400–500 DW

**This is claimed as the
first full-length book
on the bicycle.**

A Victorian pewter vase
trophy, with racing cyclist
figure and period cycle
mounted to the front, the
surround decorated in
relief with a floral butterfly
design, 10in (25.5cm) high.
£125–150 MUL

A nickel-plated
cycling trophy, c1900,
25in (63.5cm) high.
£250–300 YEST

A Britannia metal cycling
trophy, the Vivid Challenge
Cup, competed for
between 1894 and 1902,
with an associated Britannia
metal two-handled
presentation goblet and
associated ephemera,
cup 23in (58.5cm) high.
£450–550 S

EQUESTRIAN

A pair of black leather
riding boots and trees,
c1900, 20in (51cm) high.
£130–145 SPT

A Victorian silver-plated
stirrup mantel clock,
with a presentation
inscription and dated
'1884', 8½in (21.5cm) high.
£400–450 HYD

An Irish horn-handled riding crop, 1900, 29in (73.5cm) long.
£80–100 RTh

An oak horse-
measuring stick,
18thC, 72in
(183cm) long.
£150–180 Odi

▶ A Doulton Lambeth harvest jug
and two beakers, moulded in white
with hunting scenes on a brown
ground, with silver rims marked
London 1901, cups 5in (12.5cm) high.
£325–360 CoHA

A bronze figure of a huntsman,
by John Willis Good, signed,
mid-19thC, 11½in (29cm) long.
£3,500–4,000 JNic

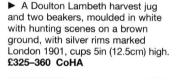

A French biscuit tin, decorated
with a polo scene, by Felix Potin,
slight wear, Paris, c1910,
15¾in (40cm) wide.
£65–80 DW

A blacksmith's painted pine
and wrought-iron trade sign,
c1860, 26in (66cm) wide.
£1,200–1,500 RYA

FISHING

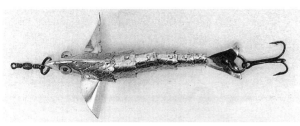

A nickel-silver 'Superior Flexible Jointed Bait', attributed to Gregory, with glass eyes, c1890, 3½in (9cm) long.
£1,500–1,800 Bon(C)

An Allcock-style flat metal bait, with twin fin painted in blue and silver herring-pattern, c1900, 4in (10cm) long.
£40–50 MUL

◀ Hardy Bros Ltd, *Hardy's Anglers' Guide*, 1930, 9 x 5in (23 x 12.5cm).
£80–100 AnS

▶ Walton and Cotton, *The Complete Angler*, published by Valentine Press, 1883, 9 x 6in (23 x 15cm).
£250–275 CBO

Eric Taverner, *Trout Fishing From All Angles*, The Lonsdale Library, No. 120 from a limited edition of 375, with mounted flies at the end, signed, c1929, in slipcase, 10 x 7in (25.5 x 18cm).
£650–700 HBo

◀ An Edwardian brass-bound pine box, for storing and carrying fishing rods, reels and equipment, 80in (203cm) long.
£340–375 GLO

◀ A stuffed and mounted bream, inscribed 'Caught by E. H. Brown, St Ives, July 20th 1927, 5lbs 14oz', in a bowfronted case, case 29in (73.5cm) wide.
£550–650 CGC

A stuffed and mounted pike in a river-bed setting, by Parker, with gilt inscription 'Pike Caught 1st Nov 1914. Wgt 13lbs', R. G. Parker of Bristol label to flat-fronted case, case 39in (99cm) wide.
£700–850 Bon(C)

A folding wooden gaff, by Bernard & Son, London, with turned handle, gaff point recess and locking collar, c1910, 46in (117cm) extended.
£120–150 OTB

A bamboo landing net, c1910,
12in (30.5cm) diam.
£65–75 SPT

An Allcock Aerial 4in alloy
casting reel, with see-
through check, 1940s,
in a cardboard box.
£200–240 MUL

An Allcock Coxon Aerial 4in reel, with wooden
star back, brown Bakelite front and rear
flanged spool, stamped 'Patent' and with
on/off check, 1910–15.
£450–550 TRM

An Eaton & Deller Perth-style 3¼in
brass and ebonite reel, late 19thC.
£200–240 Bon(C)

A C. Farlow & Co 3½in brass plate-
wind reel, with horn handle, c1890.
£75–90 TRM

A Hardy Hercules Special Pattern
4½in fly reel, with raised constant
check housing, c1890.
£320–380 Bon(C)

► A Hardy 3¼in brass and ebonite trout/light salmon fly
reel, with horn handle and nickel-silver rim bindings, c1895.
£230–275 OTB

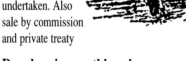

A Hardy Sea Silex 6in
duralumin sea centrepin
reel, with three-rim control,
ivorine rim brake,
compression brake
with correct patent
No.7893, 1930s.
£400–450 Bon(C)

A Hardy Perfect 3in alloy
reel, with 1896 check,
ivorine handle and
strapped rim tension
adjuster, 1896–1905.
£600–650 TRM

A Hardy Altex Mark I
2½in spinning reel, 1935.
£150–180 TRM

◄ A Heaton of
Birmingham 5in trotting
reel, with perforated drum,
raised annular line-guide
and gunmetal foot, c1900.
£140–175 OTB

An Ogden Smith of London 3in alloy Exchequer trout fly reel, with perforated drum, left-hand wind nickel-silver drum locking screw and rim tension regulator, c1935.
£40–50 OTB

A Wallace Watson Patent 4in alloy casting reel, third model, with additional brake provided by a rocking foot, c1935.
£130–160 OTB

A Bond & Son 2½in folding handle crankwind winch, with locking disc and triple-pillared cage, mid-19thC.
£400–450 Bon(C)

A Carter & Sons 3in brass crankwind winch, with triple-pillared cage, engraved, late 19thC.
£220–260 Bon(C)

A 1½in brass clamp winch, with turned ivory handle and steel collar locking screw, c1880.
£120–150 OTB

◀ A Hardy's bottle of prepared sand eels, 1920–30.
£50–60 CGC

FOOTBALL

An England International red velvet football cap, by Foster & Co, Oxford and London, the peak embroidered with '1896–97'.
£400–450 P(Ba)

A spelter figure of a footballer, early 20thC, 16in (40.5cm) high.
£900–1,000 BRT

A German porcelain figure of a young boy about to kick a ball, stamped 'Juventus', c1920, 7½in (19cm) high.
£130–150 MUL

A chrome car mascot, in the form of a footballer, on a wooden base, 1930s, 10in (25.5cm) high.
£300–330 SPT

A Carlton Ware condiment set, the carrying handle in the form of a Newcastle United footballer, with football-shaped salt cellar, pepperette and mustard pot, the stand modelled as a football pitch, 1930s, 5in (12.5cm) wide.
£250–300 AG

A silver fob, by Joseph Taylor, enamelled with a footballer in blue, green and brown, Birmingham 1881, 1in (2.5cm) wide.
£850–950 BEX

A 9ct gold medal, commemorating the *Daily Telegraph* '*Titanic* Fund' football match, Tottenham Hotspur v Woolwich Arsenal, 29th April 1912.
£4,500–5,500 S

The *Daily Telegraph* '*Titanic* Fund' football match was played at The Stadium, Shepherd's Bush, also known as Park Royal, to help raise funds for the families of the disaster and ended in a 3–0 victory for Woolwich Arsenal.

A 9ct gold medal, commemorating Sheffield Wednesday winning the First Division League Championship, the reverse inscribed 'Winners, Ellis J. Rimmer', dated '1928–29', with box.
£370–400 BKS

A Chad Valley book-shaped tin moneybox, decorated with a football scene, the red spine titled *The Sharp Shooter*, 1950s, 5½ x 4in (14 x 10cm).
£70–85 DW

A Bell china mug, commemorating Sheffield Wednesday Cup Winners 1935, the front with city crest, the reverse with the names of players and manager, 3in (7.5cm) high.
£400–450 VS

An autographed and framed photograph of the Aston Villa team, 1937–38, 9½ x 7½in (24 x 19cm).
£220–260 VS

GOLF

A gutty ball press, 1860s, 12in (30.5cm) high.
£200–240 MUL

A Ross 'Patent Home Press' ball mould/press, c1900.
£750–825 S

A silver cigarette case, presented to J. Sibson, a professional at Rushcliffe Golf Club, Nottinghamshire, 1931–33, the front and back engraved with signatures of the President and committee members, the inside scratched with the signatures of sporting and entertainment stars.
£200–240 VS

A hardback booklet, *The Golfer's Vade Mecum*, published by The Ocean Accident and Guarantee Corp, listing Open Winners, 1861–1908, rules, etiquette and full complement of empty scorecards, c1910, 3 x 2in (7.5 x 5cm).
£350–400 VS

Horace G. Hutchinson, *Golf, The Badminton Library*, published by Longmans & Co, 1902, 8 x 6in (20.5 x 15cm).
£120–140 CBO

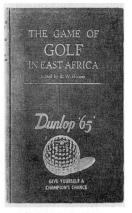

The Game of Golf in East Africa, edited by R. W. Hooper, first edition, Nairobi, 1953, in cloth with gilt.
£320–380 DW

A bronze figure of Harry Vardon by Elkington, c1905, 7in (18cm) high, later presented as a trophy.
£500–600 WaR

A pair of cold-painted bronze figures of male and female golfers, on onyx bases, c1910, 6½in (16.5cm) high.
£500–600 MUL

A chrome-plated brass car mascot, in the form of a golfer, by Desmo, c1937, 6in (15cm) high.
£160–200 WAL

Cross Reference
See Colour Review

A New Hudson Bicycle is part of every good sportsman's equipment !

The Golfer

NEW HUDSON
BICYCLE

◀ A colour poster advertising 'New Hudson Bicycle (Birmingham) for the Golfer', published by Birmingham Litho Co Printers, framed and glazed, 24 x 14½in (61 x 37cm).
£140–170 MUL

▶ A bronze golfing medallion, the centre panel enamelled in colours with a golfer, the reverse inscribed 'St Nicholas Golf Club Prestwick, Roger Jubilee Caskets Competition, Best Scratch Score', in original case by Sorley of Glasgow, hand-dated '13.6.29'.
£90–100 VS

A Standard Golf Company of Sunderland Patent Duplex RL2 model golfing iron, with aluminium head and hickory shaft, c1920.
£275–300 S

ROWING & SAILING

An Oxford Royal Regatta silver cup and cover, by Duncan Urquhart and Naphtäli Hart, engraved with grapes and vine leaves, a pair of oars and tiller, gilt interior, later monogrammed and inscribed around the foot, marked, London 1811, 13in (33cm) high.
£850–950 F&C

► An Oxford University commemorative rudder, 1886, 23in (58.5cm) long.
£450–550 DOA

◄ A New Thames Yacht Club sailing trophy, in the form of a mantel clock, the silvered dial with retailer's name E. W. Streeter, framed within a silver ship's wheel, the wood plinth with repoussé plaques of yachts and presentation inscription, mounts marked 1877, 16½in (42cm) high.
£2,000–2,400 L

An American silver rowing trophy, by Tiffany & Co, New York, applied with trophies of a crossed oar and spar behind a ribbon-tied laurel wreath, the handles formed as eagles' heads, the finial formed as two oarsmen, the whole on a japanned wood base, 1876, 35in (89cm), 157oz.
£13,000–15,000 S(S)

RUGBY

A pair of black leather rugby boots, 1940s.
£65–75 SPT

A spelter figure of a young rugby player, mounted on a naturalistic base, c1880, 11in (28cm) high.
£300–350 MUL

A white England No. 1 International jersey, the breast badge embroidered with a shield of English roses and 'Paris 1933'.
£850–950 S

A Doulton Lambeth lemonade jug, relief-decorated in brown and green, with five cameos of rugby players in action, embossed marks to base, 1883, 9in (23cm) high.
£1,300–1,500 P(Ba)

A menu card for a dinner held in honour of Cardiff City AFC winning the Welsh Cup on 1st May 1912, signed in pencil by 35 team players and guests.
£600–700 P(Ba)

◄ A Rugby League home programme, London Highfield v France at White City, 21st March 1934.
£75–90 VS

SHOOTING

An Edwardian silver tobacco box, by Horton & Allday, the hinged cover engraved with partridges in a landscape, the reverse wtih pheasants, gilt interior, Birmingham 1901, 1½in (4cm) diam.
£350–420 WW

A painted tin decoy, c1890, 21in (53.3cm) high.
£180–200 HUM

A canvas-covered cartridge case, with leather straps and brass fittings, c1890, 15in (38cm) wide.
£250–285 SPT

A Victorian oak gun rack, for seven guns, the top pierced for barrels, 36¼in (92cm) wide.
£1,400–1,700 TEN

▶ A leather leg-of-mutton gun case, c1890, 31in (78.5cm) long.
£100–125 SPT

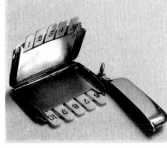

A silver butt marker, London 1925, 2in (5cm) wide.
£1,800–2,000 JBU

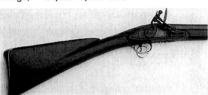

A flintlock sporting gun, by J. Wilson, with three-stage octagonal to round barrel, fully stocked with early 18thC hand-rail stock, original iron ramrod, c1820, 61½in (156cm) long.
£1,100–1,250 GV

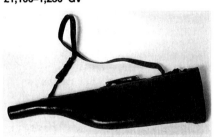

TENNIS

A box of four Dunlop tennis balls, used in the Kramer Professional Tennis Tournament at Birmingham on 13th August 1958, the inside of the box lid signed by six players, with 16 black and white photographs depicting the players, and one match ticket.
£550–600 P(Ba)

A tennis racket and leather case, with brass fittings, 1920s, 28in (71cm) wide.
£75–85 SPT

A 'Club' tennis racket, by A. W. Gamage Ltd, London, with original red natural gut strings, 1890s.
£140–170 DW

▶ An Edwardian mahogany and brass press for four tennis rackets, with brass-inlaid carrying handle and brass top locking screws.
£110–130 MUL

A Lawn Tennis Championship of Ireland silver tray trophy, by Langley Archer West, London, the border chased with leaves, flowers and scrolls, and engraved with a broad band of scrolling leaves and diaper around the central inscription, London 1895, 30¼in (77cm) wide, 160oz.
£3,000–3,500 DN

Glossary

We have defined here some of the terms that you will come across in this book. If there are any terms or technicalities you would like explained or you feel should be included in future, please let us know.

acid engraving: Technique of decorating glass by coating it in resin, incising a design and exposing the revealed areas to hydrochloric acid fumes.

agate ware: 18thC pottery, veined or marbled to resemble the mineral agate.

albarello: Pottery vessel used for storing pharmaceutical ingredients.

amboyna: Yellowish-brown burred wood imported from the West Indies and used as a veneer.

anchor escapement: Said to have been invented c1670 by Robert Hooke or William Clement. A type of escape mechanism shaped like an anchor, which engages at precise intervals with the toothed escape wheel. The anchor permits the use of a pendulum (either long or short), and gives greater accuracy than was possible with the verge escapement.

arabesque: Scrolling foliate decoration.

armoire: Large French cupboard or wardrobe, usually of monumental character.

askos: Small ancient Greek vessel to contain liquids, in the form of a closed pot with a spout and handle.

associated: Term used in antiques, in which one part of an item is of the same design but not originally made for it. See **marriage**.

automaton: Any moving toy or decorative object, usually powered by a clockwork mechanism.

barley-twist: Form of turning, popular in the late 17thC, which resembles a spiral of traditional barley sugar.

basalt(es): Black stoneware with a smooth, stone-like finish; perfected by Josiah Wedgwood.

bezel: Ring, usually brass, surrounding the dial of a clock, and securing the glass dial cover.

bisque: French term for biscuit ware, or unglazed porcelain.

blazes: Fine flutes cut in glass, with the tallest in the centre. They can also be slanting.

bombé: Outswelling, curving or bulging. Term used to describe a chest with a bulging front. In fashion from Louis XV period.

bonheur du jour: Small French writing table with a raised back comprising a cabinet or shelves.

boteh: Stylized design of afloral bush found on rugs, similar to a Paisley design.

bracket clock: Originally a 17thC clock which had to be set high up on a bracket because of the length of the weights; now sometimes applied to any mantel or table clock.

bureau de dame: Writing desk of delicate appearance and designed for use by ladies. Usually raised above slender cabriole legs and with one or two external drawers.

bureau plat: French writing table with a flat top and drawers in the frieze.

cabaret set: Tea set on a tray for three or more people.

calamander: Hardwood, imported from Sri Lanka (of the same family as ebony), used in the Regency period for making small articles of furniture, as a veneer and for crossbanding.

camaieu: Porcelain decoration using different tones of a single colour.

cameo glass: Two or more layers of coloured glass in which the top layer/s are then cut or etched away to create a multi-coloured design in relief.

An ancient technique popular with Art Nouveau glassmakers in the early 20thC.

candle slide: Wooden slide to hold a candlestick.

cartouche: Ornate tablet or shield surrounded by scrollwork and foliage, often bearing an inscription, monogram or coat-of-arms.

cased glass: One layer of glass, often coloured, sandwiched between two plain glass layers or vice versa, the outer layer engraved to create a decorative effect. An ancient technique revived in the 19thC. See **cameo glass** and **overlay**.

celadon: Chinese stonewares with an opaque grey-green glaze, first made in the Song Dynasty and still made today, principally in Korea.

cellaret: Lidded container on legs designed to hold wine. The interior is often divided into sections for individual bottles.

champlevé: Enamelling on copper or bronze, similar to cloisonné, in which a glass paste is applied to the hollowed-out design, fired and ground smooth.

chapter ring: Circular ring on a clock dial on which the hours and minutes are engraved, attached or painted.

character doll: One with a naturalistic face, especially laughing, crying, pouting, etc.

chilong: Chinese mythical dragon-type lizard.

Chinese Imari: Chinese imitations of Japanese blue, red and gold painted Imari wares, made from the early 18thC.

chinoiserie: The fashion, prevailing in the late 18thC, for Chinese-style ornamentation on porcelain, wallpapers, fabrics, furniture and garden architecture.

cistern tube: Mercury tube fitted into stick barometers, the lower end of which is sealed into a boxwood cistern.

clobbered: Term given to Chinese export blue and white ceramics which have had enamel decoration added in Europe, usually Holland.

clock garniture: Matching group of clock and vases or candelabra made for the mantel shelf. Often highly ornate.

cloisonné: Enamelling on metal with divisions in the design separated by lines of fine metal wire. A speciality of the Limoges region of France in the Middle Ages, and of Chinese craftsmen to the present day.

coin silver: Silver of the standard used for coinage, ie .925 or sterling.

coromandel: Imported wood from the Coromandel coast of India, of similar blackish appearance to calamander and used from c1780 for banding, and for small pieces of furniture.

countwheel: Wheel with segments cut out of the edge or with pins fitted to one face, which controls the striking of a clock. Also known as a locking plate.

cuerda seca: Tile-making technique, developed in Iran in the 15thC, whereby the colours of the design were separated by an oily substance which leaves a brownish outline.

cut glass: Glass carved with revolving wheels and abrasive to create sharp-edged facets that reflect and refract light so as to sparkle and achieve a prismatic (rainbow) effect. Revived in Bohemia in the 17thC, and common until superseded by pressed glass for utilitarian objects.

Cyma: Double-curved moulding. Cyma recta is concave above and convex below; cyma reversa the other way round. Also known as ogee and reverse ogee moulding. Popular with 18thC cabinet-makers.

Cymric: Trade-name used by Liberty & Co for a mass-produced range of silverware inspired by Celtic art, introduced in 1899 and often incorporating enamelled pictorial plaques.

cwpwrdd deuddarn: Welsh variety of the press cupboard with two tiers.

deadbeat escapement: Type of anchor escapement, possibly invented by George Graham and used in precision pendulum clocks.

Delft: Dutch tin-glazed earthenwares named after the town of Delft, the principal production centre, from the 16thC onwards. Similar pottery made in England from the late 16thC is also termed 'delft' or 'delftware'.

deutsche Blumen: Naturalistically painted flowers, either single or tied into bunches, used as a popular decorative motif on 18thC pottery and porcelain.

diaper: Surface decoration composed of repeated diamonds or squares, often carved in low relief.

ding: Chinese three-legged vessel.

diorama: Miniature three-dimensional scene.

dog of Fo: Buddhist guardian lion.

doucai: Decoration on Chinese porcelain using five colours.

écuelle: 17th and 18thC vessel, usually of silver, but also of ceramic, for serving soup. Has a shallow, circular bowl, two handles and a domed cover. It often comes complete with a stand.

Elastolin: German makers of composition toy soldiers and zoo figures, 1904–55.

ensi: Rug used as a tent door by Turkoman tribes.

escapement: Means or device which regulates the release of the power of a timepiece to its pendulum or balance.

famille jaune/noire/rose/verte: Chinese porcelain in which yellow, black, pink or green respectively are the predominant ground colours.

fauteuil: French open-armed drawing room chair.

fielded panel: Panel with bevelled or chamfered edges.

filigree: Lacy openwork of silver or gold thread, produced in large quantities since end 19thC.

flatware (1): Collective name for flat pottery and porcelain, such as plates, dishes and saucers.

flatware (2): Cutlery.

flow blue: Process used principally after 1840, in which powder is added to the dye used in blue and white transferware so that the blue flows beyond the edges of the transfer, making the pattern less sharply defined. Items using this process were made primarily for the American market.

fluted: Border that resembles a scalloped edge, used as a decoration on furniture, glass, silver and porcelain items.

fusee: 18thC clockwork invention; a cone-shaped drum, linked to the spring barrel by a length of gut or chain. The shape compensates for the declining strength of the mainspring thus ensuring constant timekeeping.

gadroon: Border or ornament comprising radiating lobes of either curbed or straight form. Used from the late Elizabethan period.

gilding: Process of applying thin gold foil to a surface. There are two methods. Oil gilding involves the use of linseed oil and is applied directly onto the woodwork. Water gilding requires the wood to be painted with gesso. The term is also used in ceramics, glass etc.

girandole: Carved and gilt candle sconce incorporating a mirror.

Glasgow School: Term used to describe the style developed in the late 19thC by Charles Rennie Mackintosh and his followers, a simplified linear form of Art Nouveau highly influential on Continental work of the period.

goncalo alves: Brazilian timber sometimes mistaken for rosewood.

grisaille: Monochrome decoration, usually grey, used on ceramics and furniture during the 18th and 19thC.

guéridon: Small circular table designed to carry some form of lighting.

guilloche: Pattern of twisting bands, spirals, double spirals or linked chains.

gul: From the Persian word for flower – usually used to describe a geometric flowerhead on a rug.

guttus: Ancient Greek closed vessel with a spout and handle for pouring oil into lamps.

halberd: Spear fitted with a double axe.

hard paste: True porcelain made of china stone (petuntse) and kaolin; the formula was long known to, and kept secret by, Chinese potters but only discovered in the 1720s at Meissen, Germany, from where it spread to the rest of Europe and the Americas. Recognized by its hard, glossy feel.

harewood: Sycamore which has been stained a greenish colour. It is used mainly as an inlay and was known as silverwood in the 18thC.

herati: Overall repeating design of a flowerhead within a lozenge issuing small leaves. Used in descriptions of rugs.

hiramakie: Japanese term for sponged gold applied level with the surface.

hirame: Japanese lacquer decorated with gold and silver leaf.

hongmu: Type of wood used in the manufacture of Chinese furniture.

ho-o: Mythical Chinese bird, similar to a phoenix, symbolizing wisdom and energy.

huanghuali: Type of Oriental wood, much admired for its colour.

hydria: Ancient Greek water vessel characterized by a vertical handle at the back for dipping and two horizontal handles for lifting.

Imari: Export Japanese porcelain of predominantly red, blue and gold decoration which, although made in Arita, is called Imari after the port from which it was shipped.

inro: Japanese multi-compartmental medicine or seal container, carried suspended from the sash of a kimono.

intaglio: Incised gemstone, often set in a ring, used in antiquity and during the Renaissance as a seal. Any incised decoration; the opposite of carving in relief.

ironstone: Stoneware, patented 1813 by Charles James Mason, containing ground glassy slag, a by-product of iron smelting, for extra strength.

jadeite: Type of jade, normally the best and most desirable.

Jugendstil: German Art Nouveau style.

Kakiemon: Family of 17thC Japanese porcelain decorators who produced wares decorated with flowers and figures on a white ground in distinctive colours: azure, yellow, turquoise and soft red. Widely imitated in Europe.

katana: Long Japanese sword.

kiku mon: Japanese stylised chrysanthemum.

kelim: Flat woven rug lacking a pile.

khula khud: Indo-Persian term for helmet.

kilin: Chinese mythical beast with a lion's tail, cloven hooves and the scales of a dragon.

kinrande: Japanese brocade decoration.

kiri: Japanese name for the Paulownia flower.

kirin: Japanese mythical beast.

knop: Knob, protuberance or swelling in the stem of a wine glass, of various forms which can be used as an aid to dating and provenance.

koro: Japanese incense burner.

kovsh: Russian vessel used for measuring drink, often highly decorated for ornamental purposes from the late 18thC.

kraak porselein: Dutch term for porcelain raided from Portuguese ships, used to describe the earliest Chinese export porcelain.

krater: Ancient Greek vessel for mixing water and wine in which the mouth is always the widest part.

kufic: Arabic angular script – used in rugs to refer to stylized geometric calligraphy.

lingzhi: Type of fungus or mushroom, used as a motif on Chinese works of art.

Lithyalin: Polished opaque glass resembling hardstones, patented by Friedrich Egermann in 1829 at his factory in Haida, northern Bohemia.

loaded: In silverware, a hollow part of a vessel, usually a candlestick, filled with pitch or sand for weight and stability.

Long Eliza: Elongated female figure found on Kangxi blue and white export porcelain. The name derives from the Dutch 'lange lijsen'.

lunette: Semi-circular decorative motif popular for carved friezes in the Jacobean and Victorian periods.

made up: Piece of furniture that has been put together from parts of other pieces of furniture. See **marriage**.

maiolica: Tin-glazed earthenware produced in Italy from the 15thC to the present day.

majolica: Heavily-potted, moulded ware covered in transparent glazes in distinctive, often sombre colours, developed by the Minton factory in the mid-19thC.

manjua: Japanese bun filled with sweet bean paste, now applied to the shape of a *netsuke*.

marriage: Joining together of two unrelated parts to form one piece of furniture. See **associated** and **made up**.

merese: Flat disc of glass which links the bowl and stem, and sometimes the stem and foot, of a drinking glass.

mihrab: Prayer niche with a pointed arch; the motif which distinguishes a prayer rug from other types.

millefiori: Multi-coloured, or mosaic, glass, made since antiquity by fusing a number of coloured glass rods into a cane, and cutting off thin sections; much used to ornament paperweights.

nashiji: Multitude of gold flakes in Japanese lacquer.

netsuke: Japanese carved toggles made to secure *sagemono* ('hanging things') to the *obi* (waist belt) from a cord; usually of ivory, lacquer, silver or wood, from the 16thC.

niello: Black metal alloy or enamel used for filling in engraved designs on silverware.

oinochoe: Small ancient Greek jug with handles.

ojime: Japanese word meaning bead.

okimono: Small, finely carved Japanese ornament.

ormolu: Strictly, gilded bronze but used loosely for any yellow metal. Originally used for furniture handles and mounts but, from the 18thC, for inkstands, candlesticks etc.

overlay: In cased glass, the top layer, usually engraved to reveal a different coloured layer beneath.

overstuffed: Descriptive of upholstered furniture where the covering extends over the frame of the seat.

palmette: In rugs, a cross-section through a stylized flowerhead or fruit.

papier mâché: Moulded paper pulp, suitable for japanning and polishing, used for small articles such as trays, boxes, tea caddies, and coasters.

pâte-de-cristal: Glass that is crushed into fine crystals and and then bound together so that it can be moulded rather than having to be worked in its molten state.

pâte-de-verre: Translucent glass created by melting and applying powdered glass in layers or by casting it in a mould.

pâte-sur-pâte: 19thC Sèvres porcelain technique, much copied, of applying coloured clay decoration to the body before firing.

penwork: Type of decoration applied to japanned furniture, principally in England in the late 18th/early 19thC. Patterns in white japan were applied to a piece which had already been japanned black, and then the details and shading were added using black Indian ink with a fine quill pen.

pier glass: Mirror designed to be fixed to the pier, or wall, between two tall window openings, often partnered by a matching pier table. Made from mid-17thC.

pietra dura: Italian term for hard stone, applied to a mosaic pattern of semi-precious stones and marble.

plate: Old fashioned term, still occasionally used, to describe gold and silver vessels; not to be confused with Sheffield plate, or plated vessels generally, in which silver is fused to a base metal alloy.

plique-à-jour: Enamelling technique in which a structure of metal strips is laid on a metal background to form enclosed areas which are then filled with transparent enamels. When the backing is removed, a transparent 'stained glass' effect is achieved.

pole screen: Small adjustable screen mounted on a pole and designed to stand in front of an open fire to shield a lady's face from the heat.

poudreuse: French dressing table.

poupard: Doll without legs, often mounted on a stick. Popular in 19thC.

powder flask: Device for measuring out a precise quantity of priming powder, suspended from a musketeer's belt or bandolier and often ornately decorated. Sporting flasks are often made of antler and carved with hunting scenes.

powder horn: Cow horn hollowed out, blocked at the wide end with a wooden plug and fitted with a measuring device at the narrow end, used by musketeers for dispensing a precise quantity of priming powder.

plum pudding: Type of figuring in some veneers, produced by oval spots in the wood. Found particularly in mahogany.

pressed glass: Early 19thC invention, exploited rapidly in America, whereby mechanical pressure was used to form glassware in a mould.

printie: Circular or oval scoop out of glass, sometimes called a lens.

Puritan spoon: Transitional style of silver spoon, linking early English to modern types. Similar to a slip top but with a broader stem, its name derives from its plain form.

quama: Russian dagger.

quarter-veneered: Four consecutively cut, and therefore identical, pieces of veneer laid at opposite ends to each other to give a mirrored effect.

register plate: Scale of a barometer against which the mercury level is read.

regulator: Clock of great accuracy, thus sometimes used for controlling or checking other timepieces.

rocaille: Shell and rock motifs found in rococo work.

rummer: 19thC English low drinking goblet.

ruyi: Chinese presentation sceptre.

sancai: Three colour decoration on Chinese porcelain.

sang-de-boeuf: (lit. ox-blood) A bright red glaze used extensively on Chinese ceramics during the Qing Dynasty.

saph: Long, narrow, multiple-niche prayer rug.

S.F.B.J.: Société de Fabrication de Bébés et Jouets; association of doll makers founded 1899 by the merger of Jumeau, Bru and others.

shamshir: Indian sword.

shaska: Russian sabre.

Shibayama: Lacquer applied with semi-precious stones and ivory.

shinshinto: Japanese term meaning 'new new', referring to edged weapons produced between 1800 and 1868.

shishi: Japanese mythical beast, a lion-dog.

shou symbol: Formal, artistic version of the Chinese character *shou*, meaning long-life.

siphon tube: U-shaped tube fitted into wheel barometers where the level of mercury in the short arm is used to record air pressure.

soft paste: Artificial porcelain made with the addition of ground glass, bone-ash or soapstone. Used by most European porcelain manufacturers during the 18thC. Recognized by its soft, soapy feel.

spadroon: Cut-and-thrust sword.

spandrel: Element of design, closing off a corner.

spelter: Zinc treated to look like bronze and much used as an inexpensive substitute in Art Nouveau appliqué ornament and Art Deco figures.

spontoon: Type of halberd often carried by junior infantry officers and senior non-commissioned officers.

standish: Silver inkstand.

strapwork: Repeated carved decoration suggesting plaited straps.

stumpwork: Embroidery which incorporates distinctive areas of raised decoration, formed by padding certain areas of the design.

sugán: Twisted lengths of straw: referring to Irish country chairs which have seats of this type.

susani: Central Asian hand-embroidered bridal bed-cover.

takamakie: Technique used in Japanese lacquerware in which the design is built up and modelled in a mixture of lacquer and charcoal or clay dust, and then often gilded.

tanto: Japanese dagger.

Taotie: Chinese mythical animal which devours wrong-doers.

tazza: Wide but shallow bowl on a stem with a foot; ceramic and metal tazzas were made in antiquity and the form was revived by Venetian glassmakers in 15thC. Also made in silver from 16thC.

teapoy: Piece of furniture in the form of a tea caddy on legs, with a hinged lid opening to reveal caddies, mixing bowl and other tea drinking accessories.

tear: Tear-drop shaped air bubble in the stem of an early 18thC wine glass, from which the air-twist evolved.

tester: Wooden canopy over a bedstead supported on either two or four posts. It may extend fully over the bed, known as a full tester, or only over the bedhead half, known as a half tester.

tête-à-tête: Tea set for two people.

thuyawood: Reddish-brown wood with distinctive small 'bird's-eye' markings, imported from Africa and used as a veneer.

timepiece: Clock that does not strike or chime.

tin glaze: Glassy opaque white glaze of tin oxide; re-introduced to Europe in 14thC by Moorish potters; the characteristic glaze of delftware, faïence and maiolica.

togidashi: Japanese laquer technique in which further layers are added to *hiramakie* (qv) and then polished flush with the original surface.

tombak: Alloy of copper and zinc.

touch: Maker's mark stamped on much, but not all, early English pewter. Their use was strictly controlled by the Pewterer's Company of London: early examples consist of initials, later ones are more elaborate and pictorial, sometimes including the maker's address.

transfer-printed: Ceramic decoration technique perfected mid-18thC and used widely thereafter for mass-produced wares. An engraved design is transferred onto a slab of glue or gelatin (a bat), which was then laid over the body of the vessel, leaving an outline. This was sometimes coloured in by hand.

tsuba: Guard of a Japanese sword, usually consisting of an ornamented plate.

Tudric: Range of Celtic-inspired Art Nouveau pewter of high quality, designed for mass-production by Archibald Knox and others, and retailed through Liberty & Co.

tulipwood: Yellow-brown wood with reddish stripe, imported from Central and South America and used as a veneer and for inlay and crossbanding.

tyg: Mug with three or more handles.

verge escapement: Oldest form of escapement, found on clocks as early as 1300 and still in use in 1900. Consisting of a bar (the verge) with two flag-shaped pallets that rock in and out of the teeth of the crown or escape wheel to regulate the movement.

vernier scale: Short scale added to the traditional 3in (7.5cm) scale on stick barometers to give more precise readings than had previously been possible.

verre églomisé: Painting on glass. Often the reverse side of the glass is covered in gold or silver leaf through which a pattern is engraved and then painted black.

vesta case: Ornate flat case of silver or other metal for carrying vestas, an early form of match. Used from mid-19thC.

vitrine: French display cabinet which is often of bombé or serpentine outline and ornately decorated with marquetry and ormolu.

Vitruvian scroll: Repeated border ornament of scrolls that resemble waves.

WMF: Short for the German Württembergische Metallwarenfabrik, one of the principal producers of Art Nouveau silver and silver-plated objects, early 20thC.

wucai: Type of five-colour Chinese porcelain decoration.

yen yen: Chinese term for a long-necked vase with a trumpet mouth.

Directory of Specialists

If you wish to be included in next year's directory, or if you have a change of address or telephone number, please contact Miller's Advertising Department by April 2001. We advise readers to make contact by telephone before visiting a dealer, therefore avoiding a wasted journey.

20thC Design
London
Zoom, 312 Lillie Road,
Fulham SW6 7PS
Tel: 07000 ZOOM 2000
Mobile: 0958 372975

Antiques Dealers' Association
Kent
West Kent Antique Dealers'
Association
Tel: 01959 569408
www.wkada.co.uk

Oxfordshire
Thames Valley Antique
Dealers' Association (TVADA)
The Old College,
Queen Street,
Dorchester-on-Thames,
Oxon OX10 7HL
Tel/Fax: 01865 341639
antiques@tvada.co.uk

Wiltshire
Internet Antique Dealers'
Association (I-ADA)
Tel: 01722 336869
info@I-ADA .com
www.I-ADA.com

Antiquities
Dorset
Chris Belton, PO Box 356,
Christchurch BH23 1XQ
Tel: 01202 478592

Architectural Antiques
Cheshire
Nostalgia,
Hollands Mill,
61 Shaw Heath,
Stockport SK3 8BH
Tel: 0161 477 7706

Devon
Ashburton Marbles,
Grate Hall, North Street,
Ashburton TQ13 7DU
Tel: 01364 653189

Gloucestershire
Reclamation Services Ltd,
Catbrain Quarry,
Painswick Beacon,
Above Paradise,
Painswick GL6 6SU
Tel: 01452 814064
www.recserv.demon.co.uk

Somerset
Wells Reclamation & Co,
Coxley, Nr Wells BA5 1RQ
Tel: 01749 677087

Surrey
Drummond's Architectural
Antiques,
The Kirk Patrick Buildings,
25 London Road (A3),
Hindhead GU26 6AB
Tel: 01428 609444

Yorkshire
Architectural & Historical
Salvage, Spa Street,
Ossett, Wakefield WF5 0HJ
Tel: 01924 262831

Arms & Militaria
Cheshire
Armourer – The Militaria
Magazine, Published by
Beaumont Publishing Ltd,
1st floor Adelphi Mill,
Bollington SK10 5JB
Tel: 01625 575700
editor@armourer.co.uk
www.armourer.co.uk
*A bi-monthly magazine for
military antique collectors
and military history
enthusiasts, offering
hundreds of contacts for
buying and selling, articles
on all aspects of militaria
collecting plus the dates
of UK militaria fairs and
auctions. Available on
subscription*

Gloucestershire
Q&C Militaria,
22 Suffolk Road,
Cheltenham GL50 2AQ
Tel: 01242 519815
Mobile: 0378 613977

Lincolnshire
Garth Vincent,
The Old Manor House,
Allington,
Nr Grantham NG32 2DH
Tel: 01400 281358

Surrey
West Street Antiques,
63 West Street,
Dorking RH4 1BS
Tel: 01306 883487

Sussex
Wallis & Wallis,
West Street Auction
Galleries, Lewes BN7 2NJ
Tel: 01273 480208

West Midlands
Weller & Dufty Ltd,
141 Bromsgrove Street,
Birmingham B5 6RQ
Tel: 0121 692 1414

Yorkshire
Andrew Spencer Bottomley,
The Coach House,
Thongs Bridge,
Holmfirth HD7 2TT
Tel: 01484 685234

Asian Works of Art
Buckinghamshire
Glade Antiques,
PO Box 939,
Marlow SL7 1SR
Tel: 01628 487255

London
David Bowden,
12 The Mall, Upper Street,
Islington N1 0PD Tel: 020
7226 3033

Barographs
Somerset
Richard Twort
Tel/Fax: 01934 641900
Mobile: 07711 939789

Barometers
Berkshire
Alan Walker,
Halfway Manor,
Halfway,
Nr Newbury RG20 8NR
Tel: 01488 657670

Somerset
Knole Barometers,
Bingham House, West
Street, Somerton TA11 7PS
Tel: 01458 241015
Mobile: 07785 364567

West Yorkshire
Weather House Antiques,
Kym S. Walker,
Foster Clough,
Hebden Bridge HX7 5QZ
Tel: 01422 882808/886961

Wiltshire
P. A. Oxley,
The Old Rectory, Cherhill,
Nr Calne SN11 8UX
Tel: 01249 816227

Beds
Greater Manchester
Victorian Imports,
Prestwich Antiques,
371/373 Bury New Road,
Prestwich M25 1AW
Tel: 0161 798 0911/
0161 773 0500

Wales
Seventh Heaven,
Chirk Mill, Chirk, Wrexham,
County Borough LL14 5BU
Tel: 01691 777622

Worcestershire
S. W. Antiques,
Abbey Showrooms,
Newlands, Pershore WR10 1BP
Tel: 01386 555580

Billiard Tables
Berkshire
William Bentley Billiards,
Standen Manor Farm,
Hungerford RG17 0RB
Tel: 01672 871214

Surrey
Academy Billiard Co,
5 Camphill Industrial Estate,
Camphill Road,
West Byfleet KT14 6EW
Tel: 01932 352067

Books
Kent
The Chaucer Bookshop,
6–7 Beer Cart Lane,
Canterbury CT1 2NY
Tel: 01227 453912
chaucerbooks@canterbury.
dialnet.com
www.chaucer-
bookshop.co.uk/main.html

Middlesex
John Ives, 5 Normanhurst
Drive, Twickenham TW1 1NA
Tel: 020 8892 6265
Reference books

Surrey
David Aldous-Cook,
PO Box 413,
Sutton SM3 8SZ
Tel: 020 8642 4842
*Reference books on antiques
and collectables*

USA
Art Book Services,
c/o Antique Collectors' Club
Market Street Industrial Park,
Wappinger Falls,
New York 12590
Tel: 914 297 0003
www.ArtBookServices.com

Wiltshire
Dominic Winter Book
Auctions,
The Old School,
Maxwell Street,
Swindon SN1 5DR
Tel: 01793 611340

Boxes & Treen
Berkshire
Mostly Boxes,
93 High Street, Eton,
Windsor SL4 6AF
Tel: 01753 858470

London
Coromandel
Tel: 020 8543 9115
Mobile: 07932102756

Gerald Mathias,
Antiquarius,
135 King's Road,
Chelsea SW3 4PW
Tel: 020 7351 0484

Somerset
Alan Stacey,
Boxwood Antique Restorers.
Appointment only
Tel: 01963 33988
*Cabinet-making, polishing,
carving and specialists in
tortoiseshell, ivory and
mother-of-pearl on boxes,
caddies and furniture.
See our advertisement in
Boxes (colour) section*

British Antique Furniture Restorers' Association
BAFRA Head Office,
The Old Rectory,
Warmwell,
Dorchester,
Dorset DT2 8HQ
Tel: 01305 854822
Fax: 01305 852104

Bedfordshire
Duncan Michael Everitt,
DME Restorations Ltd,
11 Church Street,
Ampthill MK45 2PL
Tel: 01525 405819
Fax: 01525 756177
dme.rest@dial.pipex.com
www.dmerestoration.co.uk
*A full restoration service
of furniture.*

Berkshire
Ben R. W. Norris,
Knowl Hill Farm,
Knowl Hill, Kingsclere,
Newbury RG20 4NY
Tel: 01635 297950
*Gilding, carving &
architectural woodwork*

Cambridgeshire
Ludovic Potts, Unit 1 & 1A,
Haddenham Business Park,
Station Road, Ely CB6 3XD
Tel: 01353 741537
*Traditional repairs, boulle,
walnut, oak, veneering,
upholstery, cane, rush
& gilding*

Devon
Tony Vernon,
15 Follett Road, Topsham,
Exeter EX3 0JP
Tel: 01392 874635
*All aspects of conservation
and restoration including
gilding, carving, upholstery,
veneering and polishing.
Included on the
Conservation Register of
the Conservation Unit
of the Museums and
Galleries Commission*

Dorset
Michael Barrington,
The Old Rectory, Warmwell,
Dorchester DT2 8HQ
Tel: 01305 852104
*The conservation and
restoration of antique & fine
furniture & clocks. Clock
dials and movements,
barometers, upholstery,
mechanical music, automata
and toys, antique metalwork
ferrous and non-ferrous*

Richard Bolton,
Meadow Court,
Athelhampton House,
Dorchester DT2 7LG
Tel: 01305 848346
*All aspects of furniture
restoration. Tuition available*

Philip Hawkins,
Glebe Workshop, Semley,
Shaftesbury SP7 9AP
Tel: 01747 830830
hawkinssemley@hotmail.com
Oak & country furniture

Essex
Clive Beardall,
104B High Street,
Maldon, CM9 5ET
Tel: 01621 857890
Furniture

Gloucestershire
Alan Hessel, The Old Town
Workshop, St George's
Close, Moreton-in-Marsh
GL56 0LP
Tel: 01608 650026

Stephen Hill,
Brewery Antiques,
2 Cirencester Workshops,
Brewery Court,
Cirencester GL7 1JH
Tel: 01285 658817
Mobile: 0976 722028

Andrew Lelliott,
6 Tetbury Hill, Avening,
Tetbury GL8 8LT
Tel: 01453 835783

*Restoration and conservation
of fine furniture and clock
cases. Matching mouldings –
bespoke fine quality mouldings
for all woodworkers.
Included on the
Conservation Unit register*

Hampshire
John Hartley,
Johnson's Barns,
Waterworks Road, Sheet,
Petersfield GU32 2BY
Tel: 01730 233792
*Comprehensive furniture
restoration. Large workshops*

David C. E. Lewry,
Wychelms, 66 Gorran
Avenue, Rowner,
Gosport PO13 0NF
Tel: 01329 286901
Furniture

Hertfordshire
John B. Carr,
Charles Perry Restorations
Ltd, Praewood Farm,
Hemel Hempstead Road,
St Albans AL3 6AA
Tel: 01727 853487
*Specialists in restoration and
conservation*

Clifford J. Tracy Ltd,
Unit 3 Shaftesbury Industrial
Centre, Icknield Way,
Letchworth SG6 1HE
Tel: 01462 684855
*Restoration of antique
furniture, marquetry, inlaid
ivory, brass and tortoiseshell,
woodturning, polishing,
gilding, general cabinet-
making and complete
re-upholstery service.
Worm-infested furniture
is guaranteed clear by
non-toxic methods.
Free estimates.
Our own transport for
collections and delivery*

Kent
Timothy Akers,
The Forge, 39 Chancery Lane,
Beckenham BR3 6NR
Tel: 020 8650 9179
www.akersofantiques.com
*Longcase and bracket
clocks, cabinet-making,
French polishing*

Benedict Clegg,
Rear of 20 Camden Road,
Tunbridge Wells TN1 2PT
Tel: 01892 548095

Bruce Luckhurst,
Little Surrenden Workshops,
Ashford Road,
Bethersden,
Ashford TN26 3BG
Tel: 01233 820589
restoration@woodwise.
newnet.uk
www.bruceluckhurst.co.uk
One-year course available

Lancashire
Eric Smith Antique
Restorations,
The Old Church,
Park Road, Darwen BB3 2LD
Tel: 01254 776222
*Furniture, vernacular furniture,
longcase clocks. Registered
with museums & galleries.
Commissions London*

London
Oliver Clarke,
Heritage Restorations,
96 Webber Street SE1 0QN
Tel: 020 7928 3624
*Restoration – 18th & 19thC
furniture specialist*

William Cook, 167 Battersea
High Street SW11 3JS
Tel: 020 7736 5329

Robert H. Crawley,
Aberdeen House,
75 St Mary's Road,
Ealing W5 5RH
Tel: 020 8566 5074

Sebastian Giles,
Sebastian Giles Furniture,
11 Junction Mews W2 1PN
Tel: 020 7402 1535
Comprehensive

Rodrigo Titian, Titian Studio,
318 Kensal Road W10 5BN
Tel: 020 8960 6247
enquiries@titianstudios.co.uk
www.titianstudios.co.uk
*Carving, gilding, lacquer,
painted furniture and French
polishing. Caning & rushing*

Norfolk
Michael Dolling,
Church Farm Barns,
Glandford, Holt NR25 7JR
Tel: 01263 741115

Roderick Nigel Larwood,
The Oaks, Station Road,
Larling, Norwich NR16 2QS
Tel: 01953 717937
*Restorers of fine antiques
and traditional finishers*

Scotland
William Trist,
135 St Leonard's Street,
Edinburgh EH8 9RB
Tel: 0131 667 7775
Fax: 0131 668 4333
*Antique furniture restoration.
Cabinet & chairmakers, cane
& rush seating, upholstery*

Shropshire
Richard A Higgins,
The Old School, Longnor,
Nr Shrewsbury SY5 7PP
Tel: 01743 718162
*Furniture, clocks, movements,
dials & cases, casting, plating,
boulle, gilding, lacquerwork,
carving, period upholstery*

Somerset
Stuart Bradbury,
M. & S. Bradbury,
The Barn, Hanham Lane,
Paulton, Bristol BS39 7PF
Tel: 01761 418910
*Antique furniture conservation
& restoration*

Robert P. Tandy,
Unit 5, Manor Workshops,
West End, Nailsea,
Bristol BS48 4DD
Tel: 01275 856378
*Traditional antique furniture
restoration & repairs.*

Surrey
David J. Booth, 9 High St,
Ewell, Epsom KT17 1SG
Tel: 020 8393 5245
*Restoration & large
showrooms*

Michael Hedgecoe,
21 Burrow Hill Green,
Chobham,
Woking GU24 8QS
Tel: 01276 858206

Gavin Hussey,
4 Brook Farm,
Clayhill Road,
Leigh RH2 8PA
Tel: 01306 611634/
0411 281661
Antique restoration

Timothy Naylor,
The Workshop,
2 Chertsey Road,
Chobham,
Woking GU24 8NB
Tel: 01276 855122

Sussex
Simon Paterson,
Whitelands,
West Dean,
Chichester PO18 0RL
Tel: 01243 811900
*Boulle-work, marquetry,
clock case & general
restoration & repair*

Albert Plumb,
Albert Plumb Furniture Co,
Briarfield,
Itchenor Green,
Chichester PO20 7DA
Tel: 01243 513700
*Cabinet-making,
upholstery*

West Midlands
Phillip Slater,
93 Hewell Road,
Barnt Green,
Birmingham B45 8NL
Tel: 0121 445 4942
Inlay work, marquetry

Wiltshire
William Cook,
High Trees House,
Savernake Forest,
Nr Marlborough
SN8 4NE
Tel: 01672 513017

Yorkshire
Rodney F. Kemble,
16 Crag Vale Terrace,
Glusburn,
Nr Keighley BD20 8QU
Tel: 01535 636954/633702
*Furniture and small
decorative items*

Cameras
Lincolnshire
Antique Photographic
Company Ltd
Tel: 01949 842192
alpaco@lineone.net
www.thesaurus.co.uk/cook

Carpets
Gloucestershire
Samarkand Galleries,
7–8 Brewery Yard,
Sheep Street,
Stow-on-the-Wold
GL54 1AA
Tel: 01451 832322
mac@samarkand.co.uk
www.samarkand.co.uk
*Antique rugs from
Near East & Central Asia.
Antique nomadic weavings.
Decorative carpets. Tribal
artefacts. Contact: Brian
MacDonald FRGS*

Ceramics
Surrey
Julian Eade.
Tel: 020 8394 1515
Mobile: 0973 542971
*Doulton Lambeth
stoneware and Burslem
wares. Royal Worcester,
Minton and Derby*

Clocks
Bedfordshire
James B. Chadburn,
37 Stewkley Road,
Wing LU7 0NJ
Tel: 01296 681750
*Fine antique clocks
and barometers and
restoration*

Cheshire
Coppelia Antiques,
Holford Lodge,
Plumley Moor Road,
Plumley WA16 9RS
Tel: 01565 722197

Devon
Musgrave Bickford Antiques,
15 East Street, Crediton
EX17 3AT
Tel: 01363 775042

Essex
It's About Time,
863 London Road,
Westcliff on Sea SS0 9SZ
Tel: 01702 472574

Village Clocks,
Eastwood House,
32 Eastwood Drive,
Highwood,
Colchester CO4 4EB
Tel: 01787 375896

Gloucestershire
Jeffrey Formby,
Orchard Cottage,
East Street, Moreton-in-
Marsh GL56 0LQ
Tel: 01608 650558

Grandfather Clock Shop,
Styles of Stow, The Little
House, Sheep Street,
Stow-on-the-Wold GL54 1JS
Tel: 01451 830455

Jillings Antique Clocks,
Croft House, 17 Church St,
Newent GL18 1PU
Tel: 01531 822100
Mobile: 0973 830110

Greater Manchester
Northern Clocks,
Boothsbank Farm, Worsley,
Manchester M28 1LL
Tel: 0161 790 8414

Hampshire
Bryan Clisby,
Antique Clocks at Andwells
Antiques, High Street,
Hartley Wintney RG27 8NY
Tel: 01252 842305

Clock-Work-Shop
(Winchester),
6A Parchment Street,
Winchester SO23 8AT
Tel: 01962 842331

Kent
Campbell & Archard Ltd,
Lychgate House, Church
Street, Seal TN15 0AR
Tel: 01732 761153

Gem Antiques,
28 London Road,
Sevenoaks TN13 1AP
Tel: 01732 743540

Gaby Gunst, 140 High
Street, Tenterden TN30 6HT
Tel: 01580 765818

The Old Clock Shop,
63 High Street,
West Malling ME19 6NA
Tel: 01732 843246

Derek Roberts,
25 Shipbourne Road,
Tonbridge TN10 3DN
Tel: 01732 358986

London
Chelsea Clocks & Antiques,
Stand H3-4, Antiquarius Market,
135 Kings Road SW3 4PW
Tel: 020 7352 8646

The Clock Clinic Ltd,
85 Lower Richmond Road
SW15 1EU
Tel: 020 8788 1407

Pendulum, King House,
51 Maddox Street W1R 9LA
Tel: 020 7629 6602

Roderick Antiques Clocks,
23 Vicarage Gate W8 4AA
Tel: 020 7937 8517

W. F. Turk, 355 Kingston
Road, Wimbledon Chase
SW20 8JX
Tel/Fax: 020 8543 3231

Norfolk
Keith Lawson L.B.H.I.,
Scratby Garden Centre,
Beach Road, Scratby,
Great Yarmouth NR29 3AJ
Tel: 01493 730950

North Yorkshire
Botany Bay Antiques,
8 Grape Lane, Whitby
Tel: 01947 602007
botanybay@madasafish.com
www.botanybayantiques.co.uk

Oxfordshire
Craig Barfoot,
Antique Clocks, Tudor House,
East Hagbourne OX11 9LR
Tel: 01235 818968
Mobile: 07710 858158

Republic of Ireland
Jonathan Beech,
Westport, Co. Mayo
Tel: 00 353 98 28688

Scotland
John Mann, Antique Clocks,
The Clock Showroom,
Canonbie, Near Carlisle,
Galloway DG14 0SY
Tel: 013873 71337/71828
johnmannantiqueclocks.co.uk

Shropshire
The Curiosity Shop,
127 Old St, Ludlow SY8 1NU
Tel: 01584 875927

Somerset
Kembery Antique Clocks,
Bartlett Street Antiques
Centre, 5 Bartlett Street,
Bath BA1 2QZ
Tel: 0117 956 5281/
0850 623237

Staffordshire
Essence of Time,
Tudor of Lichfield Antique
Centre, Bore Street,
Lichfield WS13 6LL
Tel: 01543 263951/
01902 764900
Mobile: 07944 245064

Surrey
The Clock House,
75 Pound Street,
Carshalton SM5 3PG
Tel: 020 8773 4844

The Clock Shop,
64 Church Street,
Weybridge KT13 8DL
Tel: 01932 840407/855503

E. Hollander,
1 Bennetts Castle,
89 The Street, Capel,
Dorking RH5 5JX
Tel: 01306 713377
Clock restoration

Horological Workshop,
204 Worplesdon Road,
Guildford GU2 9UY
Tel: 01483 576496

Sussex
Sam Orr,
Antique Clocks,
36 High Street,
Hurstpierpoint,
Nr Brighton BN6 9RG
Tel: 01273 832081

Warwickshire
Summersons,
172 Emscote Road,
Warwick CV34 5QN
Tel/Fax: 01926 400630
www.summersons.com
*Complete restoration of
antique clocks & barometers,
dial restoration, cabinet-work
& French polishing, wheel
cutting, parts made, clock
hands cut, fretwork,
silvering/ gilding, polishing/
laquering, restoration parts
& materials, insurance
valuations, free estimates
and advice.*

West Midlands
Woodward Antiques,
14 High Street,
Tettenhall,
Wolverhampton WV6 8QT
Tel: 01902 745608

Wiltshire
P. A. Oxley,
Antique Clocks,
The Old Rectory, Cherhill,
Nr Calne SN11 8UX
Tel: 01249 816227

Allan Smith Clocks,
Amity Cottage,
162 Beechcroft Road,
Upper Stratton,
Swindon SN2 6QE
Tel: 01793 822977
Mobile: 0378 834342

Yorkshire
Brian Loomes,
Calf Haugh Farm,
Pateley Bridge HG3 5HW
Tel: 01423 711163

Time & Motion, 1 Beckside,
Beverley HU17 0PB
Tel: 01482 881574

Comics
London
Comic Book Postal Auctions
Ltd, 40–42 Osnaburgh Street
NW1 3ND
Tel: 020 7424 0007

Commemorative ware
North Yorkshire
Botany Bay Antiques,
8 Grape Lane,
Whitby YO22 4BA
Tel: 01947 602007
botanybay@madasafish.com
www.botanybayantiques.co.uk

Decorative Arts
Cheshire
Bizarre,
116 Manchester Road,
Altrincham WA14 4PY
Tel: 0161 926 8895
Art Deco furniture

Gloucestershire
Ruskin Decorative Arts,
5 Talbot Court,
Stow-on-the-Wold,
Cheltenham GL54 1DP
Tel: 01451 832254
*Decorative Arts 1860–1930.
Arts & Crafts, Art Nouveau
and Art Deco items.
Cotswold School Movement,
Guild of Handicraft,
Gordon Russell, Gimson,
the Barnsleys, etc.*

Greater Manchester
A. S. Antiques,
26 Broad Street, Pendleton,
Salford M6 5BY
Tel: 0161 737 5938

Kent
Delf Stream Gallery, 14 New
Street, Sandwich CT13 9AB
Tel: 01304 617684

Lincolnshire
Art Nouveau Originals,
Stamford Antiques Centre,
The Exchange Hall,
Broad St, Stamford PE9 1PX
Tel: 01780 762605

London
20th Century Glass,
Kensington Church Street
Antique Centre, 58–60
Kensington Church Street
W8 4DB
Tel: 020 7938 1137
Tel/Fax: 020 7729 9875
Mobile: 07971 859848
*Glass. Open Thurs, Fri & Sat
12–6pm or by appointment*

Art Furniture,
158 Camden St NW1 9PA
Tel: 020 7267 4324

Art Nouveau Originals
C1900, 11 Camden
Passage, Islington N1 8EA
Tel: 020 7359 4127
Mobile: 077 74 718096

Artemis Decorative Arts Ltd,
36 Kensington Church Street
W8 4BX
Tel: 020 7376 0377/
020 7937 9900

Sylvia Powell, Decorative
Arts, 18 The Mall,
Camden Passage N1 0PD
Tel: 020 7354 2977
Doulton

Rumours, 4 The Mall,
Upper Street, Camden
Passage, Islington N1 0PD
Tel: 020 7704 6549/
07836 277274/
07831 103748
Moorcroft

Shapiro & Co, Stand 380,
Gray's Antique Market,
58 Davies Street W1Y 1LB
Tel: 020 7491 2710

Surrey
Gooday Gallery,
14 Richmond Hill,
Richmond TW10 6QX
Tel: 020 89408652
Mobile: 077101 24540
*Art Nouveau, Art Deco,
Tribal Art and post-war
Modernism 1890–1980*

Sussex
Art Deco Etc,
73 Upper Gloucester Road,
Brighton BN1 3LQ
Tel: 01273 329268
Decorative Arts ceramics

Dolls
North Yorkshire
Botany Bay Antiques,
8 Grape Lane, Whitby
Tel: 01947 602007
botanybay@madasafish.com
www.botanybayantiques.co.uk

Ephemera
Nottinghamshire
T. Vennett-Smith,
11 Nottingham Road,
Gotham NG11 0HE
Tel: 0115 983 0541

Exhibition & Fair Organisers
Surrey
Cultural Exhibitions Ltd,
8 Meadrow,
Godalming GU7 3HN
Tel: 01483 422562

Exporters
Devon
McBains of Exeter, Exeter
Airport, Clyst, Honiton,
Exeter EX5 2BA
Tel: 01392 366261

Pugh's Farm Antiques,
Pugh's Farm, Monkton,
Nr Hontion EX14 9QH
Tel: 01404 42860

Nottinghamshire
Antiques Across the World,
James Alexander Buildings,
London Road/Manvers
Street, Nottingham NG2 3AE
Tel: 0115 979 9199

Suffolk
Wrentham Antiques,
40–44 High St, Wrentham,
Nr Beccles NR34 7HB
Tel: 01502 675583

Sussex
International Furniture
Exporters, The Old Cement
Works, South Heighton,
Newhaven BN9 0HS
Tel: 01273 611251

The Old Mint House,
High Street,
Pevensey BN24 5LF
Tel: 01323 762337

Fans
London
L & D Collins
Tel: 020 7584 0712

Fishing
Hampshire
Evans & Partridge,
Agriculture House,
High Street,
Stockbridge SO20 6HF
Tel: 01264 810702

Kent
Old Tackle Box, PO Box 55,
Cranbrook TN17 3ZU
Tel/Fax: 01580 713979

London
Angling Auctions,
PO Box 2095, W12 8RU
Tel: 020 8749 4175

Shropshire
Mullock & Madeley,
The Old Shippon,
Wall-under-Heywood,
Church Stretton SY6 7DS
Tel: 01694 771771

Furniture
Argentina
Antiguedades La Rueda,
Av. Rivdavia 7901(1407)
Capital Federal,
Buenos Aires
Tel/Fax: 005 4 11 4612 8668
info@larueda.com
www.larueda.com

Bedfordshire
Transatlantic Antiques Ltd,
101 Dunstable Street,
Ampthill MK45 2JT
Tel: 01525 403346

Berkshire
Hill Farm Antiques, Hill Farm,
Shop Lane, Leckhampstead,
Nr Newbury RG20 8QG
Tel: 01488 638541
Dining tables

The Old Malthouse,
15 Bridge Street,
Hungerford RG17 0EG
Tel: 01488 682209

Cumbria
Anthemion, Bridge Street,
Cartmel, Grange-over-Sands
LA11 7SH
Tel: 015395 36295
Mobile: 0468 443757

Derbyshire
Spurrier-Smith Antiques,
28, 30, 39 Church Street,
Ashbourne DE6 1AJ
Tel: 01335 343669/342198

Essex
F. G. Bruschweiler (Antiques)
Ltd, 41–67 Lower Lambricks,
Rayleigh SS6 7EN
Tel: 01268 773 761

Gloucestershire
Berry Antiques,
3 High Street,
Moreton-in-Marsh GL56 0AH
Tel: 01608 652929

Hertfordshire
Collins Antiques,
Corner House,
Wheathampstead
AL4 8AP
Tel: 01582 833111

Kent
Douglas Bryan Antiques,
The Old Bakery,
St Davids Bridge,
Cranbrook TN17 3HN
Tel: 01580 713103
Oak & country

Lennox Cato,
1 The Square, Church St,
Edenbridge TN8 5BD
Tel: 01732 865988
Mobile: 07836 233473

Flower House Antiques,
90 High Street,
Tenterden TN30 6HT
Tel: 01580 763764

Heirloom Antiques,
68 High Street,
Tenterden TN30 6AU
Tel: 01580 765535

Pantiles Spa Antiques,
4, 5, 6 Union House,
The Pantiles,
Tunbridge Wells TN4 8HE
Tel: 01892 541377

Gillian Shepherd,
Old Corner House Antiques,
6 Poplar Road,
Wittersham,
Tenterden TN30 7PG
Tel: 01797 270236

Sutton Valence Antiques,
Unit 4 Haslemere,
Parkwood Estate,
Maidstone
ME15 9NL
Tel: 01622 675332

Lincolnshire
Lindsey Court Antiques,
Lindsey Court,
Horncastle
LN9 5DH
Tel: 01507 527794

Norman Mitchell,
47a East Street,
Horncastle
Tel: 01507 525532

Seaview Antiques,
Stanhope Road,
Horncastle LN9 5DG
Tel: 01507 524524

London
Adams Rooms Antiques
& Interiors,
18–20 The Ridgeway,
Wimbledon Village
SW19 4QN
Tel: 020 8946 7047
Chairs

Antique Warehouse,
9–14 Deptford Broadway
SE8 4PA
Tel: 020 8691 3062

Oola Boola,
166 Tower Bridge Road
SE1 3LS
Tel: 020 7403 0794/
020 8693 5050
Mobile: 0956 261252

Georg S. Wissinger Antiques,
Georgian House Antiques,
166 Bermondsey Street
SE1 3TQ
Tel: 020 7407 5795

 Buxton

The 37th Buxton Antiques Fair
12th - 19th May 2001
The Pavilion Gardens,
Buxton, Derbyshire

 Surrey

The 33rd Surrey Antiques Fair
5th - 8th October 2000
Guildford Civic ,
Guildford, Surrey

Established Antiques Fairs
of distinction and high
repute offering pleasure to
both lovers and
collectors of craftsmanship
and fine works of art.
For further information and
complimentary tickets,
please contact:

CULTURAL EXHIBITIONS LTD.
8 Meadrow, Godalming, Surrey GU7 3HN
Telephone: Godalming 01483 422562

Robert Young Antiques,
68 Battersea Bridge Road
SW11 3AG
Tel: 020 7228 7847
Country furniture

Middlesex
Robert Phelps Ltd,
133–135 St Margaret's Rd,
East Twickenham
TW1 1RG
Tel: 020 8892 1778/7129

Northamptonshire
Paul Hopwell,
30 High Street,
West Haddon NN6 7AP
Tel: 01788 510636
Oak & Country furniture

Mark Seabrook Antiques,
9 West End,
West Haddon NN6 7AY
Tel: 01788 510772
Mobile: 0370 721931
Oak & country

Nottinghamshire
Newark Antiques
Warehouse,
Old Kelham Road,
Newark NG24 1BX
Tel: 01636 674869
enquiries@newarkantiques.
co.uk
www.newarkantiques.co.uk

Oxfordshire
The Chair Set,
18 Market Place,
Woodstock OX20 1TA
Tel: 01428 707301
Chairs

Rupert Hitchcox Antiques,
The Garth,
Warpsgrove,
Nr Chalgrove,
Oxford OX44 7RW
Tel: 01865 890241

Georg S. Wissinger Antiques,
Georgian House Antiques,
21 & 44 West Street,
Chipping Norton,
Oxon OX7 5EU
Tel: 01608 641369

Somerset
Geoffrey Breeze Antiques,
6 George Street,
Bath BA1 2EH
Tel: 01225 466499

Granary Galleries,
Court House,
Ash Priors,
Nr Bishops Lydeard,
Taunton TA4 3NQ
Tel: 01823 432402/
432816

Suffolk
Hubbard Antiques,
16 St Margaret's Green,
Ipswich IP4 2BS
Tel: 01473 226033

Surrey
Dorking Desk Shop,
41 West Street,
Dorking RH4 1BU
Tel: 01306 883327
Desks

J. Hartley Antiques Ltd,
186 High Street,
Ripley GU23 6BB
Tel: 01483 224318

The Refectory,
38 West Street,
Dorking RH4 1BU
Tel: 01306 742111
*Oak & country, refectory
table specialist*

Richmond Hill Antiques,
82 Hill Rise,
Richmond TW10 6UB
Tel: 0208 940 5755

Ripley Antiques,
67 High Street,
Ripley GU23 6AN
Tel: 01483 224981

Anthony Welling,
Broadway Barn,
High Street,
Ripley GU23 6AQ
Tel: 01483 225384
Oak & country furniture

Sussex
British Antique Replicas,
School Close,
Queen Elizabeth Avenue,
Burgess Hill RH15 9RX
Tel: 01444 245577

Dycheling Antiques,
34 High Street, Ditchling,
Hassocks BN6 8TA
Tel: 01273 842929
Chairs

Jeroen Markies Antiques Ltd,
16 Hartfield Road,
Forest Row RH18 5HE
Tel: 01342 824980

Stable Antiques,
Adrian Hoyle,
98a High Street,
Lindfield RH16 2HP
Tel: 01444 483662
Regency furniture

Wales
Country Antiques (Wales),
Castle Mill, Kidwelly,
Carmarthenshire SA17 4UU
Tel: 01554 890534
Oak

Russell Worby,
Welsh Oak & Country
Furniture, PO Box 43,
Colwyn Bay LL29 8WS
Tel: 01492 512794
*Welsh country furniture.
Open any time by
appointment only*

Warwickshire
Apollo Antiques Ltd,
The Saltisford,
Birmingham Road,
Warwick CV34 4TD
Tel: 01926 494746

Coleshill Antiques & Interiors,
12–14 High Street,
Coleshill B46 1AZ
Tel: 01675 467416

Don Spencer Antiques,
36A Market Place,
Warwick CV34 4SH
Tel: 01926 407989/499857
Desks

West Midlands
Martin Taylor Antiques,
140B Tettenhall Road,
Wolverhampton WV6 0BQ
Tel: 01902 751166/
0836 636524

Wiltshire
Cross Hayes Antiques,
Unit 6 Westbrook Farm,
Draycot Cerne,
Chippenham SN15 5LH
Tel/Fax: 01249 720033
Eve: 01666 822062
www.crosshayes.co.uk

Yorkshire
David South,
Kings House,
15 High Street,
Pateley Bridge,
Harrogate HG3 5AP
Tel: 01423 712022
Furniture & upholstery

Glass
Somerset
Somervale Antiques,
6 Radstock Road,
Midsomer Norton,
Bath BA3 2AJ
Tel: 01761 412686

Icons
London
Iconastas,
5 Piccadilly Arcade SW1
Tel: 020 7629 1433
Russian and Soviet art

Jewellery
London
Wimpole Antiques,
Stand 349,
Grays Antique Market,
South Molton Lane W1Y 2LP
Tel: 020 7499 2889

Marine
Hampshire
Mariner's Antiques,
Dolphin Quay Antiques
Centre, Queen Street,
Emsworth PO10 7BU
Tel: 07710 330700
01420 476718
www.mariner's-antiques.com
*Specialists in marine
paintings & prints, Royal
Navy & shipping line
memorabilia, nautical books,
ship models and nautical
antiques*

Shropshire
Mark Jarrold
Tel/Fax: 01584 841210
Mobile: 07776 193193
mark.jarrold@btinternet.com
Marine Instruments

Markets & Centres
Berkshire
Stables Antiques Centre,
1a Merchant Place
(off Friar Street),
Reading RG1 1DT
Tel: 0118 959 0290
*Open 7 days a week. Over
40 dealers on two floors.
Near station and car parks*

Buckinghamshire
Marlow Antique Centre,
35 Station Road,
Marlow SL7 1NW
Tel: 01628 473223
*Over 25 Dealers.
Mon–Sat 10am–5.30pm
Sun 11am–4.30pm.
Specializing in furniture,
china, glass, cuff links,
pens. A good secondhand
book dept. Warm & friendly
atmosphere.
Trade welcome.*

Derbyshire
Chappells & The Antiques
Centre, King Street,
Bakewell DE45 1DZ
Tel: 01629 812496
Fax: 01629 814531
www.chappells-
antiques.co.uk
*30 established dealers (incl.
BADA & LAPADA members)
of quality antiques and
collectables 17th–20thC.
Tea and coffee house.
Open Mon–Sat 10am–5pm.
Sun 11am–5pm. Closed
Christmas Day, Boxing Day
& New Year's Day. Ring
for brochure, directions
& parking information*

Duesbury's Antiques Centre,
220 Siddals Road,
Derby DE1 2QE
Tel: 01332 370151
www.antiquesplus.co.uk
*Mon–Sat 10am–5.00pm,
Sun 11am–4pm*

Essex
Debden Antiques,
Elder Street,
Saffron Walden CB11 3JY
Tel: 01799 543007
Fax: 01799 542482
*Mon–Sat 10am–6pm Bank
Hols 11am–4pm. 30 quality
dealers in a stunning 17thC
Essex barn. Large selection
of 16th–20thC oak, mahogany
and pine furniture, water-
colours and oil paintings,
rugs, ceramics, silver and
jewellery. Plus garden
furniture and ornaments in
our lovely courtyard*

Gloucestershire
Cirencester Arcade
& Ann's Pantry,
25 Market Place,
Cirencester GL7 2NX
Tel: 01285 644214
Fax: 01285 651267
*Antiques, gifts, furnishings,
etc. Restaurant/tea rooms,
private room for hire.
Over 60 traders*

Hampshire
Dolphin Quay Antique
Centre, Queen Street,
Emsworth PO10 7BU
Tel: 01243 379994/379998
*Open 7 days a week
(including Bank Holidays)
Mon–Sat 10am–5pm, Sun
10am–4pm. Marine/Naval
antiques, paintings, water-
colours, prints, antique clocks,
Decorative Arts, furniture,
sporting apparel, luggage,
specialist period lighting,
conservatory/garden antiques,
antique pine furniture*

Herefordshire
Ross On Wye Antiques
Gallery, Gloucester Road,
Ross-on-Wye HR9 5BU
Tel: 01989 762290
Closed Sundays

Kent
Copperfields Antiques
& Craft Centre, 3c–4
Copperfields, Spital Street,
Dartford DA9 2DE
Tel: 01322 281445
Open Mon–Sat 10am–5pm

Antiques, bygones, collectables, stamps, Wade, Sylvac, Beswick, Royal Doulton, Victoriana, Art Deco, 1930s–60s, clocks, crafts, hand-made toys, dolls' houses & miniatures, jewellery, glass, china, furniture, Kevin Francis character jugs, silk, lace and more

Lancashire
GB Antiques Ltd,
Lancaster Leisure Park,
(the former Hornsea Pottery),
Wyresdale Road,
Lancaster LA1 3LA
Tel: 01524 844734
Over 140 dealers in 40,000 sq. ft. of space. Porcelain, pottery, Art Deco, glass, books and linen, mahogany, oak and pine furniture. Open 7 days a week 10am–5pm

Kingsmill Antique Centre,
Queen Street, Harle Syke,
Burnley BB10 2HX
Tel: 01282 431953
Open 7 days 10am–5pm, 8pm Thurs. 8,500 sq ft. Trade welcome

Lincolnshire
Hemswell Antique Centre,
Caenby Corner Estate,
Hemswell Cliff,
Gainsborough DN21 5TJ
Tel: 01427 668389

London
Atlantic Antiques Centres,
Chenil House, 181–183
Kings Road SW3 5EB
Tel: 020 7351 5353

Bourbon-Hanby Antiques
Centre, 151 Sydney Street,
Chelsea SW3 6NT
Tel: 020 7352 2106

Norfolk
The Antique Shop,
8 White Hart St,
Thetford IP24 1AD
Tel: 01842 755511

Oxfordshire
Antiques on High,
85 High St, Oxford OX1 4BG
Tel: 01865 251075
Open 7 days, 10am–5pm. Sundays & Bank Holidays 11am–5pm. 35 dealers with a wide range of quality stock

Chipping Norton Antiques
Centre, Ivy House,
Middle Row, Market Place,
Chipping Norton OX7 5NA
Tel: 01608 644212

Shropshire
Bridgnorth Antique Centre,
High Town, Whitburn Street,
Bridgnorth WV16 4QT
Tel: 01746 768055
Open 7 days 10am–5.30pm

Whitchurch Antique Centre,
Heath Road, Prees Heath,
Whitchurch SY13 2AD
Tel: 01948 662626

Staffordshire
Tutbury Mill Antiques Centre,
Tutbury Mill Mews, Tutbury
DE13 9LU
Tel: 01283 520074
www.antiquesplus.co.uk

Mon–Sat 10.30am–5.30pm
Sun 12–5pm

Suffolk
Puritan Values at the Dome
Art & Antiques Centre,
St Edmunds Business Park,
St Edmonds Road,
Southwold IP18 6BZ
Tel: 01502 722211
Fax: 01520 722734
www.dome-art.freeserve.co.uk
*7,500 sq. ft. of space.
Open 7 days 10am–6pm.
Specializing in the Arts and
Crafts movement. Largest
collection in the world*

Sussex
Church Hill Antiques Centre,
6 Station Road,
Lewes BN7 2DA
Tel: 01273 474 842

Wales
Afonwen Craft & Antique
Centre, Afonwen,
Caerwys, Nr Mold,
Flintshire CH7 5UB
Tel: 01352 720965
*Open all year Tues–Sun
9.30am–5.30pm, closed
Mon, open Bank Holidays.
The largest antiques & craft
centre in North Wales.
14,000 sq ft of showrooms,
antiques, fine jewellery,
furniture, fine jewellery.
Licensed restaurant*

Offa's Dyke Antique Centre,
4 High Street, Knighton,
Powys LD7 1AT
Tel: 01547 520145

Romantiques Antique
Centre, Bryn Seion Chapel,
Station Road, Trevor,
Nr Llangollen LL20 7PF
Tel: Day 0378 279614
Eve 01978 752140

Warwickshire
Barn Antiques Centre,
Station Road, Long Marston,
Nr Stratford-upon-Avon
CV37 8RB
Tel: 01789 721399
*Open 7 days 10am–5pm.
Large selection of antique
furniture, antique pine, linen
and lace, old fireplaces and
surrounds, collectables,
pictures and prints, silver,
ceramics & objet d'arts*

Granary Antiques Centre,
Ansley Road (B4114),
Nuneaton CV10 0QL
Tel: 024 76395551
*(Part of Hoar Park Craft
Village). Tues–Sun and Bank
Holidays 10am–5pm. Porcelain,
pottery, kitchenalia, collectables,
Victorian and Edwardian
furniture. Mason's Ironstone*

Yorkshire
Cavendish Antique
& Collectors Centre,
44 Stonegate, York YO1 8AS
Tel: 01904 621666
*Open 7 days 9am–6pm.
Over 50 dealers*

The Court House,
2–6 Town End Road,
Ecclesfield, Sheffield
Tel: 0114 257 0641

Sheffield Antiques Emporium
& The Chapel, 15–19 Clyde
Road, (off Broadfield Road),
Heeley, Sheffield S8 0YD
Tel: Emporium: 0114 258 4863
Chapel: 0114 258 8288
*Over 70 dealers. Collectables,
furniture, pictures, books,
militaria, linen, kitchenalia,
china, Art Deco, clocks,
silver and silver plate, etc.
Open 7 days, Mon–Sat
10am–5pm, Sundays & Bank
Holidays 11am–5pm*

Stonegate Antiques Centre,
41 Stonegate, York YO1 8AW
Tel: 01904 613888
Fax: 01904 644400
*Open 7 days 9am–6pm.
Over 110 dealers on 2 floors*

Miniatures
Gloucestershire
Judy & Brian Harden
Antiques, PO Box 14,
Bourton-on-the-Water,
Cheltenham GL54 2YR
Tel: 01451 810684
Portrait miniatures

Money Boxes
Yorkshire
John & Simon Haley,
89 Northgate,
Halifax HX1 1XF
Tel: 01422 822148

Musical Instruments
Nottinghamshire
Turner Violins, 1–5 Lily
Grove, Beeston NG9 1QL
Tel: 0115 943 0333

Packers & Shippers
Dorset
Franklin, Alan, Transport,
26 Blackmoor Road,
Ebblake Industrial Estate,
Verwood BH31 6BB
Tel: 01202 826539

Paperweights
Cheshire
Sweetbriar Gallery,
Robin Hood Lane,
Helsby WA6 9NH
Tel: 01928 723851

Pianos
Gloucestershire
Piano-Export, Bridge Road,
Kingswood, Bristol BS15 4FW
Tel: 0117 956 8300

Kent
Period Piano Company,
Park Farm Oast, Hareplain
Road, Biddenden,
Nr Ashford TN27 8LJ
Tel: 01580 291393
*Specialist dealer and restorer
of period pianos*

Pine
Cumbria
Ben Eggleston Antiques,
The Dovecote, Long Marton,
Appleby CA16 6BJ
Tel: 01768 361849
Trade only

Essex
English Rose Antiques,
7 Church Street,
Coggeshall CO6 1TU
Tel: 01376 562683
*Large selection of English
and Continental pine furniture*

Gloucestershire
Parlour Farm Antiques,
Unit 12b Wilkinson Road,
Love Lane Industrial Estate,
Cirencester GL7
Tel: 01285 885336
Mobile: 0374 280982

Hampshire
Pine Cellars, 39 Jewry St,
Winchester SO23 8RY
Tel: 01962 777546/867014

Kent
Glassenbury Antique Pine,
Glassenbury Timber Yard,
Iden Green, Goudhurst,
Cranbrook TN17 2PA
Tel: 01580 212022

Old English Pine,
100 Sandgate High Street,
Sandgate,
Folkestone CT20 3BY
Tel: 01303 248560

Up Country,
The Old Corn Stores,
68 St John's Road,
Tunbridge Wells TN4 9PE
Tel: 01892 523341

Lancashire
David Roper Antiques,
Hill View Farm, Gill Lane,
Longton, Preston PR4 4ST
Tel: 01772 615366/611591
Mobile: 07803 134851
*Mostly English 18th, 19th
and early 20thC pine and
country furniture, decorative
accessories, collectables.
No reproductions*

Netherlands
Jacques Van Der Tol,
Antiek & Curiosa,
Antennestraat 34,
1322 A E Almere-Stad
Tel: 00 313 653 62050

Republic of Ireland
Delvin Farm Antiques,
Gormonston, Co Meath
Tel: 00 353 1 841 2285

Somerset
East Street Antiques,
42 East Street,
Crewkerne TA18 7AG
Tel: 01460 78600

Gilbert & Dale Antiques,
Old Chapel, Church Street,
Ilchester, Nr Yeovil BA22 8ZA
Tel: 01935 840464
Painted pine & country

Westville House Antiques,
Littleton, Nr Somerton
TA11 6NP
Tel: 01458 273376

Staffordshire
Johnson's, 120 Mill Street,
Leek ST13 8HA
Tel: 01538 386745
*English & French country
furniture. Unique objects &
decorative accessories.
Most items 18th & 19thC.
Open 9am–5pm Mon–Sat.
Export trade welcome*

Surrey
Grayshott Pine,
Crossways Road, Grayshott,
Hindhead GU26 6HF
Tel: 01428 607478

Sussex
Bob Hoare, Antiques,
Unit Q, Phoenix Place,
North St, Lewes BN7 2DQ
Tel: 01273 480557

Ann Lingard, Ropewalk
Antiques, Ropewalk,
Rye TN31 7NA
Tel: 01797 223486

Graham Price,
Unit 4, Chaucer Industrial
Estate, Dittons Road,
Polegate BN26 6JD
Tel: 01323 487167

Wales
Pot Board, 30 King Street,
Carmarthen, Wales SA31
1BS Tel: 01267 236623

Wiltshire
North Wilts Exporters,
Hill House, Brinkworth
SN15 5AJ
Tel: 01666 510876

Pine & Country Furniture
Oxfordshire
Julie Strachey,
Southfield Farm, North Lane,
Weston-on-the-Green
OX6 8RG
Tel: 01869 350833
*Antique farm & country
furniture in pine, oak, etc.
Ironwork & interesting pieces
for the garden (no repro).
By appointment.
Junction 9 M40 2 miles*

Porcelain
Bedfordshire
Transatlantic Antiques Ltd,
101 Dunstable Street,
Ampthill MK45 2JT
Tel: 01525 403346

Gloucestershire
Clive & Lynne Jackson.
Tel: 01242 254375
Mobile: 0410 239351
Parian ware

Hampshire
Goss & Crested China
Centre & Museum,
incorporating Milestone
Publications, 62 Murray Rd,
Horndean PO8 9JL
Tel: (023) 9259 7440
Goss & crested china

Northern Ireland
Marion Langham,
Claranagh, Tempo,
County Fermanagh BT94 3FJ
Tel: 028 895 41247
ladymarion@btinternet.co.uk
Belleek

London
Marion Langham.
Tel: 020 7730 1002
Belleek

Shropshire
Teme Valley Antiques,
1 The Bull Ring,
Ludlow SY8 1AD
Tel: 01584 874686

Somerset
Andrew Dando, 4 Wood
Street, Queen Square,
Bath BA1 2JQ
Tel: 01225 422702

Sussex
Jupiter Antiques, PO Box 609,
Rottingdean BN2 7FW
Tel: 01273 302865
*English porcelain from 18thC
factories, Royal Worcester
and Royal Crown Derby*

Pottery
Berkshire
Special Auction Services,
The Coach House, Midgham
Park, Reading RG7 5UG
Tel: 0118 971 2949
*Commemoratives, pot lids,
Prattware, fairings, Goss
and crested, Baxter and
Le Blond prints*

Buckinghamshire
Gillian Neale Antiques,
PO Box 247,
Aylesbury HP20 1JZ
Tel: 01296 423754/
07860 638700
Blue & white ware

Kent
Gillian Shepherd,
Old Corner House Antiques,
6 Poplar Road, Wittersham,
Tenterden TN30 7PG
Tel: 01797 270236
Blue & white transferware

London
Jonathan Horne,
66 Kensington Church Street
W8 4BY
Tel: 020 7221 5658

Rogers de Rin,
76 Royal Hospital Road
SW3 4HN
Tel: 020 7352 9007
Wemyss

Tyne & Wear
Ian Sharp Antiques,
23 Front Street,
Tynemouth NE30 4DX
Tel: 0191 296 0656

Wales
Islwyn Watkins,
Offa's Dyke Antique Centre,
4 High Street, Knighton,
Powys LD7 1AT
Tel: 01547 520145

Warwickshire
Paull's of Kenilworth,
Beehive House,
125 Warwick Road,
Old Kenilworth CV8 1HY
Tel: 01926 855253
Mason's Ironstone

Publications
London
Antiques Trade Gazette,
115 Shaftesbury Avenue
WC2H 8AD
Tel: 020 7930 9958

West Midlands
Antiques Magazine,
H.P. Publishing, 2 Hampton
Court Road, Harborne,
Birmingham B17 9AE
Tel: 0121 681 8000

Restoration
London
Oliver Clarke,
Heritage Restorations,
96 Webber Street SE1 0QN
Tel: 020 7928 3624
18th & 19thC furniture

Northamptonshire
Leather Conservation,
The University College
Campus, Boughton Green
Road, Moulton Park,
Northampton NN2 7AN
Tel: 01604 719766
*Conservation and restoration
of leather screens, wall
hangings, car, carriage and
furniture upholstery, saddlery,
luggage, firemens' helmets
etc. Included on the Register
maintained by the
Conservation Unit of the
Museum and Galleries
Commission.*

Lyden Antique Restoration
Ltd, 48 Hesketh Road,
Yardley Gobion NN12 7TS
Tel: 01604 631234
www.lyden.co.uk

Rock & Pop
Cheshire
Collector's Corner,
PO Box 8,
Congleton CW12 4GD
Tel: 01260 270429

Rocking Horses
Essex
Haddon Rocking Horses Ltd,
5 Telford Road,
Clacton-on-Sea CO15 4LP
Tel: 01255 424745
millers@rockinghorses.uk.com
www.rockinghorses.uk.com

Scientific Instruments
Cheshire
Charles Tomlinson, Chester
Tel/Fax: 01244 318395
charles.tomlinson@lineone.net
http://website.lineone.net/-
charles.tomlinson

Scotland
Early Technology,
Monkton House,
Old Craighall, Musselburgh,
Midlothian EH21 8SF
Tel: 0131 665 5753

Services
London
Invaluable/Thesaurus
www.invaluable.com

Wiltshire
SimplyAntiques.com
Tel: 01722 340347
enq@SimplyAntiques.com
www.SimplyAntiques.com
Buy and sell on the net

Worcestershire
Retro Products,
Matthew House,
Hoo Farm Industrial Estate,
Worcester Road,
Kidderminster DY11 7RA
Tel: 01562 865435
Fittings and accessories

Silver
Bedfordshire
Transatlantic Antiques Ltd,
101 Dunstable Street,
Ampthill MK45 2JT
Tel: 01525 403346

Gloucestershire
Corner House Antiques,
High Street,
Lechlade GL7 3AE
Tel: 01367 252007

London
Daniel Bexfield,
26 Burlington Arcade,
W1V 9AD
Tel: 020 7491 1720

The Silver Fund Ltd,
40 Bury Street,
St James's
SW1Y 6AU
Tel: 020 7839 7664

Shropshire
Teme Valley Antiques,
1 The Bull Ring,
Ludlow SY8 1AD
Tel: 01584 874686

Sports & Games
Nottinghamshire
T. Vennett-Smith,
11 Nottingham Road,
Gotham NG11 0HE
Tel: 0115 983 0541

Teddy Bears
Oxfordshire
Teddy Bears of Witney,
99 High Street,
Witney OX8 6LY
Tel: 01993 702616/706616

Textiles
Somerset
Julia Craig,
Bartlett Street Antiques
Centre,
5–10 Bartlett Street,
Bath BA1 2QZ
Tel: 01225 448202/310457
Mobile: 07771 786846

Toys
Middlesex
Hobday Toys
Tel: 01895 636737

Sussex
Wallis & Wallis,
West Street Auction
Galleries,
Lewes BN7 2NJ
Tel: 01273 480208

Yorkshire
John & Simon Haley,
89 Northgate,
Halifax HX1 1XF
Tel: 01422 822148

Tunbridge Ware
Kent
Bracketts,
Auction Hall,
The Pantiles,
Tunbridge Wells TN1 1UU
Tel: 01892 544500

Watches
London
Pieces of Time,
(1–7 Davies Mews),
26 South Molton Lane
W1Y 2LP
Tel: 020 7629 2422

Yorkshire
Harpers Jewellers Ltd,
2/6 Minster Gates,
York YO1 7HL
Tel: 01904 632634

Wine Antiques
Buckinghamshire
Christopher Sykes,
The Old Parsonage,
Woburn, Milton Keynes
MK17 9QM
Tel: 01525 290259

Directory of Auctioneers

Auctioneers who hold frequent sales should contact us by April 2001 for inclusion in the next edition.

London

Academy Auctioneers & Valuers,
Northcote House, Northcote
Avenue, Ealing W5 3UR
Tel: 020 8579 7466
www.thesaurus.co.uk/academy/

Bloomsbury Book Auctions,
3/4 Hardwick Street,
Off Rosebery Avenue EC1R 4RY
Tel: 020 7833 2636

Bonhams, Montpelier Street,
Knightsbridge SW7 1HH
Tel: 020 7393 3900

Bonhams, 65–69 Lots Road,
Chelsea SW10 0RN
Tel: 020 7393 3900

Brooks (Auctioneers) Ltd,
81 Westside SW4 9AY
Tel: 020 7228 8000

Christie's South Kensington Ltd,
85 Old Brompton Road SW7 3LD
Tel: 020 7581 7611

Dix-Noonan-Webb,
1 Old Bond Street W1X 3TD
Tel: 020 7499 5022

Glendinings & Co,
101 New Bond Street W1Y 9LG
Tel: 020 7493 2445

Lloyds International Auction
Galleries, 118 Putney Bridge Road
SW15 2NQ
Tel: 020 8788 7777
www.lloyds-auction.co.uk

Lots Road Galleries, 71–73 Lots Rd,
Chelsea SW10 0RN
Tel: 020 7351 7771

Onslow's, The Depot,
2 Michael Road SW6 2AD
Tel: 020 7371 0505
Mobile 07831 473400

Phillips, 101 New Bond St W1Y 0AS
Tel: 020 7629 6602

Phillips Bayswater,
10 Salem Road W2 4DL
Tel: 020 7229 9090

Sotheby's, 34–35 New Bond
Street W1A 2AA
Tel: 020 7293 5000

Spink & Son Ltd, 69 Southampton
Row, Bloomsbury WC1B 4ET
Tel: 020 7563 4000

Bedfordshire

BBG Wilson Peacock,
26 Newnham Street,
Bedford MK40 3JR
Tel: 01234 266366

Berkshire

Chancellors, R. Elliott,
32 High Street, Ascot SL5 7HG
Tel: 01344 872588

Dreweatt Neate,
Donnington Priory, Donnington,
Newbury RG13 2JE
Tel: 01635 553553
fineart@dreweatt-neate.co.uk

Buckinghamshire

Amersham Auction Rooms, 125
Station Road, Amersham HP7 0AH
Tel: 01494 729292
www.thesaurus.co.uk/amersham

Bosley's, 42 West Street,
Marlow SL7 2NB
Tel: 01628 488188

Bourne End Auction Rooms,
Station Approach,
Bourne End SL8 5QH
Tel: 01628 531500

Hamptons, 10 Burkes Parade,
Beaconsfield HP9 1PD
Tel: 01494 672969

Cambridgeshire

Cheffins Grain & Comins, 2 Clifton
Road, Cambridge CB2 4BW
Tel: 01223 213343

Cheshire

Dockree's, Cheadle Hulme Centre,
Clemence House, Mellor Road,
Cheadle Hulme SK8 5AT
Tel: 0161 485 1258

Halls Fine Art Auctions, Booth
Mansion, 30 Watergate Street,
Chester CH1 2LA
Tel: 01244 312300/312112

Maxwells of Wilmslow, 133a
Woodford Road, Woodford SK7 1QD
Tel: 0161 439 5182

Phillips North West, New House,
150 Christleton Road,
Chester CH3 5TD
Tel: 01244 313936

Wright Manley,
Beeston Castle Salerooms,
Tarporley CW6 9NJ
Tel: 01829 262150

Cornwall

Martyn Rowe,
Truro Auction Centre, City Wharf,
Malpas Road, Truro TR1 1QH
Tel: 01872 260020

Cumbria

Penrith Farmers' & Kidd's plc,
Skirsgill Salerooms,
Penrith CA11 0DN
Tel: 01768 890781

Phillips Carlisle,
48 Cecil Street, Carlisle CA1 1NT
Tel: 01228 42422

Thomson, Roddick & Laurie,
24 Lowther St, Carlisle CA3 8DA
Tel: 01228 28939/39636

Derbyshire

Neales, The Derby Saleroom,
Becket Street, Derby DE1 1HW
Tel: 01332 343286

Devon

Bearnes, St Edmund's Court,
Okehampton Street, Exeter EX4 1DU
Tel: 01392 422800

Bearnes, Avenue Road,
Torquay TQ2 5TG
Tel: 01803 296277

Bonhams West Country,
Devon Fine Art Auction House,
Dowell Street, Honiton EX14 8LX
Tel: 01404 41872

Phillips, Alphin Brook Road,
Alphington, Exeter EX2 8TH
Tel: 01392 439025

Plymouth Auction Rooms,
Edwin House, St John's Road,
Cattedown, Plymouth PL4 0NZ
Tel: 01752 254740

Rendells, Stonepark,
Ashburton TQ13 7RH
Tel: 01364 653017
www.rendells.co.uk

Dorset

Cottees of Wareham, The Market,
East Street, Wareham BH20 4NR
Tel: 01929 552826

Dalkeith Auctions, Dalkeith Hall,
Dalkeith Steps,
Rear of 81 Old Christchurch Road,
Bournemouth BH1 1EW
Tel: 01202 292905

Hy Duke & Son, Dorchester Fine
Art Salerooms, Dorchester DT1 1QS
Tel: 01305 265080

Phillips Sherborne,
Long Street Salerooms,
Sherborne DT9 3BS
Tel: 01935 815271

Riddetts of Bournemouth,
177 Holden Hurst Road,
Bournemouth BH8 8DQ
Tel: 01202 555686

Essex

BBG Ambrose, Ambrose House,
Old Station Road,
Loughton IG10 4PE
Tel: 020 8502 3951

Cooper Hirst Auctions,
Granary Saleroom, Victoria Road,
Chelmsford CM2 6LH
Tel: 01245 260535

Saffron Walden Auctions,
1 Market Street,
Saffron Walden CB10 1JB
Tel: 01799 513281

G. E. Sworder & Sons
14 Cambridge Road,
Stansted Mountfitchet CM24 8BZ
Tel: 01279 817778

Trembath Welch, The Old Town
Hall, Great Dunmow CM6 1AU
Tel: 01371 873014

Gloucestershire
Bristol Auction Rooms,
St John's Place, Apsley Road,
Clifton, Bristol BS8 2ST
Tel: 0117 973 7201
www.bristolauctionrooms.co.uk

Cotswold Auction Company Ltd,
The Coach House, Swan Yard,
9–13 Market Place,
Cirencester GL7 2NH
Tel: 01285 642420

Mallams, 26 Grosvenor Street,
Cheltenham GL52 2SG
Tel: 01242 235712

Moore, Allen & Innocent,
The Salerooms, Norcote,
Cirencester GL7 5RH
Tel: 01285 646050
surveyors@mooreallen.co.uk

Specialised Postcard Auctions,
25 Gloucester Street,
Cirencester GL7 2DJ
Tel: 01285 659057

Tayler & Fletcher,
London House, High Street,
Bourton-on-the-Water, Cheltenham
GL54 2AP
Tel: 01451 821666

Wotton Auction Rooms,
Tabernacle Road,
Wotton-under-Edge GL12 7EB
Tel: 01453 844733

Greater Manchester
Bonhams, St Thomas's Place,
Hillgate, Stockport SK1 3TZ
Tel: 0161 429 8283

Capes Dunn & Co,
The Auction Galleries,
38 Charles Street,
Off Princess Street M1 7DB
Tel: 0161 273 6060/1911

Hampshire
Evans & Partridge,
Agriculture House, High Street,
Stockbridge SO20 6HF
Tel: 01264 810702

Jacobs & Hunt,
26 Lavant Street,
Petersfield GU32 3EF
Tel: 01730 233933

George Kidner, The Old School,
The Square, Pennington,
Lymington SO41 8GN
Tel: 01590 670070
info@georgekidner.co.uk

May & Son, 18 Bridge Street,
Andover SP10 1BH
Tel: 01264 323417 & 363331
mayandson@enterprise.net

D. M. Nesbit & Co,
Fine Art and Auction Department,
Southsea Salerooms, 7 Clarendon
Road, Southsea PO5 2ED
Tel: 023 9286 4321
nesbits@compuserve.com

Odiham Auction Sales,
The Eagle Works, Rear of Hartley
Wintney Garages, High Street,
Hartley Wintney RG27 8PU
Tel: 01252 844410
auction@dircon.co.uk

Phillips Fine Art Auctioneers,
54 Southampton Road,
Ringwood BH24 1JD
Tel: 01425 473333

Phillips of Winchester,
The Red House, Hyde Street,
Winchester SO23 7DX
Tel: 01962 862515

Romsey Auction Rooms,
86 The Hundred, Romsey SO51 8BX
Tel: 01794 513331

Herefordshire
Morris Bricknell, Stuart House,
18 Gloucester Road,
Ross-on-Wye HR9 5BU
Tel: 01989 768320

Russell, Baldwin & Bright,
Ryelands Road,
Leominster HR6 8NZ
Tel: 01568 611122
fineart@rbbm.co.uk
www.rbbm.co.uk

Nigel Ward & Co,
The Border Property Centre,
Pontrilas HR2 0EH
Tel: 01981 240140

Williams & Watkins, Ross Auction
Rooms, Ross-on-Wye HR9 7QF
Tel: 01989 762225

Hertfordshire
Brown & Merry,
Tring Market Auctions,
Brook Street, Tring HP23 5EF
Tel: 01442 826446
sales@tringmarketauctions.co.uk
www.tringmarketauctions.co.uk

G. E. Sworder incorporating
Andrew Pickford, The Hertford
Saleroom, 42 St Andrew Street,
Hertford SG14 1JA
Tel: 01992 583508

Humberside
Dickinson Davy & Markham,
Wrawby Street, Brigg DN20 8JJ
Tel: 01652 653666

Kent
Bracketts, Auction Hall, Pantiles,
Tunbridge Wells TN1 1UU
Tel: 01892 544500

Canterbury Auction Galleries,
40 Station Road West,
Canterbury CT2 8AN
Tel: 01227 763337

Mervyn Carey, Twysden Cottage,
Benenden, Cranbrook TN17 4LD
Tel: 01580 240283

Gorringes, 15 The Pantiles,
Tunbridge Wells TN2 5TD
Tel: 01892 619670

Hogben Auctioneers,
Fine Art Auction Rooms, Unit C,
Highfield Estate, Off Warren Road,
Folkestone CT20 1JB
Tel: 01303 246810

Ibbett Mosely, 125 High Street,
Sevenoaks TN13 1UT
Tel: 01732 452246/456731

Lambert & Foster, 77 Commercial
Road, Paddock Wood TN12 6DR
Tel: 01892 832325

Lambert & Foster, 102 High Street,
Tenterden TN30 6HT
Tel: 01580 762083

B. J. Norris, The Quest,
West Street, Harrietsham,
Maidstone ME17 1JD
Tel: 01622 859515

Phillips Fine Art Auctioneers,
49 London Road,
Sevenoaks TN13 1AR
Tel: 01732 740310

Lancashire
Smythe's, 174 Victoria Road West,
Cleveleys FY5 3NE
Tel: 01253 852184

Leicestershire
Gildings,
64 Roman Way,
Market Harborough LE16 7PQ
Tel: 01858 410414

Heathcote Ball & Co,
Castle Auction Rooms,
78 St Nicholas Circle,
Leicester LE1 5NW
Tel: 0116 253 6789
heathcote-ball@clara.co.uk
www.heathcote-ball.clara.co.uk

Lincolnshire
Marilyn Swain Auctions,
The Old Barracks,
Sandon Road,
Grantham NG31 9AS
Tel: 01476 568861

Merseyside
Cato Crane & Co,
Liverpool Auction Rooms,
6 Stanhope Street,
Liverpool L8 5RF
Tel: 0151 709 5559
www.catocrane.co.uk

Worralls, 13–15 Seel Street,
Liverpool L1 4AU
Tel: 0151 709 2950

Norfolk

Garry M. Emms & Co Ltd,
t/a Great Yarmouth Salerooms,
Beevor Road
(off South Beach Parade),
Great Yarmouth NR30 3PS
Tel: 01493 332668/720179

Thomas Wm. Gaze & Son,
Diss Auction Rooms,
Roydon Road, Diss IP22 3LN
Tel: 01379 650306
www.twgaze.com

G. A. Key, Aylsham Salerooms,
8 Market Place, Aylsham NR11 6EH
Tel: 01263 733195
www.aylshamsalerooms.co.uk

Knight's, Cuckoo Cottage, Town
Green, Alby, Norwich NR11 7HE
Tel: 01263 768488

Northamptonshire

Merry's Auctioneers,
Northampton Auction & Sales
Centre, Liliput Road, Brackmills,
Northampton NN4 7BY
Tel: 01604 769990

Northumberland

Louis Johnson Auctioneers,
63 Bridge St, Morpeth NE61 1PQ
Tel: 01670 513025

Nottinghamshire

Bonhams, 57 Mansfield Road,
Nottingham NG1 3PL
Tel: 0115 947 4414

Arthur Johnson & Sons Ltd,
Nottingham Auction Centre,
Meadow Lane, Nottingham NG2 3GY
Tel: 0115 986 9128
auctions@a-johnson.co.uk

Mellors & Kirk,
The Auction House,
Gregory Street, Lenton Lane,
Nottingham NG7 2NL
Tel: 0115 979 0000

Neales, 192 Mansfield Road,
Nottingham NG1 3HU
Tel: 0115 962 4141

Phillips, 20 The Square,
Retford DN22 6XE
Tel: 01777 708633

T. Vennett-Smith, 11 Nottingham
Road, Gotham NG11 0HE
Tel: 0115 983 0541

Oxfordshire

Dreweatt Neate Holloways,
49 Parsons Street,
Banbury OX16 8PF
Tel: 01295 817777
ccovacic@dreweatt-neate.co.uk
www.dreweatt-neat.co.uk

Mallams, 24 St Michael's Street,
Oxford OX1 2EB
Tel: 01865 241358

Phillips, 39 Park End Street,
Oxford OX1 1JD
Tel: 01865 723524

Simmons & Sons, 32 Bell Street,
Henley-on-Thames RG9 2BH
Tel: 01491 571111

Soames County Auctioneers,
Pinnocks Farm Estates, Northmoor
OX8 1AY
Tel: 01865 300626

Shropshire

Halls Fine Art Auctions,
Welsh Bridge, Shrewsbury SY3 8LA
Tel: 01743 231212

Somerset

Clevedon Salerooms, Herbert
Road, Clevedon BS21 7ND
Tel: 01275 876699

Gardiner Houlgate, The Old
Malthouse, Comfortable Place,
Upper Bristol Road, Bath BA1 3AJ
Tel: 01225 447933

Greenslade Taylor Hunt Fine Art,
Magdalene House, Church
Square, Taunton TA1 1SB
Tel: 01823 332525

Lawrence Fine Art Auctioneers,
South Street, Crewkerne TA18 8AB
Tel: 01460 73041

Phillips, 1 Old King Street,
Bath BA1 2JT
Tel: 01225 310609

Richards, The Town Hall,
The Square, Axbridge BS26 2AR
Tel: 01934 732969

Staffordshire

Louis Taylor Auctioneers &
Valuers, Britannia House,
10 Town Road, Hanley,
Stoke-on-Trent ST1 2QG
Tel: 01782 214111

Wintertons Ltd, Lichfield Auction
Centre, Wood End Lane, Fradley,
Lichfield WS13 8NF
Tel: 01543 263256

Suffolk

Dyson & Son, The Auction Room,
Church Street, Clare,
Sudbury CO10 8PD
Tel: 01787 277993
info@dyson-auctioneers.co.uk
www.dyson-auctioneers.co.uk

Lacy Scott and Knight,
Fine Art Department,
The Auction Centre,
10 Risbygate Street,
Bury St Edmunds IP33 3AA
Tel: 01284 763531

Olivers, Olivers Rooms,
Burkitts Lane, Sudbury CO10 1HB
Tel: 01787 880305

Phillips, 32 Boss Hall Road,
Ipswich IP1 59J
Tel: 01473 740494

Surrey

Chancellors, 74 London Road,
Kingston-upon-Thames KT2 6PX
Tel: 020 8541 4139

Ewbank, Burnt Common Auction
Room, London Road, Send,
Woking GU23 7LN
Tel: 01483 223101

Hamptons International,
Baverstock House,
93 High Street, Godalming GU7 1AL
Tel: 01483 423567
fineart@hamptons-int.com
www.hamptons.co.uk

Lawrences Auctioneers,
Norfolk House, 80 High Street,
Bletchingley RH1 4PA
Tel: 01883 743323

John Nicholson,
The Auction Rooms,
Longfield, Midhurst Road,
Fernhurst GU27 3HA
Tel: 01428 653727

Phillips Fine Art Auctioneers,
Millmead, Guildford GU2 5BE
Tel: 01483 504030

Richmond & Surrey Auctions,
Richmond Station,
Old Railway Parcels Depot,
Kew Road,
Richmond TW9 2NA
Tel: 020 8948 6677

P. F. Windibank,
The Dorking Halls, Reigate Road,
Dorking RH4 1SG
Tel: 01306 884556/876280
sjw@windibank.co.uk
www.windibank.co.uk

Sussex

John Bellman Auctioneers,
New Pound Business Park,
Wisborough Green,
Billingshurst RH14 0AZ
Tel: 01403 700858
jbellman@compuserve.com

Burstow & Hewett, Abbey Auction
Galleries and Granary Salerooms,
Lower Lake, Battle TN33 0AT
Tel: 01424 772374

Peter Cheney,
Western Road Auction Rooms,
Western Road,
Littlehampton BN17 5NP
Tel: 01903 722264/713418

Denham's, The Auction Galleries,
Warnham, Horsham RH12 3RZ
Tel: 01403 255699/253837
denhams@lineone.net

Eastbourne Auction Rooms,
Auction House, Finmere Road,
Eastbourne, BN22 8QL
Tel: 01323 431444

Gorringes Auction Galleries,
Terminus Road,
Bexhill-on-Sea TN39 3LR
Tel: 01424 212994

Gorringes Auction Galleries,
15 North Street,
Lewes BN7 2PD
Tel: 01273 472503
auctions@gorringes.co.uk
www.gorringes.co.uk

Graves, Son & Pilcher,
Hove Auction Rooms,
Hove Street, Hove BN3 2GL
Tel: 01273 735266

Edgar Horn, Fine Art Auctioneers,
46–50 South Street,
Eastbourne BN21 4XB
Tel: 01323 410419
www.edgarhorns.com

Raymond P. Inman,
The Auction Galleries, 35 & 40
Temple Street, Brighton BN1 3BH
Tel: 01273 774777
www.raymondinman.co.uk

Lewes Auction Rooms
(Julian Dawson), 56 High Street,
Lewes BN7 1XE
Tel: 01273 478221
www.lewesauctions.com

Phillips Chichester,
Baffins Hall, Baffins Lane,
Chichester PO19 1UA
Tel: 01243 787548

Rye Auction Galleries,
Rock Channel, Rye TN31 7HL
Tel: 01797 222124

Sotheby's Sussex, Summers
Place, Billingshurst RH14 9AD
Tel: 01403 833500

Rupert Toovey & Co Ltd,
Star Road, Partridge Green H13 8RA
Tel: 01403 711744
www.rupert-toovey.com

Wallis & Wallis, West Street
Auction Galleries, Lewes BN7 2NJ
Tel: 01273 480208

Worthing Auction Galleries Ltd,
Fleet House, Teville Gate,
Worthing BN11 1UA
Tel: 01903 205565
worthing-auctions.co.uk
www.worthing-auctions.co.uk

Warwickshire
BBG Locke & England,
18 Guy Street, Leamington Spa
CV32 4RT
Tel: 01926 889100
www.auctions-online.com/locke

West Midlands
Biddle and Webb Ltd,
Ladywood, Middleway,
Birmingham B16 0PP
Tel: 0121 455 8042
antiques@biddleandwebb.
freeserve.co.uk

Frank H Fellows & Sons,
Augusta House,
19 Augusta Street, Hockley,
Birmingham B18 6JA
Tel: 0121 212 2131

Phillips,
The Old House,
Station Road, Knowle,
Solihull B93 0HT
Tel: 01564 776151

Walker, Barnett & Hill,
Waterloo Road Salerooms,
Clarence Street,
Wolverhampton WV1 4JE
Tel: 01902 773531

Weller & Dufty Ltd,
141 Bromsgrove Street,
Birmingham B5 6RQ
Tel: 0121 692 1414
wellerdufty@freewire.co.uk
www.welleranddufty.co.uk

Wiltshire
Henry Aldridge & Son,
Devizes Auction Rooms,
1 Wine Street, Devizes SN10 1AP
Tel: 01380 729199

Swindon Auction Rooms,
The Planks (off The Square),
Old Town, Swindon SN3 1QP
Tel: 01793 615915

Dominic Winter Book Auctions,
The Old School,
Maxwell Street,
Swindon SN1 5DR
Tel: 01793 611340

Woolley & Wallis,
Salisbury Salerooms,
51–61 Castle Street,
Salisbury SP1 3SU
Tel: 01722 424500

Worcestershire
Philip Laney,
The Malvern Auction Centre,
Portland Road, off Victoria Road,
Malvern WR14 2TA
Tel: 01684 893933

Philip Serrell,
The Malvern Saleroom,
Barnards Green Road,
Malvern WR14 3LW
Tel: 01684 892314

Yorkshire
Boulton & Cooper,
St Michaels House,
Market Place,
Malton YO17 0LR
Tel: 01653 696151

H C. Chapman & Son,
The Auction Mart,
North Street,
Scarborough YO11 1DL
Tel: 01723 372424

Cundalls,
15 Market Place,
Malton YO17 7LP
Tel: 01653 697820

Dee, Atkinson & Harrison,
The Exchange Saleroom
Driffield YO25 7LJ
Tel: 01377 253151
exchange@dee-atkinson-harrison
www.dee-atkinson-harrison.co.uk

David Duggleby,
The Vine St Salerooms,
Scarborough YO11 1XN
Tel: 01723 507111
auctions@davidduggleby.
freeserve.co.uk
www.thesaurus.co.uk/david-
duggleby

Andrew Hartley,
Victoria Hall Salerooms,
Little Lane, Ilkley LS29 8EA
Tel: 01943 816363
ahartley.finearts@talk21.com

Lithgow Sons & Partners,
Antique House,
Station Road, Stokesley,
Middlesbrough TS9 7AB
Tel: 01642 710158/710326

Malcolms No1 Auctioneers
& Valuers, The Chestnuts,
16 Park Avenue,
Sherburn-in-Elmet,
Nr Leeds LS25 6EF
Tel: 01977 684971

Morphets of Harrogate,
6 Albert Street,
Harrogate HG1 1JL
Tel: 01423 530030

Phillips Leeds,
17a East Parade, Leeds LS1 2BH
Tel: 0113 2448011

Tennants,
The Auction Centre,
Harmby Road, Leyburn DL8 5SG
Tel: 01969 623780

Tennants,
34 Montpellier Parade,
Harrogate HG1 2TG
Tel: 01423 531661

Republic of Ireland
James Adam & Sons,
26 St Stephen's Green,
Dublin 2
Tel: 00 3531 676 0261

Hamilton Osborne King,
4 Main Street,
Blackrock, Co. Dublin
Tel: 353 1 288 5011
blackrock@hok.ie
www.hok.ie

Mealy's,
Chatsworth Street,,
Castle Comer, Co Kilkenny
Tel: 00 353 56 41229

Whyte's Auctioneers,
30 Marlborough St, Dublin 1
Tel: 00 353 1 874 6161

Scotland
Christie's Scotland Ltd,
164–166 Bath Street,
Glasgow G2 4TG
Tel: 0141 332 8134

Macgregor Auctions,
56 Largo Road, St Andrews,
Fife KY16 8RP
Tel: 01334 472431

McTear's Fine Art
Auctioneers and Valuers,
Argyll & Clyde Rooms,
The Skypark, 8 Elliot Place,
Glasgow G3 8EP
Tel: 0141 221 4456
enquiries@mctears.co.uk
www.mctears.co.uk

Phillips Scotland,
65 George Street,
Edinburgh EH2 2JL
Tel: 0131 225 2266

Phillips Scotland,
207 Bath Street, Glasgow G2 4HD
Tel: 0141 221 8377

Sotheby's,
112 George Street,
Edinburgh EH2 4LH
Tel: 0131 226 7201

Thomson Roddick & Medcalf,
60 Whitesands,
Dumfries DG1 2RS
Tel: 01387 255366

Thomson Roddick & Medcalf,
20 Murray Street,
Annan DG12 6EG
Tel: 01461 202575

Wales
Peter Francis,
Curiosity Sale Room,
19 King Street,
Carmarthen SA31 1BH
Tel: 01267 233456
peterfrancis@valuers.fsnet.co.uk
www.peterfrancis.co.uk

Morgan Evans & Co Ltd,
30 Church Street,
Llangefni, Anglesey,
Gwynedd LL77 7DU
Tel: 01248 723303/421582
llangefni@morganevans.demon.
co.uk
www.property-wales.co.uk/
morganevans

Phillips Cardiff,
7–8 Park Place,
Cardiff CF10 3DP
Tel: 029 2039 6453

Rogers Jones & Co,
33 Abergele Road,
Colwyn Bay LL29 7RU
Tel: 01492 532176
www.rogersjones.ukauctioneers.
com

Wingetts Auction Gallery,
29 Holt St, Wrexham, Clwyd,
Flintshire LL13 8DH
Tel: 01978 353553
auctions@wingetts.co.uk
www.wingetts.co.uk

Australia
Leonard Joel Auctioneers,
333 Malvern Road,
South Yarra, Victoria 3141
Tel: 03 9826 4333
decarts@ljoel.com.au or
jewellery@ljoel.com.au
www.ljoel.auemail

Phillips Sydney,
162 Queen Street,
Woollahra, Sydney NSW 2025
Tel: 00 612 9326 1588

Phillips,
Level 1, 1111 High Street,
Armadale 3143, Melbourne,
Victoria NSW 2025
Tel: (613) 9823 1949

Austria
Dorotheum,
Palais Dorotheum, A-1010 Wien,
Dorotheergasse 17
Tel: 0043 1 515 600

Channel Islands
Bonhams & Martel Maides Ltd,
Allez St Auction Rooms,
29 High Street, St Peter Port,
Guernsey GY1 4NY
Tel: 01481 713463/722700

Bonhams & Langlois,
Westaway Chambers,
39 Don Street, St Helier,
Jersey JE2 4TR
Tel: 01534 22441

China
Sotheby's,
Li Po Chun Chambers,
18th Floor, 189 Des Vouex Road,
Hong Kong
Tel: 852 524 8121

Germany
Auction Team Köln,
Postfach 50 11 19, 50971 Köln
Tel: 00 49 0221 38 70 49
auction@breker.com

Hermann Historica OHG,
Postfach 201009, 80010 Munchen
Tel: 00 49 89 5237296

Sotheby's,
Mendelssohnstrasse 66
D-60325 Frankfurt-am-Main
Tel: 00 49 69 74 07 87

Sotheby's,
Odeonsplatz 16,
D-80539 München 49
Tel: (89) 291 31 51

Monaco
Sotheby's Monaco,
Le Sporting d'Hiver,
Place du Casino 98001 Cedex
Tel: 00 377 93 30 8880

Netherlands
Sotheby's Amsterdam,
De Boelelaan 30
1083 HJ Amsterdam
Tel: 00 31 20 550 22 00

Van Sabben Poster Auctions,
Oosteinde 30, 1678 HS Oostwoud
Tel: 00 31 229 20 25 89

Sweden
Bukowskis, Arsenalsgatan 4,
Stockholm SE111 47
Tel: 08 614 08 00
info@bukowskis.se
www.bukowskis.se

Switzerland
Phillips,
Kreuzstrasse 54, 8008 Zürich
Tel: 00 41 1 252 69 62

Phillips Geneva,
9 rue Ami-Levrier,
CH-1201 Geneva
Tel: 00 41 22 738 07 07

Sotheby's,
13 Quai du Mont Blanc,
CH-1201 Geneva
Tel: 00 41 22 908 4800

Sotheby's Zurich,
Gessneralee 1, CH-8021 Zürich
Tel: 00 41 1 226 2200

USA
Butterfield & Butterfield,
220 San Bruno Avenue,
San Francisco CA 94103
Tel: 00 1 415 861 7500

Du Mouchelle Art Gallery,
409 East Jefferson Avenue, Detroit
MI 48226
Tel: 00 1 313 963 6255

New Orleans Auction Galleries,
801 Magazine Street,
AT 510 Julia, New Orleans,
Louisiana 70130
Tel: 00 1 504 566 1849

Phillips New York, 406 East 79th
Street, New York NY10021
Tel: 00 1 212 570 4830

Skinner Inc, 357 Main Street,
Bolton MA 01740
Tel: 00 1 978 779 6241

Skinner Inc, The Heritage
On The Garden, 63 Park Plaza,
Boston MA 02116
Tel: 001 617 350 5400

Sloan's, C G Sloan & Company
Inc, 4920 Wyaconda Road,
North Bethesda MD 20852
Tel: 00 1 301 468 4911/669 5066

Sloan's Auctioneers & Appraisers,
Miami Gallery, 8861 NW
18th Terrace, Suite 100,
Miami, Florida 33172
Tel: 00 1 305 592 2575/800 660 4524

Sotheby's, 215 West Ohio Street,
Chicago, Illinois 60610
Tel: 00 1 312 670 0010

Sotheby's, 9665 Wilshire
Boulevard, Beverly Hills,
California 90212
Tel: (310) 274 0340

Sotheby's, 1334 York Avenue,
New York NY 10021
Tel: 00 1 212 606 7000

Treadway Gallery Inc and
John Toomey Gallery,
Treadway Gallery Inc,
2029 Madison Road, Cincinnati,
Ohio 45208
Tel: 001 513 321 6742

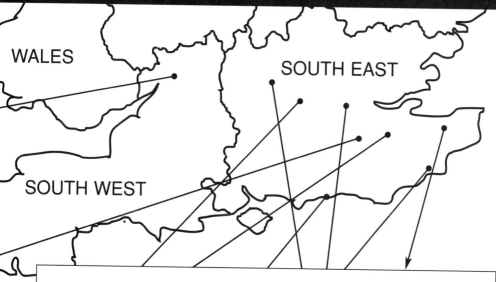

WALES

SOUTH EAST

SOUTH WEST

WALES

SOUTH EAST

SOUTH WEST

MAY & SON

(Established 1925)
Auctioneers & Estate Agents
Monthly catalogued auctions of Antiques & Collectables
Periodical Specialist Sales
Thesaurus Auction Contributor – House Clearances &
Removals

No Trade items entered   No Buyers Premium

Good friendly Auctions with fascinating and interesting items

Viewing & Catalogues from 18 Bridge Street, Andover, Hants
Tel: 01264 323417 Fax: 01264 338841

EWBANK
FINE ART AND GENERAL
AUCTIONEERS & VALUERS

Antiques and Fine Art
Auctioneers

Valuations for
Probate, Insurance
and Family Division

House clearances arranged

Burnt Common Auction Rooms
London Road, Send, Woking GU23 7LN
Tel: 01483 223101 · Fax: 01483 222171

Out of town location fronting the A3 halfway
between Guildford and M25

MEMBERS OF THE SOCIETY OF FINE ART AUCTIONEERS

COOPER HIRST AUCTIONS
Chartered Surveyors
Auctioneers and Valuers

★ REGULAR ANTIQUE SALES
★ HOUSEHOLD FURNITURE AND EFFECTS –
  Every TUESDAY at 10.00am (Viewing from 8.30am)
★ TIMBER, BUILDING MATERIALS, DIY, PLANT,
  MACHINERY AND VEHICLES. Every FRIDAY at
  10.00am (Viewing from 8.30am)
★ BANKRUPTCY AND LIQUIDATION SALES
★ VALUATIONS OF ANTIQUES, FINE ART AND
  OTHER CHATTELS FOR ALL PURPOSES
★ HOUSE CLEARANCES, REMOVALS AND
  LONG/SHORT TERM STORAGE

THE GRANARY SALEROOM
VICTORIA ROAD, CHELMSFORD
Tel: 01245 260535 Fax: 01245 345185

Trembath Welch
Chartered Surveyors, Auctioneers, Estate Agents
Incorporating J. M. WELCH & SON
Established 1886
DUNMOW SALEROOMS

Office at: The Old Town Hall
Great Dunmow
Essex CM6 1AU
Tel: 01371 873014 Fax: 01371 878239

Fortnightly Auction Sales: Including Victorian and Edwardian furniture, effects, collectors' items
and contemporary furniture and furnishings. 11 a.m. start.

Quarterly Antique Auction Sales: Including period furniture, silver, china, glass, jewellery, paintings, prints,
clocks, etc.
Catalogues available for both sales
Valuations conducted for Probate, Insurance and Sale
Trembath Welch a Local Firm with National Connections

WEST MIDLANDS

WALES

SOUTH EAST

SOUTH WEST

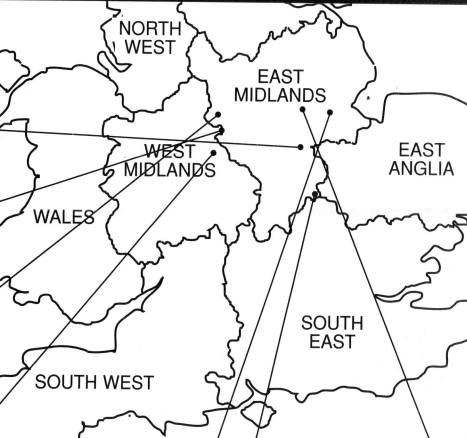

NORTH WEST

EAST MIDLANDS

WEST MIDLANDS

EAST ANGLIA

WALES

SOUTH EAST

SOUTH WEST

MARILYN SWAIN

REGULAR ANTIQUE & FINE ART SALES

FORTNIGHTLY SALES OF VICTORIAN & LATER FURNITURE

VALUATIONS FOR ALL PURPOSES

MEMBERS OF THE SOCIETY OF FINE ART AUCTIONEERS

THE OLD BARRACKS, SANDON ROAD, GRANTHAM, LINCS
TEL: 01-476-568861

MERRY'S
AUCTIONS
A trading division of Northamptonshire Auctions plc

Northampton's Longest Established Auctioneers
with
Purpose Built Modern Auction Rooms
Free on-site parking
Licensed Bar/Cafeteria
holding
Fortnightly Two-day Auctions of
Victorian and later furniture and effects
and
Bi-monthly Antique and Fine Art Sales

Free Pre-sale Inspection and Advice
Full House Clearance Service
with inventory

All enquiries to Denise Cowling FGA

Northampton Auction & Sales Centre
Liliput Road, Brackmills, Northampton NN4 7BY
Tel: 01604 769990 Fax: 01604 763155

EST NEALES 1840
LEADING INDEPENDENT FINE ART AUCTIONEERS

The Real Alternative
to London for the
Sale of your
Antiques and Works of Art

*A telephone call is all that is necessary to
obtain helpful specialist advice and valuation*

0115 9624141

A George III library table attributed to Gillows of Lancaster, *c.1800*
Sold for £91,000.00

NATIONWIDE REPRESENTATION & COLLECTION
SERVICE. SALES EVERY WEEK

**Neales, 192 Mansfield Road
Nottingham NG1 3HU**

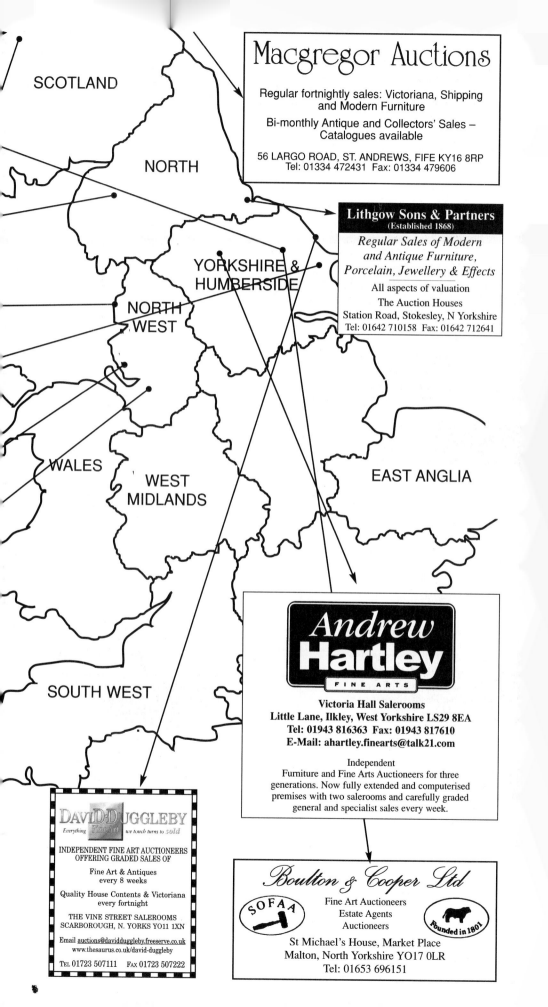

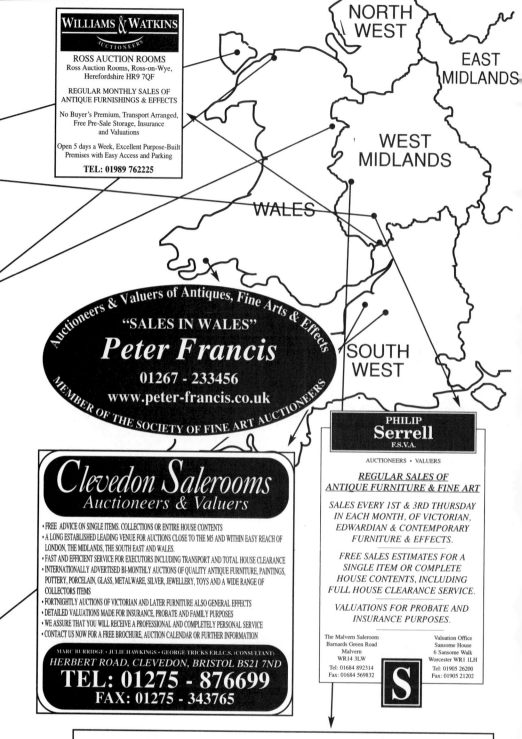

Key to Illustrations

Each illustration and descriptive caption is accompanied by a letter code. By referring to the following list of auctioneers (denoted by *) and dealers (•) the source of any item may be immediately determined. Inclusion in this edition in no way constitutes or implies a contract or binding offer on the part of any of our contributors to supply or sell the goods illustrated, or similar articles, at the prices stated. Advertisers in this year's director are denoted by †.

If you require a valuation for an item, it is advisable to check whether the dealer or specialist will carry out this service and if there is a charge. Please mention Miller's when making an enquiry. Having found a specialist who will carry out your valuation it is best to send a photograph and description of the item to the specialist together with a stamped addressed envelope for the reply. A valuation by telephone is not possible.

Most dealers are only too happy to help you with your enquiry; however, they are very busy people and consideration of the above points would be welcomed.

A&H	• †	Architectural & Historical Salvage, Spa Street, Ossett, Wakefield, Yorkshire WF5 0HJ Tel: 01924 262831
AAV	*	Academy Auctioneers & Valuers, Northcote House, Northcote Ave, Ealing, London W5 3UR Tel: 020 8579 7466 www.thesaurus.co.uk/academy/
ACT	•	Alscot Bathroom Co, The Stable Yard, Alscot Park, Stratford-upon-Avon, Warwicks CV37 8BL Tel: 01789 450 861
ADE	• †	Art Deco Etc, 73 Upper Gloucester Road, Brighton, Sussex BN1 3LQ Tel: 01273 329268
AEF	•	A & E Foster, Bucks Tel: 01494 562024
AG	*	Anderson & Garland (Auctioneers), Marlborough House, Marlborough Crescent, Newcastle-upon-Tyne, Tyne & Wear NE1 4EE Tel: 0191 232 6278
AH	* †	Andrew Hartley, Victoria Hall Salerooms, Little Lane, Ilkley, Yorkshire LS29 8EA Tel: 01943 816363, ahartley.finearts@talk21.com
AL	• †	Ann Lingard, Ropewalk Antiques, Ropewalk, Rye, Sussex TN31 7NA Tel: 01797 223486
ALA	•	Alexander Antiques, Post House, Small Dole, Henfield, Sussex BN5 9XE Tel: 01273 493121
ALiN	•	Andrew Lineham Fine Glass, The Mall, Camden Passage, London N1 8ED Tel: 020 7704 0195 Wed & Sat 01243 576241
ALS	• †	Allan Smith Clocks, Amity Cottage, 162 Beechcroft Road, Upper Stratton, Swindon, Wiltshire SN2 6QE Tel: 01793 822977 Mobile: 0378 834342
ANG	• †	Chris Belton, PO Box 356, Christchurch, Dorset, BH23 1XQ Tel: 01202 478592
ANO	• †	Art Nouveau Originals, Stamford Antiques Centre, The Exchange Hall, Broad Street, Stamford, Lincs PE9 1PX Tel: 01780 762605
AnS	•	The Antique Shop, 30 Henley Street, Stratford-upon-Avon, Warwickshire CV37 6QW Tel: 01789 292485
AnSh	•	Antique Shop, 136a High Street, Tenterden, Kent TN30 6HT Tel: 01580 764323
ANT	• †	Anthemion, Bridge Street, Cartmel, Grange-over-Sands, Cumbria LA11 7SH Tel: 015395 36295 Mobile: 0468 443757
Anth	•	Anthea, Grays Antique Market, South Molton Lane, London W1Y 2LP
ANV	•	Anvil Antiques, Cartmel, Grange-over-Sands, Cumbria LA11 6QA Tel: 015395 36362
AOT	•	Annie's Old Things, PO Box 6, Camphill, Queensland 4152, Australia Tel: 00614 12353099, annie@fan.net.au
AP	* †	GE Sworder, incorporating Andrew Pickford, The Hertford Saleroom, 42 St Andrew Street, Hertford, Hertfordshire SG14 1JA Tel: 01992 583508/501421
APC	•	Antique Photographic Company Ltd. Tel: 01949 842192, alpaco@lineone.net www.thesaurus.co.uk/cook
ARE	•	Arenski, 185 Westbourne Grove, London W11 2SB Tel: 020 7727 8599
ART	• †	Artemis Decorative Arts Ltd, 36 Kensington Church Street, London W8 4BX Tel: 020 7376 0377/020 7937 9900 Artemis.w8@btinternet.com
ASA	• †	A. S. Antiques, 26 Broad Street, Pendleton, Salford, Greater Manchester M6 5BY Tel: 0161 737 5938
ASAA	•	ASA Antiques, 5–10 Bartlett Street, Bath, Somerset BA1 2QZ Tel: 01225 421037/312781
ASH	• †	Ashburton Marbles, Grate Hall, North Street, Ashburton, Devon TQ13 7DU Tel: 01364 653189
ASM	•	Art Smith, Antiques at Wells Union, Route 1, 1755 Post Road, Wells, ME 04090 USA Tel: 207 646 6996
AXT	•	Alexis F. J. Turner, 144a Bridge Road, East Moseley, Surrey KT8 9HW Tel: 020 8542 5926
B&L	*	Bonhams & Langlois, Westaway Chambers, 39 Don Street, St Helier, Jersey JE2 4TR Tel: 01534 22441
B&R	•	Bread & Roses, Durham House Antique Centre, Sheep St, Stow-on-the-Wold, Glos GL54 1AA Tel: 01926 817342/01451 870404
BAB	•	The Barn at Bilsington, Ashford, Kent TN25 7JR Tel: 01233 720917
BAC	•	Bath Antiquities Centre, 4 Bladud Buildings, Bath, Somerset BA1 5LS Tel: 01225 460408 artefacts@bathantiquities.freeserve.co.uk
BaN	•	Barbara Ann Newman, London House Antiques, 4 Market Square, Westerham, Kent TN16 1AW Tel: 01959 564479 Mobile: 0850 016729
BB(L)	*	Butterfield & Butterfield, 7601 Sunset Boulevard, Los Angeles CA 90046, USA Tel: 00 1 323 850 7500
BB(S)	*	Butterfield & Butterfield, 220 San Bruno Avenue, San Francisco CA 94103 USA Tel: 00 1 415 861 7500
BBA	*	Bloomsbury Book Auctions, 3/4 Hardwick Street, Off Rosebery Avenue, London EC1R 4RY Tel: 020 7833 2636
BBR	*	BBR, Elsecar Heritage Centre, Wath Road, Elsecar, Barnsley, Yorkshire S74 8HJ Tel: 01226 745156
Bea(E)	*	Bearnes, St Edmund's Court, Okehampton St, Exeter, Devon EX4 1DU Tel: 01392 422800
BED	•	Johann Bedingfeld, 1 West Street, Dorking, Surrey RH4 1BL Tel: 01306 880022
BELL	•	Bell Antiques, Glos. Tel: 0121 745 9034
Ber	•	Berry Antiques, Berry House, 11–13 Stone Street, Cranbrook, Kent TN17 3HF Tel: 01580 712345
BERA	• †	Berry Antiques, 3 High Street, Moreton-in-Marsh, Glos GL56 0AH Tel: 01608 652929, chris@berryantiques.com
BEV	•	Beverley, 30 Church Street, Marylebone, London NW8 8EP Tel: 020 7262 1576
BEX	• †	Daniel Bexfield, 26 Burlington Arcade, London W1V 9AD Tel: 020 7491 1720
BG	*	Braswell Galleries, 125 West Ave, Norwalk CT06854 USA Tel: 001 203 899 7420
BGC	•	Brenda Gerwat-Clark, Granny's Goodies, G2/4 Alfie's Antique Market, 13–25 Church Street, London NW8 8DT Tel: 020 7706 4699
BHa	• †	Judy & Brian Harden Antiques, PO Box 14, Bourton-on-the-Water, Cheltenham, Glos GL54 2YR Tel: 01451 810684
BIG	*	Bigwood Auctioneers Ltd, The Old School, Tiddington, Stratford-upon-Avon, Warwickshire, CV37 7AW Tel: 01789 269415

BKS	*	Brooks (Auctioneers) Ltd, 81 Westside, London SW4 9AY Tel: 020 7228 8000
BL	• †	Brian Loomes, Calf Haugh Farm, Pateley Bridge, Yorkshire HG3 5HW Tel: 01423 711163
BLA	•	Blair Antiques, 14 Bonnethill Road, Pitlochry, Perthshire, Scotland PH16 5BS Tel: 01796 472624
BLH	*	BBG Ambrose, Ambrose House, Old Station Road, Loughton, Essex IG10 4PE Tel: 020 8502 3951
BOL	•	Bears of London, Unit 32, Bourbon Hanby Antiques Centre, 151 Sydney Street, Chelsea, London SW3 6NT Tel: 020 7795 3000 Mobile: 07957 338 668
Bon	* †	Bonhams, Montpelier Street, Knightsbridge, London SW7 1HH Tel: 020 7393 3900
Bon(C)	*	Bonhams, 65–69 Lots Road, Chelsea, London SW10 0RN Tel: 020 7393 3900
Bon(G)	*	Bonhams & Martel Maides Ltd, Allez St Auction Rooms, 29 High Street, St Peter Port, Guernsey, Channel Islands GY1 4NY Tel: 01481 713463/722700
Bon(M)	*	Bonhams, St Thomas's Place, Hillgate, Stockport, Gt. Manchester SK1 3TZ Tel: 0161 429 8283
BOR	•	Bed of Roses, 12 Prestbury Road, Cheltenham, Glos GL52 2PW Tel: 01242 231918
BOS	*	Bosley's, 42 West Street, Marlow, Bucks SL7 2NB Tel: 01628 488188
BOW	• †	David Bowden, 12 The Mall, Upper Street, Islington, London N1 0PD Tel: 020 7226 3033
BR	* †	Bracketts Auction Hall, Pantiles, Tunbridge Wells, Kent TN1 1UU Tel: 01892 544500
BRH	*	Bruun Rasmussen-Havnen, Pakhusvej 12, DK-2100, Copenhagen, Denmark Tel: +45 70 27 60 80, havnen@bruun-rasmussen.dk, www.bruun-rasmussen.dk
Bri	* †	Bristol Auction Rooms, St John's Place, Apsley Road, Clifton, Bristol, Glos BS8 2ST Tel: 0117 973 7201 www.bristolauctionrooms.co.uk
BRT	•	Britannia, Gray's Antique Market, Stand 101, 58 Davies Street, London W1Y 1AR Tel: 020 7629 6772
BrW	•	Brian Watson Antique Glass, The Grange, Norwich Road, Wroxham, Norwich, Norfolk NR12 8RX Tel: 01603 784177
BTB	•	Behind the Boxes, 98 Kirkdale, Sydenham, London SE26 4BG Tel: 020 8291 6116
BUK	*	Bukowskis, Arsenalsgatan 4, Stockholm, Sweden-SE111 47 Tel: 08 614 08 00, info@bukowskis.se
BUSH	•	Bushwood Antiques, Stags End Equestrian Centre, Gaddesden Lane, Hemel Hempstead, Hertfordshire HP2 6HN Tel: 01582 794700
BWA	•	Bow-Well Antiques, 103 West Bow, Edinburgh, Scotland EH1 2JP Tel: 0131 225 3335
BWe	* †	Biddle & Webb Ltd, Ladywood, Middleway, Birmingham, West Midlands B16 0PP Tel: 0121 455 8042, antiques@biddleandwebb.freeserve.co.uk
BYG	•	Bygones Reclamation (Canterbury), Nackington Road, Canterbury, Kent Tel: 01227 767453
ByI	•	Bygones of Ireland Ltd, Lodge Road, Westport, County Mayo Tel: 00 353 98 26132/25701
C&C	•	Cohen & Cohen, 101b Kensington Church Street, London W8 7LN Tel: 020 7727 7677
CAG	* †	Canterbury Auction Galleries, 40 Station Road West, Canterbury, Kent CT2 8AN Tel: 01227 763337
CARS	•	C.A.R.S. (Classic Automobilia & Regalia Specialists), 4–4a Chapel Terrace Mews, Kemp Town, Brighton, Sussex BN2 1HU Tel: 01273 60 1960
CAT	• †	Lennox Cato, 1 The Square, Church Street, Edenbridge, Kent TN8 5BD Tel: 01732 865988 Mobile: 07836 233473
CB	•	Christine Bridge, 78 Castelnau, London SW13 9EX Tel: 07000 445277
CBC	•	Cheshire Billiards Co, Springwood Lodge, Ermine Street, Appleby, Lincolnshire DN15 0DD Tel: 01724 852359
CBO	•	The Chaucer Bookshop, 6–7 Beer Cart Lane, Canterbury, Kent CT1 2NY Tel: 01227 453912 chaucerbooks@canterbury.dialnet.com www.chaucer-bookshop.co.uk/main.html
CBP	* †	Comic Book Postal Auctions Ltd , 40–42 Osnaburgh Street, London NW1 3ND Tel: 020 7424 0007
CCB	•	Colin C. Bowdell, PO Box 65, Grantham, Lincolnshire NG31 6QR Tel: 01476 563206
CCO	•	Collectable Costume, Fountain Antique Centre, 3 Fountain Buildings, Lansdowne Road, Bath, Somerset BA1 5DU Tel: 01225 428731
CF	•	Country Furniture, 79 St Leonards Road, Windsor, Berkshire SL4 3BZ Tel: 01753 830154
CGC	*	Cheffins Grain & Comins, 2 Clifton Road, Cambridge, Cambs CB2 4BW Tel: 01223 358731
ChA	•	Chapel Antiques, The Chapel, Chapel Place, Tunbridge Wells, Kent TN1 1YR Tel: 01892 619921, chapelplace@hotmail.com
CHAP	•	Bill Chapman, Stand 11, Bourbon Hanby Antiques Centre, 151 Sydney Street, Chelsea, London SW3 6NT Tel: 020 7352 2106
CHe/ CHE	• †	Chelsea Clocks & Antiques, Stand H3-4, Antiquarius Market, 135 King's Road, London SW3 4PW Tel: 020 7352 8646
CLE	* †	Clevedon Salerooms, Herbert Road, Clevedon, Somerset BS21 7ND Tel: 01275 876699
CoA	• †	Country Antiques (Wales), Castle Mill, Kidwelly, Carmarthenshire, Wales SA17 4UU Tel: 01554 890534
CoCo	•	Country Collector, 11–12 Birdgate, Pickering, Yorkshire YO18 7AL Tel: 01751 477481
CoHA	• †	Corner House Antiques, High Street, Lechlade, Glos GL7 3AE Tel: 01367 252007
COLL	•	Collinge Antiques, Old Fyffes Warehouse, Conwy Rd, Llandudno Junction, Wales LL31 9LU Tel: 01492 580022 Mobile: 0836 506354
CORO	• †	Coromandel, London Tel: 020 8543 9115 Mobile: 07932102756
CPA	•	Cottage Pine Antiques, 19 Broad Street, Brinklow, Nr Rugby, Warwickshire CV23 0LS Tel: 01788 832673
CRI	*	Criterion Salerooms, 53 Essex Road, Islington, London N1 2BN Tel: 020 7359 5707
CRN	•	The Crow's Nest, 3 Hope Square, opp. Brewer's Quay, Weymouth, Dorset DT4 8TR Tel: 01305 786930
CRU	•	Mary Cruz Antiques, 5 Broad Street, Bath, Somerset BA1 5LJ Tel: 01225 334174
CS	• †	Christopher Sykes, The Old Parsonage, Woburn, Milton Keynes, Bucks MK17 9QM Tel: 01525 290259
CSAC	•	Church Street Antiques Centre, 3–4 Church Street, Stow-on-the-Wold, Glos GL54 1BB Tel: 01451 870186
DA	* †	Dee, Atkinson & Harrison, The Exchange Saleroom, Driffield, Yorkshire YO25 7LJ Tel: 01377 253151, exchange@dee-atkinson-harrison, www.dee-atkinson-harrison.co.uk
DAC	•	Didcot Antiques Centre, 220 Broadway, Didcot, Oxfordshire OX11 8RS Tel: 01235 510819
DAD	•	Decorative Arts @ Doune, Stand 26, Scottish Antique and Arts Centre, By Doune, Stirling, Scotland FK16 6HD Tel: 01786 461 439 Mobile: 0378 475 974, gordonfoster@excite.co.uk fionamacsporran@btinternet.com
DaH	•	Dale House Antiques, High Street, Moreton-in-Marsh, Glos GL56 0AD Tel: 01608 650763
DAN	•	Andrew Dando, 4 Wood Street, Queen Square, Bath, Somerset BA1 2JQ Tel: 01225 422702
DBA	• †	Douglas Bryan Antiques, The Old Bakery, St David's Bridge, Cranbrook, Kent TN17 3HN Tel: 01580 713103
DD	* †	David Duggleby, Vine St Salerooms, Scarborough, Yorkshire YO11 1XN Tel: 01723 507111 auctions@davidduggleby.freeserve.co.uk www.thesaurus.co.uk/david-duggleby
DDM	*	Dickinson Davy & Markham, Wrawby Street, Brigg, Humberside DN20 8JJ Tel: 01652 653666
DeA	•	Delphi Antiques, Powerscourt Townhouse Centre, South William Street, Dublin 2 Tel: 00 353 1 679 0331
DEE	•	Dee's Antique Pine, 89 Grove Road, Windsor, Berkshire SL4 1HT Tel: 01753 865627/850926
DeG	•	Denzil Grant, Suffolk Fine Arts, Drinkstone House, Drinkstone, Bury St Edmunds, Suffolk IP30 9TG Tel: 01449 736576
Del	•	Delomosne & Son Ltd, Court Close, North Wraxall, Chippenham, Wiltshire SN14 7AD Tel: 01225 891505
DEN	* †	Denham's, The Auction Galleries, Warnham, Horsham, Sussex RH12 3RZ Tel: 01403 255699/ 253837, denhams@lineone.net

DFA	• †	Delvin Farm Antiques, Gormonston, County Meath Tel: 00 353 1 841 2285
DIA	•	Mark Diamond, London Tel: 020 8508 4479
DIC	•	D & B Dickinson, The Antique Shop, 22 & 22a New Bond St, Bath, Somerset BA1 1BA Tel: 01225 466502
DID	•	Didier Antiques, 58–60 Kensington Church Street, London W8 4DB Tel: 020 7938 2537/078 36 232634
DMa	•	David March, Abbots Leigh, Bristol, Glos BS8 Tel: 0117 937 2422
DMC	*	Diamond Mills & Co, 117 Hamilton Road, Felixstowe, Suffolk IP11 7BL Tel: 01394 282281
DN	* †	Dreweatt Neate, Donnington Priory, Donnington, Newbury, Berkshire RG13 2JE Tel: 01635 553553, fineart@dreweatt-neate.co.uk
DN(H)	*	Dreweatt Neate Holloways, 49 Parsons Street, Banbury, Oxon OX16 8PF Tel: 01295 817777 ccovacic@dreweatt-neate.co.uk www.dreweatt-neate.co.uk
DNW	*	Dix-Noonan-Webb, 1 Old Bond Street, London W1X 3TD Tel: 020 7499 5022
DOA	•	Dorchester Antiques, 3 High Street, Dorchester-on-Thames, Oxon OX10 7HH Tel: 01865 341 373
Doc	*	Dockree's, Cheadle Hulme Centre, Clemence House, Mellor Road, Cheadle Hulme, Cheshire SK8 5AT Tel: 0161 485 1258
DOL	•	Dollectable, 53 Lower Bridge Street, Chester, Cheshire CH1 1RS Tel: 01244 344888/679195
DOM	•	Peter Dome, Sheffield
DOR	•	Dorset Reclamation, Cow Drove, Bere Regis, Wareham, Dorset BH20 7JZ Tel: 01929 472200
DORO	*	Dorotheum, Palais Dorotheum, A-1010 Wien, Dorotheergasse 17, Austria Tel: 0043 1 515 600
DRA	• †	Derek Roberts, 25 Shipbourne Road, Tonbridge, Kent TN10 3DN Tel: 01732 358986
DRU	• †	Drummond's Architectural Antiques, The Kirk Patrick Buildings, 25 London Road (A3), Hindhead, Surrey GU26 6AB Tel: 01428 609444
DSG	• †	Delf Stream Gallery, 14 New Street, Sandwich, Kent CT13 9AB Tel: 01304 617684
DuM	*	Du Mouchelles, 409 East Jefferson, Detroit, Michigan 48226, USA Tel: 001 313 963 0248
DW	* †	Dominic Winter, Book Auctions, The Old School, Maxwell Street, Swindon, Wiltshire SN1 5DR Tel: 01793 611340
E	* †	Ewbank, Burnt Common Auction Room, London Road, Send, Woking, Surrey GU23 7LN Tel: 01483 223101
EH	* †	Edgar Horn's, Fine Art Auctioneers, 46–50 South Street, Eastbourne, Sussex BN21 4XB Tel: 01323 410419, www.edgarhorns.com
ELI	•	Eli Antiques, Stand Q5 Antiquarius, 135 King's Road, London SW3 4PW Tel: 020 7351 7038
EMC	•	Sue Emerson & Bill Chapman, Bourbon Hanby Antiques Centre, Shop No 18, 151 Sydney Street, Chelsea, London SW3 6NT Tel: 020 7351 1807
EON	•	Eugene O'Neill, Antique Gallery, Echo Bridge Mall, 381 Elliot Street, Newtown Upper Falls, MA 02164 USA Tel: (617) 965 5965
ESA	• †	East Street Antiques, 42 East Street, Crewkerne, Somerset TA18 7AG Tel: 01460 78600
ET	• †	Early Technology, Monkton House, Old Craighall, Musselburgh, Midlothian, Scotland EH21 8SF Tel: 0131 665 5753, michael.bennett-levy@virgin.net, www.earlytech.com
ETO	•	Eric Tombs, 62a West Street, Dorking, Surrey RH4 1BS Tel: 01306 743661
EW	•	Elaine Whobrey, Bartlett Street Antique Centre 5–10 Bartlett Street, Bath, Somerset BA12QZ Tel: 01225 466689
F&C	•	Finan & Co, The Square, Mere, Wilts BA12 6DJ Tel: 01747 861411
FA/FAG	•	Fagins Antiques, The Old Whiteways Cider Factory, Hele, Exeter, Devon EX5 4PW Tel: 01392 882062
Fai	•	Fair Finds Antiques, Rait Village Antiques Centre, Rait, Perthshire, Scotland PH2 7RT Tel: 01821 670379
FAN	•	Fantiques Tel: 020 8840 4761
FBG	*	Frank H. Boos Gallery, 420 Enterprise Court, Bloomfield Hills, Michigan 48302, USA Tel: 001 248 332 1500

FF	•	Freeforms, Unit 6 The Antique Centre, 58–60 Kensington Church Street, London W8 4DB Tel: 020 7937 9447
FHF	*	Frank H. Fellows & Sons, Augusta House, 19 Augusta Street, Hockley, Birmingham B18 6JA Tel: 0121 212 2131
FOX	•	Foxhole Antiques, Swan & Foxhole, Albert House, Stone Street, Cranbrook, Kent TN17 3HF Tel: 01580 712720
FQA	•	Scottish Antique and Arts Centre, Carse of Cambus, Doune, Perthshire, Scotland FK16 6HD Tel: 01786 841203
G(B)	* †	Gorringes Auction Galleries, Terminus Road, Bexhill-on-Sea, Sussex TN39 3LR Tel: 01424 212994
G(L)	*	Gorringes Auction Galleries, 15 North Street, Lewes, Sussex BN7 2PD Tel: 01273 472503 auctions@gorringes.co.uk, www.gorringes.co.uk
G(T)	*	Gorringes, 15 The Pantiles, Tunbridge Wells, Kent TN2 5TD Tel: 01892 619670
G&CC	• †	Goss & Crested China Centre & Museum incorporating Milestone Publications, 62 Murray Rd, Horndean, Hants PO8 9JL Tel: 023 9259 7440 info@gosschinaclub.demon.co.uk
GAK	* †	G A Key, Aylsham Salerooms, 8 Market Place, Aylsham, Norfolk NR11 6EH Tel: 01263 733195 www.aylshamsalerooms.co.uk
Gam	*	Clarke Gammon, The Guildford Auction Rooms, Bedford Road, Guildford, Surrey GU1 4SJ Tel: 01483 880915
GBr	• †	Geoffrey Breeze Antiques, 6 George Street, Bath, Somerset BA1 2EH Tel: 01225 466499
GD	• †	Gilbert & Dale Antiques, The Old Chapel, Church Street, Ilchester, Nr Yeovil, Somerset BA22 8ZA Tel: 01935 840464
GeM	• †	Gerald Mathias, Antiquarius, 135 King's Road, Chelsea, London SW3 4PW Tel: 020 7351 0484
GeW	•	Geoffrey Waters Ltd, F1–F6 Antiquarius Antiques Centre, 135–141 King's Road, London SW3 4PW Tel: 020 7376 5467
GH	*	Gardiner Houlgate, The Old Malthouse, Comfortable Place, Upper Bristol Road, Bath, Somerset BA1 3AJ Tel: 01225 447933
GHC	•	Great Haul of China, PO Box 233, Sevenoaks, Kent TN13 3ZN Tel: 01732 741484
GIO	•	Giovanna Antiques, Bourbon & Hanby Antiques Centre, Shop 16, 151 Sydney Street, London SW3 6NT Tel: 020 7565 0004
GKe	•	Gerald Kenyon, 6 Great Strand Street, Dublin 1 Tel: 00 3531 873 0625/873 0488
GLD	• †	Glade Antiques, PO Box 939, Marlow, Bucks SL7 1SR Tel: 01628 487255
Gle	*	Glendinings & Co, 101 New Bond Street, London W1Y 9LG Tel: 020 7493 2445
GLO	•	Gordon Loraine Antiques, Rait Village Antiques Centre, Rait, Perthshire, Scotland PH2 7RT Tel: 01821 670760
GLT	•	Glitterati, Assembly Antique Centre, 6–8 Saville Row, Bath, Som BA1 2QP Tel: 01225 333294
GN	• †	Gillian Neale Antiques, PO Box 247, Aylesbury, Bucks HP20 1JZ Tel: 01296 423754/07860 638700
GOL	•	The Golden Sovereign, The Copper House, Gt Bardfield, Essex CM7 4SP Tel: 01371 810507
GrD	•	Grays Dolls, Grays in the Mews, 1–7 Davies St, London W1Y 2LP Tel: 020 8367 2441/7629 7034
GRG	•	Gordon Reece Gallery, Finkle Street, Knaresborough, Yorks HG5 8AA Tel: 01423 866219
GRI	•	Grimes House Antiques, High Street, Moreton-in-Marsh, Glos GL56 0AT Tel/Fax: 01608 651029, grimes-house@cix.co.uk, www.grimeshouse.co.uk, www.cranberryglass.co.uk
GS	•	Ged Selby Antique Glass, Yorkshire. By appointment Tel: 01756 799673
GSP	*	Graves, Son & Pilcher, Hove Auction Rooms, Hove Street, Hove, Sussex BN3 2GL Tel: 01273 735266
GTH	*	Greenslade Taylor Hunt Fine Art, Magdelene Hse, Church Square, Taunton, Somerset TA1 1SB Tel: 01823 332525
GV	• †	Garth Vincent, The Old Manor House, Allington, Nr Grantham, Lincolnshire NG32 2DH Tel: 01400 281358
HA	•	Hallidays, The Old College, Dorchester-on-Thames, Oxon OX10 7HL Tel: 01865 340028/68 Mobile: 0860 625917
HAL	• †	John & Simon Haley, 89 Northgate, Halifax, Yorkshire HX1 1XF Tel: 01422 822148
Hal	*	Halls Fine Art Auctions, Welsh Bridge, Shrewsbury, Shropshire, SY3 8LA Tel: 01743 231212

Hal(C) * Halls Fine Art Auctions, Booth Mansion, 30 Watergate St, Chester, Cheshire CH1 2LA Tel: 01244 312300/312112

HALL• Hall's Nostalgia, 21 Mystic Street, Arlington, MA 02474 USA Tel: 001 781 646 7757

HAM * † Hamptons International, Baverstock House, 93 High Street, Godalming, Surrey GU7 1AL Tel: 01483 423567, fineart@hamptons-int.com www.hamptons.co.uk

HarC • Hardy's Collectables, 862 Christchurch Road, Boscombe, Bournemouth, Dorset BH7 6DQ Tel: 01202 422407/473744 Mobile: 07970 613077

HARP • † Harpers Jewellers Ltd, 2/6 Minster Gates, York YO1 7HL Tel: 01904 632634 hjewels@aol.com

HBo • Harrison's Books, Stand J20/21 Grays Mews Antiques Market, 1–7 Davies Street, London W1Y 2LP Tel: 020 7629 1374

HCH * † The Cotswold Auction Company Ltd, The Coach House, Swan Yard, 9–13 Market Place, Cirencester, Glos GL7 2NH Tel: 01285 642420

HEB • Hebeco, 47 West Street, Dorking, Surrey RH4 1BU Tel: 01306 875396 Mobile: 0410 019790

HEL • Helios Gallery, 292 Westbourne Grove, London W11 2PS Tel: 077 11 955 997 heliosgallery@btinternet.com

HEM • † Hemswell Antique Centre, Caenby Corner Estate, Hemswell Cliff, Gainsborough, Lincolnshire DN21 5TJ Tel: 01427 668389

Herm * Hermann Historica OHG, Postfach 201009, 80010 München Germany Tel: 00 49 89 5237296

HEW • Muir Hewitt, Halifax Antiques Centre, Queens Road/Gibbet Street, Halifax, Yorks HX1 4LR Tel: 01422 347377

HGh • Hungry Ghost, 1 Brewery Yard, Sheep Street, Stow-on-the-Wold, Glos GL54 1AA Tel: 01451 870101

HHO • Howard Hope, 21 Bridge Road, East Molesey, Surrey KT8 9EU Tel: 020 8941 2472/8398 7130 Mobile: 0585 543267

HOA • † Bob Hoare Antiques, Unit Q, Phoenix Place, North Street, Lewes, Sussex BN7 2DQ Tel: 01273 480557

HOB • † Hobday Toys, Middlesex Tel: 01895 636737

HofB • Howards of Broadway, 27A High Street, Broadway, Worcs WR12 7DP Tel: 01386 858924

HOK * Hamilton Osborne King, 4 Main Street, Blackrock, Co. Dublin Tel: 353 1 288 5011 blackrock@hok.ie, www.hok.ie

HON • Honan's Antiques, Crowe Street, Gort, County Galway Tel: 00 353 91 631407

HUM • Humbleyard Fine Art, Unit 32 Admiral Vernon Arcade, Portobello Road, London W11 2DY Tel: 01362 637793 Mobile: 0836 349416

HUR • Hurst Gallery, 53 Mt. Auburn Street, Cambridge, MA 02138 USA Tel: 617 491 6888 www.hurstgallery.com

HVH * Horta, Hotel de Ventes, 16 Avenue Ducpetiaux, 1060 Bruxelles Tel: 02 533 11 11

HYD * Hy Duke & Son, Dorchester Fine Art Salerooms, Dorchester, Dorset DT1 1QS Tel: 01305 265080

ICO • Iconastas, 5 Piccadilly Arcade, London SW1 Tel: 020 7629 1433, iconastas@compuserve.com

IS • † Ian Sharp Antiques, 23 Front Street, Tynemouth, Tyne & Wear NE30 4DX Tel: 0191 296 0656

IW • † Islwyn Watkins, Offa's Dyke Antique Centre, 4 High Street, Knighton, Powys, Wales LD7 1AT Tel: 01547 520145

JAA * Jackson's Auctioneers & Appraisers, 2229 Lincoln Street, Cedar Falls, IA 50613 USA Tel: 00 1 319 277 2256

JAd * James Adam & Sons, 26 St Stephen's Green, Dublin 2 Tel: 00 3531 676 0261

JaG • Japanese Gallery, 23 Camden Passage, London N1 8EA Tel: 020 7226 3347

JAK • † Clive & Lynne Jackson, Glos Tel: 01242 254375 Mobile: 0410 239351

JBe * John Bellman Auctioneers, New Pound Business Park, Wisborough Grn, Billingshurst, Sussex RH14 0AZ Tel: 01403 700858 jbellman@compuserve.com

JBU • John Bull (Antiques) Ltd, JB Silverware, 139a New Bond Street, London W1Y 9FB Tel: 020 7629 1251 Mobile: 0850 221 468 elliot@jbsilverware.co.uk, www.jbsilverware.co.uk, www.antique-silver.co.uk

JD * † Lewes Auction Rooms (Julian Dawson), 56 High Street, Lewes, Sussex BN7 1XE Tel: 01273 478221, www.lewesauctions.com

JE • † Julian Eade, Surrey Tel: 020 8394 1515 Mobile: 0973 542971

JEA • John Edwards Antiques, Worcester Antiques Centre, 15 Reindeer Court, Mealcheapen St, Worcester WR1 4DF Tel: 01905 353840 John@RoyalWorcester.freeserve.co.uk

JEB • Jenni Barke, Scottish Antique and Arts Centre, Carse of Cambus, Doune, Perthshire, Scotland FK16 6HD Tel: 01786 841203

JeF • † Jeffrey Formby, Orchard Cottage, East Street, Moreton-in-Marsh, Glos GL56 0LQ Tel: 01608 650558, www.formby-clocks.co.uk

JHa • Jeanette Hayhurst Fine Glass, 32a Kensington Church St, London W8 4HA Tel: 020 7938 1539

JHo • † Jonathan Horne, 66 Kensington Church Street, London W8 4BY Tel: 020 7221 5658 JH@jonathanhorne.co.uk, www.jonathan.co.uk

JIL • † Jillings Antique Clocks, Croft House, 17 Church Street, Newent, Glos GL18 1PU Tel: 01531 822100 Mobile: 0973 830110

JM * † Maxwells of Wilmslow, 133A Woodford Road, Woodford, Cheshire SK7 1QD Tel/Fax: 0161 439 5182

JMC • J & M Collectables, Kent Tel: 01580 891657

JMW • JMW Gallery, 144 Lincoln Street, Boston MA02111 USA Tel: 001 617 338 9097

JNic * John Nicholson, The Auction Rooms, Longfield, Midhurst Road, Fernhurst, Surrey GU27 3HA Tel: 01428 653727

JO • Jacqueline Oosthuizen, 23 Cale Street, Chelsea, London SW3 3QR Tel: 020 7352 6071

JoW • John Wade, PO Box 303, Welwyn, Hertfordshire AL6 0XL

JPr • Joanna Proops, Antique Textiles, 34 Belvedere, Lansdown Hill, Bath, Somerset BA1 5HR Tel: 01225 310795

JSM • J & S Millard Antiques, Assembly Antiques, 5–8 Saville Row, Bath, Somerset BA1 2QP Tel: 01225 469785

JuB • Julia Bennett Tel: 01279 850279

JuC •† Julia Craig, Bartlett Street Antiques Centre, 5–10 Bartlett Street, Bath, Somerset BA1 2QZ Tel: 01225 448202/310457 Mob: 07771 786846

JUP • Jupiter Antiques, PO Box 609, Rottingdean, Sussex BN2 7FW Tel: 01273 302865

JW • Julian Wood, Exeter Antique Lighting, Cellar 15, The Quay, Exeter, Devon EX2 4AY Tel: 01392 490848

JWA • J.W.A. (UK) Limited, PO Box 6, Peterborough, Cambs PE1 5AH Tel: 01733 348344

K • Kite, 15 Langton Street, London SW10 0JL Tel: 020 7351 2108 Mobile: 077 11 887120

K&D • † Kembery Antique Clocks, Bartlett Street Antiques Centre, Bath, Somerset BA1 2QZ Tel: 0117 956 5281 Mobile: 0850 623237

KB • † Knole Barometers, Bingham House West Street, Somerton, Somerset TA11 7PS Tel: 01458 241015 Mobile: 07785 364567 dccops@btconnect.com

KIE • Netsuke, Bartlett Street Antique Centre 5–10 Bartlett Street, Bath, Somerset BA1 2QZ Tel: 01225 464689

KJ • Katie Jones, 195 Westbourne Grove, London W11 2SB Tel: 020 7243 5600

KOLN * Auction Team Köln, Postfach 50 11 19, 50971 Köln, Germany Tel: 00 49 0221 38 70 49 auction@breker.com

L * Lawrence Fine Art Auctioneers, South Street, Crewkerne, Som TA18 8AB Tel: 01460 73041

L&E * BBG Locke & England, 18 Guy Street, Leamington Spa, Warwickshire CV32 4RT Tel: 01926 889100, www.auctions-online.com/locke

L&T * Lyon & Turnbull, 33 Broughton Pl, Edinburgh, Scotland EH1 3RR Tel: 0131 557 8844

LaM * La Maison, 410 St John St, London EC1V 4NJ Tel: 020 7837 6522

LAY * David Lay, ASVA, Auction House, Alverton, Penzance, Cornwall TR18 4RE Tel: 01736 361414

LBe • Linda Bee, Art Deco Stand L18–21, Grays Antique Market, 1–7 Davies Mews, London W1Y 1AR Tel: 020 7629 5921

LBO • Laura Bordignon Antiques, PO Box 14559, London SW19 5ZP Tel: 020 8241 7844 Mobile: 0378 787929

LBr • Lynda Brine, Assembly Antique Centre, 5–8 Saville Row, Bath, Somerset BA1 2QP Tel: 01225 448488

LDC • † L & D Collins, London Tel: 020 7584 0712

LeB	•	Le Boudoir Collectables, Bartlett Street Antique Centre, Bath, Somerset BA1 2QZ Tel: 01225 311061
LF	* †	Lambert & Foster, 102 High Street, Tenterden, Kent TN30 6HT Tel: 01580 763233
LHAr	•	Artifacts, USA Tel/Fax: 001 415 381 2084
LIB	•	Libra Antiques, 81 London Road, Hurst Green, Etchingham, Sussex TN19 7PN Tel: 01580 860569
LJ	*	Leonard Joel Auctioneers, 333 Malvern Road, South Yarra, Victoria 3141, Australia Tel: 03 9826 4333, jewellery@ljoel.com.au decarts@ljoel.com.au, www.ljoel.com.au
LPA	•	L.P. Furniture, (The Old Brewery), Short Acre Street, Walsall, West Midlands WS2 8HW Tel: 01922 746764
LT	* †	Louis Taylor Auctioneers & Valuers, Britannia House, 10 Town Road, Hanley, Stoke-on-Trent, Staffordshire ST1 2QG Tel: 01782 214111
LUC	•	R. K. Lucas & Son, The Tithe Exchange, 9 Victoria Place, Haverfordwest, Wales SA16 2JX Tel: 01437 762538
M	*	Morphets of Harrogate, 6 Albert Street, Harrogate, Yorks HG1 1JL Tel: 01423 530030
M&K	*	Mellors & Kirk, The Auction House, Gregory Street, Lenton Lane, Nottingham, NG7 2NL Tel: 0115 979 0000
MAG	•	Magna Gallery, 41 High Street, Oxford OX1 4AP Tel: 01865 245805
MAR	*	Frank R. Marshall & Co, Marshall House, Church Hill, Knutsford, Cheshire WA16 6DH Tel: 01565 653284
MARK	•	20th Century Marks, 12 Market Square, Westerham, Kent TN16 1AW Tel: 01959 562221, lambarda@msn.com
MB	• †	Mostly Boxes, 93 High Street, Eton, Windsor, Berkshire SL4 6AF Tel: 01753 858470
MBO	•	Michael E. Bound, Portobello Rd, London
MCA	* †	Mervyn Carey, Twysden Cottage, Benenden, Cranbrook, Kent TN17 4LD Tel: 01580 240283
MCN	•	MCN Antiques, 183 Westbourne Grove, London W11 2SB Tel: 020 7727 3796
MEA	* †	Mealy's, Chatsworth Street, Castle Comer, Co Kilkenny Tel: 00 353 56 41229
MER	•	Mere Antiques, 13 Fore Street, Topsham, Exeter, Devon EX3 0HF Tel: 01392 874224
MGC	•	Midlands Goss & Commemoratives, The Old Cornmarket Antique Centre, 70 Market Place, Warwick CV34 4SO Tel: 01926 419119
MIL	•	Milverton Antiques, Fore Street, Milverton, Taunton, Som TA4 1JU Tel: 01823 400592
MIN	•	Ministry of Pine, Timsbury Village Workshop, Timsbury Industrial Estate, Hayeswood Road, Bath, Som BA3 1HQ Tel: 01761 472297/434938
Mit	•	Mitchells, Fairfield House, Station Rd, Cockermouth, Cumbria CA13 9PY Tel: 01900 827800
MJB	*	Michael J. Bowman, 6 Haccombe House, Netherton, Newton Abbot, Devon TQ12 4SJ Tel: 01626 872890
MLa	• †	Marion Langham, London Tel: 020 7730 1002
MLL	•	Millers Antiques Ltd, Netherbrook House, 86 Christchurch Road, Ringwood, Hampshire BH24 1DR Tel: 01425 472062
MoS	•	Morgan Stobbs. By appointment. Tel: Mobile 0402 206817
MRW	•	Malcolm Russ-Welch, PO Box 1122, Rugby, Warwickshire CV23 9YD Tel: 01788 810 616
MSB	•	Marilynn and Sheila Brass, PO Box 380503, Cambridge, MA 02238-0503 USA Tel: 617 491 6064
MSW	* †	Marilyn Swain Auctions, The Old Barracks, Sandon Road, Grantham, Lincolnshire NG31 9AS Tel: 01476 568861
MTay	• †	Martin Taylor Antiques, 140B Tettenhall Road, Wolverhampton, West Midlands WV6 0BQ Tel: 01902 751166/0836 636524
MUL	• †	Mullock & Madeley, The Old Shippon, Wall-under-Heywood, Church Stretton, Shropshire SY6 7DS Tel: 01694 771771
NAW	• †	Newark Antiques Warehouse, Old Kelham Road, Newark, Notts NG24 1BX Tel: 01636 674869
NC	•	The Nautical Centre, Harbour Passage, Hope Square, Weymouth, Dorset DT4 8TR Tel: Daytime 01305 777838
NCA	•	New Century, 69 Kensington Church Street, London W8 4BG Tel: 020 7376 2810

NET	•	Nettlebed Antique Merchants, 1 High Street, Nettlebed, Henley on Thames, Oxon RG9 5DA Tel: 0370 554559/01491 642062
NEW	•	Newsum Antiques, 2 High Street, Winchcombe, Glos GL54 5HT Tel: 01242 603446 Mobile: 07968 196668
NOA	*	New Orleans Auction Galleries Inc, 801 Magazine Street, AT 510 Julia, New Orleans, Louisiana 70130 USA Tel: 001 504 566 1849
NOST	• †	Nostalgia, Hollands Mill, 61 Shaw Heath, Stockport, Cheshire SK3 8BH Tel: 0161 477 7706
NOTT	•	Notts Pine, The Old Redhouse Farm, Stratton-on-the-Fosse, Bath, Somerset BA3 4QE Tel: 01761 419911 Evening: 01761 471614
NSA	•	Nancy Stronczek Antiques, 26 Bouker Street, Greenfield, MA 01301 USA Tel: 413 774 3260 njs@crocker.com
OAS/ Odi	* †	Odiham Auction Sales, The Eagle Works, rear of Hartley Wintney Garages, High Street, Hartley Wintney, Hampshire RG27 8PU Tel: 01252 844410, auction@dircon.co.uk
OCH	•	Gillian Shepherd, Old Corner House Antiques, 6 Poplar Road, Wittersham, Tenterden, Kent TN30 7PG Tel: 01797 270236
OD	•	Offa's Dyke Antique Centre, 4 High Street, Knighton, Powys, Wales LD7 1AT Tel: 01547 528635/528940
OE	•	Orient Expressions, Assembly Antiques Centre 5–8 Saville Row, Bath, Somerset BA1 2QP Tel: 01225 313399/mob 0788 1588 314
OFM	•	Old French Mirror Company, The, Nightingales, Greys Green, Rotherfield Greys, Henley-on-Thames, Oxon RG9 4QQ Tel: /Fax 01491 629913 bridget@debreanski.freeserve.co.uk, www.frenchmirrors.co.uk
Oli	* †	Olivers, Olivers Rooms, Burkitts Lane, Sudbury, Suffolk CO10 1HB Tel: 01787 880305
OLM	•	The Old Mill, High Street, Lamberhurst, Kent TN3 8EQ Tel: 01892 891196
ONS	*	Onslow's, The Depot, 2 Michael Road, , London SW6 2AD Tel: 020 7371 0505 Mobile: 078 31 473 400
OO	•	Pieter Oosthuizen, Unit 4 Bourbon Hanby Antiques Centre, 151 Sydney Street, London SW3 6NT Tel: 020 7460 3078
OOLA	• †	Oola Boola, 166 Tower Bridge Road, London SE1 3LS Tel: 020 7403 0794/8693 5050 Mobile: 0956 261252
OT	•	Old Timers, Box 392, Camp Hill, PA 17001-0392, USA Tel: 001 717 761 1908
OTB	• †	Old Tackle Box, PO Box 55, Cranbrook, Kent TN17 3ZU Tel/Fax: 01580 713979
OTT	•	Otter Antiques, 20 High Street, Wallingford, Oxon OX10 0BP Tel: 01491 825544
P	* †	Phillips, 101 New Bond Street, London W1Y 0AS Tel: 020 7629 6602
P(B)	*	Phillips, 1 Old King Street, Bath, Som BA1 2JT Tel: 01225 310609
P(Ba)	*	Phillips Bayswater, 10 Salem Rd, London W2 4DL Tel: 020 7229 9090
P(C)	*	Phillips Cardiff, 7–8 Park Place, Cardiff, Wales CF10 3DP Tel: 029 2039 6453
P(E)	*	Phillips, Alphin Brook Road, Alphington, Exeter Devon EX2 8TH Tel: 01392 439025
P(EA)	*	Phillips, 32 Boss Hall Road, Ipswich, Suffolk IP1 59J Tel: 01473 740494
P(Ed)	*	Phillips Scotland, 65 George Street, Edinburgh, Scotland EH2 2JL Tel: 0131 225 2266
P(G)	*	Phillips Fine Art Auctioneers, Millmead, Guildford, Surrey GU2 5BE Tel: 01483 504030
P(L)	*	Phillips Leeds, 17a East Parade, Leeds, Yorkshire LS1 2BH Tel: 0113 2448011
P(NW)	*	Phillips North West, New House, 150 Christleton Road, Chester, Cheshire CH3 5TD Tel: 01244 313936
P(O)	*	Phillips, 39 Park End Street, Oxford OX1 1JD Tel: 01865 723524
P(S)	*	Phillips Fine Art Auctioneers, 49 London Road, Sevenoaks, Kent TN13 1AR Tel: 01732 740310
P(Sc)	*	Phillips Scotland, 207 Bath Street, Glasgow, Scotland G2 4HD Tel: 0141 221 8377
P(WM)	*	Phillips, The Old House, Station Road, Knowle, Solihull, W Midlands B93 0HT Tel: 01564 776151
P&T	•	Pine & Things, Portobello Farm, Campden Road, Nr Shipston-on-Stour, Warwickshire CV36 4PY Tel: 01608 663849

SLN	*	Sloan's, C G Sloan & Company Inc, 4920 Wyaconda Road, North Bethesda, MD 20852 USA Tel: 00 1 301 468 4911/669 5066
SMAM	•	Santa Monica Antique Market, 1607 Lincoln Boulevard, Santa Monica, California 90404, USA Tel: 310 314 4899
SMI	•	Janie Smithson, Lincolnshire Tel/Fax: 01754 810265 Mobile: 0831 399180
Som	•†	Somervale Antiques, 6 Radstock Road, Midsomer Norton, Bath, Somerset BA3 2AJ Tel: 01761 412686
SOO	•	Soo San, 239a Fulham Road, London SW3 6HY Tel: 020 7352 8980
SoS/ SOS	•	Styles of Stow, The Little House, Sheep Street, Stow-on-the-Wold, Glos GL54 1JS Tel: 01451 830455
SPa		Sparks Antiques. No longer trading
SPR	•	Simon and Penny Rumble, Causeway End Farm House, Chittering, Cambridgeshire CB5 9PW Tel: 01223 861831
SPT	•	Sporting Times Gone By, Warehouse (Clubhouse) Tel: 01903 731065 Mobile: 07976 942059 www.sportingtimes.co.uk
SPU	•†	Spurrier-Smith Antiques, 28, 30, 39 Church Street, Ashbourne, Derbyshire DE6 1AJ Tel: 01335 343669/342198
SQA	•	Squirrel Antiques, Scottish Antique and Arts Centre, Carse of Cambus, Doune, Perthshire, Scotland, FK16 6HD Tel: 01786 841203
STA		Michelina & George Stacpoole, Main St, Adare, Co Limerick Tel: 00 353 61 396 409
STE		Stevenson Brothers, The Workshop, Ashford Road, Bethersden, Ashford, Kent TN26 3AP Tel: 01233 820363
STS		Shaw to Shore, Church Street Antiques Centre, Stow-on-the-Wold, Glos GL54 1BB Tel: 01451 870186
SUC		Succession, 18 Richmond Hill, Richmond, Surrey TW10 6QX Tel: 020 8940 6774
SWB	•†	Sweetbriar Gallery, Robin Hood Lane, Helsby, Cheshire WA6 9NH Tel: 01928 723851
SWG	•	Swan Gallery, High Street, Burford, Oxfordshire OX18 4RE Tel: 01993 822244
SWN	•	Swan Antiques, Stone Street, Cranbrook, Kent TN17 3HF Tel: 01580 712720
SWO	*†	G. E. Sworder & Sons, 14 Cambridge Road, Stansted Mountfitchet, Essex CM24 8BZ Tel: 01279 817778
TAC		Tenterden Antiques Centre, 66–66a High Street, Tenterden, Kent TN30 6AU Tel: 01580 765655/765885
TAM	*	Tamlyn & Son, 56 High Street, Bridgwater, Somerset TA6 3BN Tel: 01278 458241
TC	•	Timothy Coward, Devon Tel: 01271 890466
TCG	•	20th Century Glass, Kensington Church Street Antique Centre, 58–60 Kensington Church Street, London W8 4DB Tel: 020 7938 1137 Tel/Fax: 020 7729 9875 Mobile: 07971 859848
TED	•†	Teddy Bears of Witney, 99 High Street, Witney, Oxfordshire OX8 6LY Tel: 01993 702616/706616
TEN	*	Tennants, The Auction Centre, Harmby Road, Leyburn, Yorkshire DL8 5SG Tel: 01969 623780
TEN	*	Tennants, 34 Montpellier Parade, Harrogate, Yorkshire HG1 2TG Tel: 01423 531661
TF	*†	Tayler & Fletcher, London House, High Street, Bourton-on-the-Water, Cheltenham, Glos GL54 2AP Tel: 01451 821666
THOM	•	S & A Thompson. Tel/Fax: 01306 711970 Mobile: 0370 882746
TMA	*†	Brown & Merry, Tring Market Auctions, Brook Street, Tring, Hertfordshire HP23 5EF Tel: 01442 826446 sales@tringmarketauctions.co.uk www.tringmarketauctions.co.uk
TMi	•	T. J. Millard Antiques, Assembly Antiques, 5–8 Saville Row, Bath, Somerset BA1 2QP Tel: 01225 448488
TOM	•†	Charles Tomlinson, Chester Tel/Fax: 01244 318395 Charles.Tomlinson@lineone.net www.lineone.net/-charles.tomlinson
TPC	•†	Pine Cellars, 39 Jewry Street, Winchester, Hampshire SO23 8RY Tel: 01962 777546/867014
TRL/ TRM	*	Thomson, Roddick & Laurie, 60 Whitesands, Dumfries, Scotland DG1 2RS Tel: 01387 255366
TRL/ TRM	*	Thomson, Roddick & Laurie, 24 Lowther Street, Carlisle, Cumbria CA3 8DA Tel: 01228 28939/39636
TWD	•	The Watch Department, 49 Beauchamp Place, London SW3 1NY Tel: 020 7589 4005 thewatchdept@virgin.net www.watchdept.co.uk
UNI	•	Unicorn Antique Centre, 2 Romney Enterprise Centre, North Street, New Romney, Kent TN28 8DW Tel: 01797 361940
VB	•	Variety Box, 16 Chapel Place, Tunbridge Wells, Kent TN1 1YQ Tel: 01892 531868
VCL	•	Vintage Cameras Ltd, 254 & 256 Kirkdale, Sydenham, London SE26 4NL Tel: 020 8778 5416/5841
VOS	*	Vost's, Newmarket, Suffolk CB8 9AU Tel: 01638 561313
VS	*†	T. Vennett-Smith, 11 Nottingham Road, Gotham, Notts NG11 0HE Tel: 0115 983 0541
WA	*†	Whyte's Auctioneers, 30 Marlborough Street, Dublin 1 Tel: 00 353 1 874 6161
WaH	•	The Warehouse, 29–30 Queens Gardens, Worthington Street, Dover, Kent CT17 9AH Tel: 01304 242006
Wai	•	Peter Wain, Glynde Cottage, Longford, Market Drayton, Shropshire TF9 3PW Tel: 01630 638358
WAL	*†	Wallis & Wallis, West Street Auction Galleries, Lewes, Sussex BN7 2NJ Tel: 01273 480208
WaR	•	Wot a Racket, 250 Shepherds Lane, Dartford, Kent DA1 2PN Tel: 01322 220619, wot-a-racket@talk21.com
WBB	•†	William Bentley Billiards, Standen Manor Farm, Hungerford, Berkshire RG17 0RB Tel: 01672 871214
WBH	*†	Walker, Barnett & Hill, Waterloo Road Salerooms, Clarence Street, Wolverhampton, West Midlands WV1 4JE Tel: 01902 773531
WeA	•	Wenderton Antiques, Kent. By appointment. Tel: 01227 720295
WEL	•†	Wells Reclamation & Co, Coxley, Nr Wells, Somerset BA5 1RQ Tel: 01749 677087
WELD	•	J. W. Weldon, 55 Clarendon Street, Dublin 2 Tel: 00 353 1 677 1638
WILL	*	Willingham Auctions, 25 High Street, Willingham, Cambridgeshire CB4 5ES Tel: 01954 261252
WilP	*	BBG Wilson Peacock, 26 Newnham Street, Bedford, Bedfordshire, MK40 3JR Tel: 01234 266366
WIM	•	Wimpole Antiques, Stand 349, Grays Antique Market, South Molton Lane, London W1Y 2LP Tel: 020 7499 2889
WL	*†	Wintertons Ltd, Lichfield Auction Centre, Wood End Lane, Fradley, Lichfield, Staffordshire WS13 8NF Tel: 01543 263256
WoR	*†	Wotton Auction Rooms, Tabernacle Road, Wotton-under-Edge, Glos GL12 7EB Tel: 01453 844733
WoW	•	Wealth of Weights, Stable Doors Market Street, Hailsham, Sussex East BN27 2AE Tel: 01323 441150 jaqui@weights.force9.co.uk
WRe	•	Walcot Reclamations, 108 Walcot Street, Bath, Somerset BA1 5BG Tel: 01225 444404
WSA	•†	West Street Antiques, 63 West Street, Dorking, Surrey RH4 1BS Tel: 01306 883487
WW	•	Woolley & Wallis, Salisbury Salerooms, 51–61 Castle Street, Salisbury, Wiltshire SP1 3SU Tel: 01722 424500
YAG	•	The York Antiques Gallery, Route 1, PO Box 303, York, ME 03909 USA Tel: 207-363-5002
YAN	•	Yanni's Antiques, 538 San Anselmo Avenue, San Anselmo, CA 94960 USA Tel: 001 415 459 2996
YC	•	Yesterday Child, Angel Arcade, 118 Islington High Street, London N1 8EG Tel: 020 7354 1601
YEST	•	Yesterday's, V.O.F. Yesterday's Maaseikerweg 202, 6006 AD Weert, The Netherlands Tel: 0475 531207
ZOOM	•†	Zoom, 312 Lillie Road, Fulham, London SW6 7PS Tel: 07000 ZOOM 2000 Mobile: 0958 372975

Index

Italic page numbers denote colour pages; **bold** numbers refer to information and pointer boxes

 *Interesting*

 *Informative*

 *Interactive*

 *Impartial*

 *Internet*

MILLER'S

going on-line in the autumn

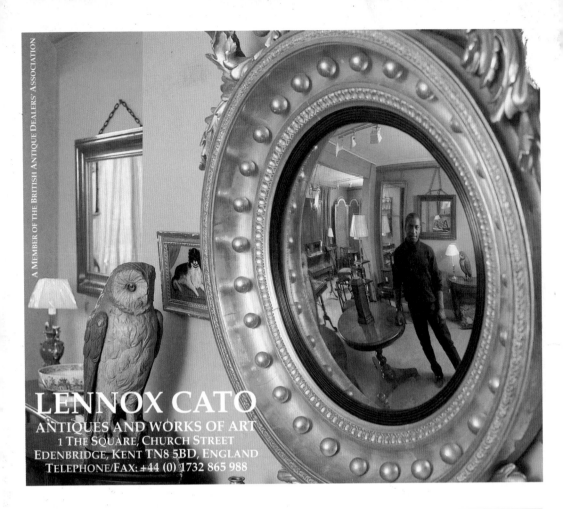
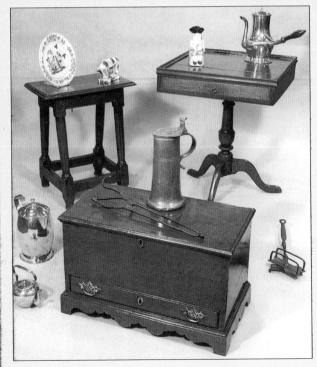